The Waite Group's
MS-DOS® Bible

RELATED TITLES

The Waite Group's Using PC-DOS™
The Waite Group

The Waite Group's MS-DOS® Developer's Guide, Second Edition
John Angermeyer, Kevin Jaeger, et al.

The Waite Group's Understanding MS-DOS®
Kate O'Day and John Angermeyer

The Waite Group's Tricks of the MS-DOS® Masters
John Angermeyer, Rich Fahringer, Kevin Jaeger, and Dan Shafer

The Waite Group's Discovering MS-DOS®
Kate O'Day

The Waite Group's MS-DOS® Papers
The Waite Group

The Waite Group's C Primer Plus, Revised Edition
Mitchell Waite, Stephen Prata, and Donald Martin

The Waite Group's Advanced C Primer ++
Stephen Prata

The Waite Group's Essential Guide to Microsoft® C
Naba Barkakati

The Waite Group's Microsoft® C Bible
Naba Barkakati

The Waite Group's Microsoft® C Programming for the PC, Revised Edition
Robert Lafore

The Waite Group's QuickC™ Bible
Naba Barkakati

The Waite Group's Essential Guide to Turbo C®
Naba Barkakati

The Waite Group's Turbo C® Bible
Naba Barkakati

The Waite Group's Turbo C® Programming for the PC, Revised Edition
Robert Lafore

For the retailer nearest you, or to order directly from the publisher, call 800-428-SAMS. In Indiana, Alaska, and Hawaii call 317-298-5699.

The Waite Group's
MS-DOS® Bible

Third Edition

Steven Simrin

HOWARD W. SAMS & COMPANY

A Division of Macmillan, Inc.
4300 West 62nd Street
Indianapolis, Indiana 46268 USA

International Standard Book Number: 0-672-22693-6
Library of Congress Catalog Card Number: 89-61437

From The Waite Group:
Development Editors: Mitchell Waite and James Stockford
Technical Reviewers: Blair Hendrickson and Harry Henderson
Chapter Opening Art: Bob Johnson

From Howard W. Sams & Company:
Acquisitions Editor: James S. Hill
Development Editor: James Rounds
Manuscript Editor: Marie Butler-Knight and Diana Francoeur
Cover Artist: Kevin Caddell
Illustrator: Wm. D. Basham
Indexer: Ted Laux
Compositor: Shepard Poorman Communications

Printed in the United States of America

Trademarks

To Benjamin, to the one to come, and to the memory of Jeb

Overview

Contents

Part 3   MS-DOS Commands   363

Part 4   Appendixes   507

A   MS-DOS Interrupts and Function Calls   509

Preface
to the First Edition

This book is about MS-DOS, the powerful disk operating system developed by Microsoft for microcomputers. MS-DOS is the manager of your computer. It is responsible for supervising the flow of information into and out of your machine and for controlling the interaction of the various parts of your computer system. This book will show you how to master MS-DOS and take advantage of its enormous capabilities. It is an easy-to-use guide, written to provide you with a ready reference to both the fundamentals and the more-advanced aspects of MS-DOS.

When I first began using MS-DOS, I quickly realized that I was virtually on my own. While it was easy to find material on the basics of MS-DOS, most advanced sources of information were hard to find and often quite sketchy in their treatment. Many questions came up for which I could find no answer. I would spend hours pouring over user's manuals, magazine articles, and how-to books. Often my searches were fruitless, and I would end up sitting in front of my computer, trying to figure things out for myself. Of course, experimenting is half the fun of using a computer, but it can be frustrating when you are in a hurry or you simply aren't in the mood for experimenting. I determined to spare others some of these "laboratory experiments" and share the results of my research.

The result has been this book. *MS-DOS Bible* is for all users of MS-DOS, from beginners to computer professionals. It begins with starting up your system and creating, editing, and managing files. It moves on to data handling and customizing your keyboard. Then it covers such advanced topics as exploring with DEBUG, using LINK, and understanding the structure of MS-DOS.

This book features:

► Learn-by-doing approach
► Jump table for quick access of specific topics
► Step-by-step tutorials

► Coverage of the basics up through advanced programming information

► Special in-depth section on MS-DOS commands

► Appendixes listing error messages, function calls and interrupts, practical batch files, and ASCII codes

MS-DOS Bible assumes no prior knowledge on your part. Each topic is discussed in a logical fashion from beginning to end, without relying on computerese. Those of you who are interested in only an overview of a topic can skim for highlights. Those who are interested in details will find them here, presented thoroughly and clearly.

Acknowledgments to the First Edition

I am grateful to all who provided assistance during the writing of *MS-DOS Bible*. In particular, I would like to thank Mike Van Horn of The Waite Group, who initially suggested that I write this book. Many thanks to Mary Johnson, also of The Waite Group, who acted as my editor. Finally, special thanks to family members and friends who gave valuable encouragement and moral support throughout the project.

Preface
to the Third Edition

When I wrote the first edition of *The Waite Group's MS-DOS Bible*, IBM PCs and PC compatibles were starting to appear in businesses and homes worldwide. With each computer came a copy of the still young MS-DOS. Things were different back then. There was little talk of TSRs, PC networks, ATs, or 386 machines. Hard disks were still somewhat of a luxury, and 640 Kbytes of memory seemed to be more than anyone could possibly ever use.

Three years later, when I wrote the second edition of *MS-DOS Bible*, MS-DOS had become the most widely used microcomputer operating system in the world. This was not surprising, given the incomparable marketing strength of IBM, but it was significant in understanding how MS-DOS had evolved over the years. Many new demands had been placed on MS-DOS. Many of these demands had not been anticipated when the operating system was first designed. In most cases, ways were found to satisfy the demands simply because the market for a solution was so strong.

The changes in the second edition of *MS-DOS Bible* mirrored the changes that occurred in MS-DOS. While the primary objective of the book continued to be to provide the reader with an up-to-date, comprehensive, easy-to-understand guide, the second edition represented a substantial rewriting of the first edition. The first four chapters were revised to more thoroughly address the issues of hard disk usage. New batch files were added to chapter 5, and the chapter on memory and disk structure became two chapters, to cover the many developments in the areas of disk media, disk formats, and memory configuration. A new chapter was added to cover terminate and stay resident programs.

Throughout the book, there was a stronger emphasis on programming. New examples showed how to use DEBUG to explore MS-DOS. Programs written in C, Pascal, and assembly language were added and thoroughly discussed. In addition, the expanded appendixes contained a primer on assembly language programming for those readers with little or no assembler experience. Part 3, "MS-DOS Commands," was revised and expanded to include all MS-DOS commands through version 3.3, and many of the examples used in the first edition were revised or replaced.

The pace of the PC and MS-DOS world continues to accelerate rapidly—thus the need for a third edition of *MS-DOS Bible*. MS-DOS 4.0 is a major advance over the previous versions of DOS. To accommodate the increased use of the mouse and the increased preference for a window-type interface, DOS 4.0 provides DOSSHELL, a customizable menu and file management system. To accommodate the increasing number of applications using the EMS 4.0 expanded memory scheme, DOS 4.0 includes an EMS 4.0 expanded memory driver. Because of growing disk storage requirements, DOS 4.0 supports hard disk partitions larger than 32 Mbytes in size.

Each of these topics is covered in this edition. In addition, three new chapters have been added. The first new chapter, on system configuration, discusses how you can modify and extend DOS to suit your needs and preferences. With the vast array of hardware devices available for use with PC computers, an understanding of system configuration is critical. The second new chapter covers the use of DOSSHELL. The chapter explains all aspects of the interface, from simply using it to programming it. The third new chapter covers expanded memory. The chapter discusses what expanded memory is, why it is necessary, how you use it, and how it works.

Existing chapters have been revised, some extensively. The increased prevalence of hard disk drives is probably the single most dramatic change that has occurred in PC computing since the first edition of *MS-DOS Bible* was written. Appropriately, chapter 1 now covers the topic of hard disk installation, detailing all aspects of partitioning and formatting a hard disk. Other chapters have been modified to incorporate new material. Many of the chapters contain new examples, which are even more instructive and more relevant.

The objective of *MS-DOS Bible* remains to be an easy-to-use guide to both the fundamental and advanced aspects of MS-DOS. This third edition is *still* intended for all users of MS-DOS and makes no assumptions about your previous experience with computers or MS-DOS.

Acknowledgments to the Third Edition

I would like to thank Jim Stockford of The Waite Group for the invaluable assistance, advice, and support he has provided in the production of *The Waite Group's MS-DOS Bible*. Special thanks also to Diana Francoeur for the many hours of effort which were so helpful. The assistance of Mitchell Waite, Blair Hendrickson, Jordan Breslow, Harry Henderson, and Marie Butler-Knight is also gratefully acknowledged. To Andy C., Nadine P., Chris, Bill, Nancy, Don, and the others, thank you so much for your support. Finally, the most special of thanks to my wife, Shelley, and our beloved sons, Benjamin and Jonathan, whose love and understanding made the writing of this book possible.

Steven Simrin is a veterinarian living in Kensington, California. He began working with microcomputers following graduation from veterinary school. He is currently a post-doctoral fellow at the University of California, San Francisco. His research interests include the use of computerized databases as a tool in the evaluation of medical technologies.

Introduction

This book explains the MS-DOS operating system. Its primary goal is to provide a comprehensive, easy-to-understand guide to MS-DOS. The material is presented in order from fundamental to advanced. For those readers new to MS-DOS, topics such as booting the system, using the commands, and file organization are discussed in the early chapters. Advanced topics—such as TSR programming, device drivers, DEBUG, and LINK—are discussed in the final chapters. The middle chapters cover the material needed to understand the advanced topics. Batch files, DOSSHELL, and the internal structure of MS-DOS are discussed fully, with programming examples provided.

This book is meant to be self-contained. No assumptions are made regarding the reader's level of computer expertise. Goals as diverse as maximizing your efficiency in using MS-DOS, to writing fully functional TSR programs are addressed.

All versions of MS-DOS and PC-DOS up to, and including, MS-DOS 4.01 and PC-DOS 4.01 are covered.

What Is MS-DOS?

MS-DOS stands for *Microsoft Disk Operating System*. An *operating system* is a computer program that coordinates the activities of a computer. The operating system is responsible for setting guidelines under which common computer tasks are carried out. A *disk* operating system is one that is used with disks (or diskettes). And Microsoft Corporation is the manufacturer of MS-DOS.

The three chief functions of an operating system are:

1. Transferring data between the computer and various peripheral devices (terminals, printers, floppy diskettes, hard disks, etc.). This transfer of data is called input/output, or I/O.
2. Managing computer files.
3. Loading computer programs into memory and initiating program execution.

MS-DOS handles all these duties admirably, as you will soon find out. In fact, one of the advantages of using MS-DOS is that it is simple to learn yet provides you with some very sophisticated, complex functions.

The Operating System and You

Without an operating system, a computer is like a wild, untamed beast— lightning fast, with incredible strength, but uncontrollable by humans. An operating system harnesses the speed and strength of the computer, converting its power into a useful tool.

How much you need to know about your computer's operating system depends largely on what tasks you wish to carry out. If you are primarily concerned with loading programs and copying files, you need understand only the most fundamental aspects of the operating system. On the other hand, if you are a systems programmer, you need to be familiar with the most intimate details of the operating system. Those of you who want to use the operating system to maximize the usefulness of your microcomputer are somewhere in-between.

Whichever category you fall into, the more familiar you are with your operating system, the better you can apply its capabilities to your own goals. The purpose of this book is to assist you in attaining those goals.

A Brief History of MS-DOS

The origin of MS-DOS can be traced to 1980, when Seattle Computer Products developed a microcomputer operating system for use as an in-house software development tool. Originally called QDOS, the system was renamed 86-DOS in late 1980 after it had been modified.

The rights to 86-DOS were purchased by Microsoft Corporation, which had contracted with IBM to produce an operating system for IBM's new line of personal computers. When the IBM PC hit the market in 1981, its operating system was a modified version of 86-DOS called PC-DOS version 1.0.

Shortly after the IBM PC was released, "PC-compatible" personal computers began to appear. These computers used an operating system called MS-DOS version 1.0. Microsoft had made available to the manufacturers of these machines an operating system that was a near replica of PC-DOS—the now famous MS-DOS.

The only significant difference between any of these operating systems was at the "systems level." Each operating system had to be customized for the particular machine on which it was to run. Generally speaking, these changes were apparent only to the systems programmer whose job was to "fit" the operating system to the machine. The users of the various operating systems were not aware of any significant differences.

Since the initial release of PC-DOS and MS-DOS, both operating systems have evolved along identical paths. Version 1.1 was released in 1982. The major change in 1.1 was double-sided disk drive capability. (Version 1.0 could be used only with single-sided disk drives.) Version 1.1 also allowed the user to redirect printer output to a serial port.

Version 2.0 was released in 1983. A major advancement over the earlier versions, it was designed to support a fixed (hard) disk and included a sophisticated hierarchical file directory, installable device drivers, and file handles.

MS-DOS 3.0 (released in 1984) provided improved support for fixed disks and microcomputers linked on a computer network. Subsequent versions through 3.3 (released in 1987) continued this trend.

MS-DOS 4.0, released in 1988, provides an alternative graphic user interface (DOSSHELL), an expanded memory device driver, support for hard disk partitions larger than 32 Mbytes, and several new commands and command options.

Although this book is titled "*MS-DOS Bible*," the information presented in it applies equally to PC-DOS and MS-DOS. Unless otherwise noted, the names MS-DOS, PC-DOS, and DOS are interchangeable. Versions 1.0 and 1.1 will be referred to as MS-DOS 1 or 1.X. Versions 2.0, 2.10, and 2.11 will be referred to as MS-DOS 2 or 2.X. Versions 3.0, 3.1, 3.2, and 3.3 will be referred to as MS-DOS 3 or 3.X. Versions 4.0 and 4.01 will be referred to as MS-DOS 4 and MS-DOS 4.X.

Organization and Contents of This Book

This book is divided into four parts:

- ▶ An information jump table
- ▶ Tutorials on various MS-DOS topics
- ▶ Discussions of MS-DOS commands

▶ Appendixes covering functions and interrupts, undocumented features of MS-DOS, practical batch files, code pages, assembly language programming, ASCII codes, and hexadecimal arithmetic

Part 1—Information Jump Table is a quick guide to the tutorials and command discussions. Major topics are listed alphabetically, with specific tasks or commands listed alphabetically below them.

Part 2—MS-DOS Tutorials consists of 16 chapters, arranged in order from those most fundamental to the use of MS-DOS to those required by programmers. Tutorials within the chapters provide hands-on learning aids, guiding you through the concepts presented in the chapter.

Part 3—MS-DOS Commands explains over 70 MS-DOS commands. Since MS-DOS is a "command-driven" system (it takes action in response to commands that you enter), this part emphasizes the purpose of each command and the procedure for using it.

Part 4—Appendixes contains supplemental material related to many of the topics covered in the book. Appendix A has a general introduction to the MS-DOS interrupts and function calls and then offers detailed discussions of each. Appendix B discusses some undocumented, but widely used, features of MS-DOS. Appendix C presents a simple menu-driven system that is constructed using batch files. Appendix D discusses code pages—what they are and how they are used. Appendix E is a primer on assembly language programming. It is provided so that readers with little or no assembly language experience may understand the assembly language programs presented in the book. Appendix F contains two ASCII cross-reference tables and explains hexadecimal to decimal conversion and vice-versa.

Chapter Summaries

Here is a brief summary of each of the 16 chapters covered in Part 2.

▶ **Chapter 1, Starting MS-DOS:** everything you need to know to begin using MS-DOS. Booting the system, backing up the system diskettes, and hard disk installation are covered. The important task of hard disk partitioning and formatting is covered. Use of the SELECT program to install DOS 4 is also covered.

▶ **Chapter 2, MS-DOS Files:** the fundamentals of data storage, naming and copying files.

▶ **Chapter 3, Directories, Paths, and Trees:** file management techniques, including creating directories and subdirectories and using the PATH command.

▶ **Chapter 4, MS-DOS Batch Files:** what batch files are and how to create them. How to use replaceable parameters and execute batch file commands.

▶ **Chapter 5, Configuring Your System:** how you can modify MS-DOS according to your use requirements and preferences. Use of the system files AUTOEXEC.BAT and CONFIG.SYS is discussed in this chapter.

▶ **Chapter 6, Redirection, Filters, and Pipes:** advanced data-handling features of MS-DOS.

▶ **Chapter 7, Using DOSSHELL:** a complete discussion of the use of the DOS 4 graphical user interface. The chapter also discusses the use of Program Start Commands, which allow you to customize the DOSSHELL interface.

▶ **Chapter 8, EDLIN, the MS-DOS Text Editor:** how to use EDLIN to create and modify files. Using EDLIN commands.

▶ **Chapter 9, Extended Keyboard and Display Control:** techniques for customizing your keyboard and display screen.

▶ **Chapter 10, Disk Structure and Management:** how MS-DOS organizes and manages data stored on disk, including discussion of the file directory, the file allocation table, and the MS-DOS system files.

▶ **Chapter 11, Memory Structure and Management:** how MS-DOS organizes and manages memory, including explanation of program loading, the program segment prefix, the MS-DOS environment, and memory control blocks.

▶ **Chapter 12, Expanded Memory:** a thorough overview of expanded memory: what it is, why it is necessary, how to use it, and how it works.

▶ **Chapter 13, Terminate and Stay Resident Programs:** what they are, how they function, and guidelines for "well-behaved" TSRs. A fully functional pop-up TSR is presented.

▶ **Chapter 14, MS-DOS Device Drivers:** what they are and how they function. A device driver skeleton that can be used to build a working device driver is presented.

▶ **Chapter 15, DEBUG:** exploring the inner workings of your computer, examining and modifying computer programs, and using DEBUG commands.

▶ **Chapter 16, LINK:** modifying object code into relocatable modules, combining separate object modules into a single relocatable module, and using LINK switches.

How to Use This Book

This book can be used in several ways. It can be read in order, from start to finish, or it can be read in skip-around fashion, using the Information Jump Table to locate a particular topic of interest. Experienced users of MS-DOS will probably use this latter method. The generous use of cross references throughout the book will help hit-and-miss users fill in information gaps.

Before you begin your exploration of MS-DOS, you should be aware of some of the conventions used in this book.

Screen Output and User Input

Unless noted otherwise, text identical to that appearing on the computer screen is printed in a special typeface:

```
Current date is Tue 7-08-1987
Enter new date: _
```

Note that the underscore character (_) indicates the position of the cursor.

Text that you are to type (user input) is shown in an italicized version of the same special typeface:

```
Current date is Tue 7-08-1987
Enter new date: 6/01/1989
```

If you are entering information from a tutorial, be sure to type it exactly as shown, including blank spaces and punctuation marks.

Some characters cannot be printed in italic type. These are:

asterisk (*)

backward slash (\)

caret (^)

double quotation mark (")

forward slash (/)

greater than (>)

hyphen (-)

left bracket ([)

less than (<)

plus (+)

right bracket (])

single quote (')

vertical bar (¦)

When these special characters are used in MS-DOS commands and programs, they will be shown within an italicized command, such as

```
C>dir¦find "-88 "
```

The characters ¦, ", and - do not appear to be italicized, but regard them as if they were and enter them along with the rest of the command.

Note that in EDLIN, the MS-DOS text editor (chapter 8), the asterisk is used as a prompt; and in DEBUG, an MS-DOS utility (chapter 15), the hyphen is used as a prompt. For example, in the following EDLIN command

    *2L

you would not enter the * because it is the EDLIN prompt; you would enter only 2L. The same is true for DEBUG commands:

    -d

All you enter is d.

Commands

Special command keys are shown with an initial capital letter, like this: Esc, Del, Alt. The carriage return is indicated as Enter. Commands using control characters are shown as Ctrl-D, Ctrl-N. On screen, such commands are represented as ^d, ^n. This is the same as Ctrl-D and Ctrl-N in this book's notation. In either case, you press the Ctrl key and the letter simultaneously. You do not have to shift to capitalize the letter.

Entering commands into your computer is easy. When you see the MS-DOS prompt (A> or C>), simply type the command and press Enter to signal MS-DOS that you are finished. On some keyboards, the Enter key may appear as Return or ↵. In any case, you must press the Enter key in order for the computer to respond.

Commands may be entered in uppercase letters, lowercase letters, or a combination. It makes no difference to MS-DOS. This book shows commands entered in lowercase, since that is the way most people will enter them. In typing your command, be sure to include all punctuation and blank spaces as shown. Always leave a space between the command and the drive indicator and between a command and a filename. If you don't, MS-DOS may become confused and not execute your command properly.

Do not type a lowercase "L" for the number 1, and do not use an uppercase "O" for a zero. MS-DOS does not recognize one for the other. If you have entered a command and it doesn't work, check your typing. You may have made a typing error or failed to enter the appropriate punctuation or spacing.

A Word about Disks and Diskettes

Throughout this book we will be discussing MS-DOS operations that utilize data stored on floppy diskettes and hard (fixed) disks. Unless otherwise noted, the word "disk" will refer to both floppy diskettes and hard disks.

P A R T

1

Information Jump Table

HOWARD W. SAMS & COMPANY

ʄʄʄ

Bookmark

DEAR VALUED CUSTOMER:

Howard W. Sams & Company is dedicated to bringing you timely and authoritative books for your personal and professional library. Our goal is to provide you with excellent technical books written by the most qualified authors. You can assist us in this endeavor by checking the box next to your particular areas of interest.

We appreciate your comments and will use the information to provide you with a more comprehensive selection of titles.

Thank you,

Vice President, Book Publishing
Howard W. Sams & Company

COMPUTER TITLES:

Hardware
- ☐ Apple 140
- ☐ Macintosh I01
- ☐ Commodore I10
- ☐ IBM & Compatibles I14

Business Applications
- ☐ Word Processing J01
- ☐ Data Base J04
- ☐ Spreadsheets J02

Operating Systems
- ☐ MS-DOS K05
- ☐ OS/2 K10
- ☐ CP/M K01
- ☐ UNIX K03

Programming Languages
- ☐ C L03
- ☐ Pascal L05
- ☐ Prolog L12
- ☐ Assembly L01
- ☐ BASIC L02
- ☐ HyperTalk L14

Troubleshooting & Repair
- ☐ Computers S05
- ☐ Peripherals S10

Other
- ☐ Communications/Networking M03
- ☐ AI/Expert Systems T18

ELECTRONICS TITLES:
- ☐ Amateur Radio T01
- ☐ Audio T03
- ☐ Basic Electronics T20
- ☐ Basic Electricity T21
- ☐ Electronics Design T12
- ☐ Electronics Projects T04
- ☐ Satellites T09

- ☐ Instrumentation T05
- ☐ Digital Electronics T11

Troubleshooting & Repair
- ☐ Audio S11
- ☐ Television S04
- ☐ VCR S01
- ☐ Compact Disc S02
- ☐ Automotive S06
- ☐ Microwave Oven S03

Other interests or comments: _____

_____

Name_____

Title _____

Company _____

Address _____

City _____

State/Zip _____

Daytime Telephone No. _____

A Division of Macmillan, Inc.

4300 West 62nd Street Indianapolis, Indiana 46268

22693

Bookmark

BUSINESS REPLY CARD

FIRST CLASS   PERMIT NO. 1076   INDIANAPOLIS, IND.

POSTAGE WILL BE PAID BY ADDRESSEE

HOWARD W. SAMS & CO.
ATTN: Public Relations Department
P.O. BOX 7092
Indianapolis, IN 46209-9921

HOWARD W. SAMS
& COMPANY

Information Jump Table

To use this table, first find the major topic you are interested in; then locate the specific task or command that you wish to perform. Both major topics and specific tasks or commands are listed alphabetically.

Batch Files

Code Pages

Commands

► Deleting a file (DEL)   *409–410*

► Displaying the directory (DIR)   *26–28, 419–422*

► Displaying a file's contents (TYPE)   *501*

► Entering a command   *6–7, 366–369*

► Erasing a file (ERASE)   *426–427*

► Formatting a disk (FORMAT)   *29–30, 434–440*

► Internal vs external commands   *365–366*

► Removing a subdirectory (RMDIR)   *68, 485*

► Renaming a file (REN)   *478–479*

► Specifying a search path (PATH)   *68–70, 466–468*

► Time setting (TIME)   *23, 498–499*

► Wildcards in commands   *54–55*

Note: See the table of contents for a complete list of MS-DOS commands.

The Environment

► Adjusting the environment size   *235–237*

► Batch files and the environment   *91–93*

► Description of MS-DOS environment   *235–238*

► Parents, children, and their environment   *237–238*

Files

► Batch files   *73–93, 579–583*

► COM and EXE files   *427–428*

► Displaying the contents of a file   *501*

► File allocation table (FAT)   *201, 209–213, 217–219*

► File directories   *57–71, 204–209, 214–217*

► File management   *58–71, 219–222*

► Filenames and filename extensions   *50–52*

► System files   *201–204, 226–227, 436–437*

Hard (Fixed) Disk

► Booting with a hard disk   *20–26, 37–38*

► Extended DOS partition   *32*

Memory under MS-DOS

MS-DOS (General Information)

Peripheral Devices/Device Drivers

Procedures

Programming under MS-DOS

► Interrupts and function calls   *509–572*
► Terminate and stay resident programming   *267–296*
► Undocumented features of MS-DOS   *573–577*

System Configuration

► Role of AUTOEXEC.BAT   *110–112*
► Role of CONFIG.SYS   *100–110*
► Use of SELECT for system configuration   *39–47*
► What is system configuration?   *39, 96*

Utility Programs

► BACKUP   *40–41*
► DEBUG   *319–352*
► DISKCOPY   *26–29, 424–425*
► EDLIN   *155–178*
► FDISK   *31–37, 41–42*
► FORMAT   *29–38, 434–440*
► LINK   *353–362*
► MEM   *452–455*
► MODE   *456–465*
► RESTORE   *43, 482–484*
► SELECT   *39–47, 486–488*
► SYS   *497–498*
► XCOPY   *503–506*

Wildcards

► Substituting "*" for a group of characters   *55*
► Substituting "?" for a single character   *54*

2

MS-DOS Tutorials

- ► Starting MS-DOS
- ► MS-DOS Files
- ► Directories, Paths, and Trees
- ► MS-DOS Batch Files
- ► Configuring Your System
- ► Redirection, Filters, and Pipes
- ► The DOSSHELL Interface
- ► EDLIN, the MS-DOS Text Editor
- ► Extended Keyboard and Display Control
- ► Disk Structure and Management
- ► Memory Structure and Management
- ► Expanded Memory
- ► Terminate and Stay Resident Programs
- ► MS-DOS Device Drivers
- ► DEBUG
- ► LINK

1

Starting MS-DOS

Booting MS-DOS
Backing Up the System Diskette
Formatting a Diskette
Changing Disk Drives
Installing MS-DOS on a Hard Disk
Automated Installation and Configuration

This chapter explains how to start using MS-DOS. The chapter covers a fairly wide range of material, primarily because of the variety of needs which must be addressed.

When MS-DOS was first released, each user received a single 5¼-inch floppy diskette, which contained a copy of the entire operating system. Very few of the early PC-type computers had hard disk drives. Therefore, the first books on using MS-DOS (including the first edition of *MS-DOS Bible*) assumed that everyone would be using a system with one or two 5¼-inch floppy diskette drives and no hard drive.

The situation has changed dramatically over the years. Most MS-DOS computers now have one or more hard drives. Some systems have 5¼-inch floppy drives; others have 3½-inch floppy drives. Some systems have both. There are also five different types of 5¼-inch diskettes (160 Kbytes, 180 Kbytes, 320 Kbytes, 360 Kbytes, and 1.2 Mbytes) and two different types of 3½-inch diskettes (720 Kbytes and 1.44 Mbytes). Of these, the most widely used are the 360-Kbyte (the standard 5¼-inch double density diskette used in XT-type computers), the 1.2-Mbyte (the 5¼-inch high density diskette used in AT-type computers), and the 1.44-Mbyte (the 3½-inch diskettes introduced in the PS/2 line of computers).

There are now four major versions of MS-DOS (referred to as MS-DOS 1, 2, 3, and 4). Each major version has several minor versions—for example, MS-DOS 3.30 and MS-DOS 4.01. Versions 3 and 4 are generally distributed on two or more diskettes. Most suppliers offer these versions of the operating system on both 5¼-inch and 3½-inch diskettes.

If you are new to MS-DOS, you may find this combination of different diskette types and different MS-DOS versions a little overwhelming. Be assured, though, that long-time users of MS-DOS are also somewhat overwhelmed (and often frustrated) by this situation. A significant portion of the personal computer industry exists solely to service the needs created by this situation (for example, suppliers of equipment to facilitate the transferring of data between machines with different types of disk drives).

This chapter will tell you how to get going with MS-DOS, regardless of the MS-DOS version you are using, regardless of the type of diskette drive(s) on your computer, and regardless of the presence or absence of a hard disk drive on your system.

The chapter begins by discussing how to load MS-DOS into your computer's memory (a process referred to as booting). The next section discusses the important task of making backup copies of your MS-DOS system diskettes. You should make your backups before doing anything else with MS-DOS. The chapter's third section discusses how to install MS-DOS on a hard disk drive. *Installation* is the process whereby MS-DOS is copied from your floppy diskette(s) onto the hard disk. You can then put the diskettes away for safe keeping and subsequently use the hard disk copy of the operating system. The final section of this chapter discusses SELECT, a program supplied with PC-DOS 4 which automates the installation process.

MS-DOS *files* and *disk directories* are mentioned throughout this chapter. You may want to briefly refer to chapters 2 and 3 as you are reading this chapter, for a quick introduction to these two important concepts. Two files with special meaning to MS-DOS are named AUTOEXEC.BAT and CONFIG.SYS. The role of these files is discussed fully in chapter 5.

Booting MS-DOS

MS-DOS is supplied on one or more floppy diskettes, which come with your computer or can be purchased from a software vendor. When your computer is turned on, MS-DOS is loaded into the computer's memory through a process called *booting*. The events that occur during the booting process are discussed in chapter 11. This section describes the steps that you need to take the first time you "boot up" MS-DOS.

In order for a diskette to be used to boot MS-DOS, the diskette must contain a set of *system files*. If your version of MS-DOS is supplied on more than one diskette, it is possible that not all of the diskettes are "bootable." Please refer to the manual supplied with your version of MS-DOS to determine which diskette is used for booting.

Before turning on your computer, place the boot diskette in drive A. Please refer to the manual supplied with your computer, or contact your computer supplier, if you are uncertain as to the location of drive A. Figure 1-1 illustrates the insertion of a 5¼-inch diskette into drive A. Notice that the diskette is held with the label facing up and toward the user as it is inserted. When using a 3½-inch disk drive, the diskettes are inserted in a similar fashion. The major difference between using 3½-inch and 5¼-inch diskettes is that, with the larger diskettes, you must close a door on the drive following insertion.

Figure 1-1. Major components of typical microcomputer system.

After the diskette is properly inserted, go ahead and turn on your computer. For a time it may appear that little if anything is happening. Actually, a series of checks is being run to verify that all is well inside your computer. Eventually the *cursor*, the small flashing light that marks your place on the screen, will appear. You will hear some whirring and clicking from the disk drive, and the drive's indicator light will flash on. The light indicates that MS-DOS is being loaded from the diskette into computer memory.

Setting the Date

Now that MS-DOS has been loaded into memory, you are ready to set the date. Your display screen should look something like this:

```
Current date is Tue 1-01-1980
Enter new date: _
```

In the last line of the display, MS-DOS prompts you to enter a new date (today's date). The date that you enter will be used by MS-DOS as a *date stamp* to help identify all files stored on disk during the current work session. Having to enter a date may seem inconvenient to you, but that date might be important months from now when you are trying to locate a file.

Notice that the second to the last line of the display shows the "current date." This is the date that MS-DOS was manufactured and first stored on a disk. This date will be displayed each time that you boot MS-DOS.

To enter the new date, follow these steps:

1. Type the number of the current month; for example, 01 = January, 02 = February, etc. The leading zero in the number may be omitted (January, for example, may be entered as "1" or "01").
2. Type a dash (-), slash (/), or period (.) to separate the month from the day.
3. Type the number of the day of the month. Again, a leading zero may be omitted.
4. Type a dash (-), slash (/), or period (.) to separate the day from the year.
5. Type the year. MS-DOS will accept any year in the range 1980 through 2099. You do not have to type all four digits of the year, only the last two (1990 may be entered as either "1990" or "90").
6. Press the Enter key.

The new date should appear on the screen:

```
Current date is Tue 1-01-1980
Enter new date: 10/30/90      ←Enter
```

After you press Enter, MS-DOS checks to make sure that the date you have specified is valid (the screen will display the message `Invalid date` if it is not) and then stores the date in memory. The date is stored in memory only while your computer is turned on. When you switch off the power, the date is lost and must be reentered the next time you boot the system.

Setting the Time

Once you have entered a valid date, MS-DOS prompts you to enter the new time (the present time). The time that you enter will be used by MS-DOS as a *time stamp* to help identify all files stored on disk during the current work session. Like entering the date, entering the time may seem to be a nuisance, but you may be glad you did six months from now.

```
Current date is Tue 1-01-1980
Enter new date: 10/30/90
Current time is: 0:01:01.58
Enter new time: _
```

Notice that the "current time" is displayed in the second to the last line. This is the time of day that MS-DOS was manufactured and first stored on a disk. It will be displayed each time that you boot MS-DOS.

To enter the new time, follow these steps:

1. Type the hour of the day. Any number in the range 01 through 24 is valid. A leading zero may be omitted (01 and 1 are both valid).
2. Type a colon (:) to separate the hours from the minutes.
3. Type the minutes. A leading zero is optional.
4. (Optional) Type a colon followed by the seconds. After entering the seconds, you may specify hundredths of a second by typing a period (.) and the hundredths of the second.
5. Press the Enter key.

The new time should appear on the screen:

```
Current date is Tue 1-01-1980
Enter new date: 10/30/90
Current time is: 0:01:01.58
Enter new time: 9:40      ←Enter
```

After you have pressed Enter, MS-DOS checks to make sure that the time you have specified is valid (the screen will display the message `invalid time` if it is not) and then stores the time in memory. The time is updated several times a second by your computer's internal timer. The current time is stored in memory only while your computer is turned on. When you switch off the power, the time is lost.

If it has a battery powered clock card, your computer will maintain the current date and time while it is turned off. When you subsequently turn your computer back on, the correct date and time will be displayed. The date and time will not be correct if your computer does not have a battery powered clock.

The System Prompt

Once a valid date and time have been entered, MS-DOS displays its *system prompt* (**A>**). Notice that a blinking cursor follows the **A>** prompt. The prompt and the blinking cursor are your signal from MS-DOS that it is ready for use:

```
Current date is Tues 1-01-80
Enter new date: 10/30/90
Current time is: 0:01:01.58
Enter new time: 9:40

The COMPAQ Personal Computer MS-DOS
Version 3.30

(C) Copyright Compaq Computer Corp. 1982, 1987
(C) Copyright Microsoft Corp. 1981, 1987

A> _
```

The MS-DOS Command Line

MS-DOS is a *command-driven* operating system. This means that there is a set of commands that you use to tell the operating system what tasks you wish it to perform. To enter a command, type its name on the MS-DOS *command line*.

The command line is indicated by the system prompt. MS-DOS stores everything you type after the system prompt, until you press the Enter key, as part of the command line. Only when you press the Enter key does MS-DOS begin to analyze what you have typed.

The command line has two parts, the *head* and the *tail*. The head is the name of a command or other program you wish to run. The tail is separated from the head by a space character. When MS-DOS analyzes the command line, it treats the text preceding the first space character as the head and looks for a command or program with a name that matches the head. MS-DOS saves everything that follows the first space character (no matter what you type) as the tail. When MS-DOS loads the command or program with the matching name, it "passes" the tail to that program. It is the job of the program, not MS-DOS, to process the command line tail. For instance, if you type "Willy don't you weep" on the command line, MS-DOS will look for a program named WILLY and pass "don't you weep" to WILLY for processing.

Each MS-DOS command is designed to do a certain job, and part of its design allows you to control it in various ways, depending upon what options and parameters it has been designed to accept from the command line tail. In order to use an MS-DOS command, you simply have to learn its name and what it will accept on the command line tail. Some commands work without needing any information from the command line tail. Other commands require additional information, such as the name of a disk drive, a file, or a directory. Many commands are designed to respond to *options*, otherwise known as *switches*, which generally take the form of a slash character followed by a single letter—for example, */s*.

Date and Time Defaults

While entering the new date and time is a good work habit, there may be occasions when you decide not to enter the date and time. If so, simply press the Enter key. The date and time will be set to the *default values,* the preset values used by MS-DOS unless you specify otherwise. In this case, the default values are the "current" date and time that are displayed by MS-DOS each time you boot the system. There is no correlation between these values and the date and time that you are actually using the computer. If you choose the default values, the screen will leave a blank in place of the new time and date:

```
Current date is Tues 1-01-80
Enter new date:      ←Enter
Current time is: 0:01:01.58
Enter new time:      ←Enter

The COMPAQ Personal Computer MS-DOS
Version 3.30

(C) Copyright Compaq Computer Corp. 1982, 1987
(C) Copyright Microsoft Corp. 1981, 1987

A> _
```

Date and Time Stamps

While MS-DOS is running, the computer's internal timer is used to update the present time, changing the value that is stored in memory several times a second. MS-DOS will also update the present date whenever the time reaches midnight (24:00:00.00).

When MS-DOS stores a file on a disk, the current date and time are stored on the disk along with other information about the file. These date and time stamps can be viewed by using the DIR command (more about DIR later). Date and time stamps can help you keep track of when a file was created or last modified but only if you entered the correct date and time when you booted MS-DOS.

Rebooting with Ctrl-Alt-Del

The procedure just described for booting MS-DOS is known as a *cold boot* because it began with the computer turned off. However, MS-DOS can also be started (or restarted) with the computer turned on. Naturally, this is known as a *warm boot*.

With the computer running, place your MS-DOS system diskette in drive A, close the drive door, and press the Ctrl-Alt-Del keys simultaneously. MS-DOS will be loaded (or reloaded) into memory. Just as it does for a cold boot, MS-DOS will prompt you to enter the current date and time.

Backing Up the System Diskette

If you are using MS-DOS for the first time, you should make a *backup copy,* or duplicate, of your system diskette before proceeding any further. The method used to make a backup depends on whether your system has two floppy disk drives or just one floppy disk drive. We will describe the method for two-drive systems first.

Note: If your system has a hard disk, determine whether it has one or two floppy disk drives and then use the appropriate method. In hard disk systems, it is especially important that you back up the system diskette before using the hard disk, since you might inadvertently erase the system diskette when setting up the hard disk.

MS-DOS uses a program called DISKCOPY.COM to copy diskettes. The program is supplied as a file on one of the MS-DOS system diskettes. The first step in backing up your system diskettes is to find the diskette that contains DISKCOPY.COM.

The MS-DOS command DIR (for DIRectory) is used to display the names of the files contained on a diskette. The command

dir a: /w

tells MS-DOS to display the names of the files on the diskette in drive A using the wide (/w) format. The wide format simply allows more filenames to be displayed at one time.

With the diskette you used to boot the system in drive A, go ahead and enter **dir a:** /w. Throughout this book, the word "enter" means to type the text that is indicated and then press the Enter key. You should see something like this after entering the command:

```
A>dir a: /w

Volume in drive A has no label
Directory of  A:\

COMMAND  COM  ANSI      SYS  COUNTRY  SYS  DISPLAY  SYS  DRIVER    SYS
FASTOPEN EXE  FDISK     COM  FORMAT   COM  KEYB     COM  KEYBOARD  SYS
MODE     COM  NLSFUNC   EXE  PRINTER  SYS  REPLACE  EXE  SELECT    COM
SYS      COM  VDISK     SYS  XCOPY    EXE  EGA      CPI  LCD       CPI
4201     CPI  5202      CPI
        22 File(s)        9216 bytes free

A>
```

What you see is the list of the names of the files contained on the boot diskette. It is likely that the actual list displayed on your system will differ somewhat from this list. That simply means that the diskette used to boot your computer contains a different set of files than the diskette used in this example.

We are looking for the file DISKCOPY.COM and it is not contained in the above listing. If the listing on your screen does contain the entry DISKCOPY COM, then you have the diskette you need. Otherwise, replace the diskette in drive A with another of the MS-DOS system diskettes and re-enter the command **dir a: /w**. Repeat the process until you find the file DISKCOPY.COM. In the following listing, the entry for DISKCOPY.COM appears in the second column of the third row:

```
A>dir a: /w

Volume in drive A has no label
Directory of  A:\

APPEND   EXE  ASSIGN    COM  ATTRIB    EXE  BACKUP   COM  BASIC    COM
BASICA   COM  CHKDSK    COM  COMMAND   COM  COMP     COM  DEBUG    COM
DISKCOMP COM  DISKCOPY  COM  EDLIN     COM  FIND     EXE  FORMAT   COM
GRAFTABL COM  GRAPHICS  COM  JOIN      EXE  LABEL    COM  MORE     COM
PRINT    COM  RECOVER   COM  REPLACE   EXE  RESTORE  COM  SHARE    EXE
SORT     EXE  SUBST     EXE  TREE      COM  XCOPY    EXE  BASIC    PIF
BASICA   PIF  MORTGAGE  BAS
        32 File(s)       43008 bytes free

A>
```

The disk copying process can begin once you have located DISKCOPY. COM. You will need one blank diskette for each MS-DOS system diskette. The blank diskettes must be the same size as the system diskettes, and the storage capacity of the blank diskettes must be the same as or greater than each of the system diskettes. The blank diskettes are referred to as the *target diskettes*. The original system diskettes are referred to as the *source diskettes*.

Instead of using blank diskettes as targets, you can use diskettes that contain files which you no longer need. *All existing files* on the target diskettes *will be destroyed* by the backup process. You can use the DIR command to make sure that prospective target diskettes do not contain any files that you want to save (chapter 2 explains how to copy a file that you want to save from one diskette to another).

Copying Diskettes on Two-Drive Systems

If your computer has two floppy diskette drives of the same size, you begin the disk copying process by entering the command **diskcopy a: b:**. MS-DOS will respond with the following message:

```
Insert SOURCE diskette in drive A:

Insert TARGET diskette in drive B:

Press any key to continue . . .
```

The source is the MS-DOS system diskette that is currently in disk drive A. Insert one of your target diskettes in drive B and press any key. MS-DOS will make an exact copy of the source diskette on the target.

When the copying process is completed, MS-DOS will display the following query:

```
Copy another diskette (Y/N)?
```

Press y if MS-DOS is supplied on more than one system diskette. You will be prompted to insert the next system diskette as the source and another blank diskette as the target. Repeat the process until you have made backup copies for each of the MS-DOS system diskettes. Press **n** in response to the above query after you have copied the final system diskette.

You should use the backup system diskettes for your future work with MS-DOS. Place the original system diskettes somewhere where they will be safe, and use them only to make additional backup copies as you need them.

Copying Diskettes on One-Drive Systems

If your computer has a single floppy diskette drive, begin the disk copying process with the same command used on two-drive systems: **diskcopy a: b:**. Now though the operating system displays the following:

```
Insert SOURCE diskette in drive A:

Press any key to continue . . .
```

the diskette containing DISKCOPY.COM is your source, so go ahead and press any key. MS-DOS will read from the diskette and then display the following:

```
Insert TARGET diskette in drive A:

Press any key to continue . . .
```

This is your prompt to remove the source diskette and insert the target diskette. This process is called *disk swapping*. MS-DOS will prompt you to repeat the swapping process until the target diskette contains a complete copy of the source diskette.

When the copying process is completed, MS-DOS will display the following query:

```
Copy another diskette (Y/N)?
```

Press y if MS-DOS is supplied on more than one system diskette. You will be prompted to insert the next system diskette as the source and another blank diskette as the target. Repeat the process until you have made backup copies for each of the MS-DOS system diskettes. Press **n** in response to the above query after the final system diskette has been copied.

You should use the backup system diskettes for your future work with MS-DOS. Place the original system diskettes somewhere where they will be safe and use them only to make additional backup copies as you need them.

Computers with 5¼-inch and 3½-inch Disk Drives

On systems with both a 5¼-inch disk drive and a 3½-inch disk drive, one of the drives will be assigned drive letter A and the other letter B. On these systems, the command "diskcopy a: b:" will not work, because the drives are not the same size. Instead, you must use the command "diskcopy a: a:" (or "diskcopy b: b:"). MS-DOS will prompt you to swap diskettes as described in the section headed "Copying Diskettes on One-Drive Systems."

Formatting a Diskette

Before a diskette can store data that is usable by MS-DOS, it must be *formatted*. During formatting, the diskette is divided into parcels called *sectors*, which are readable by MS-DOS. Formatting also analyzes the diskette for defects and sets up a file directory. Most (but not all) versions of MS-DOS will automatically format a diskette, if necessary, when the DISKCOPY command is used to back up a diskette.

If you use an unformatted diskette for your system backup, and your version of MS-DOS does not automatically format with DISKCOPY, MS-DOS will display the following message:

```
Disk error reading drive A
Abort, Retry, Ignore?
```

Insert the system diskette containing the file FORMAT.COM in drive A (use the DIR command to locate the file). Enter **format a:**. MS-DOS will prompt you as follows:

```
A>format a:      ←Enter
Insert new diskette for drive A:
and strike any key when ready
```

Remove the system diskette from drive A, and replace it with the diskette that is to be formatted. Formatting destroys all existing data on a diskette so make sure that the diskette does not contain any data that you will need later on. (If you want to abort the formatting process at this point, press Ctrl-C.) Press any key to format the diskette in drive A. MS-DOS will tell you when formatting is complete:

```
Formatting...Format complete

  362496 bytes total disk space
  362496 bytes available on disk

Format another (Y/N)?n     ←you press "n"
A>
```

The formatted diskette can now be removed from drive A and may be used to store data.

Changing Disk Drives

Most MS-DOS commands involve storing and/or retrieving data on a disk. You can specify which drive MS-DOS is to use by including the letter designator of the appropriate drive in the MS-DOS command. If you do not specify a drive in the command, MS-DOS assumes that the disk is in the *default drive*.

MS-DOS displays the letter of the *current* default drive in the system prompt. When you start MS-DOS from a diskette, the A drive is the default and MS-DOS displays the prompt **A>**.

To change the default drive, type the letter of the drive you wish to be the new default, type a colon, and then press Enter:

```
A>b:     ←Enter
B>
```

The colon tells MS-DOS that "b" refers to a disk drive. If you omit the colon, MS-DOS will assume that "b" is a command and will try to execute it. The default drive will come on for a second or two, and MS-DOS will search for command "b". When no command named "b" is found, MS-DOS will display an error message and then prompt you to enter another command:

```
A>b
Bad command or file name
A>
```

Installing MS-DOS on a Hard Disk

Most people using MS-DOS will want to *install* the operating system on their hard disk. Installation is the process of copying the MS-DOS *system files* and the MS-DOS *external files* from the system diskettes onto the hard disk. The system files are the files required to make the hard disk bootable. The external files contain the MS-DOS *utility programs*. DISKCOPY.COM and FORMAT.COM are examples of MS-DOS external files.

A hard disk must be partitioned and formatted before MS-DOS can be installed on it. The MS-DOS program used to partition hard disks is called FDISK.

Disk Partitions and FDISK

A hard disk consists of a stack of *platters*. Each platter has two surfaces used to store data. Each platter surface is divided into a series of concentric circles called *tracks*. All tracks of equal diameter are grouped together to form a *cylinder*. The outermost group of tracks on each platter forms cylinder 0, the second-outermost forms cylinder 1, and so on.

Before a hard disk can be used, contiguous cylinders must be grouped together to form *partitions*. Each partition "belongs" to a particular operating system. This means that for each partition there is only one operating system that can store files in that partition. Most people just have partitions that belong to MS-DOS on their hard disks, but partitions for XENIX, CP/M, and other operating systems can coexist on a single hard disk, right along with one or more MS-DOS partitions.

FDISK, the MS-DOS utility program used to establish hard disk partitions, has evolved considerably over the years. The MS-DOS 2.X version of FDISK allows just a single MS-DOS partition on each hard disk. The partition is limited to 32 Mbytes of storage capacity.

The MS-DOS 3.0–3.2 versions of FDISK allow each hard disk to have up to four MS-DOS partitions. Each partition is assigned its own drive letter, and partitions are still limited to 32 Mbytes.

The MS-DOS 3.3 version of FDISK allows you to create a *primary* and *extended* MS-DOS partition on each hard disk. The primary partition is still limited to 32 Mbytes, but there is no limit to the size of the extended partition. The extended partition may be divided into multiple *logical drives*, each logical drive being assigned its own drive letter. Each hard disk must have one primary partition. Use of the PC-DOS 3.3 version of FDISK is illustrated below.

The MS-DOS 4.X version of FDISK can be used to create a single partition as large as the disk's total storage capacity. Removal of the 32-Mbyte limitation is one of the major enhancements of MS-DOS 4.X. Use of the 4.X version of FDISK is discussed in the final section of this chapter.

Starting FDISK

The example presented here uses the PC-DOS 3.30 version of FDISK to partition a previously nonpartitioned 40-Mbyte hard disk. Users of 3.3 and previous versions of MS-DOS can follow the same procedure. (Version 4 adds additional capabilities to this command.) Two 20-Mbyte partitions are created. If you are using a version other than PC-DOS 3.30, your screens may differ somewhat from those presented here. Nonetheless, the general concepts presented are applicable to all versions of FDISK.

Start FDISK by first locating the backup system diskette containing the file FDISK.COM. Recall that the DIR command is used to obtain a listing of the files contained on a diskette. Go ahead and enter **fdisk** once you have located FDISK.COM. The program will start and you will see a display similar to this:

```
IBM Personal Computer
Fixed Disk Setup Program Version 3.30
(C)Copyright IBM Corp. 1983,1987

FDISK Options

Current Fixed Disk Drive: 1

Choose one of the following:

     1. Create DOS partition
     2. Change Active Partition
     3. Delete DOS partition
     4. Display Partition Information


Enter choice: [1]


Press ESC to return to DOS
```

This is the FDISK Options menu. The first time you use FDISK, your objective is to create a partition for use by DOS. Before proceeding, though, a word of warning. You must be VERY careful when using FDISK. It is possible to wipe out an entire partition of data with FDISK. If you are uncertain about what is happening, press the Esc key until you return to the DOS command prompt (**A>**).

Entering "1" will cause FDISK to display the Create DOS Partition menu, shown below:

```
Create DOS Partition

Current Fixed Disk Drive: 1

1. Create Primary DOS partition
2. Create Extended DOS partition


Enter choice: [1]

Press ESC to return to FDISK Options
```

Creating Partitions

All hard disks partitioned with the 3.3 and 4.X versions of FDISK are required to have one primary DOS partition. Choose selection "1" from the Create DOS Partition menu and FDISk will display the Create Primary DOS Partition menu:

```
Create Primary DOS Partition

Current Fixed Disk Drive: 1
  :
  :
Do you wish to use the maximum size
for a DOS partition and make the DOS
partition active (Y/N).........? [n]
```

As you can see, FDISK wants to know if it should create the largest DOS partition possible. Because the example is being carried out on a 40-Mbyte drive, the largest possible primary partition is 32 Mbytes (remember that this example is using PC-DOS 3.30, which has a 32-Mbyte limit). However, it has been decided to divide the drive into two 20-Mbyte partitions. Therefore, we do not want the largest possible partition so "n" is entered in response to the question. This produces the following:

```
Create Primary DOS Partition


Current Fixed Disk Drive: 1


Total disk space is  976 cylinders.
Maximum space available for partition
is  771 cylinders.

Enter partition size...........: [ 488]


No partitions defined

Press ESC to return to FDISK Options
```

There are a total of 976 cylinders on the 40-Mbyte disk. A maximum of 771 cylinders may be used for the primary DOS partition (this corresponds to a 32-Mbyte partition). The number 488 is entered on the `Enter partition size` line, because we want the new partition to occupy one-half of the disk's total capacity (20 Mbytes is one-half of 40 Mbytes, and 488 cylinders is one-half of 976 cylinders). FDISK will display the updated partition information after the size of the primary partition has been specified:

```
Create Primary DOS Partition

Current Fixed Disk Drive: 1

Partition Status   Type  Start  End Size
  C: 1             PRI DOS    0  487 488
```

Press the Esc key to return to the FDISK Option menu, enter 3 ("Create DOS partition"), and then enter 2. FDISK will display the Create Extended DOS Partition menu:

```
Create Extended DOS Partition

Current Fixed Disk Drive: 1

Partition Status   Type  Start  End Size
  C: 1             PRI DOS    0  487 488


Total disk space is  976 cylinders.
Maximum space available for partition
is  488 cylinders.

Enter partition size...........: [ 488]
```

FDISK displays the current partition information and states that 488 cylinders are available to use as a partition. This represents the remaining half of the disk's storage capacity. This is the default size for the extended partition, so pressing the Enter key is all that is required. FDISK will automatically display the updated partition information:

```
Create Extended DOS Partition

Current Fixed Disk Drive: 1

Partition Status   Type  Start  End Size
  C: 1             PRI DOS    0  487  488
     2             EXT DOS  488  975  488



Extended DOS partition created

Press ESC to return to FDISK Options
```

Once the extended partition has been created, FDISK will prompt you to define the extended partition's logical drives:

```
Create Logical DOS Drive(s)



No logical drives defined


Total partition size is  488 cylinders.

Maximum space available for logical
drive is  488 cylinders.

Enter logical drive size........: [ 488]


Press ESC to return to FDISK Options
```

An extended partition consists of one or more logical drives. Each logical drive has a unique drive letter assigned to it. In the example, we want the entire extended partition to be a single logical drive, so we simply press the Enter key. This creates a single logical drive that is 488 cylinders in size. FDISK displays the updated information:

```
Create Logical DOS Drive(s)

Drv Start End  Size

D:  488   975  488

All available space in the Extended DOS
partition is assigned to logical drives.


Logical DOS drive created, drive letters
changed or added
Press ESC to return to FDISK Options
```

FDISK also tells us that the entire extended partition is to be referred to using drive letter D.

Activating the Primary DOS Partition

After the partitions have been defined, one of them must be designated as being "active." The active partition is the partition that is read during the boot-up process. Only one partition on the disk is active at a time. On systems where the hard disk contains more than one operating system, the active partition determines which operating system boots up when the computer is turned on.

You activate the primary DOS partition by first returning to the FDISK Options menu (press Esc to return) and then pressing 2 ("Change Active Partition"). FDISK displays the Change Active Partition menu:

```
Change Active Partition

Current Fixed Disk Drive: 1

Partition Status   Type  Start  End Size
  C: 1             PRI DOS    0  487  488
     2             EXT DOS  488  975  488



Total disk space is  976 cylinders.

Enter the number of the partition you
want to make active...............: [1]
```

We want to activate partition number 1, so a "1" is entered on the Enter the number line. FDISK updates the partition information:

```
Change Active Partition

Current Fixed Disk Drive: 1
```

```
Partition Status   Type  Start  End Size
   C: 1       A    PRI DOS    0  487  488
      2            EXT DOS  488  975  488


Total disk space is  976 cylinders.
```

Notice that the **Status** column for partition 1 now contains an **A**, indicating that partition 1 is active.

Once the primary partition is activated, you can quit FDISK by pressing the Esc key two times. FDISK will prompt you to reboot your computer.

Upon rebooting, you are ready to format the hard disk and then install DOS. Before leaving our discussion of FDISK, however, let us mention the other selections available on the FDISK Options menu.

Other FDISK Options

In addition to creating and activating DOS partitions, there are three other actions that you can take from the FDISK Options menu.

You can use FDISK to delete existing DOS partitions. Remember that all data in a partition is lost when the partition is deleted. If the disk contains an extended DOS partition, that partition must be deleted before the disk's primary DOS partition can be deleted.

The size of an existing partition cannot be changed. You must delete the existing partition and then create a new partition.

You can also use FDISK to simply display the current partition information. It is probably a good idea to display the partition information before making any changes with FDISK. This will help you avoid making costly mistakes.

FDISK examines and modifies the partition information of one hard disk at a time. If your computer has more than one hard drive, a fifth option ("Select Next Fixed Disk Drive") will be displayed in the FDISK Option menu. This option directs FDISK to move on and access the partition information of the next drive in the system.

Formatting the Hard Disk

Two logical drives were created in the above example using FDISK. The logical drive in the primary DOS partition is referred to as logical drive C; the logical drive in the extended partition is referred to as logical drive D. Each logical drive must be *formatted* before it can be used by DOS.

If you reformat a drive that already contains some data, the existing data becomes unavailable to DOS. While it is possible to retrieve data from accidentally reformatted drives using programs such as Norton Utilities, PC-Tools, and Mace Utilities, such situations are to be avoided. These programs are very good, but trying to rescue data from a reformatted hard disk is strenuous, time consuming, and often not completely successful. *Be very careful whenever you are formatting a hard disk drive!*

FORMAT is the DOS utility program used to format both floppy diskettes and hard disks. Using the DIR command, locate the backup system diskette that contains the file FORMAT.COM. The examples that follow use FORMAT to format drive C.

The command to format drive C is "format c:", but we are going to want drive C to be bootable. This means that DOS will automatically be loaded into memory from drive C each time the computer is turned on. In order to accomplish this, we need the command "format c: /s". The "/s" is a *command switch* which tells DOS to format drive C and also make it bootable by placing a copy of the DOS system files on the drive. The example below illustrates the use of FORMAT. The example assumes that a backup system diskette containing the file FORMAT.COM is in drive A.

```
A>format c: /s      ←enter command
WARNING, ALL DATA ON NON-REMOVABLE DISK      ←DOS issues warning
DRIVE C: WILL BE LOST!
Proceed with Format (Y/N)?y

Format complete
System transferred

   21170176 bytes total disk space
      79872 bytes used by system
      30720 bytes in bad sectors
   21059584 bytes available on disk


   A>
```

Notice that FORMAT issues a warning and asks if you want to proceed before it begins to format. You should enter **n** if you are at all uncertain about what you are doing.

The message **System transferred** indicates that the files required for booting have been copied to drive C. The final four lines report the following:

1. The total storage space on disk drive C
2. The amount of storage used by the system files
3. The amount of storage unavailable for use ("bad sectors"—most disks have some)
4. The amount of storage currently available on disk drive C

Drive C is now ready for use by DOS. It is also bootable so that it can be used to start up DOS.

Drive D also needs to be formatted before it is usable. This is done with the command "format d:" because there is no need for drive D to be bootable.

Automated Installation and Configuration

The topic of system configuration is covered in chapter 5, but needs to be mentioned briefly here. *Configuration* is essentially a customization of DOS. You customize the operating system according to your own preferences and use patterns. Information regarding configuration is stored in two special files named CONFIG.SYS and AUTOEXEC.BAT. The remainder of this chapter discusses a DOS utility program named SELECT, which can be used to automatically install DOS and create CONFIG.SYS and AUTOEXEC.BAT files.

SELECT is a program provided with MS-DOS 4 that provides an automated method for installing and configuring the operating system. While you can install MS-DOS 4 in the conventional, nonautomated fashion described earlier in this chapter, using SELECT facilitates the process, especially for those users who are inexperienced in installing and configuring DOS. SELECT asks you a series of questions regarding your use of MS-DOS. The program uses your responses to create the files CONFIG.SYS and AUTOEXEC.BAT.

As an example of what SELECT can do for you, here is the CONFIG.SYS file which SELECT automatically created on my computer:

```
BREAK=ON
BUFFERS=20
FILES=8
LASTDRIVE=E
SHELL=C:\DOS\COMMAND.COM /P /E:256
DEVICE=C:\DOS\ANSI.SYS
INSTALL=C:\DOS\FASTOPEN.EXE C:=(50,25)
```

Here is the AUTOEXEC.BAT created by SELECT:

```
@ECHO OFF
SET COMSPEC=C:\DOS\COMMAND.COM
VERIFY OFF
PATH C:\DOS
APPEND /E
APPEND C:\DOS
PROMPT $P$G
VER
DOSSHELL
```

SELECT and Hard Disk Installation

If you are installing MS-DOS on a hard disk, SELECT will determine if the hard disk already contains a primary DOS partition. If a primary partition does not exist, SELECT will use FDISK to create a primary partition. SELECT will instruct FDISK to create the largest possible partition or, if you prefer, to create a smaller partition according to your specification.

If a primary DOS partition already exists, SELECT will install MS-DOS on that partition without disturbing your non-DOS files.

A problem arises if your hard disk has an existing primary DOS partition and you want to use the 4.X version of FDISK to create a primary partition larger than 32 Mbytes. The remainder of this section discusses how to preserve the data in an existing partition and then create a new partition with FDISK. You may skip this material and go on to the section titled "Starting SELECT" if you will not be modifying a DOS partition.

BACKUP

If your hard disk has an existing DOS partition and you want to create a larger partition, you must first delete the existing partition. Because this will destroy any data in the partition, you may want to use the DOS program named BACKUP to preserve the partition's contents. If you are not concerned with saving the contents of an existing DOS partition, you may skip ahead to the discussion of FDISK.

BACKUP is used to create *archival* copies of files. In this example, BACKUP is used to store the archival files on floppy diskettes. If you are going to follow this procedure, make sure that you have an adequate supply of floppy diskettes. Do not use floppies that have files in their root directories, because BACKUP will erase these files.

Boot your computer using the MS-DOS 4 diskette labeled "Install" (or the equivalent diskette if you are using another implementation of DOS 4.X). When the booting process is completed, MS-DOS will display this message:

```
Insert SELECT diskette in drive A:

Press Enter to continue installing DOS,
or press Esc to exit.
```

Press the Esc key and then replace the "Install" diskette with the diskette labeled "Select". Enter the command **dir /w** to make sure that the file BACKUP.COM is on the diskette. Once you have verified that you have the right diskette, enter the following command:

```
A>backup c:\*.* a: /s
```

This example assumes that the primary DOS partition is assigned drive letter C and that drive A will hold the floppies used in the backup procedure.

When you enter the above command, DOS will read the file BACKUP.COM into memory and then issue the following message:

```
Insert backup diskette 01 in drive A:

WARNING! Files in the target drive
A:\ root directory will be erased
Press any key to continue . . .
```

Label a diskette 01, place it in drive A, and press any key. BACKUP will begin to copy the contents of the DOS partition to the diskette. The following message will be displayed when the diskette's capacity is reached:

```
Insert backup diskette 02 in drive A:

WARNING! Files in the target drive
A:\ root directory will be erased
Press any key to continue . . .
```

Label another diskette 02 and place the diskette in drive A. Repeat the process, numbering and inserting a fresh diskette as prompted. MS-DOS will display the system prompt (**A>**) when the backup process has been completed. Set aside the labeled diskettes for later use.

If your hard disk also has an extended DOS partition, you will have to repeat the backup process for each logical drive in the extended partition. When the entire backup process is completed, you are ready to use FDISK.

FDISK—Version 4.X

Use of the FDISK program was discussed, along with illustrative examples, earlier in this chapter. Use of the 4.X version of FDISK is essentially identical.

The MS-DOS 4 version of FDISK is supplied on the diskette labeled "Install". Place the diskette in drive A and enter **fdisk**. The program will start by displaying the FDISK Options menu, which is nearly identical to the menu illustrated earlier in this chapter.

The first task in using FDISK is to delete the existing DOS partition(s). If you have an extended partition, it must be removed before you remove the primary DOS partition.

Once the existing partitions are deleted, you can create the new partition. From the FDISK Options menu, select "Create DOS Partition or Logical DOS Drive" and then select "Create Primary DOS Partition". At this point, the program asks if you want to create the largest possible primary partition. The partition is created and automatically activated if you enter "y". The program displays the following if you enter "n":

```
Create Primary DOS Partition

Current fixed disk drive: 1
```

```
    Total disk space is    41 Mbytes (1 Mbyte = 1048576 bytes)
    Maximum space available for partition is    41 Mbytes (100%)

Enter partition size in Mbytes or percent of disk space (%) to
create a Primary DOS Partition..................................:
[  41]


    No partitions defined



    Press Esc to return to FDISK Options
```

The essential difference between this display and others discussed previously is that partition size can be specified in Mbytes or percentage of disk space, rather than as a range of cylinders.

If you choose to specify a partition size (rather than having the program automatically create the largest possible partition) you must go on to activate the partition. You can also create an extended partition if you have any remaining disk space. DOS will prompt you to reboot the system when you quit FDISK.

FORMAT—Version 4.X

Use of the 4.X version of FORMAT is identical to that described for earlier versions of the program. If you are using MS-DOS 4, FORMAT.COM comes on the diskette labeled "Install".

You will have to format your new DOS partition(s) before you can store any files on it. The following example illustrates how to format drive C so that it is bootable. The example assumes that the file FORMAT.COM is on the diskette in drive A:

```
A>format c: /s


WARNING, ALL DATA ON NON-REMOVABLE DISK
DRIVE C: WILL BE LOST!
Proceed with Format (Y/N)?y


Format complete
System transferred


Volume label (11 characters, ENTER for none)? mini


    42366976 bytes total disk space
      110592 bytes used by system
       92160 bytes in bad sectors
    42164224 bytes available on disk


        2048 bytes in each allocation unit
```

```
          20588 allocation units available on disk

     Volume Serial Number is 2221-14D4

     A>
```

Notice that the 4.X version of FORMAT assigns a serial number to each disk (or diskette) that it formats. The new partition is now ready for use. The first thing you might want to do is use the DOS program RESTORE to retrieve files that were saved from the old partition using the BACKUP program.

RESTORE

Place the diskette with the file RESTORE.COM in drive A. If you are using MS-DOS 4, this will be the diskette labeled "Select". Enter the command:

```
A>restore a: c:\*.* /s
```

DOS will display the following message:

```
Insert backup diskette 01 in drive A:
Press any key to continue . . .
```

Insert the backup diskette labeled "01" and press any key. DOS will copy the files back to the hard disk and prompt you when it is time to insert each of the backup diskettes. When the process is completed, all of the files from the original partition will be back on the hard disk, and the directory structure that existed will still be intact. You can now go on to use the SELECT program to install DOS 4 on the new partition.

Starting SELECT

Start SELECT by inserting the "Install" diskette into drive A. Turn on the computer or press Ctrl-Alt-Del to reboot. You must boot from the floppy, because SELECT will only run under DOS 4.

The menu-driven installation and configuration procedure that SELECT presents is straightforward but somewhat awkward, requiring an excessive amount of disk swapping. The program operates by presenting you with a series of menus. The menus are referenced by the titles displayed at the top of the screen.

PC-DOS vs. MS-DOS

The SELECT installation program described here is the version provided in PC-DOS 4.01. IBM (bless their hearts) has designed this implementation of SELECT so that it refuses to recognize hard disks that contain MS-DOS.

If you try to run SELECT on a computer with MS-DOS on the hard disk,

SELECT hums along for a while, then gives you a meaningless message stating that "an error" has occurred. SELECT then quits without giving you the slightest clue as to what went wrong.

You can get IBM's SELECT to work with a hard disk containing MS-DOS by modifying the hard disk's boot sector. Doing this requires a disk utility program such as Norton Utilities (the DOS utility program DEBUG will also work, but it is MUCH riskier and not recommended). Boot your computer using the MS-DOS on the hard disk. Use your disk utility program to examine the contents of the boot sector (sector 0). The bytes at offsets 3 through 7 in the sector form the following sequence:

4D 53 44 4F 53.

These hexadecimal numbers represent the ASCII values for the letter sequence "MSDOS". Use your disk utility program to change bytes 3 through 7 so that they form the following sequence:

49 42 4D 20 20.

These hexadecimal numbers represent the letter sequence "IBM" followed by two blanks.

After the change is made, reboot your computer using the DOS 4 "Install" diskette in drive A. The SELECT utility will now work with your hard disk. You may get another error message, but this will occur after DOS 4 has been installed and configured. Ignore the error and reboot DOS 4 from your hard disk. All will be well.

Alternatively, you can back up the contents of your MS-DOS hard disk as described above using BACKUP. Reformat your hard disk using the IBM version of FORMAT and then use RESTORE to put your file back on the hard disk. This method is more laborious than modifying the boot sector, but it is less risky, particularly if you do not have an appropriate disk utility program.

Using SELECT

The first three screens that SELECT presents greet you and provide some general information. SELECT warns you to have available one to four blank diskettes. The actual number of diskettes required depends on the type of storage device on which DOS 4 is to be installed. Most users will be installing DOS 4 onto a hard disk drive, in which case a single blank diskette is required.

SELECT also informs you about the role of various keys. The most important keys are **Enter**, which generally advances you to the next screen; **Esc**, which generally returns you to the previous screen; and **F1**, which provides a help facility. The help facility has some "intelligence" in that it is aware of what you were doing when help was requested.

Balancing Memory

Proceed through the first set of screens by pressing the Enter key and swapping diskettes as instructed. The first functional screen you will come to is headed "Specify Function and Workspace". This screen lets you determine the amount of memory that will be dedicated to DOS. You may choose one of three options.

If you select "Minimum DOS function; maximum program workspace", SELECT will configure your system so that DOS occupies approximately 80 Kbytes of memory. SELECT will place the following statement in the CONFIG.SYS file that it is creating:

```
FILES=8
```

If you select "Balance DOS function with program workspace", SELECT will configure your system so that DOS occupies approximately 90 Kbytes of memory. SELECT will place the following statements in CONFIG.SYS:

```
BUFFERS=20
FILES=8
INSTALL=C:\DOS\FASTOPEN.EXE C:=(50,25)
```

If you select "Maximum DOS function; minimum program workspace", SELECT will configure your system so that DOS occupies approximately 110 Kbytes of memory. SELECT will place the following statements in CONFIG.SYS:

```
BUFFERS=25,8
FCBS=20,8
FILES=8
INSTALL=C:\DOS\FASTOPEN.EXE C:=(150,150)
```

You can see that more memory is dedicated to DOS in going from minimum to maximum DOS function. The configuration commands listed above are each discussed in chapter 5.

After you have made your selection for DOS function level, press the Enter key. The SELECT utility will present the next screen.

Country Specific Information

This "Select Country and Keyboard" screen lets you select the formats used by DOS for the following:

date and time
currency symbols
capitalization rules

> sorting order
>
> character sets

Most users in the United States will want to select choice 1, the predefined country and keyboard information. Select choice 2 if the predefined information is not suitable. You will be presented with a list of countries. Choose the country most appropriate for your needs. Please refer to appendix D for additional information on the use of non-U.S. country information.

Location of System Directory

The next two screens let you specify the drive and subdirectory location for the DOS system files. SELECT will use the information you enter to create a PATH statement, which it will place in the AUTOEXEC.BAT file. The role of the PATH statement is discussed in chapter 3.

Printer Configuration

The next series of screens lets you configure DOS to use a printer. A selection of printers from which you can choose will be presented. SELECT will also prompt you for information about how the printer is connected to the computer. The information you enter is used in setting up a PRINT command in the AUTOEXEC.BAT file. SELECT will put the appropriate MODE command in AUTOEXEC.BAT if you specify that the printer is connected to a serial port.

The PC-DOS version of SELECT will list only IBM printers. If you have a non-IBM printer, check its documentation to see what IBM printers it emulates, and choose the appropriate one from the list.

Installation Options

Following the presentation of the printer screens, SELECT will ask if you wish to "accept the configuration" or "review, change or add" to it. Choosing the latter will display a listing of configuration options. Next to each option is a "yes" or a "no", which indicates whether or not the SELECT utility decided that the option should be supported on your system. SELECT makes its decisions based on the type of hardware it detects in your system, along with the responses that you provide to the program. You can override SELECT's options, but often it makes no sense to do so. For example, you would not want expanded memory supported if your system does not have an expanded memory card.

The Configuration Files

Once you accept the configuration options, the SELECT utility is ready to create the new configuration files. DOS 4 is just like the earlier versions of DOS in that configuration information is stored in the files CONFIG.SYS and AUTOEXEC.BAT. However, SELECT does not create these files; rather, it creates files named CONFIG.400 and AUTOEXEC.400. SELECT does this so that it will not override any previously existing CONFIG.SYS and AUTOEXEC.BAT files.

After the SELECT utility has created CONFIG.400 and AUTOEXEC.400, it signals you that its work is done. You are instructed to remove the system diskettes and reboot the system.

Final Points

Upon completion of its work, SELECT instructs you to remove all diskettes and reboot your system (assuming, of course, that you installed DOS 4 on a hard disk). The commands in CONFIG.400 and AUTOEXEC.400 have no effect when you reboot. Guided by the concepts presented in chapter 5, you will have to use a text word processor (such as EDLIN, the DOS text editor discussed in chapter 8, or any word processor operating in text mode) to examine the contents of your old CONFIG.SYS file and the new CONFIG.400 file. If there are commands that you wish to keep from your original files, combine them with the text in the CONFIG.400 file to make a new CONFIG.SYS file. Similarly, if you wish to keep commands from your old AUTOEXEC.BAT file, combine them with the text in the AUTOEXEC.400 file as a new AUTOEXEC.BAT file. Following these combinations, reboot your system. This time, the new configuration commands will be in effect when the system comes up.

2

MS-DOS Files

Filenames and Extensions
File Specifications
Copying a File
Wildcards

One of the chief responsibilities of an operating system is the management of computer files. A *computer file* is similar to any other type of file in that it is a collection of related information stored in one place. Unlike paper files, which are stored in filing cabinets or desk drawers, computer files are stored on disks. They are then loaded into the computer's memory when the information they contain is to be used. The operating system controls both the storing and the loading of computer files.

This chapter will explain how files are named and what information MS-DOS needs to know about files in order to work with them. The procedures for copying files and for using "wildcards" in files are also explained.

If your computer has a hard disk, you may want to skim this chapter and the next before installing MS-DOS on your hard disk. Installation of MS-DOS is covered in chapter 1.

Filenames and Extensions

Each MS-DOS file has a *filename* and an optional *filename extension*. MS-DOS uses these names to differentiate one file from another. Some filenames and extensions, such as those for the files on the operating system diskette, are preassigned; others are assigned by you. Filenames and extensions are usually chosen so that they are descriptive of the information in the file. Extensions are used to indicate the *type* of file, such as a data file or a text file. Extensions also help to distinguish closely related files; for example, a personal letters file as opposed to a business letters file.

When MS-DOS stores a file on a disk, it automatically stores the file's filename and extension in an area of the disk called the *file directory*. To view filenames and extensions, insert one of your backup MS-DOS diskettes in drive A and enter **dir /w**:

```
A>dir /w


 Volume in drive A has no label
 Volume Serial Number is 203D-10CC
 Directory of  A:\

COMMAND  COM  ASSIGN   COM  ATTRIB   EXE  BASIC   COM  BASICA  COM
COMP     COM  DEBUG    COM  DISKCOMP COM  EDLIN   COM  FILESYS EXE
FIND     EXE  IFSFUNC  EXE  JOIN     EXE  LABEL   COM  MEM     EXE
MODE     COM  MORE     COM  MORTGAGE BAS  SHARE   EXE  SORT    EXE
SUBST    EXE  TREE     COM  XCOPY    EXE
        23 File(s)       30208 bytes free

A>
```

The command **dir /w** directs MS-DOS to display the filenames and extensions of the files in the current directory of the default drive. The concept of current directory is discussed in the following chapter. The default drive in the example is drive A (as indicated by the command line prompt **A>**). The display that you obtain may differ somewhat from that presented above.

The first filename and extension is `COMMAND COM`, the second `ASSIGN COM`, and so on. The last line indicates that there are 23 files in the directory and that the diskette has 30208 bytes of storage space that are free.

Note on Examples

Because this chapter's purpose is to introduce the fundamental concept of MS-DOS files, all of the examples presented assume that MS-DOS is not yet installed on a hard disk. The MS-DOS command line is represented by `A>`, indicating that drive A is the current drive. Of course, the examples assume that you have made backup copies of your MS-DOS system diskettes. Refer to chapter 1 for details on making backups.

MS-DOS has specific rules for naming files. Each filename in the same directory must be unique. In other words, the filename *and* its extension cannot be the same as another filename and extension already in use in that directory. For example, you cannot give the name "letters.per" to two files; MS-DOS becomes confused and does not know which "letters.per" file you are referring to. You can, however, use the same filename but different extensions. For example, you could name your file of business letters "letters.bus" and your file of personal letters "letters.per". A few filenames are reserved by MS-DOS for its exclusive use. These are the names of MS-DOS program files and commands and the abbreviations for devices (such as "PRN" for printer). Check your user's guide for a list of reserved names. Filenames must take the form:

filename.*extension*

The *filename* is one to eight characters in length. The *extension*, which is optional, is one to three characters in length. A period (.) is used to separate the filename from the extension. If you accidentally enter a filename with more than eight characters and you do not enter an extension, MS-DOS will automatically place a period after the eighth character, use the next three characters as the extension, and disregard the remaining characters. If you enter a filename with more than eight characters and you also enter an extension, MS-DOS signals an error. If your extension has more than three characters, MS-DOS ignores the extra characters.

MS-DOS allows only certain characters to be used in filenames and extensions. These are:

letters of the alphabet
numbers 0 through 9
special characters $ # & @ ! % ( ) - { } ' _ ' ^ ~

MS-DOS treats uppercase and lowercase letters alike, so you may use any combination of capital and lowercase letters in filenames and extensions. In this book, filenames discussed in the text will be lowercased and enclosed in quotation marks (the "letters.per" file).

File Specifications

In order for MS-DOS to work with a file, it must know the file's filename and filename extension. In addition, it must know which disk drive contains the file. A disk drive is specified by a letter, called a *drive designator*. The first disk drive is specified by a drive designator of "A:" and is called "drive A." The second drive has a drive designator of "B:" and is called "drive B." A hard disk is usually specified as "C:" and is called "drive C."

The drive designator combines with the filename and the extension to form the *file specification*, or *filespec* for short. The filespec contains the drive designator followed by the filename and filename extension (if there is an extension). For example, if a file with the filename "instruct" and the extension "txt" were located on disk drive A, its complete filespec would be "A:instruct.txt" (or "a:instruct.txt").

Copying a File

One of the most frequently performed tasks of an operating system is the copying of computer files stored on floppy disks. An experienced user routinely copies all valuable computer files at regular intervals. That way, if one copy of the file is damaged or destroyed, a backup is available.

The procedures for copying a file differ slightly, depending on whether your system has one or two floppy disk drives. The following sections will first describe the procedure for copying a file with a two-drive system and then describe the procedure for a one-drive system.

In copying a file, the first drive is called the *source drive* and the second the *target drive*. As you may recall from chapter 1, the same terminology is used for disks. The disk containing the original file is the *source disk,* while the disk receiving the copy is the *target disk.*

Two-Drive Systems

To copy a file using a two-drive system, insert the source diskette (the diskette containing the file to be copied) in drive A. Place the formatted target diskette in drive B. (Refer to chapter 1 for help in formatting a diskette.)

In the example shown here, the file "instruct.txt" is on the diskette in drive A. To copy the file onto the diskette in drive B, type the word **copy**, then type the filespec of the file to be copied, and finally type the filespec of the copy:

```
A>copy a:instruct.txt b:instruct.txt
```

Press Enter. The copying process will start, and MS-DOS will display a message when the copying is completed.

```
1 File(s) copied
A>
```

Hard Drive Systems

When copying a file to a hard drive, you need to use the drive letter of the hard drive in the filespec of the copy. For example, to copy "instruct.txt" from drive A to a hard disk with drive letter C, enter the following command

A>*copy a:instruct.txt c:instruct.txt*

You may leave out the drive letter specifier for the source file if the source is only the default disk drive. Similarly, you may leave out the drive letter specifier of the target if the default drive is to be the target.

One-Drive Systems

To copy a file using a one-drive system, insert the source diskette into the system drive. Type **copy**, then type the filespec of the file to be copied, and finally type the filespec of the copy:

A>*copy a:instruct.txt b:instruct.txt*

Press Enter. MS-DOS will store as much of the file in memory as possible. The following message will then be displayed:

```
Insert diskette for drive B: and strike
any key when ready
```

This is MS-DOS's way of telling you that the system drive is now *logical* drive B (see the DEVICE command in Part 3 for a discussion of physical and logical drives). It is also your cue to insert into the system drive the formatted target diskette (the diskette on which the file copy will be written). Refer to chapter 1 if you need help in formatting diskettes.

Note: The preceding message may be displayed before the red light on the disk drive goes off. If so, wait until the light goes off before you change diskettes.

Once the diskette for logical drive B is in place, press any key to continue the operation. MS-DOS will write to the disk that portion of the file previously stored in memory. If the memory is not large enough to hold the entire file, MS-DOS will display the following message:

```
Insert diskette for drive A: and strike
any key when ready
```

This message says that the system drive is now logical drive A. Remove the target diskette and insert the diskette containing the original file. Strike any key. Continue to follow MS-DOS's instructions. Remember that the original file is on the diskette "for drive A" and the copy is on the diskette "for drive B." MS-DOS will tell you when the copy procedure has been completed:

```
1 File(s) copied
A>
```

Once the file has been copied, you may use the COMP command (see Part 3) to verify that an accurate copy of the file has been made.

Wildcards

Wildcards are special symbols (sometimes called *global characters*) that are used to stand for one or more specific characters in a filename or extension. MS-DOS provides two wildcard symbols that you may use to specify files in MS-DOS commands—the question mark and the asterisk.

The question mark (?) is used to represent a *single character* in a filename or extension, while the asterisk (*) is used to represent a *group of characters* in a filename or extension. You will find wildcards are very handy, especially in the DIR, COPY, ERASE, and RENAME commands, because these commands frequently refer to groups of files.

The "?" Wildcard

Imagine that you have a diskette containing several files, including these four:

        last.txt
        list.txt
        lost.txt
        lust.txt

Let's say that you wanted to copy each of these files. There are two ways you could accomplish this. You could use the COPY command four times, specifying a different file each time; or you could use COPY one time, using a wildcard character in the filespec. If you chose the second way, your command would look like this:

```
A>copy a:l?st.txt b:l?st.txt
```

The **?** in the second position of the filename indicates that the second character is wild. MS-DOS is instructed to execute the command on all files on the diskette in drive A that have an "l" as the first character in the filename, an "s" as the third character, a "t" as the fourth character, and a filename extension of ".txt". Any character in the second position is acceptable according to this command.

The "*" Wildcard

Using an "*" in a filename or filename extension tells MS-DOS that all characters in the position of the "*" are wild. In addition, all characters to the right of the "*" are wild. As an example, let's say that you want to refresh your memory regarding the files in the system diskette. In particular, you want to see which system files have a filename beginning with "f" and a filename extension of ".com". Insert your working system diskette in drive A and enter the following command (refer to Part 3 of this book for a complete discussion of DIR):

```
A>dir f*.com/w
FORMAT   COM           FDISK        COM
       2 File(s)                 84992 bytes free
```

MS-DOS interprets the filespec **f*.com** to mean any file that has a filename beginning with "f" and a filename extension of ".com". The **/w** simply directs MS-DOS to display only the filenames and directory names.

A filespec may contain more than one wildcard character. For example, "f*.com" is equivalent to f???????.com. In the following example, wildcards are used in the filespec to indicate that all the files on the diskette in drive A should be copied onto the diskette in drive B:

```
A>copy a:*.* b:*.*
```

Don't be afraid to experiment with wildcards in MS-DOS commands. They can be a tremendous timesaver once you are familiar with their use. A word of caution though: ***Make sure that you have backup copies of any important files before you start playing with wildcards***. It's very easy for even an experienced MS-DOS user to inadvertently wipe out many hours of work with a misplaced wildcard.

3

Directories, Paths, and Trees

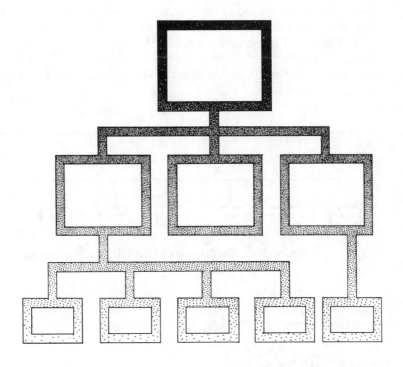

File Management
Setting Up a Hierarchical File System

Chapter 2 covered the basics of what a file is, how it is named, and the information that MS-DOS needs to know about a file in order to use it. Chapter 2 also explained some basic procedures for copying files. This chapter will discuss the way files are managed by MS-DOS.

If your computer has a hard disk, you may want to skim this chapter and chapter 2 before installing MS-DOS on your hard disk. Hard disk installation is discussed in chapter 1.

File Management

The basis of file management is the *file directory*. The file directory is an area on the disk that is set aside during the formatting process. The file directory serves as a table of contents for the files stored on the disk. For each file stored, there is a corresponding entry in the file directory.

Each entry in the file directory stores a filename and a filename extension. The entry also contains the time and date that the file was created or last modified, the file's size in bytes, and other information that MS-DOS needs in using the file. The structure of file directories is covered in much more detail in chapter 10.

Figure 3-1 illustrates a simple directory and file system. All of the files are on a single level relative to the file directory. Such an arrangement is called *nonhierarchical*. Versions of MS-DOS prior to 2.0 use a nonhierarchical file system.

Figure 3-1. Nonhierarchical file management system.

The single biggest change implemented in MS-DOS 2.0 was the introduction of a *hierarchical* file system. Such a system is essential in managing the large number of files stored on hard disks.

Hierarchical File Systems

It is not unusual for hard disks to store hundreds or even thousands of files. Handling such a large number of files requires a more efficient storage and retrieval system than that used by nonhierarchical systems.

MS-DOS 2.0 and subsequent versions use a hierarchical file system (figure 3-2). In this type of system, files and groups of files are divided into a series of levels, beginning with the file directory at the uppermost level. The file directory is called the *root directory* because all the other levels branch out from it. The file directory can contain the names of single files as well as

Figure 3-2. Single files and subdirectory.

other directories. These directories are called *subdirectories* and can themselves contain the names of files or other subdirectories. By grouping related files into their own directory, the time necessary to search for a particular file on a disk is shortened. Each succeeding level within the hierarchy is referenced relative to the root directory (see figure 3-3).

Figure 3-3. Hierarchical file management system.

When you use the DIR command to list the contents of the root directory, DOS will display both filenames and subdirectory names. For each file, the directory entry will show the filename and extension, the size of the file in bytes, and the time and date when the file was created or last modified. Files that are subdirectories are signified by the notation " < DIR >" for directory. MS-DOS will also show the total number of files (including subdirectories) and the number of free bytes remaining on the disk.

The number of entries that the root directory can hold is limited. On single-sided, 5¼-inch diskettes, the limit is 64 files and/or subdirectories. On double-sided, 5¼-inch diskettes, the limit is 112. On high density (1.2-Mbyte) 5¼-inch diskettes, the limit is 224. A 720-Kbyte, 3½-inch diskette has a limit of 112. A 1.4 Mbyte, 3½-inch diskette has a limit of 128 entries.

Note: From this point on, the word "directory" will refer to both a root directory and a subdirectory. Any comments that relate to one but not the other will be qualified.

Trees

The file arrangement used in MS-DOS 2.X, 3.X, and 4.X is described as *tree-structured*. In this case, however, the "tree" happens to be upside down, with the root (directory) at the top. Each branch coming out of the root corresponds to an entry, either a file or a subdirectory (a group of related files). Secondary branches arise from each subdirectory in level 1, tertiary branches arise from subdirectories in level 2, and so on.

This tree-structured arrangement allows each subdirectory and its entries to be treated as though there were no other data stored on the disk. This can make life much more tolerable when you are dealing with a hard disk containing several hundred files. Let's look at a typical example of the use of trees.

Suppose that you are using a word processing program to write a book. Each chapter in the book is stored as a file on a disk. Suppose that you also do some computer programming. On the same disk you store a program that you are writing. Finally, just to complicate things, suppose you also store on the disk a program and some data that you use in your business.

Figure 3-4 shows how you might structure these files. Notice that the root directory contains four entries: the MS-DOS file COMMAND.COM and three subdirectories named WRITE, PROGRAMS, and BUSINESS. The subdirectory WRITE itself contains three entries: a file named "wp.exe" and two subdirectories, LETTERS and BOOK.

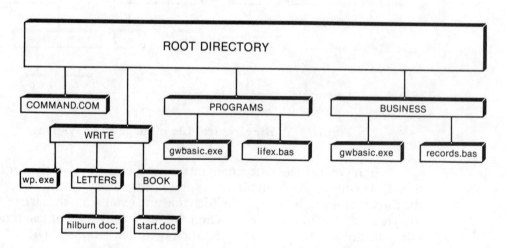

Figure 3-4. Tree-structured arrangement of files.

The subdirectory LETTERS has one entry: a file named "hilburn.doc". The subdirectory BOOK also has one entry: a file named "start.doc". The subdirectory PROGRAMS contains two files: "gwbasic.exe" and "lifex.bas"; as does the subdirectory BUSINESS: "gwbasic.exe" and "records.bas".

By structuring your data in this way, the files are separated into functional groups. For example, the subdirectory WRITE contains the word processing program ("wp.exe") and the documents that have been created by that program. These documents have been placed in separate subdirectories according to their subject matter. The subdirectory PROGRAMS contains the BASIC interpreter and one BASIC program. The subdirectory BUSINESS holds a second copy of the BASIC interpreter and a BASIC program used in business.

Setting Up a Hierarchical File System

This section will explain how the file structure shown in figure 3-4 was created. Along the way, it will discuss the commands used by MS-DOS to manage a hierarchical file system.

The examples presented show how to set up a file system on a hard disk with drive letter C. It is assumed that the hard disk has previously been partitioned and formatted (see chapter 1) for use by MS-DOS. The commands discussed here can also be used with floppy diskette files.

Paths

A *path* is the course that must be followed to get from one directory to another. For example, consider the subdirectory BOOK in figure 3-4. Suppose that you want to travel from the root directory to BOOK. What path would you take? Starting at the root directory, you would pass through the subdirectory WRITE and from there to the subdirectory BOOK.

In the same way, MS-DOS 2.X, 3.X, and 4.X find a file by taking a particular path to the directory containing that file. You tell MS-DOS which path to take by specifying the start of the path and the subdirectories to use. The path from the root directory to BOOK is:

ROOT DIRECTORY→WRITE→BOOK

This list of names is called a *path specifier.* When entering a path specifier in an MS-DOS command, use a backslash (\) to separate one directory from another. In entering the path specifier, do not enter "ROOT DIRECTORY". The root directory is represented by the first backslash. The path specifier from the root directory to BOOK is therefore:

\write\book

Creating a Subdirectory

With drive C as the default directory, enter the command **dir**. Your display screen will look something like this:

```
C>dir
```

```
Volume in drive C has no label
Directory of C:\

COMMAND  COM  25307   3-17-90   12:00p
        1 File(s)   10510200 bytes free
```

The line `Directory of C:\` tells you that MS-DOS is displaying the names of the entries in the root directory (\) of the disk in drive C. In this case, the root directory contains only one entry, the MS-DOS file COMMAND.COM.

Now we will begin expanding the directory to include some subdirectories. The MS-DOS command MKDIR (MaKe DIRectory) is used to create a subdirectory. Let's use MKDIR to create the three subdirectories WRITE, PROGRAMS, and BUSINESS.

Before we do that though, let's go over the rules for naming subdirectories, just in case you want to make up your own subdirectory names. Subdirectory names can be up to eight characters long, with an optional extension of three characters. Each subdirectory must have a name that does not match the name of any file or subdirectory contained in the same directory. The valid characters used in the name are the same as those for filenames.

To create a subdirectory, type **mkdir** (or **md** for short) and then type the path specifier of the subdirectory being created. In entering your command, you may omit the path if the new subdirectory will be entered in the *current directory*. The current directory is the directory in which you are now working. (We will discuss the current directory in more detail later in this section.)

Now we are ready to create the subdirectory WRITE. Type **mkdir** (or **md**) followed by a backslash to indicate that the subdirectory will be an entry in the root directory; then type the name of the new subdirectory:

```
C>mkdir \write
```

When you press Enter, MS-DOS will create the new subdirectory. In a similar fashion, you can create the subdirectories PROGRAMS and BUSINESS:

```
C>mkdir \programs
C>mkdir \business
```

Now let's enter the DIR command to see what MS-DOS has done:

```
C>dir
 Volume in drive C has no label
 Directory of C:\

COMMAND  COM   25307   3-17-90   12:00p
WRITE          <DIR>          9-17-90   11:42a
```

```
PROGRAMS      <DIR>      9-17-90   11:43a
BUSINESS      <DIR>      9-17-90   11:44a
         4 File(s)    10505080 bytes  free
```

If you are following along on your computer, the size of your COM-MAND.COM file may not be 25,307 bytes. The date/time stamps on your disk will certainly differ from those shown here. The important points are that three subdirectories have been created and that they are entered in the root directory. The subdirectories are identified by the label `<DIR>`. Notice that creating three subdirectories used up 5,120 bytes of disk space. (Compare the number of free bytes before and after the subdirectories were created.)

Changing the Current Directory

A path tells MS-DOS the route to take to a particular directory. If an MS-DOS command does not specify a path, MS-DOS will attempt to execute the command in the current directory. At any given time, each drive on the system has a current directory.

The MS-DOS command CHDIR (CHange DIRectory) is used to change a drive's current directory. To use CHDIR, type **chdir** (or **cd** for short) followed by the path specifier of the desired directory.

In this tutorial, the current directory on drive C is the root directory. Entering the CHDIR command without any specifiers causes MS-DOS to display the path specifier of the current directory. Type **chdir**:

```
C>chdir
C:\
```

The backslash means that the root directory is the current directory on drive C.

We can make WRITE the current directory by including the path specifier to WRITE in the CHDIR command:

```
C>chdir \write
```

The first directory in a path specifier may be omitted if it is the current directory. Since the preceding command was invoked while the root directory was the current directory, the command could have been entered as:

```
C>chdir write
```

To verify that WRITE is now the current directory, type **chdir** without a path specifier. MS-DOS will display the path to the current directory:

```
C>chdir
C:\WRITE
```

A Word about Parents

All subdirectories are entries in another directory. WRITE, PROGRAMS, and BUSINESS are entries in the root directory. A directory is said to be the *parent directory* of the subdirectories that it contains as entries. The root directory is the parent directory of WRITE, PROGRAMS, and BUSINESS.

Putting Files into a Subdirectory

Now that WRITE is the current directory, let's put some files in it. We will start off by putting a copy of the file "wp.exe" in WRITE. This is done simply by making a copy of the file. Place a diskette with the file "wp.exe" in drive A and enter the following command:

```
C>copy a:wp.exe c:
```

A Typical Setup

A typical way to set up directories on a hard disk is to create a subdirectory named \DOS to store the MS-DOS utility files (such as FORMAT.COM, EDLIN.COM, and MORE.COM). Another subdirectory named \SYS is created to store the MS-DOS device drivers (such as VDISK.SYS and ANSI.SYS). Many users also put the MS-DOS files with the extension CPI in subdirectory \SYS. You may also want to create a subdirectory named \PRGMS to hold your application programs. You might want a separate subdirectory in \PRGMS for each application program. In general, minimizing the number of files in the hard disk's root directory makes navigation through the disk's contents much easier.

This command instructs MS-DOS to copy the file "wp.exe" to drive C. Since no paths were included in the command, MS-DOS will look for "wp.exe" in the current directory on drive A (in this case the root directory) and copy it to the current directory on drive C. WRITE is the current directory on drive C, so "wp.exe" will be copied into WRITE.

The MKDIR command can be used to create a subdirectory in WRITE. Recall that to use this command you must type **mkdir** (or **md**) followed by the path to the new subdirectory.

The current directory is WRITE, so the path to the subdirectory LETTERS (see figure 3-4) is WRITE\LETTERS. But, remember that the first directory in a path may be omitted when it is the current directory. Therefore, to create LETTERS, enter the following command:

```
C>mkdir letters
```

The subdirectory BOOK is created in the same way:

```
C>mkdir book
```

Now that we have established our three subdirectories, let's place some files in them. Notice that the subdirectory LETTERS in figure 3-4 contains the file "hilburn.doc". However, before we enter "hilburn.doc" in LETTERS, let's make LETTERS the current directory:

```
C>cd letters
```

Now place a diskette with the file "hilburn.doc" in drive A and enter:

```
C>copy a:hilburn.doc c:
```

Next we will copy the file "start.doc" into the subdirectory BOOK. Let's begin by making BOOK the current directory. Recall that the current directory is LETTERS. The path from LETTERS is WRITE\BOOK. But entering the command "cd write\book" results in an **Invalid directory** message. The reason for this is that WRITE is the parent directory of LETTERS. The parent of a directory is represented in MS-DOS commands by two periods (..). The path specifier from LETTERS to BOOK is therefore "..\book". To make BOOK the current directory, enter the following command:

```
C>cd ..\book
```

Note that this command could also have been entered as "cd \write \book".

Now we can copy "start.doc" into BOOK by inserting a diskette with "start.doc" in drive A and entering:

```
C>copy a:start.doc c:
```

Before going any further, let's step back and see what we have accomplished. First, though, we will make WRITE the current directory. WRITE is the parent directory of the current directory (BOOK), so we can make WRITE the current directory by entering:

```
C>cd ..
```

Note that this command could also have been entered as "cd \write".

To make sure that WRITE is now the current directory, type **cd** without a path specifier. MS-DOS will display the path from the root directory to the current directory:

```
C>cd
C:\WRITE
```

Let's use the DIR command to display the contents of the current directory:

```
C>dir

 Volume in drive C has no label
 Directory of   C:\WRITE

 .              <DIR>      9-17-90    11:42a
 ..             <DIR>      9-17-90    11:42a
 WP      EXE    72960      6-20-85     5:02p

 LETTERS        <DIR>      9-17-90     2:00p
 BOOK           <DIR>      9-17-90     2:00p
         5 File(s)     10262392 bytes free
```

Notice that the first two lines contain periods rather than names. The single period (.) in line 1 designates the current directory. The two periods in line 2 represent the parent directory of the current directory. The next three lines show the file and subdirectories that have been entered in WRITE.

Completing the remainder of the file structure shown in figure 3-4 is simply a matter of repeating some of our previous steps. First, the root directory is made the current directory:

```
C>cd \
```

Then the subdirectories PROGRAMS and BUSINESS are created as entries in the root directory:

```
C>md programs
C>md business
```

Next the current directory is changed to PROGRAMS. A diskette with the files "gwbasic.exe" and "lifex.bas" is placed in drive A, and the files are copied into PROGRAMS:

```
C>cd programs
C>copy a:gwbasic.exe c:
C>copy a:lifex.bas c:
```

The current directory is then changed to BUSINESS. A disk containing the files "gwbasic.exe" and "records.bas" is placed in drive A, and the files are copied into BUSINESS:

```
C>cd \business
C>copy a:gwbasic.exe c:
C>copy a:records.bas c:
```

This completes the construction of the directory and file structure shown in figure 3-4.

Looking at the Tree

As the number of files and subdirectories on a disk increases, the organization of the disk becomes more and more complex. TREE is an MS-DOS command that is used to construct a map of a disk's tree structure. To demonstrate this command, place your working system diskette in drive A, making sure that the file TREE.COM is on the working system diskette. Enter the command **a:tree c:/f**. This command tells MS-DOS to display the tree of directories found on fixed (hard) disk C. The /f switch directs MS-DOS to list the files on the fixed disk as well.

```
C>a:tree c:/f

TREE: Full-disk sub-directory listing - Version 3.30
Copyright (C)1987 XYZ Data Systems, Inc.

C:\COMMAND.COM                              17664 bytes
C:\WRITE
C:         \WP.EXE                          72960 bytes
C:         \LETTERS
C:                 \HILBURN.DOC              4608 bytes
           1 file(s)
C:         \BOOK
C:               \STARTING.DOC              15360 bytes
     3 file(s)
C:\PROGRAMS
C:         \GWBASIC.EXE                     57344 bytes
C:         \LIFEX.BAS                        7808 bytes
     2 file(s)
C:\BUSINESS
C:         \GWBASIC.EXE                     57344 bytes
C:         \RECORDS.BAS                      9088 bytes
     2 file(s)
     4 file(s)
                    10109816 bytes free
                    10592256 bytes total
End of listing
```

Verify for yourself that this listing contains all the information in figure 3-4. Notice that it also contains the size of each file on the disk. In PC-DOS 4.0, you can specify the listing of a specific directory and its subdirectories; to do so, follow the drive letter with the pathname for the directory.

Removing a Subdirectory

The MS-DOS command RMDIR (ReMove DIRectory), RD for short, is used to remove a subdirectory from a disk. To use RMDIR, type **rmdir** (or **rd**) and then type the path to the subdirectory. However, before you can remove the subdirectory, you must empty it of any files and/or subdirectories that it contains.

Suppose that you want to remove the subdirectory BOOK from the hard disk (figure 3-4). The first step is to erase all the files entered in BOOK. This can be accomplished by using the MS-DOS command ERASE and the wildcard *.* (see chapter 2). After you enter the following command, MS-DOS will ask if you are sure that you want to erase all the files in the specified subdirectory:

```
C>erase \write\book *.*
Are you sure? (Y/N) y
```

Since you responded "yes," MS-DOS erased the files in BOOK, and the subdirectory can now be removed by entering:

```
C>rmdir \write\book
```

The PATH Command

An *executable file* is a set of directions that the computer executes in order to perform a specific task. An executable file may be an application program (such as a word processing program), an external MS-DOS command (such as TREE), or a batch file (see chapter 5). When you enter the name of an executable file, MS-DOS looks for the file in the current directory. The PATH command is used to tell MS-DOS where to look for an executable file that is not in the current directory.

To use the command, type **path** followed by the path(s) that you want MS-DOS to follow in its search for the executable file. If you want to specify more than one path, separate the paths with semicolons. If you enter PATH without any parameters, MS-DOS will display the command paths that were set the last time the PATH command was used. If you enter PATH followed by just a semicolon, MS-DOS will cancel the command paths that were set by the previous PATH command. The following example sets up a DOS search path so that the operating system searches for files in the subdirectories C:\DOS, C:\SYS, and C:\PRGMS:

```
C>path c:\dos;c:\sys;c:\prgms
```

Using the Search Path

Pretend that you are using a word processing program to write several different types of documents. Let's say that you are writing a computer book, a novel, personal letters, business letters, save-the-whales letters, and miscellaneous letters. Let's also say that you are a very prolific writer. You have already written 30 chapters in both the computer book and the novel, and you have a total of 400 letters that are evenly divided among the personal, business, whale, and miscellaneous categories. Each of your chapters and each of your letters is saved as one file on your hard disk. That's a total of 460 files just for your word processor. How can you use MS-DOS to organize these files?

There is no single right way to organize any hard disk system. The best approach is to try something out, see if you like it, and change it if you don't. Here is one way you might organize your files. Create a separate subdirectory for each of the different categories of word processing documents. These subdirectories will be entered in the root directory of the hard disk. Into each subdirectory enter the corresponding documents. Finally, enter a copy of the file "wp.exe" (the word processing program) in the root directory. Figure 3-5 shows how the files might be structured on your imaginary hard disk.

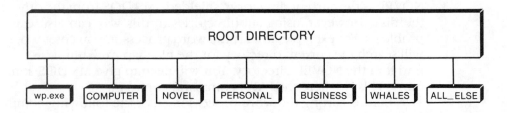

Figure 3-5. Organizing files by grouping them into subdirectories.

In a typical computer work session, you might sit down to do some work on your novel. You might want to quickly review some of the already completed chapters and then revise your latest chapter. For the time being, you aren't concerned about your 100 save-the-whales letters or anything else on the hard disk that is not part of your novel.

First, make NOVEL the current directory on drive C:

```
C>cd \novel
C>
```

Now, if you want a list of the chapters that you have written, all you have to do is type **dir/w**, the MS-DOS command for displaying a directory of filenames. Only the files in the NOVEL subdirectory will be displayed. (See Part 3 for a discussion of DIR.)

```
C>dir /w

Volume in drive C is HARD_DISK
Directory of C:\novel

  .           ..               CHAPT01 DOC CHAPT02 DOC CHAPT03 DOC
CHAPT04 DOC CHAPT05 DOC CHAPT06 DOC CHAPT07 DOC CHAPT08 DOC
CHAPT09 DOC CHAPT10 DOC CHAPT11 DOC CHAPT12 DOC CHAPT13 DOC
CHAPT14 DOC CHAPT15 DOC CHAPT16 DOC CHAPT17 DOC CHAPT18 DOC
CHAPT19 DOC CHAPT20 DOC CHAPT21 DOC CHAPT22 DOC CHAPT23 DOC
CHAPT24 DOC CHAPT25 DOC CHAPT26 DOC CHAPT27 DOC CHAPT28 DOC
CHAPT29 DOC CHAPT30 DOC
       32 File(s)  352224 bytes free

C>
```

If you want to copy all the chapters of your novel onto a diskette in drive B, simply type **copy *.doc b:**. Only the chapters of your novel will be copied; the other files on the disk will not.

The preceding example showed you how designating the subdirectory NOVEL as the current directory "shielded" MS-DOS from the other files on the disk. However, using subdirectories in this way can also cause some problems. For example, to start the word processor, you enter **wp**. MS-DOS will search the current directory for the file "wp.exe" but won't be able to find it in the NOVEL directory. You will need to give MS-DOS some directions. This is where the PATH command comes in.

Before starting the word processor, enter the following command:

```
C>path c:\write
```

This command tells MS-DOS that if it can't find an executable file in the current directory, it should look in the directory C:\WRITE. MS-DOS will now be able to load and execute the word processing program when you enter "wp".

The APPEND Command

PATH will direct MS-DOS only to executable files. Executable files have a filename extension of COM, EXE, or BAT. PATH will not direct application programs to data files. For example, many programs come with on-line help files. If the program is running and it needs to access a help file, the information provided by PATH is of no value since the help file is not executable.

The APPEND command, implemented in MS-DOS 3.2, 3.3, and 4.X, is designed to eliminate this problem. APPEND is used just like PATH. For example, the following command is valid:

```
append c:\programs
```

This command tells MS-DOS to look in the directory PROGRAMS when searching for both executable and nonexecutable files.

APPEND is a very valuable command, and it is discussed more thoroughly in Part 3 of this book. Part 3 also discusses some annoying bugs in APPEND that you should know about before using this command.

4

MS-DOS Batch Files

Computers are useful tools because they are capable of performing repetitive tasks without getting bored. Computers can maintain the same level of efficiency regardless of how many times they carry out the same task. Computer users, on the other hand, become bored rather easily when performing repetitive tasks, and a bored computer user tends to be inefficient and error-prone.

One repetitive task that computer users are often faced with is entering a series of commands over and over again. If you find yourself in this situation, don't despair, because MS-DOS offers a way out. It allows you to take a series of commands and store them in a special kind of file called a *batch file*. This "batch" of MS-DOS commands can then be used over and over again, always producing the same result. This chapter will explain batch files and show you some MS-DOS features that can be used in conjunction with batch files. (See appendix C for examples of batch files used to implement a menu-driven disk maintenance system.)

What Is a Batch File?

A *batch file* is a text file (ASCII file) that contains a sequence of MS-DOS commands. The rules for naming a batch file are the same as those for other files, with the exception that a batch file must have a filename extension of .BAT (BATch).

Executing the commands in a batch file is easy. You simply give MS-DOS a *start command* by typing the filename of the batch file and pressing the Enter key. When you enter the name of the batch file, MS-DOS searches the disk in the specified (or default) drive for the file. If MS-DOS does not find the file in the drive's current directory, the search is extended to any directories specified by the PATH and APPEND commands. (Both of these commands are discussed in Part 3.)

When MS-DOS locates the batch file, the first command in the file is loaded into memory, displayed on the screen, and executed. This process is repeated until all of the commands in the batch file have been executed.

Execution of a batch file can be halted at any time by pressing the Ctrl-Break key combination. If you press Ctrl-Break, MS-DOS will ask you the following question:

```
Terminate batch job (Y/N)? _
```

If you enter "Y", execution of the batch file will be stopped and the MS-DOS prompt will be displayed. Entering "N" will stop only the command currently being executed. Execution will continue with the next command in the batch file.

Creating a Batch File

You can create a batch file by using a word processor to create an ASCII (plain text) file. Refer to your word processor's manual under "ASCII files" or "DOS text files" for details. You can also use EDLIN, the MS-DOS text editor, which is discussed in chapter 8. A third way to create batch files is by entering the text directly from the command line. This method will now be discussed.

The MS-DOS device name for the keyboard is "CON" (CONsole). (MS-DOS device names are discussed in chapter 6.) To copy the input from the keyboard to a file, type **copy con:**, followed by the filename and filename extension of the file being created. For example, to create a batch file named "sample.bat", enter:

```
C>copy con: sample.bat
```

Then enter the MS-DOS commands that will make up the batch file. After entering the last command, press Ctrl-Z (or press the F6 function key) and then press Enter. The file will be stored on the disk in the default drive with the name "sample.bat". If there is an existing file named "sample.bat" in the current directory of the default drive, it will be replaced by the new file.

Batch files can be used to make automatic backup copies of important files. The command "xcopy *.doc a: /m" instructs MS-DOS to make a copy of all files with an extension of DOC that have the archive attribute set. The command also instructs MS-DOS to clear each file's attribute after the copy is made. As is discussed in chapter 10 and Part 3, the operating system sets a file's archive attribute each time the file is modified. Therefore, the effect of "xcopy *.doc a: /m" is to copy those DOC files in the current directory that have been modified since they were last copied. This handy command can be combined with the command for starting a word processor batch file:

```
C>copy con c:\batch\write.bat
wp
xcopy *.doc a: /m
^Z        ←press Ctrl-Z and Enter

C>
```

The listing creates a batch file named "write.bat" and stores it in directory C:\BATCH. The batch file is executed by entering **write** at the MS-DOS command line. The DOS search path should contain "c:\batch" so that "write" will start, regardless of which directory is current.

The batch files begin by executing the "wp" command. This starts the word processor. The command assumes that the DOS search path contains the directory holding the word processor's files. Of course, the command also assumes that "wp" starts the word processor. You will need to modify this if your word processor is started with another command.

The batch file is set up so that the command "xcopy *.doc a: /m" is automatically executed when the word processor program terminates. All of the modified document files (assumed to have the extension DOC) are copied to the current directory of the diskette in drive A. Thus "write.bat" provides an automatic backup facility for word processing document files.

Replaceable Parameters

Batch file commands may contain one or more *replaceable parameters*. A parameter is a command item that gives additional information to MS-DOS, such as the name of the file on which the command is to be performed. A *replaceable* parameter is a variable that is replaced with a string of characters (such as a filename). A batch file replaceable parameter is written as a percentage sign (%) followed by a single digit. Up to ten different replaceable parameters may be included in a batch file. You specify the character string that is to be substituted for each replaceable parameter when the batch file is called up in the batch file start command.

Substitution of character strings for the replaceable variables takes place according to the order in which the character strings are included in the start command. The first string is substituted for the replaceable variable %1, the second string is substituted for %2, and so on. MS-DOS automatically substitutes the file specification of the batch file for the replaceable variable %0.

Replaceable variables increase the flexibility of batch files. As an example, we will create a batch file with the DOS command TYPE. TYPE is used to view a text file's contents. One problem with TYPE is that if the text file is large, the contents will scroll off the screen before you have a chance to view it. You can overcome this problem by "piping" the output of TYPE to the MS-DOS *filter* named MORE. Piping and filters are discussed in chapter 6, but basically what happens is that when you pipe output into MORE, the output is displayed one screenful at a time. Therefore, the command "type bigfile.txt | more" will display the contents of "bigfile.txt" one screenful at a time (the "|" symbol creates the pipe).

We can put this command in a batch file. Let us call it "display.bat":

```
C>copy con c:\batch\display.bat
type bigfile.txt | more
^Z

C>
```

Now the command "display" will display "bigfile.txt" one screenful at a time. In order for the batch file to operate correctly, either the APPEND search path must contain the directory storing "bigfile.txt", or the file must be in the current directory. The batch file also assumes that the directory holding the file MORE.COM (an external DOS file) is contained in the DOS search path.

A major limitation of "display.bat" is that it can only be used to display "bigfile.txt". The batch file can be modified, using replaceable parameters, so that it can display any text file:

```
C>copy con c:\batch\display.bat
type %1 ¦ more
^Z


C>
```

Now the command to start the batch file is "display *filename*" where *filename* is the complete filename (filename and filename extension, separated by a period) of any text file. When the batch file executes, the filename is substituted for replaceable parameter %1 and the file's contents are displayed one screenful at a time.

Wildcards and Replaceable Variables

The character strings included in a batch file start command can include the MS-DOS wildcards ? and *. When a string containing a wildcard is specified for a replaceable variable, the batch file command containing the variable is executed one time for each file that matches the string. Consider the following batch file:

```
C>copy con: c:\batch\display2.bat
copy %1 con:
^Z

        1 File(s) copied
```

This batch file copies a file (represented by the replaceable parameter %1) to the display screen (con). The file to be copied is specified in the start command. When the specified file is found, its contents are displayed on the screen.

Notice that this file has been given the name "display2.bat". If the file had been named "display.bat", it would have written over the existing file named "display.bat".

Start the batch file with the command **display2 *.txt**. MS-DOS will search the current directory for each file matching the wildcard ("*.txt") and display each file's contents. Please refer to chapter 2 for more information on the use of wildcards.

Occasionally, one of the filenames in a batch file will contain a percentage sign. To prevent MS-DOS from confusing the filename with a replaceable parameter, type the sign two times when listing the file. For example, if you want to include the file "hiho%.txt" in a batch file, it should be listed as "hiho%%.txt".

PAUSE

The PAUSE command can be used in a batch file when you want to temporarily suspend execution of the batch file. When MS-DOS encounters PAUSE, it ceases execution of the batch file and displays the following message:

```
Strike a key when ready...
```

Pressing any key, except the Ctrl-C combination, will resume execution of the batch file.

Pressing Ctrl-C causes MS-DOS to display the message:

```
Abort batch job (Y/N)? _
```

Entering "Y" terminates batch file execution. Entering "N" resumes execution of the batch file.

As you will see in the next example, the PAUSE command can be used to allow you time to change disks during batch file execution. The following batch file automatically makes two copies of a file. The original file, the first copy, and the second copy can each be assigned any valid filename and filename extension that you wish. The two copies will be on different disks. The batch file will pause after making the first copy so that a second disk can be put in drive A:

```
C>copy con: c:\batch\copytwo.bat*
wp.exe
copy %1 a:%2
pause
copy %1 a:%3
^Z

        1 File(s) copied
```

To execute this batch file, type **copytwo**, followed in order by the filename and filename extension of the file to be copied, the filename and filename extension of the first copy, and the filename and filename extension of the second copy. Execution of the batch file begins when you press Enter:

```
C>copytwo new.doc old1.doc old2.doc

C>WP.EXE
```

This command loads and executes the word processor. When control is returned to MS-DOS, execution of the batch file continues:

```
C>COPY NEW.DOC A:OLD1.DOC
        1 File(s) copied

C>PAUSE
Strike any key when ready ...5

C>COPY NEW.DOC A:OLD2.DOC
        1 File(s) copied
```

Again, notice that the string characters in the start command replaced the variables in the batch file. After the first copy ("old1.doc") is made, the PAUSE command temporarily halts batch file execution. This allows you to put a new disk in the A drive. Batch file execution continues when a key (the "5" in this case) is pressed. The file is copied a second time ("old2.doc"), completing execution of the batch file.

The PAUSE command may also be used to display messages. When PAUSE is entered in a batch file, it can be followed by a character string. The string may be up to 121 characters long. The string will be displayed when the batch file is executed:

```
C>copy con: copytwo.bat
wp.exe
copy %1 a:%2
pause put disk number2 in drive a
copy %1 a:%3
^Z
        1 File(s) copied
```

The only difference between this batch file and the one in the previous example is that a message will be displayed when the PAUSE command is executed:

```
C>COPY NEW.DOC A:OLD1.DOC
        1 File(s) copied

C>PAUSE PUT DISK NUMBER 2 IN DRIVE A
Strike any key when ready ... 5
```

```
C>COPY NEW.DOC A:OLD2.DOC
        1 File(s) copied
```

REM

The REM (REMark) command can be used to display a message during the execution of a batch file. Enter **rem** in the batch file, followed by the message that will be displayed. The message can be up to 123 characters long. For example, enter the following:

```
C>copy con: copytwo.bat
wp.exe
rem making copy number 1
copy %1 a:%2
pause put disk number 2 in drive a
rem making copy number 2

copy %1 a:%3
^Z
        1 File(s) copied
```

The REM commands will help you follow the batch file's execution:

```
C>REM MAKING COPY NUMBER 1

C>COPY NEW.DOC A:OLD1.DOC
        1 File(s) copied

C>PAUSE PUT DISK NUMBER 2 IN DRIVE A
Strike any key when ready ...5

C>REM MAKING COPY NUMBER 2

C>COPY NEW.DOC A:OLD2.DOC
        1 File(s) copied
```

If the REM message includes any of the symbols "¦", "<", or ">", enclose the entire message in quotation marks, as in the following:

```
C>rem "dir > foo"
```

This will prevent MS-DOS from getting confused about the role of the special symbol(s). Each of these symbols is discussed fully in the following chapter.

ECHO

As you have already seen, under normal circumstances MS-DOS displays the commands in a batch file on the screen immediately before it executes them. With the ECHO command, you can control whether or not the commands are displayed.

To use ECHO in a batch file, type **echo**, followed by either **on** or **off**. ECHO ON causes MS-DOS commands to be displayed in the normal fashion. ECHO OFF suppresses the display of all MS-DOS commands including REM commands. However, ECHO OFF does not suppress any messages that are produced while commands are being executed.

If there is no ECHO command in a file, the default state is ECHO ON. ECHO is automatically turned ON when a batch file is terminated. Entering ECHO without any parameters causes MS-DOS to display the current ECHO state (ON or OFF). The following batch file demonstrates the use of ECHO:

```
C>copy con: c:\batch\example1.bat
rem this message will be displayed
rem since echo is on
echo off                                    ←ECHO is turned off
rem this message will not be displayed
rem since echo is now off
echo                                        ←ECHO state is displayed
echo on                                     ←ECHO is turned on
rem echo is back on
echo                                        ←ECHO state is displayed
^Z
          1 File(s) copied

C>example1

C>REM THIS MESSAGE WILL BE DISPLAYED

C>REM SINCE ECHO IS ON

C>ECHO OFF
ECHO is off

C>REM ECHO IS BACK ON

C>ECHO
ECHO is on
```

In the preceding example, the first two REM commands are displayed, since ECHO is initially in the default ON state. The third command in the batch file turns ECHO OFF, so the next two REM commands are not displayed. The sixth command (ECHO) verifies that the ECHO state is OFF. The seventh command then turns ECHO back ON, and the final REM command is displayed. The last command in the file (ECHO) verifies that ECHO is back ON.

If a message is entered in a batch file following ECHO, the message will be displayed regardless of the ECHO state:

```
C>copy con: c:\batch\example2.bat
echo off
rem this message will not be displayed
echo but this one will be
echo on
rem this will be displayed
echo so will this ... twice
^Z
        1 File(s) copied

C>example2

C>ECHO OFF
BUT THIS ONE WILL BE

C>REM THIS WILL BE DISPLAYED

C>ECHO SO WILL THIS ... TWICE
SO WILL THIS ... TWICE
```

The first command in this batch file turns ECHO OFF. With ECHO OFF, the first REM command is not displayed. The third command in the file is an ECHO command. Since ECHO is OFF, the command is not displayed, but the message within the ECHO command (**THIS WILL BE DISPLAYED**) *is* displayed. The fourth command in the file turns ECHO ON so that the following REM command is displayed. The final command in the file is an ECHO command. Since ECHO is ON, this command is displayed, and then the message within the command is displayed again.

Using ECHO to Send a Blank Line to the Screen

Often the text on a display screen is easier to read if it is occasionally interspersed with a blank line. With this in mind, it would be nice if ECHO could be used to send a blank line to the screen. Unfortunately, no simple way exists to do this for all versions of MS-DOS.

The command "ECHO " (ECHO followed by two spaces) will send a blank line to the screen under MS-DOS 2.X, but not 3.X or 4.X. The command "ECHO." (ECHO followed by a period) will send a blank line to the screen under 3.X and 4.X, but not 2.X. You have to be tricky if you want something that works under both versions.

The command "ECHO ^H" (ECHO followed by a space and a Ctrl-H character) will send a blank line to the screen under 2.X, 3.X, and 4.X. This method requires that the ANSI.SYS device driver (chapter 9) be installed. Many word processors allow you to place control characters in a text file. If you do not have a word processor with this capability, use your word processor to enter "ECHO *". Then use DEBUG (chapter 15) to replace the * with a Ctrl-H character. Ctrl-H is the same as the backspace character (ASCII value 008).

Suppressing ECHO OFF

MS-DOS 3.3 and 4.X allow you to suppress the display of a line in a batch file by preceding the line with an "at" character (@). One place where this is useful is in suppressing the display ECHO OFF at the start of a batch file. As an example, no display is generated from the following batch file:

```
@echo off
rem this is a test
```

Without the @, the ECHO OFF command will be displayed.

Those using MS-DOS 3.2 or earlier versions can employ a trick to make it appear as though ECHO OFF is not displayed. To begin, you must have ANSI.SYS installed as the keyboard device driver. (See chapter 9 for an explanation of how to do this.) Then, start your batch file with the following two lines:

```
echo off
echo ^[[s^[[1A^[[K^[[u
```

Note that each ^[is a single escape character, not two separate characters. Most word processors allow you to place escape characters in a text file. You can also use DEBUG (chapter 15) to replace dummy characters with escape characters (escape characters have ASCII value 1BH). If you refer to table 9-1, you will see that the second ECHO command is a sequence of instructions for ANSI.SYS. The screen device driver is instructed to:

^[[s	Save the current position of the cursor.
^[[1A	Move the cursor up one line.
^[K	Erase from the cursor to the end of the line.
^[[	Restore the cursor to its original position.

In this way, "echo off" is displayed on the screen but is erased before it can be read.

GOTO

The GOTO command is used to transfer control within a batch file. GOTO directs the batch file to jump to a labeled line within the batch file. A *line label* in a batch file consists of a colon (:) followed by up to eight characters. For example, enter the following:

```
C>copy con: example3.bat
rem this is the first line
rem this is the second line
goto four
rem this is the third line
:four
rem this is the fourth line
^Z
        1 File(s) copied

C>example3

C>REM THIS IS THE FIRST LINE
C>REM THIS IS THE SECOND LINE

C>GOTO FOUR

C>REM THIS IS THE FOURTH LINE
```

The first two commands in the batch file are executed. Execution then jumps to the :four label and continues with the final command in the batch file.

The label in a GOTO command can be a replaceable variable. This allows the execution of the batch file to jump to a line that is determined by a parameter included in the batch file start command. The following example shows how this works:

```
C>copy con: example3.bat
goto %1
:one
rem this is one
goto finish
:two
rem this is two
goto finish
:three
rem this is three
```

```
:finish
^Z
        1 File(s) copied

C>example3 three

C>GOTO THREE

C>REM THIS IS THREE
```

When this batch file is called up, the character string `three` is included in the start command. When the first command in the batch file is executed, `THREE` replaces the variable `%1`. Execution then jumps to the label `:three`. The REM command (`this is three`) is executed. The final line in the batch file is another line label. Line labels are not displayed during batch file execution.

IF

You can use the IF command to create commands in a batch file that will be executed if a specified condition is true. There are three types of conditions that IF can test: IF EXIST, IF String1==String2, and IF ERRORLEVEL.

IF EXIST

The first condition is called the EXIST condition. This conditional statement checks to see if a specified file exists. If the file exists, the condition has been met and the command will be executed. Consider the following command in a batch file:

```
if exist somefile.dat type somefile.dat
```

In executing this command, MS-DOS determines first if the file "somefile.dat" exists on the default drive. Then, if the file exists, MS-DOS executes the command to type the file. If "somefile.dat" does not exist, MS-DOS skips to the next batch command.

IF may be used to check for files on a drive other than the default. Simply precede the file specified in the IF command with the appropriate drive letter designator (such as A: or B:).

IF can check for files only in the current directory of a drive. To check a directory other than the current one, you must first make that directory the drive's current directory. Directories are discussed in chapter 3.

IF *String1==String2*

The second type of condition that may be tested by an IF statement is whether two character strings are identical. Consider the following batch file:

```
C>copy con: example4.bat
echo off
if %1==roses goto roses
if %1==candy goto candy
if %1==perfume goto perfume
echo you are in big trouble
goto finish
:roses
echo you sent roses. how thoughtful.
goto finish
:candy
echo you sent candy. how sweet.
goto finish
:perfume
echo you sent perfume. how romantic.
:finish
^Z
        1 File(s) copied

C>example4 perfume

C>ECHO OFF
YOU SENT PERFUME. HOW ROMANTIC.
```

Each of the IF statements compares a replaceable variable to a character string. Note that the IF statements use double equal signs (==). The string parameter that is included in the batch file start command replaces the variable in each IF statement. When the condition tested by an IF statement is true, the command contained in that statement is executed; in this case, execution branches to the PERFUME line label.

Notice that this batch file begins with the command `echo off`. This results in a screen display that is much less cluttered and easier to read.

IF ERRORLEVEL *n*

ERRORLEVEL is a system variable maintained by MS-DOS and used to monitor error conditions. Many of the MS-DOS commands set ERRORLEVEL if an error is encountered during execution of the command. The type of error encountered determines the value to which ERRORLEVEL is set. Application programs can also use DOS service functions 31H and 4CH to set ERRORLEVEL (see appendix A). The statement

IF ERRORLEVEL *n command*

tells MS-DOS that if ERRORLEVEL is equal to or greater than *n*, execute *command*. Refer to the discussion of the individual MS-DOS commands for details on how they set ERRORLEVEL.

IF NOT

An IF NOT statement can also test to see if a condition is false. Consider the following statement:

```
if not exist somefile.bak copy somefile.txt somefile.bak
```

This statement tests for the nonexistence of a file. If the file does not exist, the MS-DOS command within the IF statement is executed. IF NOT may be used to test any condition that may be tested with IF.

FOR

The FOR command allows a batch file command to be executed repeatedly on a set of specified parameters. The syntax (or rules) of FOR is a little involved, so let's begin with an example:

```
for %%a IN (file1 file2 file3) DO del %%a
```

As you can see from the example, a FOR statement begins with the word `for`, followed by a dummy variable. The dummy variable must be preceded by two percentage signs (`%%`). The variable is followed by the word `IN`, which must be entered in uppercase. `IN` is followed by the set of parameters on which the command is to operate. The set of parameters is usually a list of files. In our example, three files are specified as parameters. The set of parameters is followed by `DO`, which must also be entered in uppercase. `DO` is followed by the command that is to be executed. In the example, the command `del %%a` is executed three times, deleting sequentially the files `file1`, `file2`, and `file3`

A FOR statement is useful when you want to execute a command on a group of files that cannot be specified with wildcards. Suppose that three text files named "example1.bat", "program.txt", and "letter" existed on a disk and that you wanted a printed copy of each file. You could enter the command "copy example.bat prn", sit back and wait while the file is being printed, enter the same command for "program.txt", wait again, and then enter the command for "letter". If you do this, you will spend a lot of time sitting around, waiting for the computer to print each file.

The following command, included in a batch file, will perform the same task without all that wasted time:

```
for %%a IN (example.bat program.txt letter) DO copy %%a prn
```

The three text files will be printed, and you had to enter only one command.

FOR commands are not limited to use in batch files. They can be used as standard MS-DOS commands and will execute repeatedly on a set of parameters. When FOR commands are used in this fashion, the dummy variable is preceded by only one percentage sign.

Any file specified as a parameter in a FOR command must be located in the current directory of the specified or default disk drive. Current directories are discussed in chapter 3.

SHIFT

The SHIFT command allows you to specify more than ten parameters in a batch file start command. Recall that a batch file can normally contain up to ten replaceable variables. A list of character strings, included in the start command, sequentially replaces the variables as the batch file is executed. The first string specified replaces the variable %1, the second string replaces %2, and so on. The replaceable variable %0 is reserved for the file specification of the batch file.

The SHIFT command "shifts" the parameters one position to the left. The first parameter in the start command replaces %0, the second parameter replaces %1, and so on. Each time a SHIFT command is executed, the parameters shift one position to the left. The following batch file should help clarify the use of SHIFT:

```
C>copy con: example6.bat
echo off
echo %0 %1 %2 %3 %4 %5 %6 %7 %8 %9
shift
echo %0 %1 %2 %3 %4 %5 %6 %7 %8 %9
shift
echo %0 %1 %2 %3 %4 %5 %6 %7 %8 %9
shift
echo %0 %1 %2 %3 %4 %5 %6 %7 %8 %9
^Z
        1 File(s) copied

C>example6 00 01 02 03 04 05 06 07 08 09 10

C>ECHO OFF
EXAMPLE6 00 01 02 03 04 05 06 07 08
```

```
00 01 02 03 04 05 06 07 08 09
01 02 03 04 05 06 07 08 09 10
02 03 04 05 06 07 08 09 10
```

The batch file echoes the current values of the variables four times. The first time, %0 is "EXAMPLE6", %1 is "00", and so on. After one SHIFT, %0 is "00", %1 is "01", and so on. Notice that after the third SHIFT, only nine of the variables have a value. (For another, more practical, application of SHIFT, refer to the batch file presented at the end of this chapter.)

CALL

The concept of *modular programming* is widely accepted by computer programmers. Modular programming refers to the practice of dividing a computer program into small modules, each module being responsible for a single function (such as performing a calculation or copying a file). Programmers try to write modules that are reusable, meaning that a module written for one program can be reused in another program. This saves programmers from having to "reinvent the wheel" each time they write a program. The other big attraction of modular programming is that small modules are easy to debug, unlike large programs which can be very difficult to debug. Programmers use existing modules by issuing a "call." A *call* is a command to invoke a module.

Batch file programming lends itself well to the development of reusable batch file modules. Unfortunately, with versions of MS-DOS prior to 3.3, it is cumbersome to call a batch file module. To illustrate the problem, let's see what happens when the following two batch files are executed:

```
C>copy con one.bat
echo starting one
two
echo ending one
^Z
     1 File(s) copied

C>copy con two.bat
echo starting two
echo ending two
^Z
     1 File(s) copied
```

Now here is what happens when we call ONE.BAT:

```
C>one

C>echo starting one
```

```
starting one

C>two

C>echo starting two
starting two

C>echo ending two
ending two

C>
```

ONE.BAT echoes its starting message and then calls TWO.BAT. TWO.BAT displays its starting and ending messages, and its execution terminates. However, control is then passed to DOS (rather than back to ONE.BAT), and ONE.BAT's ending message does not get displayed. This failure to display ONE.BAT's ending message can be overcome with a small modification of ONE.BAT, namely, the use of the CALL command to execute TWO.BAT.

```
C>copy con one.bat
echo starting one
call two
echo ending one
^Z
     1 File(s) copied
```

Now we can see that control returns to ONE after TWO is executed:

```
C>one

C>echo starting one
starting one

C>call two

C>echo starting two
starting two

C>echo ending two
ending two

C>echo ending one
ending one
```

See the last section of this chapter, "Using Environment Variables," for another example using CALL.

CALL can also be used to invoke batch files with DOSSHELL Program Start Commands. Program Start Commands are discussed in chapter 7.

Calling Batch File Modules without CALL

CALL is implemented in MS-DOS 3.3 only. Batch files running under earlier versions of MS-DOS can call other batch files by loading a *secondary command processor* and having the secondary command processor execute the second batch file. The following version of ONE.BAT works under versions 2.X and 3.X of MS-DOS. See the discussion of COMMAND in Part 3 for details on the use of a secondary command processor.

```
C>copy con one.bat
echo starting one
rem
rem The command "command /c two" invokes a secondary command processor
rem which loads two.bat. When two.bat terminates execution, control
rem is passed back to one.bat.
rem
command /c two
echo ending one
^Z
    1 File(s) copied
C>
```

Using Environment Variables

Batch files running under MS-DOS 3.X and 4.X can access and modify the MS-DOS environment variables (the environment and environment variables are discussed in chapter 11). To reference an environment variable from within a batch file, use the variable's name preceded and followed by a percentage sign. Thus, if a batch file contains the command "ECHO %PATH%", the current directory search path is displayed.

The following batch file, ADD2PATH.BAT, can be used to append additional search paths to the current PATH variable. The batch file is called with a command having this format:

add2path newpath1;newpath2;newpath3 . . .

where each "newpath" is a search path (for example, a:\subdir2\subdir2). The batch file loops one time for each newpath entered on the command line. Each loop appends the replaceable variable %1 to the end of PATH. The SHIFT command then moves the next newpath on the command line into variable %1. The command that is after the loop label checks to see if the end of the command line has been reached. Notice the double quotes around %1.

```
echo off
echo ^[[s^[[1A^[[K^[[u
rem
rem                         ADD2PATH.BAT
rem
rem This batch file adds a search path to an existing PATH variable.
rem The syntax for using ADD2PATH is as follows:
rem
rem             ADD2PATH newpath1;newpath2 ...
rem
rem Each "newpath1", "newpath2", etc., specifies a new search
rem path, which is added to the existing PATH variable. The
rem "newpath's" may be separated by a semicolon, space, tab,
rem or equal sign.
rem
rem The batch file uses "%path%" to access the current PATH
rem variable and append the newpaths to it. The total number
rem of characters that may be added to the PATH variable is
rem limited by 2 factors: (1) Each time ADD2PATH is invoked,
rem there is a limit on the number of characters that can be
rem entered on the command line, and (2) there is a limit on
rem the number of characters that can be stored in the DOS
rem environment (see chapter 12 of MS-DOS Bible). DOS will display:
rem
rem             Out of environment space
rem
rem if the limit is reached.
rem
rem ADD2PATH "loops" one time for each new path specifier
rem entered, exiting after all have been processed.
rem The new PATH variable is displayed when execution
rem terminates.
rem
rem NOTE: The echo commands at the start of this batch file
rem require ANSI.SYS to work correctly. See chapter 8 of
rem MS-DOS Bible.
rem
:loop
rem exit if all parameters have been read
if "%1"=="" goto exit
rem append %1 to existing path
set path=%path%;%1
rem shift parameters one to left
shift
goto loop
:exit
echo PATH=%path%
echo.
```

ADD2PATH.BAT is useful if you want to add information to the end of PATH without having to enter the existing path string on the command line.

If you want to modify PATH from the command line (using "SET PATH="), you are limited by the 149-character restriction imposed by MS-DOS's keyboard buffer. Therefore, you may not be able to set as long a PATH variable as you would like. Using ADD2PATH.BAT, you are limited only by the size of your DOS environment (the size of which can be adjusted, see chapter 11).

ADD2PATH.BAT is also useful for adding search paths that you do not ordinarily use but need for a particular application. The following batch file could be used to initialize MS-DOS to use such an application.

```
echo off
rem                 WP_INIT.BAT
rem
rem A batch file to initialize MS-DOS to use "WP"
rem
rem Append WP's directory to PATH
call add2path \wp
rem
rem Set up working directories
c:
cd \letters\aug_81
cd a:\letters\aug_81
rem
rem Load the word processor
wp
rem
rem copy any new or modified files upon exit
xcopy *.* a: /m
```

5

Configuring Your System

System Parameters   CONFIG. SYS
Installable Device Drivers   AUTOEXEC.BAT

The dictionary defines *configuration* as the "arrangement of parts." System configuration refers to the arrangement of parts in a computer system. In this chapter we take a somewhat narrower perspective and discuss the configuration of DOS. Specifically, we look at how you, as the person using the operating system, can configure it to install and use a RAM disk drive, speed up disk access, use a mouse or other peripheral device, and, in general, modify the function of the system in a way that is optimal for your needs.

DOS is configured in two ways:

1. By assigning values to a set of variables known as the DOS *system parameters*
2. By installing *device drivers*

This chapter begins by discussing what these terms mean.

DOS configuration is generally carried out through the use of two special files: CONFIG.SYS and AUTOEXEC.BAT. A discussion of the use of these files makes up the majority of this chapter.

System Parameters

Each system parameter is identified by a predefined name (see table 5-1). Each parameter has a *value* which can be specified by the user. Some parameters have numeric values (such as 10 or 50); others have character string values (such as "no" or "c:\;c:\dos"). Most of the parameters have a *default value*, which is the value DOS assigns to a parameter if none is specified by the user. Each parameter's value has some influence on the manner in which DOS operates. The use of each of the system parameters listed in table 5-1 is discussed in this chapter.

System parameters are generally assigned a value by using an *assignment statement*. Each assignment statement consists of the parameter's name, followed by an equals sign (=), followed by the value assigned to the parameter. For example, the value for the system parameter BREAK can be set as follows:

```
C>break=on
```

or

```
C>break=off
```

The system parameter FILES is assigned a value of 50 as follows:

```
C>files=50
```

Most of the system parameters listed in table 5-1 may have values assigned to them *only* through the use of assignment statements contained in a special file named CONFIG.SYS. Much more will be said about this file later in this chapter.

Table 5-1. DOS System Parameters

Parameter Name	Function
BREAK	Controls the frequency with which DOS checks for Ctrl-Break
BUFFERS	Sets the number of disk buffers
COUNTRY	Specifies country-specific formatting information
FCBS	Sets the number of file control blocks
FILES	Sets the number of available file handles
INSTALL	Specifies a memory resident program that is to be loaded (MS-DOS 4.X)
LASTDRIVE	Specifies the total number of logical drives on the system
SHELL	Specifies which command processor is to be used
STACKS	Specifies the number of stacks available to handle hardware interrupts
SWITCHES	Specifies that enhanced keyboards are to behave like conventional keyboards (MS-DOS 4.X)
VERIFY	Specifies that each write to a disk is to be verified for accuracy

Environment Variables

The DOS *environment* is a block of computer memory that stores a list of *environment variables*. Environment variables are similar to system parameters in that their values affect the operating system's behavior. Values are assigned to environment variables from the command line or within a batch file, *not* from statements contained in CONFIG.SYS.

PATH, APPEND, COMSPEC, and PROMPT are predefined environment variables that have special meaning to DOS.

The value assigned to the PATH variable, along with the value assigned to the APPEND variable, specifies the directories in which DOS is to search for files not located in the current directory. You assign a value to the PATH variable by typing **path**, followed by an equals sign (=), followed by the directories to be searched. The directories are separated by semicolons. As an example, the following statement directs DOS to search the directories C:\PRGMS\WORD, C:\DOS, and C:\UTILS for files not located in the current directory:

```
C>path=c:\prgms\word;c:\dos;c:\utils
```

You can assign a value to the APPEND variable in a similar fashion. The value of the PATH and APPEND variables can be changed from the command line or from within a batch file.

The value assigned to the COMSPEC variable specifies where DOS is to locate the special file COMMAND.COM when a part of that file, known as the *transient portion*, needs to be reloaded into memory. DOS automatically assigns a value to COMSPEC during the boot-up process. You can change the value of the COMSPEC variable by using the SET command. As an example, the following command sets COMSPEC to a value of "c:\dos":

```
C>set comspec=c:\dos
```

The value assigned to the PROMPT variable determines the system prompt that is displayed at the DOS command line. You can assign a value to the variable by typing **prompt** followed by the character string that you wish to appear as a prompt. DOS provides a set of special characters that can be used to specify a prompt. For example, if the PROMPT variable has the value "pg", the system prompt consists of the drive letter of the default disk drive, followed by a colon, followed by the path to the current directory, followed by the ">" symbol. See the discussion of PROMPT in Part 3 for further information on the PROMPT special characters.

Creating User-Defined Environment Variables

You can use the SET command to create *user-defined* environment variables. Many application programs require the use of such variables. For example, some compilers are programmed to search the DOS environment for the user-defined variable LIB. The value assigned to the variable tells the compiler where to look for its library files. Prior to using the compiler, the user must assign a value to LIB as follows:

```
C>set lib=c:\lib
```

In a similar fashion, you can use the SET command to change the value of an existing environment variable.

You can delete a user-defined environment variable by assigning a value of null (no value) to the variable. As an example, the following command removes LIB from the environment:

```
C>set lib=
```

You can display all of the environment variables, along with the value assigned to each, by entering the command SET. The following example illustrates.

```
C:\>set
COMSPEC=C:\
```

```
PATH=C:\;C:\DOS
PROMPT=$P$G
HERCGB102=true
PCPLUS=C:\PRGMS\PCPLUS\

C:\>
```

Installable Device Drivers

In computer jargon the terms *peripheral device* and *I/O device* both refer to any hardware component that is external to memory and the central processing unit (CPU). The most common devices are keyboards, monitors, disk drives, printers, modems, and mice.

Computer devices either send input to memory and the CPU (keyboard, mouse), receive output from memory and the CPU (printer, monitor), or both send input and receive output (disk drives, modems).

Each device uses its own *communications protocol* when communicating with the computer. The protocol specifies how the device is to respond when it receives a certain signal from the computer. For example, a disk drive will begin to spin when it receives a certain specific signal from the computer, and the disk drive will send the computer a block of data when it receives another specific signal. Similarly, other devices carry out their special functions in response to specific signals from the computer.

The communications protocol for each device is specified in a computer program called a *device driver*. Because each type of device has its own communications protocol, each device requires its own device driver.

Standard Device Drivers

All versions of DOS contain a set of standard device drivers, which are built into the system. These include drivers for the keyboard, monitor, floppy disk drive, and line printer. Hard drive device drivers are also built into DOS 2.0 and subsequent versions. These device drivers are automatically loaded into memory and are available for use each time the system is booted up.

Installable Device Drivers

As DOS has become more popular, the variety of devices used by computers running DOS has increased dramatically. RAM disk drives, EGA monitors, VGA monitors, mice, laser printers, plotters, CD ROM readers, network interface cards, and expanded memory boards all require device driver support. DOS does not provide this support directly. Rather it provides a standard method by which the manufacturers of these devices may install their own device drivers into DOS. This ability to utilize *installable device drivers* greatly extends the capabilities of DOS and DOS computers.

Installable device drivers control communications between the computer and devices that do not have standard device drivers. They also can be used to replace standard drivers. The set of standard drivers is loaded into memory whenever DOS boots up. However, if an installable device driver for a standard device (such as the keyboard) is loaded into memory, the installable driver is used instead of the standard driver. This comes about as follows. DOS constructs a list that contains information about each device driver currently in memory. All of the installable device drivers are listed ahead of the standard device drivers. When DOS needs the services of a driver for a particular device (say the keyboard), it scans down this list until it finds the first entry for a driver of the device. Since the installable devices are listed first, the installable device driver is used instead of the standard device driver. This section discusses how to use installable device drivers. Refer to chapter 14 for a discussion of the structure of MS-DOS device drivers.

Device Statements

Most devices are supplied with a floppy diskette that contains the required installable device driver. The driver is designed by the device's manufacturer specifically for use with the particular device.

Installable device drivers are loaded into memory through the use of *device statements*. A device statement consists of the word "device", followed by an equals sign (=), followed by the file specifier of the device driver. All device statements *must* be placed in a special file named CONFIG.SYS. Device statements cannot be entered from the command line or placed in batch files. CONFIG.SYS is discussed in the following section.

The following is an example of a device statement. The statement instructs DOS to load the device driver named ANSI.SYS into memory. The driver is located on the C drive, in the directory \DOS.

```
C>device=c:\dos\ansi.sys
```

Most device drivers have a filename extension of SYS. ANSI.SYS is an installable device driver for the keyboard and display monitor. ANSI.SYS can be used to control the cursor's position on the screen, clear the screen display, control the display attributes, set the display mode, and reassign values to individual keys on the keyboard. Use of ANSI.SYS is discussed in chapter 9.

CONFIG.SYS

The first section in this chapter discussed *assignment statements*, which are used to assign values to DOS system parameters, and *device statements*, which are used to load installable device drivers into memory. Most assignment statements and *all* device statements must be used as entries in a special file named CONFIG.SYS. This section discusses CONFIG.SYS. A sample file that contains two assignment statements and one device statement is created. This section also discusses the way in which the statements contained in CONFIG.SYS are read by DOS.

Creating CONFIG.SYS

CONFIG.SYS is a DOS text file. This means that CONFIG.SYS can be created or modified using EDLIN or any word processor operating in text mode. CONFIG.SYS can also be created directly from the keyboard. Be careful, though, because the method, which is illustrated below, will overwrite an existing CONFIG.SYS file.

```
C:\>copy con config.sys
break=on
files=20
device=c:\dos\vdisk.sys
^Z
        1 File(s) copied

C:\>
```

The command `copy con config.sys` directs DOS to copy the keyboard input (the keyboard has the device name "con") into a new file named CONFIG.SYS.

The first line in the new file is an assignment statement that assigns a value of "on" to the system parameter BREAK. The value of BREAK determines the frequency with which DOS checks to see if the Ctrl-Break key combination has been pressed. Checking occurs more frequently when BREAK is set to "on".

The second line in CONFIG.SYS is an assignment statement that sets the FILES parameter to have a value of 20. The value of FILES determines the number of file handles available to the system. Most programs written to run under DOS versions 2, 3, and 4 require one file handle for each file that is open.

The third line in the new file is a device statement that loads the device driver named VDISK.SYS. VDISK.SYS is a device driver for a RAM drive. A RAM drive is a portion of computer memory that stores files in much the same manner as a conventional disk drive. Access times are much shorter on a RAM drive because memory, rather than a conventional disk drive, is being read. The other difference between RAM drives and conventional drives is that the files stored in RAM drives are volatile. This means that the files disappear when the computer is turned off.

Returning to the example presented above, entering Ctrl-Z (or pressing the F6 function key) signals DOS that the input for CONFIG.SYS is complete. DOS subsequently writes the new file to the disk and then displays the command line prompt. The statements in the new CONFIG.SYS are ready to be executed when DOS is subsequently rebooted.

You can use the EDLIN text file editor (or any other text base's editor) as an alternative to the "copy con config.sys" command. EDLIN allows you to modify an existing file; "copy con" does not. Despite what many people say about it, EDLIN is convenient for creating and modifying short text files. If you do a lot of "quick and dirty" text editing, you should consider trying it. Use of EDLIN is discussed in chapter 8.

Executing the Statements in CONFIG.SYS

During the boot-up process, DOS checks to see if a file named CONFIG.SYS is stored *in the root directory* of the boot drive. If so, DOS reads each of the statements in CONFIG.SYS, loads the specified device drivers, and assigns values to the specified system parameters. If the root directory does not contain CONFIG.SYS, DOS uses the standard device drivers and sets the system parameters to their default values.

The statements in CONFIG.SYS are read at boot time only. The statements cannot be executed from the DOS command line nor can they be executed as part of a batch file. If the contents of CONFIG.SYS are modified, none of the changes go into effect until DOS is subsequently rebooted.

Up to this point, the information presented in this chapter has provided a general view of the role of DOS system parameters, installable device drivers, and the CONFIG.SYS file. The role of each of the system parameters is discussed in the following section.

Roles of the System Parameters

A general discussion of the DOS system parameters was presented at the beginning of this chapter. This section discusses the role of each of the parameters. The value of each of the system parameters is set using assignment statements contained in CONFIG.SYS. Additionally, BREAK and VERIFY may be assigned values using assignment statements contained in batch files or entered at the command line.

BREAK

The **BREAK** parameter (DOS versions 2, 3, and 4) lets you control the manner in which DOS checks to see if Ctrl-Break has been pressed.

The Ctrl-Break key combination is a signal to DOS to stop whatever it is doing (such as executing a command or running a program), display the system's command line prompt, and wait for the user to enter a command. Thus, Ctrl-Break acts as a sort of emergency brake on the system.

If the BREAK parameter is assigned a value of "on", DOS checks in a continuous fashion for Ctrl-Break. If BREAK is assigned a value of "off", DOS only checks for Ctrl-Break when keyboard, printer, display screen, or serial port I/O occurs. "On" and "off" are the only values that may be assigned to BREAK.

If you are running programs that have long periods of disk access (such as database applications or program compiling), it may be advantageous to have BREAK set to "on". The disadvantage of BREAK being "on" is that the system runs somewhat slower, because DOS is always checking for Ctrl-Break.

Most commercial application programs "trap" Ctrl-Break. This means that the programs recognize when Ctrl-Break has been pressed and intercept the signal before it gets to DOS. In such cases, the application program determines what action is taken when Ctrl-Break is pressed. The value of the BREAK parameter does not affect these programs.

The BREAK parameter is unusual in that its value can be set with a statement in CONFIG.SYS, a statement contained in a batch file, or a statement entered at the DOS command line. The default value for BREAK is "off". You can enter **break** (without additional parameters) to see the BREAK parameter's current value.

BUFFERS

The **BUFFERS** parameter (DOS versions 2, 3, and 4) is used to set the number of *disk buffers*. You may be able to speed up your system by setting BUFFERS to the appropriate value.

A disk buffer is an area of computer memory which stores data that is read from a disk. Each buffer stores 512 bytes. When a program requests some data that is stored on a disk, DOS first determines which disk sector is storing the data. The operating system then checks the disk buffers to see if one of them already holds the contents of the required sector. If so, no additional access to the disk is required. If none of the buffers contains the sought-after data, DOS reads the entire sector containing the data into one of the disk buffers. Thus, even if the application program requests only a 128-byte block of data, the entire 512-byte sector that contains the data is read into memory.

Increasing the number of disk buffers will increase the number of disk sectors that DOS can store in memory at any one time. This will reduce the number of disk accesses required, thereby improving program execution time. The degree of improvement depends primarily on the pattern of disk access required by the program. If disk access tends to follow a random pattern, as would be the case in querying a large database, increasing the number of disk buffers should significantly improve performance. Alternatively, if disk access is primarily sequential, as is the case with most word processing applications, simply increasing the number of disk buffers will generally not result in as dramatic an improvement in performance. The DOS 4.X version of BUFFERS does support a second parameter, which is used to specify the number of *look-ahead* sectors. Use of this parameter can improve the performance of programs that perform a large amount of sequential disk access.

Each disk buffer requires a total of 528 bytes of memory. Therefore, a trade-off exists wherein increasing the number of buffers decreases the amount of memory available for application programs. If your system has less than 256 Kbytes of RAM, a large number of buffers (more than 15) may slow your programs down.

Many application programs recommend a minimum number of buffers for optimal program performance. It is often beneficial to experiment with the number of disk buffers you use. Database applications generally do well with about 20 disk buffers. Programs that perform sequential disk access generally do well with 10–15 disk buffers. Bear in mind that the more buffers there are in the system, the longer it will take DOS to search all the buffers.

The default value for BUFFERS is 2 unless any of the following conditions hold:

Default Value of

3	If the system diskette drive is >360 Kbytes
5	If memory size is >128 Kbytes
10	If memory size is >256 Kbytes
15	If memory size is >512 Kbytes

You can set the BUFFERS parameter to any value in the range 1–99. Disk buffers can be placed in expanded memory with DOS 4 (see discussion of BUFFERS in Part 3 for details). If expanded memory is used, the BUFFERS parameter can have a value up to 10,000.

COUNTRY

The value of the **COUNTRY** parameter (DOS versions 3 and 4) determines which country-specific format is used for the date, time, currency, and other parameters. The value need be set only if a non-U.S. format is required. Please refer to appendix D for additional information on the use of code page switching and the use of non-U.S. formats.

FCBS

The **FCBS** parameter (DOS versions 3 and 4) is used to limit the number of *file control blocks* that are available at any one time. A file control block (FCB) is an area of memory that stores information about files which have been opened by DOS. Generally speaking, only programs written for DOS 1.X use file control blocks. Programs written for later versions of DOS use file handles.

Experience with computer networks has shown that a large number of FCBs can degrade the performance of a network of DOS computers. Therefore, the parameter FCBS is implemented in DOS 3 and 4 to limit the number of FCBs that can be used at any one time.

Use of the FCBS parameter requires that network file sharing be implemented. *Network file sharing* describes the situation where computers on a network have the ability to directly access the files of other computers on the network. File sharing is implemented through the network operating system. File sharing can also be implemented using the DOS command SHARE. The value of the FCBS parameter has no effect if file sharing is not implemented. You can disregard this parameter unless you are receiving error messages indicating a lack of file control blocks.

FILES

The value of the **FILES** parameter (DOS versions 2, 3, and 4) sets the number of *file handles* that are available at any one time. The FILES parameter is set to a default value of 8 if no value is specified for it in CONFIG.SYS.

Most programs written to run under DOS 2, 3, and 4 require one file handle for each open file. Many commercial programs require several files to be open at a single time. In order to use these programs you must set the FILES parameter to a certain minimum value. As an example, the spell checker of Microsoft Word 4.0 requires 15 file handles. The spell checker will not run if FILES has a value less than 15.

Generally the application program determines whether the value of FILES is too low. Thus, the error message displayed varies depending on the particular application. In general, if you try to run a program and you get a message such as `Increase FILES` or `No free file handles`, you should increase the value of the FILES parameter by modifying CONFIG.SYS and rebooting your system. Setting FILES equal to 20 will accommodate most DOS applications.

The maximum value for FILES is 255. No more than 20 file handles can be used by a given program.

INSTALL

INSTALL (DOS 4) is not a system parameter, because it does not have a value assigned to it. Rather, it is a DOS command that can be used to load into memory the following "DOS extensions":

FASTOPEN.EXE

KEYB.COM

NLSFUNC.EXE

SHARE.EXE

Once they are loaded, these extensions remain in memory as a functional component of DOS.

INSTALL is discussed here because its use and command structure are similar to the use and structure of assignment statements. The use is similar because INSTALL can only be used in CONFIG.SYS. The structure is similar because an "install statement" begins with **install**, followed by an equals sign (=), followed by the path and filename of the DOS extension that is being installed. For example, the following statement is used to install the

FASTOPEN extension. The file FASTOPEN.EXE is stored on the C drive, in directory \DOS.

```
C>install=c:\dos\fastopen.exe c:=(50,25)
```

FASTOPEN is a DOS 4 utility that improves file access time by storing file directory information in memory. Its use, and use of the other extensions mentioned above, is discussed in Part 3.

Any of the DOS extensions that can be loaded with INSTALL can also be loaded from AUTOEXEC.BAT or the DOS command line. The advantage in using INSTALL is that DOS allocates memory to the extensions in a more orderly fashion than when the other loading methods are used.

LASTDRIVE

The value of the **LASTDRIVE** parameter (DOS versions 3 and 4) sets the highest drive letter available for use by the system. DOS ignores LASTDRIVE if it is set to a value that is less than the number of physical drives on the system. For example, if a computer has two floppy drives and one hard drive, DOS will ignore the statement "lastdrive=B".

Any RAM drives, multiple partition drives, network drives, or logical drives created with DOS commands SUBST or JOIN must be taken into account when setting the LASTDRIVE parameter. For example, if a computer has two floppy drives, one hard drive with two DOS partitions, a RAM drive, and two logical drives, LASTDRIVE must be set to a value of "G" or greater.

The primary purpose of the LASTDRIVE parameter is to support local area networks. In a network environment, the DOS command SUBST is often used to make a subdirectory on one computer appear to be a disk drive on another computer. Each of these *virtual disk drives* requires a unique drive letter. The value of the LASTDRIVE parameter determines how many drive letters (and thereby how many virtual drives) a computer can have. If you are using a network, the network documentation will probably suggest a value for LASTDRIVE.

SHELL

The **SHELL** parameter (DOS versions 2, 3, and 4) was originally implemented to allow users to load and use a command processor other than COMMAND.COM. While some people may actually be using SHELL for this purpose, it is most commonly used for two other purposes.

You can use the SHELL parameter to specify for use a copy of the COMMAND.COM file that is located somewhere other than in the root directory of the boot drive. This is most important in DOS 4, where the DOS SHARE facility is required when using disk partitions larger than 32 Mbytes in size. In such cases, the SHELL parameter must be initialized to load a copy of COMMAND.COM that is stored in the same subdirectory as the file SHARE.EXE. For example, if the file SHARE.EXE is stored in the directory C:\DOS, the following assignment statement must be placed in CONFIG.SYS:

```
C>shell=c:\dos\command.com /p
```

The SELECT program, which is used to install DOS 4 (see chapter 1), automatically makes this entry for you if you are using a partition larger than 32 Mbytes.

The second common use of the SHELL parameter is to increase the size of the DOS environment. The environment, which was discussed earlier in this chapter, has a default size of 160 bytes. An assignment statement of the following form can be used to create a larger environment:

```
C>shell=c:\dos\command.com /e:xxxx
```

The **xxxx** specifies the environment size. In DOS 3.1, **xxxx** specifies the number of 16-byte blocks (paragraphs) in the environment. In DOS 3.2 and subsequent versions, **xxxx** specifies the actual number of bytes in the environment (the number is automatically rounded up to the nearest multiple of 16). You should increase the size of the DOS environment if you get an **Out of environment space** message.

STACKS

Use the **STACKS** parameter (DOS versions 3.2, 3.3, and 4) to set the number and size of the *stacks* that DOS uses to handle *hardware interrupts*. A hardware interrupt is a signal generated by a device (such as the keyboard or a disk drive) that tells DOS the device needs attention. When this happens, DOS must stop what it is doing and take care of ("service") the device. But DOS cannot simply abandon whatever it is working on. It must save some information, so that it may resume its work after the hardware device is serviced. This required information is saved in a portion of memory called a stack.

Hardware interrupts can be *nested*. This means that when one interrupt is being serviced, another interrupt can occur. When the second is being serviced, a third can occur, and so on. The pool of stacks required in servicing these interrupts can become exhausted if the interrupts occur in rapid enough succession.

If there is an inadequate number of stacks, the computer will display a message like **Internal Stack Failure, System Halted** and freeze up. It will be necessary to switch the computer off and then back on to restart it. If this should occur, use the STACKS parameter to increase the number and/or the size of the available stacks.

Computers with 8088 or 8086 CPUs default to a STACK value of 0,0 (0 stacks of size 0 bytes). Under these conditions, hardware interrupts are handled in a somewhat different fashion than outlined above.

Computers with 80286 or 80386 CPUs default to a STACK value of 9,128 (9 stacks of size 128 bytes). 8088 and 8086 computers are also given 9 stacks of 128 bytes if the CONFIG.SYS file contains the statement "stacks=".

Reasonable guidelines for using the STACKS parameter are as follows:

▶ Increase the number of stacks to 15 if you get a message indicating stack failure.

▶ Increase the number to 20 if the error persists.

▶ Increase the stack size to 256 bytes if the error still persists.

Something is wrong if you still get an error. Try to determine which application(s) cause the error and contact your computer's manufacturer for advice.

SWITCHES

The SWITCHES parameter (DOS version 4) is used to control the activity of enhanced keyboards. These newer keyboards have some keys (F11 and F12 function keys, and a set of cursor keys separate from the number pad) that are not found on the older keyboards. Naturally, the new keys generate scan codes not generated by the older keys. (All keys generate a *make scan code* when pressed and a *break scan code* when released. The make and break scan codes are unique for each key.)

Some application programs are unable to process the scan codes generated by the newer keys. In such cases, these scan codes may confuse the program or even cause the system to crash. This problem can be avoided by setting the SWITCHES parameter to equal "/K". This instructs DOS to simply ignore the scan codes generated by the new keys.

VERIFY

DOS performs a series of checks to verify that each disk write is performed correctly when the VERIFY parameter is set to equal "on". You can set the value of VERIFY from the DOS command line or within a batch file in versions 2 and 3. In DOS version 4 you can set VERIFY either from the command line, within a batch file, or with a statement contained in CONFIG.SYS. Because DOS disk writes are generally very accurate, setting VERIFY to "on" usually accomplishes nothing, other than slowing DOS down.

Using CONFIG.SYS—A Working Example

Now that all of the system parameters have been discussed, let us take a look at a typical CONFIG.SYS file. Listing 5-1 is the CONFIG.SYS file I used while writing this book. We will go through and discuss it line by line.

Listing 5-1. A typical CONFIG.SYS file.

```
break=on
files=20
device=c:\dos\vdisk.sys
buffers=20
lastdrive=e
```

```
shell=c:\dos\command.com /p /e:256
device=c:\sys\emm.sys
device=c:\dos\ansi.sys
install=c:\dos\fastopen.exe c:
```

The first three lines in listing 5-1 were discussed earlier in the section headed "Creating CONFIG.SYS."

The line `buffers=20` sets the number of disk buffers. Most of my work is word processing; therefore, I should expect my system to primarily perform sequential disk access. Twenty disk buffers is a lot for sequential access, and it may be more than I actually need. But I am satisfied with my system's performance; the large number of buffers does not seem to be slowing things down.

The line `lastdrive=e` specifies that the system may have up to five disk drives. My system has two floppy drives, a hard disk, and a RAM disk. With LASTDRIVE set to "e" I can add at most one more drive. Remember that this is any type of drive, including logical drives. Therefore, I would need to change the value of LASTDRIVE if I wanted to create two logical drives (say, with the SUBST command).

The assignment statement `shell=c:\dos\command.com /p /e:256` performs two functions. First, it tells DOS to load the copy of COMMAND.COM that is stored in subdirectory \DOS on drive C. This is necessary because SHARE.EXE is in the same subdirectory. In order to implement the DOS 4 support for large disk partitions, COMMAND.COM must be loaded from the subdirectory containing SHARE.EXE.

The second function of the SHELL assignment statement is to increase the size of the DOS environment. The statement specifies an environment size of 256 bytes.

The next two lines in listing 5-1 are device statements. The first statement specifies loading of the driver EMM.SYS. This is the device driver for the expanded memory board in my system. See the accompanying box for an overview of expanded memory.

The next device statement instructs DOS to load the ANSI.SYS device driver. Use of this driver is discussed in chapter 9.

The final statement in listing 5-1 installs the program FASTOPEN in memory. The parameter `c:`, which is located at the end of the command, specifies that information for the directories on drive C is to be stored in memory.

This concludes the discussion of listing 5-1. Before ending our discussion of CONFIG.SYS, the following points are worth repeating:

1. CONFIG.SYS must be in the root directory of the boot drive.
2. Most of the commands used in CONFIG.SYS cannot be used in batch files or entered at the DOS command line.
3. Any changes made to CONFIG.SYS do not take effect until the system is subsequently rebooted.

An Overview of Expanded Memory

The term *expanded memory* refers to a technique that has been developed to overcome DOS' 640-Kbyte memory limitation. Use of expanded memory requires special expanded memory hardware and an expanded memory device driver. Generally, the same manufacturer develops and supplies both the hardware and the driver.

The expanded memory device driver, also called the expanded memory manager or EMM, is used just like the other device drivers discussed in this chapter. The EMM is installed in memory using a device statement contained in CONFIG.SYS. The function of the EMM is to provide a communications protocol between the computer and the expanded memory hardware.

PC-DOS version 4 comes with two expanded memory device drivers. XMA2EMS.SYS is a driver for IBM expanded memory hardware. XMAEM.SYS is a driver for 80386 machines, which allows those machines to emulate the function of an 80286 expanded memory card. Details on the use of these drivers are presented under the discussion of DEVICE in Part 3 of this book.

Non-IBM expanded memory hardware requires non-IBM drivers. The machine used in writing this book has an Everex expanded memory card. The driver for the card is a file named EMM.SYS. The file is stored in directory \SYS on drive C. Thus, the command to load the expanded memory driver on my machine is

```
device=c:\sys\emm.sys.
```

Expanded memory is covered much more thoroughly in chapter 12.

AUTOEXEC.BAT

The AUTOEXEC.BAT file is similar to CONFIG.SYS in that it is also a text file that is automatically read by DOS during the boot-up process (CONFIG.SYS is read and executed before AUTOEXEC.BAT). AUTOEXEC.BAT also must be stored in the root directory of the boot drive if it is to be executed automatically. Like CONFIG.SYS, AUTOEXEC.BAT allows you to configure DOS to suit your particular needs.

But AUTOEXEC.BAT is very different from CONFIG.SYS. AUTOEXEC.BAT is a batch file (see chapter 4) and it may contain any batch file command. Upon booting, MS-DOS executes the commands in the AUTOEXEC.BAT file, but you can invoke the sequence of commands in AUTOEXEC.BAT at any time by typing **autoexec** on the command line.

The sequence of commands in the AUTOEXEC.BAT file is used to perform a set of tasks that you wish to be executed each time the system is booted. Typical uses include setting the DOS search path, initializing environment variables required by programs, setting the system prompt, and starting up an application program. AUTOEXEC.BAT is also generally used to perform certain types of system initialization such as redirecting parallel printer output to a serial port or initializing the DOS print spooler.

DOS will not prompt for the date and time during boot-up if AUTOEXEC.BAT is present (unless the file contains the command DATE and/or the command TIME).

Listing 5-2 contains the AUTOEXEC.BAT file on the computer used in the writing of this book. The contents of the file illustrate some typical uses of AUTOEXEC.BAT.

Listing 5-2. A typical AUTOEXEC.BAT file.

```
path=c:\prgms\word;c:\procomm;c:\dos;c:\utils;c:\bat
mode com2:300,n,8,1,p
mode lpt1:=com2
print /d:lpt1
prompt=$p$g
set pcplus=c:\procomm\
set hercgb102=true
set lib=c:\lib
cd c:\books\dos
word config
xcopy *.* b: /m
```

The first line in listing 5-2 sets the DOS search path. This is the list of directories that DOS searches when it cannot find a file in the current directory.

The directory c:\prgms\word contains the files for my word processor. The directory c:\procomm contains the files for the communications package that I use. The directory c:\dos contains the DOS files. The directory c:\utils contains the Norton Utilities along with other utility programs that I have acquired. Finally, the directory c:\bat contains all my batch files.

When setting up your search path, remember that DOS searches the subdirectories in the order in which you list them. Therefore, the subdirectories that you use most should be listed first, and those that you use least should be listed last.

The next line in listing 5-2 sets the system prompt so that it displays the currently active directory. This is helpful as an aid in remembering where you are currently located within the directory hierarchy.

The next three lines are SET commands that create and assign values to three environment variables. The variable pcplus is required by my communications software. The variable hercgb102 is required for my word processor to work properly. The variable lib is required by my C compiler. What, if any, environment variables you require, and the values to which they must be set, are determined by the application software that you are using. Refer to the software documentation for information specific to your applications.

The next line in the AUTOEXEC.BAT file in listing 5-2 is a CD command. The command sets the subdirectory **\books\dos** on drive C as the active directory. The next command (**word config**) starts up the word processor, instructing it to load a document file named "config".

The final command in listing 5-2 is automatically executed upon exiting from the word processor. The XCOPY command checks each file in the current directory and determines which files have the archive attribute set. Those files with a set attribute are copied to drive B and the attribute is cleared. (The **/m** parameter instructs XCOPY to check the archive attribute.) Since DOS sets a file's archive attribute each time the file is modified, this final command in the AUTOEXEC.BAT file automatically makes a backup copy of any document files that I have worked on.

C H A P T E R

6

Redirection, Filters, and Pipes

Standard Input and Standard
   Output Devices
Reserved Device Names
Redirecting an MS-DOS
   Command

Filters
Pipes
Redirection versus Piping

Input and *output* are the processes through which computers receive and send data. Versions 2.X, 3.X, and 4.X of MS-DOS allow you to modify these processes through the use of some sophisticated data management techniques known as *redirection, filtering,* and *piping.* You can use these techniques and their associated MS-DOS commands to build your own information pipeline. Like a plumber, you can redirect the flow of information from one place to another, have the information modified through a filter, and then pipe the output to a final destination. This chapter will explain how to use these special techniques with MS-DOS 2.X, 3.X, and 4.X.

Standard Input and Standard Output Devices

As you know from your own experience, most of the time you use the keyboard to enter data into your computer, and during most operations this data is sent to the display screen for your viewing. The keyboard is therefore the *standard input device,* and the display screen or monitor is the *standard output device.*

MS-DOS 2.X, 3.X, and 4.X allow you to specify a device, other than the standard input device, as the source of input data. Similarly, you can specify a device, other than the standard output device, as the destination of output data. These input and output devices are called *peripheral devices* because they are hardware that is external to the microcomputer.

Reserved Device Names

When you designate an input or output device different from the standard one, you must give MS-DOS the correct name for that peripheral device. Each device, such as a printer or modem, has a standard name recognized by MS-DOS and reserved for use with that device only. There is even a dummy device for testing purposes. Table 6-1 lists the device names and the peripheral devices to which they refer.

Table 6-1. MS-DOS Reserved Names for Peripheral Devices

Reserved Name	Peripheral Device
AUX	First asynchronous communications port
COM1, COM2, COM3, COM4	Asynchronous communications ports 1 through 4
CON	Keyboard and display screen (CONsole)
LPT1, LPT2, LPT3	First, second, and third parallel printers
NUL	Dummy device (for testing)
PRN	First parallel printer

Redirecting an MS-DOS Command

The output of an MS-DOS command can be redirected to a device, other than the standard output device, by entering an MS-DOS command, followed by " > " (the symbol for redirected output), followed by the name of the device that is to receive the output (see figure 6-1).

Let's look at an example using the MS-DOS command TYPE, which is

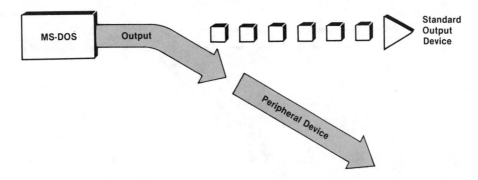

Figure 6-1. Redirection of output (>).

used to display the contents of a file on the screen. When the command **type myfile** is entered, the contents of "myfile" can be viewed on the display screen. Enter the following command to redirect output to the printer. Be sure to turn your printer on first or your system will "hang" until you do.

```
C>type myfile > prn
```

Because you used PRN—the reserved device name for the parallel printer—in your command, MS-DOS recognizes that the output of "type myfile" is to be redirected to the printer. No screen display results from this command.

In addition to the devices listed in table 6-1, MS-DOS also recognizes files as peripheral devices. This means that you can redirect output to an MS-DOS file. For example, the following command stores the output of the command DIR in a file named "dir.lst":

```
C>dir > dir.lst
```

If a file named "dir.lst" already exists on the disk in the default drive, it will be overwritten by this command. The data already in the file will be lost, replaced by the output of the command.

By using the symbol " > >", you can append output from a command to the end of an existing file. For example:

```
C>dir >> dir.lst
```

This command will add the output of the DIR command to the end of an existing file named "dir.lst". If there is no existing file with that name, a file will be created that contains the output of the DIR command.

So far we have been talking about redirected output. However, input can be redirected too (see figure 6-2). As you might expect, the symbol for redirection of input (<) is the opposite of the one for redirection of output. The next section will show you how redirection of input can be used with filters.

Figure 6-2. Redirection of input (<).

Filters

A *filter* is an MS-DOS command (or a computer program) that accepts data from an input device, rearranges or "filters" the data, and then outputs the filtered data to the designated output device. MS-DOS 2.X, 3.X, and 4.X contain three filter commands: SORT, FIND, and MORE. As we discuss these commands, we will also elaborate on the concept of redirection.

SORT

The SORT command reads lines of text from the standard input device (the keyboard), sorts the lines, and then writes the sorted results to the display screen. SORT is also used, much more commonly, to sort lines contained in text files. Redirection of the standard input is used to send the text file's contents to SORT. The sorted results are sent to the standard output (the display screen).

In the discussion of SORT that follows, we will use the contents of a file named "sample.txt" for demonstration purposes. We will begin the discussion by first using TYPE to view the unsorted contents of "sample.txt". The examples which follow assume that "sample.txt" is in the current directory of drive C.

```
C>type sample.txt
0006    acme rents       100 broadway ave      oakland
0003    flint's bbq      6609 shattuck ave     oakland
0004    cody's books     2460 telegraph ave    berkeley
0005    uc theater       2036 university ave   berkeley
0001    pegasus books    1855 solano ave       albany
0002    mountain travel  1215 irving st        san francisco

C>
```

Each line in the file is made up of four columns, which are respectively an account number, the name of a business, the business street address, and the city address.

SORT is an external MS-DOS command. This means that either the file SORT.EXE must be in the current directory or the directory containing SORT.EXE must be in the DOS search path.

The input redirection symbol (<) is used to send the contents of a text file to SORT. SORT sorts the lines in the file according to the first character on each line and sends the results to the display screen:

```
C>sort < sample.txt
0001    pegasus books    1855 solano ave        albany
0002    mountain travel  1215 irving st         san francisco
0003    flint's bbq      6609 shattuck ave      oakland
0004    cody's books     2460 telegraph ave     berkeley
0005    uc theater       2036 university ave    berkeley
0006    acme rents       100 broadway ave       oakland

C>
```

The SORT command switch /+n can be used to sort according to the character in any position on the line. In the following example, SORT is used to sort the lines according to the business name. The first character in the business name is the eighth character on the line.

```
C>sort /+8 < sample.txt
0006    acme rents       100 broadway ave       oakland
0004    cody's books     2460 telegraph ave     berkeley
0003    flint's bbq      6609 shattuck ave      oakland
0002    mountain travel  1215 irving st         san francisco
0001    pegasus books    1855 solano ave        albany
0005    uc theater       2036 university ave    berkeley

C>
```

SORT treats tabs as a single character. Therefore if your columns are aligned with tabs, SORT will probably appear to be confused, because it won't be comparing the characters you expect. For example, in "sample.txt", if the columns were aligned with tabs, SORT might not align the address for "acme rents" with the address for "mountain travel". SORT is really for use only with text files that have columns (or fields) aligned using spaces.

SORT can also sort in reverse order using the /r switch. The following example sorts the lines in the file in reverse order according to the twenty-fifth character on each line (the first digit in the street address).

```
C>sort /r /+25 < sample.txt
0003    flint's bbq      6609 shattuck ave      oakland
```

```
0004    cody's books      2460 telegraph ave    berkeley
0001    pegasus books     1855 solano ave       albany
0005    uc theater        2036 university ave   berkeley
0002    mountain travel   1215 irving st        san francisco
0006    acme rents        100 broadway ave      oakland

C>
```

Notice that where the characters in the position of comparison are identical, a comparison is made at the next position.

The output from SORT can be redirected to another device such as the printer (using "> PRN") or to a text file. The following listing shows how the result of the previous example could be redirected to a file named "address.txt":

```
C>sort /r /+25 < sample.txt > address.txt

C>
```

FIND

The FIND command searches a line of standard input for a specified sequence of characters. The line is echoed to the display screen if it contains the sequence. FIND is also used, much more commonly, to find the lines in a text file that contain a specific character sequence.

FIND is an external MS-DOS command. The requirements for its use are identical to those described above for SORT. The examples that follow use the text file "sample.txt", which is displayed above.

FIND is used by entering **find**, followed by the sequence of characters on which to base the search, followed by the name of the text file to be searched. The sequence of characters must be enclosed in quotation marks. FIND reads lines of text from the standard input device (the keyboard) if a filename is not specified. The following example looks for the line of text that contains the sequence "flint's":

```
C>find "flint's" sample.txt

---------- SAMPLE.TXT
0003    flint's bbq       6609 shattuck ave     oakland

C>
```

FIND can also be used to locate the lines that do not contain a sequence of characters. The following example demonstrates how the /v switch can be used to locate the businesses not in "berkeley".

```
C>find /v "berkeley" sample.txt
```

```
---------- SAMPLE.TXT
0006    acme rents       100 broadway ave     oakland
0003    flint's bbq      6609 shattuck ave    oakland
0001    pegasus books    1855 solano ave      albany
0002    mountain travel  1215 irving st       san francisco
```

```
C>
```

The /c switch displays a count of the lines in a text file that contain the specified sequence. The following example counts the number of businesses in "oakland":

```
C>find /c "oakland" sample.txt
```

```
---------- SAMPLE.TXT: 2
```

```
C>
```

The /n switch can be used to display the lines found, along with a line number that identifies the line's position in the file:

```
C>find /n "books" sample.txt
```

```
---------- SAMPLE.TXT
```

```
[3]0004    cody's books     2460 telegraph ave   berkeley
[5]0001    pegasus books    1855 solano ave      albany
```

```
C>
```

As was illustrated with SORT, the output from FIND can be redirected to a text file.

MORE

The MS-DOS command MORE is a filter that displays one screenful of data at a time. MORE is an external MS-DOS command. This means that MORE is not stored in memory when MS-DOS is booted. Therefore, in order to use MORE, a disk containing the file MORE.COM must be in the current directory of one of the system drives. In the following examples, MORE.COM and "sample.txt" are located in the current directory of drive C.

Data is input to MORE by redirection:

```
C>more < sample.txt
```

This command redirects the data in the file "sample.txt" as input to the filter

MORE. MORE outputs the data, 23 lines at a time, to the standard output device. When the screen is filled, the prompt **-- MORE --** is displayed. Pressing any key gives another filled screen of data. The process is repeated until the entire file has been displayed.

The output from MORE may be redirected to a device other than the standard output device. The following command sends 23 lines of "sample.txt" at a time to the printer:

```
C>more < sample.txt > prn
```

The prompt **-- More --** will also be sent to the printer.

Pipes

Pipes are connections between two programs or two commands or a command and a program. Pipes allow data that is output from one program to be redirected as input to a second program (see figure 6-3).

**Figure 6-3. Piping a command's output as input
for a second command.**

The MS-DOS symbol for a pipe is a vertical bar (¦). To redirect the output from one command (or program) to another, type the first command, followed by a vertical bar, followed by the second command.

Consider the following command:

```
C>dir ¦ find "-85 "
```

This command directs MS-DOS to send the output of the DIR command (usually sent to the display screen) as input to the FIND filter. FIND searches each line of the input for the character string "-85 ". The result is that all the files in the current directory with a 1985 date stamp are displayed on the screen. (Date stamps are discussed in chapter 1.) Any files with a filename or filename extension containing "-85" would also be displayed.

A command may contain more than one pipe. In the preceding command, the output of the FIND filter is sent to the screen. The output can be redirected with another pipe:

```
C>dir ¦ find "-85 " ¦ sort /+14
```

Now, the output of the FIND command is piped to the SORT filter, which sorts the 1985 files according to their size (the 14th column of each line). The sorted output is sent to the display screen. Try this command with one of your own files. Remember that FIND and SORT are external MS-DOS commands; therefore, the files FIND.EXE and SORT.EXE must be in the current directory of the specified (or default) drive.

Redirection versus Piping

The difference between redirection and piping can be a little confusing. Redirection refers to the modification of input from, or output to, peripheral devices (see table 6-1 and figures 6-1 and 6-2). Piping refers to the conversion of the output from an MS-DOS command or computer program into the input for another command or program (figure 6-3).

We'll try to clarify with one more example:

```
C>sort /+6 < sample.txt ¦ find "book" > bookstor.lst
```

The first part of the command (**sort /+6 < sample.txt**) redirects the file as input to SORT. The output from the SORT program is piped to the FIND program. The output from the program is redirected to the file "bookstor.lst".

Redirection and piping are not restricted to MS-DOS commands. Any program that runs under MS-DOS can be written to support redirection and piping. For example, many of the public domain DOS utility programs (such as the ubiquitous WordStar file strippers) support these features.

7

The DOSSHELL Interface

Starting DOSSHELL
Using DOSSHELL
Modifying DOSSHELL.BAT

A *shell* is a computer program that interprets your requests to run other computer programs. Another term for shell is *command interpreter*. The standard DOS shell is the program COMMAND.COM. Broadly speaking, COMMAND.COM provides support for the DOS *command line interface*. The command line is indicated by the familiar **C>**, which stares at the user whenever DOS is waiting for a command to be entered.

The command line interface is often criticized as being "awkward" and "nonintuitive" to use. Systems with a command line interface require you to type the exactly correct command. If you make a mistake, the system refuses to operate or misfires. A command line interface generally offers little in the way of clues as to your choice of possible commands or their correct spelling and syntax (not to mention command options, switches, and other possible parameters).

Many people feel that a *graphically based interface*, as employed by the Apple Macintosh, is easier to use. Graphically based interfaces display to the user a visual representation of the choice of possible commands. The user has the capability to "pick and choose" a command to be executed. The term "pick" means that by using some type of input device (most often a mouse or the cursor keys) the user can move the cursor or a highlight bar from one command to another. The term "choose" means that the user can execute a command by first "picking" it and then pressing a specific key (typically the Enter key or a button on the mouse).

Some users actually prefer the command line interface. Typically these are experienced computer users who want maximum control of their machines. Nonetheless, the trend in personal computing is clearly headed toward graphically based interfaces. DOS 4 follows this trend with the implementation of a "more friendly" user interface called DOSSHELL. Many users will find DOSSHELL a significant improvement over the standard DOS command line.

This chapter begins with a discussion of some basic facts about DOSSHELL, for users who want to begin using the new interface right away. The second section, the majority of the chapter, discusses in detail the structure, appearance, and use of the DOSSHELL interface. The second section also explains how you can extend the interface to suit your particular needs. The chapter's third and final section explains the role of the DOSSHELL.BAT batch file in configuring the DOSSHELL interface. The chapter assumes that you are familiar with the coverage of files and directories in chapters 2 and 3.

Starting DOSSHELL

To use DOSSHELL you must have the files DOSSHELL.BAT, SHELLB.COM, SHELLC.EXE, SHELL.MEU, DOSUTIL.MEU, SHELL.HLP, and SHELL.CLR. If you are using a mouse, you may also need one of these files: PCIBMDRV.MOS, PCMSDRV.MOS, or PCMSPDRV.MOS (refer to "Using a

Mouse with DOSSHELL" on page 126). All of these files, with the exception of DOSSHELL.BAT, are supplied on the DOS 4 system diskettes.

The installation program SELECT (discussed in chapter 1) copies the above mentioned files to the directory containing the DOS system files, and then creates a DOSSHELL.BAT file. When SELECT completes the installation process, you can start DOSSHELL by entering **dosshell** at the DOS command line.

If you are installing DOS 4 manually (without SELECT), you can copy the above mentioned files (except DOSSHELL.BAT) from your system diskettes to the directory in which you are storing the other DOS system files. You can then use EDLIN or another text editor to create DOSSHELL.BAT.

Use of EDLIN to create the file DOSSHELL.BAT is illustrated below. The example assumes that the DOS system files are stored in C:\DOS and that the DOS search path contains the directory holding EDLIN.COM. You can copy the commands in the example to produce a working DOSSHELL.BAT batch file. This will allow you to begin using the interface right away. Discussion of the commands contained in DOSSHELL.BAT will be delayed until the end of this chapter.

```
C:\DOS>edlin dosshell.bat              ←start EDLIN
New file
*i                                     ←enter "i"
        1:*@shellb dosshell            ←DOSSHELL command
        2:*@if errorlevel 255 goto end ←DOSSHELL command
        3:*:common                     ←DOSSHELL command
        4:*@break=off                  ←DOSSHELL command
        5:*@shellc /tran/color/menu/   ←enter
           mul/snd/meu:shell.meu/        all
           clr:shell.clr/prompt/         of this
           maint/exit/swap/date          as one line.
        6:*:end                        ←DOSSHELL command
        7:*@break=on                   ←DOSSHELL command
        8*:^Z                          ←enter Ctrl-Z
*e                                     ←enter "e"

C:\DOS>
```

Once DOSSHELL.BAT is created, the DOSSHELL interface is started by entering *dosshell* at the DOS command line. However, you may have to modify your DOS search path before the interface will start up.

DOSSHELL and the DOS Search Path

It is generally convenient to be able to start DOSSHELL without changing the current directory. For example, if the current directory on drive C is \BOOKS\DOS and DOSSHELL.BAT is stored in \DOS, it would be convenient to immediately start DOSSHELL without having to change directories. In order to do this, the DOS search path must contain the directory storing the files used by DOSSHELL. In addition, you must use the APPEND command to specify the directory containing these files.

The DOS search path is the list of directories that DOS searches if it cannot find a file in the current directory. You set the search path by typing **path** followed by the directories to be searched. The directories are separated by semicolons. For example, the command "path c:\prgms\word;c:\dos" (or "path=c:\prgms\word;c:\dos") tells DOS to look in the directories C:\PRGMS\WORD and C:\DOS for any files it cannot find in the current directory.

Some programs cannot use the information contained in the DOS search path. The APPEND command was implemented to provide these programs with a list of directories to search when looking for files not stored in the current directory. You set APPEND's search path by typing **append** followed by the directories to be searched. The directories are separated by semicolons.

If the files used by DOSSHELL are in the directory C:\DOS, the following two commands allow you to start the DOSSHELL interface without changing the current directory:

```
path c:\dos
append c:\dos
```

Unfortunately, APPEND causes problems for some applications. For example, if you modify a file that was accessed using the APPEND search path, the file may be copied to the current directory, rather than back to the directory containing the original file. The original file will remain unchanged. If programs begin to behave erratically, APPEND may be the culprit. In such cases it often is necessary to avoid using APPEND. This makes the DOSSHELL interface available only when the directory storing its required files is made current.

As an alternative to relying on PATH and APPEND, you can place a CD command in DOSSHELL.BAT to make the directory containing the DOSSHELL files the current directory. Then, whenever you enter "dosshell", that directory becomes the current directory and DOSSHELL works fine. The problem with this approach is that you end up in that directory when you quit DOSSHELL.

Using a Mouse with DOSSHELL

PC-DOS 4.01 comes with three mouse device drivers. PCIBMDRV.MOS is for the IBM mouse. PCMSDRV.MOS is for the Microsoft serial mouse. PCMSPDRV.MOS is for the Microsoft bus mouse. These drivers operate only when DOSSHELL is running. Other applications still require the original driver supplied by the mouse's manufacturer.

The SELECT installation program automatically sets up the DOSSHELL.BAT file so that the new driver appropriate for your system is loaded each time DOSSHELL is started. If your mouse does not work when DOSSHELL is running, chances are the driver installed is interfering with the mouse's regular driver. To correct the problem, examine the contents of DOSSHELL.BAT. You will see a line that looks something like this:

```
@shellc /tran/color/menu/mul/snd/meu:shell.meu/clr:shell.clr
        /prompt/mos:pcmsdrv.mos/maint/exit/swap/date
```

Delete the `/mos:pcmsdrv.mos` and restart DOSSHELL. The regular driver will now work when DOSSHELL is running.

Using DOSSHELL

This discussion on the use of the DOSSHELL interface is divided into four sections. The first section discusses the terms *DOSSHELL program* and *DOSSHELL program group*. You need to understand what these terms mean in order to follow the remainder of the discussion. The second section introduces the DOSSHELL interface and discusses the various components of the interface. Terms used in describing user interactions are defined in this section. The third section contains a detailed tutorial on the use of the DOSSHELL interface. The built-in capabilities of the interface are all presented and discussed. The final section of the discussion shows how you can write your own DOSSHELL programs to extend the capabilities of the DOSSHELL interface.

DOSSHELL Programs and Program Groups

In order to use the DOSSHELL interface effectively, you must understand what the term *DOSSHELL program* means. A DOSSHELL program is not an application program or a DOS command. Rather, a DOSSHELL program is more like a batch file, because each DOSSHELL program contains one or more batch file commands. In addition, a DOSSHELL program may contain one or more *Program Start Commands*, which are used to control the manner in which a user interacts with the DOSSHELL program. Each DOSSHELL program has a *program name* that is used to identify it. DOSSHELL programs are executable only when using the DOSSHELL interface. They are not executable from the command line or from a batch file.

DOSSHELL programs are grouped together in *DOSSHELL program groups*. Each program group also has a name that is used to identify it. As we will see shortly, you execute a DOSSHELL program by first displaying on the screen the program group that contains the program you want to execute.

The *Main Program Group* is the program group that is displayed each time the interface is started up. The Main Program Group serves as a sort of "home base" for the DOSSHELL interface. It is a convenient place to return whenever you need to set your bearing straight.

In addition to containing individual DOSSHELL programs, the Main Program Group can contain other program groups. These program groups are called *subgroups*. You can display the names of the DOSSHELL programs contained in a subgroup by selecting the subgroup's name from the Main Program Group display. Subgroups contain only DOSSHELL programs. They cannot contain other program subgroups.

The DOSSHELL Display

Upon starting, DOSSHELL presents you with the **Main Program Group** screen. This is the DOSSHELL home base mentioned above. The screen is displayed in either graphics (figure 7-1A) or text (figure 7-1B) mode, depending on the type of video display hardware being used.

Graphics and Text Modes

EGA and VGA monitors display in graphics mode; other monitors display in text mode. EGA and VGA monitors can be made to display in text mode through use of the /TEXT parameter, which is discussed at the end of this chapter. The major differences between graphics mode and text mode are:

1. Graphics mode uses an arrow to represent the position of the mouse; text mode uses a small rectangle (refer to the upper left-hand corner of figures 7-1A and B).

2. Graphics mode provides scroll bars for use with the mouse; text mode does not.

3. Graphics mode uses icons to convey information; text mode does not use icons.

4. Text mode is generally faster.

The remaining illustrations in this chapter are in graphics mode; however, the information presented is applicable for text mode unless otherwise noted.

Components of the Main Program Group Screen

Referring to figures 7-1A and 7-1B, the bar across the top of the screen displays the current date, the text "Start Programs", and the current time. As you shall see, "Start Programs" indicates that you can start DOSSHELL programs from this screen.

The second line on the screen is the **action bar**, which contains the text "Program", "Group", and "Exit". The right side of the action bar contains the text "F1=Help". You can press the F1 key at any time to obtain context-sensitive help. This means that the help provided is relevant to the task you are currently trying to perform.

The contents of the Main Program Group are listed on the left side of

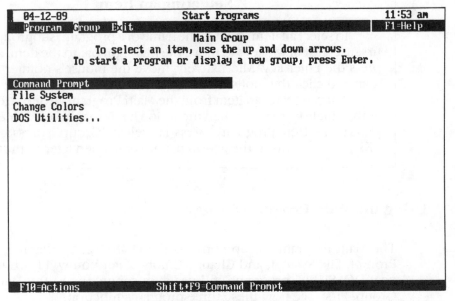

(A) *DOSSHELL in graphics mode.*

(B) *DOSSHELL in text mode.*

Figure 7-1. The Main Program Group screen is displayed in either graphics or text mode.

the screen, starting about a third of the way down. "Command Prompt", "File System", and "Change Colors" are the names of the DOSSHELL programs contained in the Main Program Group. "DOS Utilities" is the name of a program subgroup contained in the Main Program Group. The name of a subgroup is always followed by an ellipsis (. . .) to indicate that it is a subgroup name rather than a DOSSHELL program name.

The bottom line of the Main Program Group display lists some "hot" keys that are active for this screen. The F10 function key toggles the action bar on and off. The action bar toggle is on when one of the items ("Program", "Group", or "Exit") is displayed with a reverse video highlight bar. You can select (see the following box) an item from the action bar with a single keystroke when the toggle is set to "on".

The other hot key combination indicated at the bottom of the screen is Shift-F9, which executes the DOSSHELL program named Command Prompt. You can use the Command Prompt program to "jump" from the DOSSHELL interface to the command line interface. Once at the command line, you can execute DOS commands and application programs in the conventional fashion. DOSSHELL does not terminate when you execute the Command Prompt program. Instead it remains suspended in memory, ready to resume action when you type "exit" on the command line.

Selecting an Item

To select an item, such as the name of a program, subgroup, or file, first use the cursor keys to move the highlight bar to the item, and then press the Enter key. Alternatively, move the mouse's pointer over the item and click the mouse's left-most button two times.

You can select an item from the Main Program Group's action bar with a single keystroke when the action bar is toggled on. For example, press **p** to select "Program"; press **g** to select "Group"; press **x** to select "Exit". The items in the action bar are explained later in the chapter.

Using the Main Program Group

The Main Program Group contains the DOSSHELL programs Command Prompt, File System, and Change Colors. Later you will learn how to add new DOSSHELL programs and program subgroups to the Main Program Group. First, see how these three programs function.

Command Prompt

As discussed above, you can use the DOSSHELL program Command Prompt to "jump" from the DOSSHELL interface to the command line interface. You can execute Command Prompt by pressing the Shift-F9 key combination, or by selecting "Command Prompt" from the Main Program Group's list of program names. Remember that you return to the DOSSHELL interface by typing **exit** on the command line.

File System

File System is a DOSSHELL program that lets you execute, print, move, copy, delete, and rename files. You can also use the File System program to modify a file's attributes. Finally, File System allows you to delete, rename, and create file directories. Use of File System to perform each of these functions is described in this section. The section begins with some basic information about techniques and terminology.

File System Basics

Start using File System by selecting it from the Main Program Group's screen (figures 7-1A and B). This will present the File System screen (figure 7-2). The top line of the File System screen displays the date and time. The second line, referred to as the File System action bar, contains the items "File", "Options", "Arrange", and "Exit". Select "Exit" to return to the Main Program Group screen.

As is the case with the Main Program Group's action bar, the File System's action bar is toggled on and off with the F10 key. You can select an action bar item with a single keystroke when the action bar is toggled. You can also use the mouse to select an item on the action bar.

```
 04-12-89                      File System              10:13 am
 File  Options  Arrange  Exit                          F1=Help
 Ctrl+letter selects a drive.
 [==]A   [==]B   [==]C   [==]D   [==]E   [==]F

 C:\
       Directory Tree                           *.*
                                   +                                    +
 ✓C:\          ☝                   ▲  ▤012345  .678        109  06-17-88  ▲
  ├─DOS                               ▤AUTOEXEC.400        122  12-19-88
  ├─BATCH                             ▤AUTOEXEC.BAK         63  11-28-88
  ├─UTILS                             ▤AUTOEXEC.BAT         95  12-15-88
  │ └─INSET                           ▤COMMAND .COM     37,637  06-17-88
  ├─PRGMS                             ▤CONFIG  .400        145  12-19-88
  │ ├─TOPS                            ▤CONFIG  .BAK         73  04-12-89
  │ │ └─ATALK                         ▤CONFIG  .SYS        121  04-12-89
  │ ├─MOUSE                           ▤CONFIG2 .SYS        321  04-12-89
  │ ├─PAINT                           ▤DATA            11,397  11-29-88
  │ ├─WORD                            ▤IBMBIO  .COM     32,816  08-03-88
  │ ├─PROCOMM                         ▤IBMDOS  .COM     36,000  08-03-88
  │ └─WINDOWS                         ▤NEWCONFI           303  10-28-88
  │   └─PIF                         ▼
  ├─PCVI                             ▼
  └─LIB                              +                                    +
 F10=Actions   Shift+F9=Command Prompt
```

Figure 7-2. The File System screen. Drive C is currently selected.

Immediately below the action bar you can see an area that lists the disk drives on the system. In graphics mode, icons representing disk drives are displayed in this area. This area is referred to as the *drive selection area*.

Below the drive selection area, the screen is divided into two columns. A directory tree is displayed on the left. A listing of files is displayed on the right.

Move the highlight bar from the drive selection area to the directory tree, then to the listing of files, then to the action bar, then back to the drive selection area, by repeatedly pressing the tab key.

The icon or drive letter of the *currently selected drive* is highlighted when the highlight bar is in the drive selection area. The currently selected drive is the drive currently being accessed by the DOSSHELL interface. The directory tree and the listing of files on the lower portion of the screen represent a portion of the contents of the currently selected drive.

You change the currently selected drive by pressing simultaneously the Ctrl key and a letter key. For example, you make drive D the currently selected drive by pressing Ctrl-D.

The *currently selected directory* is highlighted when the highlight bar enters the area containing the directory tree. The currently selected directory contains the files whose names are displayed in the listing on the right side of the screen.

Change the currently selected directory by moving the highlight bar to the desired directory and then pressing the Enter key. The listing of files on the right side of the screen is updated to reflect the change of directories.

Only one disk drive and one file directory are currently selected at any one time. In contrast, one or more files may be currently selected at a given time. To select a file, use the tab to move the highlight bar to the column on the right, and move the highlight over the desired filename. Press the space bar to select a file. Press the space bar again to "deselect" a file. Using a mouse, you can point and click to select and deselect.

In graphics mode, selected files are represented by a highlighted file icon. Figure 7-3A shows three files as currently selected. In text mode, selected files are indicated by an arrowhead to the left of the selected filename.

The contents of the directory tree can be scrolled up and down if the tree is too large to fit in the space provided. Similarly, the listing of files can be scrolled up and down if the listing is too large to fit in the space provided. Left and right columns can be scrolled up and down.

In graphics mode, there are single arrows and double arrowheads immediately to the right of the directory tree. Use the mouse to click on the up (or down) arrow to scroll the directory tree up (or down) one line at a time. Click on the double up (or down) arrowheads to scroll the directory tree up (or down) fifteen lines at a time. Similarly, use the arrow and arrowheads to the far right of the screen to scroll the list of files up and down.

There is also a *slider box* between the up and down arrowheads, which can be used for scrolling in either direction. Move the mouse's pointer to the slider box, hold down the left mouse button, and move the slider box in the direction you want to scroll (see figure 7-3B).

In text mode, up and down arrows provide the scrolling mechanism. Scrolling with the up and down cursor keys is also supported in both types of display modes.

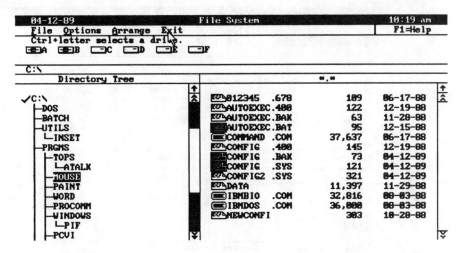

(A) *The files AUTOEXEC.BAK, CONFIG.BAK, and CONFIG.SYS are currently selected.*

(B) *Using the slider box to scroll the directory tree.*

Figure 7-3. Selecting files from the directory.

Most of the action in the File System program takes place by first selecting "Files" on the action bar. A pop-up box appears when this item is selected (see figure 7-4). This box is referred to as the *Files pop-up box*.

The last two items in the Files pop-up box are "Select all" and "Deselect all". "Select all" lets you select all of the files in the currently selected directory. It is useful for performing global operations such as moving all files from one subdirectory to another. "Deselect" lets you deselect all files currently selected. To protect against inadvertent file deletion, make it a habit to deselect all files prior to performing a file deletion.

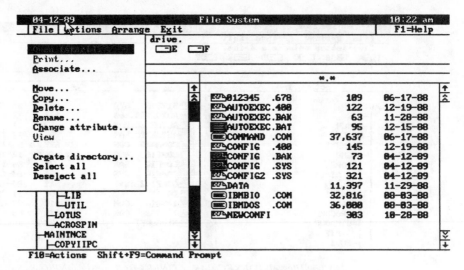

Figure 7-4. The Files pop-up box.

This concludes the discussion of the basic techniques and terminology relevant to using the File System program. The time has come to start using the program.

Additional Tips and Techniques

Underlined Letters   Many items appearing in the DOSSHELL interface have one of their letters underlined. You can select these items by pressing the key corresponding to the underlined letter. For example, if the Files pop-up box is displayed, you can press "s" to select "Select all".

Horizontal Scrolling   Many of the boxes used to enter text are too small to hold all of the characters that can potentially be entered in the box. The contents of these boxes automatically scroll as you enter more characters. The boxes also have horizontal arrows, which you can use to scroll the contents for reading. Refer to figure 7-6 for an example of this.

Escaping   Most boxes and screens allow you to escape by pressing the Esc key. This cancels any commands that you entered in the screen or box.

Running Executable Files

There are three ways to start an executable file (application program, external DOS command, batch file) from the File System screen. The first way is to move the highlight bar to the appropriate filename and press Enter. The second way is to use the mouse to double click on the filename. The third way is to select a file (described under "File System Basics") and then open the Files pop-up box. After the box is opened, select the "Open (start)" field to execute the program.

Regardless of the method used, the Open File box always appears (figure 7-5). Use the "Options" field of this box to enter any parameters required by the program. Up to 128 characters may be entered. In figure 7-5, the user has entered `c:\prgms\test.com`, so that when the "Enter" field in the lower left of the box is selected (or if the user presses the Enter key), the complete command passed to DOS is

```
debug c:\prgms\test.com
```

The program DEBUG then executes in the standard fashion, as if the user had typed `debug c:\prgms\test.com` on the command line.

The system will prompt you to press the Enter key to return to DOSSHELL when the program terminates its execution.

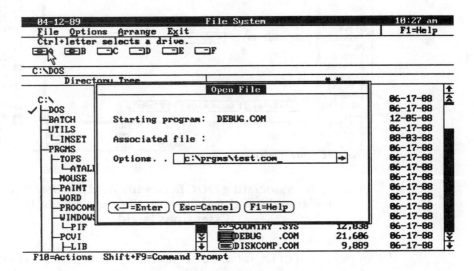

**Figure 7-5. Using the Open File box to pass the parameter
"c:\prgms\test.com" to DEBUG.COM.**

Printing a File

Select the "Print" field in the Files pop-up box to print all files currently selected. This field is available only if the DOS print spooler has previously been installed with the DOS command PRINT. If necessary, you can press Shift-F9 to jump to the command line, execute PRINT, then type **exit** to return to the DOSSHELL interface. The "Print" field will then be available for you to use.

Associating Filename Extensions with a Program

The File pop-up box can be used to link (or associate) files that use a particular filename extension to a file that is an executable program. As an example, the word processor used in writing this book is an executable file named WORD.COM. The document files created by the word processor have the filename extension DOC. Instructing the DOSSHELL interface to associate DOC files with WORD.COM means that selecting a DOC file automatically starts WORD.COM. The word processor, in turn, automatically loads the selected DOC file.

In figure 7-6, the file WORD.COM is currently selected. The File pop-up box has been opened and "Associate" has been selected. This opens the Associate File box shown in the figure.

Figure 7-6. Associating DOC files with WORD.COM. Note the horizontal scrolling arrow on the right side of the "Extensions" field.

An extension of DOC has been entered by the user (up to twenty separate extensions may be entered). When the user selects "Enter" (or presses the Enter key), another box appears, which asks if DOSSHELL should "prompt for options".

If the user selects "1", DOSSHELL will prompt for additional program parameters each time a DOC file is selected. No prompting will occur if "2" is selected.

Once the association is made, selection of any file with an extension of DOC will automatically start WORD.COM.

Moving Files

DOSSHELL provides you with the capability to move files from one directory to another. It is important to realize that move is actually a copy followed by a deletion of the original file.

The first step in moving files is to select the files that you want moved.

Use "Select all" in the Files pop-up box (figure 7-4) to move all files in a directory. Next, select "Move" from the Files pop-up box; this opens the Move File box. The names of the selected files appear in the "From" field. Enter the destination directory in the "To" field.

You can configure DOSSHELL so that you simply select the destination directory rather than having to type it in. Refer to the following section titled "Options" for information on the configuration process.

Copying Files

Copying files is similar to moving them. First select the files to be copied; use " Select all" in the Files pop-up box to copy all files in a directory. The Copy field is selected. Next select "Copy" from the Files pop-up box that opens the Copy File box. The names of the selected files appear in the "From" field. Enter the destination directory in the "To" field. If only a single file is selected, a different filename can be appended to the destination directory, thus renaming the file in the process. If you select more than one file, the copies must have the same names as the originals.

Deleting and Renaming Files

To delete files, first select the files to be deleted and then select the "Delete" field from the Files pop-up box. As previously mentioned, it is good practice always to deselect all files before you select the files that you want to delete. This will prevent any inadvertent deletions.

You can configure DOSSHELL to prompt you to confirm all file deletions. Refer to the section titled "Options" for information on configuring.

Renaming files is similar to the operations previously described. Select the files that you want to rename. Next select "Rename" from the Files pop-up box, opening the Rename File box. Then enter a new filename for each selected file.

Deleting and Renaming Directories

The procedures for deleting and renaming directories are similar to the same procedures for files. You can select only one directory at a time. You can delete and rename directories only when no files are currently selected. Directories must be empty before you can delete them. As is the case with file deletion, you can configure DOSSHELL so that directory deletion requires user confirmation. Refer to the section headed "Options" for details.

Changing Attributes

You can modify file attributes with the "Change attribute" field of the Files pop-up box. First, select the files to be modified, then select "Change attribute". The Change Attributes box will appear, asking if the selected files are to be modified one at a time or all at once.

If you choose one at a time, the filename for each selected file will be displayed along with the current status of the file's hidden, read-only, and archive attributes. Use the cursor keys and the space bar to modify the attributes as you desire, then press the Enter key. The filename of the next selected file will be displayed and you can repeat the process.

If you choose to modify all files at once, simply use the cursor keys and space bar to set the desired attributes and then press Enter. The attributes of the selected files will all be modified to the same setting.

Refer to chapter 10 and Part 3 for a discussion of DOS file attributes.

Viewing a File

Select "View" from the Files pop-up box to browse through the contents of a previously selected file. The browsing facility is available only if exactly one file is currently selected.

File View is useful in examining text files. One screen of text is displayed at a time. You can scroll up or down through the file using the PgUp and PgDn keys.

File View can also be used to examine binary files (figure 7-7A). No comparable facility is available from the DOS command line, because the TYPE command is not designed to handle binary files. A very nice feature of File View is its ability to toggle the display from an ASCII format to a hexadecimal format (figure 7-7B). Press F9 to change the format. The hexadecimal display format is most useful when examining the contents of a binary file.

Creating a Subdirectory

To create a subdirectory use the "Create directory" field of the Files pop-up box. The subdirectory created will be located in the currently selected directory. For example, you must select the directory C:\ as the currently selected directory in order to create the directory C:\DIR1.

Options

The second field on the File System action bar is titled "Options" (figure 7-2). Selecting this field produces the Options pop-up box. The three functions accessed from this box are "Display Options", "File Options", and "Show Information".

Display Options Selecting "Display Options" produces the Display Options box (figure 7-8). The settings displayed in this box let you control the listing of filenames, which appears on the right side of the screen. In figure 7-8, "Name" is set to *.*, which requests the system to display all files in the currently selected directory. You can narrow the listing to display only a subset of the files. For example, enter *.DOC in the "Name" field to list all files with a filename extension of DOC.

You can sort the filename listing using one of five criteria:

► Filename

► Filename extension

► File date stamp

► File size

► Physical location of each file on the disk

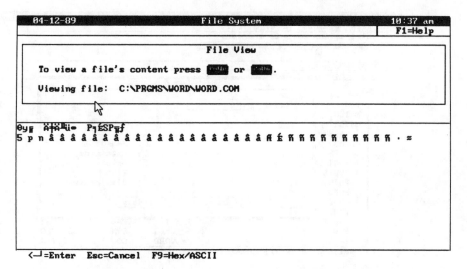

(A) *Using File View to view a binary file in ASCII mode.*

(B) *Viewing a binary file in hexadecimal format. The left-most column is the offset address into the file. The middle four columns contain the file's byte values in hexadecimal format. The right-most column is a text display of the file's contents. Non-alphanumeric bytes are represented by a period.*

Figure 7-7. Using File View to view a text or binary file.

Change the criterion by clicking with the mouse on the criterion of choice. Alternatively, press the tab key to move from the "Name" field to the "Sort by" list, then use the cursor keys to select the criterion.

File Options   Use the File Options box to set three parameters. Con-**firm on delete** instructs the system to ask you to confirm each file deletion. Confirmation is required when the box is marked or, in text mode, when the

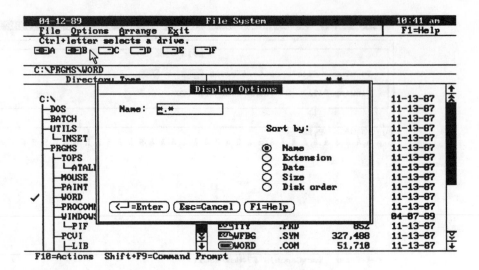

Figure 7-8. The Display Options box.

arrowhead is present. Similarly, **Confirm on replace** determines whether or not the system will ask you to confirm file replacements. Change settings by clicking with the mouse on the line of text. Alternatively, move the highlight bar to the line and change the status by pressing the space bar.

The third parameter that you can set from this box is **Select across directories**. Normally, files are deselected when a change is made in the currently selected directory. If "Select across directories" is turned on, files remain selected when a change is made in directory selection. This can be useful when you are moving or copying files from one directory to another.

As an example, say that you have selected a group of files from a directory for moving. Normally, you will have to type the name of the destination directory in the Move File box. If "Select across directories" is turned on, there is a quicker way. After selecting the files, select the destination directory before opening the Move File box. When you open the box, the system will automatically enter the destination directory name in the "To" field.

Show Information The third field in the Options pop-up box generates the Show Information box (figure 7-9). This box contains information about the most recently selected file, the total number of files currently selected, the currently selected directory, and the currently selected disk drive.

Arrange

Select "Arrange" on the File System action bar to modify the overall display format of the File System screen. Selection of "Arrange" produces the Arrange pop-up box. This box contains three potential selections.

"**Single file list**" is the format used in the previous examples presented in this chapter. A single directory tree, representing the directory structure

```
 04-12-89                    File System                   10:44 am
 File  Options  Arrange  Exit                            F1=Help
Ctr┌─────Show Information─────┐
 A │                          │
   │  File                    │
C:\P│    Name  : WORD.COM      │                    *.*
   │    Attr  : ...a           │
   │  Selected            C    │
C:\ │    Number:           0    │  OUTLINE .STY      1,024   11-13-87
├─D │    Size  :           0    │  POSTSCRL.INI     10,434   11-13-87
├─B │  Directory               │  POSTSCRL.PRD     16,350   11-13-87
├─U │    Name  : WORD          │  POSTSCRP.INI     10,434   11-13-87
 L │    Size  :   2,063,936    │  POSTSCRP.PRD     16,350   11-13-87
├─P │    Files :        44      │  README  .DOC      6,638   11-13-87
   │  Disk                    │  SAMPLE  .STY      1,024   11-13-87
   │    Name  : PCAT_COLOR     │  SEMI    .STY      1,536   11-13-87
   │    Size  :  21,344,256    │  SIDEBY  .STY      1,024   11-13-87
✓  │    Avail :   6,670,336    │  SPELL-AM.EXE    111,948   11-13-87
   │    Files :       684      │  SPELL-AM.HLP      3,715   11-13-87
   │    Dirs  :        32      │  SPELL-AM.LEX    175,173   11-13-87
   │                          │  TEST    .PIX     10,235   04-07-89
   │ ┌Esc=Cancel┐ ┌F1=Help┐   │  TTY     .PRD        852   11-13-87
   │ └──────────┘ └───────┘   │  WFBG    .SYN    327,488   11-13-87
 ─LIB└──────────────────────────┘  WORD    .COM     51,710   11-13-87
 F10=Actions  Shift+F9=Command Prompt
```

**Figure 7-9. The Show Information box. In this example,
WORD.COM is the most recently selected file, WORD is the
selected directory, and PCAT__COLOR is the selected disk drive.**

on the currently selected disk drive is displayed. A single file list containing the name of each file in the currently selected directory is also displayed.

"**Multiple file list**" lets you split the screen horizontally to display a directory tree and a file list for the two most recently selected disk drives (figure 7-10A).

"**System file list**" lets you display all of a disk's files regardless of subdirectories (figure 7-10B).

The "System file list" option is useful for finding all occurrences of a file on a disk. To do this, first select "System file list" from the Arrange pop-up box; then open the Display Options box (figure 7-8). Enter the desired filename in the "Name" field (wildcards are acceptable) and select "Enter". All occurrences of the file will be listed. To see the directory location of each listing, highlight the particular entry.

This completes the discussion of the File System program. Press F3 for a quick return to the Main Program Group's screen (figures 7-1A and B). From this point, the discussion will proceed to a discussion of the DOSSHELL program Change Color and the program subgroup DOS Utilities.

Change Colors

Change Colors is a DOSSHELL program that lets you change the color scheme of the DOSSHELL display. This program only runs on systems with color monitors.

Select "Change Colors" from the DOSSHELL Main Program Group screen (figure 7-1). Four color combinations are available; from these you may choose one. View the available choices by repeatedly pressing the right

```
 04-12-89                    File System                10:46 am
  File  Options  Arrange  Exit                          F1=Help
 Ctrl+letter selects a drive.
 ▭A  ▭B  ▭C  ▭D  ▭E  ▭F

 C:\PRGMS\WORD

        Directory Tree                          *.*
 ┌PRGMS                     ↑          SPELL-AM.LEX   175,173  11-13-87  ↑
 │ ├TOPS                    ⌃          TEST    .PIX    18,235  04-07-89  ⌃
 │ └ATALK                              TTY     .PRD       852  11-13-87
 ├MOUSE                                WFBG    .SYM   327,488  11-13-87  ⌄
 ├PAINT                    ⌄           WORD    .COM    51,718  11-13-87  ↓
✓├WORD                      ↓

 ▭A  ▭B  ▭C  ▭D  ▭E  ▭F

        Directory Tree                          *.*
✓┌D:\                       ↑          CML0200 .HCL     6,944  04-18-88  ↑
 ├CRS                       ⌃          GCLISP  .EXE   146,944  04-18-88  ⌃
 │ ├EMR11                              TOTAL           45,583  01-30-89
 │ ├EMR12                              VDF0200 .VDW     1,616  04-18-88
 │ ├EMR13                   ⌄                                            ⌄
 │ └EMR14                   ↓                                            ↓
 F10=Actions   Shift+F9=Command Prompt
```

(A) *Multiple file list display.*

```
 04-12-89                    File System                10:49 am
  File  Options  Arrange  Exit                          F1=Help
 Ctrl+letter selects a drive.
 ▭A  ▭B  ▭C  ▭D  ▭E  ▭F

 C:\PRGMS\PAINT
                                                *.*
 File                          AUTOEXEC.400      122  12-19-88  10:05am  ↑
   Name : BIT16X14.FNT         AUTOEXEC.BAK       63  11-28-88  10:09am  ⌃
   Attr : ...a                 AUTOEXEC.BAT       95  12-15-88   5:01pm
 Selected     D    C           AUTOEXEC.BAT       18  11-06-85  12:34pm
   Number:    0    2           AUTOIN  .COM      142  12-08-86   7:08pm
   Size :       7,548         BACKUP  .COM    33,754  06-17-88  12:00pm
 Directory                     BASIC   .COM     1,065  06-17-88  12:00pm
   Name : PAINT                BASIC   .PIF      369  11-12-87   1:11pm
   Size :     479,246         BASICA  .COM    36,285  06-17-88  12:00pm
   Files :         63          BASICA  .PIF      369  11-12-87   1:11pm
 Disk                          BEDROOM .FIL    7,432  04-04-88   6:34am
   Name : PCAT_COLOR           BEDROOM .PAS    4,692  04-04-88   6:34am
   Size : 21,344,256          BEEP    .COM    2,604  01-21-86   3:10pm
   Avail :  6,670,336         ▓BIT16X14.FNT    7,426  08-30-85   1:43pm▓
   Files :        684          BIT16X16.FNT    8,450  08-30-85   1:43pm  ⌄
   Dirs :          32                                                    ↓
 F10=Actions   Shift+F9=Command Prompt
```

(B) *System file list display. All files on the disk are listed. This particular listing is sorted by file size.*

Figure 7-10. Multiple and System file list options in the Arrange pop-up box.

and left cursor keys. Press the Enter key to select the combination currently being displayed. Press the Esc key to select the color scheme that was active prior to starting the Change Color program.

DOS Utilities

DOS Utilities is a DOSSHELL program subgroup that is selectable from the Main Program Group screen (figure 7-1). Recall that a subgroup is a collection of one or more DOSSHELL programs.

DOS Utilities contains DOSSHELL programs that perform the following tasks:

1. Copy diskettes (using the DOS command DISKCOPY).
2. Compare the contents of two diskettes (using the DOS command COMP).
3. Back up the contents of a fixed (hard) disk (using the DOS command BACKUP).
4. Restore the contents of a fixed (hard) disk (using the DOS command RESTORE).
5. Set the system time and date (using the DOS commands TIME and DATE).
6. Format a disk or diskette (using the DOS command FORMAT).

This section discusses and demonstrates each of these DOSSHELL programs.

Notice that each of the DOSSHELL programs presented in this section uses one or more DOS commands. This is similar to the situation in which a batch file may contain a set of DOS commands. In fact, with the exception of GOTO commands, a DOSSHELL program may contain any valid batch file command. In discussing DOSSHELL programs, it is important to recognize the difference between a DOSSHELL program (such as Disk Copy) and a DOS command (such as DISKCOPY) contained in the program.

Selecting "DOS Utilities . . . " from the Main Program Group screen produces the DOS Utilities screen. This screen lists the six DOSSHELL programs mentioned above. You can press the Esc key to return to the Main Program Group screen.

To start any of these DOSSHELL programs, move the highlight bar to the name of the desired program and press the Enter key. Alternatively, a program can be started by using the mouse pointer to double click on the program's name.

Disk Copy

Selecting the DOSSHELL Disk Copy program produces the Diskcopy Utility pop-up box. The system asks you to enter the drive letters for the source and destination diskettes. The program executes the DOS command DISKCOPY with default parameters "a: b:". You can change the defaults from the keyboard. Press the Enter key to execute the program. Press Esc to cancel the program.

Disk Compare

Selecting the DOSSHELL Disk Compare program produces the Diskcomp Utility pop-up box. The system asks you to enter the drive letters for the diskettes to be compared. The program executes the DOS command DISKCOMP with default parameters "a: b:". You can change the defaults from the keyboard. Press the Enter key to execute the program. Press the Esc key to cancel the program.

Backup Fixed Disk

Selecting the DOSSHELL Backup Fixed Disk program produces the Backup Utility pop-up box. The system asks you to enter the source and destination drives. The program executes the DOS command BACKUP with default parameters "c:*.* a: /s". You can change the defaults from the keyboard. Press the Enter key to execute the program. Press the Esc key to cancel the program.

Restore Fixed Disk

Selecting the DOSSHELL Restore Fixed Disk program produces the Restore Utility pop-up box. The system asks you to enter the source and destination drives. The program executes the DOS command RESTORE with default parameters "a: c:*.* /s". You can use the keyboard to change the defaults. Press the Enter key to execute the program. Press the Esc key to cancel the program.

Set Date and Time

Selecting the DOSSHELL Set Date and Time program produces the Set Date and Time Utility pop-up box. The system first asks you to enter a new date. No default parameters are provided. After pressing the Enter key, the system then asks you to enter the new time. Press the Enter key to complete the program. The system will prompt you again if either the date or time are specified in an invalid format. Press the Esc key to terminate the program.

Format

Selecting the DOSSHELL Format program produces the Format Utility pop-up box. The system asks you to enter the drive to format. The program executes the DOS command FORMAT with default parameter "a:". You can use the keyboard to change the default. Press the Enter key to execute the program. Press the Esc key to cancel the program.

This completes the discussion of DOSSHELL programs contained in the DOS Utilities subgroup. The following section discusses how to create new DOSSHELL programs and program subgroups.

DOSSHELL Programming

DOSSHELL programs are actually enhanced batch files. All batch file statements, other than GOTO, are usable in DOSSHELL programs.

As you have seen, a DOSSHELL program is started by selecting the program name on the display screen. You have also seen that selecting a DOSSHELL program name generates a pop-up box, which can be used to pass parameters to the program. These pop-up boxes are generated using a set of commands called *Program Start Commands* or PSCs.

In this section you will see how to create DOSSHELL programs using standard batch file commands and PSCs. The batch file commands control program actions. The PSCs control the appearance and behavior of the program's pop-up box.

Creating a New DOSSHELL Program

You have seen that DOSSHELL programs are placed in program groups. The example presented in this section will show how a new DOSSHELL program is added to the DOS Utilities program group.

Starting at the Main Program Group screen (figure 7-1), select "DOS Utilities"; this will produce the DOS Utilities screen.

The first step you take in creating a new DOSSHELL program is to select "Program" from the action bar of the program group (in this case, DOS Utilities) that will contain the new program. This selection produces a pop-up box that offers the selections "Start", "Add", "Change", "Delete", and "Copy". Selection of "Add" produces the Add Program box, which is used to create new DOSSHELL programs.

The Add Program box contains four fields. Use the tab key or the Enter key to move from one field to the next. You are required to enter information into the "Title" and "Commands" fields when creating a new DOSSHELL program. Use of the "Help text" and "Password" fields is optional.

Use the "Title" field to specify the name of the DOSSHELL program you are creating. The new program name will appear on the display screen along with the names of other programs in the same program group. In figure 7-11, a program name of Memory Check has been entered in the "Title" field. You may enter up to 40 characters in the "Title" field.

```
┌────────────────────────────────────────────────────────────────┐
│ 04-12-89              Start Programs                 11:17 am    │
│ Program  Group  Exit                                  F1=Help    │
│                     DOS Utilities...                             │
│         To select an item, use the up and down arrows.           │
│      To start a program or display a new group, press Enter.     │
│                                                                  │
│ Set Date and Time                                                │
│ Disk Copy            ┌──────── Add Program ────────┐             │
│ Disk Compare         │                             │             │
│ Backup Fixed Dis│ Required                         │             │
│ Restore Fixed D:│                                  │             │
│ Format          │  Title . . . .  │Memory Check  │→││             │
│                 │                                  │             │
│                 │  Commands  . .  │mem │pause_     │→││             │
│                 │                                  │             │
│                 │ Optional                         │             │
│                 │                                  │             │
│                 │  Help text . .  │            │→│ │             │
│                 │                                  │             │
│                 │  Password  . .  │            │   │             │
│                 │                                  │             │
│                 │ (Esc=Cancel) (F1=Help) (F2=Save) │             │
│                 └──────────────────────────────────┘             │
│                                                                  │
│   F10=Actions  Esc=Cancel  Shift+F9=Command Prompt               │
└────────────────────────────────────────────────────────────────┘
```

Figure 7-11. Creating a new DOSSHELL program. Refer to explanation in text.

Use the "Commands" field to enter the commands that make up the program. These are the commands that will be executed when the program's name is selected.

In figure 7-11, the DOS command MEM has been entered. The command PAUSE has also been entered. This will prevent the display that is generated by MEM from disappearing before you have a chance to read it. The two commands are separated by the " || " character, which is generated by pressing the F4 function key.

You may enter up to 500 characters in the "Commands" field. A little later you will see how PSCs are also used in the "Commands" field.

Use the "Help text" field to create a help facility for the new program. This is the text that will be displayed when the program is selected and the user presses the F1 function key. You may enter up to 478 characters of text in this field.

You can use the "Password" field to specify a password that must be typed before the new program can be used. You may enter up to 8 characters of text in this field.

The "Help Text" and "Password" fields will not be used in the program presented here.

Press the F2 function key (or select "Save") to save the new program. This adds the program's name to the names of DOSSHELL programs in the program group.

Now that you have seen how a DOSSHELL program is created, it is time to learn how to modify an existing program.

Modifying a DOSSHELL Program

Change an existing DOSSHELL program as follows:

1. Move the highlight bar to the program's name.
2. Select "Program" from the screen's action bar.
3. Select "Change".

This will produce the Change Program box. The box contains the same fields as the Add Program box. The current content of each field is displayed. Change the program by modifying one or more fields. Press F2 to record the changes.

Figure 7-12 shows a Change Program box being used to modify Memory Check. The first change to notice is the square brackets placed immediately after "mem". The square brackets signal DOSSHELL to generate a pop-up box before executing the MEM command. The pop-up box allows the user to type in parameters that will be passed to MEM.

The second change to notice is the pipe symbol ("|") followed by the DOS command "MORE". This change causes DOS to display the output from MEM one screen at a time. This is useful because the parameters /DEBUG and /PROGRAM cause MEM to generate a display that otherwise scrolls off the screen.

The square brackets are actually the simplest form of PSCs, because

```
 04-12-89              Start Programs             11:20 am
 Program  Group  Exit                            │ F1=Help
                      DOS Utilities...
            To select an item, use the up and down arrows.
        To start a program or display a new group, press Enter.

 Set Date and Time
 Disk Copy          ┌──────── Change Program ────────┐
 Disk Compare       │                                │
 Backup Fixed Dis   │ Required                        │
 Restore Fixed D    │                                │
 Format             │   Title . . . .  [ Memory Check    ]→│
 Memory Check       │                                │
                    │   Commands  . .  [ mem[] pause ! more ]→│
                    │                                │
                    │ Optional                        │
                    │                                │
                    │   Help text . .  [           ]→│
                    │                                │
                    │   Password  . .  [       ]     │
                    │                                │
                    │ ( Esc=Cancel ) ( F1=Help ) ( F2=Save ) │
                    └────────────────────────────────┘

 F10=Actions  Esc=Cancel  Shift+F9=Command Prompt
```

Figure 7-12. Modifying the DOSSHELL program Memory Check.

their presence is responsible for the pop-up box. Soon you will see how to modify the pop-up box by placing additional PSCs between the square brackets. First, though, it is necessary to take a look at the standard pop-up box.

Calling Batch Files from DOSSHELL Programs

Batch files can be executed from DOSSHELL programs using the CALL command. CALL returns control to DOSSHELL upon execution of the batch file.

Figure 7-13 shows the pop-up box generated by Memory Check. You can use the parameters field in the box to type parameters that will be passed along to the MEM command. The parameters are passed to MEM because the square brackets in figure 7-12 come right after "mem". Press the Enter key to continue execution of Memory Check.

Often it is convenient to have a default parameter automatically entered when the pop-up box appears. You saw examples of this in the discussion of the DOS Utility programs. You have the ability to do this in your own DOSSHELL programs through the use of PSCs.

Program Start Commands (PSCs)

You saw in the last section that square brackets cause DOSSHELL to generate a pop-up box prior to executing a command. The square brackets are the simplest form of PSCs.

```
04-12-89                    Start Programs                    11:22 am
 Program  Group  Exit                                         F1=Help
                        DOS Utilities...
            To select an item, use the up and down arrows.
          To start a program or display a new group, press Enter.

 Set Date and Time
 Disk Copy
 Disk Compare
 Backup Fixed Disk
 Restore Fixed Disk
 Format
 Memory Check              ┌──────────── Program Parameters ────────────┐
                           │                                             │
                           │  Type the parameters, then press Enter.     │
                           │                                             │
                           │  Parameters . . ┌──────────┐            ➡   │
                           │                 └──────────┘                │
                           │                                             │
                           │  (◄─┘=Enter) (Esc=Cancel) (F1=Help)         │
                           └─────────────────────────────────────────────┘
 ─────────────────────────────────────────────────────────────────────
 F10=Actions   Esc=Cancel   Shift+F9=Command Prompt
```

Figure 7-13. A standard program parameters pop-up box.

The pop-up box can be modified by placing additional PSCs between the square brackets. Most of the PSCs begin with a forward slash (/) that is followed by a letter. For example, "/D" is a PSC that automatically enters a default parameter in the pop-up box's parameter field.

Figure 7-14 illustrates use of the "/D" PSC. The Change Program box is used to modify Memory Check. The following text has been placed between the square brackets:

```
/D "/debug"
```

The **/D** is a PSC that instructs DOSSHELL to automatically enter the text that follows in the parameter field of the pop-up box.

A pair of brackets may enclose more than one PSC. Each batch file command in a DOSSHELL program can have its own set of PSCs. Each batch file command's PSCs are enclosed in a pair of square brackets immediately following the command.

Each of the DOSSHELL PSCs is discussed below. The PSCs appear in bold type. A few additional examples on the use of PSCs are provided. Unless otherwise noted, a PSC must be entered between a pair of square brackets.

[/T"Title"]   The text that appears at the top of a pop-up box is called the *title*. The standard title is "Program Parameters". This PSC is used to replace the standard title. The title may contain up to 40 characters. For example, the following command would place the title "Memory Check" at the top of the Memory Check pop-up box:

```
mem[/D "/debug" /T "Memory Check"]
```

```
┌─────────────────────────────────────────────────────────────────┐
│ 04-12-89              Start Programs               11:27 am       │
│ Program  Group  Exit                              │ F1=Help │    │
│                     DOS Utilities...                             │
│              To select an item, use the up and down arrows.      │
│           To start a program or display a new group, press Enter.│
│                                                                  │
│ Set Date and Time                                                │
│ Disk Copy           ┌──────────Change Program──────────┐         │
│ Disk Compare        │                                   │         │
│ Backup Fixed Dis    │ Required                          │         │
│ Restore Fixed D     │                                   │         │
│ Format              │   Title . . . .  [Memory Check  →]│         │
│ Memory Check        │                                   │         │
│                     │   Commands  . .  [mem[/d "/debug"]| mor→]│   │
│                     │                                   │         │
│                     │ Optional                          │         │
│                     │                                   │         │
│                     │   Help text . .  [              →]│         │
│                     │                                   │         │
│                     │   Password  . .  [      ]         │         │
│                     │                                   │         │
│                     │ (Esc=Cancel) (F1=Help) (F2=Save)  │         │
│                     └───────────────────────────────────┘         │
└─────────────────────────────────────────────────────────────────┘
   F10=Actions  Esc=Cancel  Shift+F9=Command Prompt
```

**Figure 7-14. Adding a PSC to Memory Check. The PSC /D '' /
debug'' has been entered between the square brackets.**

Compare this command to the PSC in figure 7-14.

[/I"Instruction"]   The text between the quotes replaces the instruction line ("Type the parameters, then press Enter.") in the standard pop-up
box. The instruction line may contain up to 40 characters.

[/P"Prompt"]   The text between the quotes replaces the prompt line
("Parameters . . . ") in the standard pop-up box. The prompt line may contain up to 20 characters.

[/F"File specifier"]   The text between the quotes specifies a disk file.
The command immediately preceding the brackets executes only if the file
exists. The default drive is assumed if no drive is specified. The current directory is assumed if no directory is specified.

[%n]   *n* represents an integer from 1 to 10. Each n represents one of
the parameters entered in the parameters field of the pop-up box. For example, consider the following command:

```
copy *.[%1] *. [%2]
```

A DOSSHELL program with this command executes as follows:

1. A pop-up box is displayed. The first parameter entered is assigned to
   variable %1. If a second parameter is entered, it is assigned to %2.
2. A second prompt panel is displayed. If only one parameter was entered
   for the first panel, the first parameter for this second panel is assigned
   to %2.

3. The command copies each file that has a filename extension matching the first parameter.

4. Each copy is given a filename extension matching the second parameter. As is the case with commands entered at the DOS command line, the command will fail and an error message will be displayed if the total number of parameters entered does not equal two.

%n   *n* is an integer from 1 to 10, as in the previous PSC. The difference here is that %n appears outside of the brackets and it must follow a previous occurrence of %n *inside* the brackets. The second occurrence of %n is assigned the same value as the first occurrence. Consider this example:

```
if exists [%1] type %1
```

A DOSSHELL program with this command is executed as follows:

1. A prompt panel is displayed, and the first parameter entered is assigned to variable %1.

2. The `if exists` clause checks to see if a file with a name matching the parameter exists.

3. If the file exists, its contents are displayed on the screen with the type command.

[/D"Text"]   The text between the quotes defines a default value. The default may be up to 128 characters in length. Press the Enter key if the default is correct; otherwise, enter a new parameter from the keyboard. See figure 7-14 for an example.

[/D"%n"]   *n* is an integer from 1 to 10 . A value previously assigned to %n is used as a default. A value must have previously been assigned to %n.

[/R]   This PSC instructs DOSSHELL to immediately erase the entire default parameter if any key other than Enter is pressed. This can give the editing process a cleaner appearance.

[/L"n"]   *n* is an integer from 1 to 128. It specifies the maximum number of characters that can be typed into the pop-up box's parameter field. The default limit is 128 characters.

[/M"e"]   Executes the command only if the parameter entered specifies an existing file.

/#   Substitutes the drive letter of the drive used to start DOSSHELL, followed by a colon. This PSC must be outside the brackets.

/@   Substitutes the path from the root to the directory that contains the file used to start DOSSHELL. The substitution omits the initial "\". This PSC must be outside the brackets.

Modifying Program Groups

To delete a program from a program group, first select the program. Then select "Programs" from the action bar; from the resulting box, select "Delete".

To copy a program from one program group to another, first select the program. Then select "Programs" from the action bar; from the resulting box, select "Copy". The system will prompt you to display the destination group, then to press the F2 function key to complete the copy.

The programs Command Prompt, File System, and Change Colors are special. They cannot be deleted from the Main Program Group or copied to a subgroup. However, DOSSHELL can be modified so that a different main group is activated upon start-up. Refer to the discussion in the next section for details.

To add a program subgroup to the Main Program Group, select the "Group" field from the action bar and then select "Add". This will produce the Add Group box. The Add Group box has "Title", "Help text", and "Password" fields, just like the Add Program box. Refer to the discussion on creating a DOSSHELL program for information on the use of these fields.

The Add Group box contains a "Filename" field instead of a "Commands" field. This field specifies the filename of the file that will store information about the group. The file is automatically given an extension of MEU.

Entries for the "Title" and "Filename" fields are required in order to create a subgroup. Entries for the "Help text" and "Password" fields are optional.

Modifying DOSSHELL.BAT

DOSSHELL.BAT is the batch file used to start the DOSSHELL interface. This section discusses the parameters that can be used in DOSSHELL.BAT to configure the DOSSHELL interface.

The discussion centers around the DOSSHELL.BAT file created by the SELECT installation program (listing 7-1). The DOSSHELL.BAT file created by SELECT on your system may differ somewhat from the file presented here. However, the similarities will far outweigh the differences, and the points made here will apply to all versions of DOSSHELL.BAT. The numbers on the left side of each line in listing 7-1 are for reference only.

Listing 7-1. DOSSHELL.BAT file created by SELECT.

```
1    @C:
2    @CD C:\DOS
3    @SHELLB DOSSHELL
4    @IF ERRORLEVEL 255 GOTO END
5    :COMMON
6    @BREAK=OFF
7    @SHELLC /MOS:PCIBMDRV/TRAN/DOS/COLOR/MUL/MENU/SND
     /MEU:SHELL.MEU/CLR:SHELL.CLR/PROMPT/MAINT/EXIT
     /SWAP/DATE
```

```
8       :END
9       @BREAK=ON
```

The @ before each command suppresses output to the video display. Lines 1 and 2 establish the default drive and the current directory on that drive. These commands are necessary if the DOS search path does not contain the name of the directory containing the DOSSHELL files, *or* if the AP-PEND command has not previously been invoked to specify the path to the directory containing the DOSSHELL files. If BOTH of these conditions are met, then DOSSHELL can run regardless of which drive is the default and which directory is current.

Line 3 loads the resident portion of the DOSSHELL interface. The resident portion remains in memory at all times. The command also specifies the name of the batch file used to start DOSSHELL (in this case, DOSSHELL.BAT). In a networking environment, it may be desirable to have separate start-up files for each node on the network. In each of these start-up files, `shellb dosshell` should be changed to `shellb filename`, where `filename` is the name of the start-up file.

Line 4 instructs DOS to terminate execution of the batch file if an error is encountered in loading the resident component of DOSSHELL.

The `:common` label provided in line 5 is required. It tells the DOSSHELL interface where to begin re-executing, whenever the transient component of the interface is reloaded (as occurs when EXITing from Command Prompt).

Line 6 (`break=off`) suppresses checking for Ctrl-C while the command in line 7 is being executed.

The command in line 7 loads the transient portion of DOSSHELL. SHELLC.EXE is the file that contains the transient portion. The parameters that follow `shellc` are responsible for configuring DOSSHELL. Each of these parameters, including those not shown in listing 7-1, is discussed below.

The `:end` label in line 8 is required for proper operation of DOSSHELL.

DOSSHELL Configuration Parameters

The DOSSHELL configuration parameters give you some control over DOSSHELL's behavior. Each of the configuration parameters begins with a forward slash. Refer to listing 7-1 for an illustration of how the configuration commands are used.

Each of the available configuration commands is discussed in this section. The commands appear in bold type.

/ASC: *<filename>*.ASC   Specifies the filename of the file that stores program association information. The file is given a filename extension of ASC. The default filename is SHELL. Program association is discussed in the "File System" section of this chapter.

/B:n   *n* is an integer that specifies the number of Kbytes in the buffer used by the File System program. DOSSHELL uses all available memory for the buffers if no value is specified. You should specify an amount of memory for use by the buffers if you choose to run DOSSHELL in resident mode (see /TRAN below).

CLR: *<filename>*.CLR   Specifies the filename of the file containing information on DOSSHELL's current color selection. The file is automatically given a filename extension of CLR. SHELL is the default filename.

/COLOR   Activates the Change Color program. The Change Color title will still be listed on the Main Program Group screen if this parameter is deleted. Refer to the discussion of /MEU (below) to see how you can change the programs listed on the Main Program Group screen.

The next three parameters each specify a different display mode. They are valid only for specific types of display hardware.

/CO1   Specifies 16-color display mode, with 640x350 resolution, 80 columns by 25 rows. Valid for EGA and VGA only.

/CO2   Specifies 2-color display mode, with 640x480 resolution, 80 columns by 30 rows. Valid for VGA only.

/CO3   Specifies 16-color display mode, with 640x480 resolution, 80 columns by 30 rows. Valid for VGA only.

/COM2   Specifies that the DOSSHELL mouse is connected at the COM2 serial port. COM1 is the default if this parameter is not specified.

/DOS   Activates the File System program. The File System title will still be listed on the Main Program Group screen if this parameter is deleted. Refer to the discussion of /MEU (below) to see how you can change the programs listed on the Main Program Group screen.

/EXIT   This parameter activates the "Exit" field on the Main Program Group's action bar. "Exit" still appears on the bar if this parameter is omitted, but selection of the field generates an error message.

/LF   This parameter activates the second mouse button and deactivates the first mouse button. This parameter is provided for the convenience of left-handed users.

/MAINT   This parameter activates the "Program" and "Group" fields on the Main Program Group's action bar. The fields still appear on the bar if this parameter is omitted, but an error message is generated if the user attempts to use these fields to add or change programs or groups.

/MENU   This parameter is required if any functions of DOSSHELL, other than the File System, are to be made available. File System remains available if this parameter is deleted.

MEU: *<filename>*.MEU   Specifies the filename of the file containing information about the DOSSHELL Main Program Group. This is the program group that is displayed when DOSSHELL is started. The default filename is SHELL. The file is automatically given a filename extension of MEU. This parameter must be changed to obtain a Main Program Group screen that does not list the programs Command Prompt, Change Colors, and File System.

Change this parameter by first creating a subgroup within the original Main Program Group. You must specify a filename for the new subgroup. Then change the /MEU parameter to specify the filename of the newly created subgroup. The new subgroup will come up as the Main Program Group when DOSSHELL is restarted.

/MOS:<*mouse device driver*>   Specifies a device driver for use by the DOSSHELL mouse where <*mouse device driver*> is either PCIBMDRV.MOS (IBM mouse driver), PCMSDRV.MOS (Microsoft serial mouse driver), or PCMSPDRV.MOS (Microsoft bus mouse driver). The installed driver is active only when DOSSHELL is running. The DOSSHELL mouse driver may interfere with a factory supplied driver. Delete this parameter if your mouse does not work with DOSSHELL, but otherwise functions normally. This should allow your mouse to work with DOSSHELL and also reduce the amount of memory taken up by DOSSHELL.

/MUL   Specifies that the File System is to use two buffer systems. Information about two disk drives is maintained when a two-buffer system is specified.

/PROMPT   Activates the Command Prompt program in the Main Program Group screen. The "Command Prompt" title will still be listed on the Main Program Group screen if this parameter is deleted. Refer to the discussion of /MEU to see how you can change the programs listed on the Main Program Group screen.

/TEXT   Provides text mode support for CGA and monochrome displays.

/TRAN   Specifies that DOSSHELL is to operate in transient mode. In transient mode, most of the memory used by DOSSHELL is freed up when DOSSHELL is not running. DOSSHELL remains resident in memory at all times if this parameter is omitted. If you choose to keep DOSSHELL resident, you should use the /B:n parameter to limit the amount of memory used by the File System buffers.

/SND   Activates the sound capability of DOSSHELL.

/SWAP   Activates memory swapping. With memory swapping activated, the contents of the File System buffers are saved in a disk file whenever an application program is run or control is passed to the DOS command line. This capability decreases the transition time in returning to DOSSHELL.

8

EDLIN, the MS-DOS Text Editor

Creating a File with EDLIN
Modifying an Existing File with EDLIN
Ending EDLIN
EDLIN Commands

EDLIN is a line-oriented text editor that comes with MS-DOS. Given the current proliferation of high-powered processors, you may never need to use EDLIN. EDLIN is definitely not a word processor, or even close to it. If you are doing any sort of document preparation, use a word processor or other editing program, rather than EDLIN. However, if you want a handy tool to write batch files and CONFIG.SYS files, EDLIN is just what you need.

Creating a File with EDLIN

To create a new file with EDLIN, enter **edlin** and the filespec of the file that you are creating (filespecs are discussed in chapter 2). After you press Enter, DOS will load EDLIN into memory, and EDLIN will take control. EDLIN will search the specified or default drive for the filename that was entered in the start command. If it cannot find the file, EDLIN displays the message **New file** and then displays its prompt (*) to indicate that an EDLIN command may be entered:

```
C>edlin newfile.txt

New file
*
```

> The examples presented in this chapter assume that MS-DOS can locate the file EDLIN.COM. For this to occur, either EDLIN.COM must be stored in the current directory of drive C or the PATH command must specify the directory containing EDLIN.COM. Current directories and PATH are discussed in chapter 3.

Modifying an Existing File with EDLIN

To modify a file that already exists, the file EDLIN.COM must be in drive C. Enter the EDLIN start command by typing **edlin** and the filespec of the existing file. When you press Enter, MS-DOS will search the specified or default directory for the file. If it finds the file, the file will be loaded into memory until available memory is 75% full. If the entire file is loaded, EDLIN displays the message **End of input file** and then displays its prompt (*) to indicate that an EDLIN command may be entered:

```
C>edlin oldfile.txt
End of input file
*
```

If the entire file cannot be loaded into memory, EDLIN will load lines until memory is 75% full but will not display a message. The * prompt appears when EDLIN is ready to accept a command.

The B Option

If you use the method just described to load an existing file with EDLIN, the load will stop when EDLIN encounters the first Ctrl-Z character in a file's text. The Ctrl-Z character is an end-of-file marker, indicating the end of a text file. If you wish to edit a file containing embedded Ctrl-Z characters, add /b to the end of the EDLIN start command. For example:

```
C>edlin oldfile.txt/b
```

EDLIN will load the entire file regardless of any embedded end-of-file markers.

Ending EDLIN

When you have finished editing a file, you can exit from EDLIN by entering the END command **e**. The original file (if it existed) is renamed with the extension ".BAK" to indicate that it is a backup file, and the edited file is stored on the disk specified in the initial EDLIN start command. After the file has been saved, EDLIN terminates and the MS-DOS **C>** prompt is displayed.

If you decide not to save the file that you have been editing, enter the QUIT command **q**. EDLIN will display a prompt asking if you want to abort the editing session. If you enter "y" (or "Y"), the original file (if one existed) is saved with its original filename. No .BAK file is created, and control is returned to MS-DOS. If you enter "n" (or "N"), the editing session will continue. Both the END and QUIT commands will be covered in more detail later in the chapter.

The following section will discuss each of the EDLIN commands, beginning with the most frequently used ones. Table 8-1 provides an alphabetical summary of the commands.

EDLIN Commands

Before you start using the individual EDLIN commands, you need to know the conventions or rules used by EDLIN. EDLIN commands are invoked by typing a letter and pressing Enter. In addition, most EDLIN commands either allow or require that one or more numbers be included as command parameters. When a command contains more than one number, the numbers must be separated by a comma or a space. In certain instances, a comma is required. These instances will be pointed out in the discussion of the individual commands.

EDLIN does not differentiate between uppercase and lowercase letters.

For example, you can invoke the QUIT command by entering "Q" or "q". It makes no difference to EDLIN.

EDLIN designates a particular line in the file being edited as the *current line*. The current line serves as a sort of bookmarker that allows EDLIN to keep track of where it is in a file. When EDLIN displays a portion of a file, the current line has an asterisk following the line number.

The pound sign (#) may be used to refer to the last line of a file that is in memory. This can be useful when you want to perform a task involving the last line of a file but you do not know the last line number. For example, the command "50,# d" will delete everything from line 50 to the end of the file.

It is possible to refer to line numbers relative to the current line. The minus sign (−) is used to indicate a line *before* the current line. The plus sign (+) is used to indicate a line *after* the current line. As an example, the command "−5,+5 L" will list the 5 lines before the current line, the current line, and the 5 lines after the current line.

More than one EDLIN command may be entered at a time. With some exceptions, which will be noted, one command can follow another without any special delimiting characters. For example, the command "1,10 d 1,10L" deletes the first 10 lines of a file and then lists the new lines 1 through 10.

Control characters may be entered in a text file by typing "i" (for INSERT) and then pressing Ctrl-V and typing the desired control character in uppercase. For example, to enter Ctrl-Z, type "i", press Ctrl-V, and then type capital Z.

Table 8-1. Summary of EDLIN Commands

Command	Purpose	Format
(A)PPEND (page 173)	Adds a specified number of lines from disk to the file being edited in memory	[*number*] a [*number*]
(C)OPY (page 175)	Copies a range of lines to a specified location in a file	,,*line* c [*line1*],,*line* c [*line1*], [*line2*],*line* c [*line1*],[*line2*],*line, count* c
(D)ELETE (page 167)	Deletes a range of lines	d [*line1*] d ,[*line2*] d [*line1*],[*line2*] d
EDIT (page 165)	Edits a line of text	[*line*]
(E)ND (page 173)	Ends EDLIN and saves the edited file	e

Table 8-1. (cont.)

Command	Purpose	Format
(I)NSERT (page 160)	Inserts lines of text	i [*line*] i
(L)IST (page 162)	Lists lines of text	L [*line1*] L ,[*line2*] L [*line1*],[*line2*] L
(M)OVE (page 174)	Moves a range of lines to a specified location	,,*line* m [*line1*],,*line* m ,[*line2*],*line* m [*line1*],[*line2*],*line* m
(P)AGE (page 177)	Lists lines of text	p [*line1*] p ,[*line2*] p [*line1*],[*line2*] p
(Q)UIT (page 174)	Ends EDLIN and does not save the edited file	q
(R)EPLACE (page 171)	Replaces all occurrences of a string in a specified range with a second string	r [*line1*] r ,[*line2*] r [*line1*],[*line2*] r [*line1*],[*line2*] r [*string1*] F6 [*string2*] [*line1*],[*line2*] ? r [*string1*] Ctrl-Z [*string2*]
(S)EARCH (page 169)	Searches a specified range of lines in order to locate a string	s [*line1*] s ,[*line2*] s [*line1*],[*line2*] s [*line1*],[*line2*] s [*string*] [*line1*],[*line2*] ? s [*string*]
(T)RANSFER (page 178)	Merges the contents of a specified file with the file being edited	t [*filespec*] [*line*] t [*filespec*]
(W)RITE (page 172)	Writes a number of lines from memory to disk	w [*number*] w

Note: Italics indicate items that you must supply. Items in square brackets are optional.

INSERT

The INSERT command is used to insert lines of text into the file being edited. To invoke the command, enter **i** (or **I**) when you see the EDLIN prompt (*). In the following example, INSERT is used to add text to a new file. Starting with the MS-DOS prompt (**C>**), type **edlin** followed by the name of the file that will be created ("demo1.txt"). EDLIN will display its prompt (*) to indicate that it is ready to accept a command:

```
C>edlin demo1.txt
New file
*
```

The message **New file** tells you that no file named "demo1.txt" exists on the default disk. Following the * prompt, enter the letter **i** to begin the INSERT command. EDLIN will respond by displaying **1:***, which is the signal to enter the first line of text.

Each line of text may hold up to 253 characters. To terminate a line, press Enter. EDLIN will insert the ASCII characters for carriage return and line feed at the end of the line. These two characters do not appear on the display screen.

Each time you press Enter, EDLIN stores a line of text in memory and then displays the next line number. You may enter another line of text or end the INSERT command by pressing the Ctrl-Break key combination.

The following example shows how lines of text could be entered in "demo1.txt". If you decide to enter these lines on your computer, press Enter to end each line of text (lines 1 through 11).

```
C>edlin demo1.txt
New file
*i
  1:*This is how you would create a new text file with EDLIN.
  2:*Enter "i" in response to the EDLIN prompt. EDLIN displays
  3:*"1:*". This is your signal to enter the first line of text.
  4:*You may enter up to 253 characters in a line.
  5:*          ←to skip a line press Enter
  6:*To end a line, press Enter. EDLIN will store the line of
  7:*text in memory and display the next line number. You may
  8:*enter another line of text or terminate the INSERT command.
  9:*To terminate, press Ctrl-Break.
 10:*When a command is terminated, EDLIN displays its prompt
 11:*and waits for you to enter another command.
 12:*
 13:*^C      ←you press Ctrl-Break

  *           ←EDLIN displays its prompt and waits for your next command
```

Text is inserted before the *current line* when you enter "i" with no other parameters. The current line is the last line in the file that was modified. In the preceding example, line 13 is the current line. Enter i to insert text beginning at line 13:

```
*i
13:*!!!!!!!!!!!!!!!!!!!!!!!!!!!!!!!!!!!!!!!!!!!!!!!!!!!!!!!!!!!!
14:*These 3 lines are being inserted at lines 13, 14, and 15.
15:*!!!!!!!!!!!!!!!!!!!!!!!!!!!!!!!!!!!!!!!!!!!!!!!!!!!!!!!!!!!!
16:*^C

*
```

You can use the LIST command (enter uppercase L) to display a portion of the file:

```
*L
  5:
  6:To end a line, press Enter. EDLIN will store the line of
  7:text in memory and display the next line number. You may
  8:enter another line of text or terminate the INSERT command.
  9:To terminate, press Ctrl-Break.
 10:When a command is terminated, EDLIN displays its prompt
 11:and waits for you to enter another command.
 12:
 13:!!!!!!!!!!!!!!!!!!!!!!!!!!!!!!!!!!!!!!!!!!!!!!!!!!!!!!!!!!!
 14:These 3 lines are being inserted at lines 13, 14, and 15.
 15:!!!!!!!!!!!!!!!!!!!!!!!!!!!!!!!!!!!!!!!!!!!!!!!!!!!!!!!!!!!

*
```

To suspend scrolling while using LIST, press Ctrl-NumLock. To resume scrolling, press any key. Press Ctrl-Break to terminate the listing. (For more about LIST, see the next section.)

You may specify the line at which text insertion is to begin by preceding the letter "i" with a line number. In this way, text can be inserted between existing lines in the file. Lines following the insertion will be renumbered. For example:

```
*11i
 11:*++++++++++++++++++++++++++++++++++++++++++++++++++++
 12:*These 3 lines are being inserted starting at line 11.
 13:*++++++++++++++++++++++++++++++++++++++++++++++++++++
 14:*^C

*
```

The command "5L" tells EDLIN to display the file beginning with line 5:

```
*5L

5:
6:To end a line, press Enter. EDLIN will store the line of
7:text in memory and display the next line number. You may
8:enter another line of text or terminate the INSERT command.
9:To terminate, press Ctrl-Break.
10:When a command is terminated, EDLIN displays its prompt
11:++++++++++++++++++++++++++++++++++++++++++++++++++++++
12:These 3 lines are being inserted starting at line 11.
13:++++++++++++++++++++++++++++++++++++++++++++++++++++++
14:and waits for you to enter another command.
15:
16:!!!!!!!!!!!!!!!!!!!!!!!!!!!!!!!!!!!!!!!!!!!!!!!!!!!!!!!!!!!
17:These 3 lines are being inserted at lines 13, 14, and 15.
18:!!!!!!!!!!!!!!!!!!!!!!!!!!!!!!!!!!!!!!!!!!!!!!!!!!!!!!!!!!!

*
```

In the preceding example, three lines have been inserted beginning at line 11. Note that the line numbers following the insertion have been automatically renumbered.

If you precede the letter "i" with a number that is greater than the highest-existing line number in the file or if you specify "#" as the line number, the insertion begins following the last line of the file stored in memory.

LIST

The LIST command (enter uppercase L) is used to display a specific range of lines in a file. We will demonstrate this command by using EDLIN to work on the following file:

```
1: This is line 1.
2: This is line 2.
3: This is line 3.
  .
  .
  .
14: This is line 14.
15* This is line 15.
16: This is line 16.

  .
  .
  .
24: This is line 24.
25: This is line 25.
26: This is line 26.
```

The current line (the last line modified by EDLIN) is denoted by an asterisk. In the preceding example, line 15 is the current line. Using the LIST command will not change the current line.

If you enter "L" without any line numbers, EDLIN will display the 11 lines before the current line, the current line, and the 11 lines after the current line, for a total of 23 lines—the maximum number that can be listed at any one time:

```
*L
  4: This is line 4.
  5: This is line 5.
  6: This is line 6.
  .
  .
  .
 14: This is line 14.
 15:*This is line 15.
 16: This is line 16.
  .
  .
  .
 24: This is line 24.
 25: This is line 25.
 26: This is line 26.


*
```

If there are fewer than 11 lines before the current line, extra lines are displayed after the current line so that a total of 23 lines is displayed.

To list a particular range of lines, specify the starting and ending line numbers of the range in your LIST command. The numbers must be separated by a comma or a space and must precede the letter "L". To list lines 1 through 4, enter:

```
*1,4L
  1: This is line 1.
  2: This is line 2.
  3: This is line 3.
  4: This is line 4.


*
```

If you precede the LIST command with only one number, the listing will begin at that line number. A total of 23 lines will be listed. In the following example, the 23 lines from lines 2 through 24 are listed:

```
*2L
  2: This is line 2.
```

```
      3:*This is line 3.
         .
         .
  ♠      .
     23: This is line 23.
     24: This is line 24.


  *
```

If you precede the LIST command with a comma and a line number, the listing will begin 11 lines before the current line and end at the line number that is included in the command:

```
*,16L
   4: This is line 4.
   5: This is line 5.
      .
      .
      .
  14: This is line 14.
  15:*This is line 15.
  16: This is line 16.


  *
```

If the line you specify is more than 11 lines before the current line, the display is the same as if you had entered only "L":

```
*,2L
   4: This is line 4.
      .
      .
      .
  15:*This is line 15.
      .
      .
      .
  26: This is line 26.


  *
```

You can use the LIST command to obtain a printout of a portion or all of a text file. Try printing out one of the preceding examples. Turn on your printer and press the Ctrl-PrtSc key combination. Then enter the appropriate LIST command. The display that appears on your screen will be sent to the printer.

The display will start to scroll off the screen if you list more than 24 lines. To suspend the listing, press the Ctrl-NumLock key combination. The listing will continue when you press any key. To terminate the listing, press the Ctrl-Break combination.

EDIT

The EDIT command is used to edit a line of text. To specify the line to be edited, simply enter its line number. To specify the current line, enter a period (.). To specify the line following the current line, press Enter.

When you specify a line for editing, EDLIN displays the line number and the text of that line. The line number is then repeated on the line below. For example:

```
*6
    6:*The old gray mare, she ain't what she used to be.
    6:*
```

To edit a line, simply type the new text. The edited line is placed in the file and becomes the current line when you press Enter. If you decide to retain the original line without any changes, press Esc or Ctrl-Break instead of Enter. Pressing Enter with the cursor at the beginning of the line has the same effect as pressing Esc or Ctrl-Break.

If you include the EDIT command on a line with one or more other EDLIN commands, you must use semicolons to separate the commands on the line. For example, the command "22;1,5 d" will first edit line 22 and then delete lines 1 through 5.

When you specify a line for editing, the text of that line forms the *template*. The template is the current structure of the line that is stored by MS-DOS. As the line is edited, the template is modified to reflect the editing changes.

MS-DOS Editing Keys

The MS-DOS editing keys may be used to edit the template. These keys consist of the F1, F2, F3, F4, and F5 function keys, plus the Ins and Del keys.

The **F1 function key** displays one character in the template. By repeatedly pressing the F1 key (or the → key in some computers) you can cause all or part of the template to be displayed:

```
6:*The old gray mare, she ain't what she used to be.    ←template
6:*The old gray mare, she ain't what                     ←press F1 33 times
```

The last line will be placed in the file and will become the current line if Enter is pressed. If Esc is pressed, a backslash (\) will be displayed and the changes entered in the second line will be cancelled:

```
6:*The old gray mare, she ain't what she used to be.    ←template
6:*The old gray mare, she ain't what                     ←press F1 33 times;
                                                          press Esc
```

The **F3 function key** displays the template from the position of the cursor to the end of the line:

```
6:*The old gray mare, she ain't what she used to be.    ←template
6:*The old gray mare, she ain't what she used to be._   ←press F3 once
```

The **F2 function key** copies the template up to the first occurrence of a specified character. Nothing is copied if the character specified is not in the template. The last line in the following display is obtained by first pressing the F2 key and then pressing the comma (,) key. The template is copied up to, but not including, the first comma:

```
6:*The old gray mare, she ain't what she used to be.    ←template
6:*The old gray mare_                                   ←press F2 once;
                                                          enter comma
```

The **F4 function key** skips over a template until it encounters a specified character. No characters are skipped if the specified character is not present in the template. In the next example, the F4 key is pressed and then the "s" key is pressed. This deletes the characters in the template up to the first "s". The F4 key does not display any text. To display the new template, press the F3 key:

```
6:*The old gray mare, she ain't what she used to be.    ←template
6:*She ain't what she used to be._                      ←press F4, "s",
                                                          and F3
```

The **Ins key** can be used to insert text into the template. Pressing Ins one time turns the insert mode on. Pressing it a second time turns the insert mode off.

When the insert mode is on, any characters that you type are inserted into the template. These characters do not replace characters already in the template. When the insert mode is off, any characters that you type replace characters in the template.

In the following example, the F1 key is pressed three times. The Ins key is then pressed to turn on the insert mode. Five characters (4 letters and a blank) are inserted into the template. The remainder of the template is then copied with the F3 key:

```
6:*The old gray mare, she ain't what she used to be.       ←template
6:*The very old gray mare, she ain't what she used to be._ ←press F1, Ins,
                                                             "very", and
                                                             F3
```

The **Del key** can be used to skip over one character in the template at a time.

```
6:*The old gray mare, she ain't what she used to be.    ←template
6:*The old gray mare, he ain't what she used to be.     ←press F1 20 times;
                                                          press Del, F3
```

The **F5 function key** moves the line that is currently being displayed into the template without entering it in the file. An "@" character is displayed to indicate that the new line is now in the template. Once you have entered F5, you can proceed to edit the new template. Pressing Enter stores the new template in the file.

In the next example, a new line of text has been added. The F5 key is then pressed to store the new line as the template. The new template can be edited using the techniques described in this section. The original line of text remains in the file as the current line if Enter is pressed immediately after F5 is pressed:

```
6:*The old gray mare, she ain't what she used to be.    ←template
6:*And now for something completely different@          ←type new template;
                                                          press F5
```

Right now you are probably thinking that it is more trouble than it is worth to memorize the functions of the different editing keys. Typing in new lines of text seems to require less thought than remembering which key does what. However, if you spend some time working with the editing keys, you will find that EDLIN will become more productive for you.

DELETE

The DELETE command is used to delete a range of lines. The line following the deleted range becomes the current line. The current line and any subsequent lines are renumbered following a deletion.

To use DELETE, enter **d** (or **D**) in response to the EDLIN prompt. The current line will be deleted:

```
        1: This is line 1.
        2: This is line 2.
        3: This is line 3.
        4: This is line 4.
        5:*This is line 5.
        6: This is line 6.

*d
*L
        1: This is line 1.
        2: This is line 2.
        3: This is line 3.
        4: This is line 4.
```

```
        5:*This is line 6.
    *
```

In the preceding example, the current line was initially line 5. When "d" was entered, the current line was deleted and the line after the deleted line became the current line. The line following the deleted line was renumbered.

You can specify a range of lines to be deleted by including the beginning and ending line numbers of the range in the DELETE command. The two numbers must be separated by a comma or a space. The line following the deleted range will become the current line:

```
    1: This is line 1.
    2: This is line 2.
    3: This is line 3.
    4: This is line 4.
    5:*This is line 6.

*2,4d
*L
    1: This is line 1.
    2:*This is line 6.
*
```

Lines 2 through 4 have been deleted, and what was originally line 6 is now the current line.

DELETE can be used to delete a range of lines from the current line through a specified line. The command starts with a comma followed by the last line in the range to be deleted. The first line following the deleted range becomes the current line:

```
    1: This is line 1.
    2: This is line 6.
    3: This is line 7.
    4:*This is line 8.
    5: This is line 9.
    6: This is line 10.

*,5d
*L
    1: This is line 1.
    2: This is line 6.

    3: This is line 7.
    4:*This is line 10.


*
```

The range of lines starting with the current line (line 4) and ending with line 5 has been deleted. The line following the deleted range has become the current line.

SEARCH

The SEARCH command (enter s or S) searches a range of lines for a specified character string. The first line found to contain the character string becomes the current line.

The SEARCH command can include the starting and ending line numbers of the range to be searched. Line numbers must be separated by a comma or a space. The command can also include the character string that is to be the object of the search. The string is specified with its first character in the position immediately following the "s". The string is terminated by pressing Enter.

In the following example, the SEARCH command searches the block of text beginning at line 2 and ending at line 6 for the character string "and". If the string is found within the block, EDLIN will display the first line on which it is located:

```
    1: This is a demonstration file that will be used
    2: to show how the SEARCH command operates. The
    3: SEARCH command can be very handy. Imagine that
    4: you are writing a paper and you realize that you
    5: have been misspelling the word "gigolo." You could
    6: use the SEARCH command to locate the gigolos in
    7: your paper.

*2,6 sand
    2: to show how the SEARCH command operates. The


*
```

The search began at line 2. The string "and" was located in line 2 as part of the word "command." Line 2 is now the current line, since it was the first line found to contain the string.

Entering "s" by itself causes EDLIN to search for the last string that was specified with a SEARCH or REPLACE command. The search begins at the line following the current line and ends with the last line of the file that is stored in memory. We can illustrate this application of SEARCH by continuing with the previous example.

Line 2 is the current line, and the last string entered was "and". If we enter "s", EDLIN will begin searching at line 3 for "and":

```
*2,6 sand
    2: to show how the SEARCH command operates. The
```

```
*s
    3: SEARCH command can be very handy. Imagine that

*s
    4: you are writing a paper and you realize that you

*s
    6: use the SEARCH command to locate the gigolos in

*s
Not found


*
```

The command "s" was used three times to find the string "and". The string was found in lines 3, 4, and 6. None of the lines in the file beyond line 6 contained the string. Therefore, the fourth time that "s" was entered, EDLIN replied **Not found**.

Rather than reenter "s" each time to continue searching, you can enter a question mark immediately before the letter "s". EDLIN will display the prompt **O.K.?** when it finds a line containing the character string specified in the command. If you respond "y" or press Enter, the line found becomes the current line and the search ends. Pressing any other key continues the search. Once all of the lines within the range have been searched, the **Not found** message is displayed:

```
*2,6? sand
    2: to show how the SEARCH command operates. The
O.K.? n
    3: SEARCH command can be very handy. Imagine that
O.K.? n
    4: you are writing a paper and you realize that you
O.K.? y


*
```

The string was found in three lines. Each time, EDLIN asked if the search should be ended. The search was ended at line 4 when the response was "y".

Both the starting and ending line numbers of the range to be searched can be omitted from the SEARCH command. If the starting number line is omitted, the search begins at the line following the current line. If the ending line number is omitted, the search ends at the last line of the file that is in memory. The ending line number must be preceded by a comma if the starting line number is omitted and the ending line number is specified.

If the SEARCH command is entered on a line along with other EDLIN commands, the string in the command may be terminated by pressing Ctrl-Z rather than Enter.

REPLACE

The REPLACE command (enter **r** or **R**) is used to search a specified range of lines for a character string and replace that string with a second character string. The first string is replaced at each location that it occurs within the specified range. The last line changed by REPLACE becomes the current line.

The starting and ending line numbers of the range to be searched may be specified in the REPLACE command. Line numbers must be separated by a comma or a space. The character string to be replaced and the replacement character string may also be specified in the command. The two strings must be separated by Ctrl-Z.

In the next example, lines 2 through 4 are searched for the string "you". When the string is located within the range, it is replaced with "we":

```
1: This is a demo file to show how the REPLACE command
2: works. REPLACE can be very handy. Imagine that you
3: are writing a paper and you realize that you have
4: misspelled "gigolo" as "jiggloh." You could use the
5: REPLACE command to locate the jigglohs in your paper
6: and replace them with gigolos.

*2,4 ryou^Zwe
2: works. REPLACE can be very handy. Imagine that we
3: are writing a paper and we realize that you have
3: are writing a paper and we realize that we have
*
```

Notice that the two strings in the command are separated by **^Z**. This character can be entered by pressing the F6 function key or by pressing the Ctrl-Z key combination. If you have modified your function keys (see chapter 9), you will have to use the Ctrl-Z combination.

Each time that "you" is located within the specified range, it is replaced with "we". Each time a line is changed, it is displayed. Notice that line 3 is displayed two times since "you" is replaced twice. Line 4 contains the string "You". However, "You" is *not* replaced because REPLACE differentiates between uppercase and lowercase letters.

As with the SEARCH command, you can use a question mark with RE-PLACE. The question mark is included immediately before the "r". EDLIN will display the prompt **O.K.?** each time that a line is modified. If you respond by pressing "y" or Enter, the suggested modification is made. The modification is discarded if you press any other key in response to the prompt. In either case, the search continues through the entire range specified in the command. The following example demonstrates this, beginning where the last example ended:

```
    2: works. REPLACE can be very handy. Imagine that we
    3: are writing a paper and we realize that you have
    3: are writing a paper and we realize that we have

*2,4? rwe^Zyou
    2: works. REPLACE can be very handy. Imagine that you
O.K.? y
    3: are writing a paper and you realize that we have
O.K.? y
    3: are writing a paper and you realize that you have
O.K.? y


*
```

You may omit from the command both the starting and ending line numbers of the range to be searched. The search begins with the line after the current line if you omit the starting line number. The search ends with the last line in memory if you omit the ending line number. If you specify only the ending line number in the command, the line number must be preceded by a comma.

One or both of the character strings may be omitted from the REPLACE command. If you omit the second string, EDLIN deletes all occurrences of the first string within the specified range. The first string must end with ^Z. If you omit both strings, EDLIN will reuse the search string of the most recent SEARCH or REPLACE command and the replace string of the last RE-PLACE command.

If you include the REPLACE command on a line with one or more other EDLIN commands, the replace string can be terminated by pressing Ctrl-Z rather than Enter.

WRITE

When EDLIN begins to work on an existing file, its first task is to load the file into computer memory. EDLIN will fill up to 75% of available memory with the file. EDLIN displays the message **End of input file** followed by the EDLIN prompt if memory is large enough to accommodate the entire file at one time. If the file is too large to be loaded into memory at one time, EDLIN loads a portion of the file and displays only the prompt.

If a file is larger than 75% of memory, the WRITE command (enter w or W) can be used to write a number of lines from memory to a disk. This frees a portion of memory so that additional lines in the file may be loaded into memory using the APPEND command. The WRITE command is meaningful only if the file you are editing is too large to fit in memory.

The WRITE command writes text to the disk beginning with line number 1. You can specify the number of lines to be written by preceding the letter "w" with a number. The next example writes the first 100 lines in memory to the disk that was specified in the EDLIN start command:

*100 w
*

If you do not specify the number of lines to be written (entering only "w"), EDLIN writes lines until 25% of available memory is occupied by the file. No action is taken if less than 25% of available memory is occupied by the file. After the lines are written, all lines remaining in memory are renumbered so that the first remaining line in memory becomes number 1.

APPEND

The APPEND command (enter a or A) is used to add a number of lines to the EDLIN file currently in memory. This command is used after a portion of memory is made available with the WRITE command. The APPEND command is meaningful only if the file being edited is too large to fit in memory. Refer to the previous discussion of the WRITE command for information on when to use the WRITE and APPEND commands.

The APPEND command adds lines of the file to memory starting at the end of the lines already in memory. You can specify how many lines are to be added to memory by preceding the letter "a" with a number. The following example adds 100 lines of a file to the portion of the file already in memory:

*100 a
*

If you do not specify the number of lines to be added, lines are added until available memory is 75% full. No action is taken if available memory is already 75% full. (If necessary, you can use the WRITE command to free a portion of memory.)

The message **End of input file** is displayed when the APPEND command has read the last line of the file into memory.

END

The END command (enter e or E) terminates EDLIN, saves the edited file, and returns control to MS-DOS. The edited file is saved by writing it to the disk and file specified in the EDLIN start command. As you may recall, the original unedited file is saved and given the extension "BAK". However, a .BAK file will not be created if you are creating a new file with EDLIN rather than modifying an existing file.

If the disk specified in the EDLIN start command does not have enough free space to save the entire edited file, only a portion of the file is saved. The saved portion is given a filename extension of "$$$", and the remainder of the edited file is lost. The original unedited file is stored with its original extension.

QUIT

The QUIT command (enter q or Q) is used to terminate EDLIN and return control to MS-DOS. The changes made during the editing session are not saved, and no .BAK file is created. QUIT is used only when you want to discard all of the changes made in an EDLIN session.

When you enter the command "q", EDLIN displays a prompt asking if you want to end the editing session and return to MS-DOS. A response of "y" terminates EDLIN and returns control to MS-DOS. All changes made during the EDLIN session are discarded. Only the original unedited file is saved. A response of "n" returns control to EDLIN, which displays its prompt and waits for you to enter another command.

MOVE

The MS-DOS 2.X and subsequent versions of EDLIN include a MOVE command. With MOVE, you can transfer a range of lines in a text file from one location to another. The first line moved becomes the current line. Lines are renumbered according to the direction of the move.

The starting and ending lines of the block to be moved may be specified in the MOVE command. The block is moved ahead of a third line, which must be specified in the command. All numbers in the command must be separated by commas.

In the next example, lines 2 through 5 are moved ahead of line 9. The first line moved (line 2) becomes the current line, and the lines are renumbered:

```
 1: This is line 1.
 2: This is line 2.
 3: This is line 3.
 4: This is line 4.
 5:*This is line 5.
 6: This is line 6.
 7: This is line 7.
 8: This is line 8.
 9: This is line 9.
10: This is line 10.

*2,5,9 m
*L
 1: This is line 1.
```

```
 2: This is line 6.
 3: This is line 7.
 4: This is line 8.
 5:*This is line 2.
 6: This is line 3.
 7: This is line 4.

 8: This is line 5.
 9: This is line 9.
10: This is line 10.


       *
```

You may omit the first line in the block from the command. If you do this, the block will start at the current line. You can also omit the last line in the block. In this case, the block that is moved will end at the current line.

Consider the command ",,1 m". The starting line number has been omitted, so the block to be moved begins at the current line. The ending line number has also been omitted, so the block to be moved ends at the current line. In other words, the block to be moved consists of one line— the current line. The command instructs EDLIN to move the current line ahead of line number 1. The commas must be included in this command.

COPY

The COPY command (enter c or C) is included in the MS-DOS 2.X, 3.X, and 4.X versions of EDLIN. This command is used to duplicate a range of lines.

You may specify the beginning and ending lines of the range to be copied by including the beginning and ending line numbers in the COPY command. The command must include a line number to specify where the copy will be located. All line numbers must be separated by a comma or a space. The first line copied becomes the current line:

```
 1: This is line 1.
 2: This is line 2.
 3: This is line 3.
 4: This is line 4.
 5:*This is line 5.
 6: This is line 6.
 7: This is line 7.

*1,2,6 c
*L
 1: This is line 1.
 2: This is line 2.
 3: This is line 3.
```

```
4: This is line 4.
5: This is line 5.
6:*This is line 1.
7: This is line 2.
8: This is line 6.
9: This is line 7.
*
```

In the example, the range of lines beginning with line 1 and ending with line 2 is copied ahead of line 6.

A range of lines can be copied more than one time by including a *count* in the command. The *count* is inserted between the line number that specifies where the copy is to be located and the letter "c". For example, if you wanted to copy lines 1 and 2 twice, you would enter the command "1,2,6,2 c". Compare this to the command in the previous example, which copied the lines one time. As in the previous example, if no *count* is included in the command, the range of lines is copied one time.

The starting and/or ending line numbers of the range to be copied may be omitted from the COPY command. The command assumes the omitted line(s) to be the current line:

```
1: This is line 1.
2: This is line 2.
3:*This is line 3.
4: This is line 4.
5: This is line 5.
6: This is line 6.
7: This is line 7.

*1,,6 c
*L
1: This is line 1.
2: This is line 2.
3: This is line 3.
4: This is line 4.
5: This is line 5.
6:*This is line 1.
7: This is line 2.
8: This is line 3.
9: This is line 6.
10: This is line 7.
*
```

In the example, the range of lines beginning with line 1 and ending with the current line is copied ahead of line 6. The first line copied becomes the current line.

PAGE

The PAGE (enter **p** or **P**) command is included in the MS-DOS 2.X, 3.X, and 4.X versions of EDLIN. The PAGE command lists lines of a file. Its actions are similar to those of the LIST command, with one important difference. The LIST command does not change the current line; the PAGE command does. The significance of this difference will be demonstrated in the next example.

The beginning and ending line numbers of the block of lines to be listed can be specified with the PAGE command:

```
*1,5 p
    1: This is line 1.
    2: This is line 2.
    3: This is line 3.
    4: This is line 4.
    5:*This is line 5.

*
```

If you omit the first line number of the block to be listed, the command assumes that the first line is the current line plus one. The usefulness of the PAGE command stems from the fact that the last line listed becomes the current line.

Continuing with the previous example, we find that the current line is line 5. If we invoke the PAGE command without specifying a starting line, the listing will begin with line 6. If we do not specify an ending line number, 23 lines will be listed. The last line listed becomes the current line:

```
*p
    6: This is line 6.
    7: This is line 7.
    :
    :
   27: This is line 27.
   28:*This is line 28.

*
```

In this fashion, we could continue to enter the command "p", paging through the file 23 lines at a time. Try doing this with the LIST command. Repeatedly entering the letter "L" will repeatedly list the same 23 lines. The reason is that LIST does not change the current line.

TRANSFER

The TRANSFER command (enter t or T) is included in the MS-DOS 2.X, 3.X, and 4.X versions of EDLIN. The TRANSFER command merges the contents of a specified file with the file being edited.

You can specify the location at which the merged file is inserted into the file being edited by including a line number in the TRANSFER command. The merged file will be inserted ahead of the specified line. If you do not specify a line number, the merged file is inserted ahead of the current line. As an example, the command "100 t b:demo.txt" merges the file on drive B named "demo.txt" with the file being edited. "Demo.txt" is inserted ahead of line 100 in the file being edited.

The file being merged must be located in the current directory of the specified or default drive. The current directory cannot be changed while EDLIN is running. Refer to chapter 3 for a discussion of current directories.

9

Extended Keyboard and Display Control

Using ANSI.SYS
Keyboard Reassignment
Screen Control

The ANSI.SYS file is an enhanced keyboard and display device driver supplied with DOS versions 2, 3, and 4. This chapter discusses the ways in which you can employ the enhanced support of the ANSI.SYS console driver.

As with other installable device drivers, you must explicitly configure your system in order to use ANSI.SYS. For example, if the ANSI.SYS file is in your C:\DOS directory, the device driver is installed by including the following statement in your CONFIG.SYS file:

```
device=c:\dos\ansi.sys
```

Remember that in order to use ANSI.SYS, you must reboot after changing CONFIG.SYS.

ANSI.SYS Flags

The DOS 4 version of ANSI.SYS has three optional flags that may be used in the device statement used to load the driver.

The /k flag lets you configure ANSI.SYS so that it cannot reassign the extended function keys F11 and F12 (key reassignment is discussed later in this chapter).

The /x flag lets you configure ANSI.SYS so that it can distinguish enhanced cursor keys from numeric pad cursor keys. To illustrate, if your CONFIG.SYS file contains the statement

```
device=c:\dos\ansi.sys /x
```

then reassignment of the numeric pad up arrow key does not reassign the enhanced up arrow key.

The /l flag lets you configure ANSI.SYS so that it attempts to maintain the current number of rows on the display screen. Some application programs attempt to reset the display to the default of 25 rows. If the /l flag is included in the ANSI.SYS device statement, the driver will use the MODE command in an attempt to override such programs.

Using ANSI.SYS

Data entered from the keyboard is sent to the computer as a sequence of ASCII characters. When ANSI.SYS is installed, it processes all character sequences sent from the keyboard. ANSI.SYS recognizes certain character sequences as being *command sequences*. Command sequences direct ANSI.SYS to modify keyboard input or to modify display screen output (figure 9-1). All ANSI.SYS command sequences begin with an *escape character* whose ASCII value is 27 (see appendix F for ASCII values). ANSI.SYS command sequences are not displayed on the screen.

ANSI.SYS can perform four types of commands: control cursor position, erase all or part of the display screen, reassign character strings to individual keys on the keyboard, and set display modes and attributes. Tables 9-1

Figure 9-1. ANSI.SYS receives input from the keyboard and sends output to the display screen.

through 9-5 give the individual commands, the corresponding command sequences, and a brief explanation of each command.

Table 9-1. ANSI.SYS Commands for Controlling Cursor Position

Command Name	Command Sequence	Description
Cursor position	ESC[#; #H	Moves the cursor to a specified position on the display screen. The position is specified by the *#* parameters. The first parameter specifies the line number, and the second parameter specifies the column number of the cursor position. The cursor will move to the home position if no position is specified. The command sequence must end with an uppercase "H".
Cursor up	ESC[#A	Moves the cursor up a number of lines without changing columns. The value of *#* determines the number of lines moved. The default is one. The command sequence must end with an uppercase "A".
Cursor down	ESC[#B	Moves the cursor down a number of lines without changing columns. The value of *#* determines the

Table 9-1. (cont'd)

Command Name	Command Sequence	Description
		number of lines moved. The default is one. The command sequence must end with an uppercase "B".
Cursor forward	ESC[#C	Moves the cursor forward without changing lines. The value of # determines the number of columns moved. The default is one. The command sequence must end with an uppercase "C".
Cursor backward	ESC[#D	Moves the cursor backward without changing lines. The value of # determines the number of columns moved. The default is one. The command sequence must end with an uppercase "D".
Horizontal/ vertical position	ESC[#; #f	Has function identical to cursor position command. Command sequence must end with a lowercase "f".
Save cursor position	ESC[s	Saves, in memory, the current position of the cursor. The position of the cursor can be restored with the restore cursor position command. The command sequence must end with a lowercase "s".
Restore cursor position	ESC[u	Restores the cursor to the position it occupied when the previous save cursor position command was issued. The command sequence must end with a lowercase "u".
Device status report	ESC[6n	Requests that ANSI.SYS issue a cursor position report. The command sequence must end with a lowercase "n".
Cursor position report	ESC[#; #R	Reports the current position of the cursor. The first parameter is the current line. The second parameter is the current column. ANSI.SYS issues a cursor position report in response to a device status report.

Table 9-2. ANSI.SYS Commands for
Erasing the Display Screen

Command Name	Command Sequence	Description
Erase display	ESC[2J	Erases entire display and positions the cursor at the home position. The command sequence must end with an uppercase "J".
Erase line	ESC[K	Erases from the cursor to the end of the line. The command sequence must end with an uppercase "K".

Table 9-3. ANSI.SYS Commands for
Controlling Display Screen Attributes

Command Name	Command Sequence	Description
Set graphics rendition	ESC[#; . . . ;#m	Sets the screen display attributes. The command sequence may contain one or more of the parameters that are listed below. The command sequence must end with a lowercase "m".

Attribute Parameters	*Meaning*
0	All attributes off. Normal display.
1	High intensity display on.
4	Underscore on. Underscore will not work with a color display.
5	Blink on.
7	Reverse video on.
8	Concealed on. No display.
30	Black foreground.
31	Red foreground.
32	Green foreground.
33	Yellow foreground.
34	Blue foreground.
35	Magenta foreground.
36	Cyan foreground.
37	White foreground.
40	Black background.
41	Red background.
42	Green background.

Table 9-3. (cont'd)

Attribute Parameters	Meaning
43	Yellow background.
44	Blue background.
45	Magenta background.
46	Cyan background.
47	White background.

Table 9-4. ANSI.SYS Commands for Setting Display Mode

Command Name	Command Sequence	Description
Set mode	ESC[=#h	Sets display mode according to the parameter (#) specified. Command sequence must end with a lowercase "h". (See the section "Screen Control" later in this chapter for more information on the display mode.)
Reset mode	ESC[=#l	Resets display mode according to the parameter (#) specified. Equivalent to set mode except for parameter 7, which turns end-of-line wrap off. Command sequence must end with a lowercase "l".

Mode Parameters	Meaning
0	40x25 black and white.
1	40x25 color.
2	80x25 black and white.
3	80x25 color.
4	320x200 color.
5	320x200 black and white.
6	640x200 black and white.
7	End-of-line wrap turned on.

Mode parameters 14 through 19 are supported in DOS 4.0 and subsequent versions only.

14	640x200 color
15	640x350 mono (EGA)
16	640x350 color (EGA)
17	640x480 color (VGA)

Table 9-4. (cont'd)

Mode Parameters	Meaning
18	640x480 color (VGA)
19	320x200 color

Table 9-5. ANSI.SYS Commands for Controlling Keyboard Reassignment

Command Name	Command Sequence	Description
Keyboard reassignment	ESC[#; # . . . ;# p or ESC[#;"string";p	Reassigns a character string to the key specified by the first ASCII code (#) in the sequence. The character string is determined by the remaining ASCII codes in the sequence. If the first ASCII code is a zero, the second ASCII code in the sequence determines which function key is assigned the character string. (See the section "Keyboard Reassignment" later in this chapter.)

An Example

The erase display command (table 9-2) is coded by the ASCII character sequence ESC [2 J. Note that "ESC" refers to the escape character—a single ASCII character—and not the three characters "E", "S", and "C". The display screen is erased when the sequence ESC [2 J is sent to ANSI.SYS. This sounds simple, and it is, except for one problem. All ANSI.SYS commands begin with an escape character, and sending an escape character to the display screen may require some special tactics.

Unless your system is one of those made by a few certain suppliers, you cannot use the Esc key to enter an escape character. In most machines, pressing Esc causes MS-DOS to cancel the current line being entered and skip to the next line. You can verify this by entering **copy con:** to try to create a text file containing the erase display command:

```
C>copy con: erase.txt
\         ←pressing Esc displays a "\" and causes MS-DOS to skip to the next line
[2J
```

```
^Z
        1 File(s) copied

C>type erase.txt
[2J
```

The **type** command displays the file that was created. As you can see, the file did not begin with an ESC character. The **type** command would have erased the display screen if the file had contained the complete sequence for the erase display command.

Consider yourself fortunate if your system allows you to enter the escape character from the keyboard; entering ANSI.SYS commands will be much easier for you. For example, a file that erases the display screen could be created as follows:

```
C>copy con: erase.txt
^[[2J        ←pressing Esc displays the ^[, which represents the ESC character
^Z
        1 File(s) copied
```

Getting ESC into a File

One way to insert an escape character into a file is to create the file with a dummy character in place of the escape character. Once the file is created, you could use the MS-DOS utility program DEBUG to replace the dummy character with an escape character (see chapter 15). However, there is an easier way.

You can use the MS-DOS command PROMPT to enter an escape character in a text file. PROMPT is used to change the MS-DOS system prompt. Simply enter **prompt**, followed by the new system prompt. For example, if you wanted to change the system prompt to "ROCK AND ROLL", you could do it by entering the following command:

```
C>prompt ROCK AND ROLL
ROCK AND ROLL _
```

ROCK AND ROLL is now the system prompt, and MS-DOS will display it whenever it is ready to accept a command.

The PROMPT command is discussed in Part 3. Of interest to us now is the fact that we can place an escape character in the system prompt by including "$e" in the PROMPT command. Suppose that the current system prompt is the default prompt (**C>**) and that the following command is entered:

```
C>prompt $e[2J
```

What happens? Remember that MS-DOS sends all screen output to the ANSI.SYS black box (figure 9-1). When MS-DOS is ready to display the prompt, it sends the system prompt, as output, to ANSI.SYS. Since this system prompt begins with ESC [, ANSI.SYS recognizes the output as a command sequence, and the specified command is executed. In this case, the screen is cleared. The system prompt (**ESC [2 J**) is not displayed, since ANSI.SYS does not display command sequences. The screen simply goes blank each time that MS-DOS calls for a system prompt. While a screen that constantly blanks out is of limited value, this example does show how the prompt command can be used to send an escape character to ANSI.SYS.

The examples in this chapter will use the PROMPT command to enter the escape character, since most suppliers of MS-DOS do not include direct keyboard entry of ESC. However, if you are one of the lucky ones, you do not have to resort to this rather awkward technique when using ANSI.SYS.

The remaining sections of this chapter will present some examples of how ANSI.SYS can be used for more practical modifications to MS-DOS.

Keyboard Reassignment

The ANSI.SYS device driver can be used to reassign values to individual keys on the computer keyboard (table 9-5). Like all ANSI.SYS command sequences, *reassignment sequences* begin with the ESC character followed by a left bracket ([ ). The left bracket is followed by the ASCII code (see appendix F) of the key that is to have a new value assigned to it. For example, if you wanted to assign a new value to the "a" key, the command sequence would begin with ESC [97.

The first ASCII code is followed by one or more additional ASCII codes. The key indicated by the first code takes on the values of the remaining ASCII codes in the command sequence. All ASCII codes are separated by semicolons. The command sequences for keyboard reassignment are terminated by a "p". You must use a lowercase "p".

Let's say that you want to reassign "apple" to the "a" key. When you press "a", you want "apple" to be displayed on the screen. The command sequence used is ESC [97 followed by the ASCII values for "a", "p" (twice), "l", and "e". The command sequence is terminated by a lowercase "p". The entire command sequence would be:

```
esc[97;97;112;112;108;101p
```

Now we will add the command "prompt $e" to generate the ESC character. Let's put everything together. Enter the following command to turn your "a" into an "apple":

```
C>prompt $e[97;97;112;112;108;101p
```

Does it work? Press the "a" key; you should get "apple". If you don't, you may not have installed ANSI.SYS. Refer to the beginning of this chapter if you need help in installing ANSI.SYS. The other point to remember is that a new value has been assigned to lowercase "a" only. Pressing the key for the uppercase letter will still give "A". If you try this example on your computer, you will notice that no system prompt is displayed. This is because the prompt is now an ANSI.SYS command sequence and command sequences are not displayed. To get the familiar C> back, enter:

```
prompt
C>
```

You can get your "a" back by sending the sequence ESC [97; 97p to ANSI.SYS:

```
C>prompt $e[97;97p    ←reassigns the letter a to the "a" key
prompt                ←resets the prompt to C
C>
```

In the previous example, we entered a series of ASCII values to be assigned to the "a" key. However, a keyboard reassignment command sequence can also contain the actual character string that you want to assign to a key. Instead of entering the ASCII value for each letter in "apple", you can enter the string "apple". Begin the control sequence as before, but replace the series of ASCII values with the string "apple". The string must be enclosed in quotation marks. The following sequence turns "a" to "apple":

```
esc[97;"apple"p
```

The two methods just discussed may be combined. The following sequence will also turn "a" to "apple":

```
esc[97;"appl";101p
```

Function Keys

ANSI.SYS will reassign a string to one of the function keys (F1–F10) when the first ASCII code in a reassignment sequence is zero. The second ASCII code in the command sequence determines which key is reassigned. The following sequence reassigns the string "dir" to the F1 function key:

```
esc[0;59;"dir"p
```

This sequence can be sent to ANSI.SYS with the following command:

```
C>prompt $e[0;59;"dir"p
prompt

C>
```

Appendix F has a complete list of the extended ASCII codes for the 40 function keys (unshifted, shifted, Ctrl-shifted, and Alt-shifted). The next section will give you more examples of how strings can be reassigned to function keys.

Some Useful Applications of Keyboard Reassignment

Keyboard reassignment can be used to assign frequently entered commands to individual keys. Commands so assigned could then be entered with a single keystroke. Up to 128 characters may be reassigned to a single key.

Let's say that you use your computer for word processing and BASIC programming. To load your word processor, you have to type "wp". To load your BASIC interpreter, you have to type "gwbasic". You could save yourself some typing by reassigning each of these commands to a function key.

We will illustrate by first reassigning "gwbasic" to the F2 function key. The F2 key has an extended ASCII code of 0,60 (see appendix F); therefore, the reassignment code sequence will begin with ESC [0,60. The character string reassigned to the function key can be specified in the command sequence:

```
esc[0;60;"gwbasic"
```

This command sequence tells ANSI.SYS to display "gwbasic" when the F2 key is pressed. A carriage return must be requested before MS-DOS will load "gwbasic". This can be accomplished by including the ASCII code for carriage return (13) in the command sequence. The complete command sequence for key reassignment is terminated with a lowercase "p":

```
esc[0;60;"gwbasic";13p
```

Again, we use the command "prompt $e" to send an ESC character to the ANSI.SYS device driver:

```
C>prompt $e[0;60;"gwbasic";13p    ←this sends the command sequence
prompt                            ←this resets the prompt to default

C>
```

The BASIC interpreter will now be loaded when you press the F2 key.

We can assign "wp" to the F3 function key (ASCII code 0,61) by entering the following command:

```
C>prompt $e[0;61;"wp";13p
prompt

C>
```

Let's also assign the MS-DOS command DIR and the /w switch to the F1 function key (ASCII code 0,59):

```
C>prompt $e[0;59;"dir/w";13p
prompt

C>
```

Let's put all of these reassignment commands into a single batch file. If the file is given the name AUTOEXEC.BAT, it will automatically execute when MS-DOS is booted. We will also include the TIME and DATE commands in the batch file so that the time and date will be set when MS-DOS boots.

```
C>copy con: autoexec.bat
date
time
rem
rem reassign f1
prompt $e[0;59;"dir/w";13p
rem
rem reassign f2
prompt $e[0;60;"gwbasic";13p
rem
rem reassign f3
prompt $e[0;61;"wp";13p
rem
rem return prompt to default (C>)
prompt
^Z
        1 File(s) copied

C>
```

This batch file will automatically execute if it is in the root directory of the boot disk. The reassignments we entered will take effect once the file has been executed.

Screen Control

You can use the ANSI.SYS device driver to control cursor position and set display mode and attributes. The command sequences for screen control are listed in tables 9-2 through 9-5.

This section will show you how ANSI.SYS can be used to control the display screen by modifying the batch file used in the preceding discussion of key reassignment. We will add a PROMPT command to the end of the file that will send a series of display command sequences to ANSI.SYS. These commands will modify the display screen. When the batch file terminates, the system prompt will consist of these display commands. The commands will be sent to ANSI.SYS each time that the prompt is displayed. The screen modifications will be displayed each time MS-DOS requests that the system prompt be displayed.

The commands placed in the batch file will instruct ANSI.SYS to perform the following tasks: move the cursor to the home position (first line, first column), clear any text in the first line, switch to the high-intensity display mode, display three messages on the first line, move the cursor to the first column of the 25th line, display a prompt, return to the normal display mode, and, finally, clear line 25 of any text to the right of the prompt. Sounds complicated, but it can all be accomplished with one PROMPT command.

The first task that we want to accomplish is move the cursor to the home position. Table 9-1 shows the ANSI.SYS command sequences that control the cursor. The cursor position command is ESC [#;# H. Remember that the # symbols represent parameters. The first parameter is the line number, and the second parameter is the column number of the screen location where the cursor is to be located. The cursor will be moved to the home position if no parameters are included in the command sequence. The cursor position command must be terminated by an uppercase "H". Therefore, the first screen control command sequence that we will send to ANSI.SYS is ESC [H (move cursor to home position).

Next, we want ANSI.SYS to erase the first line on the display screen. This is accomplished with the sequence ESC [K (table 9-2). The command sequence must end with an uppercase "K".

The next command sequence will switch the display mode to high intensity. This is accomplished with the command sequence ESC [1m (table 9-4). A lowercase "m" is required.

So far our command series consists of three command sequences:

The ESC character will be sent to ANSI.SYS by using the "prompt $e" command; therefore, the three ANSI.SYS commands can be sent with the following command:

```
prompt $e[H $e[K $e[1m
```

After the cursor has been positioned, the line cleared, and the high-intensity mode set, we want ANSI.SYS to display a message. Since we will be using a PROMPT command to send the commands, we can simply include the message as part of the prompt:

```
prompt $e[H $e[K $e[1m directory-f1
```

Next, we want ANSI.SYS to advance the cursor eight spaces and then display another message. The cursor forward command advances the cursor. The command sequence is ESC [# C, where the # symbol represents the number of spaces forward that the cursor will be moved. The default value for # is one. The command sequence to move the cursor forward eight spaces is ESC [8C. The command must end with an uppercase "C":

```
prompt $e[H $e[K $e[1m directory-f1 $e[8C basic interpreter-f2
```

After displaying the second message, we want ANSI.SYS to advance the cursor eight more spaces and display a third message:

```
prompt $e[H $e[K $e[1m directory-f1 $e[8C basic interpreter-f2
$e[8C word processor-f3
```

After displaying the third message on the first line, we want ANSI.SYS to move the cursor to the first column in line 25. Again, we will use the cursor position command sequence (ESC [#;# H); this time we will specify some parameters:

```
prompt $e[H $e[K $e[1m directory-f1 $e[8C basic interpreter-f2
$e[8C word processor-f3 $e[25;1H
```

With the cursor at line 25, column 1, we will have ANSI.SYS display a prompt, return to the regular display mode, and clear line 25 of all text beyond the prompt:

```
prompt $e[H $e[K $e[1m directory-f1 $e[8C basic interpreter-f2
$e[8C word processor-f3 $e[25;1H ENTER COMMAND: $e[0m $e[K
```

If we make this PROMPT command the last command in a batch file, the system prompt at the end of the batch file execution will be the sequence of messages and ANSI.SYS commands and prompts that we have just discussed. Each time MS-DOS calls for a system prompt, ANSI.SYS will execute the commands and display the messages and prompts.

To get a better idea of what we are talking about, let's use EDLIN to modify this same batch file. (See the preceding section on keyboard reassignment for the original batch file, and see chapter 8 for a discussion of EDLIN commands.)

```
C>edlin autoexec.bat        ←edit file created in previous section
End of input file           ←EDLIN responds that the file has been loaded
*L                          ←enter "L"; EDLIN will display file

    1:*DATE
    2: TIME
    3: REM
```

```
 4: REM REASSIGN F1
 5: PROMPT $e[0;59;"DIR/W";13p
 6: REM
 7: REM REASSIGN F2
 8: PROMPT $e[0;60;"GWBASIC";13p
 9: REM
10: REM REASSIGN F3
11: PROMPT $e[0;61;"WP";13p
12: REM
13: REM RETURN PROMPT TO DEFAULT (C>)
14: PROMPT
```
*   ←EDLIN waits for the next command

The first step in modifying the batch file is to remove the lines that reset the system prompt to the default. This is accomplished by deleting the last three lines of the file:

12,14d   ←delete lines 12–14
1L   ←enter 1L to list file starting with line 1

```
 1:*DATE
 2: TIME
 3: REM
 4: REM REASSIGN F1
 5: PROMPT $e[0;59;"DIR/W";13p
 6: REM
 7: REM REASSIGN F2
 8: PROMPT $e[0;60;"GWBASIC";13p
 9: REM
10: REM REASSIGN F3
11: PROMPT $e[0;61;"WP";13p
```
*

Now we want to put into the file the PROMPT command that does all the wonderful things we have just described. We will also put some "rem" statements in the batch file to explain what is going on.

12i   ←enter 12i to insert text beginning at line 12
```
12:*rem       ←type a line of text and press Enter
13:*rem the following prompt command instructs ansi.sys to
14:*rem perform several functions:
15:*rem move cursor to home, clear first line, set display mode to
16:*rem hi intensity, print 3 messages at top of screen, move cursor
17:*rem to line 25 column 1, print a prompt, reset display mode to
18:*rem normal intensity, and clear right side of line 25.
19:*rem
```

```
   20:*prompt $e[H $e[K $e[1m directory-f1 $e[8C basic interpreter-f2
$e[8C word processor-f3 $e[25;1H ENTER COMMAND: $e[0m $e[K
   21:*^Z      ←enter Ctrl-Z to terminate the INSERT command
*
```

The final line added to the batch file will be the MS-DOS command CLS. This command will clear the display screen:

```
*21i                ←enter 21i to insert text beginning at line 21
   21:*rem
   22:*rem the next command clears the screen. the batch file will
   23:*rem then terminate and return control to ms-dos.
   24:*cls
   25:*^Z            ←enter Ctrl-Z to terminate INSERT command
*1L                  ←enter 1L to display file
    1: DATE
    2: TIME
    3: REM
    4: REM REASSIGN F1
    5: PROMPT $e[0;59;"DIR/W";13p
    6: REM
    7: REM REASSIGN F2
    8: PROMPT $e[0;60;"GWBASIC";13p
    9: REM
   10: REM REASSIGN F3
   11: PROMPT $e[0;61;"WP";13p
   12: rem
   13: rem THE FOLLOWING PROMPT COMMAND INSTRUCTS ANSI.SYS TO
   14: rem PERFORM SEVERAL FUNCTIONS:
   15: rem MOVE CURSOR TO HOME, CLEAR FIRST LINE, SET DISPLAY MODE TO
   16: rem HI INTENSITY, PRINT 3 MESSAGES AT TOP OF SCREEN, MOVE CURSOR
   17: rem TO LINE 25 COLUMN 1, PRINT A PROMPT, RESET DISPLAY MODE TO
   18: rem NORMAL INTENSITY, AND CLEAR RIGHT SIDE OF LINE 25.
   19: rem
   20: PROMPT $e[H $e[K $e[1m DIRECTORY-F1 $e[8C BASIC INTERPRETER-F2
$e[8C WORD PROCESSOR-F3 $e[25;1H ENTER COMMAND: $e[0m $e[K
   21: rem
   22: rem THE NEXT COMMAND CLEARS THE SCREEN. THE BATCH FILE WILL
   23: rem THEN TERMINATE AND RETURN CONTROL TO MS-DOS.
   24: CLS
*e                   ←enter "e" to save the file and exit EDLIN
C>
```

The AUTOEXEC.BAT file is now stored in the root directory of the boot disk, and it will automatically execute when MS-DOS is booted. Let's try it out. Press the Ctrl-Alt-Del key combination to reboot the system. AUTOEXEC.BAT should begin execution, prompting you to enter the date and time. The first three PROMPT commands reassign character strings to the F1, F2, and F3 function keys. The fourth PROMPT command sets the screen control sequence. The CLS command clears the screen, and the batch file terminates, returning control to MS-DOS.

MS-DOS signals that it is ready to accept another command by displaying the system prompt. In this case, the system prompt is the screen control sequence that was the final PROMPT command in the batch file.

Figure 9-2 shows the appearance of the display screen upon conclusion of batch file execution. This display is the current system prompt. MS-DOS commands can be entered in the normal fashion. The commands "dir/w", "gwbasic", and "wp" may be entered simply by pressing function keys F1, F2, and F3. The screen control sequence will be executed each time that MS-DOS is ready to accept another command. The system prompt can be changed at any time by using the PROMPT command.

```
DIRECTORY-F1   BASIC INTERPRETER-F2   WORD PROCESSOR-F3




















ENTER COMMAND:
ENTER COMMAND:
```

Figure 9-2. The appearance of the display screen after AUTOEXEC.BAT has been executed.

Note: MS-DOS displays the system prompt twice at the end of a batch file. Because of this, the bottom line in figure 9-2 (**ENTER COMMAND:**) will be displayed twice when the system first boots. Each subsequent display of the system prompt will display **ENTER COMMAND:** one time. You can avoid this minor annoyance by modifying the last PROMPT command in AUTOEXEC.BAT. The underscore indicates the modified portion.

```
prompt $e[H $e[K $e[1m directory-f1 $e[8C basic interpreter-f2 $e[8C word
processor-f3 $e[24;1H $e[K $e[25;1H ENTER COMMAND: $e[0m  $e[K
```

10

Disk Structure and Management

In this chapter we will look at the internal structure of disks used by MS-DOS. We will also discuss how the operating system keeps track of files on a disk as well as how the contents of a file are accessed. Throughout this chapter, the word "disk" refers to both fixed disks and floppy diskettes unless specified otherwise.

This chapter does not contain any material needed for the routine use of MS-DOS. The material presented is intended for those readers who want a more thorough understanding of the operating system. Some familiarity with hexadecimal arithmetic and assembly language programming will be helpful but is not essential.

Structure of MS-DOS Disks

The next sections discuss the way that MS-DOS stores and retrieves data from disks. The roles of the boot record, file directory, and file allocation table are examined. Several examples are presented that use DEBUG to examine disk structure.

Tracks and Sectors

Before MS-DOS can store data on a disk, the disk's surface must be subdivided into tracks and sectors. *Tracks* are a series of concentric circles that cover the surface of a disk (figure 10-1). The outermost track on a disk is track 0, the neighboring track is track 1, and so on. On a double-sided diskette, the sides are also assigned numbers. The first side is side 0; the second side is side 1.

Each track is divided into a series of wedges called *sectors* (figure 10-2). Sectors are also numbered. The first sector on a track is number 1; the second, number 2; and so on. Sectors typically have a storage capacity of 512 bytes. Multiplying the number of bytes per sector by the number of sectors per track yields the number of bytes per track. Multiplying the number of bytes per track by the total number of tracks yields the total storage capacity.

Floppy Diskettes

Standard 5¼-inch diskettes have either 8 or 9 sectors per track. The 8-sector-per-track format was used in MS-DOS 1.X. The 9-sector-per-track format was introduced in MS-DOS 2.0 and continued through MS-DOS 3.3. Both formats use 40 tracks per diskette side. MS-DOS 2.X and subsequent versions can use diskettes with the 8-sector format. MS-DOS 1.X cannot use diskettes with the 9-sector format.

Quad-density 5¼-inch diskettes have 15 sectors per track and 80 tracks per side. Quad-density diskettes require quad-density drives and are supported by MS-DOS 3.X and 4.X only.

In addition to the standard and high-density 5¼-inch diskettes, MS-DOS 3.X and 4.X also support 3½-inch diskettes with 80 tracks per side

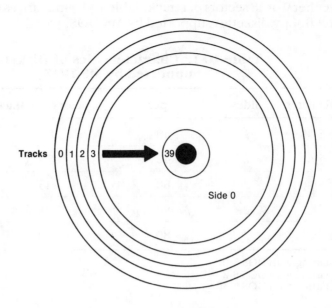

Figure 10-1. Each disk surface is divided into a series of concentric circles called *tracks*.

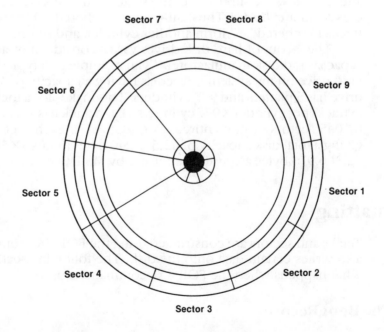

Figure 10-2. Each track is divided into *sectors* (8 sectors per track for MS-DOS 1.X, 9 for MS-DOS 2.X, 3.X, and 4.X).

and either 9 or 18 sectors per track. Table 10-1 summarizes the characteristics of the floppy diskettes supported by MS-DOS.

**Table 10-1. Characteristics of Diskettes
Supported by MS-DOS**

Diameter	Sides	Tracks per Side	Sectors per Track	Capacity
5¼″	1	40	8/9	160K/180K
5¼″	2	40	8/9	320K/360K
5¼″	2	80	15	1.2M[1]
3½″	2	80	9	720K[2]
3½″	2	80	18	1.44M[3]

[1]Starting with DOS 3.0
[2]Starting with DOS 3.2
[3]Starting with DOS 3.30

Hard Disks

Hard disks consist of one or more *platters*. Each platter has two surfaces on which data is stored. MS-DOS divides the surface of each platter into tracks, and the tracks are subdivided into sectors. All tracks that have the same radius form a *cylinder*. Thus, all tracks numbered "0" form a cylinder, all tracks numbered "1" form another cylinder, and so on.

The layout of hard disk drives varies considerably, according to disk capacity and disk manufacturer. As an example of a typical hard drive, the hard drive on my system is listed as having a capacity of 42.5 Mbytes. The drive has 5 platters and 977 cylinders. This makes for a total of 4,885 tracks (5 tracks per cylinder×977 cylinders). Each track has 17 sectors, so there are 83,045 sectors on the entire disk (4,885×17). Each sector has 512 bytes, giving a total disk capacity of 42,519,040 bytes (83,045×512). Of this total, 42,366,976 bytes are available for use by MS-DOS.

Formatting

Tracks and sectors are constructed using the FORMAT command. FORMAT also writes certain data onto the disk. The following sections will discuss what happens when the FORMAT command is used.

The Boot Record

FORMAT places a copy of the MS-DOS *boot record* in sector 1, track 0, side 0 on every disk that is formatted. The boot record consists of (1) a table containing information about the disk and (2) machine language code that loads IO.SYS and MSDOS.SYS (discussed under "System Files") into memory. The first 4 bytes in the boot record contain a machine language instruction telling the computer to jump to a certain offset in the boot record to find loading code. The table containing the disk-specific information is stored between the jump instruction and the loading code.

File Allocation Table and File Directory

FORMAT also constructs the *file allocation table* (FAT) and the *file directory*. As we will see shortly, both of these structures are intimately involved in accessing files stored on the disk. MS-DOS maintains two copies of the FAT on each disk, ostensibly because the FAT is so important that a second copy is available should the first be damaged. However, MS-DOS never uses the second copy of the FAT.

Standard 5¼-inch, 8-sector-per-track diskettes have a 1-sector FAT. Standard 5¼-inch, 9-sector-per-track diskettes have a 2-sector FAT. High density (1.2-Mbyte), 5¼-inch diskettes have a 7-sector FAT. 720-Kbyte, 3½-inch diskettes have a 3-sector FAT. 1.44-Mbyte, 3½-inch diskettes have a 12-sector FAT. The 42.5-Mbyte hard drive on my computer has an 81-sector FAT.

Standard 5¼-inch, single-sided diskettes have a 4-sector file directory. Standard 5¼-inch, double-sided diskettes have a 7-sector file directory. High-density (1.2-Mbyte), 5¼-inch diskettes have a 14-sector file directory. 720-Kbyte, 3½-inch diskettes have a 7-sector file directory. 1.44-Mbyte, 3½-inch diskettes have an 8-sector file directory. Most hard drives have a 32-sector file directory.

Table 10-2 lists the physical location of the boot record, FAT, and file directory on 5¼-inch and 3½-inch diskettes. Figure 10-3 illustrates the arrangement of these structures on a standard 5¼-inch diskette.

System Files

The /s switch directs FORMAT to place a copy of the *system files* on the disk being formatted. The three MS-DOS system files are IO.SYS, MSDOS.SYS, and COMMAND.COM. In PC-DOS, IO.SYS is called IBMBIO.COM and MSDOS.SYS is called IBMDOS.COM. The system files must be stored on any disk that will be used to boot the system. FORMAT places these files in a particular physical location on the disk in a particular order.

IO.SYS is stored on the disk immediately after the last sector of the file directory. IO.SYS consists of the operating system's default *device drivers*. A device driver is a computer program that serves as the interface between the operating system and a peripheral device (device drivers are discussed in chapter 14). Since IO.SYS interacts directly with the hardware, it is highly system-specific and is generally implemented by the computer's manufacturer.

MSDOS.SYS is stored on the disk immediately after the last sector of IO.SYS. MSDOS.SYS forms the kernel of MS-DOS. MSDOS.SYS receives all

Table 10-2. Location of Boot Record, FAT, and File Directory on 5¼" and 3½" Diskettes

	5¼", 8 Sectors/Track Diskettes		5¼", 9 Sectors/Track Diskettes		5¼", 15 Sectors/Track Diskettes	3½" Diskettes	
	Single-Sided Diskette	Double-Sided Diskette	Single-Sided Diskette	Double-Sided Diskette		720-Kbyte	1.44-Mbyte
Boot Record	Sector 1 Track 0	Sector 1 Track 0 Side 0	Sector 1 Track 0	Sector 1 Track 0 Side 0	Sector 1 Track 0 Side 0	Sector 1 Track 0 Side 0	Sector 1 Track 0 Side 0
FAT, 1st Copy	Sector 2 Track 0	Sector 2 Track 0 Side 0	Sectors 2–3 Track 0 Side 0	Sectors 2–3 Track 0 Side 0	Sectors 2–8 Track 0 Side 0	Sectors 2–4 Track 0 Side 0	Sectors 2–7, 16–18* Track 0 Side 0
FAT, 2nd Copy	Sector 3 Track 0	Sector 3 Track 0 Side 0	Sectors 4–5 Track 0 Side 0	Sectors 4–5 Track 0 Side 0	Sectors 9–15 Track 0 Side 0	Sectors 5–7 Track 0 Side 0	Sectors 4–15 Track 0 Side 1
File Directory	Sectors 4–7 Track 0	Sectors 4–7 Track 0 Side 0	Sectors 6–9 Track 0	Sectors 6–9 Track 0 Side 0	Sectors 1–14 Track 0 Side 1	Sectors 8–9 Track 0 Side 0	Sectors 8–15 Track 0 Side 0
	Sectors 1–3 Track 0 Side 1	Sectors 1–3 Track 0 Side 1	Sectors 1–3 Track 0 Side 1	Sectors 1–3 Track 0 Side 1		Sectors 1–5 Track 0 Side 1	

*Sectors 1–3, Track 0, Side 1 also included in first copy of FAT.

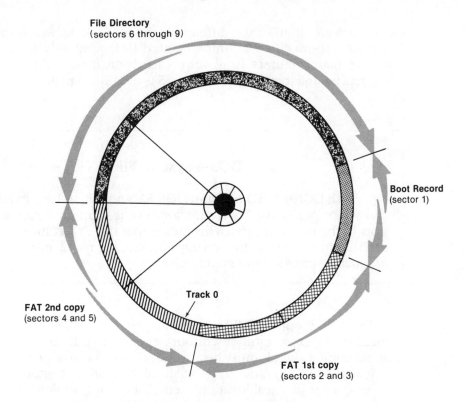

Figure 10-3. Layout for track 0 of boot record, FAT, and file directory on standard 5¼-inch, single-sided, 9-sector/track diskette.

requests for service functions (such as opening and reading a file) and channels the requests to IO.SYS. The protocol for communication between MSDOS.SYS and IO.SYS is identical from system to system. Therefore, MSDOS.SYS is said to be *hardware independent.*

COMMAND.COM is the MS-DOS *command interpreter*. The command interpreter serves as the interface between the operating system and the user. COMMAND.COM displays the system prompt, accepts commands from the keyboard and processes the commands so that they can be executed. COMMAND.COM consists of three components: a resident component, a transient component, and an initialization component. The role of the three components is discussed in chapter 11.

Interchangeability of System Files

Generally, any implementation of DOS that is designed to run on a specific computer brand will run on any compatible computer. For example, PC-DOS will run on any truly compatible machine, as will COMPAQ's version of MS-DOS, as will Cordata's version. The only area where the various implementations are significantly different is the IO.SYS file. Recall that IO.SYS is a hardware-specific file, implemented independently by each of the computer manufacturers. However, the hardware used by the different manufacturers is similar enough that IO.SYS is usually compatible across brand lines.

DOS 4 System Files

With DOS 4.X, IO.SYS and DOS.SYS no longer have to be in certain sector positions. Their directory entries can go in any available slots in the root directory. This means that the SYS command can be used to put the system files on any disk that has room, even if it wasn't originally formatted as a system disk.

Due to this compatibility, users can generally switch from one implementation of DOS to another without tremendous difficulty. However, anyone planning a switch must bear in mind that the size of the system file (particularly IO.SYS) varies from one implementation to another. Problems may arise if the physical location used to store one implementation of the system files is not large enough to store another implementation of the system files. In addition, some programs with automatic installation procedures assume a specific size for the system files. The installation procedures may fail if these assumptions are not correct.

Examining the File Directory and the FAT

The first part of this section takes a detailed look at the structure and use of the file directory and file allocation table. The second part of this section contains a description of how to use DEBUG to load the contents of the file directory and FAT into memory so that they might be examined.

File Directory

The *file directory* serves as the table of contents for a disk. For every file on the disk, there is a corresponding entry in the disk's file directory. Figure 10-4 illustrates the structure of a file directory entry. Each entry is composed of 32 bytes. The 32 bytes are partitioned into eight fields, each field containing information used by MS-DOS in file management. Table 10-3 lists the fields in a file directory entry and describes the information stored in each field.

Figure 10-4. Structure of entry in file directory.

Table 10-3. Breakdown of Bytes in a File Directory Entry

Byte(s)	Purpose
0–7	***Filename.*** The filename is padded with blank characters if it has fewer than 8 characters. The following values have special significance if they are the first byte in the filename field:
	00H The file directory entry has never been used. When MS-DOS sees 00H in this field, it skips over the entire entry. This can speed up performance.

Table 10-3. (cont'd)

Byte(s)	Purpose
E5H	The file that corresponds to this entry has been "erased." The file is not actually erased, however. The only change in this first byte is the filename field of the directory. Programs that recover "erased" files take advantage of this fact. On MS-DOS 1 disks, E5H may also indicate that the directory entry has not been used.
2EH	The file corresponding to this directory entry is another directory (or a subdirectory). If the second entry in this field is also 2EH, bytes 26–27 will contain the cluster of the directory's parent. The parent is the root directory if bytes 26 and 27 equal zero. (Clusters are discussed later in this chapter.)
8–10	***Filename extension.*** The field is padded with blank characters if the extension has fewer than three characters.
11	***File attribute.*** The file attribute is determined by the bit pattern of byte 11. The file has the attribute associated with a bit if that bit is set to equal 1. The file does not have the attribute if the bit equals 0.

Bit	File Attribute If Bit Set (Equals 1)
1	Hidden file. The file will not be listed when a DIR command is issued. (See the following box, "Modifying the Hidden File Attribute.")
2	System file. System files are used by MS-DOS during booting.
	The following bit settings are not valid for MS-DOS 1 disks:
0	Read only file. Any attempt to write to the file will generate an error message.
3	Volume label. Setting this bit tells MS-DOS that the characters in the filename and filename extension fields of this directory entry form the volume label for the disk. All other fields in this directory entry are irrelevant. This entry must be located in the root directory, and there can be only one such entry per disk.
4	Subdirectory. The directory entry corresponds to a subdirectory if this bit is set.
5	Archive. This bit is set if the file has been revised but not copied by the BACKUP command. Backing up a file clears the archive bit.

Byte(s)	Purpose
12–21	***Reserved.*** These bytes are reserved by MS-DOS. Look for them to be used in later versions of MS-DOS.

Table 10-3. (cont'd)

Byte(s)	Purpose
22–23	***Time stamp.*** The time that the file was created or last modified. Byte 23 contains bits 8–15. Byte 22 contains bits 0–7. Bits 11–15 are the binary representation of the hour of the day (0–23). Bits 5–10 are the binary representation of the minutes (0–59). Bits 0–4 are the binary representation of the number of 2-second increments.
24–25	***Date stamp.*** The date that the file was created or last modified. Byte 25 contains bits 8–15. Byte 24 contains bits 0–7. Bits 9–15 are the binary representation of the year less 1980 (1980 = 0). Bits 5–8 are the binary representation of the month (1–12). Bits 0–4 are the binary representation of the day of the month (0–31).
26–27	***Starting cluster.*** The starting cluster tells MS-DOS where to look on the disk for the start of the file. Clusters are discussed in the following section of this chapter.
28–31	***File size.*** The first word (bytes 28 and 29) contains the low-order portion of the file size. The second word (bytes 30–31) contains the high-order portion. Both words store the least-significant byte first.

Later in this chapter we will use DEBUG to see what an actual file directory looks like.

Modifying the Hidden File Attribute

The MS-DOS command ATTRIB (see Part 3) allows you to modify a file's read-only and archive attributes. However, ATTRIB does not provide for modification of the hidden file attribute. In listing 10-1, which follows, DEBUG is used to write two assembly language programs. HIDE.COM will allow you to set the hidden file attribute. UNHIDE.COM will allow you to clear the hidden file attribute. Enter **hide** [*filename.ext*] to set the hidden file attribute. Enter **unhide** [*filename.ext*] to clear the attribute. Note that files with the system attribute set will remain hidden after clearing the hidden attribute. You will need to clear both the hidden and system attributes to unhide these files. To create the programs in listing 10-1, enter the commands printed in italic type. Do not enter the explanatory comments, which are preceded by a semicolon.

Listing 10-1. HIDE.COM and UNHIDE.COM, Two Assembly Language Programs for Setting and Clearing the Hidden File Attribute (see table 10-3)

```
C>debug
-a
68D8:100 mov cx,[0080]                ;length of command tail
68D8:104 xor ch,ch                    ;clear high byte
68D8:106 dec cx                       ;ignore space in command tail
68D8:107 mov si,0082                  ;point to 1st letter in filename
68D8:10A mov di,0159                  ;point to buffer
68D8:10D repnz movsb                  ;move command tail to buffer
68D8:10F mov byte ptr [di],00         ;append 00 to filename in buffer
68D8:112 mov dx,0159                  ;point to 1st letter in buffer
68D8:115 mov ax,4300                  ;get file attribute function
68D8:118 int 21                       ;call MS-DOS
68D8:11A jc 012c                      ;jump if error
68D8:11C or cx,0002                   ;set hidden file bit
68D8:120 mov ax,4301                  ;set file attribute function
68D8:123 int 21                       ;call MS-DOS
68D8:125 jc 012c                      ;jump if error
68D8:127 mov dx,0135                  ;point to success message
68D8:12A jmp 012f
68D8:12C mov dx,0143                  ;point to error message
68D8:12F mov ah,09                    ;display string function
68D8:131 int 21                       ;call MS-DOS
68D8:133 int 20                       ;program terminate
68D8:135        ←press Enter
-e 135 'File hidden' 0d 0a '$' 'Unable to hide file' 0d 0a '$'
-f 159 L40 00                         ;start of buffer
-n hide.com
-rcx
CX 0000
:60
-w 100
Writing 0060 bytes
-a 10a
68D8:10A mov di,0174
68D8:10D        ←press Enter
-a 112
68D8:112 mov dx,0174
68D8:115        ←press Enter
-a 11c
68D8:11C and cx,fffd                  ;change fffd to fff9 for system files
68D8:120        ←press Enter
-a 12c
68D8:12C mov dx,0150
4f68D8:12F      ←press Enter
-e 135 'Hidden attribute removed' 0d 0a '$'
-e 150 'Unable to remove hidden attribute' 0d 0a '$'
```

```
-f 174 L40 00
-n unhide.com
-rcx
CX 0060
:1b4
-w 100
Writing 01B4 bytes
-q

C>
```

File Allocation Table

While the file directory serves as a disk's table of contents, the *file allocation table* (FAT) serves as a roadmap around the disk. For each file on the disk, there is a series of entries in the FAT telling MS-DOS where the file's contents are physically located.

MS-DOS divides a file's contents into *clusters*. Table 10-4 lists the number of adjoining sectors that form a cluster on the most commonly used types of disks. The cluster size on a fixed disk depends on how the disk was partitioned.

Table 10-4. Sectors per Cluster for Various Disk Types

Disk Type	Sectors per Cluster
Standard Single-sided	1
Standard Double-sided	2
Quad-density	1
10-Mbyte hard disk (single partition)	8
42.5-Mbyte hard disk (single partition)	4

Clusters are numbered according to their physical location on the disk. The first cluster starts with the sector immediately following the last sector of the file directory. The second cluster follows the first and so on.

On single-sided diskettes, cluster numbers increase going from one sector to the next along a track. When the final sector on a track is reached, the next cluster is the first sector on the following track (see figure 10-5).

On double-sided diskettes, clusters increase along a track on side 0, continue on the same track on side 1, and then continue on the following track on side 0 (see figure 10-6).

MS-DOS uses two techniques for reading the FAT's contents. The first, generally used on disks with storage capacity of less than 20 Mbytes, is the more complicated. The second, generally used on large-capacity storage devices, will be easy to understand after you've read an explanation of the first technique.

Figures 10-5 and 10-6 show that standard diskettes contain over 300 clusters. Each entry in the FAT must point to one of these clusters, so each FAT entry must be able to take on at least 300 values. A single byte can take on only 256 values (00H–FFH), so a single byte is not adequate as a FAT entry. A 2-byte number can take on up to 65,536 values (0000H–FFFFH). Since this quantity is much more than is needed, the designers of MS-DOS decided that they could save some disk space by making each FAT entry 1.5 bytes in length (000H–FFFH). A little odd, but it works well in the computer and is really not too difficult to understand. In addition, the 4,096 values that are possible with 1.5 bytes are adequate for the FATs of quad-density diskettes (2,371 clusters) and 10-Mbyte fixed disks (2,587 clusters).

Figure 10-5. Layout of boot record, FAT, file directory, and clusters on a 9-sector, *single-sided* diskette.

The first step MS-DOS takes in using the FAT is to obtain the file's first cluster number stored in bytes 26 and 27 of the file's directory entry (figure 10-7A). To find the file's second cluster number, MS-DOS takes the first cluster number and multiplies it by 1.5. The integer portion of the resulting product is then taken as an offset into the FAT (figure 10-7B).

The word (2 bytes) at the calculated offset is then modified as follows: If the first cluster number was odd, the three high-order hexadecimal digits are taken as the next cluster number. If the first cluster number was even, the three low-order hexadecimal digits are taken as the next cluster number (figure 10-7C).

Figure 10-6. Layout of boot record, FAT, file directory, and clusters on a 9-sector, *double-sided* diskette.

File Directory

(A) *Bytes 26 and 27→starting cluster number.*

File Allocation Table

(B) *Starting cluster number × 1.5 = product. Integer portion of product = offset into FAT of 2nd cluster number (*).*

Word at Calculated Offset into FAT = XX′YY′

2nd cluster = **XX′Y**
(1st cluster odd)

OR

2nd cluster number = **X′YY′**
(1st cluster even)

XX′YY′

(C) *Word at calculated offset is modified.*

Figure 10-7. The steps taken by MS-DOS in using the FAT.

To find the file's next cluster, MS-DOS multiplies the second cluster number by 1.5. It takes the integer portion of the product as an offset into the FAT and then takes the word at the calculated offset. The high-order digit is discarded if the second cluster number was even. If the second cluster number was odd, the low-order digit is discarded. The resulting three-digit hexadecimal number is the next cluster number.

This process is repeated until the resulting three-digit hexadecimal number is in the range FF8–FFF. A number in this range indicates that the end of the file has been reached. Don't get discouraged if this process seems somewhat confusing. The example in the following section should help to clarify it.

The procedure used on large storage devices is similar but more straightforward. On these large devices, there are more than 4,096 clusters, so a 1.5-byte number is not adequate. FAT entries on these devices are 2 bytes. The first cluster number is read from the directory. Now the cluster number is multiplied by 2 and the product taken as an offset into the FAT. The 2-byte word stored at this location is the next cluster number. The low-order byte is stored first, the high-order byte second.

Table 10-5 summarizes how the values stored in the FAT are interpreted.

**Table 10-5. Interpretation of Values for 1.5-Byte (XXX) and
2-Byte (XXXX) FAT Entries**

Value	Meaning
(0)000	Cluster available
(F)FF0–(F)FF6	Reserved cluster
(F)FF7	Bad cluster
(F)FF8–(F)FFF	Last cluster of file
(X)XXX	Cluster belongs to a chain

Large Partitions Using DOS 4

MS-DOS 4.X breaks the 32-Mbyte limitation on the size of the primary DOS partition. Cluster numbers remain 2 bytes in length. Therefore, there is still a limit of 65,536 clusters. Large partitions are supported by simply increasing the size of each cluster.

For partitions larger than 32 Mbytes, clusters are 4 sectors (2,048 bytes) in size. This allows for partitions as large as 128 Mbytes. For partitions larger than 128 Mbytes, clusters are 8 sectors (4,096 bytes) in size. This allows for partitions as large as 256 Mbytes. For partitions larger than 256 Mbytes, clusters are 16 sectors (8,192 bytes) in size. This allows for partitions as large as 512 Mbytes.

Because a cluster is the minimum amount of disk space that can be allocated to a file, an increase in the cluster size results in a larger amount of wasted disk space.

Exploring with DEBUG

In this section, we will use the MS-DOS utility DEBUG to examine the file directory and FAT of a typical MS-DOS diskette. You can follow along on your own computer if you wish. Before you do that, you may want to refer to chapter 15 for a detailed discussion of DEBUG and the DEBUG commands.

The demonstration uses a copy of the MS-DOS 3.3 system diskette (360-Kbyte, 5¼-inch, double-sided, 9-sector-per-track). Instructions are provided to perform the demonstration with a 5¼-inch, 1.2-Mbyte diskette and with a 3½-inch diskette.

Looking at the File Directory

Boot your system if you have not already done so. When the system prompt appears, type **debug** and press Enter. MS-DOS will load DEBUG, and DE-BUG will take control. The DEBUG prompt (a hyphen on most systems) tells you that DEBUG is loaded and ready to go:

```
-C>debug
```

MS-DOS uses the term *relative sector* to describe a sector's position relative to sector 1, track 0, side 0. Sector 2, track 0, side 0 is relative sector 1, and so on, up to sector 9, track 0, side 0, which is relative sector 8.

DEBUG uses these relative sector numbers to read disk sectors into memory. We will begin by loading the first sector of the file directory into memory. Because we are using a 9-sector-per-track, 5¼-inch diskette, we can see from table 10-2 that we want to read in sector 6, track 0, side 0. This corresponds to relative sector number 5. The following command tells DE-BUG to load into memory location CS:100 the contents from drive A (drive number 0), absolute sector 05. The **01** specifies that DEBUG is to read in one sector only.

```
-L CS:100 0 05 01
-
```

If you are using a 5¼-inch, 1.2-Mbyte diskette, change the **05** to **0F**. If you are using a 3½-inch diskette (either 720-Kbyte or 1.44-Mbyte), change the **05** to **07**. Change the **0** to **1** if you are using drive B instead of drive A. The remaining DEBUG commands used in this section will be the same regardless of the diskette type you are using.

The following DEBUG command will display the first 48 bytes of the sector that was just loaded into memory. The initial portion of the dump, the portion that we will examine, is the first entry in the disk's file directory. If you want a printout of the display, press the Ctrl-PrtSc before entering the command (make sure that your printer is turned on).

```
-d CS:100 L30
0976:0100  49 4F 20 20 20 20 20 20-53 59 53 27 00 00 00 00   IO      SYS'....
0976:0110  00 00 00 00 00 00 43 4E-65 08 02 00 E4 13 00 00   ......CNs...d...
0976:0120  4D 53 44 4F 53 20 20 20-53 59 53 27 00 00 00 00   MSDOS   SYS'....
```

The numbers to the far left are memory addresses that may differ from system to system. The middle portion of the display is called a *memory dump.* The contents of memory are displayed in hexadecimal numbers.

Let's examine the dump closely:

Filename and extension (offset 0–7 and 8–10). The underlined portion of the display on the left side comprises the first 8 bytes of the dump.

These 8 bytes make up the *filename* field of the first entry in the file directory. Notice that the 8-character filename field has been padded with blanks. The ASCII representation of the dump is the underlined portion on the right side of the screen. We can see that the filename is "IO".

The 3 bytes following the filename field (**53 59 53**) make up the *filename extension* field. In the right-hand column, we can see that the extension is "SYS".

Attribute (offset 11). Following the filename extension field is the *attribute* field. The attribute field is interpreted according to its bit pattern.

```
-d CS:100 L30
0976:0100  49 4F 20 20 20 20 20 20-53 59 53 27 00 00 00 00   IO      SYS'....
0976:0110  00 00 00 00 00 00 43 4E-65 08 02 00 E4 13 00 00   ......CNs...d...
0976:0120  4D 53 44 4F 53 20 20 20-53 59 53 27 00 00 00 00   MSDOS   SYS'....
```

In the preceding example, the field contains a value of 27H, which translates to the following bit pattern:

Bit:	7 6 5 4	3 2 1 0
Value:	0 0 1 0	0 1 1 1

Bits 0, 1, 2, and 5 have been set to equal 1. This tells us that the file IO.SYS has the attributes read only, hidden, system, and archive (see table 10-3).

Reserved (offset 12–21). The 10 bytes (all 00H) that follow the attribute field form the *reserved* field of the file directory entry. This field has been reserved by the makers of MS-DOS.

Time (offset 22–23). The next 2 bytes (**43 4E**) form the *time stamp* field. The time that the file was created or last modified is stored as the bit pattern of these two bytes.

```
-d CS:100 L30
0976:0100  49 4F 20 20 20 20 20 20-53 59 53 27 00 00 00 00   IO      SYS'....
0976:0110  00 00 00 00 00 00 43 4E-65 08 02 00 E4 13 00 00   ......CNs...d...
0976:0120  4D 53 44 4F 53 20 20 20-53 59 53 27 00 00 00 00   MSDOS   SYS'....
```

MS-DOS stores the 2 bytes of the preceding example in reverse order; thus, the bit pattern of the hexadecimal word (2 bytes) is 4E 43. The bit pattern is as follows:

	1 1 0 0	1 1 1 0	0 1 0 0	0 0 1 1
Bit	15 14 13 12	11 10 9 8	7 6 5 4	3 2 1 0
	⊢——— Hour ———⊣	⊢—— Minute ——⊣	⊢— Seconds —⊣

Bits 11–15 store the binary representation of the hour of the day. These 5 bits store a value of 1 + 8, or 9. Bits 5–10 store the minutes in binary. In this exam-

ple, the minutes value is $2+16+32=50$. Bits 0–4 hold the seconds in 2-second intervals. In this case, the number of 2-second intervals is $1+2=3$.

Putting all of this information together, we can tell that the file was created or last modified at 9:50:06 in the morning (to the closest 2 seconds).

Date (offset 24–25). The bit pattern of the *date stamp* field stores the date that the file was created or last modified.

```
-d CS:100 L30
0976:0100  49 4F 20 20 20 20 20 20-53 59 53 27 00 00 00 00   IO      SYS'....
0976:0110  00 00 00 00 00 00 43 4E-65 08 02 00 E4 13 00 00   ......CNs...d...
0976:0120  4D 53 44 4F 53 20 20 20-53 59 53 27 00 00 00 00   MSDOS   SYS'....
```

Again, the bytes are stored in reverse order, so in this example we want the bit pattern of the hexadecimal word 08 65.

```
          0  0  0  0      1  0  0  0    0  1  1  0     0  1  0  1
    Bit  15 14 13 12     11 10  9  8    7  6  5  4     3  2  1  0
    |————— Year —————|  |-Month-|  |—— Day ——|
```

Bits 9–15 store the year (less 1980). In this case, the year stored is 4, which means that IO.SYS was created or last modified in $4+1980=1984$. Bits 5–8 store the month in binary. Here, the month is $1+2=3$. The day is stored in bits 0–4. The day is $1+4=5$. Thus, the date stamp is March 5, 1984. Putting this information together with the time information, we know that IO.SYS was created or modified on March 5, 1984 at approximately 9:50:06 in the morning.

Starting cluster (offset 26–27). The hexadecimal word at offset 26–27 holds the starting cluster number of IO.SYS. Again, the word is stored in reverse order, so the starting cluster number is 00 02. We will see how MS-DOS uses this number shortly.

```
-d CS:100 L30
0976:0100  49 4F 20 20 20 20 20 20-53 59 53 27 00 00 00 00   IO      SYS'....
0976:0110  00 00 00 00 00 00 43 4E-65 08 02 00 E4 13 00 00   ......CNs...d...
0976:0120  4D 53 44 4F 53 20 20 20-53 59 53 27 00 00 00 00   MSDOS   SYS'....
```

File size (offset 28–31). This field contains the file size stored as a 4-byte hexadecimal number. MS-DOS stores the bytes in reverse order, with the low-order byte stored first and the high-order byte stored last. The size of IO.SYS is 00 00 13 E4 (hex), or decimal 5,092 bytes.

```
-d CS:100 L30
0976:0100  49 4F 20 20 20 20 20 20-53 59 53 27 00 00 00 00   IO      SYS'....
0976:0110  00 00 00 00 00 00 43 4E-65 08 02 00 E4 13 00 00   ......CNs...d...
0976:0120  4D 53 44 4F 53 20 20 20-53 59 53 27 00 00 00 00   MSDOS   SYS'....
```

This concludes our examination of an MS-DOS file directory. Next, we will use DEBUG to examine the FAT and see how MS-DOS uses the FAT, along with the starting cluster number, to keep track of a file.

Loading the FAT

Returning to figure 10-6, we can see that on a double-sided, 9-sector diskette, the first sector of the first FAT copy is stored at side 0, track 0, sector 1. This is relative sector 1 and can be loaded into memory location CS:300 with the DEBUG command "L CS:300 0 01 01". (The commands in this section work with all types of diskettes.) To follow along with this tutorial, you should have DEBUG running and your backup system diskette in drive A. Refer to the discussion of the file directory if you need some help getting started. Enter the following command:

```
-L CS:300 0 01 01
```

When the disk drive turns off, enter:

```
-d CS:300 L20
```

DEBUG will display:

```
0976:0300   FD FF FF 03 40 00 05 60-00 FF 8F 00 09 A0 00 0B   }...@..'......
0976:0310   C0 00 0D E0 00 0F 00 01-11 20 01 13 40 01 15 60   @..'.......@..'
```

This is a dump of the first 32 bytes of the FAT. The first byte in the FAT is set according to the type of disk media on which the FAT is stored (table 10-6). In this case, the medium is a double-sided, 9-sector diskette. Thus, the first byte in the FAT is the hexadecimal number FD; the second and third bytes in the FAT are always FFH.

Table 10-6. Value of First Byte in FAT According to Type of Storage Media

First Byte in FAT	Type of Media
FF	Double-sided, 8 sectors/track diskette
FE	Single-sided, 8 sectors/track diskette
FD	Double-sided, 9 sectors/track diskette
FC	Single-sided, 9 sectors/track diskette
F9	Double-sided, 15 sectors/track diskette
F8	Hard disk

Looking at the FAT

In the previous section, we saw that the starting cluster number for the file IO.SYS was hexadecimal 02 (02H). Here is how MS-DOS uses the FAT to determine the second cluster number of IO.SYS. MS-DOS starts by taking the first cluster number (02) and multiplying it by 1.5. It uses the product (3) as a pointer into the FAT. Then, MS-DOS examines the 2-byte word located at the calculated offset:

```
-d CS:300 L20
0976:0300  FD FF FF 03 40 00 05 60-00 FF 8F 00 09 A0 00 0B   }...a..'......
0976:0310  C0 00 0D E0 00 0F 00 01-11 20 01 13 40 01 15 60   a..'......a..'
```

In this example, the bytes **03 40** are at offset 3 in the FAT. Since MS-DOS stores bytes in reverse order, the 2 bytes are interpreted as 4003H. MS-DOS uses 1.5 bytes for each FAT entry, so 1.5 bytes must be extracted from this 2-byte number. The extraction is performed as follows: If the previous cluster number (2 in this case) was even, MS-DOS discards the high-order digit of the 2-byte number. If the previous cluster number was odd, MS-DOS discards the low-order digit of the 2-byte number.

In our example, the previous (first) cluster number was 2, which is even. Thus, we discard the high-order digit of 4003 to yield 003. This is the second cluster number. MS-DOS computes the third cluster number of IO.SYS by multiplying 3—the previous (second) cluster number—times 1.5. The product is 4.5. MS-DOS throws away the .5 and uses 4 as an offset into the FAT:

```
-d CS:300 L20
0976:0300  FD FF FF 03 40 00 05 60-00 FF 8F 00 09 A0 00 0B   }...a..'......
0976:0310  C0 00 0D E0 00 0F 00 01-11 20 01 13 40 01 15 60   a..'......a..'
```

The 2 bytes at offset 4 in the FAT are **40 00**. MS-DOS reads them as the 2-byte number 0040H. Since the previous (second) cluster number—3— was odd, MS-DOS discards the low-order digit of 0040 to yield 004, which is the third cluster number of IO.SYS.

In a similar fashion, MS-DOS will compute the fourth cluster number of IO.SYS as 5 and the fifth cluster number as 6. Let's see what happens when MS-DOS computes the sixth cluster number. The previous (fifth) cluster number was 6. Multiplying 6 times 1.5 equals 9. The 2 bytes at offset 9 in the FAT are **FF** and **8F**:

```
-d CS:300 L20
0976:0300  FD FF FF 03 40 00 05 60-00 FF 8F 00 09 A0 00 0B   }...a..'......
0976:0310  C0 00 0D E0 00 0F 00 01-11 20 01 13 40 01 15 60   a..'......a..'
```

MS-DOS forms the 4-byte number 8FFFH from these 2 bytes. The previous cluster number (6) was even, so MS-DOS throws out the high-order digit (8) to give the 1.5-byte number FFFH. MS-DOS reads any value in the range FF8–FFF as an end-of-file marker; therefore, FFFH tells MS-DOS that the last cluster of IO.SYS has been reached.

Without the FAT, MS-DOS would find itself adrift in a sea of clusters, unable to access any files. In fact, the FAT is so important to the operation of MS-DOS that each disk contains two copies of the FAT. Ostensibly, this second copy serves as a backup if the first is damaged. However, for reasons known only to the designers of MS-DOS, the second copy of the FAT is never used.

MS-DOS File Management

MS-DOS employs two techniques in managing files. The first technique, using data structures called *file control blocks* (FCBs), was implemented in MS-DOS 1. When MS-DOS was first developed, CP/M was the predominant operating system being used on microcomputers. FCBs were implemented specifically to provide some compatibility with CP/M files. When a hierarchical file structure was introduced in MS-DOS 2, a new technique for managing files was implemented. This technique utilizes a *file handle* and does not require the use of FCBs. File handles are patterned after the file management technique used by the UNIX operating system. This section discusses FCBs and file handles.

Structure of the File Control Block

The *file control* block is a 36-byte block of computer memory. The FCB, which is required for file management in MS-DOS 1, contains ten individual fields. Table 10-7 shows the ten fields and the purpose of each.

The *extended FCB* is used by MS-DOS to create files with a particular attribute or to search the file directory for such files. As table 10-8 shows, the extended FCB consists of a standard FCB with a 7-byte *header*. The bytes of the header are referenced by negative offsets relative to byte 00 of the standard FCB.

Table 10-7. Breakdown of File Control Block

Offset (Hex)	Purpose
00	***Disk drive number.*** Set by the programmer.
	0 default drive
	1 drive A
	2 drive B

Table 10-7. (cont'd)

Offset (Hex)	Purpose
	3 drive C etc.
01–08	*Filename of file to be created, written, or read.* Set by the programmer. The field must be padded with blanks if the filename has fewer than 8 characters. The field may contain a valid device name (excluding the optional colon).
09–0B	*Filename extension.* Set by the programmer. The field must be padded with blanks if the extension has fewer than 3 characters.
0C–0D	*Current block number.* A block consists of 128 records. The size of a record is determined by bytes 0EH and 0FH of the FCB. A block is numbered according to its position relative to the start of the file. The current block number is set to zero by MS-DOS when a file is opened. Sequential read and write operations use the current block number and the current record number (FCB byte 20H) to locate a particular record.
0E–0F	*Logical record size.* An "open file" operation assigns a value of 80H to this field.
10–13	*File size in bytes.* When MS-DOS opens a file, it extracts the file's size from the file directory and stores the value in this field. The low-order word is stored in bytes 10H and 11H; the high-order word in 12H and 13H. This value should **not** be modified by the programmer.
14–15	*Date file was created or last modified.* Also extracted from directory during an "open." This value should **not** be modified by the programmer.
16–1F	*Reserved for use by MS-DOS.* This value should **not** be modified by the programmer.
20	*Current relative record number.* This field contains the relative record number (0–127) within the current block (FCB bytes 0CH–0DH). This field is not initialized by an "open" operation.
21–24	*Random record number.* This field is used for "random" reading and writing of files. Records are numbered according to their position relative to the first record in the file. The first record is random number 0.

Table 10-8. Breakdown of Extended FCB Header

Offset (Hex)	Purpose
−07	***A flag byte set to FFH,*** indicating the beginning of an extended FCB header.
−06 to −02	***Reserved by MS-DOS.***
−01	***Attribute of file to be created or searched for:***
	02H Hidden file
	04H System file
	00H Other file

Using an FCB

MS-DOS 1 requires you to set up an FCB for a file before any operations can be performed on that file. Once the FCB is set up in memory, you must place the FCB's segment address in the DS register and the FCB's offset address in the DX register. The DS and DX registers then act as a pointer directing MS-DOS to the FCB.

With DS:DX pointing to the FCB, you must place the value of the desired service function (see appendix A) in the AH register, initialize any other registers required by that particular service function, and then direct MS-DOS to execute an interrupt type 21 (hex). Interrupt 21 is the MS-DOS *function dispatcher* that tells MS-DOS to execute the service specified by the value in the AH register. The MS-DOS service functions are used to perform the nuts and bolts operations in a computer program.

When a computer program issues a call for interrupt 21, control will pass from the computer program to MS-DOS. The service function will operate on the file specified by the FCB and then return control to the calling program. Execution of the program will then continue in the normal fashion.

As we have seen, a big drawback in using the MS-DOS 1 file management functions is the requirement that a valid FCB be established for each file read or written. MS-DOS 2 effectively removed this annoyance with the implementation of file handles.

File Handles

MS-DOS versions 2.X and subsequent versions provide a group of file management service functions that do not require the use of FCBs. Before a file is opened or created, a character string is placed in memory that specifies the drive, path, filename, and extension of the file. The DS and DX registers are then used to point to this string and the *create* (DOS function 3CH) or the *open* (DOS function 3DH) function is called. The function returns a 16-bit file handle in the AX register. The file handle is then used for any subsequent access to the file; no FCB is used. MS-DOS takes care of the messy details. The programmer simply keeps track of which file handle belongs to which file.

MS-DOS versions 2.X, 3.X, and 4.X provide support for FCBs; therefore, programs written to execute under MS-DOS 1.X will run under 2.X and subsequent versions. Programs that utilize file handles will not run under MS-DOS 1.X.

11

Memory Structure
and Management

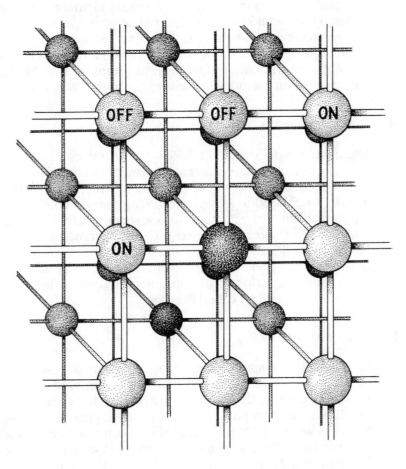

The purpose of the next three chapters is to give you a thorough understanding of how memory is organized and controlled in MS-DOS computers. This chapter is an overview, discussing structure and process in general terms. Chapter 12 extends the discussion to expanded memory, and chapter 13 then applies this information to terminate and stay resident computer programs.

Computer Memory

Computer memory consists of a large number of individual memory elements, each of which stores 1 byte of data. Each element is assigned a unique numerical address, and the elements are ordered according to these addresses. The first memory element is assigned address 0, the next is assigned address 1, and so on up to the last memory element whose address is determined by the total number of individual elements in the computer's memory. For reasons we won't go into here, memory addresses are generally given in hexadecimal numbers. In this book, hexadecimal numbers are always labeled with an uppercase *H*, for example 10H. Figure 11-1 illustrates the structure of memory in a computer with 1 Mbyte of memory.

Memory Segments

The central processing unit (CPU) in MS-DOS computers divides memory into blocks called *segments*. Each segment occupies 64 Kbytes of memory. The CPU contains four *segment registers*, which are internal storage devices used to store the addresses of selected memory segments. The four segment registers are given the names CS (code segment), DS (data segment), SS (stack segment), and ES (extra segment). The CPU contains several other registers. For now, we'll just mention IP (instruction pointer) and SP (stack pointer). IP is used with CS to keep track of which memory address stores the next executable instruction of the computer program. SP is used with SS to access a portion of memory called the *stack*.

Accessing Memory

In MS-DOS computers, memory locations are accessed by combining the contents of a segment register with the contents of one of the other registers. For example, the program instruction to be executed is accessed by combining the contents of the CS and IP registers (the combination of CS and IP is written "CS:IP"). After the instruction is retrieved from memory and executed, the IP register is incremented so that CS:IP points to the next instruction to be executed.

The manner in which register contents are combined places an upper limit on the amount of memory that is addressable by the computer hardware. MS-DOS was originally designed to run on computers with an Intel 8088 CPU. Each 8088 register stores a 16-bit number. The 8088 combines

**Figure 11-1. Memory map for a computer with
1 megabyte of memory.**

the 16-bit number from a segment register (such as CS) with the 16-bit number from another register (such as IP) to produce a 20-bit memory address. This limits the amount of memory addressable by the 8088 to 2^{20} bytes, or 1 Mbyte.

Since the birth of MS-DOS, 8088 computers have been succeeded by 80286 and 80386 computers. These computers are capable of addressing more than 1 Mbyte of memory. However, the 1-Mbyte limitation is still built into MS-DOS. This limitation is one of the major restrictions of the operating system.

The memory diagram shown in figure 11-1 illustrates an additional restriction on usable memory. Memory addresses starting at A0000H are reserved for use by the system's video display and ROM (read only memory). This memory is not available for use by programs. Therefore, user programs are restricted to the 640-Kbyte range 00000H–9FFFFH. In chapter 12, we will discuss how this constraint has been overcome through the implementation of *expanded memory*.

Booting MS-DOS

The booting process consists of reading into memory the boot record and the files IO.SYS, MSDOS.SYS, and COMMAND.COM (see chapter 10).

When the computer is first turned on (or restarted), control is passed to an address in ROM (read only memory) that checks to see if the disk has a valid boot record. If a valid record is found, it is loaded into memory, and control of the computer is passed to it.

When the boot record receives control, it checks to see if IO.SYS and MSDOS.SYS are the first two files stored on the disk. If they are, the two files are loaded into the low end of memory, and control is passed to an initialization module contained in IO.SYS. If the two files are not on the disk in the appropriate physical location, the following message is displayed:

```
Non system disk
Replace and press any key
```

> In versions of DOS prior to 3.3, IO.SYS and MSDOS.SYS must be stored in contiguous sectors. This restriction does not hold in DOS 3.3 and subsequent versions of the operating system.

The initialization module passes control to MSDOS.SYS, which initializes a disk buffer and a file control block area that are used in executing service routines. MSDOS.SYS also determines the computer's equipment status and performs any necessary hardware initialization. MSDOS.SYS then passes control back to the IO.SYS initialization module.

The initialization module checks to see if there is a CONFIG.SYS file (discussed in chapter 9) in the root directory of the boot disk. If there is, and if it contains any instructions about installable device drivers, the specified drivers are installed in memory.

Next, the initialization module issues a call to DOS function 4BH, which invokes the DOS program loader. The loader, also called EXEC, is responsible for loading a program into memory and passing control to the program. In this case, the initialization module directs EXEC to load COM-

MAND.COM. EXEC can be directed to load a different command interpreter through the use of the SHELL command (see Part 3).

Recall from chapter 10 that COMMAND.COM consists of three parts: an initialization portion, a resident portion, and a transient portion. The resident portion is loaded by EXEC and is responsible for loading the transient portion. The resident portion also contains the routines that handle input and output errors, as well as routines that handle int 22H (terminate address), int 23H (Ctrl-Break), and int 24H (critical error).

The initialization portion of COMMAND.COM is loaded into memory immediately above the resident portion. This portion of the command interpreter processes AUTOEXEC.BAT files (see chapter 4). The initialization portion also prompts you for time and date. It is then discarded.

The transient portion of COMMAND.COM is loaded into the high end of memory. This portion of the command interpreter displays the system prompt, contains the internal system commands, and loads and executes external commands and executable files. As its name implies, the transient portion may be overwritten during the execution of a program. When a program terminates, the resident portion of COMMAND.COM determines if the transient portion has been overwritten and reloads it if necessary.

Once the transient portion of COMMAND.COM has been installed, the system prompt is displayed, indicating that the booting process has been completed and that MS-DOS is ready to accept a command. Figure 11-2 illustrates the structure of computer memory at the completion of the booting process.

Program Segment Prefix

Before loading any program (including COMMAND.COM), EXEC locates the lowest available segment in memory. This segment is designated the program segment. Beginning at offset 00 in the program segment, EXEC constructs a *program segment prefix* (psp). This program segment prefix is a 256-byte (100H) block of memory that serves as an area of communication between MS-DOS and the executing program. Once the psp is constructed, EXEC loads the program beginning at offset 100H in the program segment.

Table 11-1 describes the fields of the psp. Note that several of the fields described are not officially documented by either IBM or Microsoft. However, these fields seem to have served the same function from MS-DOS 2.0 through MS-DOS 3.3, and the descriptions presented in table 11-1 are widely accepted by DOS program developers.

The segment address of the psp is sometimes referred to as the *process identifier*, or *PID*. Each program running on a computer is called a process and is identified by a unique PID. On MS-DOS computers, the PID and the psp segment address are identical. When MS-DOS was first implemented, it was used on relatively small personal computers that were never running

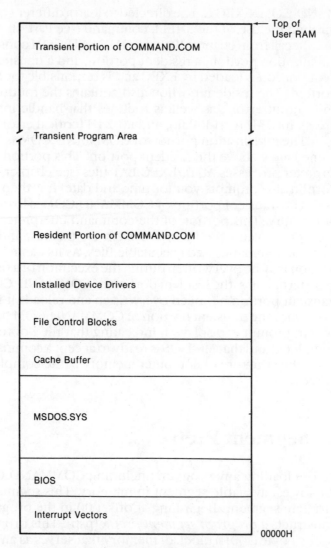

Figure 11-2. Configuration of computer memory immediately after MS-DOS is booted (exact memory addresses vary according to system configuration).

Table 11-1. Breakdown of Program Segment Prefix

Offset (hex)	Purpose
00–01	***Program terminate.*** The first two bytes of the psp are always CD and 20. These two hexadecimal numbers code for the MS-DOS interrupt "program terminate" (INT 20H). See appendix B for a discussion of MS-DOS interrupts.

Table 11-1. (cont'd)

Offset (hex)	Purpose
02–03	***Top of memory.*** These 2 bytes store, in reverse order, the starting segment address of any memory that MS-DOS has not allocated to the executable file. Since MS-DOS generally allocates all available memory to an executable file, these 2 bytes normally contain the address of the "top of memory."
04	***Byte of 00.*** Although officially documented as "reserved," this field is not currently in use.
05–09	***Function dispatcher.*** A long call to the MS-DOS function dispatcher. This field is implemented to provide compatibility with CP/M programs. New programs should not use this field to call the function dispatcher. The first byte in this field is the op-code for a long call. The second and third bytes store, in reverse order, the offset of the function dispatcher. This number also represents the number of bytes that are available in the program's code segment. The fourth and fifth bytes of the field store, in reverse order, the segment address of the function dispatcher. The function dispatcher is discussed in appendix A.
0A–0D	***Terminate address.*** These 4 bytes store, in reverse order, the default address that receives control when a program terminates execution. The value stored here preserves the default so that it can be restored, if necessary, when the program terminates.
0E–11	***Ctrl-Break exit.*** These 4 bytes store, in reverse order, the default address that receives control when Ctrl-Break is pressed. The value stored here preserves the default so that it can be restored, if necessary, when the program terminates.
12–15	***Critical error exit.*** These 4 bytes store, in reverse order, the default address that receives control when a critical error is encountered. The value stored here preserves the default so that it can be restored, if necessary, when the program terminates. See appendix A for a discussion of critical errors.
16–17	***psp of parent.*** This field stores in reverse order, the segment address of the parent's psp. For example, if COMMAND.COM uses EXEC to load an application program, then this field of the application's psp will contain the segment address of COMMAND.COM's psp.

Table 11-1. (cont'd)

Offset (hex)	Purpose
	THE COMMAND.COM shell that was loaded during booting has no viable parent. Therefore, this field in COMMAND.COM's psp stores its own segment address.
	The use of this field is undocumented by Microsoft and IBM. Officially the field is "reserved."
18–2B	*File handle alias table*. These 20 bytes are used to store the file handles that belong to this process. The byte at a given entry contains FFH if the corresponding handle is not in use by the process. A value other than FFH represents an offset into DOS's master file table, which contains the file-specific information. The size of this master table is set with the FILES=*nnn* command.
	The first 5 bytes in this field are reserved for the standard input, standard output, standard error, standard auxiliary, and standard printer devices. If any of these devices are redirected, the corresponding entry in this table will be changed by MS-DOS.
	The size of this table limits a process to 20 file handles. However, it is possible to create a table with more than 20 bytes and use it as a handle alias table. This can be accomplished by: (1) storing the size of the new table at offset 32H in the psp, (2) storing the offset and segment addresses of the new table at offset 34H of the psp, and (3) copying the contents of the old alias table into the new alias table.
	The use of this field is not documented by Microsoft or IBM. Officially the field is "reserved."
2C–2D	*Environment address.* These bytes store the segment address, in reverse order, of the program's environment. Refer to this chapter's discussion of the environment.
2E–31	*Reserved by MS-DOS*.
32–33	*Size of file handle alias table*. This 2-byte word stores the size of the process's file alias table. Current implementations of MS-DOS set the value of this field to 20. See the description of psp offset field 18H–2BH.
	The use of this field is undocumented by Microsoft and IBM. Officially this field is "reserved".
34–37	*Address of file handle alias table.* The first 2 bytes of this field store, in reverse order, the offset address of the

Table 11-1. (cont'd)

Offset (hex)	Purpose
	file handle alias table. The second 2 bytes of this field store, in reverse order, the alias table's segment address. Current implementations of MS-DOS store the alias table at PSP:0018H. See the description of psp offset field 18H–2BH.
	The use of this field is undocumented by Microsoft and IBM. Officially the field is "reserved."
37–4F	***Reserved by MS-DOS.***
50–52	***Function dispatcher, return.*** This field contains the bytes CD 21 CB—the machine code for a call to the function dispatcher followed by a FAR return.
53–5B	***Reserved by MS-DOS.***
5C–6B	***File control block.*** This default file control block is used if the first command line parameter following the program name is a filename.
6C–7B	***File control block.*** This default file control block is used if the second command line parameter following the program name is a filename.
7C–7F	***Reserved by MS-DOS.***
80–FF	***Command tail, DTA.*** The first byte stores the length of the command line's parameter string. The parameter string (command tail) is stored beginning at byte 2 of this field. The entire field also serves as a default disk transfer area. This field is used if the program requires but does not establish a DTA. When the field is used in this fashion, the command tail is overwritten.

more than one program (process) at a time. The current MS-DOS computers are quite different in this respect: it is not unusual for them to have one or more resident programs (such as Sidekick) while running the user's application program. In the environment, the concept of processes is very important, as is an understanding of the location, structure, and function of the psp. Processes and PIDs are discussed later in this chapter under "Memory Allocation."

MS-DOS 3.0 (and subsequent versions) implement DOS function 62H. This function can be called by a program to obtain the segment address of its psp. Appendix A contains a Turbo Pascal program that demonstrates the use of function 62H.

For the 2.X versions of DOS, there is an undocumented DOS function that can be used to obtain the psp's segment address. Function 51H (which is also implemented in 3.X and 4.X) returns the address in the BX register. Listing 11-1 is a Turbo Pascal program that demonstrates the use of function 51H. See appendix A for a general discussion on the use of the DOS functions.

DOS function 50H is available to set the current psp. This function is implemented in MS-DOS 2.X and subsequent versions, but its use is not officially documented. Despite this lack of sanction by IBM and Microsoft, function 50H is widely used in resident programs. When a resident program receives control (as when a "hot" key is pressed), DOS keeps the psp of the application program as the current psp. Function 50H may be used to tell DOS that the resident's psp is the current psp. Similarly, when the resident passes control back to the application program, function 50H may be used to reset the application's psp as current.

Listing 11-1. PsPeep, a Turbo Pascal Program Demonstrating the Use of Function 51H

```
program PsPeep;

{This program displays information about its psp using
MS-DOS function 51H. 51H is an undocumented function that is
identical to the MS-DOS 3.X function 62H. The difference is
that 51H is also implemented in MS-DOS 2.X.}

type
    registers = record
                ax,bx,cx,dx,bp,si,di,ds,es,flags: integer;
                end;
    HexString = string[4];
var
    dosreg  : registers;
    psp_seg : integer;

function hex (i : integer) : HexString;
{Converts decimal to hex string}
const
    h : array[0..15] of char = '0123456789ABCDEF';
var
    low,high : byte;
begin
    low  := Lo(i);
    high := Hi(i);
    hex  := h[high shr 4]+h[high and $F]+h[low shr 4]+h[low and $F];
end;

function VerNum : integer;
{This function returns the version of DOS being used.}
```

```
begin
      dosreg.ax:= $3000;              {Set AH to 30H.}
      MsDos(dosreg);                  {Call DOS}
      VerNum:= Lo(dosreg.ax);         {Major number in AL}
end;

procedure GetPsp;
{Uses DOS service function 51H to obtain the segment address
of the program's psp}
begin
      dosreg.ax := $5100;
      MsDos(dosreg);
      psp_ := dosreg.bx;
      writeln('PSP: ',hex(psp_seg));
end;

procedure TermAddr;
{Displays segment:offset address of termination handler}
begin
      write('Termination address: ');
      write(hex(MemW[psp_seg:$0c]));
      writeln(':',hex(MemW[psp_seg:$0a]));
end;

procedure ParentPsp;
{Displays psp of this program's parent. The purpose of offset
is not officially documented}
begin
      writeln('Parent PSP: ',hex(MemW[psp_seg:$16]));
end;

procedure EnvSeg;
begin
      write('Environment begins at: ');
      writeln(hex(MemW[psp_seg:$2c]),':0000');
end;

procedure FileHandles;
{Displays information about the file handle alias table. The format
for alias table is not officially documented.}
var
      AliasSeg,AliasOff,FileCnt,
      i,j                            : integer;

begin
      AliasSeg := MemW[psp_seg:$36];
      AliasOff := MemW[psp_seg:$34];
      write('Handle alias address: ');
      writeln(hex(AliasSeg),':',hex(AliasOff));
      write('Size of alias table: ');
      writeln(MemW[psp_seg:$32],' bytes');
```

```
        FileCnt := 0;
        for i := 0 to (MemW[psp_seg:$32] - 1) do
        begin
            j := Mem[psp_seg:$18 + i];
            if not (j in [$FF, 0..2]) then
                FileCnt := FileCnt + 1;
        end;
        writeln('Number of open file handles: ',FileCnt);

    end;

    procedure GoPeep;
    begin
        TermAddr;
        ParentPsp;
        EnvSeg;
        FileHandles;
    end;

    {Program starts here.}
    begin
        if VerNum < 2 then
            writeln('DOS 2.0 or later required.')
        else begin
            GetPsp;
            GoPeep;
        end;
    end.
```

Executable Files

All programs written to run under MS-DOS go through a process called *link-ing* (see chapter 16). The linker evaluates the program and determines where in memory the different parts of the program are to be located relative to one another. The linker then stores this information in a header located at the front of the program file. All files produced by the linker have a filename extension of ".EXE" and are called EXE files.

EXE files that meet three requirements may be converted to COM files. The requirements for a COM file are: (1) the program and all of its data must occupy less than 64 Kbytes; (2) the program's code, data, and stack must all reside in the same memory segment; and (3) the first executable instruction of the program must be at offset 100H within the file. If an EXE file meets all of these requirements, it can be converted to a COM file by using the MS-DOS utility EXE2BIN. COM files do not contain a header.

MS-DOS always loads COM files beginning at offset 100H in the program segment, immediately following the psp. The starting address of the program segment is placed in all four segment registers, and a value of 100H is placed in the IP register. The SP register is set to point to the top of the program segment. MS-DOS then places 2 bytes of 00H at the top of the stack and passes control to the instruction at CS:100.

When an EXE file is loaded, the file's header is placed in memory beginning at offset 100H in the program segment. The remainder of the file is then relocated in memory according to the information contained in the header. The CS, IP, SS, and SP registers are initialized according to information in the header. The DS and ES registers are set to point to the start of the psp, control is passed to the instruction pointed to by CS:IP, and program execution commences.

The Environment

Any program running under MS-DOS may use EXEC to load and run another program. When this occurs, the program calling EXEC is referred to as the *parent* and the program loaded by EXEC is referred to as the *child*. The child inherits many items from its parent, including a block of memory called the *environment*.

The environment consists of a series of statements having the form

environment variable=some string of characters

An environment statement serves to communicate information to both MS-DOS and application programs. For example, the statement "PATH=*search path*" tells MS-DOS which directories to search for files; the statement "COMSPEC=*d*:[*path*]" tells MS-DOS where to locate the transient portion of COMMAND.COM; and the statement "LIB=[*path*]" tells the compiler where to look to locate library files used in compiling programs.

The statements within the environment are separated from each other by a byte of value 00H. The final statement in the environment is followed by 2 bytes storing 00H. In MS-DOS 3 and 4, the 2 bytes of 00H are followed by a word count and by the drive, path, filename, and filename extension of the program that owns the environment. As we discussed earlier in this chapter, offset 2CH in the program's psp stores the segment address of the program's environment.

Environment Size

The environment may be up to 32 Kbytes long. As part of the standard booting process, COMMAND.COM receives an environment that is 160 bytes long. An environment of this size can fill up quickly, in which case MS-DOS will display the message: `Out of environment space`.

Users of MS-DOS 3.1 and subsequent versions can increase the size of the environment passed to COMMAND.COM by including the following command in the CONFIG.SYS file:

shell=[*d*:][*path*]command.com /p /e:*xxxx*

Refer to the discussion of SHELL in Part 3 for details on the use of this command.

Users of MS-DOS 2.X and 3.0 can also change the size of the environment, but it is necessary to use DEBUG to modify the contents of COMMAND.COM (DEBUG is thoroughly discussed in chapter 15). Place your working system diskette in drive A and enter the following command:

```
A> debug a:command.com
```

This command instructs MS-DOS to load DEBUG and tells DEBUG to load COMMAND.COM. You will want to use DEBUG to search for the portion of code within COMMAND.COM that sets the default size of the environment. When you see the DEBUG prompt (−), enter the following command:

```
-s 100 L 4500 BB 0A 00 B4 48 CD 21
```

DEBUG will search COMMAND.COM until it finds the appropriate sequence of machine code. When the code is found, DEBUG will display the address at which it is located. You should see something like this:

```
39D3:0ECE
-
```

The precise address on your machine will probably differ from the one in this example. The next step is to unassemble the machine code. Enter the following command (again, the address you use will probably differ from the one used in the example):

```
-u 39d3:0ece
39D3:0ECE BB0A00        MOV     BX,000A
39D3:0ED1 B448          MOV     AH,48
39D3:0ED3 CD21          INT     21
39D3:0ED5 E890F7        CALL    0668
39D3:0ED8 E8DCF7        CALL    06B7
39D3:0EDB 89166909      MOV     [0969],DX
39D3:0EDF A16709        MOV     AX,[0967]
39D3:0EE2 2D5900        SUB     AX,0059
39D3:0EE5 90            NOP
39D3:0EE6 A3B10B        MOV     [0BB1],AX
39D3:0EE9 E861F3        CALL    024D
39D3:0EEC 8916B70B      MOV     [0BB7],DX
-
```

The instruction **MOV BX,000A** sets the number of paragraphs (16-byte blocks) given to the environment. As you can see, the default is 10 (000AH) paragraphs. The following command changes the code so that 64 (0040H) paragraphs are set aside for the environment. Feel free to choose a smaller or larger number for your environment size. Remember that you are limited to 32 Kbytes and that DEBUG operates with hexadecimal numbers. By the way, 32 Kbytes is actually 32,768 bytes, or 2048 paragraphs.

```
-a 39d3:0ece
39D3:0ECE mov bx,0040
39d3:0ED1      ←press Enter
-
```

Since we are changing the contents of COMMAND.COM, it is a good idea to unassemble the changed code just to check our work.

```
-u 39d3:0ece
39D3:0ECE BB4000      MOV      BX,0040
39D3:0ED1 B448        MOV      AH,48
39D3:0ED3 CD21        INT      21
39D3:0ED5 E890F7      CALL     0668
39D3:0ED8 E8DCF7      CALL     06B7
39D3:0EDB 89166909    MOV      [0969],DX
39D3:0EDF A16709      MOV      AX,[0967]
39D3:0EE2 2D5900      SUB      AX,0059
39D3:0EE5 90          NOP
39D3:0EE6 A3B10B      MOV      [0BB1],AX
39D3:0EE9 E861F3      CALL     024D
39D3:0EEC 8916B70B    MOV      [0BB7],DX
-
```

Now enter w to write the modified file back to the disk. Then enter q to leave DEBUG. Test to see if COMMAND.COM has been successfully patched by using the diskette in drive A to reboot your system. If your system boots, copy COMMAND.COM into the root directory of the boot drive.

Passing an Environment to a Child

Before calling EXEC, the parent must set up a *pointer* to the environment block that the child will inherit. A pointer is a variable that stores an address in memory. In this case, the pointer stores the address of the first byte in the environment. The parent can create an environment of any size (up to 32 Kbytes) using the memory allocation function (see the following discussion). However, when control passes from the child back to the parent, the parent's environment will be unchanged from what it was originally. Therefore, the parent cannot use this mechanism to change the size of its own environment.

The parent can pass to the child an exact duplicate of its own environment by setting the pointer to equal zero. Any modifications that the child performs on its environment are strictly local: they have no effect on the parent's environment.

It is possible for a child to modify its parent's environment. One way is to have the child locate its parent's psp from offset 16H in its own psp. Once the parent's psp is located, the parent's environment address can be read from offset 2CH.

The parent's environment can also be accessed by using the memory control blocks discussed in the next section.

Memory Allocation

One of the most critical jobs of any operating system is managing computer memory. The operating system must constantly be aware of which portions of memory are being used and which portions are available. There are three fundamental requests that an operating system must be able to service in performing memory management: (1) requests for allocations of blocks of memory, (2) requests to modify the size of previously allocated blocks of memory, and (3) requests to release (deallocate) previously allocated blocks of memory.

MS-DOS carries out these tasks using functions 48H (allocate memory), 49H (release memory), and 4AH (modify memory allocation). If you refer back to the previous section where COMMAND.COM was patched to modify the environment size, you will see that function 48H was used to allocate a block of memory for the environment.

The first paragraph in each allocated memory block is set aside for the *memory control block* (mcb). The first byte of a memory control block is either 4DH or 5AH. If the first byte is 4DH, then the mcb is an internal member of the chain that links all of the mcb's. If the first byte of the mcb is 5AH, the mcb is the final mcb in the chain.

The second and third bytes of the memory control block store, in reverse order, the process identifier (PID) of the program that owns the memory block. Recall from the psp discussion that the PID is identical to the segment address of the program's psp.

The fourth and fifth bytes in the mcb store, in reverse order, the number of paragraphs in the allocated block of memory. Adding this number to the address of the current mcb gives the address of the next mcb in the chain.

As we mentioned earlier, MS-DOS supplies three functions to use in accessing mcb's. Direct manipulation of the mcb's is strongly discouraged by Microsoft and IBM. There is no way that programs can coexist unless programmers leave the mcb's alone and let DOS worry about them. Having said that, there is no reason why a programmer should not be able to look at the mcb's and use the information they contain.

Unfortunately, there is no documented way of accessing the mcb's. Even the mcb structure just described is not officially documented. Fortunately, there is a way (undocumented) to get at the mcb's: DOS function 52H. This function returns a pointer to the first mcb in the allocated chain. Once the first link is found, it is possible to traverse the entire chain.

Let's use DEBUG to see how the previous information can be used. Start DEBUG (**debug**) and wait for the prompt (−). When the prompt appears, invoke DEBUG's assembler by entering **a 100**. You should see something like this:

```
-a 100

1259:0100      ←press Enter
```

Now enter the following assembly language commands:

```
1259:0100 mov ah,52

1259:0102 int 21

1259:0104      ←press Enter


-
```

Next, enter **g 104**. This tells DEBUG to execute the assembly language commands entered and to stop at offset 104H.

```
-g 104

AX=5200 BX=0026 CX=0000 DX=0000 SP=FFEE BP=0000 SI=0000 DI=0000
DS=1259 ES=022B SS=1259 CS=1259 IP=0104  NV UP EI PL NZ NA PO NC
1259:0104 6F      DB    6F
```

DEBUG just called DOS function 52H. Function 52H returned the memory address in ES and BX. The 2-byte word at ES:BX −2 is the segment address of the first mcb in the allocation chain. The next DEBUG command displays the word at ES:BX −2:

```
-d es:0024 L2

022B:0020      73 09                        s.
```

This dump tells us that the first mcb is stored at address 0973:0000. Remember that mcb's always start at offset 0000 in a segment. We can now look at the first mcb:

```
-d 973:0 l10

0973:0000 4D 08 00 EF 02 07 03 00-36 C6 06 08 03 00 36 C7  M.......6.....6.
```

The first byte in the preceding dump is reassuring, since the first byte in each mcb must be either 4DH or 5AH. The second and third bytes store, in reverse order, the PID (psp segment address) of the process that owns this block of memory. MS-DOS always assigns PID 0008 to the block containing the CONFIG.SYS device drivers.

To find the next mcb, add the 2-byte word formed by the fourth and fifth bytes to the segment address of this mcb. DEBUG's hexadecimal calculator is useful for this:

```
-h 973 2ef

0C62 0684
```

The first number is the sum; the second number is the difference.

The next mcb is at the paragraph following 0C62:0000:

```
-d c63:0 L10

0C63:0000 4D 64 0C D3 00 EA 75 07-3B FD 73 19 AA EB F3 4E   Md....u.;.s....N
```

The preceding display is the mcb for the second block of memory in the chain. This is the memory block used by COMMAND.COM. The second and third bytes tell us that COMMAND.COM's psp starts at address 0C64:0000. Let's take a look at the psp's contents.

```
-d c64:0

0C64:0000 CD 20 00 80 00 9A F0 FE-1D F0 B2 02 64 0C 3C 01   ..........d.<.
0C64:0010 64 0C 56 05 64 0C 64 0C-01 03 01 00 02 FF FF FF   d.V.d.d.........
0C64:0020 FF FF FF FF FF FF FF FF-FF FF FF FF 3C 0D 1D 08   ............<...
0C64:0030 64 0C 14 00 18 00 64 0C-FF FF FF FF 00 00 00 00   d.....d.........
0C64:0040 00 00 00 00 00 00 00 00-00 00 00 00 00 00 00 00   ................
0C64:0050 CD 21 CB 00 00 00 00 00-00 00 00 00 00 20 20 20   .!...........
0C64:0060 20 20 20 20 20 20 20 20-00 00 00 00 00 20 20 20    .....
0C64:0070 20 20 20 20 20 20 20 20-00 00 00 00 00 00 00 00   ........
```

This is the beginning of COMMAND.COM's psp. We can use it to obtain the segment address of COMMAND.COM's environment block (offset 2CH). Thus, knowing how to get at the mcb's and traverse them allows us access to COMMAND.COM's environment. Any changes in this environment block will be passed on to all programs loaded by COMMAND.COM.

C H A P T E R

12

Expanded Memory

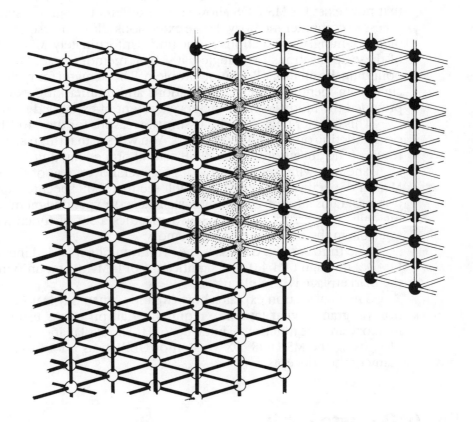

Expanded memory is the name of a method developed to overcome the memory limitation of MS-DOS computers. The structure and use of expanded memory is the subject of this chapter.

MS-DOS computers are limited to 640 Kbytes of usable main memory. When MS-DOS was first introduced, most observers felt that 640 Kbytes was more than enough memory for a personal computer. After all, earlier personal computers were limited to 64 Kbytes of memory, so 640 Kbytes seemed like more memory than any reasonable person would require.

What has happened, though, is that as computer applications have become more sophisticated, the memory limitation has become a significant problem. Large application programs, device drivers, and TSR utilities all require large amounts of memory.

More significantly, the multitasking operating system "extensions" (such as Microsoft Windows and Quarterdeck Office Systems' DESQView) that now exist for MS-DOS allow several different programs simultaneous access to computer memory. These extensions allow the use of many large, memory-hungry applications at one time. Unfortunately, MS-DOS limits all of these applications to a single 640-Kbyte memory space, thereby compounding the memory limitation problem. The demand for better performance from memory-hungry applications and multitasking extensions has provided the motivation for the development of expanded memory.

This chapter begins by discussing the reasons for the 640-Kbyte memory restriction on MS-DOS computers. You will see that this restriction is the result of the limitations of the 8088 central processing unit.

The following section provides a general overview of the Expanded Memory Specification (EMS). You will see that EMS specifies that application programs and the operating system access expanded memory by issuing calls to interrupt 67H. EMS also specifies a set of functions that are available in the use of expanded memory.

The third section discusses the evolution of expanded memory, from LIM 3.2 through LIM 4.0 The significance of LIM 4.0 as a unifying force in the marketplace is also discussed.

The final section explains how expanded memory is used by application programs, what tasks are required of all programs using expanded memory, and the function of interrupt 67H. The explanation includes examples, using the MS-DOS 4.X version of DEBUG as a tool to demonstrate many of the concepts.

The 640-Kbyte Limit

All computers access memory through their central processing unit (CPU). All CPUs contain *internal registers* that are used to store data. All CPUs also have an *address space* that determines how much memory the CPU can address or access.

One type of data used by the CPU is the *memory address*. Memory addresses specify physical locations in computer memory. The larger the internal registers, the larger the memory addresses they can store. Therefore, the size of the CPU's internal registers determines the size of the CPU's address space.

8088/86 Computers

The original IBM PC and PC-compatible computers contain an 8088/86 CPU. The 8088/86 is a "16-bit" CPU. This means that the CPU's internal registers can store numbers that are 16 bits (2 bytes) in length. The largest 16-bit number contains 16 ones, which is equivalent to the hexadecimal number FFFFH, or the decimal number 65,535 ($2^{16}-1$).

The 8088/86 addresses memory by combining a 16-bit *segment address* with a 16-bit *offset address* to form a 20-bit *physical address*. The two addresses are combined by shifting the segment address one place to the left and adding the offset address to it. As an example, if one CPU register stores a segment address of 1234H, and another register stores an offset address of 4321H, the two addresses are combined as follows:

$$\begin{array}{ll} 1234 & \leftarrow \text{16-bit segment address shifted to left} \\ \underline{4321} & \leftarrow \text{16-bit offset address} \\ 16661 & \leftarrow \text{20-bit physical address} \end{array}$$

The largest 20-bit number (in hexadecimal notation) is FFFFFH, which is equivalent to decimal 1,048,575 or $2^{20}-1$. This number represents the limit on the 8088/86's address space, which by convention is said to be 1 megabyte or 1 Mbyte.

Operating systems and application programs that run on PC and PC-compatible computers cannot access the entire 1-Mbyte address space. The reason for this is that the high end of the address space is used to store the ROM BIOS and provide address space for interface cards that support video display, local area networks, and other peripheral devices (see figure 11-1). The result is that only 640 kilobytes (640 Kbytes) of the 1-Mbyte address are available for use by operating system and application programs.

From this discussion you can see that the 640-Kbyte limitation is due to design features of MS-DOS which were implemented to accommodate the 8088/8086 hardware. If the hardware had been accommodated differently, MS-DOS could have been designed to access more than 640 Kbytes.

80286 and 80386 Computers

Because MS-DOS was written to run on 8088/86 machines, the operating system was unable to utilize the larger address space of the newer generations of IBM and IBM-compatible computers. These computers contain 80286 and 80386 CPUs, which have 32-bit internal registers that can address much larger memory spaces. But in order to maintain compatibility with the 8088 machines, the newer versions of MS-DOS continue to use 16-bit segment and offset addresses. MS-DOS application programs that run on the newer and potentially more powerful machines are thus burdened by the memory limitation of the original PC and PC compatibles.

IBM and Microsoft have developed OS/2, an operating system that can utilize the larger address space of 80286 and 80386 computers. OS/2 does have the capability to run programs written for MS-DOS, but only one MS-DOS program can run at a time and it is limited to 640 Kbytes of memory. OS/2 programs that utilize the larger address must be written specifically for OS/2.

Expanded memory, on the other hand, allows a program such as Windows or DESQView to run several standard MS-DOS applications at one time without being restricted to 640 Kbytes of memory.

Fundamentals of Expanded Memory

Expanded memory allows the CPU to access more memory than is contained in the CPU's address space, through a technique called *memory bank switching*. The principle is simple. A large amount of external memory (or other storage media) exists that cannot be directly accessed by the CPU. A block of the CPU's conventional memory is designated as a *window*. Some mechanism is implemented whereby a portion (or bank) of the external memory is *mapped* to the window. When the CPU reads from the window, it is actually reading a portion of the contents of the external memory. The application program can change the mapping to suit its needs so that different blocks of the external memory are mapped to the window. The result is that the CPU can access a large amount of external memory, although only a portion of the external memory is accessible at any one time. Figure 12-1 illustrates the concept of memory bank switching.

Expanded Memory Terminology

Once you understand the principle of memory bank switching, you understand most of what is going on with expanded memory. Expanded memory uses its own conventions and terminology, which will now be presented and then used in the remainder of this chapter.

Both the window and the external memory are divided into 16-Kbyte blocks called *pages*. As you will see later in this chapter, a page is the basic EMS unit of allocation.

The window of main memory is called the *page frame*. The page frame resides in conventional memory and is directly accessible by the CPU.

Logical memory refers to the expanded memory that is not directly

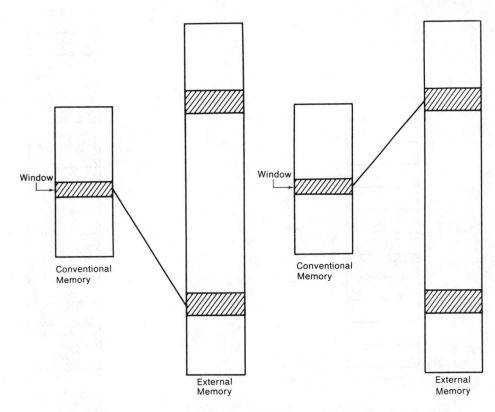

Figure 12-1. Memory bank switching. A block of conventional memory is designated as the "window." A portion of external memory is "mapped" into the window. The mapping varies over time.

accessible by the CPU. A portion of this memory is mapped to the window at a time. Expanded memory is divided into 16-Kbyte *logical pages*.

Physical memory is the memory contained in the page frame. Physical memory is divided into 16-Kbyte blocks called *physical pages*. Figure 12-2 illustrates the components of expanded memory.

The Expanded Memory Specification

The *Expanded Memory Specification (EMS)* is a document that specifies the components and behavior of expanded memory. The document defines the terms *page*, *page frame*, *logical memory*, and *physical memory*. The document also defines an *Expanded Memory Manager (EMM)*, which serves as the interface between expanded memory and application programs. The EMM is a device driver that must receive, interpret, and execute specific task requests received from the operating system and application programs.

The EMS says nothing about the way in which expanded memory is to

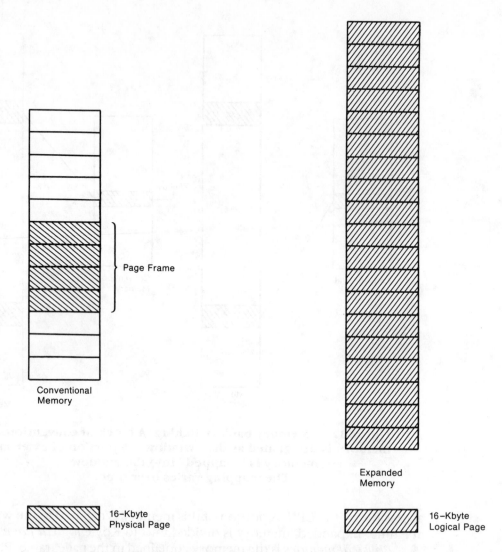

Figure 12-2. The page frame resides in conventional memory and consists of four 16-byte physical pages. Expanded memory consists of 16-Kbyte logical pages.

be implemented. For example, the EMS does not specify the design of expanded memory boards. In fact, expanded memory can be implemented entirely in software that swaps pages between a disk and the page frame.

Expanded Memory Implementation

Before turning to some of the specifics of what the EMS *does* say, let us discuss some of the different techniques used to implement expanded memory.

Expanded Memory Boards

Expanded memory boards use internal registers, which are controlled by software, to map a set of logical pages to the page frame. Mapping changes can be executed very quickly because all that is required is a changing of the value stored in one or more of the internal registers.

Alternatives to Expanded Memory Boards

Extended memory is standard computer memory that lies outside the 1-Mbyte address space. Extended memory can exist either on the motherboard or on standard memory expansion cards.

Extended memory can be used by some utilities, such as VDISK.SYS. You can also use extended memory to emulate an expanded memory board, provided you have an *expanded memory emulator*. The emulator is a computer program that works by swapping data between the page frame and extended memory. Expanded memory emulation is much slower than expanded memory boards because data must be physically moved between the page frame and extended memory.

There are some software packages that move data between the page frame and a disk drive. This type of expanded memory emulation is *very* slow, but it can provide an adequate environment to develop expanded memory applications. Usually the cost of a software emulator is much less than the cost of an expanded memory board and the memory chips needed to populate it. If the emulator adheres to the EMS, then applications developed with it will work with any implementation of expanded memory.

80386 Computers

The 80386 CPU contains sophisticated memory management hardware that allows it to use conventional memory to emulate an expanded memory board. Expanded memory implemented in this fashion is as fast as or faster than expanded memory boards.

An example of 80386 emulation is the device driver XMAEM.SYS, which comes with PC-DOS 4.X. The driver uses a portion of the PS/2 Model 80's standard memory to emulate an IBM PS/2 80286 Expanded Memory Adapter/A. Use of XMAEM.SYS is discussed below.

The Evolution of Expanded Memory

There have been three significant versions of the Expanded Memory Specification. The Lotus/Intel/Microsoft Expanded Memory Specification version 3.2 (LIM EMS 3.2) was the first specification of expanded memory and was widely used and supported. The AST Research/Quadram/Ashton-Tate Enhanced Expanded Memory Specification (AQA EEMS) was an enhanced specification that was upwardly compatible with LIM EMS 3.2. The most recent specification is LIM EMS 4.0, which incorporates the enhancements of AQA EEMS along with its own additional enhancements. These three versions of the expanded memory specification are discussed in this section.

LIM EMS 3.2

The LIM EMS 3.2 was published in September 1985. It defined a protocol for using up to 8 Mbytes of expanded memory. In addition to the concepts of page, page frame, logical page, and physical page, which are discussed in the previous section, LIM EMS 3.2 specifies that the page frame is 64 Kbytes in size and resides in conventional memory somewhere above the 640-Kbyte line and below the 1-Mbyte line. The four 16-Kbyte physical pages in the page frame are identified by the numbers 0–3.

An application program may *allocate* a block of one or more 16-Kbyte expanded memory pages at a time. Allocation simply means that the pages are "claimed" by the application and "marked" as being in use. Each allocated block is assigned a unique number, called the *handle*. The application program uses a handle when it needs to reference a specific allocated block of expanded memory.

AQA EEMS

A limitation of the LIM EMS 3.2 is that the 64-Kbyte page frame allows only four logical pages of expanded memory to be mapped to the page frame at a time. AQA EEMS removes this restriction by allowing up to sixty-four logical pages to be mapped into conventional memory at a time.

Notice that 64 times 16 Kbytes (the size of one logical page) is 1 Mbyte. Thus, AQA EEMS allows the entire MS-DOS address space to be used in the page frame. Memory below the 640-Kbyte line is called *mappable conventional memory*. This memory is generally only used for mapping by programs such as DESQView and Windows 2.0, which use mappable conventional memory to swap *executable code* in and out of the page frame. Most application programs using expanded memory use memory above 640 Kbytes for mapping.

LIM EMS 4.0

LIM EMS 4.0, which was published in August 1987, incorporates the enhancements of AQA EEMS and provides some additional enhancements of its own. LIM EMS 4.0 allows up to 32 Mbytes of expanded memory to be addressed by application programs. EMS 4.0 supports page frames larger than 64 Kbytes. However, memory boards originally designed for EMS 3.2 can only provide 64-Kbyte page frames, even if the boards are controlled by a 4.0 driver.

The significance of LIM EMS 4.0 is that it has been widely recognized as *the* standard specification for expanded memory. Most major software and hardware manufacturers have stated that they will use LIM EMS 4.0 in their future expanded memory products. Even AST, Quadram, and Ashton-Tate (the force behind AQA EEMS) have endorsed LIM EMS 4.0.

In what is perhaps the ultimate indication that LIM EMS 4.0 is accepted as standard, IBM includes XMA2EMS.SYS, a LIM 4.0 expanded memory manager, as a standard component of PC-DOS 4.X.

Using Expanded Memory

Application programs utilize expanded memory by issuing calls to the *expanded memory functions*. Programs access these functions via interrupt 67H. The use of interrupt 67H is similar to the use of interrupt 21H (the MS-DOS function dispatcher). An application program selects expanded memory functions by placing the appropriate function number in the AH register. Other registers are initialized as required by the particular function being called. The application program then calls interrupt 67H, which invokes the Expanded Memory Manager (EMM). The EMM carries out the requested function and then returns control to the application program.

The expanded memory functions report an error condition by returning a non-zero value in the AH register. A return value of zero in AH indicates that the function executed successfully.

This section discusses steps carried out by application programs in using expanded memory. You will see how interrupt 67H is used. You will also see how to use the MS-DOS 4.X version of DEBUG to gain a better understanding of expanded memory.

Appendix A contains information on interrupts and function calls that is directly applicable to the material in this section. Appendix E contains a primer on assembly language programming that you may find useful in following the examples presented below. Use of DEBUG is covered in chapter 15.

The Required Steps

To use expanded memory, the first thing an application program must do is to *check for the presence of expanded memory*. Obviously, no program can use expanded memory if it is not installed and functioning.

A program must determine *which version of expanded memory* is installed on the machine. If EMS 3.2 is installed, programs cannot request functions only implemented in EMS 4.0 .

A program must determine *how much expanded memory is available* for its use. The program may need to modify its behavior according to the amount of available memory.

A program must determine *the starting address of the expanded memory page frame* and then *allocate* a portion of expanded memory for its use. Allocation means that the memory is marked as being in use by the program.

Before a program can gain access to expanded memory, it must *map a portion of the allocated expanded memory into the page frame*. A *mapping* defines the portion of expanded memory that is currently being viewed through the page frame "window."

Once a mapping is established, the program may *read from* or *write to* expanded memory. A mapping also allows a program to *execute code* stored in expanded memory.

When a program is finished using expanded memory, it should return or *deallocate* the memory it was using, so that the memory becomes available to other programs.

We will now discuss how each of these steps is carried out.

Checking for Expanded Memory

All programs must check to see that the EMM is installed and functioning before issuing a call to interrupt 67H. The system will most likely crash if the call is made and the EMM is not present. This can happen because interrupt 67H has no meaning to the operating system; it must be defined by the EMM or some other program (see box).

Other Programs Using Interrupt 67H

Some other commercial device drivers, such as the driver for AST's PC-NET II adapter card, also use interrupt 67H. Most EMMs provide a mechanism called *chaining*, which allows the EMM to peacefully co-exist with such drivers. Refer to the documentation provided with your expanded memory board for information on implementing chaining.

There are two widely accepted methods available to check for the presence of the EMM. The first method is called the *Open Handle Method* and is performed as follows:

1. The application issues a call to MS-DOS function 3DH, asking the operating system to open a file named "EMMXXXX0." The program specifies that the "file" is to be opened in read-only mode. (Use of MS-DOS function 3DH, as well as other MS-DOS functions discussed in this chapter, is discussed in appendix A.)

2. The function call is successful if the carry flag is clear on return, in which case the AX register holds the file handle. The call is unsuccessful if the carry flag is set on return, in which case the operating system

was either unable to find "EMMXXXX0" or was unable to assign it a file handle.

3. If the call to function 3DH was successful, use MS-DOS function 44H, subfunction 0, to determine if the file handle returned for "EMMXXXX0" refers to a file or a device driver. If, on return, bit 7 of the DX register is set, then the handle refers to a device driver indicating that the EMM is installed.

4. If the EMM is installed, use MS-DOS function 44H, subfunction 7, to determine if the EMM is ready to operate. The EMM is ready if, on return, AL contains the value FFH.

5. Use MS-DOS 3EH to close the file opened in step 1 above. The application program will not need the file handle in order to use the EMM.

The second way to check for the presence of the EMM is called the *Get Interrupt Vector Method*. The method is as follows:

1. Use MS-DOS function 35H to obtain the memory address of the handler for interrupt 67H. The function returns the handler's segment address in the ES register.

2. If the EMM is installed, the string "EMMXXXX0" will be stored in the interrupt handler's segment, beginning at offset address 0AH.

The following assembly language code illustrates this technique. In this example and the examples that follow, comments following the arrows are for explanation only. They are not meant to be entered.

```
string1 db      ''EMMXXXX0''
;
mov     ah,35h          ←request DOS function 35h
mov     al,67h          ←handler address for int 67h
int     21h             ←call DOS
;
mov     di,0ah          ←ES:DI points to test string
push cs
pop     ds              ←make DS=CS
lea     si,string1      ←DS:SI points to "EMMXXXX0"
mov     cx,8            ←compare 8 bytes
repz cmpsb              ←compare the strings
jnz     bad_emm         ←compare failed
jmp     good_emm        ←compare succeeded
```

The first line in the listing defines the test string for which the code will look.

The next group of three instructions calls DOS function 35H requesting the address of the handler for interrupt 67H. Upon return, the ES register contains the handler's segment register.

The final group of instructions compares the string at es:000a with "EMMXXXX0". The instruction `repz cmpsb` compares 8 pairs of bytes. The instruction terminates with the zero flag set to "nz" if a nonmatching pair is found. The two strings are equal if the flag is set to "zr" upon completion of the compare operation.

The program may go on to use interrupt 67H once it has determined that the EMM is installed.

Getting the EMM Version Number

To obtain the version number of the installed EMM, use expanded memory function 46H. In assembly language, the call looks like this:

```
mov ah,46h
int 67h
```

On return, the upper 4 bits in the AL register store the major version number. For EMS 3.2, the major version number is 3; for EMS 4.0, the major version number is 4.

Determining How Much Expanded Memory Is Available

Expanded memory function 42H is used to obtain both the total number of expanded memory pages and the number of unallocated pages. In assembly language, the call looks like this:

```
mov ah,42h
int 67h
```

On return, the DX register contains the total number of expanded memory pages, and the BX register contains the number of unallocated pages. The unallocated pages are the pages available for use by the program.

Determining the Page Frame's Segment Address

Expanded memory function 41H is used to obtain the page frame's segment address. In assembly language, the call looks like this:

```
mov ah,41h
int 67h
```

On return, the BX register contains the page frame's segment address.

As you saw earlier in this chapter, the page frame serves as a "window" into extended memory. All access to expanded memory is through the page frame. Therefore, the application program must know where in conventional memory the page frame is located.

EMS 4.0 supports page frames larger than 64 Kbytes. The page frame may consist of 16-Kbyte pages that are not contiguous with one another. An application can use the EMS 4.0 function 58H, subfunction 1, to determine the total number of pages in the page frame (the total is returned in CX). Using that number, the program can use function 58H, subfunction 0, to populate an array with the segment address of each page in the page frame.

Allocating Expanded Memory Pages

The next step for a program is to request that the EMM allocate a set of unallocated expanded memory pages to the program.

Expanded memory function 43H is used to allocate a set of expanded memory pages. Prior to the call, the program places the number of 16-Kbyte pages that it wishes to allocate in the BX register. If a program wanted to allocate two expanded memory pages, the call would look like this:

```
mov bx,02h
mov ah,43h
int 67h
```

On return from function 43H, the DX register contains the *handle*. The handle is a number that is used to reference the set of pages that were just allocated. It is comparable to the *file handle* that is returned by MS-DOS function 3DH.

Mapping Logical Pages to the Page Frame

Once expanded memory pages have been allocated, they must be *mapped* to the page frame in order for an application program to access them. Pages that have been mapped in can be mapped out, but remain allocated. We will say more about this when we discuss context switching.

Handles are assigned a set of one or more logical pages. Each page in a set has a logical page number. The first page in a set has a logical page number of 0, the second a logical number of 1, and so on. Thus, each expanded memory page that has been allocated is uniquely identified by a handle number and logical page number.

Each physical page in the page frame is uniquely identified by a physical page number. The first page in the page frame has a physical page number of 0, the second a number of 1, and so on.

Expanded memory function 44H is used to map expanded memory pages into the page frame. Before calling function 44H, place the handle associated with the expanded memory page in the DX register, and the page's logical page number in the BX register. You specify a page in the page frame by placing a physical page number in the AL register.

In the following example, the expanded memory page with handle number 1, logical page 0 is mapped into physical page 0 of the page frame:

```
mov dx,01h     ←handle number
mov bx,00h     ←logical  page
mov al,00h     ←physical  number
mov ah,44h
int 67h
```

Exploring Expanded Memory with DEBUG

The MS-DOS 4.X version of the DEBUG utility has four commands that are used to examine and manipulate expanded memory. In the remainder of this chapter, we will use these new DEBUG commands, along with some other capabilities of the utility, to illustrate how expanded memory functions. Unfortunately, some vendors (particularly IBM) have decided not to include DEBUG as a standard component of DOS 4.X. These vendors require that you purchase the DOS Technical Reference in order to obtain DEBUG.

The objective in what follows is not to demonstrate that DEBUG can be used to write programs that use expanded memory. Rather, the objective is to use DEBUG to gain a better understanding of expanded memory so that you can go on to write such programs.

The DEBUG commands that manipulate expanded memory only work if the EMM is installed. In addition, calling interrupt 67H without the EMM installed may cause your machine to crash. Consider this to be your warning before trying to execute the examples that follow.

Starting DEBUG

We begin our DEBUG expedition by first starting DEBUG and then using the 4.X command "xa" to allocate two sets of expanded memory pages. Refer to chapter 15 if you need help starting DEBUG.

```
C:\BOOKS\DOS>debug          ←start DEBUG
-xa 1                       ←allocate a page
Handle created = 0001       ←it gets handle number 1
-xa 1                       ←allocate a second page
Handle created = 0002       ←it gets handle number 2
-
```

After DEBUG is started, the command **xa 1** directs the EMM to allocate one page of expanded memory (the format for the command is "xa *n*", where *n* is the number of expanded memory pages to be allocated).

The message **Handle created = 0001** is DEBUG's way of telling you that the page has been allocated and assigned to handle number 1. Similarly, a second page is allocated and assigned to handle number 2.

The "xs" command displays information about the current status of expanded memory:

```
-xs
Handle 0000 has 0000 pages allocated
Handle 0001 has 0001 pages allocated
Handle 0002 has 0001 pages allocated

Physical page 00 = Frame segment C400
Physical page 01 = Frame segment C800
Physical page 02 = Frame segment CC00
Physical page 03 = Frame segment D000

    2 of a total   40 EMS pages have been allocated
    3 of a total   FF EMS handles have been allocated
-
```

DEBUG tells you that handle 1 and handle 2 each have one page allocated (handle 0 is used by the EMM and is not available to application programs).

DEBUG gives you the segment address of the four physical pages making up the page frame. In this case, the 16-Kbyte pages are contiguous with each other.

DEBUG also tells you that two out of a total 40H expanded memory pages are allocated, and three out of a total FFH expanded memory handles have been allocated.

The DEBUG command "xm" can be used to map an expanded memory page into the page frame. The format for the command is "xm *lpage ppage handle*" where *lpage* is the logical page number of the expanded memory page to be mapped in, *ppage* is the physical page number of a page in the page frame, and *handle* is the number of the handle associated with the expanded memory page.

Figure 12-3 illustrates the current configuration of expanded memory. Two expanded memory pages have been allocated: one to handle 1 and one to handle 2. Neither of the pages has been mapped into the page frame.

In what follows, the "xm" command is used to map handle 1's page into the page frame:

```
-xm 0 0 1
Logical page 00 mapped to physical page 00
-
```

The command states that logical page 0 (the first zero), which is contained in the set identified by handle 1, is to be mapped into physical page 0 (the second zero). This changes the configuration of expanded memory to that illustrated in figure 12-4.

Once an expanded memory page has been mapped into the page frame, it may be read from or written to as though it were conventional

**Figure 12-3. Two logical pages have been allocated. One page is
allocated to handle 1; one page is allocated to handle 2.**

memory. An application program can access the data in the page frame using
a far (segment and offset) pointer.

Writing to and Reading from the Page Frame

We will use DEBUG to write some data to the page frame and then read it
back. If you look back to the "xs" command that was previously issued, you
will see that physical page 0 in the page frame begins at segment address
C400H. The following example uses DEBUG's "f" command to write data to
the page frame:

```
-f c400:0 L80 ''1''
-
```

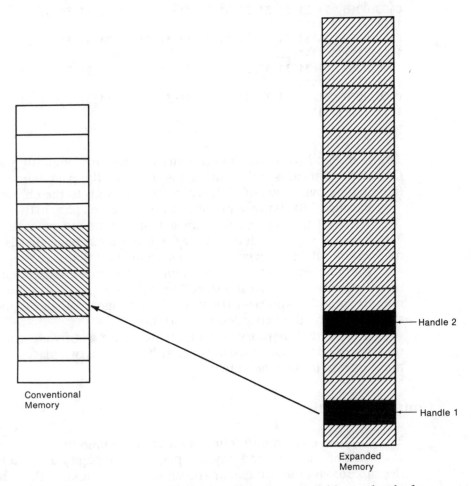

Figure 12-4. Logical page 0, handle 1 is mapped into physical page 0 of the page frame.

The command says to (f)ill memory, starting at address C400:0000, and continuing for a length of 80 bytes, with the character "1". You can use the "d" command to examine the effect of this command:

```
-d c400:0
c400:0000  31 31 31 31 31 31 31 31-31 31 31 31 31 31 31 31
1111111111111111
c400:0010  31 31 31 31 31 31 31 31-31 31 31 31 31 31 31 31
1111111111111111
c400:0020  31 31 31 31 31 31 31 31-31 31 31 31 31 31 31 31
1111111111111111
c400:0030  31 31 31 31 31 31 31 31-31 31 31 31 31 31 31 31
1111111111111111
```

```
C400:0040  31 31 31 31 31 31 31 31-31 31 31 31 31 31 31 31
1111111111111111
C400:0050  31 31 31 31 31 31 31 31-31 31 31 31 31 31 31 31
1111111111111111
C400:0060  31 31 31 31 31 31 31 31-31 31 31 31 31 31 31 31
1111111111111111
C400:0070  31 31 31 31 31 31 31 31-31 31 31 31 31 31 31 31
1111111111111111
-
```

The command (d)umps the contents of memory beginning at address C400:000. You can see that the first 80 bytes of the page frame have been filled with a byte value of 31H, which corresponds to the character "1".

Because C400 is the segment address of the first page in the page frame, the "1"s in the previous example are actually written to expanded memory. The location in expanded memory is the logical page that is currently mapped into the first page of the page frame (see figure 12-5).

If expanded memory is implemented with an expanded memory board, the data is physically stored in only one place—on the expanded memory board. It appears to be stored in the page frame due to the status of the registers on the expanded memory board.

If expanded memory is implemented with a software emulator that uses extended memory, then the data is physically in two places: in extended memory and in the page frame.

Context Switching

The *mapping context* is the current state of mappings between logical pages in expanded memory and physical pages in the page frame. At times, it is desirable to save the context, or a portion of the context, so that it might later be restored. For example, a large spreadsheet using expanded memory could easily have more data than could fit in the 64-Kbyte page frame at one time. The spreadsheet can map a portion of expanded memory into the page frame, read from and write to the page frame, and then, before mapping in another portion of expanded memory, save the mapping context. The spreadsheet can then recall the first portion of expanded memory by restoring the saved mapping context.

We will return to DEBUG to illustrate the concepts of mapping context and context saving. A final word of caution before we proceed though. The next example will call interrupt 67H from DEBUG. If your system does not have EMM installed and you issue a call to interrupt 67H, your system will either crash or do something totally unpredictable. So don't try this example unless EMM is installed.

Expanded memory function 47H is used to save a portion of the mapping context. Prior to calling the function, place the appropriate handle number in the DX register. The call then saves a record of the mapping context that exists for that handle.

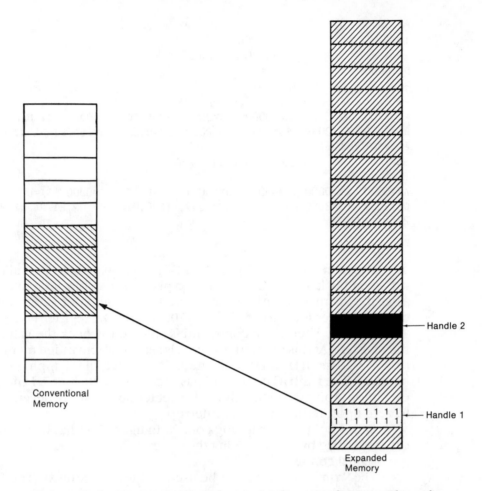

Figure 12-5. Data written to a page in the page frame ends up in a logical page in expanded memory.

Take a look back at figure 12-5. A mapping exists between the single logical page assigned to handle 1 and physical page 0 in the page frame. This mapping context can be saved with the following code:

```
mov dx,01h
mov ah,47h
int 67h
```

This code can be executed from DEBUG as follows:

```
-a                    ←start DEBUG's assembler
2059:0100 int 67
i]2059:0102           ←press Enter
-rax                  ←set the AX register
```

```
AX 0000
:4700              ←AX=4700h
-rdx               ←set the DX register
DX 0000
:1                 ←DX=01h
-r                 ←check machine's state
AX=4700  BX=0000  CX=0000  DX=0001  SP=FFEE  BP=0000  SI=0000  DI=0000
DS=2059  ES=2059  SS=2059  CS=2059  IP=0100   NV UP EI PL NZ NA PO NC
2059:0100 CD67          INT     67
-p                 ←execute interrupt 67h

AX=0000  BX=0000  CX=0000  DX=0001  SP=FFEE  BP=0000  SI=0000  DI=0000
DS=2059  ES=2059  SS=2059  CS=2059  IP=0102   NV UP EI PL NZ NA PO NC
2059:0102 1F            POP     DS
-
```

The example begins by starting DEBUG's assembler. This allows us to use assembly language mnemonics to place executable code into memory. After the instruction int 67h is entered, the assembler is terminated and the AX register is set to a value of 4700H. The DX register is then set to a value of 01H. Then the r command is entered to check the value of all of the registers. At this point, the system is set to call expanded memory function 47H. The 01H in DX tells the EMM to save the mapping context of handle 1. The DEBUG command p is used to execute int 67H and then halt execution. You can tell that the call executed successfully because AH is set to zero upon return from the interrupt.

At this point, the mapping context in figure 12-5 has been saved. This can be verified by first changing the context and then attempting to restore the original context.

The "xm" command can be used to alter the context. The following command changes the context to that illustrated in figure 12-6:

```
-xm 0 0 2
-
```

The command states that logical page 0 (the first zero), which is contained in the set identified by handle 2, is to be mapped into physical page 0.

The next two commands fill the first 80 bytes of the page frame with the character "2" and then display the results:

```
-f c400:0 l80 '2'
-d c400:0
C400:0000  32 32 32 32 32 32 32 32-32 32 32 32 32 32 32 32
2222222222222222
C400:0010  32 32 32 32 32 32 32 32-32 32 32 32 32 32 32 32
2222222222222222
C400:0020  32 32 32 32 32 32 32 32-32 32 32 32 32 32 32 32
2222222222222222
```

```
C400:0030  32 32 32 32 32 32 32 32-32 32 32 32 32 32 32 32
2222222222222222
C400:0040  32 32 32 32 32 32 32 32-32 32 32 32 32 32 32 32
2222222222222222
C400:0050  32 32 32 32 32 32 32 32-32 32 32 32 32 32 32 32
2222222222222222
C400:0060  32 32 32 32 32 32 32 32-32 32 32 32 32 32 32 32
2222222222222222
C400:0070  32 32 32 32 32 32 32 32-32 32 32 32 32 32 32 32
2222222222222222
-
```

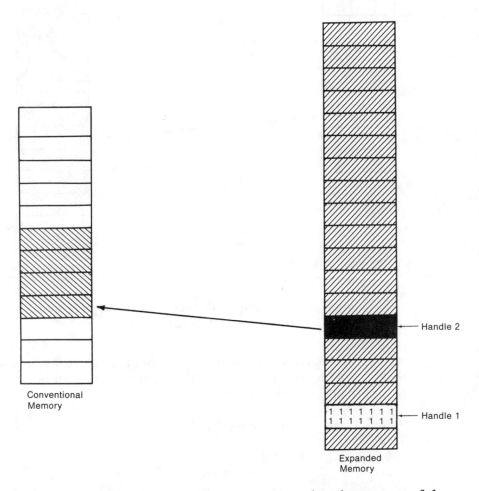

Figure 12-6. A new mapping context. Note that the content of the page belonging to handle 1 is preserved.

Figure 12-7 illustrates the configuration of expanded memory at this point.
Expanded memory function 48H is used to restore a mapping context.
Prior to the call, a handle number is placed in the DX register. The function

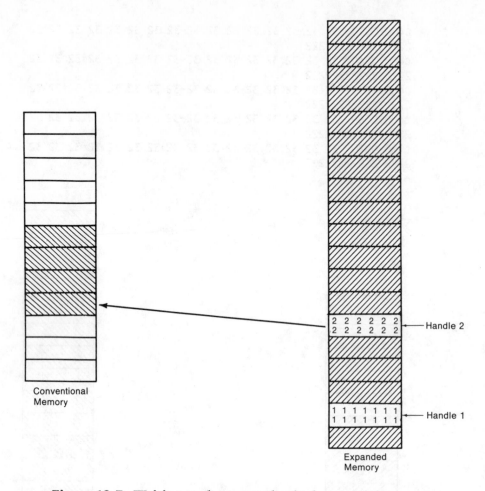

Figure 12-7. Writing to the same physical page under a new mapping context.

restores the handle's previously saved mapping context. We can use DEBUG to illustrate the use of function 48H. The following example is a continuation of the previous example:

```
-rip              ←set the IP register
IP 0102
:100              ←IP=100H
-rax              ←set the AX register
AX 0000
:4800             ←AX=4800H
-r                ←check machine's state
AX=4800  BX=0000  CX=0000  DX=0001  SP=FFEE  BP=0000  SI=0000  DI=0000
DS=5E2F  ES=5E2F  SS=5E2F  CS=5E2F  IP=0100    NV UP EI PL NZ NA PO NC
5E2F:0100 CD67          INT     67
-p                ←restore context
```

```
AX=0000  BX=0000  CX=0000  DX=0001  SP=FFEE  BP=0000  SI=0000  DI=0000
DS=5E2F  ES=5E2F  SS=5E2F  CS=5E2F  IP=0102     NV UP EI PL NZ NA PO NC
5E2F:0102 5D              POP      BP
-d c400:0      ←check context restored
C400:0000  31 31 31 31 31 31 31 31-31 31 31 31 31 31 31 31
1111111111111111
C400:0010  31 31 31 31 31 31 31 31-31 31 31 31 31 31 31 31
1111111111111111
C400:0020  31 31 31 31 31 31 31 31-31 31 31 31 31 31 31 31
1111111111111111
C400:0030  31 31 31 31 31 31 31 31-31 31 31 31 31 31 31 31
1111111111111111
C400:0040  31 31 31 31 31 31 31 31-31 31 31 31 31 31 31 31
1111111111111111
C400:0050  31 31 31 31 31 31 31 31-31 31 31 31 31 31 31 31
1111111111111111
C400:0060  31 31 31 31 31 31 31 31-31 31 31 31 31 31 31 31
1111111111111111
C400:0070  31 31 31 31 31 31 31 31-31 31 31 31 31 31 31 31
1111111111111111
-
```

The example begins by resetting the IP register so that it points to the int 67H instruction at offset address 100H. The value of AX is then set to 4800 in order to call function 48H. The machine's state is then checked and, as you can see, DX is still set to 01H. Thus, things are set to restore the previously saved mapping context of handle 1. The **p** command executes int 67H and the **d c400:0** command verifies that the context of handle 1 has been restored (figure 12-8).

EMS 4.0 implements expanded memory function 4EH, which allows an application program to save the mapping context for the entire page frame. This provides a considerable improvement over function 47H, which can only save the context of one handle at a time.

Deallocating Pages

An application program must deallocate its expanded memory pages when it is done using them. This makes the pages available for use by other applications. A well-designed program will deallocate its expanded memory programs even when it terminates in an abnormal fashion (such as when the user presses Ctrl-Break).

Expanded memory function 45H is used to deallocate pages. Prior to the call, place a handle number in the DX register. The function deallocates the expanded memory pages that correspond to the handle number.

The MS-DOS 4.X version of DEBUG uses the "xd" command to deallocate pages. The format for the command is

xd *handle*

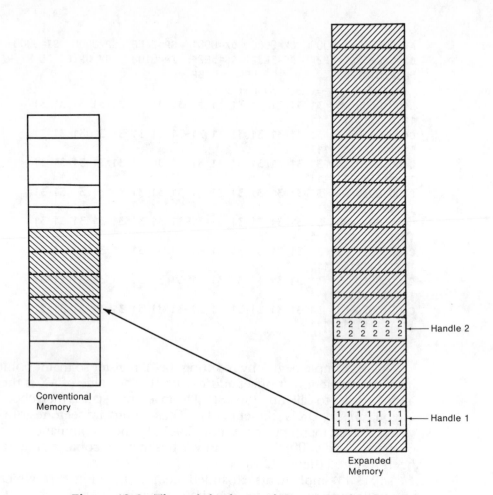

Conventional
Memory

Handle 2

Handle 1

Expanded
Memory

Figure 12-8. The original mapping context is restored.

EMS 4.0 Enhancements

All of the expanded memory functions used in this chapter's tutorial are
implemented in EMS 3.2 and 4.0. The discussion has mentioned some enhanced functions (4EH and 58H) that are only implemented in EMS 4.0. This
section discusses some other enhancements provided by EMS 4.0.

Executing Code in Expanded Memory

Prior to EMS 4.0, it was a bit of a chore for the application programmer to
link code in conventional memory to code in expanded memory. It could be
done, but it was difficult. EMS 4.0 made the process much easier by implementing expanded memory functions 55H and 56H.

Function 55H is called *Alter Page Map and Jump*. When this function
is called, a new page map is mapped into the page frame and control is

passed to the address specified by the application. Unlike the other expanded memory functions, this function does not return control to the calling application. It is up to the code that received control to return control to the caller. Details on the use of function 55H are too involved to be presented here. Interested readers should consult the references mentioned at the end of this chapter.

Function 56H is named *Alter Page Map and Call*. When the function is called, a new page map is mapped into the page frame and program execution branches to an address specified by the application program. The function terminates when the called code issues a *far return*. Execution returns to the calling application, and the old page map is mapped into the page frame. Readers interested in the details of using function 56H should consult the references mentioned at the end of this chapter.

Moving/Exchanging Blocks of Memory

EMS 4.0 function 57H allows an application program to move data between expanded memory and conventional memory. Moving may also be carried out between two locations in conventional memory or two locations in expanded memory. Up to 1 Mbyte may be moved with a single call to this function.

Support for Advanced Hardware Features

EMS 4.0 provides support for a set of advanced hardware features that are just starting to appear on a new generation of expanded memory boards. The newer boards have *multiple sets of mapping registers*, which allow context switches to be performed almost instantly. The boards also have *DMA registers*, which preserve the mapping context so that DMA can be carried out. DMA stands for Direct Memory Access and refers to the process whereby certain tasks, such as reading data from a disk, can be performed without tying up the CPU. EMS 4.0 function 5BH is implemented to support both multiple mapping registers and DMA registers.

Another new hardware feature allows expanded memory boards to preserve a mapping context when a warm boot of the machine occurs (such as when the user presses Ctrl-Alt-Break). EMS 4.0 function 5CH is provided to support such hardware. The function serves to warn the system that a warm boot is about to occur.

Conclusion

The purpose of this chapter has been to convey an understanding of what expanded memory is and how it operates. The examples provide some insight into how application programs use expanded memory. Many details concerning expanded memory have not been covered in this chapter. The interested reader is referred to *The Waite Group's MS-DOS Developer's Guide, Second Edition* for a more detailed examination of programming with expanded memory. You can obtain a free copy of LIM EMS 4.0 by contacting Intel Corporation (in the USA call 800-538-3373; elsewhere call 503-629-7354).

13

Terminate and Stay Resident Programs

TSRs—An Overview
TSRs—Guidelines for a Peaceful Coexistence
POPCLOCK—An Example of a TSR

Programs that remain loaded in memory after their execution terminates are called *terminate and stay resident* (TSRs). There are many types of TSRs, ranging from MS-DOS utilities such as PRINT.COM and APPEND.EXE to the popular "pop-up" utilities such as Sidekick. This chapter discusses the way in which TSRs are constructed. The first section describes, in a very general way, fundamental techniques for keeping a program resident after execution and subsequently accessing the program so that it can be reexecuted. The second section discusses in some detail the important issues that must be addressed when writing a well-behaved TSR. Finally, a working TSR program, "POPCLOCK" (see page 285), is presented and discussed in the third section of the chapter.

The material presented requires an understanding of interrupts and the MS-DOS function calls. Appendix A contains an introductory discussion on interrupts. The MS-DOS interrupts and function calls that are used extensively in this chapter are also discussed in appendix A.

The TSR presented at the end of this chapter is written in assembly language. Some familiarity with assembly language programming will be useful in getting the most out of the program discussion. Those readers with little or no experience with assembly language are referred to the assembly language primer in appendix E.

TSRs—An Overview

TSR programs generally consist of two components. The first component initializes the TSR and instructs MS-DOS on how to reexecute the TSR. This portion of the TSR is executed one time when the program is loaded into memory. The second component of a TSR is the part of the program that is run each time the TSR executes. It is this portion of the TSR that must remain accessible to MS-DOS. The relation between these two components is the topic of the following discussion.

Loading a TSR

When MS-DOS loads a program for execution, the operating system allocates all available memory to the program. Most programs keep all of the memory they are allocated until it is time to terminate execution. These programs then terminate by issuing a call to interrupt 20H or DOS function 4CH, either of which directs MS-DOS to deallocate all of the program's memory and make it available for use by other programs (see figure 13-1).

Just like other programs, TSRs are loaded into memory and allocated all available memory. However, TSRs terminate by issuing a call to DOS function 31H rather than interrupt 20H or DOS function 4CH. Function 31H is used because it allows the TSR to specify an amount of memory that is to remain allocated to the TSR. Prior to calling function 31H, the TSR places in the DX register the size of the memory block it wishes to retain. The size is specified in paragraphs, one paragraph being 16 bytes long. The block retained by the TSR always begins at the start of the program's psp (see figure 13-2).

As an example, let us say that a programmer has written a TSR that is 3200 bytes long. The program needs to keep 200 paragraphs of memory for

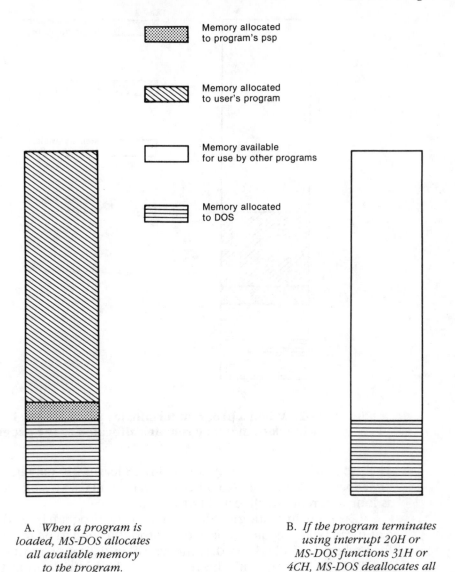

Memory allocated
to program's psp

Memory allocated
to user's program

Memory available
for use by other programs

Memory allocated
to DOS

A. *When a program is
loaded, MS-DOS allocates
all available memory
to the program.*

B. *If the program terminates
using interrupt 20H or
MS-DOS functions 31H or
4CH, MS-DOS deallocates all
memory allocated
to the program.*

**Figure 13-1. The operating system is responsible for allocating and
deallocating memory.**

itself, plus 16 paragraphs for its psp. Therefore, prior to calling function
31H, the program must store a value of 216 in DX. The following code shows
how this is carried out:

```
mov     ah,31h      ;terminate, stay resident function
mov     dx,216      ;paragraphs to remain allocated
int     21h         ;call MS-DOS
```

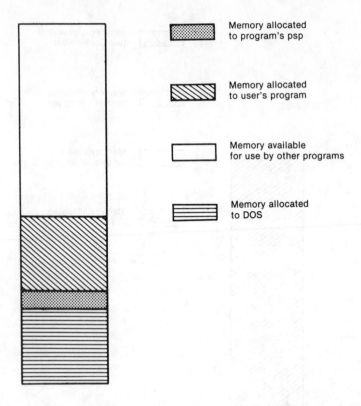

Figure 13-2. When a program terminates using MS-DOS function 31H, a block of memory remains allocated to the program.

The program terminates, but now MS-DOS leaves 216 paragraphs of memory allocated to the TSR. No other programs will use this block of memory as long as it remains allocated to the TSR.

The point in writing a TSR is that once the program is resident in memory, it can be reexecuted repeatedly without having to be reloaded. Therefore, when the TSR is loaded, some type of initialization must occur so that the TSR can subsequently be reexecuted. This initialization typically involves a modification of the interrupt vector table.

Modifying the Interrupt Vector Table

Associated with each interrupt is an *interrupt vector* and an *interrupt handler*. The interrupt handler is program code that is responsible for processing the interrupt request. The handler may be supplied by the operating system, the ROM BIOS, or (as will be described) an application program.

The interrupt vector is a pointer to the interrupt handler. Each interrupt vector is stored in the operating system's *interrupt vector table*. Each entry in the interrupt vector table consists of the segment and offset address of the corresponding interrupt handler.

MS-DOS function 35H is used to obtain an interrupt vector. For example, if a programmer wishes to determine the memory address of the handler for interrupt 9, he or she would use MS-DOS function 35H. Prior to calling the function, an interrupt number is placed in the AL register. On return, ES:BX contains the interrupt vector. The following listing uses DEBUG to demonstrate the use of DOS function 35H:

```
C>debug

-a                              ;start DEBUG assembler
1226:0100 mov ah,35             ;request function 35h
1226:0102 mov al,9             ;return vector for int 9
1226:0104 int 21               ;call MS-DOS
1226:0106      ←press Enter

-g 106                          ;execute, stop at offset 106
AX=3509 BX=E987 CX=0000 DX=0000 SP=FFEE BP=0000 SI=0000 DI=0000
DS=1226 ES=F000 SS=1226 CS=1226 IP=0106  NV UP EI PL NZ NA PO NC

1226:0106 6D        DB       6D
-q

C>
```

On return from the function call, ES:BX contains the vector for interrupt 9.

The interrupt vector table is modified by using MS-DOS function 25H. This function is used by a programmer who writes an interrupt handler to replace the one provided by the operating system or the ROM BIOS. Prior to calling the function, the segment:offset address of the new handler is placed in DS:DX and the corresponding interrupt number is placed in AL. The following code modifies the interrupt table so that the vector for interrupt 9 will point to address 1010:2234:

```
mov ah,25h       ;request function 25h
mov al,9         ;modify vector for int 9
mov ds,1010h     ;segment of new handler
mov dx,2234h     ;offset of new handler
int 21h          ;call MS-DOS
```

During initialization, a TSR uses functions 25H and 35H to establish the conditions under which the TSR is reexecuted. For example, a pop-up TSR may be designed to execute each time that a particular key combination is pressed. The programmer might decide to modify the interrupt vector table so that the entry for interrupt 9 pointed to the TSR. Then each time a key was pressed, the TSR would begin to execute. The TSR would check to see which key combination had been pressed. If the appropriate combination had been pressed, the TSR would pop up. However, if any other key combination were detected, the TSR would pass control to the old interrupt 9 handler and that handler would process the keyboard input in the standard fashion. The following pseudocode shows how this would be carried out:

Initialization:

　　　　　．
　　　　　．
　　　　　．

—get int 9 vector using function 35H

—save segment address of old handler

—save offset address of old handler

—reset int 9 vector with function 25H

　　—on call, DS has segment of new handler

　　—on call, DX has offset of new handler

—terminate and stay resident

New Handler:

　　　　　．
　　　　　．
　　　　　．

—determine key(s) pressed

—if "hotkey" pressed, pop up

—call old handler, using save addresses

　　　　　．
　　　　　．
　　　　　．

That, in a general sense, is how TSRs operate. Unfortunately, writing a working TSR is much more complicated. Several factors must be considered so that TSRs can peacefully coexist with MS-DOS, with the application program currently being run, and with any other TSRs that might be in memory at the same time. These considerations are discussed next.

TSRs—Guidelines for a Peaceful Coexistence

Writing a TSR is an exercise in circumventing DOS. There are two reasons why this is true. First, MS-DOS was designed to be a *unitasking* operating system. This means that MS-DOS is meant to run one program, throw it away, run another, throw it away, and so on. Asking MS-DOS to supervise more than one program at a time is beyond the operating system's capabilities. The programmer must circumvent this deficiency to get a working TSR.

The second reason why TSRs require a circumvention of MS-DOS is that TSR programmers must utilize features of MS-DOS that are not officially documented by Microsoft or IBM. Utilization of undocumented features is always a risky proposition, but for the time being TSR programmers have no other choice. They must rely on their own wits, as well as the wits of their fellow programmers, in unraveling the features of MS-DOS needed to write properly behaved TSRs. Recently, however, Microsoft, for the first time, published a set of guidelines for TSRs, including official documentation of many of the features presented in this chapter.

Some of the features of MS-DOS presented here remain undocumented, but all are well known and used by most programmers writing TSRs. Therefore, they can be considered reliable until proved otherwise. Unfortunately, it must be added that all undocumented features must be used cautiously and at the programmer's own risk. Since there is no official documentation of what the features do, programmers have nothing to fall back on if the features behave in an unexpected fashion. Programmers must also bear in mind that Microsoft and IBM have repeatedly stated that any or all of the undocumented features of MS-DOS may not be supported in future versions.

With that disclaimer out of the way, let us continue with the discussion of TSRs. There are three areas of consideration that must be addressed by TSR programmers. The first area relates to the manner in which the interrupt vector table is modified. Any modification of the table must utilize a technique called *chaining*. Chaining preserves the integrity of the system that existed prior to modification of the interrupt table.

The second area of consideration for the TSR programmer centers around the problem of *reentry*. Problems with reentry result from MS-DOS's deficiency in preserving its current state when an interrupt occurs. Getting around the reentry problem requires heavy reliance on undocumented MS-DOS features.

The third area of consideration for the TSR programmer involves TSRs' access to files. As will be discussed, TSRs must make special adjustments if they will be accessing files through the use of file handles.

Chaining

Whenever a TSR modifies the interrupt vector table, it is essential that the program "chains" onto the old interrupt handler. *Chaining* is the process by which the new interrupt handler always issues a call to the old interrupt handler. The new handler accomplishes this by using a pointer to the old handler. The pointer is usually saved during initialization of the TSR. Chaining is illustrated in figure 13-3.

Chaining is necessary if TSRs are to coexist with each other. To understand why, consider what would happen if two TSRs were loaded into memory. If both of the TSRs modified the same interrupt vector, then the vector would end up pointing to whichever TSR was loaded into memory last. If this TSR did not chain to the first TSR, the first TSR would never execute. Chaining must be implemented so that TSRs can execute regardless of the loading order.

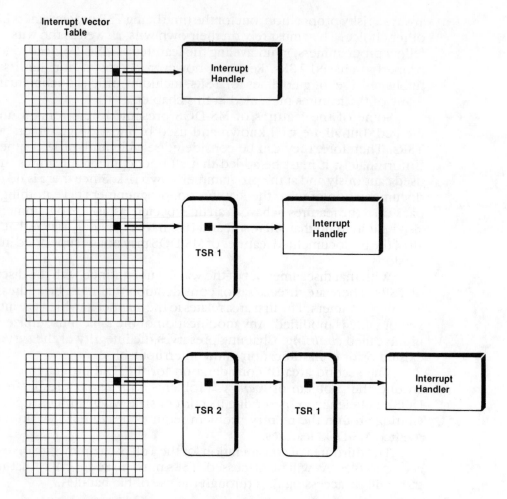

Figure 13-3. Chaining ensures that all handlers are serviced.

The Problem of Reentry

Whenever a program issues a DOS function call, the operating system is said to be *entered*. If an interrupt occurs while MS-DOS is entered, and the interrupt handler issues a function call, MS-DOS is said to be *reentered*. Reentry can cause MS-DOS to crash flat on its face. Therefore, precautions must be taken to see that reentry occurs only under certain circumstances. To understand further what reentry is and how it can be controlled, we need to discuss MS-DOS's internal stacks.

The Internal MS-DOS Stacks

MS-DOS maintains three internal stacks that it uses to process function calls. Stack number 1 is used to process requests for DOS function 00H and all DOS functions above and including function 0DH. Stack number 1 is also used to process requests for interrupt 25H (absolute disk read), interrupt 26H (absolute disk write), and interrupt 28H (discussed in the following section).

Stack number 2 is used to process requests for MS-DOS functions 01H through 0CH. In MS-DOS 2.X, stack number 2 is also used by DOS functions 50H (set process id) and 51H (get process id). As you will see later in this chapter, this causes problems for programs running under 2.X.

Stack number 3 is used by MS-DOS while it determines which of the other stacks to use in processing a function request. Stack number 3 is also used to process requests for function 59H (get extended error information). Finally, stack number 3 is used in place of stack number 2 if MS-DOS is called from a critical error handler (more on this later).

MS-DOS has no mechanism for preserving the contents of its internal stacks. Therefore, when MS-DOS is reentered, all three of the internal stacks are vulnerable. If the reentry call utilizes an internal stack that contains information MS-DOS still needs, the operating system will probably crash.

There are two undocumented features that are utilized in dealing with the reentry problem. The first involves reading a counter that is incremented when MS-DOS is entered, and decremented when it is exited. The second undocumented feature is an interrupt that is generated by MS-DOS when it is safe to use two of the internal DOS stacks.

The INDOS Flag

MS-DOS maintains an internal counter that the operating system increments each time MS-DOS is entered, and decrements each time it is exited. This counter has been given many names, but, since the counter is not documented, none of them are official. Most commonly, the counter is called the "INDOS FLAG," even though it is not really a flag (which is either set or clear) but is a counter (which can have any nonnegative value).

TSR programs locate the INDOS flag using (undocumented) DOS function 34H. On return from this call, the ES register contains the flag's segment address, and the BX register contains the flag's offset address. Function 34H should be executed when the TSR is initialized and the flag's address stored in variables local to the TSR. Then, when the TSR is reexecuted, the status of the flag can be determined directly, without using function 34H. This is important because calling function 34H can result in reentry and system failure.

There is some confusion as to the true significance of the INDOS flag. Before we get into the details of using the flag, it is important to recognize its major limitation. Whenever the MS-DOS prompt is displayed, the INDOS flag is nonzero. Therefore, if a TSR program executes only when INDOS equals zero, the program will not function when the MS-DOS prompt is displayed. Some additional way is needed to activate a TSR. The way most commonly used is interrupt 28H.

Interrupt 28H

If the INDOS flag is set, and MS-DOS is processing a call for any of functions 01H through 0CH, interrupt 28H is generated by MS-DOS at a rate of 18.2

times per second. Since functions 01H through 0CH all use DOS stack number 2, interrupt 28H is a signal that it is safe to use stacks 1 and 3.

When a TSR is accessed via interrupt 28H, MS-DOS functions 01H through 0CH cannot be called, since interrupt 28H ensures only that stacks 1 and 3 are safe. In fact, interrupt 28H ensures that stack 2 is not safe, so calling functions 01H through 0CH almost guarantees a crash if the TSR was activated by interrupt 28H.

The problem with using only interrupt 28H for access to the TSR is that many application programs do not issue calls for DOS functions 01H through 0CH. Therefore, interrupt 28H is not generated when these applications are running. Another interrupt must be used to activate the TSR from these applications. The handler for this interrupt must check INDOS before executing the TSR, since nothing is known about the status of the MS-DOS stacks when the interrupt is invoked.

The author's experience with TSRs indicates that any MS-DOS function can be called from a TSR if the INDOS flag equals zero. However, if the TSR is activated by interrupt 28H, the INDOS flag will not equal zero, and the system will probably crash if functions 01H through 0CH are used. Since functions 01H through 0CH can be replaced by ROM BIOS calls, the simplest solution is not to use functions 01H through 0CH in a TSR.

Critical Error

A *critical error* occurs when a peripheral device is needed by MS-DOS but the device is not available. Typical situations causing critical error are open drive doors or printers that are off-line.

When a critical error occurs, MS-DOS sets a *critical error flag* and invokes interrupt 24H. Interrupt 24H is a call to the critical error handler that is responsible for recovering from the critical error. Most users of MS-DOS are familiar with the **Abort, Retry, Fail?** message, which is displayed by the critical error handler when a drive door is left open.

Executing a TSR while a critical error is being processed can cause the system to crash. Therefore, prior to executing a TSR, the status of the critical error flag should be checked. If the flag is clear, then execution can proceed. The address of the critical error flag is obtained by using (undocumented) DOS function 5DH, subfunction 6. On return from the call, ES contains the flag's segment address, and BX contains its offset. This function is demonstrated as part of the program presented at the end of this chapter.

Programmers must also consider how their TSR will handle critical errors. The simplest course is to make no provisions for critical error. In that case, the TSR will rely on the critical error handler for the program that was interrupted by the TSR. Such an arrangement will suffice if a TSR does not perform disk I/O. However, if you are writing a TSR that performs disk I/O, you should consider writing a critical error handler for the TSR. Each time the TSR is activated, change the interrupt 24H vector to point to the new handler. Each time the TSR terminates, change the vector so that it points to the old handler.

File Handles and TSRs

Whenever MS-DOS loads a program into memory, it assigns the program a *process id*. In all cases, the process id is nothing more than the segment address of the program's psp. The current process id is the id of the program currently running. MS-DOS stores this id internally and uses it when a program accesses a file through the use of file handles. Recall from chapter 11 that each program stores a list of file handles in its psp. When MS-DOS receives a request to access a file, the operating system sees which process id is current and looks in the corresponding psp to locate the file handle.

Unfortunately, when a TSR executes, MS-DOS does not change the current process id. The operating system considers the application that was running to be the current one. It is the responsibility of the programmer to make the TSR current. The TSR is made current as follows:

1. MS-DOS function 51H is used to obtain the current id. This is the id of the program that was running when the TSR was invoked. The function returns the id in BX. The id is saved for later use.

   Function 51H is not documented but is implemented in MS-DOS 2.X, 3.X, and 4.X. It is identical to the documented function 62H that is implemented in MS-DOS 3.X.

2. MS-DOS function 50H is used to set the current id equal to the TSR's psp address. Function 50H is another undocumented DOS function. Prior to calling the function, BX is set to equal the psp address. This can be accomplished by pushing CS to the stack and popping BX.

   Once the TSR is made current, it can use the file handles that are stored in its psp.

3. Prior to returning to the application, the TSR uses function 50H to restore the current id to the value it had before executing the TSR.

As we mentioned earlier, functions 50H and 51H use DOS stack number 2 under MS-DOS 2.X. This causes a serious problem, as it groups these two functions with functions 01H through 0CH. If we stick by the guidelines discussed previously, functions 50H and 51H should be avoided in TSRs running under MS-DOS 2.X. Fortunately, there is a way to fool MS-DOS and get around this problem.

When the critical error flag is set, MS-DOS thinks a critical error is being processed. Under these conditions MS-DOS uses stack number 3 in place of stack number 2. Thus, a TSR running under MS-DOS 2.X can set the critical error flag, use functions 50H and 51H, and then clear the critical error flag.

POPCLOCK—An Example of a TSR

POPCLOCK.ASM (listing 13-1) is a TSR program that implements a pop-up clock. Once the program is loaded, the clock will pop up whenever the left and right shift keys are simultaneously depressed. POPCLOCK runs under MS-DOS 2.0 and later versions. POPCLOCK works with monochrome, CGA, and EGA adapters, although the clock will not pop up if the display is in graphics mode.

POPCLOCK is presented to illustrate the points about TSRs that are discussed in this chapter. As you can see from the length of listing 13-1, even simple TSRs such as POPCLOCK tend to be long programs. It is important to recognize, however, that a lot of the code in POPCLOCK is generic, in the sense that it can be used again in other programs. Therefore, once you have the code for one TSR, much of the work for subsequent TSRs is already done.

To make our discussion more manageable, we will divide POP-CLOCK.ASM into four parts and discuss each separately. The four parts are: lines 22–72, lines 73–202, lines 203–483, and lines 484–589.

Lines 22–72 of the listing declare the variables used by the program. These variables will be explained as they are used.

Lines 73–202 make up the new interrupt handlers used by POP-CLOCK. The program uses new handlers for the following interrupts:

Interrupt	Function
8H	Timer
9H	Keyboard hardware
10H	ROM BIOS video service
13H	ROM BIOS disk service
28H	MS-DOS scheduler

Lines 203–483 form the main portion of the TSR. This is the code that is executed each time the clock pops up.

Lines 484–589 make up the initialization portion of POPCLOCK. This section of code is executed once at load time and then discarded.

We will discuss the initialization portion of the program first, followed by the handlers, and then the main portion of the TSR.

Initialization

POPCLOCK is executed as a COM file; therefore, the first executable instruction in the program must be at offset 100H. The directive **org 100h** ensures that this is the case. The first instruction (line 20 of the listing) is a jump to **init**. Initialization begins (lines 495–498) by using MS-DOS function 34H to obtain the segment and offset address of the INDOS flag. The address is stored using two variables local to the program.

Next, the address of the critical error flag is obtained using DOS function 5DH, subfunction 6. The offset is saved in local variable **errflag_off**. Notice that it is necessary to restore DS on return from the call. This is because the segment address of the error flag is returned in DS. Saving the segment address is not required, since the critical error flag and the INDOS flag are always located in the same segment (in fact, the critical error flag is sometimes called INDOS2).

Lines 529–574 reset the interrupt vector table. For each of the interrupt vectors modified (8H, 9H, 10H, 13H, and 28H), function 35H is used to retrieve the original vector value, each original value is saved as two variables, and function 25H is then used to reset the vector so that it points to the new handler. Let's walk through the first one to clarify this.

In line 531, a value of 35H is placed in AH and a value of 08H is placed in AL. This indicates a request for MS-DOS function 35H (get interrupt vector) and specifies the vector for interrupt 8H. The segment address contained in the vector is returned in ES, the offset in BX. These values are saved as local variables in lines 533 and 534.

In line 536, a value of 25H is placed in AH and a value of 08H placed in AL. This indicates a request for DOS function 25H (set interrupt vector) and specifies the vector for interrupt 8H. Prior to the call, the offset value for the new vector is placed in DX and the segment value in DS. The procedure **new8_hndlr** (line 76) is the new handler for interrupt 8H. Therefore, we want DX to store the offset of **new8_hndlr** and DS to store the segment. Notice that it is not necessary to place the segment address in DS, since DS already points to the correct segment. On return from the call, **new8_hndlr** is the new handler for interrupt 8H.

The process just described is repeated for the other interrupts used by the TSR. The program then displays a message stating that POPCLOCK is installed (lines 578–580). Notice that in the initialization portion of the program there is no concern about using MS-DOS functions 01H through 0CH. This is because during initialization the TSR owns the show. MS-DOS treats it like any other program. It is only when the TSR reexecutes by way of the modified interrupt table that issues of reentry must be considered.

Once the loaded message is displayed, initialization is complete and the program is ready to terminate but remain resident (lines 582–587). As we mentioned earlier in the chapter, DOS function 31H requires that the amount of memory that is to remain allocated to the program be specified in DX. In order to determine how much memory is required, a dummy variable (line 482) is placed at the end of the portion of the program that is to remain resident. The number of bytes to save is simply the difference between the dummy variable's offset minus the offset of the start of the program. Adding 15 bytes rounds the block up to the next highest paragraph. In line 585, the block size is divided by 16 to give the number of paragraphs to keep. Finally, the AX register is set to request function 31H, and MS-DOS is called. The call now returns control back to MS-DOS, and POPCLOCK is resident in memory. Notice that the initialization portion of the code loses its memory allocation. The program is written this way because the initialization code is not needed after the program is loaded.

The Interrupt Handlers

Once initialization is completed, all of the new interrupt handlers are active. We will now discuss them one at a time, starting with the simplest and working our way up.

Interrupt 10H

The new handler for interrupt 10H is listed in lines 146–152. Recall that int 10H is the ROM BIOS video service. The purpose of the new handler is to set a flag each time int 10H is called. The flag will ensure that the clock does not pop up while a call to the video service is in progress. Such an event, if allowed to occur, could make a mess of the screen.

The new handler also chains to the old handler. This has to be done or the video service requests would not be processed. Before calling the old int 10H handler, the new handler must push the flags register to the stack (line 147). This is necessary because the original int 10H handler thinks it is being called by way of an interrupt rather than a procedure call. Therefore, the final instruction in the original handler is `iret` rather than `ret`. Recall that an `iret` instruction pops the segment address, the offset address, and the flags from the stack. If the flags were not pushed, something else would be popped, the stack would be out of sync, and some sort of system failure would no doubt ensue.

After pushing the flags, the handler increments `video_flag` and then chains to the original handler. On return, `video_flag` is decremented. The new handler then terminates with an `iret` instruction.

Interrupt 13H

The new handler (lines 157–165) for interrupt 13H (ROM BIOS disk service) is almost identical to the new handler for interrupt 10H. In this case, `disk_flag` is set each time the handler is called. This will ensure that no pop-ups occur while the disk is being accessed. Such an event could confuse the system, and data might be lost in the process.

There are some differences in `new13_hndlr` that should be explained. The original 13H handler sets the flag register according to the outcome of the service request. The new handler is written so that this information can be transmitted back to the original caller. First, notice that the flags are pushed in line 161. This is necessary because the decrement in the next line may affect the flags. After the decrement, the flags are popped and a `ret 2` is issued. This instruction tells MS-DOS to return to the caller and discard 2 bytes from the stack. But notice that `new13_hndlr` is declared as a `far` procedure. This means that when the `ret` is issued, MS-DOS pops a segment and offset address from the stack. The 2 bytes thrown away are the flags register, which was pushed when the new int 13H handler was originally called.

Interrupt 9H

Interrupt 9H is an interrupt generated by the hardware each time that a key is pressed or released. The new handler (lines 122–141) chains to the old handler, then uses function 2 of interrupt 16H to determine if the right and left shift keys are depressed. This function reads the byte at address 0000:0417H and stores the value in AL. This byte is set as follows:

If This Key Is Depressed	This Bit Is Set
Insert	7
Caps Lock	6
Num Lock	5
Scroll Lock	4
Alt	3
Ctrl	2
Left Shift	1
Right Shift	0

On return from the call to interrupt 16H, the handler executes **and al, 0fh** (line 130). This clears all the bits in AH and leaves AL unchanged. The next line compares the value in AL to 3. AL will equal 3 if the right and left shift keys are depressed. This is the signal to pop the clock. If the compare is false, the hot keys have not been pressed, so the handler jumps to the exit (line 133).

If the compare was true, the handler must continue. In line 135 the handler checks the value of **running_flag**. This flag is set by the main portion of the TSR each time that the clock is popped. The flag is cleared when the TSR exits. Therefore, if **running_flag** is set (not equal to zero), the clock is already popped and the handler exits. If **running_flag** is equal to zero, the clock is not currently popped. In this case, the handler sets **hotkey** equal to 18. The handler then exits (line 140) by an **iret**. The variable **hotkey** signals the handlers for interrupts 8H and 28H that the hot key combination has been pressed. The reasons for setting **hotkey** equal to 18 are discussed next.

Interrupt 8H

Interrupt 8H is the hardware timer interrupt. It is generated by the system's timer chip 18.2 times a second. Once POPCLOCK is loaded into memory, the new handler for interrupt 8H (lines 76–117) is called 18.2 times a second.

The first thing the new handler does is chain to the old handler (lines 77–78). The new handler then checks to see if **hotkey** equals zero. If it does, the handler exits.

If **hotkey** is nonzero, the new handler checks to see if **video_flag** or **disk_flag** are nonzero. Recall that these flags are set and cleared in the new handlers for interrupts 10H and 13H. If either of these flags is nonzero, we do not want to pop the clock. Accordingly, the program will jump to **dec_hkey** (line 114), and **hotkey** is decremented. Therefore, since the handler is called approximately 18 times a second, **hotkey** will remain nonzero for approximately a second if either **video_flag** or **disk_flag** is nonzero.

If both **video_flag** and **disk_flag** equal zero, the handler proceeds to the next step (line 88). The DI and ES register contents are saved, and ES:DI is set to point to the INDOS flag. If `indos` is nonzero, DI and ES are popped, `hotkey` is decremented, and the handler exited.

If `indos` equals zero, the handler proceeds. The next step is to check the critical error flag (lines 100–101). If the flag is nonzero, we do not want to pop the clock. ES and DI are popped, `hotkey` is decremented, and the handler exited.

If the critical error flag equals zero, all is clear to pop the clock. First, ES and DI are popped from the stack (lines 104–105), `hotkey` is set to zero, and `do_it` (the main portion of the TSR) is called.

Interrupt 28H

Interrupt 28H provides the other "hook" into POPCLOCK. The new handler (lines 170–201) is very similar to the new handler for interrupt 8H. The only difference is that this handler does not need to check the INDOS flag. Recall that int 28H is called only when `indos` is set. However, int 28H also indicates that it is safe to use MS-DOS as long as certain precautions are followed (i.e., stay away from DOS functions 01H–0CH).

As should ALWAYS be done, the new int 28 handler chains to the old handler. The flags `hotkey`, `video_flag`, and `disk_flag` are checked as in the int 8H handler. If these flags check out correctly, the critical error flag is checked. If the flag equals zero, all is clear to pop the clock. The `hotkey` flag is set to zero, and `do_it` is called (line 197).

Popping the Clock

The portion of the program that actually displays the clock is the procedure `do_it` (lines 206–480). It is important to bear in mind that when `do_it` gets control, the only registers whose status is known are CS and IP. The other registers, particularly the other segment registers, have the values that were being used when the hot keys were pressed. Before `do_it` can use DS, SS, or ES, the registers must be set appropriately.

The first thing `do_it` does is set `running_flag`. This prevents the int 9H handler from setting `hotkey` while the clock is popped (refer back to lines 135–136).

Next, `do_it` sets up a local stack (lines 211–217). This is necessary to avoid disturbing the MS-DOS stack. The first step in setting up a local stack is disabling the interrupts (line 211). This is important because if an interrupt occurs before both SS and SP have been reset, the system could crash. Once the interrupts are disabled, the values in SS and SP are saved in local variables, SS is set to equal CS (the local segment), and SP is set to point at the top of the local stack. Once the local stack is established, interrupts are enabled (line 217).

The contents of the MS-DOS registers are saved on the local stack (lines 219–227). Next, the ROM BIOS service is used to see if the display is in graphics mode (lines 231–236). If graphics are enabled, the program jumps to line 240, the stack is popped, the MS-DOS stack is reactivated, and the program issues a ret which sends control back to either the new int 8H handler or the new int 28H handler. The handlers then issue an iret (line 110 or 200), and POPCLOCK is exited.

If the display is not in graphics mode, it is time to display the clock. Lines 259 through 263 save the cursor's position and size so that they can be restored when POPCLOCK exits.

The ROM BIOS Video Services

Since TSRs should avoid DOS functions 01H–0CH, they must rely on the ROM BIOS video services for output to the screen. The ROM BIOS video services are accessed via interrupt 10H. Prior to the call, a function number is placed in AH. This determines which service is provided. The ROM BIOS video services used by POPCLOCK are described here. Appendix A contains additional information on the use of the ROM BIOS interrupts.

Int 10H

AH Value on Call	Function
01H	**Set cursor type**. On the call, the first 4 bits in CH store the cursor's starting line and the first 4 bits in CL store the cursor's ending line.
02H	**Set cursor position**. On the call, BH contains the page number, DH contains the *y* coordinate of the cursor, and DL contains the *x* coordinate of the cursor.
03H	**Get cursor position**. On the call, BH contains the page number. On return, CH contains the starting line of the cursor, CL contains the ending line of the cursor, DH contains the cursor's *y* coordinate, and DL contains the cursor's *x* coordinate. Note that the starting and ending line determine the cursor's size, not its position.
07H	**Scroll window down**. On the call, AL contains the number of lines to scroll, BH contains the attribute used for the blanked area, CH contains the upper left *y* coordinate of the window, CL contains the upper left *x* coordinate of the window, DH contains the lower right *y* coordinate of the window, and DL contains the lower right *x* coordinate of the window. If AL equals zero on the call, the entire window is blanked.

Int 10H (cont'd)

AH Value on Call	Function
08H	***Read attribute and character at cursor***. On the call, BH contains the page number. On return, AH contains the attribute byte and AL contains the ASCII character byte.
09H	***Write character and attribute***. On the call, AL contains the ASCII character byte, BH contains the page number, BL contains the attribute byte, and CX contains the number of times the character is to be written. The character is written at the current position of the cursor. This function does not advance the cursor.
0AH	***Write character only***. On the call, AL contains the ASCII character byte, BH the page number, BL the color byte (if in graphics mode), and CX the number of times the character is to be written.
0FH	***Get display mode***. On return, AH contains the number of character columns on the screen, AL contains the display (0–3 and 7 are text), and BH contains the active page number.

Lines 276–295 use a nested loop to save the contents of the screen that will be covered by the clock. The inner loop is traversed once for each character saved. The outer loop is traversed once for each line saved.

Lines 299–316 create the window. Interrupt 10H, function 07H is called twice to create a window with a border around it. Lines 320–366 display the text contained in lines 62–63 of the listing.

Line 371 calls the procedure `gettime` (lines 449–480), which uses DOS function 2CH to get the current time. DOS function 2CH can be used safely, since it is not in the forbidden range of 01H–0CH.

Lines 368–396 display the time (finally!!), which is stored in the variables listed in lines 64–71.

Lines 394–395 call the keyboard BIOS service to check on the keyboard's status. If no key is pressed, the service returns with the zero flag set. If this is the case, the test at line 396 is true and the time display loop is traversed again. If a key is pressed, the BIOS function returns with the zero flag clear, the test at line 396 is false, and the loop is exited. On exiting from the loop, the character input by the user is discarded so that it will not interfere with whatever program is continued when POPCLOCK terminates.

Lines 401–433 restore the screen in a manner similar to that used in saving the screen's contents. Lines 435–443 restore the cursor to the position and size it had when the clock was popped.

Finally, the jump at line 445 sends execution back to line 240. The MS-DOS registers are restored, and the MS-DOS stack is reestablished. The ret at line 255 sends things back to either the int 8H handler or the int 28H. In either case, the handler issues an iret and the program continues where it left off when the hot keys were pressed.

Listing 13-1. Pop-up Clock TSR Program

```
1    ;*************************************************************
2    ;                    POPCLOCK.ASM
3    ;
4    ; A memory-resident program that provides a pop-up clock.
5    ; DOS 2.0 or later version required.
6    ; To create an executable version of this program, enter
7    ; the following commands:
8    ;        C>masm popclock ;;;
9    ;        C>link popclock ;;;;
10   ;        C>exe2bin popclock popclock.com
11   ;        C>popclock
12   ;*************************************************************
13
14   cseg     segment          para public 'code'
15
16   assume   cs:cseg
17       org  100h ;required for COM programs
18
19   begin:
20       jmp  init
21
22   ;*************************************************************
23   ;Declare program variables
24   ;*************************************************************
25   old8_hndlr     label dword      ;old int 8h handler
26   old8_off       dw       ?
27   old8_seg       dw       ?
28   old9_hndlr     label dword      ;old int 9h handler
29   old9_off       dw       ?
30   old9_seg       dw       ?
31   old10_hndlr    label dword      ;old int 10h handler
32   old10_off      dw       ?
33   old10_seg      dw       ?
34   old13_hndlr    label dword      ;old int 13h handler
35   old13_off      dw       ?
36   old13_seg      dw       ?
37   old28_hndlr    label dword      ;old int 28h handler
38   old28_off      dw       ?
39   old28_seg      dw       ?
40
41   hotkey         db       0       ;greater than 0 if hotkey pressed
42   video_flag     db       0       ;int 10h flag
43   disk_flag      db       0       ;int 13h flag
```

```
44  running_flag   db         0       ;equals 1 if program running
45
46
47  indos_off      dw         ?       ;offset of indos flag
48  indos_seg      dw         ?       ;segment of indos flag
49  errflag_off    dw         ?       ;offset of critical error flag
50
51  cur_pos        dw         ?       ;saves cursor's position
52  cur_size       dw         ?       ;saves cursor's size
53  sp_save        dw         ?       ;stores MS-DOS stack pointer
54  ss_save        dw         ?       ;stores MS-DOS SS register
55  screen_buf     dw 174 dup(?)      ;buffer to save screen contents
56
57                 db 255 dup ("#") ;local stack
58  stk_top        db         ("#") ;top of local stack
59
60  load_msg       db "POPCLOCK Installed",0dh,0ah
61                 db "Right & left shift to activate",0dh,0ah,"$"
62  brk_msg        db "Any key to continue"
63  time_msg       db "Current time is "
64  hour10         db         ?       ;store time of day
65  hour           db         ?
66                 db         ":"
67  min10          db         ?
68  min            db         ?
69                 db         ":"
70  sec10          db         ?
71  sec            db         ?
72  dos1_msg       db         "DOS 2.X or later required",0dh,0ah,"$"
73  ;****************************************************************
74  ;New handler for int 8h (timer)
75  ;****************************************************************
76  new8_hndlr     proc       near
77     pushf                           ;simulate INT
78     call old8_hndlr                 ;chain to old handler
79
80     cmp  hotkey,0                   ;hotkey pressed?
81     je   hkey0                      ;if no, exit
82
83     cmp  video_flag,0               ;int 10h busy?
84     jne  dec_hkey                   ;if yes, dec. hotkey flag
85     cmp  disk_flag,0                ;int 13h busy?
86     jne  dec_hkey                   ;if yes, dec. hotkey flag
87
88     push di                         ;save registers
89     push es
90
91     ;check value of indos flag
92     ;
93     mov  di,indos_off               ;offset of flag
94     mov  es,indos_seg               ;segment of flag
```

```
95          cmp  byte ptr es:[di],0
96          jne  pop_stk                  ;exit if DOS busy
97
98          ;check critical error flag
99          ;
100         mov  di,errflag_off           ;offset of flag
101         cmp  byte ptr es:[di],0
102         jne  pop_stk                  ;exit if flag set
103
104         pop  es                       ;restore registers
105         pop  di
106         mov  hotkey,0                 ;clear hotkey flag
107         call do_it                    ;run program
108
109    hkey0:
110         iret
111    pop_stk:
112         pop  es
113         pop  di
114    dec_hkey:
115         dec  hotkey
116         iret                          ;return to MS-DOS
117    new8_hndlr     endp
118
119    ;****************************************************************
120    ;New handler for int 9h (keyboard hardware interrupt)
121    ;****************************************************************
122    new9_hndlr     proc      near
123         sti                           ;enable interrupts
124         pushf                         ;simulate INT
125         call old9_hndlr
126
127         push ax                       ;save ax
128         mov  ah,2                     ;get shift key status
129         int  16h                      ;call BIOS keyboard routine
130         and  al,0Fh
131         cmp  al,3                     ;right and left shift pressed?
132         pop  ax
133         jne  exit_9                   ;if no, exit
134
135         cmp  running_flag,0           ;program already running?
136         jne  exit_9                   ;if yes, exit
137
138         mov  hotkey,18                ;hotkey active
139    exit_9:
140         iret                          ;return to MS-DOS
141    new9_hndlr     endp
142
143    ;****************************************************************
144    ;New handler for int 10h (ROM BIOS video service)
145    ;****************************************************************
```

```
146   new10_hndlr    proc     near
147      pushf                      ;simulate INT
148      inc  video_flag
149      call old10_hndlr
150      dec  video_flag
151      iret
152   new10_hndlr    endp
153
154   ;****************************************************************
155   ;New handler for int 13h (ROM BIOS disk service)
156   ;****************************************************************
157   new13_hndlr    proc     far
158      pushf                      ;simulate INT
159      inc  disk_flag
160      call old13_hndlr
161      pushf                      ;protect flags
162      dec  disk_flag
163      popf                       ;restore flags
164      ret  2                     ;return to MS-DOS; discard 2 bytes
165   new13_hndlr    endp
166
167   ;****************************************************************
168   ;New handler for int 28h (DOS scheduler)
169   ;****************************************************************
170   new28_hndlr    proc     near
171      pushf                      ;simulate INT
172      call old28_hndlr           ;chain to old handler
173
174
175      cmp  hotkey,0              ;hotkey pressed?
176      je   exit28                ;if no, exit
177
178      cmp  video_flag,0          ;int 10h busy?
179      jne  exit28                ;if yes, exit
180      cmp  disk_flag,0           ;int 13h busy?
181      jne  exit28                ;if yes, exit
182
183      push di                    ;save registers
184      push es
185
186
187      ;check critical error flag
188      ;
189      mov  es,indos_seg
190      mov  di,errflag_off        ;offset of flag
191      cmp  byte ptr es:[di],0
192      pop  es                    ;restore registers
193      pop  di
194      jne  exit28
195
196      mov  hotkey,0              ;clear hotkey flag
```

```
197         call do_it                      ;run program
198
199     exit28:
200         iret                            ;return to MS-DOS
201     new28_hndlr     endp
202
203     ;****************************************************************
204     ;DO_IT -- Main portion of POPCLOCK
205     ;****************************************************************
206     do_it   proc  near
207         mov  running_flag,1             ;set running flag
208
209        ;Set up local stack and save DOS registers
210            ;
211            cli                          ;disable interrupts
212            mov  sp_save,sp              ;save MS-DOS stack pointer
213            mov  ss_save,ss              ;save MS-DOS SS register
214            push cs
215            pop  ss                      ;local stack segment
216            mov  sp,offset stk_top       ;top of local stack
217            sti                          ;enable interrupts
218
219            push ax                      ;save MS-DOS registers
220            push bx                      ;on local stack
221            push cx
222            push dx
223            push si
224            push di
225            push ds
226            push es
227            push bp
228
229        ;Check display mode, exit if in graphics mode
230            ;
231            mov  ah,0Fh                   ;get display mode function
232            int  10h                      ;call BIOS video service
233            cmp  al,3
234            jbe  get_cursor
235            cmp  al,7
236            je   get_cursor
237
238        ;Restore DOS stack and return to caller
239            ;
240     exit: pop  bp
241            pop  es
242            pop  ds
243            pop  di
244            pop  si
245            pop  dx
246            pop  cx
247            pop  bx
```

```
248        pop    ax
249
250        cli
251        mov    ss,ss_save
252        mov    sp,sp_save
253        sti
254        mov    running_flag,0      ;clear flag
255        ret                        ;return to caller
256
257    ;In text mode so continue
258        ;
259    get_cursor:
260        mov    ah,03               ;get cursor position, BH has page
261        int    10h                 ;call BIOS
262        mov    cur_pos,dx          ;save cursor's position
263        mov    cur_size,cx         ;save cursor's size
264
265    ;Save contents of window
266        ;
267        mov    ah,02               ;set cursor position
268        mov    dl,17               ;upper left of window
269        mov    dh,6
270        int    10h
271
272        push   cs
273        pop    es                  ;make es local
274        mov    di,offset screen_buf
275        mov    cx,6                ;save 6 rows
276    loop1:
277        push   cx
278        mov    cx,29               ;save 29 columns
279    loop2:
280        cld                        ;clear direction flag
281        mov    ah,8                ;read attribute and character
282        int    10h
283        stosw                      ;store in buffer
284
285        inc    dl                  ;move cursor to next column
286        mov    ah,02
287        int    10h
288        loop loop2                 ;save next character
289
290        mov    dl,17               ;move cursor to start
291        inc    dh                  ;of next row
292        mov    ah,02
293        int    10h
294        pop    cx
295        loop loop1                 ;save next row
296
297    ;make window border
298        ;
```

```
299          push  bx                   ;save page number
300          mov   ax,0700h             ;blank a window
301          mov   bh,70h               ;reverse attribute
302          mov   ch,6                 ;upper left y coordinate
303          mov   cl,17                ;upper left x coordinate
304          mov   dh,10                ;lower right y coordinate
305          mov   dl,45                ;lower right x coordinate
306          int   10h                  ;call ROM video service
307
308    ;clear window interior
309          ;
310          mov   ax,0700h             ;blank a window
311          mov   bh,07h               ;normal attribute
312          mov   ch,7                 ;upper left y coordinate
313          mov   cl,18                ;upper left x coordinate
314          mov   dh,9                 ;lower right y coordinate
315          mov   dl,44                ;lower right x coordinate
316          int   10h                  ;call ROM video service
317
318
319    ;display window contents
320          ;
321          pop   bx                   ;restore page number
322          mov   ah,02                ;position cursor
323          mov   dh,10
324          mov   dl,21
325          int   10h
326
327          mov   ah,01h               ;turn cursor off
328          mov   cx,1000h
329          int   10h
330
331          push  cs
332          pop   ds                   ;make ds local
333          mov   si,offset brk_msg    ;quit prompt
334          mov   cx,19                ;display 19 characters
335          cld                        ;forward direction
336    winloop1:
337          lodsb                      ;byte to AL
338          mov   ah,0ah               ;write character only
339          push  cx                   ;save loop counter
340          mov   cx,1                 ;output 1 time
341          int   10h
342
343          pop   cx                   ;restore loop counter
344          inc   dl
345          mov   ah,02                ;advance cursor
346          int   10h
347          loop  winloop1             ;display another character
348
349          mov   ah,02                ;position cursor
```

```
350          mov   dh,8
351          mov   dl,19
352          int   10h
353
354          mov   cx,16                ;display 16 characters
355      winloop2:
356          lodsb                      ;byte to AL
357          mov   ah,0ah               ;write character only
358          push  cx                   ;save loop counter
359          mov   cx,1                 ;output 1 time
360          int   10h
361
362          pop   cx                   ;restore loop counter
363          inc   dl
364          mov   ah,02                ;advance cursor
365          int   10h
366          loop  winloop2             ;display another character
367
368      ;display time until key pressed
369      ;
370      timeloop1:
371          call  gettime              ;get current time
372
373          mov   ah,02                ;position cursor
374          mov   dh,8
375          mov   dl,35
376          int   10h
377
378          mov   si,offset hour10
379          mov   cx,8                 ;8 characters to display
380
381      timeloop2:
382          lodsb                      ;byte to AL
383          mov   ah,0ah               ;write character only
384          push  cx                   ;save loop counter
385          mov   cx,1                 ;output 1 time
386          int   10h
387
388          pop   cx                   ;restore loop counter
389          inc   dl
390          mov   ah,02                ;advance cursor
391          int   10h
392          loop  timeloop2
393
394          mov   ah,01                ;check input status
395          int   16h
396          jz    timeloop1            ;loop if no key pressed
397
398          mov   ah,00
399          int   16h                  ;throw away input
400
```

```
401     ;restore screen and exit
402         ;
403         mov   ah,02              ;set cursor position
404         mov   dl,17              ;upper left of window
405         mov   dh,6
406         int   10h
407
408         mov   si,offset screen_buf ;start of stored display
409         mov   cx,6               ;restore 6 rows
410     loop11:
411         push  cx                 ;save outer loop counter
412         mov   cx,29              ;restore 29 columns
413     loop12:
414         cld                      ;clear direction flag
415         lodsw                    ;get character/attribute
416         mov   bl,ah              ;attribute byte
417         mov   ah,9               ;write character and attribute
418         push  cx                 ;save inner loop counter
419         mov   cx,1               ;write one time
420         int   10h                ;call BIOS
421         pop   cx                 ;restore inner loop counter
422
423         inc   dl                 ;move cursor to next column
424         mov   ah,02
425         int   10h
426         loop  loop12             ;save next character
427
428         mov   dl,17              ;move cursor to start
429         inc   dh                 ;of next row
430         mov   ah,02
431         int   10h
432         pop   cx                 ;restore outer loop counter
433         loop  loop11             ;save next row
434
435     ;restore cursor to its size and position prior to call
436         ;
437         mov   ah,1               ;restore size
438         mov   cx,cur_size
439         int   10h
440
441         mov   ah,2               ;restore position
442         mov   dx,cur_pos
443         int   10h
444
445         jmp   exit
446
447     do_it     endp               ;end of main procedure
448
449     gettime   proc  near
450
451         mov   ah,2ch             ;get time function
```

```
452        int  21h                  ;call MS-DOS
453
454    ;hours returned in ch, minutes in cl, and seconds in dh
455    ;convert these to ascii values and store
456        ;
457        mov  bl,10
458
459        xor  ah,ah
460        mov  al,ch                 ;hours
461        div  bl
462        or   ax,3030h
463        mov  hour10,al
464        mov  hour,ah
465
466        xor  ah,ah                 ;minutes
467        mov  al,cl
468        div  bl
469        or   ax,3030h
470        mov  min10,al
471        mov  min,ah
472
473        xor  ah,ah                 ;seconds
474        mov  al,dh
475        div  bl
476        or   ax,3030h
477        mov  sec10,al
478        mov  sec,ah
479        ret
480    gettime  endp
481
482    last_byte      db      "$"
483
484    ;****************************************************************
485    ;INITIALIZE -- Initializes POPCLOCK
486    ;****************************************************************
487    initialize     proc      near
488    assume  ds:cseg              ;variables in this segment
489
490
491
492
493    ;locate indos flag
494        ;
495    init:  mov   ah,34h
496        int  21h
497        mov  indos_off,bx         ;offset address of flag
498        mov  indos_seg,es         ;segment address of flag
499
500
501    ;locate critical error flag
502        ;
```

```
503          mov   ah,30h                    ;get MS-DOS version
504          int   21h
505          cmp   al,2
506          jg    call5d                    ;function 5dh implemented
507          je    calc                      ;MS-DOS 2.X, so calculate address
508   ;exit if DOS 1.X running
509          ;
510          mov   dx,offset dos1_msg
511          mov   ah,9
512          int   21h
513          int   20h                       ;return to MS-DOS
514   ;must be running 2.X so compute error flag's address
515          ;
516   calc:   mov   si,bx                    ;bx has indos flag
517          inc   si
518          jmp   save_it
519   ;locate error flag using 3.X function 5dh
520          ;
521   call5d: mov   ah,5dh                   ;MS-DOS error function
522          mov   al,6                      ;return flag address
523          int   21h                       ;call MS-DOS
524   save_it: push  cs
525          pop   ds                        ;reset ds
526          mov   errflag_off,si
527
528
529   ;Insert new handlers into interrupt chains
530          ;
531          mov   ax,3508h                  ;get int 8h vector
532          int   21h
533          mov   old8_off,bx               ;save it
534          mov   old8_seg,es
535
536          mov   ax,2508h                  ;set vector function
537          mov   dx,offset new8_hndlr
538          int   21h
539
540          mov   ax,3509h                  ;get int 09h vector
541          int   21h
542          mov   old9_off,bx               ;save it
543          mov   old9_seg,es
544
545          mov   ax,2509h                  ;set vector function
546          mov   dx,offset new9_hndlr
547          int   21h
548
549          mov   ax,3510h                  ;get int 10h vector
550          int   21h
551          mov   old10_off,bx              ;save it
552          mov   old10_seg,es
553
```

```
554          mov   ax,2510h              ;set vector function
555          mov   dx,offset new10_hndlr
556          int   21h
557
558          mov   ax,3513h              ;get int 13h vector
559          int   21h
560          mov   old13_off,bx          ;save it
561          mov   old13_seg,es
562
563          mov   ax,2513h              ;set vector function
564          mov   dx,offset new13_hndlr
565          int   21h
566
567          mov   ax,3528h              ;get int 28h vector
568          int   21h
569          mov   old28_off,bx          ;save it
570          mov   old28_seg,es
571
572          mov   ax,2528h              ;set vector function
573          mov   dx,offset new28_hndlr
574          int   21h
575
576     ;Display message then terminate but stay resident
577          ;
578          mov   dx,offset load_msg
579          mov   ah,09h
580          int   21h
581
582          ;amount of memory to retain in dx
583          mov   dx,(offset last_byte - offset cseg + 15)
584          mov   cl,4
585          shr   dx,cl                 ;convert to paragraphs
586          mov   ax,3100h              ;TSR function
587          int   21h                   ;call MS-DOS
588
589     initialize     endp
590          ;
591     cseg      ends
592        end   begin                  ;end of program
```

14

MS-DOS Device Drivers

Using Device Drivers   **Function of Device Drivers**
Structure of Device Drivers   **Device Commands**

The two essential hardware elements of a computer are the central processing unit (CPU) and computer memory. All the other hardware components (disk drives, keyboards, video displays, printers, modems, etc.) are considered external to the computer. These external components are called *peripheral devices,* or simply *devices*.

Communication between a peripheral device and the computer must be carried out according to strict guidelines determined by the computer and the particular peripheral device. For each peripheral device in a system, there is a computer program responsible for regulating the communication between that device and the computer. These computer programs are called *device drivers* (figure 14-1). This chapter will discuss MS-DOS device drivers. The major portion of the discussion will center around *installable device drivers*.

Figure 14-1. The device driver controls communication between the peripheral device and the computer.

Using Device Drivers

One of the primary roles of an operating system is to provide a set of device drivers that can be utilized by computer programs. MS-DOS provides device drivers that can be used by any program written to execute under MS-DOS. When a program running under MS-DOS needs to communicate with a peripheral device, the program tells MS-DOS which device it wants to communicate with and MS-DOS locates the proper device driver. Table 14-1 lists the standard device drivers provided with MS-DOS.

Table 14-1. Standard Peripheral Devices Supported by MS-DOS Device Drivers

Peripheral Device	Device Type*	Device Name
Console (keyboard/screen)	C	CON:
First asynchronous communications port	C	AUX: or COM1:
Second asynchronous communications port	C	COM2:
First parallel printer	C	PRN: or LPT1:
Second parallel printer	C	LPT2:
Dummy device	C	NUL:
Floppy diskette drive	B	—
Fixed disk drive	B	—

*C = character device   B = block device

Character and Block Devices

Character devices send and receive data in a serial fashion, one character at a time. Character devices include the serial and parallel ports, the keyboard, and the display screen. Every character device is assigned a *device name*. MS-DOS reserves particular names for certain character devices. These reserved names are listed in the right-hand column of table 14-1. Each character device driver controls one peripheral device.

    Block devices send and receive data in blocks. Generally each block consists of 512 bytes. Block devices include floppy diskette drives, fixed disk drives, and other mass storage devices. Block devices do not have specific names, rather they are referenced by drive designator letters (A, B, C, etc.). A single block device driver may control more than one peripheral device.

Adding a New Device

Prior to MS-DOS 2.0, there was no standardized way of adding a new device driver to the operating system. Manufacturers of peripheral devices were forced to modify the PC's BIOS (basic input output system) in order to incorporate their drivers. The problem with this approach was that modifications were often not compatible with each other. MS-DOS 2.0 changed all that with the introduction of installable device drivers.

    Installable device drivers are stored as files. The drivers are installed in memory through the use of a text file named CONFIG.SYS. CONFIG.SYS is created by the user and stored in the root directory of the disk used to boot the system. Device drivers are installed by placing the following type of statement in CONFIG.SYS:

    device=[*d:*][*path*]*filename*

During booting, MS-DOS checks to see if there is a CONFIG.SYS file. If there is, MS-DOS installs the specified device driver(s).

    Chapter 9 discusses the installation and use of ANSI.SYS, an installable console device driver that provides enhanced capabilities for the keyboard and display screen. In the remainder of this chapter, we will take a detailed look at the structure and function of device drivers. The material presented is not required for users of MS-DOS. Some familiarity with assembly language programming will be useful in following the text.

Structure of Device Drivers

MS-DOS *device drivers* are computer programs that are generally written in assembly language. Device drivers consist of three parts: a *device header*, a *strategy routine*, and an *interrupt routine*.

Device Header

The device header (figure 14-2) is an 18-byte-long data structure located at the beginning of each device driver. The device header is made up of five fields: the next header pointer, the device attribute field, the strategy routine, the interrupt routine, and the device name.

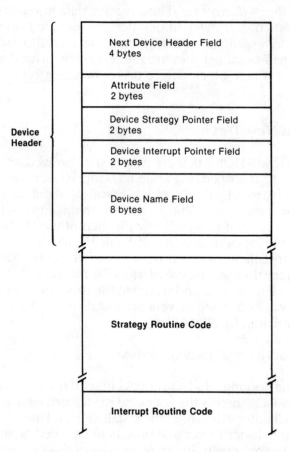

Device Header

- Next Device Header Field 4 bytes
- Attribute Field 2 bytes
- Device Strategy Pointer Field 2 bytes
- Device Interrupt Pointer Field 2 bytes
- Device Name Field 8 bytes

Strategy Routine Code

Interrupt Routine Code

Figure 14-2. Structure of MS-DOS device driver.

Next Header Pointer

The first field of the device header consists of 4 bytes that store the segment and offset addresses of the *next device header*. As we will describe, MS-DOS creates a linked list of the drivers configured into the system. This first field serves as a pointer to the device header of the next driver in the linked list (figure 14-3). The programmer sets the value of this field to −1 (4 bytes of FFH), and MS-DOS inserts the appropriate pointer values as it constructs the

Next Device Header Field		FF FF FF FF
Device Strategy Pointer Field		
Device Interrupt Pointer Field		
Device Name Field		
Strategy Routine Code		
Interrupt Routine Code		

Figure 14-3. MS-DOS sets the next device header field to contain the segment and offset addresses of the next device header.

linked list. The field retains a value of −1 in the header of the last driver in the linked list.

Device Attribute Field

The second field in the device header consists of 2 bytes that store the *device attribute* field. The bit pattern of this field is set by the programmer to contain descriptive information about the device controlled by the driver (table 14-2). The commands mentioned in table 14-2 are discussed later in this chapter.

Strategy Routine

The third field in the device header stores a 2-byte pointer to the driver's *strategy routine*. The value in this field is set by the programmer according to the strategy routine's location within the driver. The strategy routine is discussed later in this chapter.

Table 14-2. Interpretation of Bit Patterns of Device Header Attribute Field

Bit Number	Meaning
bit 15	= 1 if character device = 0 if block device
bit 14	= 1 if IOCTL is supported = 0 if IOCTL not supported
bit 13	= 1 if non-IBM format disk = 0 if IBM format disk (block devices)
bit 12	= 1 if device can handle Output Til Busy command = 0 if device cannot handle Output Til Busy command (character devices)
bit 11	= 1 if device supports Device Open, Device Close, and Removable Media commands = 0 if device does not support Device Open, Device Close, and Removable Media commands
bit 6	= 1 if device supports Get Logical Device and Set Logical Device commands = 0 if device does not support Get Logical Device and Set Logical Device commands
bit 4	= 1 if the device implements int 29H for fast console I/O = 0 if device does not implement int 29H
bit 3	= 1 if current clock device = 0 if not current clock device
bit 2	= 1 if current NUL device = 0 if not current NUL device
bit 1	= 1 if current standard output device = 0 if not current standard output device
bit 0	= 1 if current standard input device = 0 if not current standard input device

Interrupt Routine

The fourth field in the device header stores a 2-byte pointer to the driver's *interrupt routine*. The value in this field is set by the programmer according to the interrupt routine's location within the driver. The interrupt routine is discussed later in this chapter.

Device Name

The fifth field in the device header is the *device name* field. In character device drivers, this field stores the name assigned by the programmer to the device. The field is padded with blanks if the name is less than 8 characters long. A name cannot be used as both a device name and a filename. In block device drivers (which do not have device names), this field is set by the programmer to specify the number of units controlled by the driver.

Function of Device Drivers

The following paragraphs cover the installation, location, and calling of device drivers. The fields of the *request header*—a data structure serving MS-DOS and the device driver—are explained. The section ends with an assembly language program that can be expanded to form a functional device driver.

Installation

As part of the booting process, MS-DOS installs the standard (resident) device drivers, which are stored in the IO.SYS system file. Recall that MS-DOS connects the drivers via a linked list. The driver for the NUL device (the "bit-bucket") is always the first driver on the list (figure 14-4). After the resident drivers are installed, MS-DOS places in memory any installable device drivers. The installable drivers are inserted into the linked list immediately after the NUL driver (figure 14-5). All of the resident drivers remain in the linked list, downstream from the installable drivers.

Figure 14-4. Driver chain with resident drivers only.

Locating a Driver

When a computer program requests the use of a peripheral device, the program issues a call to the appropriate MS-DOS function. MS-DOS searches the linked list of drivers, starting with the NUL driver, until it locates a driver with a name field corresponding to the one supplied by the program. MS-DOS always stops at the first match. Therefore, if the linked list contains more than one driver for a particular device, MS-DOS uses the one located closest to the front of the linked list.

Once MS-DOS locates the appropriate driver, the driver must be informed of the type of service required (read, write, status check, etc.). This information is sent to the driver in the form of a *driver command*.

Figure 14-5. Driver chain with one installed driver.

There are 20 valid driver commands, each of which is assigned a unique 1-byte command code. The driver commands are discussed at the end of this chapter.

Request Header

In response to the request issued by the program, MS-DOS places a command code in a data structure called the *request header*. The request header (figure 14-6) serves as the communication area between MS-DOS and the device driver.

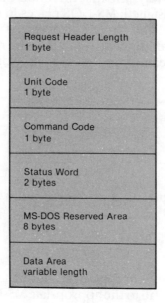

Figure 14-6. Structure of MS-DOS request header.

The first field in the request header is a single byte that stores the length of the request header. As we will discuss, the length of the request header is determined by the command code issued by MS-DOS.

The second field of the request header is a single byte that stores the *unit code*. The unit code is valid for block devices only and identifies the particular device requested. For example, if the system has two disk drives controlled by the same driver, the unit code is used to determine which drive is accessed.

The third field of the request header stores the 1-byte command code.

The fourth field of the request header stores a 2-byte *status word*. The bit pattern of this field is set by the driver to communicate information back to MS-DOS. Bit 15 of the status word is set if the driver encounters an error. Bit 9 is set to indicate a response of "busy" to a status request (command code 6). Bit 8 is set by the driver if processing required for the command code has been completed. The low-order byte (bits 0 through 7) is set to indicate the nature of any error (table 14-3).

Table 14-3. Error Codes Returned in the Low-Order Byte of Status Word

Error Code	Meaning
00	Write-protect violation
01	Unknown unit
02	Device not ready
03	Unknown command
04	CRC error
05	Bad drive request structure length
06	Seek error
07	Unknown media
08	Sector not found
09	Printer out of paper
0A	Write fault
0B	Read fault
0C	General fault
0F	Invalid disk change (MS-DOS 3.X, 4.X)

The fifth field in the request header is an 8-byte block that is reserved by MS-DOS and not available for use.

The sixth field of the request header is called the *data area*. The format and the length of the data area are dependent on the command code. As we will see, each command code has a specific set of parameters that must be set by the driver. When control passes from the driver back to MS-DOS, MS-DOS expects to find these parameters at specific locations within the request header's data area

It is important to understand that identification of the appropriate device, selection of the command code, and initialization of the request header is performed by MS-DOS in response to a function request. The programmer of the device driver need not be concerned with how MS-DOS performs these tasks. Once MS-DOS actually calls the driver, the driver is in control, and the programmer's code goes into action.

Calling the Driver

Once a request header has been properly initialized by MS-DOS, the operating system sets the ES and BX registers to point to the segment and offset addresses of the request header (segment and offset addressing is discussed in chapter 15). MS-DOS then issues a call to the driver's strategy routine.

The only function of the strategy routine is to save the segment and offset addresses of the request header in two local variables. It is the programmer's responsibility to define these variables within the driver and see that they are initialized when the driver is called. The strategy routine then passes control back to MS-DOS, which immediately calls the driver's interrupt routine.

The interrupt routine is the heart of the device driver. The first portion of the interrupt routine consists of a look-up table, constructed by the programmer, which tells the routine where to jump, according to the command code passed in the request header.

In responding to the MS-DOS request, the interrupt routine reads the command code, performs the table look-up, and passes control to the procedure that processes the particular command code. The procedure then processes the command using the fields of the request header to store information regarding the outcome of the request.

When the interrupt routine completes its work, control is returned to MS-DOS. MS-DOS determines the results of the request by inspecting the contents of the request header. MS-DOS, in turn, passes these results back to the program that initially requested access to the peripheral device.

Listing 14-1 contains an assembly language skeleton of an MS-DOS device driver. The listing can be expanded to form a functional device driver.

Listing 14-1. Skeleton for an MS-DOS Device Driver

```
;               Device Driver Skeleton
;
code_seg        segment para    public 'code'
skeleton        proc    far
                assume  cs:code_seg,es:code_seg,ds:code_seg
;
begin:
;
;Device Header
next_dev        dd      -1              ;segment:offset of next header
attrib_field    dw      8000h           ;character device
```

```
strat_ptr       dw      strategy        ;offset of strategy routine
int_ptr         dw      interrupt       ;offset of interrupt routine
name            db      'DEMO    '      ;name of driver
;
;
;Variable size area for use by driver. Store address of request
;header here.
rheader_off     dw      ?
rheader_seg     dw      ?
;
;This area can be used for other purposes as is necessary.
;
;Strategy routine                       ;called first by MS-DOS
strategy:
        mov     cs:rheader_off,bx       ;save address of request header
        mov     cs:rheader_seg,es
        ret                             ;return to MS-DOS
;
;
;Interrupt routine
interrupt:
        push    ds                      ;save MS-DOS registers
        push    es
        push    ax
        push    bx
        push    cx
        push    dx
        push    si
        push    di
;retrieve command code from request header
        mov     al,es:[bx+2]
;
;On the basis of the command code, which is now in al,
;branch to the appropriate routine and process the command.
;This area forms the meat, not the skeleton, of the driver. It
;can be coded as the programmer sees fit, as long as the
;requirements for each command code are met.
;
;
;After command is processed, exit the driver
        mov     es:word ptr [bx+3],0100h   ;set done bit in

                                           ;request header's

                                           ;status word

        pop     di                         ;restore MS-DOS stack
        pop     si
        pop     dx
        pop     cx
```

```
        pop     bx
        pop     ax
        pop     es
        pop     ds
        ret;                                    ;return to MS-DOS
;
;end of device driver
skeleton        endp
code_seg        ends
                end     begin
```

Device Commands

There are twenty command codes that a device driver may be called upon to process. This section discusses each command and lists the specific tasks to be executed for that command. Also listed are the fields of the request header's data area that must be read by the driver (on the call from MS-DOS) and set by the driver (on the return to MS-DOS).

Note: For all commands, the driver reads the request header length, the unit code (block devices only), and the command code. Also, for all commands, the driver sets the status word. Refer back to figure 14-6.

INIT (Command Code 0)

This command is invoked only at boot time when MS-DOS installs the driver. INIT performs any initialization of the device that is necessary. Of all the driver commands, only INIT may call the MS-DOS functions. INIT may use functions 01H through 0CH and function 30H only.

The driver must perform the following tasks:

1. Set the number of units controlled by the driver. This task is required for block device drivers only. This number overrides the first byte in the device name field of the device header.

2. Determine the break address. This address marks the end of the portion of the driver that remains resident in memory following execution of INIT. Since INIT is used only one time, many programmers place the code for INIT at the end of the driver. Then the portion of memory storing INIT can be released to MS-DOS following device initialization.

3. Set up a pointer to the BIOS parameter block (BPB) table. For each block device, INIT must set up in memory a BPB (see command code 2) for each type of media that can be used with the device. The BPB table contains pointers to the BPBs for a particular device. INIT returns the segment:offset pointer to the BPB table in the request header's data area.

4. Set the status word in the request header.

The driver may read the following fields in the data area:

Request Header Offset   **Description**

18–21   Offset and segment addresses of first
                    character after "=" in CONFIG.SYS
                    statement that loaded the driver. The
                    remainder of the command string may
                    be read by the driver.

22   First available drive (0 = A, etc., MS-
                    DOS 3+ only).

The driver must set the following fields in the data area:

Request Header Offset   **Description**

13   Number of units controlled by driver.

14–15   Offset address of break.

16–17   Segment address of break.

18–19   Offset address of BPB table.

20–21   Segment address of BPB table.

MEDIA CHECK (Command Code 1)

This command is valid for block devices only. Character drivers should set
only bit 8 ("done") in the request header's status word. The command is
issued to determine if the disk media on a drive has been changed. MS-DOS
issues this command before performing any disk read or write. The driver
must return one of three values:

−1   Media changed.

 0   Don't know if media changed.

 1   Media not changed.

For hard disks and RAM disks, the media cannot be changed, so the
driver can be written to always return a "Media not changed" signal. This
signal allows MS-DOS to access the disk without reading the file allocation
table (since the FAT is in memory from the previous disk access).

Since there is no foolproof way to determine if a floppy disk has been
changed, it is reasonable for drivers of devices having removable media to
always return a "Don't know" signal. The manner in which MS-DOS handles a "Don't know" signal depends on the state of the drive's file buffers.
If the buffers contain data that need to be written out ("dirty" data),
MS-DOS will assume that no disk change occurred and will write the data.

This action risks damaging the file structure of a new disk if there has been a disk swap. If the buffers do not contain dirty data, MS-DOS assumes that the media has been changed. In this case, MS-DOS invalidates the contents of any buffers associated with the drive, issues a BUILD BPB command (driver command code 2) to the driver, and reads the disk's FAT and file directory.

The driver must perform the following tasks:

1. Report the results of the media check.
2. Set the status word in the request header.

The driver may read the following fields in the data area:

Request Header Offset	Description
13	Media descriptor byte from disk's boot sector (the boot record is discussed in chapter 11).

The driver must set the following fields in the data area:

Request Header Offset	Description
14	Results of the media status check.
15–16	Offset address of the disk's volume label (MS-DOS 3.X and 4.X).
17–18	Segment address of disk's volume label (MS-DOS 3.X and 4.X).

BUILD BPB (Command Code 2)

This command is valid for block devices only. Character drivers only need set bit 8 ("done") of the request header's status word. BUILD BPB is called when MEDIA CHECK (driver command code 1) returns a "Media changed" or "Don't know" signal. The driver is responsible for locating the disk's boot sector, reading into memory the BIOS parameter block (BPB, see table 14-4), and returning to MS-DOS a pointer to the BPB. Under MS-DOS 3.X and 4.X, the driver should also store the disk's volume id label in memory.

The driver must perform the following tasks:

1. Read the new BPB into memory.
2. Return to MS-DOS a pointer to the new BPB.
3. Read the disk's volume id label into memory (MS-DOS 3.X and 4.X).
4. Set the status word in the request header.

Table 14-4. Parameters Defined in the BPB, Their Lengths and Offset Locations in the Boot Sector of the Device Media

Parameter	Length	Offset
Bytes per sector	Word	11–12
Sectors per allocation unit	Byte	13
Reserved sectors	Word	14–15
Number of FATs	Byte	16
Number of root directory entries	Word	17–18
Total sectors on media	Word	19–20
Media descriptor	Byte	21
Number of sectors occupied by a single FAT	Word	22–23

The driver may read the following fields in the data area:

Request Header Offset	**Description**
13	Media descriptor byte.
14–17	If the non-IBM format bit (bit 13) of the device header attribute field is 0, these 4 bytes store the offset and segment addresses of a buffer that holds the first sector of the disk's file allocation table (the first byte of which is the disk's media descriptor). If bit 13 of the attribute field is 1, the buffer may be used as a work area by the driver.

The driver must set the following fields in the data area:

Request Header Offset	**Description**
18–19	Offset address of the new BPB.
20–21	Segment address of the new BPB.

IOCTL INPUT (Command Code 3)

IOCTL (input/output control) functions allow programs and drivers to communicate by passing I/O control strings to one another through a memory buffer. IOCTL functions may be used with character or block devices that have bit 14 set in their device header's attribute field.

Programs utilize IOCTL functions through the use of MS-DOS function 44H. IOCTL INPUT is used to send control information from the driver to an application program. IOCTL OUTPUT is used to send control information from an application program to the driver.

The following tasks are required for driver commands IOCTL INPUT (command code 3), INPUT (command code 4), OUTPUT (command code 8), OUTPUT WITH VERIFY (command code 9), and IOCTL OUTPUT (command code 12):

1. Perform the requested input or output.
2. Set the number of bytes transferred.
3. Set the status word in the request header.

For the preceding commands, the driver may read the following fields in the request header's data area:

Request Header Offset	Description
13	Media descriptor byte.
14–15	Offset address of transfer buffer.
16–17	Segment address of transfer buffer.
18–19	Size of transfer requested (bytes for character devices, sectors for block devices).
20–21	Starting sector (block devices only).

For the preceding commands, the driver must set the following fields in the request header's data area:

Request Header Offset	Description
18–19	Actual size of transfer (bytes for character devices, sectors for block devices).
22–25	Offset and segment addresses of disk's volume id label. This field is used with command codes 4 and 8 only and only in MS-DOS 3.X and 4.X. If the driver returns error code 0FH (invalid disk change), MS-DOS can use this pointer to retrieve the label and to prompt the user to insert the corresponding disk.

INPUT (Command Code 4)

This command is used to read data from a peripheral device. See IOCTL INPUT (command code 3) for information on this command.

NONDESTRUCTIVE READ (Command Code 5)

This command is used with character devices only. Block drivers should set only bit 8 ("done") in the request header's status word. This command reads a single character from the device's buffer without removing the character from the buffer.

The driver must perform the following tasks:

1. Read a character from the device's buffer.
2. Set the status word in the request header.

The driver must set the following field in the data area:

Request Header Offset	Description
13	Character read.

INPUT STATUS (Command Code 6)

This command is used with character devices only. Block drivers should set only bit 8 ("done") in the request header's status word. This command tells MS-DOS whether or not there are any characters in the device's buffer ready to be read. If there are no characters to be read, the driver sets the busy bit (bit 9) of the request header's status word field to a value of 1. The busy bit is set to 0 if there is a character to read or if the device does not have a buffer.

The driver must perform the following task:

Set the status word in the request header.

INPUT FLUSH (Command Code 7)

This command is used with character devices only. Block drivers should set only bit 8 ("done") in the request header's status word. This command flushes the device's character buffer by reading characters from the device until the device status indicates that there are no more characters in the buffer.

The driver must perform the following task:

Set the status word in the request header.

OUTPUT (Command Code 8)

This command is used to write data to a peripheral device. See IOCTL INPUT (command code 3) for information on this command.

OUTPUT WITH VERIFY (Command Code 9)

This command is used to write data to a peripheral device. Each write is followed by a read to verify that the write was accurate. See IOCTL INPUT (command code 3) for information on this command.

OUTPUT STATUS (Command Code 10)

This command is used with character devices only. Block drivers should set only bit 8 ("done") in the request header's status word. This command checks the status of output-only device buffers (such as print buffers). The driver sets the busy bit (bit 9) of the request header's status word field to 0 if the device is idle or if the buffer is not full. The driver sets the busy bit to 1 if the device is busy or if the buffer is full.

The driver must perform the following task:

Set the status word in the request header.

OUTPUT FLUSH (Command Code 11)

This command is used with character devices only. Block drivers should set only bit 8 ("done") in the request header's status word. This command emp- ties a device's output buffer.

The driver must perform the following task:

Set the status word in the request header.

IOCTL OUTPUT (Command Code 12)

This command is used to send a control string from a program to a device driver. See IOCTL INPUT (command code 3) for information on this com- mand.

DEVICE OPEN (Command Code 13)

This command is implemented in MS-DOS 3.0 and later versions. The com- mand is invoked each time a device is opened if bit 11 of the driver's device header is set to 1. Thus, the command provides the driver with a way of tracking the number of times a device is opened. In conjunction with DE- VICE CLOSE (command code 14), this command can be used to limit the number of processes that can access a device at a given time. DEVICE OPEN can also be used to initialize character devices each time that they are used.

The driver must perform the following task:

Set the status word in the request header.

DEVICE CLOSE (Command Code 14)

This command is implemented in MS-DOS 3.0 and later versions. The com- mand is invoked each time a device is closed if bit 11 of the driver's device header is set to 1. Thus, the command provides the driver with a way of tracking the number of times a device is closed. In conjunction with DE- VICE OPEN (command code 13), this command can be used to control the number of processes that can access a device at a given time.

The driver must perform the following task:

Set the status word in the request header.

REMOVABLE MEDIA (Command Code 15)

This command is implemented in MS-DOS 3.0 and later versions. It is availa- ble only on block devices that have bit 11 of the attribute field in the device header set to 1. The command is invoked by MS-DOS each time that a program issues a call to MS-DOS service function 44H, subfunction 08H (IOCTL-removable media). The driver sets the busy bit (bit 9) of the request header's status word to 0 if the media is removable, to 1 if the media is not removable.

The driver must perform the following task:

Set the status word in the request header.

OUTPUT UNTIL BUSY (Command Code 16)

This command is implemented on MS-DOS 3.0 and later versions. It can be used with character devices that have bit 13 of the attribute field in the device header set to 1. This command sends output to the device until it receives a busy signal from the device. Its intended use is for implementing print spoolers.

The driver must perform the following tasks:

1. Report the number of characters written to the device.
2. Set the status word in the request header.

The driver may read the following fields in the data area:

Request Header Offset	Description
13	Media byte descriptor.
14–15	Offset address of memory buffer containing output data.
16–17	Segment address of memory buffer containing output data.
18–19	Number of bytes to be output.

The driver sets the following field in the data area:

Request Header Offset	Description
18–19	Number of bytes actually output.

Command Codes 17 and 18 are undefined.

GENERIC I/O CONTROL (Command Code 19)

This command is implemented in MS-DOS 3.20 and later versions. It can be used on block devices that have bit 0 set in the device header's attribute field. The purpose of this command is to provide a standard IOCTL service for block devices. The command is called when MS-DOS service function 44H, subfunction 0DH is invoked. Refer to the MS-DOS technical manual for details in implementing this command.

The driver must perform the following tasks:

1. Retrieve the major and minor function codes from the request header and verify that they are valid. For MS-DOS 3.20, the only valid major function value is 08H. The valid minor function codes are as follows:

   40H   Set device parameters.
   41H   Write logical drive track.
   42H   Format and verify logical drive track.
   60H   Get device parameters.
   61H   Read logical drive track.
   62H   Verify logical drive track.

2. Set the status word in the request header.

The driver may read the following fields in the data area:

Request Header Offset	Description
13	Major function code.
14	Minor function code.
15–16	Contents of SI register.
17–18	Contents of DI register.
19–20	Offset address of IOCTL request.
21–22	Segment address of IOCTL request.

Command codes 20, 21, and 22 are undefined.

GET LOGICAL DEVICE (Command Code 23)

This command is implemented in MS-DOS 3.20 and later versions. It is used with block devices only. Bit 6 of the attribute field in the device header must be set to 1 if this command is to be used. The command is used to determine the last logical drive letter assigned to a device.

The command must perform the following tasks:

1. Place a value in the unit code field of the request header. If the value is a nonzero number, it represents the last logical drive letter assigned to the device (0 = A, 1 = B, etc.). A zero value indicates that the device is assigned only one logical drive letter.

2. Set the status word in the request header.

SET LOGICAL DEVICE (Command Code 24)

This command is implemented in MS-DOS 3.20 and later versions. It is used with block devices only. Bit 6 of the attribute field in the device header must be set to 1 if this command is to be used. The command is used to assign a logical drive letter to a device.

The command must perform the following tasks:

1. Retrieve the unit code field of the request header. If the value represents a valid logical drive letter (0 = A, 1 = B, etc.), the logical drive letter is assigned to the device. The driver places a value of zero in the unit code field if the value passed does not represent a valid logical drive letter.

2. Set the status word in the request header.

15

DEBUG

DEBUG Commands
Introductory DEBUG
Advanced DEBUG

DEBUG is an MS-DOS utility program that allows you to examine and modify computer files and computer memory on a byte-by-byte basis.

DEBUG does not compare with powerful commercial debuggers such as CodeView, but as examples throughout this book show, DEBUG is useful for exploring the workings of DOS, for writing short assembly language programs, and for "patching" existing programs. Unfortunately, some of the later versions of DOS (such as PC-DOS 4) do not supply DEBUG as a standard part of the operating system. In order to get DEBUG with these versions, you must also obtain the diskette that comes with the system's technical reference manual.

This chapter begins with an explanation of DEBUG commands and the rules for using them. Since many of DEBUG's features require some familiarity with 8086/8088 assembly language programming, the discussion of DEBUG itself is divided into two sections. The first section, "Introductory DEBUG," explains how to use DEBUG to examine the contents of computer memory. It is written as an introduction to DEBUG and is intended for all readers who are interested in gaining some familiarity with this powerful MS-DOS utility.

"Advanced DEBUG," the second section, explains how DEBUG can be used as a tool in examining and modifying computer programs. Some familiarity with assembly language programming is helpful, but not essential, in understanding the material presented in this section.

Here is a summary of the features provided by DEBUG:

▶ Loads program files and data files into computer memory.

▶ Enters assembly language instructions directly into memory.

▶ Executes computer programs in a controlled environment.

▶ Displays the contents of a portion of computer memory in hexadecimal and ASCII formats.

▶ Changes the contents of a portion of memory.

▶ Moves blocks of data in memory to specified locations.

▶ Displays, creates, and modifies assembly language statements in memory.

▶ Follows, step by step, the execution of program instructions.

▶ Displays and modifies the contents of the CPU registers and flags.

▶ Stores the contents of a portion of computer memory on floppy and hard disks.

▶ Performs hexadecimal addition and subtraction with a built-in calculator.

DEBUG Commands

DEBUG is a command-driven program, which means that you must enter a command before DEBUG will perform an operation. DEBUG displays a prompt to notify you when it is ready to accept a command. In MS-DOS 1, the DEBUG prompt is a greater than sign (**>**). In MS-DOS 2 and subsequent versions, the DEBUG prompt is a hyphen (**−**). The examples in this chapter will use the hyphen as the DEBUG prompt.

Before we examine the DEBUG commands, we need to discuss the syntax, or rules, that must be followed when using DEBUG. All DEBUG commands begin with a letter. The letter may be entered in uppercase or lowercase. Most DEBUG commands include parameters other than the starting letter. When two consecutive parameters in a command are numbers, the numbers must be separated by a space or a comma. (All numbers used in DEBUG are hexadecimal.) In all other instances, parameters may be entered without separation.

To illustrate these rules, let's look at the following two commands, which are functionally equivalent. (Don't worry about the meaning of these commands for now.)

```
-D 100 L20
```

means the same as

```
-d100l20
```

Remember that any time consecutive parameters are hexadecimal numbers they must be separated by a comma or a space. The spaces in the following command are therefore necessary:

```
-SCS:0100 23 45 57
```

These rules will become second nature as you become familiar with the DEBUG commands. For the sake of clarity, we have inserted spaces between all parameters, though you need not use spaces except between consecutive hexadecimal numbers.

Table 15-1 is an alphabetical summary of the DEBUG commands. You can find a complete discussion of each command by referring to the page listed below each command's name.

Table 15-1. Summary of DEBUG Commands

Command	Purpose	Format
(A)SSEMBLE (page 342)	Assembles assembler statements into memory	a [*start*]
(C)OMPARE (page 347)	Compares contents of two blocks of memory	c [*start1*] [*end*] [*start2*] c [*start1*] L [*length*] [*start2*]

Table 15-1. (cont.)

Command	Purpose	Format
(D)UMP (page 325)	Displays memory contents	d d [*start*] [*end*] d [*start*] L [*length*]
(E)NTER (page 330)	Enters list of byte values and/or string characters into computer memory.	e [*start*] [*list*]
	Displays and, if desired, changes memory contents	e [*start*]
(F)ILL (page 349)	Fills block of memory with list of byte values and/ or string characters	f [*start*] [*end*] [*list*] f [*start*] L [*length*] [*list*]
(G)O (page 338)	Begins program execution	g g=[*start*] g [*breakpoint(s)*] g=[*start*] [*breakpoint(s)*]
(H)EXADECIMAL Arithmetic (page 351)	Adds and subtracts two hexadecimal numbers	h [*number1*] [*number2*]
(I)NPUT (page 358)	Reads and displays byte from a port	i [*port*]
(L)OAD (page 345)	Loads a file into memory	L L [*start*]
	Loads sector(s) into memory	L [*drive*] [*sector*] [*number*] L [*start*] [*drive*] [*sector*] [*number*]
(M)OVE (page 349)	Moves block of data from one memory location to another	m[*start1*] [*end*] [*start2*] m [*start1*] L [*length*] [*start2*]
(N)AME (page 343)	Names a file	n [*filespec*]
	Names a parameter	n [*param*]
	Names two parameters	n [*param1*] [*param2*]

Table 15-1. (cont.)

Command	Purpose	Format
(O)UTPUT (page 350)	Sends byte value out a port	o [port] [byte]
(P)roceed (page 351)	Executes a subroutine, program, loop, or interrupt	p[=address][value]
(Q)UIT (page 324)	Ends DEBUG	q
(R)EGISTER (page 332)	Displays contents of registers and status flags	r
	Displays and changes contents of a register	r [register name]
	Displays and changes status flags	rf
(S)EARCH (page 348)	Searches block of memory for list	s [start] [end] [list] s [start] L [length] [list]
(T)RACE (page 340)	Executes one machine instruction	t t=[start]
	Executes a number of machine instructions	t [number] t=[start] [number]
(U)NASSEMBLE (page 334)	Unassembles machine code	u u [start] [end] u [start] L [length]
(W)RITE (page 346)	Writes a file to disk	w w [start]
	Writes to sectors on disk	w [drive] [sector] [number] w [start] [drive] [sector] [number]
XA (page 352)	Allocates EMS pages	xa number
XD (page 352)	Deallocates an EMS handle	xd handle

Table 15-1. (cont.)

Command	Purpose	Format
XM (page 352)	Maps an expanded page into the page frame	xm *lpage ppage handle*
XS (page 352)	Displays expanded memory status	xs

Note: Italics indicate items that you must supply. Items in square brackets are optional.

Introductory DEBUG

This section will explain how to start and end DEBUG, how to use DEBUG to display memory contents, and how to enter data with DEBUG. No knowledge of assembly language programming is necessary.

Starting DEBUG

To start DEBUG, enter the command **DEBUG**. MS-DOS will load DEBUG and display a prompt (−) when DEBUG is ready to receive your command. (All of the examples in this chapter assume that drive C contains a copy of the file DEBUG.COM.)

```
C>debug
-
```

In the DEBUG start command, you may specify the file to be debugged:

```
C>debug textpro.com
-
```

The DEBUG start command must include a drive letter designator and/or a path specifier if the file to be debugged is not located in the current directory of the default drive.

Ending DEBUG

To terminate DEBUG and return control to MS-DOS, enter **q** in response to the DEBUG prompt:

```
-q
C>
```

Displaying Memory Contents

Computer memory is an aggregate of individual memory *addresses*. Addresses are physical locations within memory that store one piece (a byte) of data. Computers that use MS-DOS divide memory into *segments*. Each segment consists of 64K contiguous bytes of memory. Individual memory addresses within a segment are referred to by their *offset*. The first byte in a segment is at offset 0 within the segment, the second byte is at offset 1 within the segment, and so on. Individual memory addresses are identifiable by stating their segment and offset addresses. With this background information, let's see how the DEBUG command DUMP is used to examine computer memory.

The DUMP command (enter **d** or **D**) is used to display the contents of a selected portion of computer memory. The "dump" is displayed in both hexadecimal and ASCII format. In the following example, DEBUG is started from MS-DOS:

```
C>debug
-
```

Recall that the hyphen is DEBUG's way of telling you that it is ready to accept a command. (On some systems, the DEBUG prompt is **>**.) Let's enter "d" and see what happens:

```
C>debug
-d
0958:0100  00 00 00 00 00 00 00 00-00 00 00 00 00 00 00 00   ................
0958:0110  00 00 00 00 00 00 00 00-00 00 00 00 00 00 00 00   ................
0958:0120  00 00 00 00 00 00 00 00-00 00 00 00 00 00 00 00   ................
0958:0130  00 00 00 00 00 00 00 00-00 00 00 00 00 00 00 00   ................
0958:0140  00 00 00 00 00 00 00 00-00 00 00 00 00 00 00 00   ................
0958:0150  00 00 00 00 00 00 00 00-00 00 00 00 00 00 00 00   ................
0958:0160  00 00 00 00 00 00 00 00-00 00 00 00 00 00 00 00   ................
0958:0170  00 00 00 00 00 00 00 00-00 00 00 00 00 00 00 00   ................
-
```

The first number in the upper left corner (**0958:0100**) of the display is the memory address where the dump begins. The address is read as "segment 0958H offset 0100H." The address displayed on your computer will probably be different from the address in the example.

The first **00** following **0958:0100** indicates that a byte value of 00H is stored at memory address 0958:0100. The next **00** in the top line means that a value of 00H is stored at the following address in computer memory (0959:0101). Proceeding across the top line, we see a total of 16 **00**'s. This means that the 16 consecutive memory addresses beginning at 0958:0100 and continuing through 0958:010F all store a value of 00H.

The next seven lines (each preceded by a memory address) contain the remainder of the dump. We can see that this particular dump displays the contents of 128 consecutive memory addresses. The dump starts at address 0958:0101 and proceeds through address 0958:017F.

The dashes in the middle of each line serve as reference points. Eight of the 16 bytes on each line are to the left of the dash, and 8 are to the right. The 16 periods at the end of each line fill the space where memory contents are displayed in ASCII format. Unprintable characters are indicated by a period. We see nothing but periods, since there is no printable character with an ASCII value of 00H.

Let's try the DUMP command one more time and see what happens:

```
-d
0958:0180  00 00 00 00 00 00 00 00-00 00 00 00 00 00 00 00   ................
0958:0190  00 00 00 00 00 00 00 00-00 00 00 00 00 00 00 00   ................
0958:01A0  00 00 00 00 00 00 00 00-00 00 00 00 00 00 00 00   ................
0958:01B0  00 00 00 00 00 00 00 00-00 00 00 00 00 00 00 00   ................
0958:01C0  00 00 00 00 00 00 00 00-00 00 00 00 00 00 00 00   ................
0958:01D0  00 00 00 00 00 00 00 00-00 00 00 00 00 00 00 00   ................
0958:01E0  00 00 00 00 00 00 00 00-00 00 00 00 00 00 00 00   ................
0958:01F0  00 00 00 00 00 00 00 00-00 00 00 00 00 00 00 00   ................
-
```

Again, the screen displays all zeros and periods. But notice the memory addresses. This dump took off where the previous dump ended. What's happening?

If "d" is entered with no additional parameters, DEBUG displays (or "dumps") the contents stored in 128 consecutive memory addresses. The first byte displayed is located at the address immediately following the last byte displayed by the previous dump. If no previous DUMP command has been issued, the dump begins at the memory address used by DEBUG to load the file being debugged. (More on this in "Advanced DEBUG.")

We can tell DEBUG where to begin the dump by including an address in the command. The beginning address is specified by listing its segment and offset addresses. The two numbers are separated by a colon (:). The following command directs DEBUG to display 128 bytes of memory beginning at segment address 0958H, offset address 0000H:

```
-d 0958:0000
0958:0000  CD 20 00 20 00 9A EE FE-1D F0 34 02 68 06 62 02   M . ..n .p4.h.b.
0958:0010  68 06 E2 04 9C 05 9C 05-01 01 01 00 02 FF FF FF   h.b.............
0958:0020  FF FF FF FF FF FF FF FF-FF FF FF FF 65 06 BC 2A   ............e.<*
0958:0030  68 06 00 00 00 00 00 00-00 00 00 00 00 00 00 00   h...............
0958:0040  00 00 00 00 00 00 00 00-00 00 00 00 00 00 00 00   ................
0958:0050  CD 21 CB 00 00 00 00 00-00 00 00 00 00 20 20 20   M!K..........
0958:0060  20 20 20 20 20 20 20 20-00 00 00 00 00 20 20 20        .....
0958:0070  20 20 20 20 20 20 20 20-00 00 00 00 00 00 00 00        ........
-
```

Well, now we are getting somewhere. Notice that the dump started at the address specified in the DUMP command. Again, we have 128 consecutive bytes dumped. But this time we got something other than zeros and periods. The first byte dumped is located at memory address 0958:0000 and has a value of CDH.

Conventional ASCII values (see appendix F) fall in the range 00H to 7FH. DEBUG subtracts 80H from any byte with a value greater than 7FH and displays the character that corresponds to the resulting ASCII value. CDH minus 80H equals 4DH. 4DH is the ASCII value of the letter "M." Therefore, DEBUG displays an "M" as the first character in the ASCII portion of the dump.

The second memory location in the dump has a value of 20H. This is the ASCII value for a space, so DEBUG displays a space at the second position in the ASCII portion of the dump. The third address in the dump stores a value of 00H, which we know does not represent any printable ASCII character. DEBUG therefore prints a period at the third position of the ASCII dump.

This dump is not too exciting, as it consists of a few meaningless letters and a lot of periods. Let's try to find something more interesting to look at. We will briefly leave DEBUG and return to MS-DOS. To do this, simply enter q after the DEBUG prompt:

```
-q
C>
```

As you can tell from the MS-DOS prompt (C>), we have left DEBUG and have arrived back in MS-DOS. Before we return to DEBUG, we will use the MS-DOS text editor EDLIN to create a text file. (EDLIN is discussed in chapter 8.) If you are unfamiliar with EDLIN, just follow the instructions in the example.

The file to be created will take up about 250 bytes of disk space. In our example, the file will be stored on drive C, the default directory. Enter the following command:

```
C>edlin dbugpro.txt
```

This command tells MS-DOS to load EDLIN and instructs EDLIN to create a file named "dbugpro.txt". EDLIN will display the following message:

```
New file
*
```

EDLIN is now ready to accept a command. Type **1i** (or **1i**). Then type the text that appears in each line. Press Enter at the end of lines 1–5 and Ctrl-Z at the end of line 6:

```
C>edlin dbugpro.txt
New file
*1i
```

```
1:*++++++++++++++++++++++++++++++++++++++++++++++++++++++++++++++
2:*This text file will be used to demonstrate DEBUG.
3:*The file will be loaded into memory when DEBUG is started.
4:*DEBUG is easy to use after some practice.
5:*++++++++++++++++++++++++++++++++++++++++++++++++++++++++++++++
6:*^Z
*e      ←type "e"
C>
```

The **e** command terminated EDLIN, and the **C>** prompt tells us that we have returned to MS-DOS. "Dbugpro.txt" has been created and stored on drive C. We can now return to DEBUG and examine the newly created file. With drive C as the default directory, enter the following command:

```
C>debug dbugpro.txt
-
```

As you can see, the DEBUG prompt tells us that we are back in DEBUG and that the file "dbugpro.txt" has been loaded into memory.

Enter **d** for a dump beginning at the memory address where "dbug-pro.txt" was loaded:

```
-d
0958:0100  2B 2B 2B 2B 2B 2B 2B 2B-2B 2B 2B 2B 2B 2B 2B 2B   ++++++++++++++++
0958:0110  2B 2B 2B 2B 2B 2B 2B 2B-2B 2B 2B 2B 2B 2B 2B 2B   ++++++++++++++++
0958:0120  2B 2B 2B 2B 2B 2B 2B 2B-2B 2B 2B 2B 2B 2B 2B 2B   ++++++++++++++++
0958:0130  2B 2B 2B 2B 2B 2B 2B 2B-2B 0D 0A 54 68 69 73 20   +++++++++..This
0958:0140  74 65 78 74 20 66 69 6C-65 20 77 69 6C 6C 20 62   text file will b
0958:0150  65 20 75 73 65 64 20 74-6F 20 64 65 6D 6F 6E 73   e used to demons
0958:0160  74 72 61 74 65 20 44 45-42 55 47 2E 0D 0A 54 68   trate DEBUG...Th
0958:0170  65 20 66 69 6C 65 20 77-69 6C 6C 20 62 65 20 6C   e file will be l
-
```

Enter **d** again to continue the dump:

```
-d
0958:0180  6F 61 64 65 64 20 69 6E-74 6F 20 6D 65 6D 6F 72   oaded into memor
0958:0190  79 20 77 68 65 6E 20 44-45 42 55 47 20 69 73 20   y when DEBUG is
0958:01A0  73 74 61 72 74 65 64 2E-0D 0A 44 45 42 55 47 20   started...DEBUG
0958:01B0  69 73 20 65 61 73 79 20-74 6F 20 75 73 65 20 61   is easy to use a
0958:01C0  66 74 65 72 20 73 6F 6D-65 20 70 72 61 63 74 69   fter some practi
0958:01D0  63 65 2E 0D 0A 2B 2B 2B-2B 2B 2B 2B 2B 2B 2B 2B   ce...+++++++++++
0958:01E0  2B 2B 2B 2B 2B 2B 2B 2B-2B 2B 2B 2B 2B 2B 2B 2B   ++++++++++++++++
0958:01F0  2B 2B 2B 2B 2B 2B 2B 2B-2B 2B 2B 2B 2B 2B 2B 2B   ++++++++++++++++
-
```

In the preceding examples, each **d** command caused 128 bytes of memory to be displayed. The contents of "dbugpro.txt" were displayed in hexadecimal format at the center of the screen and in ASCII format to the right.

You may specify the start and stop addresses of a dump as follows:

```
-d 0958:01AA 01D2
0958:01AA  44 45 42 55 47 20                                DEBUG
0958:01B0  69 73 20 65 61 73 79 20-74 6F 20 75 73 65 20 61  is easy to use a
0958:01C0  66 74 65 72 20 73 6F 6D-65 20 70 72 61 63 74 69  fter some practi
0958:01D0  63 65 2E                                         ce.
-
```

The preceding dump begins at address 0958:01AA and ends at 0958:01D2. The starting and ending addresses are specified in the DUMP command. Notice that the starting address is specified by segment (0958) and offset (01AA). Only the offset (01D2) is specified for the ending address.

Addresses stored in segment registers (see "Registers and Flags" in "Advanced DEBUG") may be specified in a dump by including the register's name in the command. The following command directs DEBUG to begin a dump at the memory location whose segment address is stored in the DS register and whose offset address is 01AAH. The ending offset address is specified as 01D2H.

```
-d DS:01AA 01D2
0958:01AA  44 45 42 55 47 20                                DEBUG
0958:01B0  69 73 20 65 61 73 79 20-74 6F 20 75 73 65 20 61  is easy to use a
0958:01C0  66 74 65 72 20 73 6F 6D-65 20 70 72 61 63 74 69  fter some practi
0958:01D0  63 65 2E                                         ce.
-
```

We can leave out segment addresses altogether, entering only offset addresses. DEBUG will assume that the segment address is stored in the DS register:

```
-d DS:01AA 01D2
0958:01AA  44 45 42 55 47 20                                DEBUG
0958:01B0  69 73 20 65 61 73 79 20-74 6F 20 75 73 65 20 61  is easy to use a
0958:01C0  66 74 65 72 20 73 6F 6D-65 20 70 72 61 63 74 69  fter some practi
0958:01D0  63 65 2E                                         ce.
-
```

Finally, we can tell DEBUG the number of bytes to be dumped by following the start address with an L followed by the number of bytes to be dumped. The next command tells DEBUG to dump 41 (29H) bytes:

```
-d DS:01AA L29
0958:01AA  44 45 42 55 47 20                                DEBUG
0958:01B0  69 73 20 65 61 73 79 20-74 6F 20 75 73 65 20 61  is easy to use a
0958:01C0  66 74 65 72 20 73 6F 6D-65 20 70 72 61 63 74 69  fter some practi
0958:01D0  63 65 2E                                         ce.
-
```

Entering Data with DEBUG

The ENTER command (enter **e** or **E**) is used to place data into memory. This powerful command allows you to modify the contents of memory on a byte-by-byte basis. ENTER can be used in conjunction with the NAME and WRITE commands (see "Advanced DEBUG") to modify files and store the modified files on disk.

The command begins with the letter "e" followed by the address at which data entry will begin. DEBUG assumes that the segment address is stored in the DS register if you specify only an offset address.

Data to be entered is specified in the command as a sequence of hexadecimal numbers and/or character strings. You must separate hexadecimal numbers with a space or a comma. A string of characters must be enclosed in quotation marks. If a command contains a character string, the hexadecimal ASCII values for the characters in the string are stored in memory.

The following example demonstrates the ENTER command:

```
-e 0958:0000 20 2A 44 41 54 41 20 'IS' 20 48 45 52 45 2A 20
-
```

The preceding ENTER command instructed DEBUG to enter 16 bytes of data in memory. The data is stored at consecutive memory locations beginning at address 0958:0000. Fourteen of the bytes entered are listed in the command as hexadecimal numbers. Two of the bytes are listed as a character string ('IS').

We can use the DUMP command to display the data entered. The "L" option will tell DEBUG to dump 16 (10H) bytes of memory:

```
-d 0958:0000 L10
0958:0000   20 2A 44 41 54 41 20 49-53 20 48 45 52 45 2A 20   *DATA IS HERE*
-
```

Notice that memory addresses 0958:0007 and 0958:0008 store the hexadecimal ASCII values of the characters in the string "is". The ASCII representation of the data entered is displayed at the right.

The ENTER command can also be used to display, and optionally change, the byte value stored at an address. In this case, the command consists of the letter "e" followed by a memory address. No list of numbers or strings is included in the command. DEBUG responds by displaying the address specified and the byte value stored at that address:

```
-e 0958:0000
0958:0000   20.
```

Pressing the space bar displays the value at the next memory address:

```
-e 0958:0000
0958:0000   20. 2A.
```

The value stored at an address can be changed by entering a new hexadecimal value. Strings, however, cannot be entered when the command is used in this fashion:

```
-e 0958:0000
0958:0000  20. 2A.21
```

In the preceding example, memory address 0958:0001 originally contained a value of 2AH. The value stored at this address has been changed to 21H.

At each 8-byte boundary (an offset address ending in either 8 or 0), DEBUG displays the current address:

```
-e 0958:0000
0958:0000  20.   2A.21 44.   41.   54.   41.   20.   49.43
0958:0008  53.48 20.41 48.4E 45.47 52.45 45.44 2A.   20.
```

In the preceding example, the values stored at offset addresses 0001H and 0007H through 000DH have been changed. The values at the other addresses are unchanged.

The preceding memory address and the value stored at that address can be displayed by entering a hyphen (−). This value can be changed if desired:

```
-e 0958:0000
0958:0000  20.   2A.21 44.   41.   54.   41.   20.   49.43
0958:0008  53.48 20.41 48.4E 45.47 52.45 45.44 2A.   20.-
0958:000E  2A.
```

To terminate the command, press Enter. The reappearance of the DEBUG prompt (−) signals that DEBUG is ready to receive your next command:

```
-e 0958:0000
0958:0000  20.   2A.21 44.   41.   54.   41.   20.   49.43
0958:0008  53.48 20.41 48.4E 45.47 52.45 45.44 2A.   20.-
0958:000E  2A.21      ←press Enter
-
```

The changes made can be examined with the DUMP command:

```
-d 0958:0000 L10
0958:0000  20 21 44 41 54 41 20 43-48 41 4E 47 45 44 20 21    !DATA CHANGED!
```

Advanced DEBUG

The following discussion of the remaining DEBUG commands is written to be as self-explanatory as possible. Although some knowledge of assembly language programming would be helpful, it is not essential. Let us begin with a few general concepts before we proceed with the commands.

Registers and Flags

The heart of a microcomputer is its *central processing unit* (CPU), the portion of the computer responsible for performing all arithmetic and logical operations and controlling the flow of information throughout the system. CPUs store data in structures called *registers*. Most computers that use MS-DOS have CPUs containing 13 registers. The registers are given the names AX, BX, CX, DX, SP, BP, SI, DI, CS, DS, SS, ES, and IP. The CS, DS, SS, and ES registers are called the *segment registers*.

In MS-DOS computers, the CPU also contains nine "flags." A *flag* is a structure that is either "set" or "cleared" by different computer operations. As we shall see, DEBUG can be used to examine and modify the registers and flags.

DEBUG Initialization

When you instruct MS-DOS to start DEBUG, the operating system places the file DEBUG.COM in memory at the lowest-available memory location. DEBUG then takes control and constructs a *program segment prefix* (psp) at the lowest-available location in memory. The psp is a contiguous block of memory used by MS-DOS during program execution. The psp is 256 (100H) bytes in length. (For more on the psp, see chapter 11.)

Looking at Registers with DEBUG

The REGISTER command (enter **r** or **R**) is used by DEBUG to display and modify the contents of the CPU registers and status flags. This command also displays information about the next machine instruction scheduled for execution. Let's begin our discussion of REGISTER by starting DEBUG. With drive C as the default directory, enter the following command:

```
C>debug
-
```

DEBUG signals that it is ready to accept a command by displaying its prompt. Let's enter **r** and see what happens:

```
C>debug
-r
AX=0000  BX=0000  CX=0000  DX=0000  SP=FFEE  BP=0000  SI=0000 DI=0000
DS=0958  ES=0958  SS=0958  CS=0958  IP=0100   NV UP DI PL NZ NA PO NC
0958:0100  0000         ADD        [BX+SI],AL                     DS:0000=CD
-
```

The display shows the hexadecimal values stored in each of the 13 registers. The segment registers (DS, ES, SS, and CS) all store a value of 0958H. This number is the address of the lowest-available segment in the memory of the computer used in this example. If you are following along on your computer, the value stored in your segment registers may not equal 0958H.

The SP register has been initialized to a value of FFEEH. The IP register has been set to equal 0100H. The remaining registers have been set to equal zero.

The status of the eight flags is displayed on the right side of the second line. All flags are initially cleared by DEBUG. Table 15-2 lists the eight flags and the symbols used to indicate their status in the order that they are displayed by DEBUG.

A computer program is a sequence of *machine instructions* that the computer is to execute. Machine instructions are written in *machine code,* a series of bytes stored in memory. The machine code for the next instruction to be executed is stored in memory at the address pointed to by the CS and IP registers. In the previous example, this address is CS:IP=0958:0100.

The third line of each register display contains information about the instruction at CS:IP. The CS:IP address is displayed at the left of the third line. The next item displayed is the sequence of bytes that make up the machine instruction. In the previous example, the instruction sequence is 00H 00H (displayed as **0000**). This sequence of machine code is represented by the assembly language *mnemonic* displayed in the middle of the third row— **ADD [BX+SI], AL**. A mnemonic is a memory aid, such as an abbreviation or a code. Mnemonics are frequently used by programmers.

Table 15-2. Flags and Symbols in DEBUG

Flag Name	Set	Clear
Overflow (yes/no)	OV	NV
Direction (decrement/increment)	DN	UP
Interrupt (enable/disable)	EI	DI
Sign (negative/positive)	NG	PL
Zero (yes/no)	ZR	NZ
Auxiliary carry (yes/no)	AC	NA
Parity (even/odd)	PE	PO
Carry (yes/no)	CY	NC

In the preceding display, the instruction to be executed tells the computer to take the value stored in the AL register (the low-order byte in the AX register) and add that value to the value stored at memory address DS:0000. The resulting value is to be stored at DS:0000. The current value stored at DS:0000 is displayed at the right end of the third line.

You may alter the value stored in a register by entering "r" followed by the name of the register. The current value in the register will be displayed, and a new value can be entered. To retain the current value of the register, press Enter.

```
-r CX
CX 0000
:245D
-r
AX=0000  BX=0000  CX=245D  DX=0000  SP=FFEE  BP=0000  SI=0000 DI=0000
DS=0958  ES=0958  SS=0958  CS=0958  IP=0100   NV UP DI PL NZ NA PO NC
0958:0100 0000         ADD        [BX+SI],AL                    DS:0000=CD
-
```

Since CS:IP points to the next instruction, changing the CS and/or IP registers can have dramatic results:

```
-r IP
IP 0100
:0000
-r
AX=0000  BX=0000  CX=245D  DX=0000  SP=FFEE  BP=0000  SI=0000 DI=0000
DS=0958  ES=0958  SS=0958  CS=0958  IP=0000   NV UP DI PL NZ NA PO NC
0958:0000 CD20           INT    20
-
```

Now CS:IP points to memory address 0958:0000. The machine code sequence at this address is CD 20, which instructs the computer to execute interrupt 20.

DEBUG displays the status of the flags when the command **rf** is entered. Any or all of the flags can then be modified by entering one or more symbols (see table 15-2). The symbols may be entered in any order with or without spaces between them. In the following example, the overflow, sign, and carry flags are set:

```
-rf
NV UP DI PL NZ NA PO NC -OV NG CY
-r
AX=0000  BX=0000  CX=245D  DX=0000  SP=FFEE  BP=0000  SI=0000 DI=0000
DS=0958  ES=0958  SS=0958  CS=0958  IP=0000   OV UP DI NG NZ NA PO CY
0958:0000 CD20           INT    20
-
```

Unassembling with DEBUG

Recall that a computer program is a series of instructions stored in the computer as machine code. In machine code, each instruction to the computer consists of a sequence of one or more bytes. While machine code makes sense to a computer, it is very difficult for most people to make any sense out of it.

Because machine code is so cumbersome and difficult to work with, another low-level computer language called *assembly language* is often used instead. Assembly language programmers use symbolic instructions when writing programs. These symbols, called *mnemonics,* are easier for people to understand than machine code. For example, an assembly language programmer might use the statement "RD" for the instruction "read data." However, mnemonics don't mean a thing to computers; so before a program can be executed, the mnemonics must be converted to machine code. This conversion process is called *assembly* and is performed by a computer program called an *assembler*.

Often it is desirable to reverse the assembly process; that is, to take machine code and "unassemble" it back to the corresponding assembly language mnemonics. This process is performed by a computer program called, naturally, an *unassembler*.

The UNASSEMBLE command (enter u or U) is used to invoke DEBUG's unassembler. The command can be used to unassemble existing machine code and obtain what MS-DOS manuals term "assembler like" statements. This refers to the fact that assembly language programmers can use labels to reference specific memory locations. These labels are a tremendous help in understanding the logical flow of an assembly language program. The UNASSEMBLE command references memory locations by numerical addresses only; no labels are used. This difference can make an unassembled program listing much more difficult to follow than the original assembly language program. Nonetheless, an unassembler can be an extremely powerful aid in figuring out how a computer program works and how it can be modified.

To demonstrate DEBUG's unassembler, let's unassemble a portion of DEBUG.COM. We begin at the DOS level and instruct DEBUG to load the file DEBUG.COM. With drive C as the default directory, enter the command shown in the next example.

Note: If you follow this example on your computer and get markedly different results, you probably have a different version of DEBUG.COM. However, you can still use the concepts presented here to explore your version of DEBUG.COM.

```
C>debug debug.com
```

The appearance of the DEBUG prompt tells us that DEBUG is ready to accept a command. DEBUG has constructed a psp, at the end of which it has loaded the file DEBUG.COM. DEBUG has then stored the segment address of the psp in each of the four segment registers.

Let's begin our examination of the DEBUG.COM file by having DEBUG dump the first 80 bytes (50H) of the file. We will use the DUMP command, specifying an address at which to begin the dump. We know that DEBUG.COM has been loaded at offset address 100H in the segment containing the psp. We do not know the value of that segment, but its value, whatever it is, has been stored in the four segment registers. Therefore, we can use any of the segment registers in the DUMP command:

```
-d CS:0100 L50
096C:0100  EB 09 56 65 72 73 20 32-2E 31 30 B4 30 CD 21 86   k.Vers 2.1040M!.
096C:0110  E0 3D 00 02 73 09 BA 69-2B B4 09 CD 21 CD 20 B4   '=..s.:i+4.M!M 4
096C:0120  51 CD 21 89 1E 4F 2B BC-D4 2A A2 D5 2C B4 52 CD   QM!..O+<T*"U.4RM
096C:0130  21 8C C8 8E D8 8E C0 E8-F1 00 B0 23 BA 62 02 CD   !.H.X.@hd.O#:b.M
096C:0140  21 8C CA B8 03 2F D1 E8-D1 E8 D1 E8 D1 E8 03 D0   !.J8./QhQhQhQh.P
-
```

This dump displays the first 80 bytes of the machine code making up the program file DEBUG.COM. On the computer used in this example, the CS register has been initialized to a value of 096CH. Do not be surprised if the value of the CS register on your computer is different. This would mean only that the lowest-available segment on your computer is located at a segment address other than 096CH.

The bytes in this dump mean a lot to the computer but not much to most people. We can use the unassemble command to obtain an assembly listing of the machine code. Unassembling begins at the same address as the dump:

```
-u CS:0100
096C:0100       EB09            JMP     010B
096C:0102       56              PUSH    SI
096C:0103       65              DB      65
096C:0104       7273            JB      0179
096C:0106       2032            AND     [BP+SI],DH
096C:0108       2E              CS:
096C:0109       3130            XOR     [BX+SI],SI
096C:010B       B430            MOV     AH,30
096C:010D       CD21            INT     21
096C:010F       86E0            XCHG    AL,AH
096C:0111       3D0002          CMP     AX,0200
096C:0114       7309            JNB     011F
096C:0116       BA692B          MOV     DX,2B69
096C:0119       B409            MOV     AH,09
096C:011B       CD21            INT     21
096C:011D       CD20            INT     20
096C:011F       B451            MOV     AH,51
-
```

This is an unassembled listing of the first 33 bytes of DEBUG.COM. The first item (column 1) on each line is the starting segment and offset address of an instruction that the computer is to execute. The second item (column 2) in each line is the actual sequence of bytes that make up the machine code for the instruction. The third item (columns 3 and 4) on each line is the assembly language statement that corresponds to the machine-coded instruction.

In the first line, the instruction begins at address 096C:0100. The machine code for the instruction consists of the 2-byte sequence EBH, 09H (written as **EB09**). The corresponding assembly language statement is **JMP 010B**. Even though the meaning of this assembly language statement is not entirely obvious, you can probably guess what it means. For someone experienced in assembly language programming, this unassembled listing is an essential aid in understanding the workings of a machine language program. By the way, **JMP 010B** is an instruction to the computer telling it to jump to offset address 010BH and continue program execution with the instruction that begins at that point.

The UNASSEMBLE command can be entered with or without a starting address. If you enter only an offset address, the command assumes that the segment address is stored in the CS register. If you do not enter an address, the command assumes that the starting address is the location following the last instruction that was unassembled. If you did not issue a previous UNASSEMBLE command, unassembling begins at address CS:0100.

A range of memory to be unassembled may be specified by entering a starting address and an ending address. The ending address must be an offset address. If the end address does not correspond to the last byte in an instruction, the complete instruction is still unassembled:

```
-u CS:0100 0104
096C:0100    EB09                    JMP    010B
096C:0102    56                      PUSH   SI
096C:0103    65                      DB     65
096C:0104    7273                    JB     0179
```

The number of bytes to be unassembled may be specified with the "L" option. The default value is 32. If the final byte specified does not correspond to the final byte in an instruction, the complete instruction is still unassembled:

```
-u CS:0106 L4
096C:0106    2032                    AND    [BP+SI],DH
096C:0108    2E                      CS:
096C:0109    3130                    XOR    [BX+SI],SI
```

One final word about the UNASSEMBLE command. If you specify a starting address for the command, be certain that the address is indeed the starting point of a machine instruction. If you specify a starting address that is in the middle of an instruction, or a memory address that contains data rather than program code, the resulting unassembled list may be meaningless.

To obtain a printout of an unassembly listing, press Ctrl-PrtSc before entering your UNASSEMBLE command.

Program Execution with DEBUG

The DEBUG command GO (enter **g** or **G**) is used to execute machine language programs in a controlled environment. We will demonstrate the GO command with a short computer program that will be written using DE-BUG. To follow along, boot your system, using drive C as the default directory. After you see the prompt, start DEBUG:

```
C>debug
-
```

When the DEBUG prompt appears, carefully enter the following commands.

```
-e CS:0100 B0 01 BF 00 02 B9 1D 00 FC F2 AA B0 24
-e CS:010D AA 06 1F BA 00 02 B4 09 CD 21 CD 20
```

The preceding DEBUG commands place in memory a sequence of byte values that form a machine language computer program. When the program is executed, it will clear the display screen, print a row of happy face symbols on the screen, and then return control to DEBUG.

The UNASSEMBLE command can be used to examine the program before we execute it:

```
-u CS:100      117
0976:0100      B002              MOV      AL,01
0976:0102      BF0002            MOV      DI,0200
0976:0105      B91D00            MOV      CX,001D
0976:0108      FC                CLD
0976:0109      F2                REPNZ
0976:010A      AA                STOSB
0976:010B      B024              MOV      AL,24
0976:010D      AA                STOSB
0976:010E      06                PUSH     ES
0976:010F      1F                POP      DS
0976:0110      BA0002            MOV      DX,0200
0976:0113      B409              MOV      AH,09
0976:0115      CD21              INT      21
0976:0117      CD20              INT      20
-
```

The GO command may be entered without additional parameters. When this is done, execution begins at the instruction pointed to by CS:IP. Let's use the REGISTER command to check on the status of the registers:

```
-r
AX=0000  BX=0000  CX=0000  DX=0000  SP=FFEE  BP=0000  SI=0000 DI=0000
DS=0976  ES=0976  SS=0976  CS=0976  IP=0100    NV UP DI PL NZ NA PO NC
```

```
0976:0100 B001          MOV      AL,01
-
```

Since CS and IP are pointing to the first instruction of our program, enter **g** and see what happens:

```
-g
😊😊😊😊😊😊😊😊😊😊😊😊😊😊😊😊😊😊😊😊😊😊😊😊😊😊😊😊😊😊
```

You should see a row of 30 happy faces. DEBUG displays the following message:

```
Program terminated normally
-
```

The message **Program terminated normally** tells you that control has been passed from the program being executed back to DEBUG.

The GO command may be used to set *breakpoints*. Breakpoints are used to halt program execution at particular points in the machine code sequence. Breakpoints are set by specifying breakpoint addresses in the GO command. Up to ten breakpoints may be set in one command. DEBUG assumes that a breakpoint's segment address is stored in the CS register if you specify only an offset address in the GO command. Breakpoint addresses must be separated by a space or a comma.

When DEBUG encounters a breakpoint, program execution is halted and the contents of the registers and the status of the flags are displayed. Breakpoints can be very useful in following and/or debugging programs that contain branching logic. They can also be very useful in "sidestepping" portions of code that do not require the scrutiny of the TRACE command. (TRACE is discussed in the next section.)

The program we have written contains an instruction at offset address 0109 that is repeated 30 times during program execution. Single-stepping through this instruction eighty times with TRACE would be extremely monotonous and yield no new information about the workings of the program. Breakpoints allow us to rapidly execute the instruction, halting program execution at the instruction located at 010B.

Let's use TRACE to step through the first three instructions in the program. We will then use GO to rapidly execute the instructions at 0109. GO will set a breakpoint at address 010B.

```
-t
AX=0001  BX=0000  CX=0000  DX=0000  SP=FFEE  BP=0000  SI=0000 DI=0000
DS=0976  ES=0976  SS=0976  CS=0976  IP=0102   NV UP DI PL NZ NA PO NC
0976:0102 BF0002          MOV      DI,0200
-t

AX=0001  BX=0000  CX=0000  DX=0000  SP=FFEE  BP=0000  SI=0000 DI=0200
DS=0976  ES=0976  SS=0976  CS=0976  IP=0105   NV UP DI PL NZ NA PO NC
```

```
0976:0105 B91D00          MOV     CX,001D
-t


AX=0001  BX=0000  CX=001D  DX=0000  SP=FFEE  BP=0000  SI=0000 DI=0200
DS=0976  ES=0976  SS=0976  CS=0976  IP=0108      NV UP DI PL NZ NA PO NC
0976:0108 FC              CLD
-t


AX=0001  BX=0000  CX=001D  DX=0000  SP=FFEE  BP=0000  SI=0000 DI=0200
DS=0976  ES=0976  SS=0976  CS=0976  IP=0109      NV UP DI PL NZ NA PO NC
0976:0109 F2              REPNZ
0976:010A AA              STOSB
-g 010b


AX=0001  BX=0000  CX=001D  DX=0000  SP=FFEE  BP=0000  SI=0000 DI=0250
DS=0976  ES=0976  SS=0976  CS=0976  IP=010B      NV UP DI PL NZ NA PO NC
0976:010B B024              MOV     AL,24
-
```

The instructions at offset 0109 and 010A were actually repeated 30 times, but by setting the breakpoint we were able to zoom through them with GO.

You can use the GO command to specify the first instruction to be executed, thereby overriding the CS:IP pointer. After typing **g**, type an equal sign (=) followed by the address of what is to be the starting instruction. If you enter only an offset address, DEBUG assumes that the CS register contains the segment address.

If we were to continue the previous example by entering a "g", execution would commence with the instruction pointed to by CS:IP (0958: 010B). We can rerun the program from the start by including the starting address of the program in the GO command:

```
-g=100
```

☺☺☺☺☺☺☺☺☺☺☺☺☺☺☺☺☺☺☺☺☺☺☺☺☺☺☺☺☺☺

A row of happy faces appears, and a message is displayed, telling us that program execution has terminated and control has been returned to DEBUG.

Single-Stepping through a Program

The TRACE command (enter **t** or **T**) is used to execute machine language programs in a single-step fashion. After each instruction is carried out, the contents of the registers and the status of the flags are displayed. Each display is identical to the display that results when the REGISTER command is used. The only difference is that each time a TRACE command is entered, one instruction is executed before the next display is put on the screen.

We will demonstrate TRACE with the same program that was used to demonstrate GO. If you no longer have the program in memory, start DEBUG and enter the following commands:

```
C>debug
-e CS:0100 B0 01 BF 00 00 B9 1D 00 FC F2 AA B0 24
-e CS:010D AA 06 1F BA 00 02 B4 09 CD 21 CD 20
```

Once the program is in memory, we can begin. Let's start with a REGIS-TER command to see where we are:

```
-r
AX=0001  BX=0000  CX=0000  DX=0000  SP=FFEE  BP=0000  SI=0000 DI=0250
DS=0976  ES=0976  SS=0976  CS=0976  IP=0100    NV UP DI PL NZ NA PO NC
0976:0100 B001           MOV      AL,02
-
```

Entering a "t" executes the instruction located at CS:IP. After the in-struction is executed, the registers and flags are displayed:

```
-t
AX=0001  BX=0000  CX=0000  DX=0000  SP=FFEE  BP=0000  SI=0000 DI=0250
DS=0976  ES=0976  SS=0976  CS=0976  IP=0102    NV UP DI PL NZ NA PO NC
0976:0102 BF0002          MOV      DI,0200
-t

AX=0001  BX=0000  CX=0000  DX=0000  SP=FFEE  BP=0000  SI=0000 DI=0200
DS=0976  ES=0976  SS=0976  CS=0976  IP=0105    NV UP DI PL NZ NA PO NC
0976:0105 B91D00          MOV      CX,001D
-
```

You can use the TRACE command to specify which instruction will be executed by including the address of the instruction in the command. To specify an instruction, enter "t", followed by an equal sign (=), followed by the address of the instruction to be executed. DEBUG assumes that the in-struction's segment address is stored in the CS register if you specify only an offset address in the TRACE command:

```
-t=0100
AX=0001  BX=0000  CX=0000  DX=0000  SP=FFEE  BP=0000  SI=0000 DI=0200
DS=0976  ES=0976  SS=0976  CS=0976  IP=0102  NV UP DI PL NZ NA PO NC
0976:0102 BF0002          MOV      DI,0200
-
```

The preceding trace executed the instruction at offset 0100H. CS:IP is now pointing to the instruction at offset 0102H.

TRACE can also be used to execute more than one instruction. You simply enter the number of instructions that are to be executed. After each instruction is executed, the registers and flags are displayed. If several in-structions are executed, the display will scroll off the screen. You can sus-pend the scrolling by pressing the Ctrl-NumLock keys. To continue scrolling, press any key.

Pressing the Ctrl-C keys stops the trace, and the DEBUG prompt is displayed:

```
-t6
AX=0001  BX=0000  CX=0000  DX=0000  SP=FFEE  BP=0000  SI=0000 DI=0200
DS=0976  ES=0976  SS=0976  CS=0976  IP=0105    NV UP DI PL NZ NA PO NC
0976:0105 B91D00        MOV     CX,001D


AX=0001  BX=0000  CX=001D  DX=0000  SP=FFEE  BP=0000  SI=0000 DI=0200
DS=0976  ES=0976  SS=0976  CS=0976  IP=0108    NV UP DI PL NZ NA PO NC
0976:0108 FC            CLD


AX=0001  BX=0000  CX=001D  DX=0000  SP=FFEE  BP=0000  SI=0000 DI=0200
DS=0976  ES=0976  SS=0976  CS=0976  IP=0109    NV UP DI PL NZ NA PO NC
0976:0109 F2            REPNZ
0976:010A AA            STOSB


AX=0001  BX=0000  CX=001C  DX=0000  SP=FFEE  BP=0000  SI=0000 DI=0201
DS=0976  ES=0976  SS=0976  CS=0976  IP=0109    NV UP DI PL NZ NA PO NC
0976:0109 F2            REPNZ
0976:010A AA            STOSB


AX=0001  BX=0000  CX=001B  DX=0000  SP=FFEE  BP=0000  SI=0000 DI=0202
DS=0976  ES=0976  SS=0976  CS=0976  IP=0109    NV UP DI PL NZ NA PO NC
0976:0109 F2            REPNZ
0976:010A AA            STOSB


AX=0001  BX=0000  CX=001A  DX=0000  SP=FFEE  BP=0000  SI=0000 DI=0203
DS=0976  EX=0976  SS=0976  CS=0976  IP=0109    NV UP DI PL NZ NA PO NC
0976:0109 F2            REPNZ
0976:010A AA            STOSB
-
```

Four different instructions have been executed, but one of them was executed four times. Each time that the **REPNZ STOSB** instruction was executed, the CX register was decremented by one. The computer will execute this instruction 30 (001DH) times before it moves on to the next instruction in the program. To trace through all of that would have required a lot of time, so we stopped the trace.

Even if we entered the command "t 001D", it would take a while for all of the displays to scroll up the screen. Refer to the earlier discussion of GO breakpoints to see how you can speed up the execution of instructions that are repeated many times.

Assembling with DEBUG

The DOS 2 version, and subsequent versions, of DEBUG can be used to enter 8088/8086/8087 assembly language statements directly into memory. (DEBUG in MS-DOS 1.X does not have this capability.) The ASSEMBLE command is useful in composing short assembly language programs and in modifying existing assembly language programs. This command allows you to enter assembly language mnemonics and operands. Labels cannot be entered with the command. The advantage of using the ASSEMBLE command is that the machine code for each instruction is entered directly into memory, eliminating the need to go through an assembly process.

To use the ASSEMBLE command, enter **a** followed by the memory address of the first machine instruction to be entered. DEBUG assumes that the segment address of the instruction is stored in the CS register if you specify only an offset address. When the command is entered, DEBUG displays the start address and waits for you to enter an assembly language statement. DEBUG displays the next address in memory if the instruction entered is valid. If the instruction is not valid, DEBUG indicates the location of the error. Pressing Enter without an instruction terminates the assembly command.

We will demonstrate the ASSEMBLE command by writing a short assembly language program that may look familiar to you. If you follow the next example on your own computer, the segment addresses may not match those in the text.

```
C>debug
-a100
0976:0100 MOV AL,01
0976:0102 MOV DI,0200
0976:0105 MOV CX,001D
0976:0108 CLD
0976:0109 REPNZ STOSB
0976:010B MOV AL,24
0976:010D STOSB
0976:010E PUSH ES
0976:010F POP DS
0976:0110 MOV DX,0200
0976:0113 MOV AH,09
0976:0115 INT 21
0976:0117 INT 20
0976:0119      ←press Enter
-
```

You may have recognized this program as being the same one used earlier to demonstrate the GO and TRACE commands. Previously we created that program by entering the machine code directly into memory. This time we used DEBUG's mini-assembler to create the same program with assembly language mnemonics.

Naming a File with DEBUG

The NAME command (enter **n** or **N**) is used to specify the name of a file to DEBUG. The named file can be loaded into memory with the LOAD command or saved on a disk with the WRITE command. (LOAD and WRITE are discussed later in this chapter.)

To name a file, type **n** followed by the desired file specification. DEBUG will store the length of the file specification at offset address 0080H in the program segment prefix. The file spec itself is then stored beginning at offset 0081H. The file specification is "parsed," and the product is entered by MS-DOS at offset address 005CH in the psp.

In the following example, the NAME command is used to specify a file as "mytest1.pro". Then the DUMP command is used to see how this information is stored in memory:

```
-n mytest1.pro
-d 0050 L40
0958:0050  CD 21 CB 00 00 00 00 00-00 00 00 00 00 4D 59 54   M!K.........MYT
0958:0060  45 53 54 31 20 50 52 4F-00 00 00 00 00 20 20 20   EST1 PRO.....
0958:0070  20 20 20 20 20 20 20 20-00 00 00 00 00 00 00 00           ........
0958:0080  0B 4D 59 54 45 53 54 31-2E 50 52 4F 0D 00 00 00   .MYTEST1.PRO....
-
```

This dump begins at offset 50H in the psp. The length of the filename specified by the NAME command is stored at offset address 0080H. The file specification begins at offset 0081H. The parsed form of the file specification is stored beginning at offset 005CH. The 00H at offset 005CH indicates that any subsequent read or write of this file will be done at the default drive.

The NAME command is also used to pass filename parameters. As an example, let's say that the program "mytest1.pro" performs some operation on two data files that we will call "file1.dat" and "file2.dat". The names of these data files must somehow be passed to "mytest1.pro". If we were starting "mytest1.pro" in MS-DOS, we could pass the parameter information by entering the filenames in the start command:

```
C>mytest1.pro file1.dat file2.dat
```

If we are executing "mytest1.pro" under DEBUG, the parameters are passed using the NAME command. One or two parameters can be passed with the command. Parameters must be separated by a space or a comma:

```
-n file1.dat file2.dat
-d 0050 L50
0958:0050  CD 21 CB 00 00 00 00 00-00 00 00 00 00 4D 59 54   M!K.........FIL
0958:0060  45 31 20 20 20 44 41 54-00 00 00 00 00 46 49 4C   E1   DAT.....FIL
0958:0070  45 32 20 20 20 44 41 54-00 00 00 00 00 00 00 00   E2   DAT........
0958:0080  14 20 46 49 4C 45 31 2E-44 41 54 20 46 49 4C 45   . FILE1.DAT FILE
0958:0090  32 2E 44 41 54 0D 00 00-00 00 00 00 00 00 00 00   2.DAT..........
-
```

The information in the command is again stored starting at offset 0081H. The two parameters are parsed, and one is stored at offset 005CH and the other at 006CH. "Mytest1.pro" will look at these two addresses to find the names of the files on which it is to operate.

You will find more information on the NAME command in the following discussions of the DEBUG commands LOAD and WRITE.

Loading a File with DEBUG

The LOAD command (enter L or l) is used to load files into computer memory. The specification for the file to be loaded must be stored at offset 005CH in the program segment prefix. This is accomplished either by including the specification in the DEBUG start command or by using the NAME command.

Once the appropriate information is stored at offset 005CH, the file can be loaded by entering "L". You may enter the memory address at which loading is to begin. If you enter only an offset address, the command assumes that the segment address is stored in the CS register. If you do not enter an address, the file will be loaded at address CS:0100. Files with the extension ".COM" and ".EXE" are always loaded at CS:0100. Any address that is specified when these files are loaded is ignored.

After a file is loaded, DEBUG sets the BX and CX registers to the number of bytes loaded into memory. For .EXE and .HEX files, this number will be smaller than the size of the file. The following example loads the file "dbugpro.txt" into memory at the default address of CS: 0100:

```
C>debug
-n dbugpro.txt
-L
-r
AX=0000  BX=0000  CX=00CF  DX=0000  SP=FFEE  BP=0000  SI=0000  DI=0000
DS=0958  ES=0958  SS=0958  CS=0958  IP=0100   NV UP DI PL NZ NA PO NC
0958:0100 2A2A         SUB     CH,[BP+SI]                      SS:0000=CD
-
```

The BX and CX registers show that 207 (000000CFH) bytes have been read into memory. We could have achieved these same results by including the file specification in the DEBUG start command ("debug dbugpro.txt"). The only difference is that when the file is loaded with the LOAD command, the memory location of the load may be specified.

It is important to recognize that the LOAD command loads the file specified at offset 005CH and that this information changes each time the NAME command is used. For this reason, it is advisable to use the NAME command immediately before loading a file with the LOAD command.

LOAD can also be used to load consecutive sectors of a disk into memory. (Sectors are discussed in chapter 10.) To specify the address at which the load is to take place, use the same procedure as you did in loading a file. Then enter the number designation of the disk to be read (0=default, 1=A, 2=B, 3=C, etc.). Enter the relative number of the first sector loaded into memory and the number of sectors to be loaded. A maximum of 80H sectors can be loaded:

```
-L 0500 0 00 02
-
```

This command loads consecutive sectors of data into memory, beginning at memory address CS:0500. The sectors are loaded from the default drive. The first sector loaded is relative sector 00 (the first sector on the disk). Two (02) consecutive sectors are loaded.

Storing Data with DEBUG

The WRITE command (enter **w** or **W**) is used to store data on a disk. A valid file specification must be located at offset address 005CH into the program segment prefix before WRITE can be used. To accomplish this, either include the file specification in the DEBUG start command or use the NAME command.

Before a file can be stored, the size of the file must be specified in the BX and CX registers (a 4-byte hexadecimal number). It is good practice to check the values of the BX and CX registers (use the REGISTER command) before storing a file with the WRITE command.

You can specify the starting address in memory of the data to be written. If you specify only an offset address, DEBUG assumes that the segment address is stored in the CS register. If you do not specify an address, writing commences with the data at address CS:0100.

When a file is written, it is given the name specified at offset 005CH in the psp. If the disk already contains a file with that name, the existing file is overwritten. In order to avoid overwriting the wrong file, it is good practice to use the NAME command immediately before storing a file with the WRITE command. Files with the extension ".EXE" or ".HEX" cannot be written to disk using the WRITE command.

In the next example, the BX and CX registers are set to a value of 256 (00000100H). The NAME command is then used to set the file specification at offset address 005CH. The WRITE command writes to disk the 256 bytes starting at address CS:0100. The file is given the name "dbugtxt.pro". DEBUG then displays a message telling how many bytes have been stored:

```
-r BX
BX 0000
:0000
-r CX
CX 0000
:0100
-n dbugtxt.pro
-w
```

```
Writing 0100 bytes
-
```

You can use the WRITE command to write data to specific disk sectors. To specify the starting address of the data to be written, use the same procedure as you did earlier in writing a file. Then specify the number designation of the drive to be written to (0=A, 1=B, 2=C). Next, enter the relative disk sector at which writing is to begin. Finally, enter the number of consecutive sectors that will be written. A maximum of 80H sectors can be written.

In the following example, the data starting at address CS:0700 is written to the disk in drive B (1). The write begins at relative sector 50H (absolute sector 51H) and fills 20H consecutive sectors on the disk:

```
-w 0700 1 50 20
-
```

Writing to absolute sectors can be extremely powerful in modifying disk contents. It can also be extremely destructive if not used with caution. Double-check that all parameters are correct before you perform a sector write. Carelessness here can be very painful.

Comparing Blocks of Memory

The COMPARE command (enter c or C) is used to compare the contents of two blocks of memory. If unequal bytes are found, their addresses and the values at those addresses are displayed.

The command begins with the starting address of the first block of memory. If you enter only an offset address, DEBUG assumes that the segment address is stored in the DS register. To set the size of the blocks to be compared, enter the letter L followed by the number of bytes in each block. Then enter the starting address of the second block of memory. Again, entering only an offset address causes DEBUG to assume that the segment address is in the DS register.

In the next example, two 16-byte blocks of memory are compared. The first block begins at address CS:0000. The second block begins at CS:0030. The DUMP command is used two times to display each block. The COMPARE command is then used to display the addresses at which the blocks have unequal values:

```
-d CS:0000 L10
0958:0000  CD 20 00 20 00 9A EE FE-1D F0 34 02 68 06 62 02   M . ..N .p4.h.b.
-d CS:0030 L10
0958:0030  68 06 00 00 00 00 00 00-00 00 00 00 00 00 00 00   h...............
-c CS:0000 L10 CS:0030
0958:0000  CD  68  0958:0030
0958:0001  20  06  0958:0031
0958:0003  20  00  0958:0033
```

```
0958:0005   9A   00   0958:0035
0958:0006   EE   00   0958:0036
0958:0007   FE   00   0958:0037
0958:0008   1D   00   0958:0038
0958:0009   F0   00   0958:0039
0958:000A   34   00   0958:003A
0958:000B   02   00   0958:003B
0958:000C   68   00   0958:003C
0958:000D   06   00   0958:003D
0958:000E   62   00   0958:003E
0958:000F   02   00   0958:003F
```

The size of the blocks to be compared can also be set by including an ending offset address of the first block in the command. This offset will determine the ending address of the second block, since the blocks must be equal in size. Using this method, the preceding COMPARE command could be written as "c CS:0000 000F 0030". If no differences are found, the DEBUG prompt is displayed and another command can be entered.

Searching Memory

The SEARCH command (enter s or S) is used to search a block of memory for a list of byte values. The address at which the search is to start is included in the command. If you specify only an offset address as the start, DEBUG assumes that the segment address is stored in the DS register.

The address at which the search is to end is set in one of two ways. You can include in the command the ending address, which must be an offset address. Or you can specify the number of bytes to be searched by including in the command the letter "L", followed by the number of bytes to be searched.

Your command must include a list of byte values to be searched. The list may contain hexadecimal numbers and/or string characters. You must separate hexadecimal numbers by a space or a comma. String characters must be enclosed in quotation marks. Any string characters in the list will result in a search for the hexadecimal ASCII values of those characters.

Each time a match to the list is found, the address of the first byte of the match is displayed. If no matches are found, the DEBUG prompt is displayed and another command may be entered:

```
-s CS:0000 015F 44 4F 53 20 33 2E 33
0958:0004
-
```

This command searches the block of memory beginning at CS:0000 and ending at CS:015F for a match to the list of seven hexadecimal numbers included in the command. A match has been found starting at address CS:0004. The same command could have been entered as "s CS:0000 L160 'DOS 3.3'."

Moving Data in Memory

The MOVE command (enter **m** or **M**) moves a block of data from one memory location to another. The move overwrites any previously existing data at the destination. The command is executed in such a way that no data is lost if there is some overlap between the source and the destination. The source data is unaltered by the command unless it is overwritten.

The MOVE command must contain the starting address of the source data. If you enter only an offset address for the starting address, DEBUG assumes that the segment address is stored in the DS register.

The end address of the source data can be set in two ways. You can state in the command the end address, which must be an offset address. Or you can specify the length of the block to be moved by including in the command the letter "L", followed by a hexadecimal number.

In the following example, a dump displays a block of memory. The MOVE command is then used to move that block to another location. Another dump shows that the move was successful:

```
-d DS:0500 L20
0958:0500  CD 20 CB 00 00 00 00 00-00 00 00 00 00 00 00 00  M!K.............
0958:0510  4C 53 20 20 20 41 53 53-00 00 00 00 00 20 20 20  LS   ASS.....
-m DS:0500 051F DS:2000
-d DS:2000 L20
0958:2000  CD 20 CB 00 00 00 00 00-00 00 00 00 00 00 00 00  M!K.............
0958:2010  4C 53 20 20 20 41 53 53-00 00 00 00 00 20 20 20  LS   ASS.....
-
```

The MOVE command told DEBUG to take the block of data that starts at address DS:0500 and extends to DS:051F and move it to fill the block of memory that begins at address DS:2000. The move is actually a copy, since the original data was not altered. The same command could have been written as "m 0050 L20 2000."

Filling Memory

The FILL command (enter **f** or **F**) is used to fill a block of memory with a list of values. The command must include the starting address of the fill. If you do not state a segment address, this value is assumed to be stored in the DS register.

The address at which the fill is to end can be set in two ways. You can include in the command the end address, which must be an offset address. Or you can set the length of the block to be filled by entering in the command the letter "L", followed by a hexadecimal number.

The FILL command includes a list that will fill the memory block. The list can consist of hexadecimal numbers and/or string characters. You must separate hexadecimal numbers by a space or a comma. String characters must be enclosed in quotation marks. Hexadecimal ASCII values of string characters are stored in memory.

If the list is shorter than the block of memory to be filled, the list is repeated until the block is filled. If the list is longer than the block of memory, the list is copied until the block is filled, and the remaining characters in the list are ignored.

In this example, a portion of memory is filled with a list of values. A dump then displays that portion of memory:

```
-f DS:0100 017F 21 23 24 25
-d DS:0100 L80
0958:0100  21 23 24 25 21 23 24 25-21 23 24 25 21 23 24 25   !#$%!#$%!#$%!#$%
0958:0110  21 23 24 25 21 23 24 25-21 23 24 25 21 23 24 25   !#$%!#$%!#$%!#$%
0958:0120  21 23 24 25 21 23 24 25-21 23 24 25 21 23 24 25   !#$%!#$%!#$%!#$%
0958:0130  21 23 24 25 21 23 24 25-21 23 24 25 21 23 24 25   !#$%!#$%!#$%!#$%
0958:0140  21 23 24 25 21 23 24 25-21 23 24 25 21 23 24 25   !#$%!#$%!#$%!#$%
0958:0150  21 23 24 25 21 23 24 25-21 23 24 25 21 23 24 25   !#$%!#$%!#$%!#$%
0958:0160  21 23 24 25 21 23 24 25-21 23 24 25 21 23 24 25   !#$%!#$%!#$%!#$%
0958:0170  21 23 24 25 21 23 24 25-21 23 24 25 21 23 24 25   !#$%!#$%!#$%!#$%
```

The FILL command fills the block of memory starting at DS:0100 and ending at DS:017F with the hexadecimal numbers 21H, 23H, 24H, and 25H. The same command could have been written as "f 0100 L80 '!#$%'."

Sending Data to a Port

The microprocessor inside your computer communicates with the outside world through the use of ports. The keyboard is connected to one port, the display screen to another, the printer to another, and so on. Each port is identified by its address, just as memory locations are identified by their addresses. Port addresses are very specific for each computer. Refer to the information supplied by your computer's manufacturer for port addresses.

The microprocessor reads data from a peripheral device (such as the keyboard) by reading the data sent in from the device's port. Similarly, the microprocessor sends data to a peripheral device (such as the printer) by sending out data from the device's port.

The OUTPUT command (enter o or O) is DEBUG's way of sending a byte value to an output port. The command must include the address of the output port and the byte value to be sent. The two parameters must be separated by a space or a comma. In the following example, the byte value 3CH is sent to output port 62H:

```
-o 62 3C
-
```

Reading Data from a Port

The INPUT command (enter i or I) is used to obtain and display 1 byte of input from a specified port. The command includes the address of the port.

DEBUG then reads 1 byte from that port and displays its value on the screen. In the next example, 1 byte is read from port 62H. The value at that port (03H) is then displayed:

```
-i 62
03
-
```

Hexadecimal Arithmetic with DEBUG

The HEXADECIMAL Arithmetic command (enter h or H) is used to perform hexadecimal addition and subtraction on two numbers. The numbers can be one to four hexadecimal digits in length and must be separated in the command by a space or a comma. DEBUG adds the numbers and displays the result. DEBUG also subtracts the second number from the first and displays the result.

In the following example, 05CDH is added to 320FH, yielding a sum of 37DCH. Then 05CDH is subtracted from 320FH, yielding a difference of 2C42H:

```
-h 320F 05CD
37DC  2C42
-
```

If the second number entered is larger than the first, the difference is displayed in two's complement representation. (Refer to a text on assembly language programming for a discussion of two's complement representation.)

Proceeding through a Loop

Consider what would happen if you wanted to use DEBUG to execute an interrupt. For example, let us say that the current status of DEBUG is as follows:

```
-r
AX=3000  BX=0000  CX=0000  DX=0000  SP=FFEE  BP=0000  SI=0000  DI=0000
DS=5C35  ES=5C35  SS=5C35  CS=5C35  IP=0100   NV UP EI PL NZ NA PO NC
5C35:0100 CD21          INT    21
-
```

If you simply enter g, DEBUG will execute interrupt 21 without any problem. The problem arises when control returns from the interrupt. There is nothing to stop program execution and DEBUG will simply attempt to execute whatever instruction is located at offset address 102. More often than not, such conditions result in a system crash, which necessitates a reboot. There are ways to deal with this problem (such as entering the command "g=102"), but they place the burden of determining where execution should be halted on you.

The (P)roceed command is implemented in DOS 4 to rectify this problem. Simply enter **p** to execute an interrupt. Execution terminates upon return from the interrupt. The following example illustrates:

```
AX=3000  BX=0000  CX=0000  DX=0000  SP=FFEE  BP=0000  SI=0000  DI=0000
DS=5C35  ES=5C35  SS=5C35  CS=5C35  IP=0100   NV UP EI PL NZ NA PO NC
5C35:0100 CD21           INT    21
-p

AX=0004  BX=0000  CX=0000  DX=0000  SP=FFEE  BP=0000  SI=0000  DI=0000
DS=5C35  ES=5C35  SS=5C35  CS=5C35  IP=0102   NV UP EI PL NZ NA PO NC
5C35:0102 5B             POP    BX
-
```

The Proceed command can also be used to execute a loop of program code, a subroutine call, or a repeat string instruction. The complete syntax for the command is as follows:

p [=*address*][*value*]

The optional "=address" parameter may be a segment:offset address or simply an offset address. If no segment is specified, the address in CS is used as the segment address. The current value of CS:IP is used if no "=address" parameter is used.

The optional "value" parameter specifies the number of instructions to execute. The default for "value" is 1. In the above example, only one instruction (**INT 21**) is executed. Of course, the code of the interrupt handler is also executed. If "value" had been set to 2, then the instruction immediately following **INT 21** would also have been executed.

Using DEBUG with Expanded Memory

The DOS 4 version of DEBUG implements four commands that allow DEBUG to manipulate expanded memory. The "xa" command is used to allocate a specific number of expanded memory pages. The "xd" command is used to deallocate a set of expanded memory pages. The "xm" command is used to map an expanded memory page into conventional memory. Finally, "xs" is used to display the current status of expanded memory. Use of these commands is illustrated in chapter 12.

16

LINK

Overview of LINK
Starting LINK
LINK Switches

This chapter describes the use of the MS-DOS utility program called LINK.
LINK is used in compiling or assembling computer programs. LINK is not
supplied with all implementations of DOS. However, LINK is generally provided with the assemblers and compilers whose use requires LINK. The
material in this chapter is applicable to all versions of LINK.

Overview of LINK

Compilers and assemblers produce *object code,* a code that can be executed by a computer without undergoing further simplification. LINK is an MS-DOS utility program used to modify a collection or module of object code so that the module is relocatable. A *relocatable module* is a computer program or a computer program subroutine that will execute successfully regardless of where it is stored in computer memory.

LINK is also used to combine separately produced object modules into a single relocatable module. LINK produces a single relocatable module, called a *run file,* by combining and modifying user-specified object modules. LINK searches for the specified object modules on the specified or default disk drive. A message is displayed, directing the user to change diskettes and press Enter if LINK cannot locate a module. At the user's option, LINK will produce a list file containing information about the code in the run file. LINK will also search specified libraries for any object modules that are needed to complete the run file.

VM.TMP

LINK uses as much memory as is available in creating a relocatable module. LINK will create a temporary disk file named VM.TMP on the default drive and display the following message if the system does not have enough free memory:

```
VM.TMP has been created
```

LINK will erase any existing file named VM.TMP when it creates a temporary storage file. VM.TMP is erased when LINK ends.

Starting LINK

There are three methods for starting LINK. In each case, one of the system drives must contain the MS-DOS file LINK.EXE. In the following examples, LINK.EXE is on the default drive. LINK.EXE is not supplied with MS-DOS 3.3 and 4.X system diskettes. You must secure the "Utilities" diskette that comes with the Technical Reference manual in order to obtain the 4.X implementation of LINK.)

Starting LINK involves entering one or more filenames in response to LINK's prompts. You have the option of preceding each filename with a drive designator and/or a path specifier.

Method 1

In the first method, LINK is started by typing **link** and pressing Enter. Begin the command with the letter designator of the drive containing LINK.EXE if LINK.EXE is not on the default drive:

```
C> link
```

MS-DOS will load LINK and display a copyright message followed by the prompt:

```
Object Modules [ .OBJ]:
```

This is a prompt to enter the object module(s) that LINK will use to produce the run file (the relocatable module). Individual modules must be separated by a space or a plus (+) sign. LINK assumes that each object module has an extension of ".OBJ". Any other extension must be specified.

To illustrate, let's suppose that you have used a compiler or an assembler to create the object modules "example1.obj" and "example2.obj". To combine them into a single relocatable module, you would enter their filenames in response to the initial LINK prompt:

```
Object Modules [ .OBJ]: example1+example2
```

Since no extensions are specified, LINK assumes that the modules have an extension of ".OBJ".

LINK next prompts you to enter the name to be given to the run file:

```
Run File [EXAMPLE1.EXE]:
```

If you do not enter a filename, LINK will default to the filename of the first object module listed in the previous command. A run file must have an extension of ".EXE". Any other extension will be ignored.

When you press Enter, LINK will display the following prompt:

```
List File [NUL.MAP]:
```

Enter a filename if you want LINK to create a *list file*. The list file contains the name and size of the segments within the relocatable module. The list file will also contain any errors that are detected by LINK. (Later in the chapter, we will discuss list files again and present an example.) LINK gives the list file an extension of ".MAP" if an extension is not specified. Press Enter if you do not want a list file created.

LINK's final prompt asks you for the names of any library files to be searched for unresolved references:

```
Libraries [.LIB]:
```

Some compilers contain a default library that LINK will search if you press Enter. LINK will look for the compiler library on the default drive. If the library is not on the default drive, LINK will look for it on the drive specified by the compiler.

You may specify up to eight library files to be searched. LINK assumes an extension of ".LIB" if an extension is not specified. Individual filenames must be separated by a space or a plus sign (+). If your response to the prompt includes a drive designator, LINK will look for the listed library file(s) on the specified drive. LINK will search the drive specified by the compiler (or the default drive) if no drive designator is included.

```
Libraries [.LIB]: c:mylib+yourlib+a:hislib+c:
```

The preceding response directs LINK to search the files "mylib.lib" and "yourlib.lib" on the C drive, "hislib.lib" on the A drive, and the default library (if one exists) on the C drive.

LINK will search the library files in the order that they are listed. If there is a default library, it will be searched last. When LINK finds the module that contains the symbol it is looking for, that module is processed in the normal fashion. LINK displays a message telling you to enter a new drive designator letter when it cannot find a specified library file.

You can use a comma to end a response to a LINK prompt. When you use a comma, you can type your response to the next prompt without waiting for the prompt to be displayed:

```
Object Modules [.OBJ]: example1,
List File [NUL.MAP]: example1
Libraries [.LIB]:
```

The first command tells LINK the name of the object module. The comma following the object module tells LINK that the response to the next prompt (run file) is also entered on the first line. In this case, no name is entered for the run file, so LINK assigns the default filename to the run file. Notice that the prompt for the run file is not displayed. The last two commands tell LINK to create a list file named "example1.map" and to search the default library file.

The first two commands in the previous example could have been combined as follows:

```
Object Modules [.OBJ]: example1,,example1
Libraries [.LIB]:
```

In this example, the first command ends with two commas, followed by the name that LINK will assign to the list file. Notice that the prompt for the list file is not displayed.

If you end any of the responses to a LINK prompt with a semicolon, the remaining responses will be assigned their defaults. No further prompts will be displayed:

```
Object Modules [.OBJ]: example1;
```

This command tells LINK that "example1" is the object module. Since the command ends in a semicolon, the remaining prompts are not displayed and are assigned their defaults.

Method 2

In the second method for starting LINK, the responses to the LINK prompts can be included in the LINK start command. The responses must be listed in the order in which LINK displays the prompts (Object Modules, Run File, List File, Libraries). You must separate the responses with a comma.

LINK will prompt for any responses that were not included in the start command:

```
C>link example1,,example1

Microsoft Object Linker V2.00
(C) Copyright 1982 by Microsoft Inc.

Libraries [.LIB]:
```

The start command tells MS-DOS to load LINK. The start command also tells LINK to search for the module "example1.obj", assign the run file its default filename, and create a list file named "example1.map". Notice that the prompts for these responses are not displayed.

If you include responses to LINK prompts in the start command and if you end the command with a semicolon, any subsequent prompts will not be displayed and they will be assigned their defaults:

```
C>link example1;

Microsoft Object Linker V2.00
(C) Copyright 1982 by Microsoft Inc.
```

This start command loads LINK and tells LINK to search for "example1.obj". The three remaining prompts are not displayed and are assigned their defaults.

Method 3

The third method for starting LINK requires that a set of LINK responses be stored in a text file. These responses must be stored in the order that the LINK prompts are displayed. LINK can then be started by including the name of the text file in the LINK start command. This method is convenient when you are entering a long list of object modules. A long response to the object module or library prompt may be stored on several lines by using a plus sign (+) to continue a response onto the next line.

A text file containing a sequence of responses can be created from your keyboard. Starting at the MS-DOS command level (the DOS prompt is displayed), type **copy con:** and then type the filename of the text file that you will be creating. The filename may be preceded by a drive designator letter and/or a pathname.

In the following example, a text file named "sample1.txt" is created.

```
C>copy con: sample1.txt              ←Enter
example1+example2+example3,,;        ←Enter
^Z                                   ←you press Ctrl-Z and Enter
          1 File(s) copied
```

To start LINK with a text file, type **link**, followed by a blank space and the symbol @, followed by the filename and extension of the text file. LINK will assume that the first character in the filename is a blank if you include a space betwen the "@" and the filename of the text file:

```
C>link @sample1.txt

Microsoft Object Linker V2.00
(C) Copyright 1982 by Microsoft Inc.

Object Modules [.OBJ]: example1+example2+example3
Run File [EXAMPLE1.EXE]:
List File [EXAMPLE1.MAP]:
```

The responses to the prompts have been extracted from the file "sample1.txt". LINK automatically searches for the object modules "example1", "example2", and "example3". LINK then assigns the default filename to the run file and creates a list file named "example1.map". The library prompt is not displayed because of the semicolon at the end of the response line. LINK assigns the default response to the library prompt.

LINK Switches

LINK provides seven optional switches that you can specify when starting LINK. Each switch directs LINK to perform certain tasks when constructing a relocatable module. To specify a switch, type a forward slash (/) followed by the first letter of the switch name at the end of a response line. You may include a switch when using any of the three methods for starting LINK. Switches may be specified on any response line. Each letter specifying a switch must be preceded by a forward slash.

The /High Switch

Within each relocatable module, LINK stores information that tells MS-DOS where to load the module in computer memory. Normally, this information instructs MS-DOS to load the module at the lowest-available address in memory. The **/high switch** tells LINK to construct a module that MS-DOS will load at the highest-available memory address.

The next command directs LINK to combine the object modules "example1" and "example2" into a relocatable module. LINK will produce a run file named "example1.exe" (the default) and a list file named "example.map". The default library file will be searched. The LINK switch /high (entered as /h) directs LINK to produce a run file that MS-DOS will load at as high a memory location as possible. Enter the following command:

```
C>link example1+example2,,example1;/h
```

The /high switch should not be used when linking Pascal or FORTRAN object modules.

The /Dsallocate Switch

The **/dsallocate switch** (entered as **/d**) directs LINK to create a run file that loads all data at the high end of the data segment. If this switch is not used, LINK will create a run file that loads data at the low end of the data segment. The /dsallocate switch is required when linking Pascal or FORTRAN object modules.

The /Linenumber Switch

LINK will generate a list file when it is instructed to do so. The list file contains a list of the segments in the run file as well as each segment's relative start and stop addresses. A *segment* is a contiguous portion of the run file, which may be up to 64K bytes in length. Segments are generally used to partition a run file into functional components. Each segment within an object module is assigned to a class by the programmer. LINK combines the segments of the specified object modules according to each segment's class.

A segment's *relative start address* is the location of the first byte in a segment relative to the first byte in the run file. For example, if the first byte of a segment is the first byte of the run file, the segment's relative start address is 0. A segment's *relative stop address* is the location of the last byte in a segment relative to the first byte in the run file. For example, if the last byte of a segment is the 100th byte of the run file, the segment's relative stop address is 99 (99 bytes from the first byte in the run file).

The **/linenumber switch** (entered as **/l**) tells LINK to include in the list file the line numbers and relative addresses of the *source statements* in each object module. Source statements are the statements in a computer program in the form that they are entered by the programmer. The /linenumber switch only works with object modules produced by a compiler that numbers each source statement (such as the BASIC compiler).

The /Map Switch

Symbols (such as variable names) that are shared by two or more object modules are called *public symbols*. Symbols are designated as being "public" by the compiler or assembler used to create the modules. The **/map switch** (entered as **/m**) directs LINK to include in the list file all public symbols that are defined in the specified object modules.

The next set of commands directs LINK to create a list file named "example.map". The MS-DOS command TYPE is then used to display "example.map". Enter the following:

```
C>link example1,,example1/m

Microsoft Object Linker V2.00
(C) Copyright 1982 by Microsoft Inc.

Libraries [.LIB]:


C>type example.map
```

Start	Stop	Length	Name	Class
00000H	000C7H	00C8H	STACKSG	STACK
000D0H	000D5H	0006H	DATASG	DATA
000E0H	000F2H	0013H	CODESG	CODE

```
Origin     Group
```

Address	Publics by Name
000D:0004	AAA
000D:0002	PRICE
000D:0000	QTY

Address	Publics by Value
000D:0000	QTY
000D:0002	PRICE
000D:0004	AAA

```
Program entry point at 000E:0000
```

The first portion of the list file contains the name, class, length, and start and stop addresses of each segment in the run file.

The second section in the list file is headed `Origin Group`. A *group* consists of one or more segments contained in the specified object modules that are to be combined into a single segment in the run file. Groups are defined by the programmer during program assembly or compiling. Any groups defined by the compiler or assembler are listed here, along with their relative starting addresses (origin) within the relocatable module. The module in this example does not contain any groups.

The third section of the list file is an alphabetical listing of the public symbols contained in the object modules. The relative addresses of each symbol within the relocatable module are also listed.

The fourth section of the list file is a listing of the public symbols contained in the object modules ordered by their relative addesses within the module.

The final line in the list file gives the relative address of the run file's *entry point*. The entry point is the location of the first executable computer instruction contained in the run file.

The /Pause Switch

The /pause switch (entered as /p) is used to suspend LINK execution before the run file is written to disk. This allows you to swap disks. To demonstrate the use of the /pause switch, enter the following:

```
C>link example1,,example1/p

Microsoft Object Linker V2.00
(C) Copyright 1982 by Microsoft Inc.

Libraries [.LIB]:
About to generate .EXE file
Change disks      ←press Enter when ready
```

It is important not to remove a disk if the VM.TMP file or the list file is to be stored on it.

The /Stack:[*Number*] Switch

The *stack* is a segment within the run file that is used to store data during program execution. Compilers and assemblers provide information in the object modules that allows LINK to compute the required size of the stack. The /stack:[*number*] switch can be used to override the stack size that is indicated in the object modules.

Any hexadecimal number from 0001H to FFFFH may be specified for the size of the stack in bytes. LINK will create a stack with 0200H bytes if you specify a number less than 0200H (decimal 512). Enter the following command to create a run file with a stack that contains 0300H bytes:

```
C>link example1,,example1/s:300
```

The /No Switch

The **/no switch** (entered as **/n**) directs LINK not to search the default library file for unresolved external references. For example, if you are linking modules that were created with a Pascal compiler, you could enter "/n" at the end of a response to a LINK prompt and LINK would not search "pascal.lib" for any unresolved external references.

3

MS-DOS Commands

- APPEND
- ASSIGN
- ATTRIB
- BACKUP
- BREAK
- BUFFERS
- CALL
- CHCP
- CHDIR
- CHKDSK
- CLS
- COMMAND
- COMP
- COPY
- COUNTRY
- CTTY
- DATE
- DEL
- DEVICE

- DIR
- DISKCOMP
- DISKCOPY
- ECHO
- ERASE
- EXE2BIN
- FASTOPEN
- FCBS
- FDISK
- FILES
- FIND
- FOR
- FORMAT
- GOTO
- GRAFTABL
- GRAPHICS
- IF
- INSTALL
- JOIN

- KEYB
- KEYBxx
- LABEL
- LASTDRIVE
- MEM
- MKDIR
- MODE
- MORE
- NLSFUNC
- PATH
- PAUSE
- PRINT
- PROMPT
- RECOVER
- REM
- RENAME
- REPLACE
- RESTORE
- RMDIR

- SELECT
- SET
- SHARE
- SHELL
- SHIFT
- SORT
- STACKS
- SUBST
- SWITCHAR
- SWITCHES
- SYS
- TIME
- TREE
- TRUENAME
- TYPE
- VER
- VERIFY
- VOL
- XCOPY

MS-DOS Commands

MS-DOS is a *command-driven* operating system. In other words, when you enter a command into your computer, MS-DOS carries it out by performing the appropriate actions. This part of the book will discuss each of the MS-DOS commands, explaining their characteristics, use, and format and giving you examples of each command. The discussion of each command begins with a heading such as the one you see here:

CLS

Internal
MS-DOS 2.X, 3.X, 4.X

The first line in the heading shows the command in uppercase letters. The second line describes the command as being either an internal or an external command. *Internal* commands are those commands that have been built into MS-DOS. Whenever MS-DOS is booted, these commands are automatically loaded into memory. Internal commands are executed immediately and may be used any time you are operating in MS-DOS, without reinserting the system diskette. Some examples of internal commands are BREAK, CHDIR, COPY, CLS, TIME, and TYPE.

External commands are stored on a disk (usually the system diskette), in the form of a file, until they are needed by MS-DOS. Some examples of external commands are CHKDSK, DISKCOPY, FORMAT, PRINT, and RE-COVER. When you tell MS-DOS to execute an external command, it must load the file containing the command into memory before it can perform the command. Therefore, before you can use an external command, the file containing the command must be in a disk drive. If the external command is in the current directory of the default drive, enter the command name (along with any required parameters):

```
C>chkdsk a:
```

If the external command is in the current directory of a drive other than the default, precede the command name with the letter specifier of the appropriate drive:

```
A>c:chkdsk b:
```

If the external command is not in the current directory of a drive, precede the command name with the path specifier to the appropriate directory:

```
A>c:\dos\chkdsk b:
```

The PATH command can be used to establish a set of path specifiers for MS-DOS to use in looking for external commands. Path specifiers in this set need not be included on the command line when invoking an external command. Current directories, default drives, and path specifiers are discussed in chapters 2 and 3.

The third line in the heading tells you which version(s) of MS-DOS can execute the command. The notation "MS-DOS 2.X" refers to all versions of MS-DOS with a major version of 2 (e.g., 2.00, 2.10). Similarly, 3.X refers to all versions with a major version number of 3, and 4.X refers to all versions with a major version number of 4. Following the convention used throughout this book, the terms "MS-DOS," "DOS," and "PC-DOS" are used interchangeably, unless otherwise specified.

Command Format

Whenever MS-DOS displays the system prompt (e.g., **A>**, **B>**, **C>**), you may enter a command. However, you must use the proper *format*, or pattern, for that particular command. Let's look at some examples.

The format for the command CLS (CLear Screen) is simply "CLS". This means that to execute the command, you type **cls** and press the Enter key. Remember that you may use either uppercase or lowercase letters to type the command; MS-DOS will automatically convert all letters to uppercase.

C>*cls* ←Enter

Many MS-DOS commands require that you include one or more *parameters* when you enter the command. A parameter is an item that gives additional information to MS-DOS. In the command formats used in this book, parameters appear in lowercase italic type. The command's format will tell you which, if any, parameters are used with the command. For example, the format for the command SYS (SYStem files) is "SYS *d:*". The "*d:*" is a parameter indicating that you should specify a drive. If you do not enter a drive letter designator (for example, c: or a:), MS-DOS will use the *d*efault drive. Suppose that you wish to use drive A. Your command statement will look like this:

C>*sys a:* ←Enter

Some parameters are optional. When the parameter is enclosed in square brackets [like this], the inclusion of that parameter is optional. For example, the format for the command VOL (VOLume) is "VOL [*d:*]". Since the "*d:*" is in brackets, you may enter the command with or without the drive designator. MS-DOS will interpret the command one way if the parameter is present, another way if it is not.

Many MS-DOS 2.X, 3.X, and 4.X command formats include the word "path." *Path* is a parameter telling MS-DOS which path, or course, to take in travelling from one directory to another. In place of the word "path," you must enter the directory names, separated by a backslash (\). The directory names become the "path specifiers." Let's look at the format for the command MKDIR (MaKe DIRectory):

MKDIR [*d:*]*path*

The format tells us that the drive designator is optional, since the "*d:*" is in brackets. However, "*path*" is not in brackets, so you must enter a directory name(s). You can find more information about paths in chapter 3.

Other parameters frequently found in MS-DOS command formats are *filename* and *.ext*. When you see the words "filename" and ".ext" in the format, you must type the name of the file (up to eight characters in length) and its extension (a period and up to three characters), if there is an extension. For example, the format for the command TYPE is:

TYPE [*d:*][*path*]*filename*[*.ext*]

As you can see, this command requires a filename parameter. Optional parameters are the drive designator, path specifier, and filename extension.

Some MS-DOS commands require a *source* and a *target* file. The source contains the data to be used in executing the command. The target contains the data that is the result of command execution. You may specify multiple sources and targets with the use of wildcards, as discussed later in this introduction.

Command Notation

You have probably noticed that several kinds of typefaces and punctuation marks are used in the command formats. Items in **boldface** type are ones that must be entered. You may use either uppercase or lowercase letters in entering them. Items in *italics* are optional variables and are enclosed in square brackets [ ]. Items in ***boldface italics*** are variables that must be entered.

Include all punctuation marks as shown in the format, including commas, colons, semicolons, question marks, slashes, and quotes. Also include any parentheses and plus signs.

Items separated by a vertical bar | are either/or entries. ON|OFF means either ON or OFF. An ellipsis . . . following items means that you may repeat the items as often as needed. As mentioned before, items in square brackets are optional. Do not enter vertical bars, ellipses, or square brackets.

Wildcards

Most MS-DOS commands allow the use of *wildcards* in filenames and filename extensions. Sometimes called "global characters," wildcards replace one or more specific characters in the filename or its extension. When wildcards (? and *) are used, the command is executed once for each matching file that is found. You will find more information about wildcards in chapter 2.

Switches

Another kind of parameter found in some MS-DOS commands is a *switch*. A switch instructs MS-DOS to execute a command in a certain way. To use a switch, type a forward slash (/) followed by a letter or number. The command format will show you which, if any, switches can be used with the command. For example, here is the format for the DIR (DIRectory) command:

DIR [*d*:][*path*][*filename*][.*ext*]][/P][/W]

As you can see, DIR has two switches, /p and /w. Both are optional, since they are enclosed in brackets. Depending on which switch you select, MS-DOS will scroll the directory and pause (/p) when the screen is full, or it will list the directory in wide (/w) columns across the screen. Any switches that may be used with a particular command are explained in the discussion for that command.

Using MS-DOS on a Network

There are now many computer network packages available that will link computers running under MS-DOS. The details of setting up and starting these networks depend on the package used and will not be discussed here. Instead, we will make some general remarks about how MS-DOS commands behave on a network.

Network drives are assigned drive letters, just like drives on your own machine. Suppose that Manny and Joe are using separate computers, but both the computers are on the same network. Manny's computer has drives A, B, and C. Joe's computer also has drives A, B, and C. Manny decides that he wants to use Joe's drive C and that he (Manny) wants to call it drive D. Manny enters a command telling MS-DOS and the network software that, from now on, whenever Manny says drive D, he means Joe's drive C. To Manny, Joe's drive C is network drive D.

Most MS-DOS commands treat network drives like any other drive. For example, if Manny enters the command "dir d:", he sees the contents of Joe's drive C. However, some MS-DOS commands (see box) do not work with network drives. For most of these commands, prohibiting their use with network drives seems reasonable. Network drives are shared resources and must be used respectfully. For example, Joe probably would not appreciate it if Manny entered the command "format d:" and MS-DOS executed it. While some of the restricted commands (such as FASTOPEN and VERIFY) do not appear to pose any danger to the network drives, they may nevertheless be unusable on network drives because of implementation problems.

MS-DOS Commands That Cannot Be Used with Network Drives

CHKDSK	FASTOPEN	JOIN	SUBST
DISKCOMP	FDISK	LABEL	SYS
DISKCOPY	FORMAT	RECOVER	VERIFY

APPEND

External
MS-DOS 3.2, 3.3, 4.X

Function: Directs MS-DOS to nonexecutable files

Format: APPEND [/E] [/X]
             APPEND *d:path* [*;d:*[*path*]] . . .
             APPEND /X:ON (DOS 4.X only)
             APPEND /X:OFF (DOS 4.X only)
             APPEND /PATH:ON (DOS 4.X only)
             APPEND /PATH:OFF (DOS 4.X only)

Examples: append /x /e
             append c:\word;c:\turbo

The APPEND command provides a long awaited, much needed enhancement to the PATH command. PATH establishes a list of subdirectories for MS-DOS to search when a file is not located in the current directory. Unfortunately, the information supplied by PATH is useful only in locating files with a filename extension of EXE, COM, or BAT (executable files). The APPEND command corrects this deficiency by allowing the inclusion of nonexecutable files in a directory search path.

Many programs, particularly word processors, consist of an executable file (the "program") plus one or more nonexecutable files. A help facility is an example of a nonexecutable file. Versions of MS-DOS prior to 3.2 have no way of finding such files if the files are not located in the current directory. APPEND overcomes this limitation by providing MS-DOS with path information to all files regardless of filename extension.

The parameters used with APPEND are path specifiers separated by semicolons. APPEND allows up to 128 characters in the complete path specification.

An Example

The word processor used to write this book consists of one executable file ("wp.exe") and four nonexecutable files ("wpmsg.txt", "wpsysd.sys", "wphelp.txt", "wpque.sys"). The five files are stored in the subdirectory \WORD. APPEND is used to let MS-DOS know about the location of these files as follows:

```
C>append c:\word
```

Once the command is entered, any subdirectory can be used as the current directory, since APPEND provides the operating system with the information required to locate all of the files used by the word processor. Notice that the APPEND path specifier included a drive letter. This is a good practice to follow because it allows MS-DOS to locate files regardless of which drive is currently the default.

APPEND is a terminate and stay resident program (see chapter 13). This means that the first time you invoke APPEND, the program is read from the disk and stored in memory. APPEND then remains in memory until the system is turned off or restarted. Once loaded into memory, APPEND can be used to display, modify, or cancel the APPEND path specifier.

Displaying the APPEND Path Specifier

MS-DOS will display the APPEND path specifier in response to APPEND.

```
C>append c:\word

C>append
APPEND=c:\WORD

C>append c:\word;c:\turbo
C>append
APPEND=C:\WORD;C:\TURBO
```

Cancelling APPEND's Path Specifier

APPEND followed by a semicolon cancels the APPEND path specifier.

```
C>append
APPEND=C:\WORD;C:\TURBO

C>append ;

C>append
No Append
```

APPEND remains in memory when the path specifier is cancelled. A new specifier can be set at any time.

DOS Functions and the /X Switch

MS-DOS carries out most of its work through the use of the MS-DOS *functions*. Use of the functions is discussed in appendix A, but understanding the role of three of the functions is helpful when using the APPEND command.

EXEC

MS-DOS uses the function called EXEC to load and run executable files. You can use the /x switch, an optional APPEND parameter, to control the operating system's use of EXEC.

The /x switch allows EXEC to use the APPEND search path to locate and run executable files. The following example, using DOS 4.X, illustrates the use of the /x switch.

```
C:\>append                    ←load APPEND without /x
C:\>append c:\batch           ←set APPEND search path
C:\>test                      ←execute "test.bat"
Bad command or file name      ←EXEC can't find "test.bat"
C:\>append /x                 ←make search path available
C:\>test                      ←try "test.bat" again
TEST.BAT executed             ←EXEC can find it now
```

The first command in the example loads APPEND into memory. The command does not include the /x switch; therefore, the APPEND search path is not available to EXEC.

The second command sets the APPEND path specifier to be C:\BATCH.

The command **test** is simply a command to execute the batch file "test.bat". In the example, "test.bat" happens to be in the directory C:\BATCH. Because the APPEND search path is not available, EXEC cannot locate "test.bat" and the batch file fails to execute.

The command **append /x** makes the APPEND search path available to EXEC. EXEC locates "test.bat" and the batch file echoes a message to indicate that it has executed successfully.

FIND FIRST and FIND NEXT

DOS uses the function FIND FIRST to locate the first file in a directory that matches a wildcard specification. The function FIND NEXT is used to locate any additional files in the directory that match the wildcard. As an example, the command "copy *.bat b:" uses FIND FIRST to identify the first file in a directory that has an extension of BAT. After copying the first file, the command uses FIND NEXT to identify the next BAT file in the directory. The file is copied and FIND NEXT is used again to locate the next BAT file. The process repeats until all of the BAT files have been copied.

The /x switch controls the action taken by DOS when FIND FIRST fails to find a match in the current directory. If /x has been "set" (by executing "append /x"), FIND FIRST will look in each of the directories of the AP-PEND path specifier until it finds a match for the wildcard. If /x has not been set, FIND FIRST will send DOS a "File not found" error, and the process will terminate.

When /x is set, FIND FIRST will stop in the first directory that contains a match. FIND NEXT is then used to locate additional matches in the same directory. The process will terminate when the last file in that directory is located.

Using the /X Switch

The /x switch is more flexible in DOS 4.X than in DOS 3.2 or 3.3. In 4.X, you may enter "append /x" (or, equivalently, "append /x:on") at any time. Similarly, you can turn /x off at any time using the command "append /x:off".

In DOS 3.2 and 3.3, the /x switch can only be used the first time APPEND is invoked. Thus, if you load APPEND into memory with the command "append", the /x switch is permanently off. The only way to turn it on is to reboot the system and load APPEND with the command "append /x". Similarly, when the switch is on, the only way to turn it off is to reboot and load APPEND without using the /x.

The /E Switch

DOS normally stores the value of the APPEND path specifier at a memory location known only to the operating system. Users and application programs have no direct access to the specifier.

You can use the /e switch to direct DOS to store the APPEND path specifier as an environment variable. Environment variables are directly accessible to both users and application programs. Enter the command **set** to display the DOS environment variables.

This sounds harmless enough. Unfortunately, the /e switch causes DOS to do some very strange things. For example, if the /e switch is set and the /x switch is also set, DOS will refuse to recognize drive letter parameters in the DIR command. If drive C is the default drive and you enter the command "dir a:", DOS will display the contents of the directory on drive C.

The /e switch can be used only when APPEND is first loaded into memory.

The /Path Switch

So far you have seen how DOS uses APPEND when it is unable to locate a file. DOS normally uses APPEND whether or not a filename is preceded by a path specifier. For example, if the command "copy c:\batch\test.bat b:" is entered, and the directory C:\BATCH does not contain a file named "test.bat", DOS will use the APPEND path specifier in an attempt to locate the file.

The /path switch, available with the DOS 4.X implementation of APPEND, allows you to modify this behavior. If you enter "append /path:off" DOS will not use APPEND when a filename is preceded by a path specifier or a drive letter. For example, if you enter "append /path:off" and then try to execute the COPY command in the previous paragraph, the command will simply terminate if the directory C:\BATCH does not contain a file named "test.bat".

The command "append /path:on" reverses the effect of "append /path:off". Either of these commands may be entered at any time.

The PC-DOS 4.00 version of the /path switch contains a bug that affects the DOS batch file processor. As you have seen, if the /x switch is set to "on", DOS will use APPEND to locate batch files that are to be executed. Unfortunately, the batch file processor gets confused by the /path switch. When the switch is set to "off", DOS displays the confusing message `Batch file missing` when it attempts to execute a batch file that has been located using the APPEND path specifier.

Problems with APPEND

APPEND is a very useful command. Unfortunately, APPEND is not as well designed or well behaved as it should be. The design problem centers around the fact that any file read with the APPEND path specifier is written to the current directory. The directory setup used in writing this book illustrates the problem. The word processor is stored as \WORD\WP.EXE. The contents of this section of the book are stored as \BOOK\COMMANDS\AP-PEND.DOC. One way to set up the system is as follows:

```
C>append /e /x

C>append c:\book\commands

C>cd \word
```

With \WORD as the current directory, the word processor can be started, and, using the APPEND path specifier, the word processor can locate "append.doc" for editing. The problem is that following any changes to the file, the word processor writes "append.doc" to the current directory \WORD. The original file remains unchanged in \BOOK\COMMANDS.

Fortunately, this problem has a simple solution. I can make BOOK \COMMANDS the current directory, and use APPEND to locate "wp.exe":

```
C>append c:\word

C>cd \book\commands
```

Now any changes made to "append.doc" are stored in the original file.

I find problems like this somewhat amusing, but obviously the potential for real trouble exists. Even IBM acknowledges that a problem exists. The PC-DOS 3.30 manual states that "APPEND /X may cause problems with some applications. If you experience problems using the /X option, you may want to use the APPEND command without it." The manual goes on to say that the APPEND path specifier must be cancelled prior to using the commands BACKUP and RESTORE. In addition, the manual says that AP-PEND must be used before the ASSIGN command is used. The DOS 4.X version of APPEND has been modified to deal with some of these problems, but the use of APPEND still requires caution.

I have used APPEND while writing this book and have not experienced any serious problems. However, I back up my data frequently and always have my fingers crossed. At this point, the value of APPEND appears to out-weigh the apparent risks.

ASSIGN

External
MS-DOS 2.X, 3.X, 4.X

Function: Reassigns the disk operation drive to another drive

Format: ASSIGN [x[=]y[. . .]]

Examples: assign
assign a=c
assign a=c b=c

Note: the commands JOIN and SUBST are more flexible and are safer to use than ASSIGN. Their use is recommended as an alternative to ASSIGN.

Some computer programs will execute only on systems with a particular drive configuration. For example, a program may require that any data used in the program be located on drive A. The ASSIGN command allows you to overcome this limitation by reassigning the specified disk drive to another disk drive.

Suppose you have a program that requires data to be on drive A, but you want to keep the data on your hard disk, drive C. You can use ASSIGN to tell MS-DOS that all references to drive A are to be redirected to drive C (the hard disk). Note that you do not have to enter a colon after the drive letter when you are using the ASSIGN command:

```
C>assign a=c
```

Now each time that the program looks for data on drive A, MS-DOS will automatically redirect the program to drive C.

You may make more than one reassignment with each ASSIGN command. The following command tells MS-DOS to redirect all references for drives A and B to drive C:

```
C>assign a=c b=c
```

Entering ASSIGN with no parameters cancels any previous ASSIGN commands and you are returned to the original drive:

```
C>assign
```

ASSIGN is designed primarily for use with MS-DOS 1.X programs that are run on systems without hard disks. ASSIGN should be used only when necessary and then with caution. Reassigning a floppy disk drive to the hard disk will redirect all access of the floppy disk to the hard disk. Unless care is exercised, you can inadvertently erase all or part of the hard disk.

The makers of MS-DOS recommend that application programs be written so that the user specifies the drive configuration of the system on which the program will be run. Restricting programs to a particular configuration is discouraged.

Note that the MS-DOS commands DISKCOPY and DISKCOMP will ignore any drive reassignments made with ASSIGN. ASSIGN should not be used with BACKUP, RESTORE, LABEL, JOIN, SUBST, or PRINT because drive reassignments can confuse these commands, causing unpredictable results.

ATTRIB

External
MS-DOS 3.X, 4.X

Function: Modifies read-only and archive file attributes

Format: ATTRIB [+R (or) −R][+A (or) −A][*d*:][*path*]***filename***[.*ext*][/S]

Example: attrib +r mypro.c

MS-DOS maintains a *file attribute* for each file. The attribute contains information about how the file is stored. Each file's attribute is actually a composite of six individual characteristics that the file may or may not possess. The command ATTRIB allows you to modify two of these attributes: *read-only* and *archive*. See chapter 10 for detailed information about file attributes and for a set of programs allowing you to modify a file's hidden file attribute.

The Read-Only Attribute

MS-DOS files that possess a read-only attribute cannot be written to or erased. ATTRIB can be used to mark files as read-only, thereby protecting the files from accidental modification or erasure. The command "attrib +r *filename*" makes a file read-only. The command "attrib −r *filename*" removes read-only protection, and "attrib *filename*" displays a file's read-only status.

The following commands give the file "mypro.c" read-only status, confirm that the file is read-only, remove the read-only status, and confirm that the read-only status has been removed.

```
C>attrib +r mypro.c    ←set as read-only

C>attrib mypro.c       ←request attribute status

    R C:\MYPRO.C       ←MS-DOS displays (R = read-only)

C>attrib -r mypro.c    ←remove read-only status

C>attrib mypro.c       ←request attribute status

    c:\MYPRO.C         ←read-only removed
```

The Archive Attribute

MS-DOS turns on a file's archive attribute each time that the file is modified. In 3.2 and later versions of MS-DOS, the archive attribute can also be set by using the command "attrib +a *filename*". A file's archive attribute may be cleared with the command "attrib −a *filename*". The command "attrib *filename*" displays the status of a file's archive attribute. See the discussions of the commands BACKUP and XCOPY for information on how MS-DOS uses a file's archive attribute.

Processing Directories

ATTRIB processes files in the specified (or default) directory which match the file specified in the command line. The /s switch directs ATTRIB to also process all files in the subdirectories of the specified (or default) directory. The following example is executed with \BOOK as the default directory:

```
C>dir                            ←display contents of \BOOK

Volume in drive C is HARDDISK
Directory of C:\BOOK

.          <DIR>    3-27-90   3:52p
..         <DIR>    8-11-90   6:10p
NEW        <DIR>    8-11-90   8:10p
OLD        <DIR>    8-11-90   8:11p
MISC       DOC      3210  9-23-90  11:07a
```

```
        5 File(s)  3954688 bytes free

C>attrib *.* /s                         ←request attribute status for files in
                                          \BOOK and all subdirectories

A    C:\BOOK\NEW\ATTRIB.DOC             ←MS-DOS displays status for files in
                                          subdirectory \BOOK\NEW

A    C:\BOOK\NEW\ASSIGN.DOC

A    C:\BOOK\NEW\TMP\INTRO.DOC          ←status for files in \BOOK\NEW\TMP

A    C:\BOOK\OLD\DIR.DOC                ←status for files in \BOOK\OLD

A    C:\BOOK\MISC.DOC                   ←status for files in \BOOK
```

BACKUP

External
MS-DOS 2.X, 3.X, 4.X

Function: File backup utility

Format: **BACKUP** *d:*[*path*] [*filename*[.*ext*]] *d:*[/S] [/M] [/A]
             [/D:*mm/dd/yy*] [/T:*hh:mm:ss*] [/F]
             [/L[:[*d:*][*path*][*filename*][.*ext*]]]

Examples: backup c: a:
             backup c:*.doc a:
             backup c:\ a: /s

The BACKUP command is a DOS utility that allows you to make backup copies of disk files. While BACKUP can be used to back up individual files, its primary value is in backing up groups of files or even the entire contents of a hard disk.

Backup copies are stored in *archival* form. This means that the files are stored in a format that is specific for backup storage. They cannot be used for other purposes. Archival files are converted back into standard DOS files using the DOS RESTORE command.

The BACKUP command allows you to select files for archival storage on the basis of path specifier, filename, date stamp, and/or time stamp. You can also back up files that have been changed since they were previously backed up.

DOS 3.X and 4.X can store archive files on either floppy diskettes or hard disks. On floppy diskettes, the archive files are stored in the root directory. The BACKUP utility *erases any existing files* in the root of any floppies storing archive files (unless the /a switch is used).

On hard disks, the archive files are stored in a subdirectory named \BACKUP. The BACKUP utility *erases any existing files* in the \BACKUP directory on the hard drive storing the archive files (unless the /a switch is used). Archive files cannot be stored on the logical drive containing the original files. (A hard drive with two DOS partitions consists of two logical drives; see chapter 1.)

The DOS 2.X version of BACKUP stores archive files only on floppy diskettes. The files are stored in the root directory. The BACKUP utility *erases any previously existing files* in the root of floppies storing the archive files (unless the /a switch is used).

Many users have experienced problems trying to restore archive files that were created with an earlier version of DOS. For example, archive files created with the DOS 2.X version of BACKUP cannot be converted back to standard files with the DOS 3.X version of RESTORE. You can avoid this problem by using equivalent versions of BACKUP and RESTORE. If you want to archive some files prior to installing a new version of DOS, first boot your system using the floppy with the new DOS. Then use the new DOS version of BACKUP to create your archive files, before installing the new DOS on your system. This will guarantee that your archive files are compatible with the new version of RESTORE.

Backing Up a File

To create a backup copy of a hard disk file, first type **backup**, then type the file specification of the file you are copying, next type the drive designator (such as **a:**) of the target diskette (the floppy diskettte that will store the copy), and finally type any of the four optional switches (see the following discussions).

A *file specification* consists of a letter designating the drive holding the file, followed by the name of the path leading to the directory holding the file, followed by the filename and filename extension of the file. If the BACKUP command does not include a drive letter and path for the file to be copied, BACKUP will assume that the file to be copied is in the current directory of the default drive.

Wildcard characters (see chapter 2) may be used in the filenames and file extensions. When wildcards are used, all of the matching files in the specified (or default) directory will be backed up.

In the first example, we will use BACKUP to make a copy of the hard disk file "lotsa.dat". The backup will be stored on the target diskette in drive A.

```
C>backup c:lotsa.dat a:
```

MS-DOS beeps and displays this warning:

```
Insert backup diskette 01 in drive A:
Warning! Diskette files will be erased
Strike any key when ready
```

BACKUP will erase any data on the diskette before making the backup copy, unless you use the /a switch. This warning gives you a chance to substitute another diskette if you wish. After double-checking to make sure that you have the right diskette in drive A, go ahead and press any key. BACKUP will copy the hard disk file onto the diskette in drive A and display the following message on the screen:

```
*** Backing up files to diskette 01 ***
\a:lotsa.dat
```

Keeping Track of Your Backups

BACKUP will prompt you to insert another diskette if the backup process will exceed the capacity of the target diskette. Given the tremendous storage capacity of a hard disk, it is not uncommon to need several diskettes to finish the job. A good practice is to keep a written record of important BACKUP sessions. You can get a printed copy of the BACKUP screen display by pressing Ctrl-PrtSc before you enter the BACKUP command. All screen display will be echoed (copied) to your printer. Make sure that your printer is turned on before you press Ctrl-PrtSc. At the end of the backup session, press Ctrl-PrtSc again to stop the echoing process.

For a convenient way to automate this record-keeping process with MS-DOS 3.3, see the following discussion of the /l switch in "Other BACKUP Switches."

Backing Up a Directory

All the files in a directory will be backed up if the BACKUP command does not contain a filename. In the following example, all the files in the subdirectory SUBDIR1 will be backed up. Notice that MS-DOS lists each file in the subdirectory as it is being backed up.

```
C>backup c:\subdir1 a:

Insert backup diskette 01 in drive A:
Warning! Diskette files will be erased
Strike any key when ready

*** Backing up files to diskette 01 ***
\SUBDIR1\FILE1
```

```
\SUBDIR1\FILE2
\SUBDIR1\FILE3
\SUBDIR1\FILE4
```

Backing Up an Entire Disk

The /s switch is used with BACKUP to copy all files in a directory as well as all files in all subdirectories contained in the directory. This capability allows you to back up an entire hard disk, preserving the disk's directory structure in the process.

If you have a hard disk, it is good practice to have an archive copy of the disk's entire contents. Then, if a disaster such as accidental formatting of the disk occurs, you will be able to restore the hard disk's file contents and directory structure in a straightforward manner.

The following example shows how you can use BACKUP to archive your entire hard disk. You will have to do this if you are upgrading to DOS 4.X and wish to create a disk partition larger than 32 Mbytes. You can also use this technique if your computer currently uses MS-DOS and you want to use the SELECT program to install PC-DOS 4.X. Please refer to chapter 1 for a discussion of SELECT.

If you are upgrading to DOS 4.X, you should boot your system with the 4.X system floppy and then use the 4.X version of BACKUP to back up your entire hard disk. After archiving your files, you can reformat your hard disk with the 4.X versions of FDISK and FORMAT and then use the 4.X version of RESTORE to restore your archived files.

```
C:\>backup c:\ a: /s /l:c:\utils\backup.log

Insert backup diskette 01 in drive A:

WARNING! Files in the target drive
A:\ root directory will be erased
Press any key to continue . . .
```

The command says to create on drive A an archive file containing the contents of the root directory on drive C. The /s switch says to include all files contained in all subdirectories of the root. Thus, all files on drive C will be stored in the archive. The /l switch says to create a log file. The log file will record the names of the files stored in the archive. The log file is to have the name c:\utils\backup.log.

Once the command is entered, DOS will prompt you to insert the backup diskette in drive A. DOS will also warn you that any files contained in the root directory of drive A will be erased.

Once the backup diskette is in drive A, you can start the backup process by pressing any key. DOS will display the complete path specifier and filename of each file as it is copied to the archive file. DOS also prompts you to insert another diskette when the diskette in drive A becomes full.

Backing Up Modified Files

The /m switch is used to back up any files that have been modified since the last BACKUP session. This handy option can save you time and diskette space, since it selects only those files that need to be backed up.

Let's say that you use your hard disk to store your word processing documents. All of the documents have a filename extension of DOC. If you have several hundred document files, it can be difficult to keep track of which files need to be backed up and which files have already been backed up. But you needn't concern yourself with this problem because BACKUP and /m will take care of it for you. All you need to do is enter the following command at the end of each word processing session:

```
C>backup *.doc a:/m
```

Any document file that was modified in the work session will automatically be backed up.

Backing Up Files by Date

The /d switch is used with BACKUP to copy files that were created, or last modified, on or after a specific date. The following command will back up any files in the root directory that were created, or modified, after December 11, 1988.

```
C>backup c:\ a:/d:12-11-88
```

Backing Up Files by Time

The /t switch, implemented in MS-DOS 3.3, allows you to back up files that were created or modified after a specified time of day. The following example creates a backup of all files in the root directory that have a time stamp later than 3:00 pm. The backup copies are stored on drive A.

```
C>backup c:\*.* a:/t:15:00:00
```

Other BACKUP Switches

The /a switch allows you to add archive files to the root directory of floppies or to the \BACKUP subdirectory of hard disks without erasing pre-existing data.

The /f switch, implemented only in version 3.3, allows you to store archive files on a previously unformatted diskette. MS-DOS must be able to read the file FORMAT.COM in order to execute this option. The DOS 4.X version of BACKUP will automatically format an unformatted diskette. The /f switch is therefore not implemented in 4.X.

The /l switch, implemented in MS-DOS 3.3, directs BACKUP to create a *log file*. The log file consists of a record of all files that have been backed up, along with the date and time of the backup. The log file can be useful in keeping track of files that have been archived. You can specify a drive, path, and filename for the log file. The default is BACKUP.LOG stored in the root of the source drive.

Restrictions with BACKUP

The commands ASSIGN, JOIN, and SUBST instruct MS-DOS to redirect all references for one device to another device. For example, ASSIGN may be used to redirect all references for drive A to drive C. Each of these commands can put MS-DOS in a state that is confusing to BACKUP. The effect is that BACKUP results may be unpredictable if one of these commands has previously been used.

Another restriction in using BACKUP occurs with the APPEND command. BACKUP used in conjunction with APPEND may result in loss of data. See the discussion of APPEND for details.

BACKUP and ERRORLEVEL

ERRORLEVEL is a variable that has special meaning to MS-DOS. The value of ERRORLEVEL is set by the BACKUP command as follows:

0   BACKUP command completed in normal fashion.

1   No files were found on the hard disk that match the file(s) specified in the BACKUP command.

3   Execution of the BACKUP command was terminated by the user pressing Ctrl-Break.

4   The BACKUP command was terminated due to an error in execution.

Once the value of ERRORLEVEL has been set, ERRORLEVEL may be used in conjunction with the IF command in an MS-DOS batch file. ERRORLEVEL allows you to create batch files that are executed according to the outcome of a BACKUP command. See the discussion of the IF command for further details.

BREAK

Internal
MS-DOS 2.X, 3.X, 4.X

Function: Controls the frequency with which MS-DOS checks for Ctrl-C and Ctrl-Break.

Formats: **BREAK ON**
BREAK OFF
BREAK

Example: break on

Pressing the Ctrl-C or Ctrl-Break key combinations will generally terminate a program and return control of the computer to MS-DOS. You can use the BREAK command to control the frequency with which MS-DOS checks for these key combinations.

The command "break off" directs MS-DOS to check for Ctrl-Break and Ctrl-C only during input and output operations (such as reading the keyboard or sending characters to the display screen).

The command "break on" directs MS-DOS to check for Ctrl-Break and Ctrl-C whenever a call is made to the operating system's service functions. The service functions are discussed in appendix A, but for purposes of understanding the BREAK command you only need to know that MS-DOS checks for Ctrl-Break and Ctrl-C much more frequently when BREAK is on.

You can enter "break" (with no additional parameters) to see if BREAK is currently on or off.

You can use the BREAK command on the MS-DOS command line, in a batch file, or in the special MS-DOS file CONFIG.SYS (refer to chapter 5 for a discussion of CONFIG.SYS). When BREAK is used in CONFIG.SYS, an equal sign (=) must be placed between "break" and its parameter ("break=on" or "break=off").

BUFFERS

Internal
MS-DOS 2.X, 3.X, 4.X

Function: Establishes the number of disk buffers that MS-DOS creates in memory.

Format: BUFFERS=*xx*
BUFFERS=*xx*[,*yy*] [/X] (4.X only)
Note: BUFFERS can only be used in the file CONFIG.SYS.

Examples: buffers=5
buffers=15,5 /X

A *disk buffer* is an area of memory that MS-DOS uses to store data being written to, or read from, a disk. A buffer serves as a way station between the disk and the portion of memory storing a program's data.

MS-DOS transfers data between a disk and a buffer in 512-byte increments. To illustrate how a buffer is used, consider what happens when a program requires a 128-byte record stored on disk. MS-DOS reads a 512-byte portion of the file from the disk. Contained within these 512 bytes are the 128 bytes needed by the program. The 128 bytes are transferred to the program's data area in memory. If the program subsequently requires another 128-byte record, MS-DOS first determines if the record is already stored in a buffer. If it is, no disk access is required.

The BUFFERS command is used to establish the number of disk buffers set up by MS-DOS during booting. Increasing the number of buffers can speed program execution, but only up to a point. The more buffers that exist, the more sectors that can be stored in memory; hence, fewer accesses of the disk are necessary. However, the more buffers, the longer it takes MS-DOS to search all the buffers to see if the needed sector is already in memory. Eventually it becomes faster to access the disk than to search all the buffers.

The amount of memory taken up by the disk buffers is another consideration. Each buffer adds 528 bytes to the amount of memory taken up by MS-DOS. By increasing the amount of memory needed by MS-DOS, the amount of memory available for program data is reduced. Thus, the additional buffers can increase the frequency of disk accesses, causing the program to slow down.

If disk access tends to follow a random pattern, as would be the case in querying a large database, increasing the number of disk buffers should significantly improve performance. Alternatively, if disk access is primarily sequential, as is the case with most word processing applications, increasing the number of disk buffers will generally not result in as dramatic an improvement in performance. Chapter 5, Configuring Your System, contains additional guidelines on the use of BUFFERS.

You can use BUFFERS to set up from 1 to 99 buffers in conventional memory. In addition, the DOS 4.X version of BUFFERS allows you to create up to 10,000 buffers in expanded memory (see DOS 4.X enhancements below).

On DOS versions prior to 3.3, the default value for BUFFERS is 2. This is the number of disk buffers created if CONFIG.SYS does not contain a BUFFERS statement.

In DOS 3.3 and 4.X, the default is determined by the system's hardware. If the amount of random access memory (RAM) is less than or equal to 128 Kbytes *and* all diskette drives are less than 360 Kbytes, the BUFFERS default is 2.

If RAM is less than or equal to 128 Kbytes *and* one or more diskette drives is 360 Kbytes or greater, the BUFFERS default is 3.

If RAM is greater than 128 Kbytes and less than or equal to 256 Kbytes, the BUFFERS default is 5.

If RAM is greater than 256 Kbytes and less than or equal to 512 Kbytes, the BUFFERS default is 10.

If RAM is greater than 512 Kbytes, the BUFFERS default is 15.

Enhancements in DOS 4.X

The DOS 4.X version of BUFFERS allows you to place disk buffers in expanded memory and also to establish the size of a *read-ahead buffer*.

The /x switch tells DOS to place the disk buffers in expanded memory. You can create up to 10,000 disk buffers when the buffers are placed in expanded memory. Of course, you will need an expanded memory card and expanded memory software in order to use this option. Unfortunately, that is often not enough. Many users of PC-DOS 4.X report that the switch does not work on their systems. In general, the /x switch only operates correctly on systems with IBM expanded memory cards.

When an application program needs data on the disk, DOS determines which disk sector is storing the data. The operating system then reads that sector into memory. If the application program is primarily performing sequential readings of the disk— that is, one sector is read, followed by the adjoining sector, and so on—it is advantageous for DOS to "look ahead" and read a sequence of sectors into memory each time a disk access is performed. This reduces the total number of disk accesses required and speeds up the program's execution. Programs such as word processors, which typically perform a large amount of sequential disk access, may experience improved performance by increasing the number of look-ahead sectors.

The DOS 4.X version of BUFFERS accepts a second parameter, which allows you to establish the number of look-ahead sectors that are read into memory. You may specify a value of 1 to 8 for the number of sectors to "read ahead." All of the read-ahead sectors are placed in a single buffer. Each read-ahead sector requires 512 bytes of memory. No read-ahead buffer is created if the second parameter is not specified.

The following example illustrates the use of BUFFERS in DOS 4.X:

```
buffers=15,5 /x
```

The statement (which must be contained in the CONFIG.SYS file) creates 15 disk buffers in expanded memory. In addition, a read-ahead buffer is created that contains 5 read-ahead sectors.

CALL

Internal
MS-DOS 3.3, 4.X

Function: Allows a batch file to be called (executed) from another batch file. Control returns to the first batch file when the called batch file terminates.

Format: CALL *<filename>*

Example: call batfile2

The CALL command is a batch file command that is used to execute one batch file from within another batch file. The called batch file receives its own copy of the DOS environment, which it may modify. Control returns to the first batch file when the called batch file terminates. The environment of the calling batch file is not affected by any changes made by the called batch file to its environment. Use of the CALL command is illustrated in chapter 4, MS-DOS Batch Files.

CHCP

Internal
MS-DOS 3.3, 4.X

Function: Selects a code page for the system
Note: Please refer to appendix D for an overview of code pages and code page switching.

Format: CHCP [*xxxx*]

Examples: chcp
chcp 850

The command CHCP selects a specific code page for each device in the system which supports that code page. Prior to using CHCP, the NLSFUNC command must be invoked. The following two commands assign code page 850 to the system:

```
C>nlsfunc
C>chcp 850
```

Note that the NLSFUNC command need be invoked only one time after the system is booted.

CHCP with no parameters displays the system's currently active code page.

```
C>chcp
```

```
Active code page:   437
```

CHDIR

Internal
MS-DOS 2.X, 3.X, 4.X

Function: Changes the current directory or displays the current
           directory's path

Format: CHDIR [[*d:*]*path*]

Examples: chdir \suba1\suba2
           cd a:\subb1
           chdir
           cd

The *current directory* is the directory in which MS-DOS is currently active. At any given time, there is only one current directory for each drive in the system. You can use the command CHDIR (CHange DIRectory) to instruct MS-DOS to change the drive's current directory. You can also use CHDIR to display the path to a drive's current directory. This command can be entered as "chdir" or abbreviated as "cd".

Changing the Current Directory

To change the current directory, type **chdir** (or **cd**) and then type the path to the new current directory. Suppose that the path from the root directory to the subdirectory SUBA2 is ROOT DIRECTORY, SUBA1, SUBA2 (see figure 1). MS-DOS represents this path as \SUBA1\SUBA2. Note that the root directory is indicated by the first backward slash.

The following command will make SUBA2 the current directory of drive C:

Figure 1. File structure for root directory, SUBA1, SUBA2.

```
C>chdir \suba1\suba2
```

To change the current directory of a drive that is not the default drive, type the drive letter designator and then type the path:

```
C>cd a:\subb1
```

Displaying the Path to the Current Directory

Entering "chdir" (or "cd") with no parameters directs MS-DOS to display the path to the current directory of the default drive:

```
C>chdir
C:\SUBA1\SUBA2
```

To display the path to the current directory of a drive other than the default, type **chdir** (or **cd**), followed by the letter designator of the drive:

```
C>cd a:
A:\SUBB1
```

You can find more detailed information on directories, subdirectories, current directories, and paths in chapter 3.

CHKDSK

External
MS-DOS 1.X, 2.X, 3.X, 4.X

Functions: Analyzes the file allocation table (FAT), the directory, and any
subdirectories on a disk
Analyzes the status of computer memory

Format: **CHKDSK** [*d:*]
CHKDSK [*d:*][*filename.ext*][/F][/V] (MS-DOS 2.X, 3.X, 4.X)

Examples: chkdsk
chkdsk b:
chkdsk/f
chkdsk b:letter.doc /f/v

The CHKDSK (CHecK DiSK) command is an MS-DOS utility that checks the
condition, or status, of a disk's data. MS-DOS stores data in files on a disk. It
keeps track of the files on the disk by consulting the disk's directory and file
allocation table (FAT). CHKDSK analyzes the FAT and the disk directory (and
any subdirectories) for errors and problems. To prevent minor problems
from turning into major ones, it is a good idea to run CHKDSK occasionally
on all your hard disks and floppy diskettes. You will find more information
about the structure and role of the FAT and the file directory in chapter 10.

Using CHKDSK

Since CHKDSK is an external command, a copy of the file CHKDSK.COM
must be available to the system before you can use the command. This
means that either CHKDSK.COM must be in the current directory of the
default drive or that the location of CHKDSK.COM must have been specified by the PATH command (see the discussion of PATH).

To check a disk, type **chkdsk** and then type the letter designator of the
drive containing the disk to be checked. If you do not enter a drive letter
designator, CHKDSK will examine the disk in the default drive:

```
C>chkdsk

Volume HARDDISK created Jul 6, 1987 2:14p
10592256 bytes total disk space
   57334 bytes in 3 hidden files
  184320 bytes in 42 directories
10264576 bytes in 846 user files
   86016 bytes available on disk
```

```
524288 bytes total memory
320704 bytes free

C>
```

Since the preceding command did not include a drive letter designator, CHKDSK examined the disk in the default drive; it did not find any errors. The status report displays information about the disk and the computer memory. The first four lines report the total disk space taken up, the number of files on the diskette, and the remaining available space. The last two lines report on the amount of memory used up and the amount still available.

CHKDSK Features of MS-DOS 2.X, 3.X, and 4.X

The MS-DOS 2.X, 3.X, and 4.X versions of CHKDSK have four additional features:

1. If a filename is included in the command, CHKDSK will display the number of noncontiguous areas (sectors) on the disk that contain the named file. While files that are highly fragmented (having many noncontiguous areas) are acceptable, they can slow down system performance. If you use the wildcard *.* as a filename, CHKDSK will report on each fragmented file in the current directory. You can specify another directory by preceding the *.* with a path specifier and a backwards slash (\). A fragmented file can be copied into a contiguous area on another disk with the COPY command.

2. The /f switch instructs CHKDSK to attempt to correct any errors detected. CHKDSK always asks if it should attempt to correct any errors that it detects. However, CHKDSK makes no attempt to correct the errors if /f was not used. Unfortunately, CHKDSK cannot correct all errors. Commercial programs such as PC-Tools, Norton Utilities, and Mace Utilities contain disk sector editors and other powerful utilities that can help you correct errors reported by CHKDSK.

3. The /v switch directs CHKDSK to display the filename and path specifier of each file on the disk. A good way to find a file on a hard disk is to "pipe" the output of "chkdsk /v" to the FIND command as follows:

```
chkdsk c: /v | find filename
```

Piping of DOS commands is discussed in chapter 6.

4. You can redirect the status report and any messages to a disk file by using the following command:

```
C>chkdsk b: > file
```

Note: Do not use the /f switch in the CHKDSK command if you are redirecting CHKDSK's output.

CHKDSK Error Messages

Allocation Error, Size Adjusted

The file's entry in the file directory indicates that the file is larger than the amount of disk space allocated for the file in the FAT. The /f switch directs CHKDSK to truncate the file so that its size matches the allocation specified by the FAT.

Cannot CHDIR to <*file specifier*>

Tree cannot be processed beyond this point The first entry in each subdirectory is given the name ".", which represents the directory itself. The second entry in each subdirectory is given the name "..", which represents the subdirectory's parent directory. CHKDSK displays this error message if either of these entries is corrupted. CHKDSK asks you if it should `Convert directory to file`. If you answer yes, the subdirectory is converted to a standard file. Recognize that this new file only contains the contents of the subdirectory. It does not contain the contents of the files listed in the subdirectory. These files become lost clusters when the subdirectory is converted. CHKDSK also asks you if it should convert these lost clusters to files ("lost clusters" are discussed below). CHKDSK does not take any action if the /f switch was not used.

Cannot CHKDSK a Network Drive (or SUBSTed or ASSIGNed Drive)

CHKDSK cannot be used to check any drives on a local area network. It also cannot be used on logical drives created with the DOS commands SUBST and ASSIGN.

Contains invalid cluster, file truncated

Same as "Allocation error, size adjusted".

<*file specifier*> contains N noncontiguous blocks

If you enter the command "chkdsk *.*", CHKDSK displays this message for each file in the current directory that is stored in noncontiguous blocks. This does not represent an error, but highly "fragmented" files can slow down disk access. Commercial programs (such as Mace UnFrag and Disk Optimizer) are available to "defrag" highly fragmented disks.

Convert directory to file (Y/N)?

This message is preceded by the name of a directory (or subdirectory) that is no longer functional because of one or more invalid entries. CHKDSK asks if you want this directory converted to a file (which could then be examined with DEBUG). If you enter "Y" (and /f was included in the CHKDSK command), the directory will be converted to a file. If you enter "N", no conversion is made.

Convert lost chains to files (Y/N)?

A *cluster* is a unit of space on a disk. The cluster is said to be "lost" when the FAT entry for the cluster is a nonzero number but the cluster does not belong to any file. A contiguous set of lost clusters is called a *lost chain*. This message asks if you want each lost chain stored in a file. If you reply "Y", MS-DOS creates a separate file for each lost chain. The files are named FILE*nnnn*.CHK, where *nnnn* is a sequential number beginning with 0000. If you reply "N", MS-DOS converts to zero the entries in the FAT that correspond to the lost chains and makes available for new files the areas in the disk occupied by the lost chains. Regardless of your reply, no changes will be written to the disk if you did not include /f in the CHKDSK command.

Disk error writing FAT *x*

CHKDSK was unable to update the FAT. The *x* will either be 1 or 2, depending on which copy of the FAT CHKDSK was trying to update.

. Entry (or .. Entry) has bad attribute (or link or size)

The first (".") or second ("..") entry in a subdirectory is defective. The 3.X and 4.X versions of CHKDSK will attempt to fix this error if the /f switch was used.

Error found, F parameter not specified
Corrections will not be written to disk

The /f switch was not included with the CHKDSK command. The results of the CHKDSK analysis will be displayed, but no changes will be written to the disk.

filename is cross-linked:
On cluster *xx*

Two files are said to be *cross-linked* when the FAT indicates that a cluster belongs to both files. The message will be displayed twice, once for each file that is cross-linked. CHKDSK does not take any action when this situation occurs. Cross-linked files can be salvaged, either partially or entirely, by copying each of the files onto another disk.

First cluster number is invalid,
Entry truncated

This message will be preceded by the name of a file. The file's first cluster, which is located in the file directory, is invalid. The file will be truncated to a length of zero if the /f parameter was included in the CHKDSK command.

Insufficient room in root directory
Erase files from root and repeat CHKDSK

CHKDSK has been instructed to convert lost chains into files. Unfortunately, there is not enough room in the root directory for all the files that CHKDSK wants to create. To solve this problem, copy the files already recovered to another diskette. Then delete the recovered files from the original diskette. Rerun CHKDSK on the original diskette to recover the remaining lost chains.

Invalid subdirectory

CHKDSK has found an invalid entry in the subdirectory that is named. CHKDSK will attempt to correct the error if the /f parameter was included in the CHKDSK command.

Probable non-DOS disk
Continue (Y/N)?

The first byte of the FAT does not contain a valid entry. CHKDSK will indicate the possible corrective measures if you reply with "Y". However, the changes will not be written to the disk if the /f parameter was not included in the CHKDSK command.

xxxxxxx bytes disk space freed

An error in the FAT has been corrected by truncating a file. The portion of the disk previously allocated to the file is now available for data storage.

xxx lost clusters found in *yyy* chains

A cluster is "lost" if the FAT entry for the cluster is a nonzero number but the cluster does not belong to any file. A contiguous group of lost clusters is called a *lost chain*. CHKDSK will ask if you want to convert each lost chain to a file or if you want to free the disk space taken up by the chains.

CLS

Internal
MS-DOS 2.X, 3.X, 4.X

Function: Clears the screen and moves the cursor to home position

Format: CLS

Example: cls

The CLS (CLear Screen) command clears the display screen and moves the cursor to the home position. CLS sends the ASCII character sequence ESC[2J to the console device driver. This is the ANSI command sequence for clearing the screen and moving the cursor to home position.

On some systems, the ANSI.SYS device driver must be installed by the user before the CLS command will operate. See chapter 9 for information on installing the ANSI.SYS device driver.

COMMAND

External
MS-DOS 2.X, 3.X, 4.X

Function: Invokes a secondary command processor

Formats: **COMMAND**[*/Cstring*][*/P*]
COMMAND[*d:*][*path*][*/C string*][*/P*][*/E:xxxxx*]   (MS-DOS 3.X,4.X)
COMMAND /MSG   (MS-DOS 4.X)

Examples: command
command /c dir
command /c do it.bat

The *command processor* serves as the interface between you and the operating system. It displays the system prompt on the screen, interprets the command you enter, and acts according to the contents of that command. The primary MS-DOS command processor is COMMAND.COM.

You can use COMMAND to invoke a secondary command processor. Invoking the command directs COMMAND to (1) load a copy of the command processor into memory and (2) pass control to the copy (the secondary command processor). MS-DOS uses the path specifier contained in the command to locate the copy of COMMAND.COM that will be loaded. If COMMAND.COM is not stored in the specified directory, or if no path specifier is included in the command, MS-DOS uses the path stored in the environment to locate COMMAND.COM.

To invoke a secondary command processor, type **command**:

    C>command

On the surface it appears as though nothing has happened, but you are now operating under the control of a secondary command processor. If you get a **Bad file or command** message, insert your working copy of the system diskette in drive A and try again.

To leave the secondary command processor and return control to the primary command processor, type **exit**:

    C>exit

Again it appears as though nothing has happened, but you are now back under the control of the primary command processor.

COMMAND Switches

Using the /c switch when you invoke a secondary command processor allows you to enter a command line:

```
C>command /c dir
```

This command tells MS-DOS to load a secondary command processor and instructs the secondary command processor to execute a DIR command.

The /c switch is occasionally used to allow a batch file to run another batch file. Starting with DOS 3.3, CALL should be used for this purpose. CALL does not require the loading of a secondary command processor.

The /p switch tells MS-DOS to keep the secondary command processor in memory even if an EXIT command is issued. The /p switch is used when increasing the size of the MS-DOS environment (see chapter 11). If both /p and /c are issued, the /p switch is ignored.

The /e:*xxxxx* switch, implemented in MS-DOS 3.1 but not documented until version 3.2, is used to set the size of the environment that is passed to the secondary command processor. If no environment size is specified, the secondary command processor inherits an environment that is the same size as the environment of the primary command processor.

In version 3.1, *xxxxx* sets the number of paragraphs (16-byte blocks) in the environment. The allowable range is 10 to 2048.

In 3.2 and later versions, *xxxxx* sets the number of bytes in the environment. The allowable range is 160 to 32,768, the environment size being rounded up to the nearest multiple of 16.

The environment variables of the primary processor are inherited by the secondary command processor. Any modifications that the secondary command processor performs on its environment variables are local. The modifications do not affect the environment variables of the primary command processor. The MS-DOS environment and environment variables are discussed in chapter 11.

The /MSG switch is implemented in DOS 4.X for use on floppy disk systems. The switch directs DOS to load error message information into memory along with the secondary command processor. This does away with the need to read a floppy disk each time an error is encountered. You do not need to use this switch on systems with a hard disk drive.

Purpose of a Secondary Command Processor

A secondary command processor allows a computer program or batch file to utilize other programs, other batch files, or MS-DOS commands. It works something like this: MS-DOS is booted, and the (primary) command processor is loaded into memory and takes control. You enter the name of the file containing a computer program; the command processor loads the program and passes control to it. Your program begins to execute and at some point loads a secondary command processor. The secondary processor receives control, at which point any program, batch file, or MS-DOS command may be executed. At some point, the secondary command processor is exited, and control returns to the original computer program (see figure 2). See chapter 4 for a discussion of the role of a secondary command processor in executing batch files.

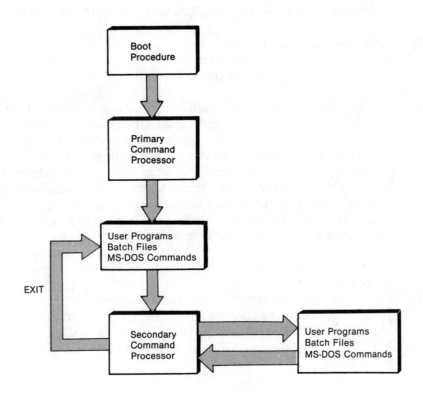

Figure 2. Loading a secondary command processor.

COMP

External
MS-DOS 1.X, 2.X, 3.X, 4.X

Function: Compares the contents of one file with the contents of
              another file

Format: COMP [*d*:][*path*][*filename*[.*ext*]][*d*:][*path*][*filename*[.*ext*]]

Examples: comp
              comp testfile.txt
              comp a:testfile.txt b:testfile.txt

Note: COMP is the file comparison utility that is included with PC-DOS (the version of MS-DOS designed for the IBM personal computer). While many other microcomputers also include a file comparison utility program, the following description and comments relate specifically to COMP, though they can be applied generally to other MS-DOS file comparison utilities.

The COMP (COMPare files) command compares files on a byte-by-byte basis. The first byte of file A is compared with the first byte of file B and so on. Any mismatches are displayed. The comparison is halted if ten mismatches are detected. COMP tells you that the `Files compare ok` if no mismatches are detected. At the completion of a comparison, you are asked if you want to compare another pair of files. No comparison is made if the files are unequal in size.

COMP is an external command; therefore, one of the disks in the system must contain a copy of the file COMP.COM. In the examples presented here, COMP.COM is stored on the C drive. If COMP.COM is not on the default drive, all commands must be preceded by the appropriate drive letter designator.

Using COMP

To compare two files, first type the name of the primary file and then type the name of the secondary file:

```
C>comp one.txt b:one.txt
```

MS-DOS responds:

```
C:ONE          .TXT and B:ONE            .TXT

Files compare ok

Compare more files (Y/N)? _
```

If you enter "Y", COMP will prompt you to enter the names of two other files to be compared. If you enter "N", the MS-DOS prompt will reappear.

COMP can compare files with different names when the files are on the same disk or on different disks. It can compare files with the same name only if they are on different disks or in different directories on the same disk.

COMP may be started without specifying one or both of the files to be compared. COMP will prompt you for the unnamed file(s):

```
C>comp

Enter primary filename
one.txt
Enter 2nd filename or drive id
b:

C:ONE      .TXT and B:ONE      .TXT

Files compare ok

Compare more files (Y/N)? _
```

Notice that only the drive designator was entered for the second file. COMP looks for a file with the same name as the first filename when the second parameter contains only a drive and/or a path.

COMP displays any mismatches between files by listing the hexadecimal offset of the mismatch(es) and the hexadecimal byte value of each file at that offset. *Offset* refers to a byte's position in the file relative to the first byte in the file. The first byte in the file is at offset 0, the second byte at offset 1, and so on.

```
C>comp one.txt two.txt

C:ONE      .TXT and A:TWO      .TXT

Compare error at offset 8
File 1 = 6B
File 2 = 6A

Compare more files (Y/N)? _
```

COMP checks to see if the final byte of each comparison is an end-of-file marker (hexadecimal 1A). If a marker is found, COMP does not take any action. If no marker is found, COMP displays the following message:

```
EOF marker not found
```

COMP determines a file's size from information stored in the file directory. Some computer programs produce directory entries that round a file's size to a multiple of 128. In these cases, COMP may read more data than what actually resides within the file. Failure to find an EOF marker may indicate that mismatches were detected beyond the end of the file.

Wildcard characters can be used to specify files for comparison. The following command tells COMP to compare all files on drive C that have a filename extension of TXT with the file on drive B having the same filename but an extension of ASM:

```
C>comp *.txt b:*.asm
```

A message will be displayed if a matching file cannot be located on drive B.

COPY

Internal
MS-DOS 1.X, 2.X, 3.X, 4.X

Functions: Copies an existing file
Combines two or more existing files into one file
Transfers data between peripheral devices and files

Format: COPY [/A][/B][*d*:][*path*]*filename*[.*ext*][/A] [/B]
[+[*d*:][*path*]*filename*[.*ext*][/A][/B] . . .] [*d*:][*path*][*filename*
[.*ext*]][/A][/B][/V]

Examples: copy file1
Copy file1+file2 b:file3
copy con: file4.txt

COPY is one of the most important MS-DOS commands. It is used primarily to make copies of existing MS-DOS files. However, COPY can also be used to combine one or more existing files into one file through a process called *concatenation*. Yet another way to use COPY is in the transfer of data between peripheral devices and files.

Copying Files

To copy a file, first type **copy** and then type the file specification of the original file (source file), followed by the file specification of the file that will contain the copy (target file). MS-DOS will make the copy and display a message telling you how many copies it has made:

```
C>copy file.txt b:file.txt
        1 File(s) copied
```

You may omit the filename of the duplicate file if it will have the same name as the original file. In such cases, the copy must be placed on a separate disk or in a separate directory on the same disk as the original file. The following command will copy "file.txt" to drive B:

```
C>copy file.txt b:
        1 File(s) copied
```

Users of MS-DOS 2.X, 3.X, and 4.X may include a path(s) for the original and/or the duplicate file(s). If one or both paths are not specified, MS-DOS will default to the current directory. The following command places a copy of "file.txt" in the subdirectory DATA on drive C. The original copy of "file.txt" is located in the current directory of drive C.

```
C>copy file.txt\data
        1 File(s) copied
```

A file may be copied to the same directory on the same disk only if the copy is given a different name:

```
C>copy file.txt file2.txt
        1 File(s) copied
```

Wildcard characters may be used with the COPY command in filenames and/or extensions. (See chapter 2 for information on MS-DOS wildcards.) The following command copies all files with an extension of DOC that are located on drive C in the subdirectory LETTERS. The copies will be placed in the subdirectory BACKUP of drive B. MS-DOS will display the name of each file as it is copied. Each copied file will have the same name as the original. At the end of the copying process, MS-DOS will display a message stating the number of files that have been copied:

```
C>copy \letters *.doc b:\\backup
COUNTRY.DOC
TICTOCK.DOC
WHATSUP.DOC
ITHURTS.DOC
QUACK.DOC
        5 File(s) copied
```

Combining Files

COPY may be used to concatenate (combine) two or more files. The files to be combined must be specified in the COPY command and separated with a plus (+) sign. The resulting file will be a combination of the specified files, and the files will be in the order in which they were listed in the command.

The next example copies the files "list1.txt" and "list2.txt" into a new file named "biglist.txt". The original files "list1.txt" and "list2.txt" are preserved. At the end of the copying process, MS-DOS states the number of copies created:

```
C>copy list1.txt+list2.txt biglist.txt
        1 File(s) copied
```

Files may be concatenated without specifying a name for the new file. If no name is specified, the new file is given the name of the first file listed for concatenation. The first file is replaced on the disk by the new file.

Wildcard characters may be used in concatenating files. The following command will combine all the files in the current directory of drive C having an extension of TXT. The combined file will be given the filename "combine.dat":

```
C>copy *.txt combine.dat
LETTER1.TXT
INSERT1.TXT
INSERT2.TXT
        1 File(s) copied
```

When concatenating with wildcards, you must specify in the COPY command the filename of the new file. Otherwise, MS-DOS will try to copy the first file listed ("letter1.txt" in the example) onto itself and the copying process will terminate.

The following command will combine each file having the form *.TXT with a matching file having the form *.DAT. If a match exists, the two files will be combined into a file named *.DOC. For example, the files "letter1.txt" and "letter1.dat" will be combined into the file "letter.doc" and so on:

```
C>copy *.txt+*.dat *.doc
LETTER1.TXT
LETTER1.DAT
LETTER2.TXT
LETTER2.DAT
ESSAY1.TXT
ESSAY2.DAT
        3 File(s) copied
```

You should be a little careful when using wildcards in combining files. Let's say that you want to combine all files having an extension of DOC into a filename "big.doc". That should be as simple as:

```
copy *.doc big.doc
```

Right? Unfortunately, it's not so simple.

As soon as the combination process begins, MS-DOS creates the file "big.doc". If there was a previously existing "big.doc", it is lost and the new "big.doc" takes its place. Once the new "big.doc" is on the scene, MS-DOS sees it as a valid *.DOC file and will entertain thoughts about adding "big.doc" to the combined file. But "big.doc" *is* the combined file. Fortunately, MS-DOS is smart enough to know not to add "big.doc" to itself. The following message is displayed:

```
Content of destination lost before copy
```

MS-DOS then proceeds on its merry way, looking for other *.DOC files and adding them to "big.doc" in the normal fashion. The preceding message will be displayed whether or not "big.doc" existed before the combining began. The problem is that if "big.doc" previously existed, it will be written over by the new "big.doc" and lost. To compound the problem, the new "big.doc" will not contain the contents of the old "big.doc".

There are two ways to avoid this problem. You can specify "big.doc" as an existing file that is to be appended to the other *.DOC files:

```
copy big.doc+*.doc
```

Or you can specify a name for the new file that does not match the wildcard filename:

```
copy *.doc big.dat
```

Using COPY to Update the Time/Date Stamp

The COPY command can be used to update the time and date stamp of a file:

```
copy anyfile.ext+,,
```

Unfortunately, if you attempt to update several time/date stamps with a single command (as in **copy *.*+,,**), MS-DOS will update only the stamp of the first file it finds that matches the wildcard.

COPY Switches

There are three optional switches that you may include in a COPY command. Two of the switches (/a and /b) control the way in which COPY reads and writes files. The third switch (/v) is used to verify the accuracy of a COPY operation.

The /a switch tells COPY to treat a file as an ASCII (text) file. If the file is to be copied, this switch tells COPY to copy the file up to, but not including, the first end-of-file marker (hexadecimal 1A). Any data after the marker is not to be copied. If the file is to be a copy, the /a switch tells COPY to add an end-of-file marker to the end of the file.

The /b switch tells COPY to treat a file as a binary file. If a file is to be copied, this switch tells COPY to copy the entire file based on the size stored in the file directory. If a file is to be a copy, the /b switch tells COPY not to place an end-of-file marker at the end of the file.

An /a or a /b switch applies to the preceding file specification and to all succeeding file specifications until another /a or /b switch is encountered. The file status is set to the default when a COPY command does not include an /a or a /b switch. For copying of files, the default file status is binary (/b). For concatenation, the default file status is ASCII (/a).

The /v switch is used to verify the accuracy of the execution of a COPY command. Verification causes the system to run more slowly. The /v parameter provides the same check on COPY as the VERIFY command.

Copying a Peripheral Device

COPY can be used to send files to peripheral devices and to transfer data between devices. The command is used in the same way as described previously, the only difference being that device names are used in place of file specifications. For example, suppose that you want to print a file named "secret.txt". All you have to do is use the COPY command and PRN, the reserved device name for the printer (see table 6-1 in chapter 6 for a list of reserved device names):

```
C>copy secret.txt prn
      1 File(s) copied
```

You can reverse the process and use COPY to send a file from a peripheral device to a file. A useful way to take advantage of this capability, and one that is utilized throughout this book, is to create a text file directly from the keyboard. The keyboard is a peripheral device with the reserved name "CON". The command "copy con filespec" tells MS-DOS to create a file from data input at the keyboard. Type your text in the normal fashion, pressing Enter at the end of each line. When the complete file has been typed, Enter Ctrl-Z and press Enter. The file will be written to the disk:

```
C>copy con: keyboard.txt
This is a sample file that is being created from
the keyboard. Ctrl-Z is typed and the Enter key is
pressed to send the file to the disk. The file can then
be viewed by entering the command TYPE KEYBOARD.TXT.
^Z

      1 File(s) copied
```

Copying between Devices

COPY can be used to send data from one peripheral device to another. The command is used just as described so far, except that one device name is included as the source of the data and a second device name is included as the recipient of the data. In the next example, COPY is used to send data from the keyboard (CON) to the printer (PRN). Press Enter at the end of each line, and press Ctrl-Z and Enter when you have entered the complete file:

```
C>copy con: prn
This is a sample file to demonstrate the use of COPY
in sending data between peripheral devices. At the end
of the input you will press Ctrl-Z and then press Enter.
This text will be sent to the printer.
^Z
        1 File(s) copied
```

Attempts to COPY a device while in binary status will generate this message:

```
Cannot do binary read from a device
```

The problem can be corrected by removing the binary switch or specifying ASCII status with the /a switch.

COUNTRY

External
MS-DOS 3.X, 4.X

Function: Specifies country-specific information such as date, time, and currency formats
Note: COUNTRY can be used in CONFIG.SYS only

Format: COUNTRY=*xxx*   (MS-DOS 3.0 through 3.2)
COUNTRY=*xxx*,[*yyy*][,[*d*:]*filename*[.*ext*]]   (MS-DOS 3.3, 4.X)

Example: country=001
country=001,437,c:\dos\country.sys

The COUNTRY command, first implemented with MS-DOS 3.0, allows you to specify certain country-specific information such as the date, the time, and currency formats.
Versions 3.0 through 3.2 use this command in a very straightforward manner. A statement of the form "country=*xxx*" is included in the CONFIG.SYS file, with *xxx* being a valid 3-digit country code. See appendix D for a listing of the valid country codes.

Use of the command is more complicated in MS-DOS 3.3 and 4.X. The format is as follows:

COUNTRY=*xxx*,[*yyy*][,[*d:*]*filename*[*.ext*]]

The *xxx* parameter remains a valid 3-digit country code. The *yyy* parameter specifies a code page. A single country has two code pages. COUNTRY determines which code page to use as the system code page. Please refer to appendix D for an overview of code pages and code page switching.

The *filename* parameter refers to the country information file (COUNTRY.SYS).

If there is no "country=" statement in CONFIG.SYS, the default country code is 001, the default code page is 437, and the default country information file is \COUNTRY.SYS.

CTTY

Internal
MS-DOS 2.X, 3.X, 4.X

Functions: Changes the standard input/output to an auxiliary console
Restores the standard input/output to the keyboard and screen

Format: **CTTY *device name***

Examples: ctty com1
ctty con

The keyboard and the display screen form the standard input/output device. This means that unless MS-DOS is instructed otherwise, it will look to the keyboard for input and will send output to the display screen. The CTTY (Change Console) command is used to make another peripheral device (such as a modem attached to an asynchronous communications port) the standard input/output device.

To use the CTTY command, type **ctty** and then type the name of the device that will be the new standard input/output device. (See chapter 6 for a list of device names reserved by MS-DOS.) The following command makes the modem attached to the first asynchronous communications port the standard input/output device:

```
C>ctty com1
```

Once this command is entered, MS-DOS will look to the port for input data. It will no longer be possible to enter data from the keyboard in the normal fashion.

The following command will restore the keyboard and display screen as the standard input/output device. The command must be entered at the current input device:

```
C>ctty con
```

CTTY allows you to use any character device as the standard input/output device. Simply type **ctty** and then type the name of the device that is defined in the device driver. (See chapter 14 for a discussion of devices and device drivers.)

One of the most useful applications of the CTTY command is to suppress all output to the screen during the execution of a batch file. As an example of where you might want to use this, consider the following batch file:

```
@echo off
copy *.* d:
```

The first line suppresses the display of the batch file commands. But `@echo off` has no effect on the screen output generated by the command `copy *.* d:`. Therefore, the name of each file will be displayed on the screen as the file is copied.

Having the filenames scroll across the screen may serve no useful purpose and might be distracting to the person using the batch file. *All* output to the display screen can be suppressed by modifying the batch file as follows:

```
@echo off
ctty nul
copy *.* d:
ctty con
```

The command `ctty nul` makes the nul device the standard input/output device. "Nul" represents a peripheral device that does nothing. Any data sent to the nul device disappears. Any attempts to read data from the nul device return nothing. By making nul the standard output device, any display intended for standard output is swallowed by "nul" and doesn't appear on the display screen.

The command "ctty nul" also turns off the keyboard. You will not be able to use your keyboard if you enter "ctty nul" from the command line. But from a batch file, you can turn both your keyboard and display screen back on with the command "ctty con". This tells DOS that the con device (keyboard and display screen) is again the standard input/output device.

DATE

Internal
MS-DOS 1.X, 2.X, 3.X, 4.X

Functions: Displays the current date known to MS-DOS
Changes the date known to MS-DOS

Format: DATE [*mm-dd-yy*]

Examples: date
date 10-30-89

The DATE command is used to display and set the current date known to MS-DOS. Each time that you create or modify a file, MS-DOS stores this date as a part of the file's entry in the disk directory.

To display the current date known to MS-DOS, type **date**. MS-DOS will display the date, including the day of the week (Mon, Tue, Wed, etc.). Then MS-DOS will ask if you want to change the current date:

```
C>date
Current date is Fri    10-28-89
Enter new date:
```

To enter a new date, use the form *mm-dd-yy* or *mm/dd/yy* where:

mm is a one- or two-digit number from 1–12,

dd is a one- or two-digit number from 1–31,

yy is a two-digit number from 80–99 or a four-digit number from 1980 to 2099.

```
C>date
Current date is Fri    10-28-89
Enter new date:10/30/89
```

If you want to leave the current date unchanged, just press Enter:

```
C>date
Current date is Mon    10-28-89
Enter new date:       ←Enter
```

You may specify the current date in the DATE command:

```
C>date 10/30/89
```

MS-DOS will prompt for another date if you enter an invalid date.

On machines with permanent clocks, the MS-DOS 3.3 and 4.X implementations of DATE reset the permanent clock's date.

DEL

Internal
MS-DOS 1.X, 2.X, 3.X, 4.X

Function: Deletes (erases) one or more files from a disk

Format: DEL [*d:*][*path*][*filename*[*.ext*]]
          DEL [*d:*][*path*][*filename*[*.ext*]] [/P] (MS-DOS 4.X)

Examples: del badfile.txt
          erase badfile.txt

The DEL (DELete) command, also known as the ERASE command, is used to remove a file(s) from a disk. To use DEL, type **del** (or **erase**) and then type the file specification of the unneeded file. (See chapter 2 for a discussion of file specifications.) If you do not include a drive designator and/or a path in the filespec, MS-DOS assumes that the file is located on the default drive and/or in the current directory. In the following example, a file in the current directory of the default drive is deleted:

```
C>del badfile.txt
```

You can delete a group of files with a single command by using wildcard characters. (See chapter 2 for a discussion of wildcards.) Use wildcards with caution, however, since it is easy to inadvertently erase files that you wanted to save. The command in the next example deletes all files in the current directory of drive B that have an extension of DOC:

```
C>del a:*.doc
```

Entering a file specification of *.* tells MS-DOS to delete all the files in the current directory. MS-DOS checks to make sure that you really want to do this:

```
C>del *.*
Are you sure (Y/N)? _
```

Type N and press Enter if you are not sure. If you are sure, type **Y**, double-check that you really are sure, say goodbye to the files, and press Enter.

MS-DOS 4.X features the /p switch, which directs the operating system to display each file's name and ask for confirmation that the file is to be deleted.

The 4.X implementation of DEL also allows you to delete the files in a directory by just specifying the directory's name. For example, if \TMP is a directory, you can delete the files in \TMP by entering the command "del \tmp". In response to this command, MS-DOS displays the message

```
All files in directory will be deleted!
Are you sure (Y/N)?
```

All files in \TMP will be deleted if you enter "y".

Actually, DEL does not remove files from a disk. It only modifies the file directory so that MS-DOS treats the files as if they did not exist. If you ever delete an important file accidentally, you may want to try to recover it with the MS-DOS utility program DEBUG. (See chapters 10 and 15 for some guidance.) There are also commercially available programs that can be used to recover erased files. The important point here is that if you think you may want to recover an erased file, **do not, under any circumstances, write any data to that disk.** If you do that, the file really does go "bye-bye."

Note that DEL cannot be used to remove a subdirectory. (See the discussion of RMDIR.) Also, DEL cannot be used to delete a file that has its read-only attribute set.

DEL should be used carefully if you use ASSIGN, JOIN, or SUBST. These commands direct MS-DOS to treat one device as if it were another. For example, ASSIGN may be used to direct all references for drive A to drive C. When conditions like this exist, it is easy to inadvertently delete files that you want to keep, so be careful.

DEVICE

Internal
MS-DOS 2.X, 3.X, 4.X

Function: Instructs MS-DOS to install a device driver
             Note: DEVICE can be used in a CONFIG.SYS file only

Format: **DEVICE=**[*d:*][*path*]***filename***[*.ext*]

Example: device=ansi.sys

The DEVICE command is used to give MS-DOS the filename(s) of any user-specified device drivers that are to be installed in computer memory. (See chapter 14 for a discussion of installable device drivers and their use.)

The DEVICE command can be used only as a statement within a CONFIG.SYS text file. The statements in CONFIG.SYS are read by MS-DOS each time that the system is booted. If any of the statements in CONFIG.SYS are

DEVICE commands, MS-DOS will store (install) in computer memory the device driver named in the command.

To enter a DEVICE command, type **device=** and then type the filename and filename extension of the device driver that is to be installed in memory. A DEVICE command can be added to an existing CONFIG.SYS file with a text editor such as EDLIN (chapter 8). A new CONFIG.SYS file can be created by using the command "copy con". (See the COPY command, "Copying between Devices.")

CONFIG.SYS must be stored in the root directory of the default drive. In the following example, ANSI.SYS and VDISK.SYS are stored in the sub-directory \DOS of drive C:

```
C>copy con: config.sys
device=c:\dos\ansi.sys
device=c:\dos\vdisk.sys
^Z        ←you press Ctrl-Z
   1 File(s) copied
```

ANSI.SYS is an installable keyboard device driver supplied with MS-DOS 2.X, 3.X, and 4.X. Use of ANSI.SYS is discussed in chapter 9. VDISK.SYS is an installable device driver for a RAM disk drive. VDISK.SYS is discussed below. This section also discusses the installable device drivers DRIVER.SYS, DISPLAY.SYS, PRINTER.SYS, XMA2EMS.SYS, and XMAEMS.SYS.

VDISK.SYS

A virtual disk, also called a RAM disk, is a portion of random access memory (RAM) that the operating system treats as a disk drive. A RAM disk is accessed with a drive specifier as if it were a conventional disk drive. The advantage of a RAM disk is that the data on the disk can be accessed much faster than data on a mechanical disk drive. The disadvantage of a RAM disk is that it is not permanent storage for data. Turning off or rebooting your system destroys the contents of the RAM disk. Any data to be saved must be copied to a mechanical disk.

VDISK.SYS is a RAM disk device driver supplied with MS-DOS 2.X, 3.X, and 4.X. It performs three functions: (1) installs the RAM disk in memory and assigns it a drive letter, (2) formats the RAM disk so that it can store files (you cannot use the FORMAT command on a RAM disk), and (3) acts as an interface between MS-DOS and the RAM disk. The syntax for installing the device driver is:

DEVICE=[*path*]**VDISK.SYS**[*vvv*][*sss*][*ddd*][[/E[*·t*]]/X[*·t*]]

The *vvv* parameter sets the size of the virtual disk in kilobytes. The allowable range is from 1 kilobyte up to the size of your system's memory. The default disk size is 64 Kbytes.

If you request too much memory for your RAM disk, VDISK will adjust your request downward to leave 64 Kbytes of memory available after the RAM disk is installed. VDISK will not install the RAM disk if less than 64 Kbytes of memory is available. If the disk size request has been adjusted, VDISK notifies you with the message **Buffer size adjusted**.

The *sss* parameter sets the number of bytes per sector on the RAM disk. Acceptable values are 128, 256, and 512. Any other value will default to 128 bytes per sector. Disk sectors are discussed in chapter 10.

The *ddd* parameter sets the number of entries allowed in the disk directory. The allowable range is 2 to 512, with a default of 64. Each directory entry requires 32 bytes. If necessary, VDISK will adjust your request size upward to fill out a complete sector. For example, if your sector size is 512, and you request 12 directory entries, VDISK will adjust upward and give you 16 directory entries ($16 \times 32 = 512$).

Each RAM disk requires 1 boot sector, 1 FAT sector, 1 directory sector, and 1 data sector. VDISK will adjust your directory entry request downward, if need be, to make room for these required sectors. Any adjustment of the number of directory entries is accompanied by the message **Directory entries adjusted**.

The /e switch directs MS-DOS to place the RAM disk in extended memory (see chapter 12). The driver itself is still stored in low memory. You may request more than one RAM disk in extended memory by placing multiple "device=vdisk.sys" commands (each with the /e switch) in your CONFIG.SYS file. Each RAM disk in extended memory may be up to 4 megabytes in size.

MS-DOS will display an **Insufficient memory** message if you use the /e switch on a machine that does not have extended memory.

The /x switch, implemented in DOS 4.X, directs the operating system to place the RAM disk in *expanded* memory. Use of expanded memory requires both an expanded memory card and an expanded memory device driver. Expanded memory is discussed in chapter 12. The PC-DOS 4.0 implementation of VDISK.SYS works in expanded memory only with an IBM expanded memory board.

If your computer has both extended and expanded memory, you may want to consider putting the RAM disk in extended memory, because there are relatively few programs running under DOS that can utilize extended memory.

The optional *:t* parameter tells MS-DOS the maximum number of sectors to transfer to extended memory or expanded memory at one time. The range is 1 to 8, with a default of 8. Try adjusting this parameter, as well as the sector size parameter, if you have trouble getting your RAM disk to work properly in expanded or extended memory.

Hardware interrupts are disabled during memory transfers between conventional and extended memory. If your RAM disk is in extended memory, it may interfere with communication programs if the value for *:t* is set too high.

The following example installs a 1000-Kbyte RAM disk:

```
device=vdisk.sys 1000 512 64 /e:4
```

The RAM disk created has a sector size of 512 bytes. The directory may contain up to 64 entries. The RAM disk is placed in extended memory. A maximum of 4 sectors is transferred to extended memory at a time.

DRIVER.SYS

DRIVER.SYS is a diskette device driver supplied with MS-DOS 3.2, 3.3, and 4.X. It is valuable for two reasons: (1) it can be used to drive all MS-DOS–supported drives (including 1.44-megabyte, 3½-inch drives) and (2) it can be used to drive "logical" as well as "physical" drives. To understand how DRIVER.SYS works, you must first understand how MS-DOS addresses disk drives.

Disk Addressing

When you switch on your computer, one of the actions that MS-DOS takes is to determine which peripheral devices are attached to the computer. After making this determination, MS-DOS reads the CONFIG.SYS file to check for any installable device drivers. During this process, MS-DOS assigns a unique drive letter to each disk drive device on the system. The first internal diskette drive is assigned A; the second, B. The letters from C on are assigned as other system drives are recognized.

On systems with only one internal diskette drive, the single drive is assigned letters A and B. The first fixed disk drive on a MS-DOS computer is always assigned drive letter C.

Disk drives are also given *physical drive numbers* The first diskette drive is assigned physical drive number 0, the second is assigned physical drive number 1, and so on for the diskette drives.

The first fixed disk on an MS-DOS computer is assigned physical drive number 128, the second is assigned 129, and so on for the fixed disks.

Physical and Logical Drives

A *physical* disk drive is a real disk drive, a piece of hardware. Its existence is totally independent of any computer.

A *logical* disk drive is a product of the logic stored inside a computer. A program (such as the operating system) tells the computer that a logical drive exists at a certain (physical) location, and the computer accepts that information. The logical drive ceases to exist when the computer is turned off.

Drive letters are used to reference logical disk drives. As discussed above, if an MS-DOS computer has one diskette drive, the drive is assigned drive letters A and B. Logical drives A and B both reside on physical drive 0.

MS-DOS assigns logical drive letters, in alphabetical order, to disk drives as each logical drive is initialized.

With this background, we can now discuss DRIVER.SYS.

Using DRIVER.SYS

The following discussion requires some knowledge of diskette structure. See chapter 10 if you are unfamiliar with this topic.

The syntax for DRIVER.SYS is:

DEVICE=DRIVER.SYS /D:*ddd*[/T:*ttt*][/S:*ss*][/H:*hh*][/C][/F:*f*]

The /D:*ddd* parameter specifies the physical drive number on which the logical diskette will reside. Allowable values are 0 to 255. As discussed, 0 to 127 refers to diskette drives and 128 to 255 refers to fixed disk drives.

The /T:*ttt* parameter specifies the number of tracks per side of the logical diskettes. Allowable values are 1 to 999. The default is 80 tracks per side.

The /S:*ss* parameter specifies the number of sectors per track of the logical diskette. Allowable values are 1 to 99. The default is 9 sectors per track.

The /H:*hh* parameter specifies the maximum number of heads. Allowable values are 1 to 99. The default is 2 heads.

The /c parameter specifies that the drive detect when the drive door has been opened and closed.

The /n parameter specifies that the physical device on which the logical device will reside be nonremovable (a fixed disk).

The /F:*f* parameter specifies the type of logical device. Allowable values and the corresponding diskette type are given in the following list. The default value is 2.

Value	Diskette Type
/f:0	160 Kbytes/180 Kbytes
	320 Kbytes/360 Kbytes
/f:1	1.2 Mbytes
/f:2	720 Kbytes
/f:7	1.44 Mbytes

Adding a Physical Drive

Let's say that you want to add an external 1.44-megabyte, 3½-inch diskette drive to a system that has one standard internal diskette drive and one fixed disk drive. Physical drive 0 is the internal diskette drive. Physical drive 1 is reserved for a second standard internal diskette. Therefore, the 3½-inch drive will be physical drive 2. The command to install an appropriate device driver is as follows (assume that DRIVER.SYS is in subdirectory C:\DOS):

```
device=c:\dos\driver.sys /d:2 /f:7
```

The **/d:2** parameter specifies physical drive number 2. The **/f:7** parameter specifies a 1.44-Mbyte diskette. Since the DEVICE command is read after drive letters A, B, and C have been assigned, the 3½-disk drive is assigned drive letter D.

Adding a Logical Drive

Sometimes it is useful to create a second logical drive on a physical drive. Assume that you have an AT computer with one 1.2-Mbyte 5¼-inch disk drive, one 3½-inch 1.44-Mbyte disk drive, and one hard disk drive. MS-DOS will assign logical drive letter A to the 5¼-inch drive, logical drive letter B to the 3½-inch drive, and logical drive letter C to the hard disk drive.

Such an arrangement can prove to be inconvenient if you perform an operation that logically requires identical disk drives. For example, say that the system diskettes are 5¼-inch and you want to create bootable 5¼-inch diskettes. If drives A and B were both 5¼-inch, you could put the system diskette in drive A, the new diskette in drive B, then enter the command "sys b:". Even if the system only had a single 5¼-inch drive (and no 3½-inch drive), the same command could still be used, because DOS would prompt you to swap diskettes. With the 3½-inch drive on the system, though, logical drive B is assigned to a separate physical drive. It is not available to the 5¼-inch drive.

The way around the problem is to use DRIVER.SYS to create a second logical drive on the 5¼-inch physical drive. The following command, when placed in CONFIG.SYS, instructs DOS to create a new logical drive on the first physical drive:

```
device=c:\sys\driver.sys /d:0 /t:80 /s:15 /h:2 /c /f:1
```

The logical drive is to be on the first physical drive (**/d:0**). It will have 80 tracks per side (**/t:80**), 15 sectors per track (**/s:15**), and two heads (**/h:2**), will detect the door opening (**/c**), and will be a 1.2-Mbyte drive (**/f:1**). Once the system is rebooted with this statement in CONFIG.SYS, the 5¼-inch drive can be referenced by using logical drive letters A and D. In this way, a 5¼-inch diskette can be made bootable with the command "sys d:".

DISPLAY.SYS

DISPLAY.SYS is a code-page-switching device driver supplied with MS-DOS 3.3 and 4.X. DISPLAY.SYS is used to implement code page switching on a display adapter. For an overview of code pages and code page switching, please refer to appendix D.

DISPLAY.SYS is installed in memory by including a statement having the following format in CONFIG.SYS:

DEVICE=[*d*:][*path*]DISPLAY.SYS CON[:]=(*type*[,[*hwcp*][,(*n,m*)]])

or

DEVICE=[*d*:][*path*]DISPLAY.SYS CON[:]=(*type*[,[*hwcp*][,*n*]])

The *type* parameter specifies the display adapter that will support code page switching. The allowable values are "EGA" and "LCD". EGA refers to both the Enhanced Graphics Adapter and the IBM PS/2 Video Display Adapter. LCD refers to the PC Convertible Liquid Crystal Display Adapter. Code page switching is not currently supported with other types of display adapters.

The *hwcp* parameter specifies the hardware code pages that are to be made available for use. Valid code page numbers are 437 (the default), 850, 860, 863, and 865. Hardware code pages are ready-to-use code pages that are stored in the display device's read-only memory (ROM). Refer to appendix D for further information on hardware code pages, including the meaning of the code page numbers.

The *n* parameter specifies the number of prepared code pages to be supported by the adapter. The allowable range is 1–12. Prepared code pages are discussed in appendix D.

The *m* parameter specifies the number of font sizes to be supported by the adapter. The Enhanced Graphics Adapter can support up to two font sizes (8×8 and 8×14). The PS/2 Display Adapter can also support up to two font sizes (8×8 and 8×16). The LCD adapter supports only one font size (8×8).

The following command illustrates the use of DISPLAY.SYS.

```
device=c:\dos\display.sys con:=(ega,437,2)
```

This command instructs MS-DOS to load the DISPLAY.SYS driver for use with the Enhanced Graphics Adapter. Along with the driver, hardware code page 437 is to be loaded. In addition, the driver is to support two prepared code pages.

PRINTER.SYS

PRINTER.SYS is another code-page-switching device driver supplied with MS-DOS 3.3 and 4.X. As its name implies, PRINTER.SYS supports code page switching on several IBM printers: the IBM Proprinter model groups 4201, 4202, 4207, and 4208, and the IBM Quietwriter III Model 5202. (The 4207 and 4208 models are supported, starting with MS-DOS 4.0.) For an overview of code page switching, please refer to appendix D.

PRINTER.SYS is installed in memory by including a statement of the following format in CONFIG.SYS:

DEVICE=[*d:*][*path*]**PRINTER.SYS** *LPT#*[:]=
(*type*[,[(*hwcp1,hwcp2*)][,*n*]])

or

DEVICE=[*d:*][*path*]**PRINTER.SYS** *LPT#*[:]=(*type*[,[*hwcp*][,*n*]])

The *LPT#* parameter is used to specify a printer device. The valid parameters are "PRN," "LPT1," "LPT2," and "LPT3."

The *type* parameter refers to the printer that will support code page switching. Use "4201" for the IBM 4201 and 4202 Proprinter, "4208" (with MS-DOS 4.X only) for the IBM Proprinter 4207 X24 and 4208 XL24, or "5202" for the IBM 5202 Quietwriter III.

The *hwcp* parameter specifies the hardware code pages that are to be made available for use. Valid code page numbers are 437 (the default), 850, 860, 863, and 865. If two or more hardware code pages are specified, they must be enclosed in parentheses. Hardware code pages are ready-to-use code pages that are stored in the printer's read only memory (ROM). Refer to appendix D for further information on hardware code pages, including the meaning of the code page numbers.

The *n* parameter specifies the number of prepared code pages to be supported by the printer. Prepared code pages are discussed in appendix D.

The following command (which must be in CONFIG.SYS) instructs MS-DOS to load the PRINTER.SYS driver for use with the Quietwriter 5202 printer. Along with the driver, hardware code page 850 is to be loaded. In addition, the driver is to support three prepared code pages.

```
device=c:\dos\printer.sys prn:=(5202,850,3)
```

XMA2EMS.SYS

XMA2EMS.SYS is an expanded memory device driver that is supplied with PC-DOS 4.X. XMA2EMS.SYS conforms to the Lotus-Intel-Microsoft Expanded Memory Specification 4.0. A complete discussion of expanded memory is presented in chapter 12. This section discusses the use of XMA2EMS.SYS. As is the case with other device drivers, XMA2EMS.SYS is written to be used with a specific piece of hardware, namely the IBM Expanded Memory Adapter. XMA2EMS.SYS probably will not work if you have another brand of expanded memory board on your system; however, the discussion of XMA2EMS.SYS is still relevant because, in general, the points covered will apply to the use of other expanded memory device drivers.

As with the other drivers discussed, XMA2EMS.SYS can only be loaded into memory with a DEVICE statement contained in the file CONFIG.SYS. There are several parameters that can be used in the DEVICE statement to control the manner in which expanded memory is implemented. Each of these parameters will now be discussed.

You can specify the memory location of a single contiguous 64-Kbyte page frame by entering **frame=** followed by the location's segment address. For example, the following statement (which must be in CONFIG.SYS) specifies that a 64-Kbyte page frame is to be located starting at segment address C000. All of the examples in this section assume that the file XMA2EMS.SYS is located in C:\SYS:

```
device=c:\sys\xma2ems.sys frame=c000
```

The default value for "frame" is D000. This means that the 64-Kbyte page frame is loaded beginning at segment address D000H, offset 0000H (D000:0000). As is discussed in chapter 12, the page frame is the area in conventional memory that serves as a window into expanded memory. In some circumstances, there may be a memory conflict between a peripheral device and the default address for the page frame. For example, it is possible that a network interface card could be located at address D000:0000. In such a situation, the default value for "frame" could be overridden, as illustrated above, and the memory conflict avoided.

Instead of a single contiguous page frame, you can specify the starting address of up to four separate physical 16-Kbyte pages. Together, these separate pages will make up the page frame. The four separate pages have the preassigned names of P0–P3. You specify a page's starting address by typing its name, an equals sign, and then the segment address of the page's starting location. As an example, the following statement specifies that four 16-Kbyte pages are to be located at segment addresses C000, C800, D000, and D800:

```
device=c:\sys\xma2ems.sys p0=c000 p1=c800 p2=d000 p3=d800
```

Use of the P0–P3 parameters is useful if conventional memory on your computer is very "crowded" and there are no contiguous 64-Kbyte blocks available. You cannot use the P0–P3 parameters if you use the "frame" parameter.

The pages P0–P3 are for use by application programs that utilize expanded memory. In addition, there are two other pages that can be specified for use by the operating system. If you specify a location for "p254", PC-DOS can use that page to run VDISK.SYS and FASTOPEN in expanded memory. If you specify a location for "p255", PC-DOS can use that page to run the BUFFERS command in expanded memory. The following example illustrates the use of these two parameters:

```
device=c:\sys\xma2ems.sys frame=c000 p254=d000 p255=d400
```

The /x:*size* switch is used to specify the number of 16-Kbyte pages of expanded memory to be used by the system. The minimum value for *size* is 4. The maximum and default value for *size* is the total amount of expanded memory contained in the system.

XMAEM.SYS

XMAEM.SYS is a device driver supplied with PC-DOS 4.X that allows the hardware of a PS/2 Model 80 to emulate an expanded memory card. If you are using XMAEM.SYS, you must load it into memory before you load an expanded memory device driver, such as XMA2EMS.SYS.

XMAEM.SYS has a *size* parameter that controls the amount of PS/2 memory to be used to emulate expanded memory. The value of *size* specifies the number of 16-Kbyte pages. The minimum value for *size* is 4. The maximum and default value for *size* is the total amount of available memory.

If you specify a value for *size* (in XMAEM.SYS), the /x:*size* switch (in XMA2EMS.SYS) will be ignored.

DIR

Internal
MS-DOS 1.X, 2.X, 3.X, 4.X

Function: Lists directory entries

Format: DIR [*d*:][*filename*[.*ext*]][/P][/W]
             DIR [*d*:][*path*][*filename*[.*ext*]][/P][/W] (MS-DOS 2.X–4.X)

Examples: dir
             dir b:
             dir b:\subdir1*.doc /w

The DIR (DIRectory) command is used to display the filename, filename extension, size, and time/date stamp of the files contained on a disk. The MS-DOS 2.X and subsequent versions of DIR also display the disk's volume identification (if one was specified when the disk was formatted) and the amount of free space remaining on the disk.

To use DIR with MS-DOS 1, simply type **dir**. Notice that if you do not enter a drive designator (such as c: or a:), MS-DOS will display the files on the default drive:

```
C>dir
FILE1       BAS       3213     10-02-89   11:42a
PROGRAM1    BAS      12674     10-09-89    9:53a
GWBASIC     EXE      57344      6-21-89   10:44a
```

```
COMMAND       COM      4879     3-11-89   11:40a
      4 File(s)
```

The first column of the display gives the name of each file. The second column gives the filename extension. The third column shows the size of the file in bytes. The fourth column shows the date that the file was created or last modified, and the fifth column shows the time that the file was created or last modified.

If you are using the DIR command with MS-DOS 2.X, 3.X, or 4.X, again simply type **dir**. The display will show the same information as the MS-DOS 1 version but will give you additional information about the disk's volume label and the space available for new files. If you do not include a path in the DIR command, MS-DOS will default to the current directory of the specified (or default) drive:

```
C>dir

    Volume in drive C is WAITE_DISK1
    Directory of C:\

COMMAND    COM    17664    3-08-89 12:00p
C                 <DIR>             1-01-86 12:07a
WS2PATH    BAT       23    10-07-89  8:18a
CONFIG     SYS      128     9-25-89  7:24p
SETCLOCK   COM      853     9-19-88  4:24p
WS                <DIR>             9-08-88  4:27p
         6 File(s)     110269 bytes free
```

In the preceding example, notice that the display shows the volume label **WAITE_DISK1** for the disk in the default drive (C:). The volume label is simply the *name* of the disk. The line **Directory of C:** tells you that the files displayed are in the root directory on drive C. Two of the directory entries contain the notation **<DIR>**. These entries represent subdirectories that are contained in the root directory. The final line says that there are 110,269 free bytes remaining on the disk.

To view the contents of a directory other than the current directory, type **dir** and then type the path to the directory:

```
C>dir \ws

    Volume in drive A is WAITE_DISK1
    Directory of C:\WS

    .            <DIR>             9-08-88  4:27p
    ..           <DIR>             9-08-88  4:27a
WS       EXE    60128     6-25-88  7:24p
WS       HLP    45853     6-25-88  7:24p
BATES    DOC     4096     9-17-89  4:27p
```

```
GILMORE    DOC     4096    9-18-89   2:15p
        6 File(s)      110269 bytes free
```

Notice the single and double periods that appear in the first two entries. These are shorthand symbols used by MS-DOS in displaying the contents of a subdirectory. The entry in the first column with a single period
represents the directory being listed. The entry with two periods represents
the listed directory's parent directory. WS is the listed directory. WS's parent
directory is the root directory. (See chapter 3 for more information about
directories, subdirectories, and parents.)

Using /P and /W with DIR

The DIR command has two optional switches. The /p switch is particularly
useful when you wish to view the contents of a large directory. When DIR is
directed to display a large number of files, the file information will scroll off
the screen faster than you can read it. You can see this by inserting a working
copy of your system diskette in drive A and entering the command **dir a:** and
pressing Enter. You will be unable to study the information before it's gone
from view. By using the /p switch, you can instruct MS-DOS to display one
"page" of file information at a time. The display will be suspended each time
that the screen is filled. The display will resume when you press any key.

The /w switch is used with DIR to display file information in the
"wide" mode. The wide mode displays the filename and filename extension
of five files on each line of the display screen. File size and file time/date
information are not displayed with the wide mode.

Using DIR to List Selected Files

You can specify a particular file in the DIR command. MS-DOS will look for
that filename and, if the file is found, will display the corresponding file
information:

```
C>dir ws2path.bat

Volume in drive C is WAITE_DISK1
Directory of C:\

WS2PATH   BAT      23    10-07-89    8:18a
        1 File(s)      110269 bytes free
```

This feature can be useful when you are looking for a specific file
among a large number of files. Let's say that you want to know if there is
a file named "letters.doc" in the subdirectory WS. You could look for the
file in two ways. You could enter the command **dir \ws** and scan the display

for "letters.doc", or you could enter the command **dir \ws letters.doc**. If you enter the second command, MS-DOS will do the scanning for you. If "letters.doc" exists, MS-DOS will display the file information. If the file does not exist, MS-DOS will let you know.

Wildcards and DIR

Using wildcard characters with DIR allows you to have MS-DOS list a specific group of files. Let's say that you want a listing of the files in the root directory of drive B that have a filename beginning with the letter "Q" and a filename extension of DOC. All you have to do is enter the following command:

```
C>dir b:\q*.doc
```

MS-DOS will pick out the files that you are looking for and display their names on the screen. (For more information on wildcards, see chapter 2.)

By eliminating the filename extension in a DIR command and entering only the filename, you can instruct MS-DOS to list all files with the specified filename. The following command directs MS-DOS to list all files in the root directory of drive B with a filename of "animals":

```
C>dir b:\animals
```

By entering the filename followed by a period and no filename extension, you can instruct MS-DOS to list all files with the specified filename and no filename extension. In the following command, MS-DOS looks for a file having the filename "animals" and no filename extension:

```
C>dir b:animals.
```

DISKCOMP

External
MS-DOS 1.X, 2.X, 3.X, 4.X

Function: Compares the contents of two floppy diskettes

Format: DISKCOMP [*d*:][*d*:]
            DISKCOMP [*d*:][*d*:][/1][/8] (MS-DOS 2.X–4.X)

Example: diskcomp a: b:

DISKCOMP (COMPare DISKette) is a utility program used to compare the contents of two floppy diskettes. DISKCOMP compares the diskettes on a sector by sector basis. It is most useful in checking the accuracy of copies made with DISKCOPY.

DISKCOMP is used for comparing diskettes only. It cannot be used with fixed disks, RAM disks, or network disks. Nor can it be used in conjunction with SUBST, ASSIGN, or JOIN.

Before using DISKCOMP, you may wish to read the discussion on diskette structure in chapter 10.

Using DISKCOMP

Since DISKCOMP is an external MS-DOS command, a copy of the file DISK-COMP.COM must be available to the system before you can use the command. This means that either DISKCOMP.COM must be in the current directory of the default drive or that the location of DISKCOMP.COM must have been specified by the PATH command (see the discussion of PATH).

If you are using a system with two diskette drives, you will save yourself a lot of diskette swapping by including two drive letter designators in the DISKCOMP command:

```
C>diskcomp c: b:
```

When you press Enter, MS-DOS will prompt you with the statements **Insert the first diskette in drive A:** and **Insert the second diskette in drive B:**. It does not matter which diskette is inserted in which drive. Once the diskettes are in place, the comparison is started by pressing any key.

If you are using a system with only one diskette drive or if you do not enter two drive letter designators in the DISKCOMP start command, MS-DOS will display a prompt telling you when to insert the first diskette and when to insert the second diskette. It is not important which diskette you designate as "first" and which you designate as "second." The important point is to keep the first and second diskettes straight after the comparison begins.

DISKCOMP compares the diskettes on a track-by-track basis. If all tracks match, MS-DOS will display the message **Diskettes compare ok**. If there is a mismatch, MS-DOS will display the track and side where the errors appear.

At the end of a comparison, DISKCOMP asks you if there are any more comparisons to perform. If you reply "Y", DISKCOMP prompts you to insert the next pair of diskettes. If you reply "N", control is returned to MS-DOS.

DISKCOMP Switches

DISKCOMP has two optional switches. The /1 switch tells DISKCOMP to compare only the first side of each diskette. The /8 switch tells DISKCOMP to compare only the first 8 sectors of each track. (See chapter 10 for a detailed discussion of tracks and sectors.)

DISKCOPY

External
MS-DOS 1.X, 2.X, 3.X, 4.X

Function: Copies the contents of one floppy diskette onto another

Format: **DISKCOPY** [*d*:][*d*:]
           DISKCOPY [*d*:][*d*:][/1] (MS-DOS 2.X–4.X)

Example: diskcopy a: b:

DISKCOPY is a utility program used to copy the contents of one floppy diskette onto another. It can be used with floppy diskettes only. MS-DOS will display an error message if you try to use DISKCOPY with a hard disk.

Using DISKCOPY

DISKCOPY is an external MS-DOS command. This means that before you can use DISKCOPY, one of the system drives must contain the file DISK-COPY.COM. In the example used here, DISKCOPY.COM is stored on drive C.
    If your system has two diskette drives, you will save yourself a lot of diskette swapping by including two drive letter designators in the DISK-COPY command.

```
C>diskcopy a: b:
```

When the command is entered, MS-DOS will load DISKCOPY.COM into memory and then prompt you to insert the source diskette in the first drive specified in the command and the target diskette in the second drive specified in the command. The *source diskette* is the diskette to be copied; the *target diskette* is the diskette that will contain the copy. Once the source and target diskettes are in place, press any key to begin the DISKCOPY process.

```
Insert source diskette in drive A

Insert target diskette in drive B

Strike any key when ready
```

If your system does not have two diskette drives or if you did not include two drive letter designators in the DISKCOPY command, MS-DOS will prompt you to insert the source and target diskettes. Remember that the source diskette is the original; the target diskette is the copy. If you get them confused, you may inadvertently erase the data stored on the original diskette. To prevent accidental erasure, you can easily write-protect the source diskette by placing a small piece of tape over the notch on the diskette's side. MS-DOS will not send data to a write-protected diskette.

At the end of the copy process, you will be asked if you wish to copy another diskette. If you reply "Y", the DISKCOPY process is repeated. If you reply "N", control is returned to MS-DOS.

The MS-DOS 2.X and later versions of DISKCOPY offer an optional /1 switch. Including the /1 switch tells DISKCOPY to copy only the first side of the source diskette.

Note: Most versions of DISKCOPY will format an unformatted target diskette.

DISKCOPY versus COPY

It is important to recognize the difference between the commands DISK-COPY and COPY. DISKCOPY begins by reading the contents of the first track off the source diskette and writing the contents to the first track of the target diskette. The contents of the second track are then read and written to the second track in the target diskette, and so on. DISKCOPY writes over all preexisting data on the target diskette.

COPY begins by reading the contents of the first sector of a file off the source diskette and writing the contents to the first available sector on the target diskette. The contents of the second sector of the file are then read and written to the next available sector on the target diskette. COPY continues in this manner until the entire file has been copied. The only preexisting data on the target diskette that is written over by COPY is the files named in the COPY command.

A file that does not occupy contiguous sectors on a diskette is called a *fragmented* file. Fragmented files can slow computer performance, since MS-DOS requires more time to read a fragmented file. It is good practice to copy a highly fragmented diskette to an empty diskette by using the command "xcopy *.* /s" (or "copy *.*") rather than using DISKCOPY. The XCOPY or COPY command will copy each of the fragmented files to contiguous sectors on the target diskette, thus improving computer performance.

ECHO

Internal
MS-DOS 2.X, 3.X, 4.X

Functions: Allows or prevents the screen display of MS-DOS commands during batch file execution
Displays messages during batch file execution

Format: ECHO [ON|OFF|*message*]

Examples: echo on
echo off
echo your message here

A *batch file* is a group of MS-DOS commands that are executed sequentially. ECHO determines whether or not the commands in a batch file are displayed on the screen during execution. ECHO can be used in the following ways:

1. **ECHO ON** tells MS-DOS to display the MS-DOS commands.
2. **ECHO OFF** tells MS-DOS to suppress display of the MS-DOS commands.
3. **ECHO [*message*]** tells MS-DOS to display [*message*]. The message will be displayed regardless of the current ECHO state.
4. **ECHO** (with no parameters) tells MS-DOS to display the current ECHO state (ON or OFF).
5. The command "echo off" is echoed on the display screen when it is executed from a batch file. In MS-DOS 3.3 and 4.X, you can suppress this echoing by replacing the command with "@echo off".

The use of ECHO in batch files is illustrated in chapter 4.

ERASE

Internal
MS-DOS 1.X, 2.X, 3.X, 4.X

Function: Erases (deletes) one or more files from a disk

Format: ERASE [*d:*][*path*][*filename*[.*ext*]]
ERASE[*d:*][*path*][*filename*[.*ext*]] [/P] (MS-DOS 4.X)

Examples: erase badfile.txt
del badfile.txt

The ERASE command is identical to the DEL command. Please refer to the DEL command for a description of ERASE.

EXE2BIN

External
MS-DOS 1.X, 2.X, 3.X, 4.X

Function: Converts EXE files to standard binary files

Format: EXE2BIN [*d*:][*path*]***filename***[.*ext*][*filespec*]

Example: exe2bin testfile

Computer programs that operate under MS-DOS are stored as either COM or EXE files (see chapter 11). EXE2BIN is an MS-DOS utility that is used to convert EXE files to COM files. You need not concern yourself with EXE2BIN unless you are assembling or compiling your own computer programs. The file EXE2BIN.EXE is not supplied with the PC-DOS 4.X system diskettes. You will have to secure a copy of the "Utilities" diskette that comes with the Disk Operating System Technical Reference manual in order to obtain the 4.X implementation of EXE2BIN.

EXE and COM Files

All EXE files contain a *header* (an area at the start of the file) that stores information about the relocatable items within the file. A *relocatable* item is a program variable whose value depends on the location at which MS-DOS loads the program in computer memory. During the loading of an EXE file, MS-DOS refers to the file's header to determine the location of each relocatable item within the file. MS-DOS then modifies the value of each relocatable item according to the memory address of the load.

COM files do not contain any relocatable items; therefore, they do not have a header. A COM file is produced by first creating an EXE file (with either an assembler or a compiler) and then using EXE2BIN to convert the EXE file to a binary file. COM files created with an assembler must begin with the statement "ORG 100H". This assembler statement tells MS-DOS to load the file at offset address 100H. A COM file is limited in size to 64 Kbytes.

Since a COM file does not have a header, converting an EXE file to a COM file will conserve computer memory. Thus, it is advantageous to convert to COM files those EXE files that do not contain relocatable items, that begin with an ORG 100H statement, and that are smaller than 64 Kbytes.

Using EXE2BIN

EXE2BIN is an external MS-DOS command. This means that before you can use EXE2BIN, the file EXE2BIN.EXE must be available to the system. Either EXE2BIN.EXE must be in the current directory of the default drive or the location of EXE2.BIN must have been specified by the PATH command (see the discussion of PATH).

To use EXE2BIN, type **exe2bin**, then type the file specification of the file to be converted, and finally type the file specification of the converted file. A filename must be specified for the file to be converted. If no filename extension is specified for the file to be converted, MS-DOS assumes that the file has an extension of EXE. A file specification for the converted file is optional. The default filename is the filename specified for the file to be converted. The default filename extension for the converted file is BIN. The current directory is used if no path is specified for the converted file.

Once you have entered the complete command, press Enter to convert the EXE file. If the EXE file conforms to the requirements of a COM file, the conversion is made and control returns to MS-DOS. The converted file can then be renamed with an extension of COM if you wish.

If the EXE file does not specify where MS-DOS is to load the file (for example, does not contain an ORG statement), EXE2BIN will convert the EXE file to a standard binary file. If such a file contains any relocatable items, MS-DOS will prompt you to enter a "fixup value." The *fixup value* is a hexadecimal number that will be the absolute memory address at which the converted file will be loaded. Such a file can be loaded only by a user application program that specifies where in memory it will be loaded. MS-DOS will be unable to load the file.

If the original EXE file specifies a loading address other than 100H, MS-DOS will display the following message:

```
Files cannot be converted
```

This message will also be displayed if the original file is not a valid EXE file.

FASTOPEN

External
MS-DOS 3.3, 4.X

Function: Provides rapid access to recently used subdirectories and files

Format: FASTOPEN *d*:[=*nnn*] . . . (use of "=" is optional)
FASTOPEN *d*:[=([*nnnn*][,*mmm*])] . . . [/X] (MS-DOS 4.X)

Example: fastopen c:=100

FASTOPEN is used to store in memory the physical disk location of recently accessed subdirectories and files. When MS-DOS needs to access a file, FASTOPEN first checks to see if the file's location is stored in memory. If it is, the file can be located very quickly.

MS-DOS locates a disk file by processing a *linked list*, which points to the file's physical location on the disk. As an example, let's consider what MS-DOS must do in order to execute the following command:

```
C>dir \subdir1\subdir2\subdir3
```

The root directory is always in a specific physical location on the disk. MS-DOS proceeds to this location and scans the root directory for an entry named SUBDIR1. This entry will contain the physical disk location of subdirectory SUBDIR1. MS-DOS proceeds to this location and scans SUBDIR1 for an entry named SUBDIR2. This entry directs the operating system to the physical location of SUBDIR2. Once SUBDIR2 is located, the location of SUBDIR3 can be read, and MS-DOS can proceed to the physical disk location of SUBDIR3. All of these steps must be carried out before the DIR command can be executed. FASTOPEN provides a way to speed up this process.

Using FASTOPEN

FASTOPEN is invoked by including on the command line the letter specifier for each hard disk on your system, followed by a number from 10 to 999. The number tells FASTOPEN how many subdirectory and file locations to store in memory for that disk. In the following example, FASTOPEN stores 100 locations for drives C and D:

```
C>fastopen c:100 d:100
```

FASTOPEN uses 34 as a default if a drive letter is not followed by a number. Each location requires 35 bytes of system memory.

Each time a file or subdirectory is accessed, FASTOPEN checks to see if the corresponding disk location is stored in memory. If not, the location is determined and stored in memory. This process continues until the number of locations stored in memory matches the number specified on the command line. Thereafter, any location placed in memory displaces the location corresponding to the least recent disk access.

The MS-DOS 4.X implementation of FASTOPEN also stores in memory a record of the disk cluster numbers of recently accessed disk files. Normally, DOS determines a file's clusters by reading the file allocation table. By storing a file's cluster sequence in a memory buffer, DOS decreases the amount of time required to access the file. Each buffer set aside to record a sequence of clusters uses 16 bytes of memory. The default value for the number of cluster sequence buffers is 34.

The 4.X version of FASTOPEN can be loaded into expanded memory by using the /x switch. If you are using PC-DOS 4.X, the /x switch only works if you are using an IBM expanded memory board and the IBM device driver XMA2EMS.SYS.

Another feature implemented in MS-DOS 4.X is the capability to load FASTOPEN into memory using an INSTALL statement contained in the CONFIG.SYS file. The following statement, when placed in CONFIG.SYS, loads FASTOPEN. When using INSTALL, the specification for FASTOPEN must include the filename extension.

```
install=c:\dos\fastopen.exe c:=(50,250)
```

FASTOPEN will set up 50 buffers to store the location of recently accessed files and directories, plus 250 buffers to store the cluster sequence of recently accessed files.

Note: FASTOPEN may be invoked one time only following system startup (you may want to include it in an AUTOEXEC.BAT file). FASTOPEN is used with hard disks only. It cannot be used with floppy disks or disks defined with the MS-DOS commands ASSIGN, JOIN, or SUBST. Nor can it be used with network drives.

FCBS

Internal
MS-DOS 3.X, 4.X

Function: Determines the number of file control blocks that may be
used when file sharing is implemented
Note: FCBS can be used in CONFIG.SYS only

Format: FCBS=*m,n*

Example: fcbs=10,5

Recall from chapter 10 that MS-DOS uses two different mechanisms to access disk files. One of these mechanisms utilizes a data structure called a *file control block* (FCB) to store information used by MS-DOS in reading and writing files. If your computer is on a network and you have implemented file sharing (see the SHARE command), MS-DOS limits the number of FCBs that can be open at one time to 4. The FCBS command allows you to increase the number of FCBs that may be open at a time.

When file sharing is *not* implemented, there is no limit on the number of available file control blocks. Therefore, the FCBS command has no effect when file sharing is not implemented.

FCBS is entered with two parameters. The first parameter determines the number of FCBs that may be open at one time. The allowable range is 1 to 255. The second parameter determines the number of FCBs that MS-DOS must leave open. As an example, suppose that CONFIG.SYS contains the following command:

fcbs=10,5

This command tells MS-DOS that up to 10 FCBs can be open. In addition, 5 FCBs are protected against automatic closure by MS-DOS. In other words, if 10 FCBs are open, and MS-DOS needs to open more FCBs, the operating system may close up to 5 FCBs but must leave the other 5 open.

If CONFIG.SYS does not contain a "fcbs=" command, a default of m=4, n=0 is set.

If MS-DOS must automatically close an FCB, it looks for the FCB that was least recently used and closes it. If MS-DOS subsequently attempts to use the closed FCB, the following error message is displayed:

```
FCB unavailable
Abort, fail?
```

FDISK

External
MS-DOS 2.X, 3.X, 4.X

Function: Configures the hard disk

Format: **FDISK**

Example: fdisk

FDISK is a utility program that is used to partition (configure) a hard disk assigned to MS-DOS. The use of FDISK is described in chapter 1.

FILES

Internal
MS-DOS 2.X, 3.X, 4.X

Function: Determines the amount of memory that is set aside for file
             handles
             Note: FILES may be used in a CONFIG.SYS file only

Format: **FILES=**xx

Example: files=25

The FILES command is used to establish the amount of memory for a control block used in managing file handles The amount of memory set aside for this purpose determines the maximum number of file handles that can exist at one time.

A *file handle* is a 16-bit number that is assigned by MS-DOS to a new file when the file is created or to an existing file when the file is opened. File handles are used by MS-DOS to keep track of the files that an application program is using at any one time. The role of file handles is discussed more fully in chapter 10.

Using FILES

A FILES command may be used only as part of a CONFIG.SYS file. CONFIG.SYS is a text file containing one or more commands that are read by MS-DOS during the booting process. Each command in CONFIG.SYS specifies certain parameters under which MS-DOS will operate. In this case, a FILES command establishes the number of file handles that may be used by MS-DOS at one time.

CONFIG.SYS can be created or modified with a text editor such as EDLIN. CONFIG.SYS can also be created by entering the command "copy con: config.sys" (see the COPY command for details).

```
C>copy con: config.sys
FILES=10
^Z        ←you press Ctrl-Z, Enter
          1 File(s) copied
```

MS-DOS will set aside memory for eight file handles if no FILES command is read during booting. For most application programs, this is sufficient. MS-DOS will display the message **No free file handles** if an application program requires more than eight file handles. MS-DOS will occupy 39 more bytes of memory for each additional file above the default value of 8.

The FILES command does not affect the number of user-specified file control blocks (FCBs) that may be set up and used with MS-DOS service functions 0FH–29H (see appendix A).

FIND

External
MS-DOS 2.X, 3.X, 4.X

Function: Searches for a specified string of text in a file or files

Format: FIND [/V][/C][/N]*string*[*filespec*][*filespec*] . . .

Examples: find "flint's" sample.txt.
                find /v "berkeley" sample.txt
                find /c "oakland" sample.txt
                find /n "books" sample.txt

FIND is an MS-DOS filter that searches the lines of one or more text files for a specified string. The specified string is enclosed on the command line in double quotes (`"like this"`). Alternatively, output from a program or another MS-DOS command can be piped through FIND. The output from FIND can be sent to the standard output or redirected to a device or a file.

FIND is an external MS-DOS command. This means that before you can use the FIND filter, a copy of the file FIND.EXE must be stored in one of the system drives.

FIND Switches

There are three optional switches for FIND. The /v switch causes FIND to display the lines in a text file that do not contain the specified string. The /c switch instructs FIND to display only a count of the number of lines in a text file that contain the specified string. The /n switch tells FIND to display the lines of a text file that contain the specified string; each line is preceded by its relative line number within the file.

Chapter 6 discusses FIND and describes MS-DOS filters, redirection, and pipes.

FOR

Internal
MS-DOS 2.X, 3.X, 4.X

Function: Executes a command repeatedly on a set of parameters

Format: **FOR** *%%variable* **IN** (*set of parameters*) **DO** *command*

Examples: for %%a IN (file1 file2 file3) DO del %%a
                for %b IN (example.bat program.txt letter) DO copy %b prn

A command can be executed repeatedly on a set of specified parameters by using the command FOR. Each FOR command begins with the word "for", followed by a dummy variable. If a FOR command is located within a batch file, the dummy variable is preceded by two percentage signs (%%). Only one percentage sign is used if the FOR command is not located in a batch file. During the execution of a FOR command, the dummy variable is sequentially replaced by each of the specified parameters.

The dummy variable is followed by the letters "IN". Both letters must be entered in uppercase. "IN" is followed by a set of parameters that must be enclosed in parentheses.

Following the set of parameters are the letters "DO", which must be entered in uppercase. "DO" is followed by the command that will be executed one time for each of the parameters in the set.

In the following example, a FOR command is used to print a copy of the files "example.bat", "program.txt", and "letter":

```
C>for %b IN (example.bat program.txt letter) DO copy %b prn

COPY EXAMPLE.BAT PRN
        1 File(s) copied

COPY PROGRAM.TXT PRN
        1 File(s) copied

COPY LETTER PRN
        1 File(s) copied
```

The use of FOR in MS-DOS batch files is discussed in chapter 5.

FORMAT

External
MS-DOS 1.X, 2.X, 3.X, 4.X

Function:	Initializes floppy diskettes and hard disks so that they can be used by MS-DOS
Formats:	FORMAT [*d:*][/S] (DOS 1.X–4.X) FORMAT[*d:*][/1][/8][/V][/B] (DOS 2.X–4.X) FORMAT [*d:*][/4] (DOS 3.X–4.X) FORMAT [*d:*][/N:*xx*/T:*yy*] (DOS 3.3–4.X) FORMAT [*d:*][/F:*size*] (DOS 4.X)
Examples:	format b: format b:/s format c:/s/v

Floppy diskettes and hard disks must be initialized before they can be used by MS-DOS. This initialization process is called *formatting* and is performed with the command FORMAT.

Formatting divides a floppy diskette or hard disk into parcels called *sectors*. Sectors are grouped together into tracks. MS-DOS assigns numbers to the sectors and tracks and uses the numbers as references to find its way around the diskette or hard disk.

Formatting places a *boot record* on each diskette and hard disk. As you might imagine, MS-DOS uses the boot record whenever it boots up. Formatting also creates a file allocation table and a disk directory on each diskette and hard disk. MS-DOS uses these structures as a table of contents to the files stored on the diskette or hard disk.

Chapter 10 contains detailed information on sectors, tracks, the boot record, the file allocation table, and the disk directory.

Using FORMAT

Formatting a diskette destroys any existing data on the diskette. Formatting a hard disk will destroy any data in the MS-DOS partition of the disk. You will need to format all new, blank diskettes that will be used by MS-DOS. You may occasionally format previously used diskettes. When you do this, make sure that you copy any files that you want to keep onto another (formatted) diskette before using FORMAT. The examples in this section show how to format a floppy diskette. The use of FORMAT to format a hard disk is nearly identical. Refer to chapter 1 for information on partitioning and formatting a hard disk.

FORMAT is an external MS-DOS command. This means that before you can begin formatting, a copy of the file FORMAT.COM must be in one of the system drives. FORMAT.COM is one of the files provided on your MS-DOS system diskette. The discussion that follows assumes that FORMAT.COM is located on a diskette in drive A.

If your system has two diskette drives, formatting is most easily accomplished by placing a working copy of your MS-DOS system diskette in drive A and the diskette to be formatted in drive B. If you are using a system with one diskette drive, insert your working copy of the system diskette in drive A. The commands that you will enter will be identical to those used on a two-drive system. MS-DOS will prompt you when it is time to change diskettes.

To begin formatting, enter the following:

```
A>format b:
```

MS-DOS will load FORMAT.COM into memory, display some information about the system manufacturer, and then issue a prompt:

```
Insert new diskette for drive B:
and strike any key when ready
```

Strike any key and formatting will begin. MS-DOS tells you that it is formatting with the following message:

```
Formatting...
```

Formatting a floppy diskette takes about one minute, so sit back and relax. MS-DOS will notify you when formatting has been completed:

```
Formatting...Format complete
```

MS-DOS will display a status report with information about the newly formatted diskette. In MS-DOS 4.0, the status report includes the total amount of disk space, the amount of available disk space, the number of bytes in each allocation unit, and the number of allocation units available on the diskette. An allocation unit (or cluster) is the minimum number of disk sectors that is allocated to a file; it varies with the type of diskette (or hard disk) used. The 4.X version of FORMAT also assigns a serial number to the diskette. The number serves no purpose other than to identify the diskette. The following is an example of a 4.X status report:

```
1213952 bytes total disk space
 107520 bytes in bad sectors
1106432 bytes available on disk

    512 bytes in each allocation unit
   2161 allocation units available on disk

Volume Serial Number is 2414-12CD
```

After displaying the status report, MS-DOS will ask if you want to format another diskette:

```
Format another (Y/N)?
```

Enter Y to format another, or N to exit FORMAT.

The System Files

The /s switch is used to add the MS-DOS system files and the file COMMAND.COM to a diskette or hard disk. The hidden MS-DOS system files have names like IO.SYS and MSDOS.SYS. These two files, along with COMMAND.COM, must be on any diskette or hard disk that will be used to boot MS-DOS. The order and the location of the system files on a diskette or hard disk are important. A diskette or hard disk may not be bootable if you simply use the command COPY to add the system files. The following command will format the diskette in drive B and instruct MS-DOS to add the system files and the COMMAND.COM file.

```
A> format b:/s
```

MS-DOS responds:

```
Insert new diskette for drive B:
and strike any key when ready

Formatting...Format complete
System transferred

    362496 bytes total disk space
     38912 bytes used by the system
    323584 bytes available on disk

Format another (Y/N)? _
```

Notice that MS-DOS includes the message: `System transferred` and that the status report contains information about the amount of disk space occupied by the system files and COMMAND.COM. If you use the command "dir b:" to examine the newly formatted diskette, the directory entry for COMMAND.COM will be displayed. No information will be displayed for the hidden system files.

Adding a Volume Label

The MS-DOS 2.X–4.X versions of FORMAT allows you to assign a *volume label,* or name, to a diskette or hard disk. A volume label serves only to identify a diskette or hard disk; it cannot be used as a parameter in any MS-DOS commands. The volume label will be displayed whenever the DIR command is used to examine the contents of a diskette or hard disk.

To assign a volume label, enter the /v switch in the FORMAT command. At the end of the formatting process, MS-DOS will prompt you to enter a volume label. A volume label can be up to 11 characters long. All characters acceptable in filenames (see chapter 2) are acceptable in volume labels.

```
A> format b:/s/v
```

MS-DOS responds:

```
Insert new diskette for drive B:
and strike any key when ready

Formatting...Format complete
System transferred
```

```
Volume label (11 characters, ENTER for none)? WAITE_DISK1

    362496 bytes total disk space
     38912 bytes used by the system
   3235684 bytes available on disk

Format another (Y/N)? _
```

You can use **dir b:** to display the volume label and directory entries of the newly formatted diskette:

```
A>dir b:

 Volume in drive B: is WAITE_DISK1
 Directory of   A:\

COMMAND  COM   15480   3-01-89  2:00a
        1 File(s)     323584 bytes free
```

The MS-DOS 4.X version of FORMAT handles volume labels a little differently. The label is specified as part of the /v switch. The following is an example:

```
format a: /v:book_backup
```

If you do not specify a volume label, MS-DOS will prompt you for one when the formatting process is complete.

Formatting 8 Sectors per Track

The MS-DOS 2 version of FORMAT will normally divide each track into 9 sectors. The MS-DOS 3 and 4 versions of FORMAT will normally divide each track into 9 or 15 sectors, depending on the type of drive holding the target diskette. The /8 switch directs FORMAT to divide each track into 9 or 15 sectors but to use only 8 of the sectors. This feature allows files on diskettes originally formatted with MS-DOS 1.X to be copied onto diskettes formatted under MS-DOS 2.X, 3.X, and 4.X.

Formatting a Single Side

FORMAT determines if the diskette to be formatted is single or double sided and accordingly formats one or two sides. However, if you include the /1 switch in the FORMAT command, only one side will be formatted, regardless of the type of diskette or diskette drive. The /1 switch can be used only with diskettes and is not available with the MS-DOS 1 version of FORMAT.

The /B Switch

Some implementations of MS-DOS 2–4 have a /b switch for FORMAT. This switch instructs FORMAT to divide each track on the diskette into 8 sectors and to allocate space on the diskette for the two hidden system files. No files are actually written to the diskette. System files can subsequently be copied to the diskette by using SYS.

The /4 Switch

The /4 switch, implemented in MS-DOS 3 and 4, allows you to format a standard diskette on a 1.2-Mbyte drive. (Use the /1 switch and the /4 switch for single-sided diskettes.) Diskettes formatted in this fashion can be used only on 1.2-Mbyte drives.

The /N:*xx* and /T:*yy* Switches

The /n and /t switches are implemented in MS-DOS 3.3 and 4.X. They are used to format a diskette at less than the maximum capacity supported by the diskette drive. The /n switch sets the number of sectors per track. The /t switch sets the number of tracks. The switches must be used together.

The /n and /t switches are implemented primarily to allow the formatting of 720-Mbyte diskettes on 1.44-Mbyte diskette drives. In the following example, it is assumed that drive D is a 3½-inch, 1.44-Mbyte drive that contains an unformatted 720-Kbyte diskette:

```
C>format d: /n:9 /t:80
```

The /F Switch

The somewhat bewildering number of FORMAT switches is the result of the variety of different types of floppy diskettes that MS-DOS may be called upon to format. For example, if you have a 1.2-Mbyte disk drive and want to format a 180-Kbyte diskette on it, you will have to enter the command "format a: /1 /4". The MS-DOS 4.X version of FORMAT makes this process somewhat easier through the use of the /f switch.

With the /f switch you do not have to know that a 180-Kbyte diskette is a single-sided (/1), normal density (/4) diskette. All you need to know is the capacity of the diskette. Then, if the capacity of the drive is the same or larger, you can use the /f switch to specify the disk's capacity. As an example, in MS-DOS 4.X, the 180-Kbyte diskette can be formatted as follows:

```
format a: /f:180
```

FORMAT and ERRORLEVEL

ERRORLEVEL is the name of a variable that is maintained by MS-DOS. The value of ERRORLEVEL is set by MS-DOS commands as a way of telling the operating system whether the command executed successfully, and if not, what went wrong. Batch files can determine the value of ERRORLEVEL by using the IF command.

The FORMAT command sets the value of ERRORLEVEL as follows:

Value	Meaning
0	FORMAT executed successfully.
3	FORMAT terminated when user pressed Ctrl-Break.
4	FORMAT terminated due to an error.
5	FORMAT terminated when user responded "N" to the warning about formatting a fixed disk.

GOTO

Internal
MS-DOS 2.X, 3.X, 4.X

Function: Transfers control to a specified location within a batch file

Format: GOTO *label*

Example: goto four

A *batch file* is a text file that contains a sequence of MS-DOS commands. Each command is entered as one line in the batch file. Lines in MS-DOS 2.X, 3.X, and 4.X batch files may be labeled. A label simply serves to identify a line. Batch file labels consist of a colon (:) followed by a string of eight or fewer characters.

GOTO directs a batch file to jump to a specific line within the file and to execute the command at that line. In this example, the GOTO command causes execution of the batch file to loop endlessly:

```
:work
rem i am working!
goto work
```

GOTO and the other batch file commands are discussed in chapter 4.

GRAFTABL

External
MS-DOS 3.X, 4.X

Function: Loads a character table into memory

Formats: **GRAFTABL**
GRAFTABL [*xxx* or /STA] (MS-DOS 3.3, 4.X)
GRAFTABL [?] (MS-DOS 4.X)

Examples: graftabl
graftabl 437

Normally, when the color/graphics adapter (CGA) is in graphics mode, the ASCII characters 128 through 255 cannot be displayed (this group of characters includes the accented letters). The GRAFTABL command is used to load into memory a character table that allows these characters to be displayed when the CGA is in graphics mode.

With the MS-DOS 3.3 and 4.X versions of GRAFTABL, the user can load a table of graphics characters that are specific to a code page. This allows the display of language-specific characters. The code page is selected by including a valid code page number on the command line. The valid numbers are 437, 860, 863, and 865. Please refer to appendix D for an overview of code pages.

Entering GRAFTABL with no parameters loads the graphics table for code page 437. You can load another graphics table by entering "graftabl xxx", where "xxx" is the number of the code page that corresponds to the table you want to load.

You can enter "graftabl /sta" to find out which code page is currently active.

In MS-DOS 4.X, you can enter "graftabl ?" to find out which code page is active as well as what other code pages are available to be loaded.

The MS-DOS 3.3 and 4.X versions of GRAFTABL return the ERRORLEVEL codes in the following list. Such codes are returned by MS-DOS commands to communicate information regarding the outcome of the commands. See chapter 4 for ways that ERRORLEVEL codes can be utilized by MS-DOS batch files.

ERRORLEVEL Code	Meaning
0	Code page successfully installed. No code page was previously installed in memory.
1	A code page was previously installed in memory. If a new code page was specified, it was successfully installed.

2	No code page was previously installed in memory. No new code page was installed.
3	Parameter not valid.
4	Incorrect version of MS-DOS

GRAPHICS

External
MS-DOS 2.X, 3.X, 4.X

Function: Prints the contents of a graphic screen display

Formats: GRAPHICS
GRAPHICS[<*printer*>][/R][/B] (DOS 3.X, 4.X)
GRAPHICS[<*printer*>][/R][/B] [/LCD] (DOS 3.3, 4.X)
GRAPHICS[<*printer*>][<*profile*>][/R][/B][/LCD]
[/PB:<*id*>] (MS-DOS 4.X)

Example: graphics color1

One of the more useful features of MS-DOS is its ability to print a full screen of text when the Shift and PrtSc keys are pressed at the same time. The command GRAPHICS expands this capability so that a graphics display can be printed by a dot matrix printer when the Shift-PrtSc combination is pressed.

GRAPHICS is another of the MS-DOS terminate and stay resident (TSR) utility programs. When the GRAPHICS command is first entered, MS-DOS reads the program into memory and keeps it there as long as the computer is running. Once GRAPHICS is installed, simply press Shift-PrtSc and GRAPHICS will go to work. Text or graphics will be printed according to the current display mode.

GRAPHICS Parameters

There are no parameters for the MS-DOS 2 version of GRAPHICS. Starting with MS-DOS 3.0, however, you may specify the type of graphics printer you are using:

Parameter	Description
GRAPHICS	IBM PC graphics printer Epson graphics printer
COLOR1	IBM PC color printer black ribbon

COLOR4	IBM PC color printer
	red, blue, green ribbon
COLOR8	IBM PC color printer
	cyan, magenta, yellow, black ribbon
COMPACT	IBM PC compact printer
	(MS-DOS 3.3 only)
THERMAL	IBM PC convertible printer
	(MS-DOS 3.3)
GRAPHICSWIDE	IBM Quietwriter—wide paper
	IBM Proprinter—wide paper

The default printer parameter is GRAPHICS.

With the /r switch, what appears as black on the screen is printed as black and what appears as white is printed as white. The default is to print black as white and white as black.

The /b switch (valid with printer parameters COLOR4 and COLOR8 only) prints the background color of the screen. The default is to not print the background.

The /lcd switch, implemented with MS-DOS 3.3, prints images as they appear on a liquid crystal display.

The MS-DOS 4.X version of GRAPHICS uses a *graphics profile* file. The graphics profile file contains instructions that guide the printer in printing the contents of the display screen. The file GRAPHICS.PRO, which comes with MS-DOS 4.X, is the standard profile file. It is the file that is used if the GRAPHICS command does not specify a *<profile>* parameter. GRAPH-ICS.PRO contains the instructions for the printers listed in the above table. Manufacturers of other printers may supply their own graphics profile file. Such a file would provide a means for GRAPHICS to be used with those printers.

MS-DOS 4.X also implements the **/PB:** *<id>* switch. Two parameters are valid for *<id>*:

▶ **LCD** for use with LCD displays (/PB:LCD is equivalent to /LCD).

▶ **STD** for use with CRT type displays (/PB:STD is the default).

The GRAPHICS command can be executed from the CONFIG.SYS file using the MS-DOS 4.X command INSTALL.

IF

Internal
MS-DOS 2.X, 3.X, 4.X

Function: Executes a command if a specified condition is true

Format: IF [NOT] *condition command*

Examples: if exist somefile.dat type somefile.dat
if %1==roses goto roses
if not exist file.bak copy file.txt file.bak

MS-DOS 2.X, 3.X, and 4.X commands can be executed on a conditional basis by including the commands in an IF statement. IF statements are generally used within a batch file. IF can check the following conditions:

IF EXIST *filespec command*   IF may be used to determine if a specific file exists in the current directory of a specified (or default) drive. The following statement directs MS-DOS to determine if a file named "somefile.dat" exists in the current directory of drive C (the default drive). If the file does exist, MS-DOS is to display (TYPE) its contents on the screen:

```
C>if exist somefile.dat type somefile.dat
```

IF *string1==string2 command*   An IF statement may be used to determine if two character strings are identical. This type of conditional statement is used to compare a string passed to a batch file as a parameter to a string specified within the batch file. The next example checks to see if batch file variable %1 is equal to the character string "roses". Execution of the batch file branches to the line labeled ":roses" if the condition is true:

```
C>if %1==roses goto roses
```

IF ERRORLEVEL *number command*   ERRORLEVEL provides a way for batch files to conditionally execute based on the outcome of an MS-DOS command or application program. ERRORLEVEL is a variable that can be set according to the outcome of a program or MS-DOS command.

The value of ERRORLEVEL can be tested with an IF statement. The command specified in the IF statement will be executed if the value of ERRORLEVEL is greater than or equal to "number". The following IF statement checks the value of ERRORLEVEL and directs MS-DOS to display the disk directory (DIR) if ERRORLEVEL is greater than or equal to 2:

```
C>if errorlevel 2 dir
```

Application programmers should refer to MS-DOS functions 31H and

4CH (appendix A) for more information on setting and reading ER-RORLEVEL.

IF NOT   The command contained in an IF NOT statement is executed if the condition tested is false. An IF NOT statement can test the same conditions as an IF statement. The following statement will check the current directory of drive C for a file named "file.bak". If the file does not exist, MS-DOS will copy the file "file.txt" and name the copy "file.bak":

```
C>if not exist file.bak copy file.txt file.bak
```

Please refer to chapter 4 for a discussion of the use of IF and IF NOT.

INSTALL

Internal
MS-DOS 4.X

Function: Load and execute DOS commands from CONFIG.SYS
*Note:*INSTALL can only be used in the file CONFIG.SYS.

Format: INSTALL=[*d:*][*path*]<*filename.ext*>[*parameters*]

Example: install=c:\dos\fastopen.exe c:=(50,250)

The MS-DOS commands FASTOPEN, GRAPHICS, KEYB, NLSFUNC, and SHARE are *memory resident* utilities. This means that the files containing these external commands remain in memory once they are loaded. They are available for use by the operating system as the need arises, without having to be reloaded from the disk.

The MS-DOS 4.X command INSTALL allows you to load and execute FASTOPEN, GRAPHICS, KEYB, NLSFUNC, and SHARE from the file CONFIG.SYS. CONFIG.SYS is a text file that must reside in the root directory of the disk used to boot MS-DOS. The statements in CONFIG.SYS are read and executed as part of the boot process. The role of CONFIG.SYS is discussed in chapter 5.

Each of the memory resident utilities mentioned can be loaded from the command line or from a batch file. However, when you use the INSTALL command to load them from CONFIG.SYS, the utilities are loaded into a lower memory address than when they are loaded from the command line or a batch file. Loading at a lower address can enhance the performance of the utility.

To use INSTALL, type **install**, followed by an equals sign (=), followed by the filename and extension of the utility, followed by any required parameters. You must include the filename extension. The filename may be preceded by a drive specifier and/or a path specifier.

The following example illustrates the use of INSTALL. Remember that the statement must be used in CONFIG.SYS.

```
install=c:\dos\fastopen.exe c:=(50,250)
```

The statement directs MS-DOS to load FASTOPEN into memory. The file FASTOPEN.EXE is located in directory C:\DOS.

Refer to the individual discussions of FASTOPEN, GRAPHICS, KEYB, NLSFUNC, and SHARE for further information on the use of these commands.

JOIN

External
MS-DOS 3.X, 4.X

Function: Creates a logical link between a disk drive and a subdirectory on another disk drive

Format: JOIN *d1*: *d2*:*directory*

Example: join a: c:\adrive

JOIN allows you to reference a disk as though the disk's contents were stored in a subdirectory on another disk. JOIN is useful if you have files located on several disks and you want to avoid changing your current drive.

Say that you have a floppy disk in drive A that contains the files "chapter1.doc", "chapter2.doc", and "chapter3.doc". Drive A can be "linked" to subdirectory ADRIVE on drive C as follows:

```
C>join a: c:\adrive

C>dir \adrive
 Volume in drive C is HARDDISK
 Directory of C:\ADRIVE

CHAPTER1 DOC   7168  6-23-89  10:22a
CHAPTER2 DOC   9259  6-23-89   5:25p
CHAPTER3 DOC   4527  6-27-89   2:20p
       5 File(s) 587760 bytes free
```

JOIN will create a subdirectory if the one specified does not exist. The subdirectory must be empty and must be located exactly one level below the root directory.

A disk drive cannot be accessed directly while it is joined to a subdirectory. In the preceding example, the command "dir a:" will result in an error message.

Displaying and Cancelling JOINs

Using JOIN displays the active links. The /d switch is used to remove a link.

```
C>join
A: => A;\ADRIVE

C>join a: /d

C>join

C>
```

Limits on JOIN

JOIN will not work if a network drive is used as a parameter. Furthermore, JOIN is not reliable when used in conjunction with the commands SUBST and ASSIGN. The commands BACKUP, RESTORE, FORMAT, DISKCOPY, and DISKCOMP should not be used while a JOIN is in effect, since these commands may perform in an unpredictable fashion when confronted with a JOIN.

KEYB

External
MS-DOS 3.3, 4.X

Function: Loads a keyboard device driver that supports non-U.S. keyboards

Formats: **KEYB**[*xx*[,*yyy*][,[*d:*][*path*]***filename***[.*ext*]]]   (MS-DOS 3.3, 4.X)
                 KEYB[*xx*[,*yyy*][,[*d:*][*path*]***filename***[.*ext*]][*/ID:zzz*]]
                 (MS-DOS 4.X)

Example: keyb
                 keyb fr,850 c:\dos\keyboard.sys

KEYB is a program provided with MS-DOS 3.30 and 4.X that loads into memory a device driver for non-U.S keyboards. It is important to differentiate KEYB from the KEYB*xx* programs supplied with versions of MS-DOS prior to 3.3. The KEYB*xx* programs are not compatible with MS-DOS 3.3 and 4.X, and KEYB can be used with MS-DOS 3.3 and 4.X only (a discussion of the KEYB*xx* programs follows this section).

KEYB is used to set the *keyboard code* and the *code page* that are active for the CON device (the combination of the keyboard and the display device).

The keyboard code determines the functional layout of the keyboard, assigning significant foreign language characters to specific keys. For example, if KEYB is used to create a functional French keyboard, pressing the "2" key displays "é" and pressing the "0" key displays "à".

Code pages are *look up* tables that are used to convert into displayable characters the numerical values by which data (including characters) is stored in a computer. Please refer to appendix D for further information on code pages.

The format for using KEYB is:

KEYB[*xx*[,[*yyy*,[[*d:*][*path*]*filename*[.*ext*]]]]]

The *xx* parameter specifies the keyboard code. The *yyy* parameter specifies a code page number. The code page number must correspond to a code page previously prepared with the MODE command (see appendix D for an explanation of the code page numbers). If a code page is not specified, KEYB uses the default code page for the country specified by the keyboard code. The following list shows the allowable combination of keyboard code and code page number parameters. See the discussion of the SELECT command for an explanation of the keyboard codes. Refer to your MS-DOS manual for elaboration on various logical keyboard layouts.

Code Page	Keyboard Code
437	US, UK, FR, GR, IT,
	SP, LA, SV, SU, NL
850	US, UK, FR, GR, IT,
	SP, LA, SV, SU, NL,
	DK, NO, PO, SF, CF,
	BE, SG
860	PO
863	CF
865	NO, DK

The *filename*[.*ext*] parameter in the KEYB command refers to the system keyboard definition file. If the filename parameter is omitted, KEYB will look in the root directory for the file KEYBOARD.SYS. Each version of KEYBOARD.SYS is specific for a version of KEYB. For example, the MS-DOS 4.X version of KEYBOARD.SYS is specific for the 4.X version of KEYB. The following command illustrates the use of KEYB:

```
keyb fr,850,c:\dos\keyboard.sys
```

This command loads into memory a driver for the French keyboard and activates code page number 850 for the CON device.

Once a driver for a non-U.S. keyboard is loaded, the user may switch to the U.S. keyboard layout by pressing Ctrl-Alt-F1. Pressing Ctrl-Alt-F2 switches to the non-U.S. layout.

Entering **keyb** (with no parameters) directs MS-DOS to display the keyboard code for whichever non-U.S. keyboard driver is currently active in memory.

The MS-DOS 4.X version of KEYB supports the /**ID:***zzz* switch. This switch is used to specify a keyboard code for those countries that have more than one keyboard layout. The values supported for *zzz* are as follows:

► When *xx* is "FR", *zzz* can be 120 or 189.
► When *xx* is "IT", *zzz* can be 141 or 142.
► When *xx* is "UK", *zzz* can be 168 or 166.

KEYB returns the following ERRORLEVEL codes. ERRORLEVEL codes are available for processing by batch files (see chapter 4).

ERRORLEVEL Code	Explanation
0	Successful execution.
1	Improper keyboard code number, code page number, or syntax.
2	Bad keyboard definition file or definition file not found.
3	Could not load driver into memory.
4	KEYB is unable to communicate with CON device.
5	Code page requested has not been prepared.
6	Code page selected is not contained in keyboard information file.
7	Incorrect version of MS-DOS.

KEYB*xx*

External
MS-DOS 3.0–3.2

Function: Installs keyboard device drivers for non-U.S.keyboard
layouts

Format: **KEYB*xx***

Example: keybfr

The KEYB*xx*.COM commands supplied with MS-DOS versions 3.0–3.2
serve as installable device drivers for creating keyboards with non-U.S. layouts. As an example, to create a keyboard with a French layout, enter the
command **keybfr**. Refer to your MS-DOS manual for further information on
the various keyboard layouts available with these commands. Note that the
files are external commands; therefore, MS-DOS must be able to locate them
on a disk before they can be executed.

The KEYB*xx*.COM files are not compatible with MS-DOS 3.3 and 4.X.
The command KEYB operates in a different manner than the KEYB*xx* commands (see the preceding KEYB command).

LABEL

External
MS-DOS 3.X, 4.X

Function: Adds, changes, or inspects a disk's volume label

Format: LABEL [*d:*][*volume label*]

Examples: label c:
label c:newlabel

A *volume label* is a string of 11 or fewer characters used to identify a diskette
or a hard disk. MS-DOS 2.X allows you to add a volume label using the FOR-
MAT command. Unfortunately, it does not allow you to modify an existing
volume label or to add a volume label to a previously formatted disk. The
LABEL command provides both of these capabilities.

LABEL, followed by a drive specifier, displays the volume label of the
specified disk. The label of the default is displayed if no drive specifier is
included. After the label is displayed, a prompt is displayed asking you to
enter a new volume label. If you just press Enter, you are asked if you wish to
delete the current volume label. The following examples illustrate the use of
LABEL:

```
C> label c:

Volume in drive C is HARDDISK

Volume label (11 characters, ENTER for none)?   ←press Enter

Delete current volume label (Y/N)?n              ←enter "n"

C>
```

You can change a volume label by including the label on the command line:

```
C> label a:book back1
```

LABEL should not be used in conjunction with ASSIGN or SUBST, since these commands can cause LABEL to act unpredictably.

LASTDRIVE

Internal
MS-DOS 3.X, 4.X

Function: Sets the last valid drive letter for the system
Note: LASTDRIVE may be used in a CONFIG.SYS file only

Format: LASTDRIVE=*drive letter*

Example: lastdrive=z

LASTDRIVE sets the number of drive letters that are valid on a system. The allowable range for *drive letter* is A through Z. The minimum acceptable value is the letter corresponding to the number of physical drives on the system (either locally or on a network). For example, if you have a system with two floppy disk drives and one hard disk drive, LASTDRIVE must be greater than or equal to C. The default value for LASTDRIVE is E.

LASTDRIVE determines the drive letters that can be assigned to logical drives created with SUBST. See the discussion of SUBST for further information.

MEM

External
MS-DOS 4.X

Function: Displays information on memory utilization

Format: MEM [/PROGRAM or /DEBUG]

Example: mem /debug

The MEM command displays information that describes the way in which computer memory is being used by MS-DOS. If you enter **mem**, with no additional parameters, MEM tells you how much used and unused memory is available in the systems. Information is displayed for conventional, extended, and expanded memory.

If you enter **mem /program**, MEM tells you which programs and installable device drivers are in memory. MEM tells you where they are loaded and how much space they occupy.

If you enter **mem /debug**, MEM also includes information regarding the standard system device drivers and any expanded memory handles.

I wish that MEM had been implemented in MS-DOS 1 rather than in MS-DOS 4. It would have made my initial education about the structure of MS-DOS much easier. For users just starting to delve into the depths of DOS, MEM gives you an opportunity to learn a lot in a hurry. For experienced DOS hackers, MEM is a very useful tool for taking a closer look at the operating system.

Listing 1 is the output generated by the command "mem /debug". Of course the actual output will vary somewhat from one system to the next. That is what makes MEM a useful utility.

The majority of the listing is divided into four columns. `Address` refers to an occupied memory address. The addresses are given in hexadecimal notation. We will refer to these addresses in the discussion of listing 1.

An Aside about Addresses

Memory addresses on MS-DOS computers are usually represented by two components: a *segment* address and an *offset* address. The segment address for each address in listing 1 is obtained by deleting the address's initial and final zeros. For example, the address 000400 has a segment address of 0040. Each of the addresses in listing 1 has an offset address of 0000.

The second column in listing 1 is headed **Name**. The entry in this column contains the name of the item that is stored in memory. The third column contains the item's **Size**, also in hexadecimal notation. The fourth column, labeled **Type**, describes the role of the item stored in memory.

Listing 1. Output Generated by MEM /DEBUG

Address	Name	Size	Type
000000		000400	Interrupt Vector
000400		000100	ROM Communication Area
000500		000200	DOS Communication Area
000700	IBMBIO	002470	System Program
	CON		System Device Driver
	AUX		System Device Driver
	PRN		System Device Driver
	CLOCK$		System Device Driver
	A: - C:		System Device Driver
	COM1		System Device Driver
	LPT1		System Device Driver
	LPT2		System Device Driver
	LPT3		System Device Driver
	COM2		System Device Driver
	COM3		System Device Driver
	COM4		System Device Driver
002B70	IBMDOS	0088A0	System Program
00B410	IBMBIO	004EA0	System Data
	ANSI	001190	DEVICE=
		000380	FILES=
		000100	FCBS=
		0029A0	BUFFERS=
		0001C0	LASTDRIVE=
		000CD0	STACKS=
0102C0	MEM	0000A0	Environment
010370	IBMDOS	000010	-- Free --
010390	SHARE	0018A0	Program
011C40	COMMAND	001640	Program
013290	COMMAND	000100	Environment
0133A0	MOUSE	0000A0	Environment
013450	MOUSE	002370	Program
0157D0	MEM	012F60	Program
028740	IBMDOS	0778B0	-- Free --

```
655360 bytes total memory
655360 bytes available
```

```
567328 largest executable program size

393216 bytes total extended memory
393216 bytes available extended memory
```

The MEM Output

Referring to listing 1, the item stored at the low end of memory (address 000000) is called **Interrupt Vector**. This is the area of memory that stores the *interrupt vector table*. Each time the hardware or software issues an *interrupt*, the operating system must determine the memory address for the handler of that type of interrupt. The function of the interrupt vector table is to store the address of each of these handlers. Each handler's address is stored at a predetermined location within the interrupt vector table. In this way, DOS knows where to look when it is trying to locate the address of a specific handler. Interrupts and interrupt handlers are discussed in appendix A.

The **ROM Communication Area**, which begins at address 000400, is also known as the *BIOS data area*. This area of memory stores data that is used by the basic input/output system (BIOS). The BIOS acts as an intermediary between the operating system and the system hardware. It is within the BIOS data area that the BIOS maintains a record of such information as how many columns and rows are on the video display and which keyboard keys are currently being pressed. Application programs can directly access this area of memory, but in general, access is carried out through the use of the *BIOS interrupts* (discussed in appendix A).

The role of the **DOS Communication Area** (address 000500) is similar to the role of the BIOS data area. It is within this area of memory that MS-DOS maintains data that it uses in carrying out certain system functions. For example, the first byte in the DOS Communication Area stores the status of the last print screen operation (the byte equals 0 if the operation was successful, 1 if the operation is in progress, and 255 if the operation failed).

The portion of memory starting at address 000700 has the name **IBMBIO** and is referred to as a **System Program**. This is the portion of memory that stores the standard system device drivers. Each of the system device drivers is listed in the **Name** column (CON, AUX, PRN, etc.). The contents of IBMBIO are stored in the PC-DOS system file IBMBIO.SYS. In MS-DOS, the equivalent file has the name IO.SYS.

The next major block of memory begins at address 002B70. This block has the name **IBMDOS** and is also referred to as a **System Program**. This block contains what is known as the operating system's *kernel*. The kernel is the portion of MS-DOS that does most of the work. Basically, the kernel receives all requests for service functions and channels them to the appropriate device driver. The kernel is stored on disk as the system file IBMDOS.SYS. In MS-DOS, the equivalent file is MSDOS.SYS.

The next block of memory, beginning at address 00B410, contains what is referred to as the *DOS extensions*. These are the installable device drivers and other items that were placed in memory when the file CON-FIG.SYS was read during the booting process. The first DOS extension in listing 1 is the device driver ANSI.SYS. The other extensions listed are five parameters that were set during the boot process. Immediately to the left of each parameter's name is the amount of memory occupied by the item specified by the parameter. This information is very useful. It allows you to view the changes that occur in your system's memory configuration as you adjust the values of the system parameters. The role of CONFIG.SYS and the system parameters is discussed in chapter 5.

The remainder of computer memory is available to application programs. The names of the programs in listing 1 are **MEM** (the DOS command that generated listing 1), **SHARE** (the DOS command SHARE, which is loaded into memory to support disk partitions larger than 32 Mbytes), **COMMAND** (the DOS command processor COMMAND.COM), and **MOUSE** (a driver for the computer's mouse). Notice that the programs are listed as type **Program**. Some of them also have an entry that is listed as type **Environment**. This is the memory address of the copy of the DOS environment that was passed to the program when it was loaded into memory.

The block of memory at address 010370 is listed as being **-- Free --**. This portion of memory contained the copy of the DOS environment that was passed to the program SHARE. Because SHARE does not use the environment, it was able to release this block of memory so that it would be available to other applications.

Address 028740 contains a large block of free memory. This is the memory that is currently available to other applications. This block's size in hexadecimal notation is 0778B0 bytes, which translates to a decimal equivalent of 489,648 bytes. The size of the MEM program is hexadecimal 012F60, which translates to 77,664. Adding 489,648 and 77,664 gives 567,312. If you add to this the free memory at address 010370 (000010 equals decimal 16), you get a total of 567,328. This is the number given in listing 1 as the **largest executable program size**.

MKDIR

Internal
MS-DOS 2.X, 3.X, 4.X

Function: Creates a subdirectory

Format: **MKDIR** [*d:*]***path***
             MD [*d:*]***path***

Examples: mkdir \write
             md b:\programs\business

The MKDIR (MaKe DIRectory) command is used to create a subdirectory.

You may enter the command as either **mkdir** or **md**. The MKDIR command may contain a drive letter designator (such as c: or a:) specifying the drive on which the subdirectory will be created. If no drive is specified, the subdirectory will be created on the default drive.

The MKDIR command must specify the path to the subdirectory being created. The first example creates a subdirectory named WRITE:

```
C>mkdir \write
```

No drive was specified in the example, which means that WRITE will be located on the default drive. The path to the new subdirectory is \WRITE. WRITE will be a subdirectory entry contained in the root directory of the default drive.

The next example creates a subdirectory named \BUSINESS:

```
C>md b: \programs\business
```

BUSINESS will be located on drive B. The path to BUSINESS is \PRO-GRAMS\BUSINESS. This means that BUSINESS is a subdirectory contained in the subdirectory PROGRAMS. PROGRAMS is, in turn, a subdirectory entry contained in the root directory of drive B.

The maximum length of the path specifier created with MKDIR is 63 characters including the "–" characters. See chapter 3 for further examples of the use of MKDIR.

MODE

External
MS-DOS 1.X, 2.X, 3.X, 4.X

Functions:
1. Sets the mode of operation of a parallel printer
2. Sets the mode of operation of a graphics/color display adapter
3. Sets protocol for an asynchronous communications port
4. Redirects parallel printer output to a serial port
5. Prepares code pages (MS-DOS 3.3, 4.X)
6. Activates code pages (MS-DOS 3.3, 4.X)
7. Displays the currently active code page (MS-DOS 3.3, 4.X)
8. Restores an active code page (MS-DOS 3.3, 4.X)

Format:
1. MODE LPT#:[*n*][,[*m*][,P]]
2. MODE *n* or MODE [*n*],*m*[,T]

3. MODE COM*n:baud*[,*parity*[,*databits*[,*stopbits*[,P]]]]
4. MODE LPT#:=COM*n*
5. MODE *device* CODEPAGE
   PREPARE=((*cplist*)[*d:*][*path*]*filename*[.*ext*])
6. MODE *device* CODEPAGE SELECT=*cp*
7. MODE *device* CODEPAGE /STATUS
8. MODE *device* CODEPAGE REFRESH

Examples:
1. mode LPT1:80,6,P
2. mode 40
   mode 80,R,T
3. mode com1:1200,N,7,1
4. mode LPT2:=com1
5. mode con codepage prepare=((805,437)c:\dos\ega.cpi)
6. mode con codepage select=850
7. mode con codepage /status

MODE is an MS-DOS utility program that is used to establish working parameters for the parallel printer and the graphics/color monitor adapter. Beginning with MS-DOS 1.1, MODE is also used to set the parameters of the asynchronous communications port.

MODE is an external command. This means that before you can use MODE, the file MODE.COM must be available to the system. Either MODE.COM must be in the current directory of the default drive or the location of MODE.COM must have been specified by the PATH command (see the discussion of PATH).

Controlling the Printer with MODE

MODE may be used to control the number of characters printed per line and the vertical spacing between lines on the parallel printer. MODE's format is as follows:

MODE LPT#: [*n*][,[*m*][,p]]

where,

is parallel printer number 1, 2, or 3,

n is characters per line (80 or 132),

m is lines printed per vertical inch (6 or 8),

p instructs MS-DOS to try again when it receives a busy signal from the printer (continuous retry on device timeout).

The following command sets parallel printer 1 to print 80 characters per line with 6 lines printed per vertical inch:

```
C>mode LPT1:80,6,p
LPT1: set for 80
Printer lines per inch set
```

The **p** tells MS-DOS to retry continuously to send data to the printer if it receives a busy signal. The retry loop can be halted by pressing Ctrl-Break.

If a parameter is omitted or if an invalid value is specified, the setting for that parameter remains unchanged.

MODE can be used to set the parameters on Epson and Epson compatible printers only. Trying this command with other printers will yield interesting but unpredictable results.

Use of the MS-DOS 4.X version of MODE in controlling the printer differs slightly from earlier versions. The format for the command is

MODE LPT# [cols=n] [lines=m] [retry=ra]

As with the earlier versions of MODE, **LPT#** may be "LPT1:", "LPT2:", or "LPT3:"; **n** may be 80 or 132; and **m** may be 6 or 8.

Allowable values for the **ra** parameter are "e" (returns an error signal when the printer is busy; this is the recommended setting for printers shared on an IBM PC Local Area Network); "b" (returns a busy signal when the printer is busy; this is compatible with the "p" parameter in earlier versions of MODE); "r" (returns a ready signal when the printer is busy; this is the recommended setting for operation compatible with previous versions of MS-DOS).

Use of "cols", "lines", and "retry" is not required if commas are used as place holders. For example, the command "mode lpt1: lines=6" can also be entered as "mode lpt1: ,6".

Graphics/Color Display Adapter

If your system is equipped with a graphics/color display adapter, you may use MODE to set the adapter's parameters. There are two formats for MODE when it is used in this fashion:

MODE n

MODE [n],m[,t]

Table 1 contains a complete listing of the parameters used with MODE to control the graphics/color display adapter. The next few examples will show you how some of the parameters can be used. Bear in mind, however, that these examples and the information in table 1 are relevant only to systems having a graphics/color display adapter.

Table 1. Parameters Used with MODE to Control the Graphics/Color Display Adapter

Parameter	Function/Value
n=40	Sets the graphics/color display adapter width to 40 characters per line.
n=80	Sets the graphics/color display adapter width to 80 characters per line.
n=BW40	Switches the active display to the color/graphics display adapter, disables the color, and sets the display width to 40 characters per line.
n=BW80	Switches the active display to the color/graphics display adapter, disables the color, and sets the display width to 80 characters per line.
n=CO40	Switches the active display to the color/graphics display adapter, enables the color, and sets the display width to 40 characters per line.
n=CO80	Switches the active display to the color/graphics display adapter, enables the color, and sets the display width to 80 characters per line.
n=MONO	Switches the active display to the monochrome display adapter. Monochrome always displays 80 characters per line.
m	Is R or L. Shifts the display right or left.
t	Requests a test pattern that is used to align the display.

The first example sets the display width to 40 characters per line:

```
C>mode 40
```

The next example switches the active display to the graphics/color display adapter, enables the color, and sets the display width to 80 characters per line:

```
C>mode co80
```

The **m** and **t** parameters are used to adjust the screen display to the right or left. The following command will shift the display one column to the right in 40-column mode and two columns to the right in 80-column mode:

```
C>mode ,r
```

The **t** parameter tells MS-DOS to display a test pattern that can be used as an aid for adjusting the screen display to the right or left. The test pattern consists of the digits 0123456789 repeated four times in the 40-column display and eight times in the 80-column display. After displaying the pattern,

MS-DOS asks if you can see the digit to the far right or the far left, depending on whether you specified right or left adjustment. The following example shows the command and the resultant display in 40-column mode:

```
C>mode ,r,t
```

This command requests a right adjustment. The screen will momentarily go blank when the command is entered; then this test pattern and prompt will appear:

```
0123456789012345678901234567890123456789
```

```
Do you see the leftmost 0? (Y/N)
```

Your display needs to be right adjusted if you do not see a 0 at the left side of the screen. If you reply "N", the display will be shifted one column to the right (two columns in 80-column mode). If you reply "Y", control is returned to MS-DOS.

The MS-DOS 4.X version of MODE also supports the following format for controlling the display screen:

MODE CON [cols=*m*] [lines=*n*]

The allowable values for **m** are 40 and 80 characters per line (EGA and VGA displays only). The allowable values for **n** are 25 and 43 for EGA, and 25, 43, and 50 for VGA. The ANSI.SYS device driver must be loaded to use MODE in this fashion.

Communications and MODE

MODE may be used to initialize an asynchronous communications port. The format for the command is:

MODE COM*n:baud*[,*parity*[,*databits*[,*stopbits*[,p]]]]

where,

> **n** is the asynchronous communications port number (1 or 2); MS-DOS 3.3 and 4.X support additional port numbers 3 and 4;
>
> **baud** is the baud rate (110, 150, 300, 600, 1200, 2400, 4800, or 9600); MS-DOS 3.3 and 4.X support an additional baud rate of 19200;
>
> *parity* is either N (none), O (odd), or E (even);
>
> *databits* are the number of bits per word (7 or 8);
>
> *stopbits* are the number of stopbits (1 or 2);

p instructs MS-DOS to try again when it receives a busy signal from the port (continuous retry on device timeout).

You must specify the baud rate when using this form of MODE. However, only the first two digits of the baud rate need be entered in the command. All other parameters have defaults that are entered by using a comma in the command. The parity default is even, the databits default is 7, and the stopbits default is 1. The stopbits default is 2 if the baud rate is set at 110.

A p tells MS-DOS to continuously retry to send data to the port if it receives a busy signal. The retry loop can be halted by pressing Ctrl-Break. The following example initializes serial port 1 with a baud rate of 1200, no parity, 8 databits, and 1 stopbit. MS-DOS echoes the parameters when the command is entered:

```
C>mode com1:12,,8,,
COM1: 1200,e,8,1,-
```

The MS-DOS 4.X version of MODE supports the following format for configuring a communications port:

MODE COMn: baud=b [parity=p] [data=d] [stop=s] [retry=ra]

The values that can be assigned to baud, parity, data, and stop are the same as in earlier versions of MS-DOS. The values that can be assigned to ra are "e" (returns an error signal when the port is busy; this is the recommended setting for printers shared on an IBM PC Local Area Network); "b" (returns a busy signal when the port is busy; this is compatible with the p parameter in earlier versions of MODE); "r" (returns a ready signal when the port is busy; this is the recommended setting for operation compatible with previous versions of MS-DOS).

Redirecting a Parallel Printer with MODE

You can use MODE to redirect parallel printer output to a serial printer that is connected to an asynchronous communications port. The asynchronous port must first be initialized according to the requirements of the serial printer. The format for redirecting is:

MODE LPT#:=COMn

where,

\# is the number of the parallel printer,
n is the number of the communications port.

In the following example, communications port 1 is initialized by the first MODE command, and output to parallel printer 1 is redirected to port 1 by the second MODE command. Notice that the port is initialized so that timeout errors are continuously retried:

```
C>mode com1:300,n,8,1,p
COM1; 300,N,8,1,P
C>mode LPT1:=com1
LPT1: redirected to COM1:
```

Code Pages and MODE

As explained in appendix D, MODE is used to generate *prepared code pages* from the code page information files supplied with MS-DOS 3.3 and 4.X. Once a prepared code page is generated, MODE may then be used to select the code page. MODE may also be used to display the set of code pages that are available for a device. Finally, MODE may be used to reestablish an active code page that has been lost. Examples will be presented for each of these applications of MODE.

Generating Prepared Code Pages

The format for generating prepared code pages is:

MODE *device* CODEPAGE PREPARE=
((*cplist*)[*d*:][*path*]*filename*[.*ext*])

The *device* parameter is the character device for which the code pages are being generated. The valid values are CON, PRN, LPT1, LPT2, and LPT3.

The *cplist* is a list of one or more valid code page numbers. These numbers are used to specify the code pages that will be prepared for the character device. Valid code page numbers are 437, 850, 860, 863, and 865. Appendix D discusses the meaning of these code page numbers.

The *filename* parameter specifies the code page information file that will be used to generate code pages. The code page information files supplied with MS-DOS 3.3 and 4.X and the devices that they support are listed in table 2.

Selecting a Code Page

Once a code page has been prepared for use, MODE may be used to select the code page. Selections make the specified code page active for the specified device. The format for code page activation is:

MODE *device* CODEPAGE SELECT=*cp*

The *device* parameter is the device for which the code page is being

Table 2. MS-DOS 3.3 and 4.X Code Page Information Files and the Devices That They Support

Device	Code Page Information File
IBM Proprinter Model 4201	4201.CPI
IBM Proprinter X24 and XL24	4208.CPI (MS-DOS 4.X only)
IBM Quietwriter III Printer Model 5202	5202.CPI
Enhanced Graphics Adapter	EGA.CPI
IBM Convertible LCD Adapter	LCD.CPI

selected. The *cp* parameter is the code page number being selected. The selected code page number must be either a previously prepared code page or a hardware code page. Hardware code pages are discussed in appendix D.

An Example Before code page switching can be implemented on a display screen, the device driver DISPLAY.SYS must be loaded into memory. Similarly, before code page switching may be implemented on a printer, the device driver PRINTER.SYS must be loaded into memory.

The following command, when placed in CONFIG.SYS, instructs MS-DOS to install DISPLAY.SYS during the booting procedure:

```
device=c:\dos\display.sys con:=(ega,,2)
```

This command tells MS-DOS to load the DISPLAY.SYS driver for use with the CON device. The parameters **(ega,,2)** instruct MS-DOS: (1) that it should enable code page switching for the Enhanced Graphics Adapter Display, (2) that none of the code pages are hardware code pages, and (3) that two of the pages are prepared code pages.

Using the **device=** statement enables code page switching. The next step is to use the MODE command to generate the prepared code pages for use by the EGA display. The following command generates code pages 437 and 850 using information in the file "ega.cpi". MS-DOS displays a message when the preparation is completed:

```
C>mode con codepage prepare=((437,850)c:\dos\ega.cpi)
Mode Prepare Codepage function completed

C>
```

Once the code pages have been generated, a particular code page may be selected using MODE. The following command selects code page number 850:

```
C>mode con codepage select=850
Mode Select Codepage function completed

C>
```

Code Page Status

The command "mode con codepage /status" directs MS-DOS to display the codepage status for the CON device. In this case the CON device is the EGA display:

```
C>mode con codepage /status
Active codepage for device CON is 850
prepared codepages:
  Codepage 437
  Codepage 850
Mode Status Codepage function completed

C>
```

Code Page Refresh

The command "mode *device* codepage refresh" reestablishes an active code page that has been lost. For example, if you turn off your printer, you may have to use this command to reestablish the active code page.

Requesting Device Status

The MS-DOS 4.X version of MODE displays the current status of a device when you enter **mode** followed by the device name. For example, the command "mode con" generates the following:

```
Status for device CON:
-----------------------
COLUMNS=80
LINES=25
Code page operation not supported on this device
```

Use the switch /sta when requesting the status of a printer—for example, "mode lpt1: /sta". The reason for this is that if you enter "mode lpt1:", any redirection for that printer will be cancelled.

You can get a status report for all devices by entering **mode** (with no additional parameters).

Setting Keyboard Typematic Rates

The MS-DOS 4.X version allows you to control the rate at which a letter is repeatedly echoed to the screen when you hold a keyboard key down. The format for the command is as follows:

MODE CON delay=*d* rate=*r*

The delay parameter controls the amount of time that the key must be held down before the repeat echoing commences. Allowable values for **d** are 1, 2, 3, and 4. The number specifies the number of ¼-second periods for the delay.

The rate parameter controls the rate of repetition once the echoing commences. The allowable range for **r** is 1 through 32. The number represents the approximate number of repetitions per second.

This use of the MODE command is not supported on all computer systems.

MORE

External
MS-DOS 2.X, 3.X, 4.X

Function: Outputs 23 lines of data at a time

Format: **MORE**

Examples: more < sample.txt
more < sample.txt > prn

MORE is an MS-DOS filter that displays data 23 lines (one full screen) at a time. A text file can be "filtered" through MORE by using the MS-DOS symbol for redirection of input **<**. The output from an application program or another MS-DOS command can also be sent through MORE by using the MS-DOS pipe feature. Output from MORE is sent to the display screen unless it is redirected to some other device (such as a file) or piped as the input to another MS-DOS command or an application program. The symbol for redirection of output is **>**.

Data filtered through MORE is sent out to the display screen (or some other device) 23 lines at a time. After each 23 lines of output, the message **-More-** appears at the bottom of the screen. Pressing any key outputs another 23 lines of data.

MORE is an external MS-DOS command. This means that before you can use the MORE filter, a copy of the file MORE.EXE must be contained in a system drive. The use of MORE is discussed in chapter 6.

NLSFUNC

External
MS-DOS 3.3, 4.X

Functions: Specifies the country information file
             Provides support for code page switching using the MS-DOS
             command CHCP

Format: NLSFUNC [[*d*:][*path*]*filename*[.*ext*]]

Examples: nlsfunc
             nlsfunc c:\dos\country.sys

The NLSFUNC command is used to specify the system's country information file. The country information file contains country-specific information such as the date, time, and currency formats.

   The NLSFUNC must be invoked before code pages can be set using the
CHCP command. Please refer to appendix D for an overview of code pages
and code page switching.

   NLSFUNC remains resident in memory once it is invoked. Therefore,
one invocation of NLSFUNC will support all subsequent invocations of
CHCP.

   If NLSFUNC is entered without specifying a country information file,
the file defined by the COUNTRY command is used as the system's country
information file.

   The format for using NLSFUNC is:

NLSFUNC [[*d*:][*path*]*filename*[.*ext*]]

The MS-DOS 4.X version of NLSFUNC may be invoked from CONFIG.SYS
by using the command INSTALL. The following example illustrates how this
can be done:

```
install=c:\dos\nlsfunc.exe c:\dos\country.sys
```

PATH

Internal
MS-DOS 2.X, 3.X, 4.X

Function: Specifies directories that MS-DOS is to search when trying to
             locate executable files

Format: PATH [[*d*:]path[;[*d*:]*path* . . .]]

Exam-   path \program1\business
ples: path b:\program2\write1;b:\program2\write2

PATH tells MS-DOS which subdirectories are to be searched if an external command or a batch file is not found in the current directory. The parameters entered in PATH are the paths to the subdirectories to be searched. (Subdirectories and paths are discussed in chapter 3.)

Consider the following situation. Suppose that you have a diskette in drive A that contains several files and a subdirectory named PROGRAM1. PROGRAM1 contains a batch file named "business.bat". Let's say that the current directory on drive C is the root directory and that you want to execute "business.bat".

To start a batch file, you simply enter the filename of the batch file. Let's see what happens when you do that:

```
C>business
Bad command or file name
```

What happened is that MS-DOS searched the current directory of drive C for "business.bat". Since the root directory is the current directory, and "business.bat" is in the subdirectory PROGRAM1, MS-DOS was unable to find the batch file. MS-DOS assumed that "business.bat" did not exist and the **Bad command or file name** message was displayed.

There are two solutions to this problem. You could change the current directory on drive C. Then MS-DOS would be able to find "business.bat" when "business" was entered. The drawback to this solution is that changing the current directory on drive C may be inconvenient. It would be to your advantage to keep the root directory as the current directory if most of the files and programs that you are using are in the root directory.

The second solution is to use PATH to tell MS-DOS where to look for "business". All you have to do is type **path** followed by the path to the directory containing "business.bat":

```
C>path \program1
```

Once PATH has been used, MS-DOS knows where to look for a command or batch file that is not in the current directory. The last PATH command entered sets the current path. MS-DOS will display the current path if you enter PATH without any parameters:

```
C>path
PATH=\PROGRAM1
```

The current path remains in effect until it is changed by another PATH command.

A PATH command may contain more than one path. Multiple paths are separated by semicolons. MS-DOS searches the paths in the order in which they are listed. In the next example, the PATH command contains two paths on drive B. Once the command has been entered, MS-DOS will look in the subdirectory WRITE1 (which is a subdirectory entry in the subdirectory

PROGRAM2) if a command or batch file is not located in the current directory. MS-DOS will then look in the subdirectory WRITE2 (another subdirectory entry in the subdirectory PROGRAM2) if the command or batch file is not contained in WRITE1.

```
C>path b:\program2\write1;b:\program2\write2
```

The current path is cancelled if you enter PATH followed by a semicolon:

```
C>path
PATH=B:\PROGRAM2\WRITE1;B:PROGRAM2\WRITE2

C>path;

C>path
No Path
```

PASUE

Internal
MS-DOS 1.X, 2.X, 3.X, 4.X

Function: Suspends execution of a batch file

Format: PAUSE [*comment*]

Example: pause

PAUSE is used to temporarily suspend the execution of a batch file. PAUSE may also be used to display a message up to 121 characters in length. The following message is displayed when MS-DOS encounters a PAUSE:

```
Strike a key when ready . . .
```

Execution of the batch file halts until you strike a key. Note that you can strike any key except Ctrl-Break. Pressing Ctrl-Break stops the process.

PAUSE is generally used in a batch file to allow you time to perform a specific task, such as inserting a diskette. You will find more information on PAUSE in chapter 4.

PRINT

External
MS-DOS 2.X, 3.X, 4.X

Function: Prints a list of files in the "background" while MS-DOS is being used to perform other tasks

Format: PRINT [[*d:*][*filename*[*.ext*]][/T][/C][/P] . . .]
PRINT [/D:*device*][/B:*buffersize*]
[/U:*busyticks*][/M:*maxticks*]
[/S:*timeslice*][/Q:*queuesize*]
[*d:*][*filename*[*.ext*]]
[/T][/C][/P] . . .] (MS-DOS 3.X and 4.X)

Examples: print file1.txt
print file?.txt
print file1.txt file2.txt/c file3.txt file4.txt

The PRINT command is a utility program that allows you to print a set of files while simultaneously using MS-DOS to perform other tasks. The printing is said to occur in the "background" while the other work that you are doing is performed in the "foreground." The MS-DOS 3.X and 4.X implementations of PRINT have several enhancements that are discussed at the end of this section.

PRINT is an external MS-DOS command. The first time you invoke the command, PRINT.COM is read from disk and installed in memory. PRINT remains resident in memory until the power is shut off.

Using PRINT

To use PRINT, simply type **print** and then type the file specifications of the files that you want to print. Each file that you enter is placed in a *queue* (list). The files in the queue are printed one at a time, according to their order in the queue. The queue may contain up to ten files at a time. A file is deleted from the queue after it has been printed.

The first time that you use PRINT in a working session, MS-DOS displays the prompt **Name of list device [PRN]:**. MS-DOS is asking you for the device name of the printer. "PRN" is the default device name that MS-DOS assigns to the parallel printer. If you want to use the default, simply press Enter. Otherwise, type the device name and press Enter. (Devices and device names are discussed in chapter 6.)

The first PRINT example instructs MS-DOS to print the files "file1.txt", "file2.txt", and "file3.txt". These files are all located in the current directory of drive C.

```
C>print file1.txt file2.txt file3.txt
Name of list device [PRN]:     ←Enter
Resident part of print installed

    C:FILE1.TXT is currently being printed
    C:FILE2.TXT is in queue
    C:FILE3.TXT is in queue

C>
```

As you can see, MS-DOS has displayed a queue status report stating the file currently being printed. The remaining files in the queue are listed in the order in which they will be printed.

MS-DOS displays its system prompt to tell you that another command may be entered. Even though the PRINT command is executing, you may enter another command while printing continues in the background. Any MS-DOS command or program can be executed while PRINT is operating in the background as long as the command or program does not use the printer being used by PRINT.

Additional PRINT commands can be entered while PRINT is executing. The effect of these subsequent commands is to either add or delete files from the queue (see the following discussion of the /c, /p, and /t switches).

You can use the wildcard characters "*" and "?" to specify a group of files in the PRINT command. The preceding example could have been entered as:

```
C>print file?.txt
```

If there are any files in the current directory of drive C that match the wildcard, other than "file1.txt", "file2.txt", and "file3.txt", those files will also be printed by the preceding command. (Wildcards are discussed in chapter 2.)

A PRINT command may specify for printing only files that are located in the current directory of each system drive. After you have issued a PRINT command, you can change the current directory on a drive. You can then issue a subsequent PRINT command that will add files contained in the new current directory to the queue. (Directories and current directories are discussed in chapter 3.)

MS-DOS will display a queue status report if you enter PRINT with no parameters:

```
C>print
```

```
C:FILE2.TXT is currently being printed
C:FILE3.TXT is in queue
```

The /C Switch

The /c switch may be used in a PRINT command to delete one or more files from the queue. The /c switch is inserted in a PRINT command immediately after a file specification. That file and all subsequent files specified in the PRINT command are then deleted from the queue.

If a command to delete a file from the queue is issued while that file is being printed, printing of the file is halted and the message "<filespec> Cancelled by operator" is sent to the printer. The printer paper then advances to the next page, and printing continues with the next file in the queue.

The following command adds "file4.txt" to the queue and deletes "file2.txt" and "file3.txt". Remember that /c affects the immediately preceding file and all subsequent files in the PRINT command.

```
C>print file4.txt file2.txt/c file3.txt
```

The /P Switch

Most MS-DOS manuals say that the /p switch is used in the PRINT command to "set the print mode." This is a little confusing. It's simpler to think of /p as turning off a previous /c switch. The /p switch is inserted in a PRINT command immediately after a file specification. That file and all subsequent files specified in the PRINT command are added to the queue.

The following command deletes "file4.txt" from the queue and adds "file5.txt" and "file6.txt" to the queue:

```
C>print file4.txt/c file5.txt/p file6.txt
```

You can see how the /p switch turns off the /c switch. If a PRINT command does not contain a /c switch, there is no need to use the /p switch.

A PRINT command can contain a second /c switch that will turn off a previous /p switch. A second /p switch can be used to turn off the second /c switch and so on.

The /T Switch

The /t switch is used with PRINT to delete all files from the queue and terminate execution of the PRINT command. The command "print /t" halts the printing process, deletes all files from the queue, sends the message "All files cancelled by operator" to the printer, and returns control of the computer to MS-DOS:

```
C>print /t
PRINT queue is empty

C>
```

MS-DOS 3.X and 4.X Enhancements

There are six PRINT switches implemented in MS-DOS 3.X and 4.X. These switches can be set only when PRINT is loaded into memory. Their use is therefore restricted to the first time the PRINT command is invoked.

The /d:*device* switch allows you to specify a valid printing device. If you do not use this switch, MS-DOS will ask you to specify a printer (as is done with the MS-DOS 2 version of PRINT).

The /b:*buffersize* switch sets the size of the print buffer. The print buffer is the area of memory that stores the file's contents prior to sending the contents to the printer. The larger the buffer, the fewer disk accesses that are necessary, and the faster the printing is completed. The default size for the print buffer is 512 bytes.

The /q:*queuesize* switch controls the number of files that may be in the printing queue at any one time. The allowable range is 1 to 32. The default is 10.

The three remaining switches control the way in which the computer's resources are shared between PRINT (the background process) and MS-DOS (the foreground process). When you are using PRINT, it may appear that the computer is doing two things at one time. Actually the computer can execute only one task (or process) at a time, but it switches between processes so rapidly that the two processes seem to execute simultaneously.

Each process is allocated a certain number of system clock ticks to perform its work. The /s:*timeslice* switch determines how many clock ticks the MS-DOS foreground process can run before giving control to the PRINT background process. The allowable range is 1 to 255 clock ticks. The default is 8.

The /m:*maxticks* switch determines how many clock ticks the PRINT process can run before giving control back to the foreground MS-DOS process. The allowable range is 1 to 255 clock ticks. The default is 2.

The /u:*busyticks* switch determines the maximum number of clock ticks that PRINT can wait if the printer is unavailable. If this amount of time elapses and PRINT is still waiting, control is returned to the foreground MS-DOS process. The allowable range for busyticks is 1 to 255 clock ticks. The default is 1.

PROMPT

Internal
MS-DOS 2.X, 3.X, 4.X

Function: Sets the MS-DOS system prompt

Format: **PROMPT** [*text*]

Example: prompt Enter Command:

A *system prompt* is a signal from MS-DOS to you that all systems are operating and that MS-DOS is ready to receive your command. The standard MS-DOS system prompt consists of an uppercase "A," "B," or "C" followed by the greater than symbol, **>**. The letter used in the prompt tells you which system drive is the current default. For example, the **C>** prompt indicates that the current default drive is drive C.

  You can use the PROMPT command to change the system prompt. Simply type **prompt** followed by the character string that you want MS-DOS to use as the new system prompt. Once you have entered the PROMPT command, the new system prompt will be displayed each time that MS-DOS is ready to accept a command. The PROMPT command will remain in effect until you issue another PROMPT or until you reboot MS-DOS. For example, if you wanted the system prompt to be **Enter Command:** instead of **C>**, you would enter the following command:

```
C>prompt Enter Command:

Enter Command:
```

The new system prompt is now **Enter Command:**. To return to the original prompt **C>**, enter **prompt** without any other text:

```
Enter Command:prompt

C>
```

MS-DOS provides a set of *meta-strings* that can be used with PROMPT to create system prompts containing special characters. A meta-string is a dollar sign ($) followed by one of eleven ASCII characters. Table 3 lists the meta-strings and the resultant characters.

  Many people find it convenient to have the prompt display the current directory on the default drive. This is accomplished by using the PROMPT command and the meta-strings $p and $g as follows:

```
C>prompt $p$g      ← enter this command
C:\BOOKS\DOS>      ← to produce this prompt
```

This prompt is so useful that many people choose to put the command "prompt pg" in their AUTOEXEC.BAT file. If you install DOS 4.0 with SELECT on a hard drive, the "prompt pg" statement is put in your AUTOEXEC.400 file, ready to be merged into AUTOEXEC.BAT. Use of SE-LECT is discussed in chapter 1.

Meta-strings may be combined with each other and with other character strings to form system prompts. In the following example, four meta-strings are used in a PROMPT command. The PROMPT command will set the system prompt to perform the following: (1) display the message **The current time is:** followed by the current time stored by MS-DOS, (2) perform a carriage return and line feed so that the cursor is at the beginning of the next line, (3) display the drive letter designator of the default drive, and (4) display a > character.

```
C>prompt $t$ $n$g

The current time is:    9:27:45.35

C>
```

Table 3. Meta-strings and the Resultant Character(s) in the System Prompt

Meta-string	Character(s)
$t	The current time stored by MS-DOS.
$d	The current date stored by MS-DOS.
$p	The current directory of the default drive; if drive C is the default and the root directory is the current directory on drive C, $p in the PROMPT command would place "C:\" in the system prompt.
$v	The version of MS-DOS being used (e.g., 3.3)
$n	The default drive.
$g	The > character.
$l	The < character.
$b	The | character.
$q	The = character.
$$	The $ character.
$h	A backspace and erasure of the previous character.
$e	The ESCape character; PROMPT and $e can be used to send an ESCape character to the ANSI.SYS device driver (see chapter 8).
$_	Carriage return plus line feed.

MS-DOS now displays the current time whenever the system prompt is displayed. Initially, you must set MS-DOS's internal clock if you want the time displayed to be the current time. (See booting MS-DOS in chapter 1 or the TIME command for details.)

The nice feature of this system prompt is that, besides displaying the current time, the prompt automatically changes when the default drive is changed:

```
C>prompt $t$ $n$g

The current time is:    9:27:45.35

C>b:

The current time is:    9:28:00.39

B>
```

RECOVER

External
MS-DOS 2.X, 3.X, 4.X

Functions: Recovers data from files that have bad sectors
Recovers data from an entire disk that has a damaged file directory
Note: RECOVER cannot be used with network drives

Format: RECOVER [*d*:][*path*]filename[.*ext*]
RECOVER *d*

Examples: recover badfile.txt
recover b:

Floppy diskettes and hard disks used by MS-DOS are divided into storage units called *sectors*. Sectors are created during the formatting process. Each sector stores 512 bytes of data. The larger the file, the more sectors required to store it.

Floppy diskettes and hard disks each contain a *file directory*. The file directory serves as MS-DOS's table of contents to the files that are contained on the floppy diskette or hard disk. The directory, which is created during formatting, is modified each time that a file is added, deleted, or modified. (For further information on sectors, file directories, and related topics, please refer to chapters 3 and 10. You should be familiar with this material before using RECOVER.)

Occasionally one or more sectors on a floppy diskette or hard disk become damaged. When this happens, MS-DOS may not be able to read the data stored in those sectors. MS-DOS will then display the following message when it comes across a sector that it cannot read:

```
Data error reading C:
Abort, Retry, Ignore?
```

The command RECOVER is used to recover data that MS-DOS is unable to read because of damaged sectors. RECOVER can be used to recover an individual file or an entire disk that is unreadable because of damaged sectors in the file directory.

When RECOVER is used on an individual file, only the data in the undamaged sectors of a file is recovered. The data in the damaged sectors is lost. The damaged sectors are labeled so that MS-DOS will not use them in the future.

Once a file has been recovered, MS-DOS will be able to read it. A recovered file will have the same filename and filename extension as the unreadable file. A recovered file will usually have some extraneous data attached at the end, since RECOVER produces files that are multiples of 512 bytes (one sector) in size.

RECOVER is limited in its ability to repair damaged files. It is also somewhat awkward to use. Commercial disk utilities, such as PC-Tools, Norton Utilities, and Mace Utilities, are more powerful and easier to use when it comes to repairing damaged files.

Recovering a File

Since RECOVER is an external command, a copy of the file RECOVER.COM must be available to the system before you can use the command. This means that either RECOVER.COM must be in the current directory of the default drive or that the location of RECOVER.COM must have been specified by the PATH command (see the discussion of PATH).

To use RECOVER, type **recover** and then type the file specification of the file to be recovered. MS-DOS will load RECOVER.COM into memory and then pause to allow you to change diskettes if necessary. Make any necessary swaps and then press any key. The specified file will be recovered. MS-DOS will display a message that tells you how many bytes from the original file have been recovered. The following is an example:

```
C>recover b:badfile.txt

Press any key to begin recovery of the
file(s) on drive B:

X        ←you press the "x" key
```

```
900 of 1412 bytes recovered

C>
```

If you use wildcard characters to specify the file, MS-DOS will recover only the first file that matches the wildcard.

Recovering a Disk

Using RECOVER to recover all the files on a disk is a drastic measure. RECOVER looks at the file allocation table to determine where each file is located on the floppy diskette or hard disk. RECOVER cannot distinguish a damaged directory entry from an undamaged entry; therefore, all files on the disk are recovered.

To recover a disk, type **recover** and then type the letter designator of the drive containing the floppy diskette or hard disk to be recovered. MS-DOS will load RECOVER.COM into memory and then pause for any necessary disk swapping. Press a key and all files on the disk will be recovered. The following is an example:

```
C>recover b:
Press any key to begin recovery of the
file(s) on drive B:



x
22 file(s) recovered
```

The first recovered file is given the name "file0001.rec", the second "file0002.rec", and so on. Any subdirectories are treated as files. All recovered files are placed in the root directory. MS-DOS will display a message if there is not enough room in the root directory for all of the recovered files. If this should happen, copy the recovered files onto another diskette and then delete them from the partially recovered disk. Run RECOVER again and there should be enough room in the root directory for the remaining unrecovered files.

Once an entire disk has been recovered, you can use the command DIR to see that all of the files have names like "file0001.rec," "file0002.rec", and so on.

REM

Internal
MS-DOS 1.X, 2.X, 3.X, 4.X

Function: Displays a message during the execution of a batch file

Formats: REM [*message*]

Examples: rename oldname.ext newname.ext
              ren format.com xformat.com

The REM (REMark) command is used to display a message or to insert comments during the execution of a batch file. At the appropriate line in the batch file, type **rem** and then type the text of the message. When the batch file is executed and the REM command is read by MS-DOS, the message contained in that line will be displayed on the screen. The message in a REM command may be up to 123 characters long. (See chapter 4 for a discussion of batch files.) In MS-DOS 4.X, REM may also be used to insert comments in the CONFIG.SYS file.

RENAME

Internal
MS-DOS 1.X, 2.X, 3.X, 4.X

Function: Renames a file

Format: **RENAME** [*d:*][*path*]*filename*[*.ext*]*filename*[*.ext*]
              REN [*d:*][*path*]*filename*[*.ext*]*filename*[*.ext*]

Examples: rename file1 file2
              ren newfile.txt oldfile.txt

RENAME (or REN) is used to change the filename and/or filename extension of an MS-DOS file. It is one of the most frequently used, and most useful, MS-DOS commands.

To change a file's name, type **rename** and then type the file specification of the file, followed by the new filename and filename extension, if any. For example, an existing file on drive A named "oldname.ext" would be renamed to "newname.ext" as follows:

```
C:>rename a:oldname.ext newname.ext
```

MS-DOS will ignore any drive letter specifier preceding the new filename and extension. MS-DOS will display an error message if a path specifier precedes the new filename and extension.

Wildcard characters may be used with RENAME (see chapter 2).

REPLACE

External
MS-DOS 3.2, 3.3, 4.X

Function: Selectively replaces or adds files

Format: REPLACE [*d:*][*path*]*filename*[.*ext*]
[*d:*][*path*][/A][/P][/R][/S][/W] (MS-DOS 3.2–4.X)
REPLACE [*d:*][*path*]*filename*[.*ext*][*d:*]
[*path*][/A][/P][/R][/S][/W][/U] (MS-DOS 4.X)

Example: replace ch1.doc c:\ /s

REPLACE is an external MS-DOS command that allows you to selectively replace or add files to a target directory. When files are being replaced, *filename*[.*ext*] in the command line specifies the files in the target directory that are to be replaced by matching files in the source directory. Only matches are replaced. When files are being added, *filename*[.*ext*] specifies the files in the source directory that are to be added to the target. Files are added only if the target does not already contain a match. The following examples demonstrate the use of the REPLACE command.

Using REPLACE

The examples given here use two directories, TMP1 and TMP2. The contents of the directories are as follows:

```
C>dir tmp1 /w

 Volume in drive C is UCSFMIS
 Directory of C:\TMP1

 .           ..          TERRY  LET  BRUCE  LET  PAPER  TXT
         5 File(s)    491520 bytes free

C>dir tmp2 /w

 Volume in drive C is UCSFMIS
 Directory of C:\TMP2
```

```
      .       ..       BRUCE   LET
          3 File(s)    491520 bytes free
```

First we will replace TMP2\BRUCE.LET with TMP1\BRUCE.LET:

```
C>replace tmp1\bruce.let tmp2

Replacing C:\TMP2\BRUCE.LET

1 file(s) replaced
```

Let's see what happens if we try to replace TMP2\TERRY.LET:

```
C>replace tmp1\terry.let tmp2

No files replaced
```

No files are replaced since TMP2 does not already contain a file named "terry.let".

The /A Switch

The /a switch is used to add new files to a target directory (as opposed to replacing existing files).

```
C>replace tmp1\terry.let tmp2 /a

Adding C:\TMP2\TERRY.LET

1 file(s) added
```

Files are added only if the target directory does not contain a match:

```
C>replace tmp1\bruce.let tmp2 /a

No files added
```

The /S Switch

The following command goes through all of the directories on drive A, replacing any copies of the file "sample.txt" that it finds.

```
C>replace sample.txt a:\ /s
```

The /s switch is used to replace all occurrences of a file in a target directory and all subdirectories contained in the target. If the root directory is the target, all occurrences of the file on the disk are replaced. The /a and /s switches cannot be used together.

Other Switches

The /p switch prompts you with `Replace <file name> (Y/N)?` for each *filename* specified as a source file.

The /r switch replaces files that have their read-only attribute set. (See ATTRIB for a discussion of the read-only attribute.)

The /w switch instructs REPLACE to wait for you to insert a diskette prior to executing the command.

The /**u** switch, implemented in MS-DOS 4.X, replaces those files in the target directory that have an updated version in the source.

REPLACE and ERRORLEVEL

The following list gives the ERRORLEVEL values returned by REPLACE. These values may then be used by batch files or programs running under MS-DOS. See chapter 4 for a demonstration of the use of ERRORLEVEL values.

ERRORLEVEL Value	Meaning
2	No source files were found.
3	Invalid source or target path.
5	An attempt was made to access a read-only file without the /r switch.
8	Insufficient memory.
11	Invalid parameters or invalid number of parameters entered on the command line.
15	Invalid drive specified.
22	Incorrect version of MS-DOS.

RESTORE

External
MS-DOS 2.X, 3.X, 4.X

Function: Restores one or more files from one disk to another disk

Format: **RESTORE d:** [*d:*][*path*][*filename*[.*ext*]][/S][/P]
RESTORE d:[*d:*][*path*[*filename*[.*ext*]][/S][/P][/B:*mm-dd-yy*]
[/A:*mm-dd-yy*][/M][/N][/L:*time*][/E:*time*]   (MS-DOS 3.3, 4.X)

Examples: restore a: \subdir1 \file.doc
restore a: \subdir2
restore a: \subdir3 /s
restore a: \subdir4*.doc /p

The RESTORE command is used to retrieve files that were stored using BACKUP. RESTORE cannot be used on any other types of files.

Since RESTORE is an external MS-DOS command, one of the system drives must contain the file RESTORE.COM before you can use RESTORE. In the following examples, it is assumed that RESTORE.COM is stored on the hard disk drive (drive C).

Restoring a File

To restore a file to the hard disk, type **restore** and then type the letter designation of the drive containing the copy of the files to be restored. You may specify the directory path on the hard disk that will contain the restored files. If you do not specify a path, the default is the current directory on the default disk. You may also specify the name of a file to be restored. If no filename is specified, all files in the specified (or default) directory are restored. When you enter a RESTORE command, MS-DOS prompts you to insert the diskette containing the files to be restored and then instructs you to press any key to restore the files to the hard disk.

In the first example, the file "file1.doc" is located in the directory SUB.DIR1. The backup copy of "file1.doc", which is stored on the diskette in drive A, is restored to the hard disk:

```
C>restore a: \subdir1\file1.doc

Insert backup diskette 01 in drive A:
Strike any key when ready

*** Files were backed up 12/11/1989 ***
```

```
*** Restoring files from diskette 01 ***
\SUBDIR1\FILE1.DOC

C>
```

Wildcard characters may be used in filenames and extensions specified in a RESTORE command. All matching files in the specified (or default) directory will be restored.

Note: MS-DOS 3.3 and 4.X allow you to restore from a hard disk, provided, of course, that the hard disk was the target of a BACKUP command.

Restoring a Directory

In the next example, all the files stored on the backup diskette that have a path of \SUBDIR1\SUBDIR2 are restored:

```
C>restore a: \subdir1\subdir2
```

Restoring All Subdirectories

You may recall from the discussion of the BACKUP command that you can back up an entire hard disk with the command "backup c:\/s". You can use the /s switch of RESTORE to restore an entire hard disk as follows:

```
restore a: c:\ /s
```

The /s switch directs RESTORE to restore all files in the directory, plus all files in all subdirectories that are descended from the directory.

Selective Restoring with /P Switch

You may not want to restore a file that has been modified since the last time it was backed up. Such a restoration would destroy any modifications in the file. Using the /p switch at the end of your command will cause MS-DOS to check to see if any of the files being restored have been modified since they were last backed up. If so, MS-DOS will warn you that a file is about to be overwritten. A prompt will appear asking you if the (modified) file should be replaced (by the unmodified version). If you respond "N", the file is not restored and processing continues in the normal fashion. If you respond "Y", the file is restored with the unmodified copy, and processing continues in the normal fashion.

The MS-DOS 3.X and 4.X versions of the /p switch also prompt you before restoring any read-only files. See the ATTRIB command for information about read-only files.

Other Switches

MS-DOS 3.3 and 4.X contain six additional switches that allow further selectivity in the restore process.

The /n switch restores files that have been deleted. The /m switch restores files that have been deleted or modified since they were backed up.

The /b:*mm-dd-yy* switch restores all files modified on or before the specified date. The /a:*mm-dd-yy* switch restores all files modified on or after the specified date.

The l:*time* switch restores files that were modified at or later than the specified time. The /e:*time* switch restores files that were modified at or earlier than the specified time.

Some Restrictions with RESTORE

RESTORE cannot be used with JOIN, ASSIGN, SUBST, and APPEND. These commands contain bugs that cause RESTORE to act in an unpredictable fashion.

RESTORE and ERRORLEVEL

ERRORLEVEL is a variable that has special meaning to MS-DOS. RESTORE will set the value of ERRORLEVEL as follows:

0   RESTORE command completed in normal fashion.

1   The backup diskette did not contain any files matching the file(s) specified in the RESTORE command.

2   Some files were not restored due to sharing conflicts.

3   Execution of the RESTORE command was terminated by the user pressing Esc or Ctrl-Break.

4   The RESTORE command was terminated because of an error in execution.

Once the value of ERRORLEVEL has been set, it may be used in conjunction with the IF command in MS-DOS batch files. ERRORLEVEL allows you to write batch files that are executed according to the outcome of a RESTORE command. (See the discussion of the IF command for further details.)

RMDIR

Internal
MS-DOS 2.X, 3.X, 4.X

Function: Deletes a subdirectory

Format: **RMDIR** [*d:*]*path*
            RD [*d:*]*path*

Exam-   rmdir \write
ples: rd b:\programs\business

The RMDIR (ReMove DIRectory) command is used to delete a subdirectory from a disk. You may enter the command as either **rmdir** or **rd**. However, before MS-DOS can carry out your command, all the files in the subdirectory must be deleted. This is a safety feature that prevents accidental loss of files.

Your RMDIR command may include a drive letter designator (such as c: or a:) that specifies the drive containing the subdirectory to be deleted. MS-DOS assumes that the subdirectory is located on the default drive if no drive is specified.

The RMDIR command must specify the path to the subdirectory that is to be deleted. In the first example, the command is used to delete the subdirectory WRITE:

```
C>rmdir \write
```

No drive is specified, so MS-DOS assumes that WRITE is located on the default drive. The path **\write** tells MS-DOS that WRITE is a subdirectory contained in the root directory of drive C.

The next example deletes a subdirectory named BUSINESS:

```
C>rd b:\programs\business
```

The command specifies that BUSINESS is located on drive B. The path **\programs\business** tells MS-DOS that BUSINESS is a subdirectory contained in PROGRAMS. PROGRAMS is a subdirectory contained in the root directory of drive B.

The current directory and the root directory of each drive cannot be deleted with RMDIR. (For more information on subdirectories, root directories, current directories, and paths and for more examples of the use of RMDIR, please refer to chapter 3.)

SELECT

External
MS-DOS 3.X, 4.X

Function: Creates a language-specific system disk

Format: SELECT *aaa yy* (MS-DOS 3.0–3.2)
              SELECT [[A: or B:][*d*:][*path*]] *xxx yy* (MS-DOS 3.3)

Examples: select 033 fr
             select a: c:\dos 033 fr

SELECT is used to create a country-specific system disk. At boot time, the new system disk will: (1) automatically load country-specific information such as the time, date, and currency formats and (2) automatically configure the keyboard according to a country-specific layout. Country-specific information and country-specific keyboard configuration are discussed under the commands COUNTRY, KEYB, and KEYB*xx*.

Note: The MS-DOS 4.X implementation of the SELECT command is used to install the operating system on a hard disk or floppy diskettes. Refer to chapter 1 for a discussion of the 4.X version of SELECT.

Versions 3.0–3.2 of MS-DOS implement SELECT in a different fashion than version 3.3 does. The following paragraphs discuss each implementation separately.

The format for SELECT in versions 3.0–3.2 is:

SELECT *aaa yy*

The *aaa* parameter is a 3-digit country code. The *yy* parameter is a valid keyboard code. The valid combinations of country code and keyboard codes are listed in table 4 at the end of this section.

This implementation of SELECT requires that a system diskette be placed in drive A to serve as the *source* in creating the new system diskette. The *target* must be another diskette that will be swapped with the source in drive A. MS-DOS executes the command by first using DISKCOPY to copy the source to the target. MS-DOS automatically formats the target if necessary. It then prompts the user to change diskettes in drive A as required. When the copy is completed, MS-DOS uses DISKCOMP to compare the target to the source. Next, a new CONFIG.SYS file is created in the root directory of the target that contains the command "country=*aaa*" where *aaa* is the country code entered on the command line. Finally, a new AUTOEXEC.BAT file is created in the root of the target. This file will load the country-specific keyboard driver when the new diskette is used to reboot the system.

The format for the MS-DOS 3.3 version of SELECT is:

SELECT [[A: or B:][*d*:][*path specifier*]] *xxx yy*

The *xxx* and *yy* parameters are the country and keyboard codes. The "A: or B:" is used to specify the drive containing the source system diskette. If no source drive is specified, SELECT uses drive A as the source. The *d:path* parameter is used to specify the destination for the MS-DOS command files on the target. If no drive for the target is specified, drive B is assumed to hold the target diskette. If no path is specified for the target system files, the files are copied to the root of the target. This implementation allows a hard disk to be the target.

The 3.3 implementation of SELECT formats the target, then uses XCOPY to copy the system files to the target. A CONFIG.SYS file is created containing the statement "country=*xxx*", and an AUTOEXEC.BAT file is created with the following commands:

```
path \;[\path specifier]
keyb yy xxx
echo off
date
time
ver
```

The [\path] parameter refers to the optional path parameter that may have been included in the SELECT command line. This is useful if you want to have your system files in a subdirectory (such as \DOS).

Table 4. Valid Combinations of Country and Keyboard Codes

Country	Country Code	Keyboard Code
Arabic	785	
Australia	061	US
Belgium	032	BE
Canada (Eng.)	001	US
Canada (Fr.)	002	CF
Denmark	045	DK
Finland	358	SU
France	033	FR
Germany	049	GR
Israel	972	
Italy	039	IT
Latin America	003	LA
Netherlands	031	NL

Table 4. (cont'd)

Country	Country Code	Keyboard Code
Norway	047	NO
Portugal	351	PO
Spain	034	SP
Sweden	046	SV
Swiss (Fr.)	041	SF
Swiss (Ger.)	041	SG
United Kingdom	044	UK
United States	001	US

SET

Internal
MS-DOS 2.X, 3.X, 4.X

Function: Places a string in the MS-DOS environment

Format: SET [*name*=[*parameter*]]

Example: set xyz=abc

The *environment* is an area of computer memory set aside by MS-DOS to store a series of ASCII strings. Each string in the environment consists of two sets of ASCII characters separated by an equals sign. The characters to the left of the equals sign are referred to as the *name,* those to the right as the *parameter.* The strings are grouped in this area so that they may be easily referenced by MS-DOS as well as by any programs that are running under MS-DOS. MS-DOS stores the segment address of the environment at offset 2CH in the program segment prefix (see appendix A).

Each string in the environment is terminated by a byte of zero. The final string is terminated by 2 bytes of zero. The first string in the environment has the name COMSPEC. The right side of the string contains the path to the file COMMAND.COM (for example, COMSPEC=\COMMAND.COM). MS-DOS also stores the last PROMPT and PATH commands issued in the environment.

The SET command is available to programmers who want to place their own strings in MS-DOS's environment. An application program could then search the environment for the string by first looking up the environment's address in the program segment prefix.

To place a string in the environment, type **set** and then type the string:

```
C>set d1=\subdir1\subdir2
```

The current set of environment strings will be displayed if SET is entered with no other parameters:

```
C>set
COMSPEC=\COMMAND.COM
PATH=\SUBDIR1
D1=\SUBDIR1\SUBDIR2
```

To delete a string from the environment, type **set** followed by the string's name followed by an equals sign:

```
C>set path=
C>set
COMSPEC=\COMMAND.COM
D1=\SUBDIR1\SUBDIR2
```

See chapter 11 for more information on the MS-DOS environment.

SHARE

External
MS-DOS 3.X, 4.X

Function: Provides support for file sharing, file locking, diskette change detection, and hard disk partitions larger than 32 Mbytes

Format: **SHARE** [/F:*xxx*][/L:*yyy*]

Example: share /f:1024 /l:20

The SHARE command is used to provide support for *file sharing* on a computer network. Computer programs that use MS-DOS function 3DH to open a computer file will store in memory a *sharing code*. The sharing code is used by the operating system to determine the type of access other programs (on the network) have to the opened file.

Once a program has gained access to a file, it may use MS-DOS function 5CH to place a "lock" on a portion of the file. A lock gives the program exclusive access to that portion of the file.

SHARE sets aside computer memory for sharing codes and locks. The /f:*xxx* flag sets aside *xxx* bytes for sharing codes. The default is 2048 bytes. Each file opened by function 3DH requires storage for its filename plus 11 bytes.

The /l:*yyy* flag sets aside memory for *yyy* file locks. The default is 20 locks.

On systems that generate a signal when the diskette door has been opened, the MS-DOS 4.X version of SHARE notifies the operating system if a diskette change has occurred. If SHARE is loaded in memory, it checks the diskette's volume label and volume serial number, and notifies the operating system if the diskette has been changed.

The MS-DOS 4.X version of SHARE is also used to support disk partitions larger than 32 Mbytes in size. If your disk drive has such a partition, you can use the MS-DOS 4.X command INSTALL to load SHARE from the CONFIG.SYS file. The following illustrates how this is done:

```
install=c:\dos\share.exe
```

The example assumes that the file SHARE.EXE is in the directory C:\DOS. During the booting process, MS-DOS will attempt to automatically load SHARE into memory if you have a disk drive with a partition larger than 32 Mbytes and you do not use INSTALL to load SHARE from CONFIG.SYS. In order for this to be accomplished, the file SHARE.EXE must be in either the root directory or the directory specified by the SHELL statement in CONFIG.SYS.

If you use SELECT to install DOS 4.0 on a hard disk that has a DOS partition larger than 32 Mbytes, SELECT will place the "install=c:\dos \share.exe" statement in your CONFIG.400 file, ready to be merged into CONFIG.SYS. Please refer to chapter 1 for a discussion of SELECT.

See appendix A for more information on MS-DOS functions 3DH and 5CH.

SHELL

Internal
MS-DOS 2.X, 3.X, 4.X

Function: Instructs MS-DOS to load a command processor
             Note: SHELL can be used in a CONFIG.SYS file only

Format: **SHELL**=[*d:*][*path*]*filename*[.*ext*]

Example: shell=custom.com

The SHELL command is a high-level command generally used only by advanced MS-DOS programmers. SHELL is used when you wish to use a command processor other than COMMAND.COM, the standard MS-DOS command processor. COMMAND.COM, which is loaded into memory during booting, serves as the link between MS-DOS and you. (See chapter 11 for details.)

The SHELL command can be used only as a statement in the CON-FIG.SYS file. A SHELL command in CONFIG.SYS alerts MS-DOS that a new command processor will be used.

In the following example, the CONFIG.SYS file is created. The SHELL command that makes up the file tells MS-DOS to load the command processor CUSTOM.COM into memory:

```
C>copy con: config.sys
shell=custom.com
^Z      ←you press Ctrl-Z
     1 file(s) copied
```

Using SHELL to Increase the MS-DOS Environment

The MS-DOS environment has a default size of 160 bytes. With MS-DOS 3.1 and subsequent versions, you can use SHELL to increase the environment's size.

The format for the SHELL statement is:

SHELL=c:\COMMAND.COM /P /E:*xxxx*

In MS-DOS 3.1, *xxxx* is the number of paragraphs (16-byte blocks) in the environment. The allowable range is 10 to 2048. In MS-DOS 3.2 and subsequent versions, *xxxx* is the actual number of bytes in the environment. The allowable range is 160 to 32,768.

Note: chapter 11 describes a way to modify the environment's size for MS-DOS versions prior to 3.1.

SHIFT

Internal
MS-DOS 2.X, 3.X, 4.X

Function: Allows you to specify more than ten batch file parameters

Format: SHIFT

Example: shift

A batch file can contain up to ten dummy variables (%0 through %9). These dummy variables may be sequentially replaced by a list of character strings included in a batch file start command. For example, %0 is replaced by the filename of the batch file, %1 is replaced by the first character string included in the start command, %2 is replaced by the second character string, and so on.

The SHIFT command "shifts" each character string one position to the left, allowing you to pass more than ten character strings to a batch file. After one SHIFT, %0 is replaced by the first character string in the start command, %1 is replaced by the second string, and so on. Each successive SHIFT moves the parameters one position to the left. The use of SHIFT is demonstrated in chapter 4.

SORT

External
MS-DOS 2.X, 3.X, 4.X

Function: Sorts data

Format: SORT [/R][/+n]

Examples: sort < records.txt
sort /+17 < records.txt
sort /r+52 < records.txt

SORT is an MS-DOS filter that reads data from an input device, sorts the data, and then writes the data to an output device. Data is sorted using the ASCII sequence (appendix F), according to the character in a specified column of each line. If no column is specified, the data is sorted according to the first character in each line.

A text file can be input to SORT by using the MS-DOS redirection symbol <. The output from an application program or another MS-DOS command can be sent to SORT as input by using the pipe feature. Output from SORT can be redirected or piped using these same features.

SORT is an external MS-DOS command. This means that a system drive must contain a copy of the file SORT.EXE before you can use the SORT filter.

SORT has two optional switches. The /r switch sorts data in reverse order. The /+n switch sorts data according to the character located in column n of each line.

Chapter 6 describes the use of SORT and discusses MS-DOS filters, redirection, and pipes.

STACKS

Internal
MS-DOS 3.2, 3.3, 4.X

Function: Allocates stack frames to handle hardware interrupts
              Note: STACKS can be used in CONFIG.SYS only

Format: STACKS=*n,s*

Example: stacks=12,256

STACKS is used to set the number and size of *stack frames* allocated by
MS-DOS to handle hardware interrupts (refer to appendix A for a discussion
of interrupts and the role that stacks play in the processing of interrupts).
The format for STACKS is:

STACKS=*n,s*

where *n* equals the number of stack frames allocated and *s* equals the size of
each stack frame in bytes. The allowable range for *n* is 8–64. The allowable
range for *s* is 32–512.

If a "stacks=" command is not included in CONFIG.SYS, MS-DOS defaults to n=0 and s=0 for PC- and XT-type machines; n=9 and s=128 for
AT- and PS/2-type machines.

You should use the STACKS command in CONFIG.SYS if you are getting an `Internal Stack Error` message.

SUBST

External
MS-DOS 3.X, 4.X

Function: Assigns a path specifier to a drive letter

Format: SUBST *d*: *d*:*path*
              SUBST *d: /d*

Example: subst e: c:\subdir1\subdir2\subdir3
              subst e: /d

The SUBST command allows you to assign a path specifier to a drive
letter. Once the assignment is made, the drive letter may be used as a substitute for the specifier. SUBST was implemented for use by programs (such as
WordStar) that cannot process path specifiers. SUBST can also save you
some typing if you are using files located at the end of a long path.

```
A>dir \tmp\tmp1\tmp2

Volume in drive A is UCSFMIS
Directory of A:\TMP\TMP1\TMP2

.            <DIR>     6-26-89   12:02p
..           <DIR>     6-26-89   12:02p
FOO  .          16    6-26-89    5:00p
     3 File(s)    308224 bytes free

A>subst e: \tmp\tmp1\tmp2

A>dir e:

Volume in drive E is UCSFMIS
Directory of E:

.            <DIR>     6-26-89   12:02p
..           <DIR>     6-26-89   12:02p
FOO             16    6-26-89    5:00p
     3 File(s)    308224 bytes free
```

The drive receiving the assignment cannot be the current drive or the drive of the path specifier. The receiving drive letter may be any letter up to the value specified by LASTDRIVE in the CONFIG.SYS file (see the discussion of the LASTDRIVE command). The default for LASTDRIVE is E. SUBST cannot be used with network drives.

Displaying and Cancelling Substitutions

SUBST displays the active substitutions. The /d switch deletes them.

```
A>subst
E: => A:TMP\TMP1\TMP2

A>subst e: /d

A>subst

A>
```

Problems with SUBST

IBM admonishes users of PC-DOS 3.3 and 4.X that SUBST should not be used with ASSIGN, BACKUP, DISKCOMP, DISKCOPY, FDISK, FORMAT, or RESTORE. Big Blue makes no elaborations, but the obvious implication is that SUBST confuses these other commands. Any system command that interferes with at least nine other commands is to be avoided. Consider staying away from SUBST until IBM and Microsoft rid it of its bugs.

SWITCHAR

Internal
MS-DOS 2.0–2.1

Function: Changes the switch character
             Note: SWITCHAR can be used in CONFIG.SYS only

Format: SWITCHAR=*character*

Example: switchar=–

The character used to separate an operating system command from an optional switch is called the *switch character*. The forward slash (/) is the standard MS-DOS switch character. Users of other operating systems (most notably UNIX) often prefer to be able to use the same switch character regardless of which operating system they are using. MS-DOS 2.0 and 2.1 implement SWITCHAR, a convenient way to change the switch character. The format for the command (which must be used in CONFIG.SYS) is:

    SWITCHAR=*character*

where *character* is the new switch character.

Changing the Switch Character in MS-DOS 3.X and 4.X

SWITCHAR is not implemented in versions of MS-DOS after 2.10. However, changing the switch character is possible in post-2.10 versions. In the following listing, DEBUG is used to create an assembly language program called "switchar.com". Refer to chapter 15 for details on using DEBUG. The program uses the undocumented MS-DOS function 37H to set the switch character to the character whose ASCII value is stored in the DL register.

```
C>debug
-n switchar.com
-a

3A3D:0100 MOV   DL,2F                  ;default switchar
3A3D:0102 CMP   BYTE PTR [0080],00     ;length of command tail
```

```
3A3D:0107 JZ    010D              ;no tail entered
3A3D:0109 MOV   DL,[0082]         ;tail entered, dl gets ASCII
3A3D:010D MOV   [012E],DL         ;copy to message string
3A3D:0111 MOV   AX,3701           ;set switchar
3A3D:0114 INT   21                ;call MS-DOS
3A3D:0116 MOV   DX,0122           ;point to message
3A3D:0119 MOV   AH,09             ;output string function
3A3D:011B INT   21                ;call MS-DOS
3A3D:011D MOV   AX,4C00           ;exit function
3A3D:0120 INT   21                ;call MS-DOS
3A3D:0122 DB    'switchar= ',AF,' / ',AE,0D,0A,'$'
3A3D:0134
-rcx
:0000
34
-w
Writing 0034 bytes
-q

C>
```

Once the program is created, the switch character is changed by entering "switchar *character*". Entering "switchar" with no parameters sets "/" as the switch character.

SWITCHES

Internal
MS-DOS 4.X

Function: Disables enhanced keyboards with applications that won't work properly with it
Note: SWITCHES is a configuration command that can only be used in CONFIG.SYS.

Format: SWITCHES=/K

Example: switches=/k

The SWITCHES command is used to control the activity of enhanced keyboards. These newer keyboards have some keys (F11 and F12 function keys, and a set of cursor keys separate from the number pad) that are not found on the older keyboards. Naturally, the new keys generate scan codes not generated by the older keys. (All keys generate a *make scan code* when pressed and a *break scan code* when released. The make and break scan codes are unique for each key.)

Some application programs are unable to process the scan codes generated by the newer keys. In such cases, these scan codes may confuse the program or even cause the system to crash. This problem can be avoided by placing the command "switches=/k" in CONFIG.SYS. This instructs DOS to simply ignore the scan codes generated by the new keys.

SYS

External
MS-DOS 1X, 2.X, 3.X, 4.X

Function: Transfers the system files to a specified disk

Format: **SYS d:** (MS-DOS 1.X–4.X)
SYS [*d:*] d: (MS-DOS 4.X)

Example: sys b:

The MS-DOS system files are two "hidden" files that form an integral part of MS-DOS. The files are described as hidden because you cannot list them with the DIR command. The system files must be contained at a specific location and in a specific order on a disk if you are to use the disk for booting. (You will find more information on the system files in chapter 10.)

The SYS (SYStem) command is used to transfer the system files to a disk. The disk receiving the files must be either a blank formatted disk, a disk that has been formatted using the command "format *d:*/s", or a disk formatted with the command "format *d:*/b". If the disk is a blank formatted one, SYS will be able to place the system files at the required location on the disk. If the disk has been formatted using either the /s or the /b switch, the required location will have been allocated for the system files. Otherwise, SYS would be unable to correctly place the files.

When transferring files with SYS, you should use your working copy of the system diskette. In the following example, a working copy of the system diskette is in drive A. With your diskette in place, type **sys** and then type the letter designator of the drive containing the disk that will receive the system files:

```
A>sys c:
```

```
System transferred
```

The MS-DOS 4.X version of SYS allows you to specify the source drive that contains the system files. For example, if drive A is the current drive and you wish to copy the system files from drive C to drive A, you could enter the following command:

```
sys c: a:
```

MS-DOS assumes that the system files are on the current drive if no drive letter is specified for the source.

Also in DOS 4.0, the system files can be copied to the destination disk as long as there are two free root directory entries and enough space on the disk to hold the files. The disk need not have old system files or have been formatted with "format /b".

TIME

Internal
MS-DOS 1.X, 2.X, 3.X, 4.X

Functions: Displays the current time known to MS-DOS
Changes the time known to MS-DOS

Format: TIME [*hh:mm:ss.xx*]

Examples: time
time 11:30

The TIME command is used to display and set the current time known to MS-DOS. When a file is created or modified, the current time known to the system is stored in the file directory. This information, along with the current date, forms the file's time-date stamp.

To display the time, type **time**. MS-DOS will display the time and ask if you want to change it:

```
C>time
Current time is 11:42:23.07
Enter new time:
```

To enter a new time, use the form *hh:mm:ss.xx*, where:

hh is a one- or two-digit number from 0–23 (hours),

mm is a one- or two-digit number from 0–59 (minutes),

ss is a one- or two-digit number from 0–59 (seconds),

xx is a one- or two-digit number from 0–99 (hundredths of a second).

DOS 4.0 allows you to add an "a" or "p" (for am/pm), so that time can be specified using a 12-hour clock as an alternative to using a 24-hour clock.

To leave the current time unchanged, simply press Enter:

```
C>time
```

```
Current time is 11:42:23.07
Enter new time:     ←you press Enter
```

The current time may be specified in the TIME command:

```
C>time 11:59
```

MS-DOS will prompt for another time if an invalid time is entered. Any fields not specified are set to zero. For example, if the time entered is 2:00, the current time is set to 2:00:00.00.

On machines with permanent clocks, the MS-DOS 3.3 and later implementations of TIME reset the permanent clock's time. Unfortunately, PC-DOS 3.3 and 4.X set only permanent clocks whose memory address is the same as IBM's clock. TIME has no effect on clocks with a different address.

TREE

External
MS-DOS 2.X, 3.X, 4.X

Function: Displays the directory paths on the specified drive

Formats: **TREE** [*d:*][/F] (MS-DOS 2.X–4.X)
TREE [*d:*][*path*][/F][/A] (MS-DOS 4.X)

Examples: tree
tree b: /f

The TREE command is used to produce a list of the directories on a disk. Each directory on the floppy diskette or hard disk is listed by its full path name. Subdirectories are grouped and listed according to the directory in which they exist.

TREE is an external MS-DOS command. This means that a copy of the file TREE.COM must be in a system drive before you can use the TREE command. To use TREE, type **tree** and then type the letter designator of the drive containing the disk to be analyzed. The default drive is assumed if no drive is specified. MS-DOS will list the files in each directory if you include the /f switch in the command.

The MS-DOS 4.X version of TREE provides the /**a** switch, which directs TREE to use an alternate character in generating its output. The switch is provided for printers that do not support the characters normally used by TREE.

The 4.X version of TREE also allows you to specify a directory path. TREE will list the directory tree starting at the end of that path. If no path is specified, the tree starting with the current directory will be displayed.

TRUENAME

Internal
MS-DOS 4.X

Function: Displays the true name of logical drives and directories
created with the commands ASSIGN, JOIN, and SUBST

Formats: TRUENAME
TRUENAME[*d:*][*path*][*filename*]

Example: truename
truename e:

The MS-DOS commands ASSIGN, JOIN, and SUBST can be used to assign
logical names to drive letters and subdirectories. For example, the SUBST
command can be used to assign the directory C:\TMP to drive letter E: as
follows:

```
C:\BOOKS\DOS>subst e: c:\tmp
```

The effect of the command is to direct all references for drive E to the directory C:\TMP. Thus, while the following command appears to be reading
drive E, it is actually reading C:\TMP.

```
C:\BOOKS\DOS>dir e:\

 Volume in drive E is MINI
 Volume Serial Number is 3C23-15F8
 Directory of  E:\


printing.
.             <DIR>      01-07-89   4:50p
..            <DIR>      01-07-89   4:50p
4U4UIKM  4U         5 01-31-89   6:16p
        3 File(s)   36536320 bytes free
```

The display says that the directory E:\ contains a file named **4U4UIKM.4U**. In
reality, the file resides in C:\TMP as the MS-DOS 4.X command
TRUENAME demonstrates:

```
C:\BOOKS\DOS>truename e:\4u4uikm.4u
C:\TMP\4U4UIKM.4U
C:\BOOKS\DOS>
```

TRUENAME (a command implemented in PC-DOS 4.0, but not documented in any of the IBM manuals) can be entered with a drive specifier, path specifier, and/or filename parameters. The command tells you where the drive, path, or file is actually located. As the following example illustrates, if you enter **truename** with no additional parameters, the command will return the true name of the current directory:

```
C:\BOOKS\DOS>e:       ← change to the "E" drive
E:\>truename          ← what is the "E" drive's true name?
C:\TMP      ← the true name
E:\>
```

TYPE

Internal
MS-DOS 1.X, 2.X, 3.X, 4.X

Function: Displays the contents of a file

Format: TYPE [*d:*][*path*]*filename*[.*ext*]

Example: type b:letter.txt

The TYPE command is used to display the contents of a file on the screen. TYPE is generally used only with text (ASCII) files. Attempts at displaying binary files can give unexpected results.

To display a file, enter **type** followed by the filespec of the desired file. MS-DOS will read the file into memory and then display it on the screen:

```
C>type b:letter.txt
```

The display will scroll off the screen if the file contains more than 23 lines. To suspend the display, press Ctrl-NumLock. Press any key to resume the display.

To obtain a printout of a file, press Ctrl-PrtSc before entering the TYPE command. This key combination tells MS-DOS to "echo" the screen display to the printer.

Wildcard characters cannot be used with TYPE.

VER

Internal
MS-DOS 2.X, 3.X, 4.X

Function: Displays the MS-DOS version number

Format: VER

Example: ver

The VER command tells you the version of MS-DOS that you are currently using. Simply type **ver** if you want MS-DOS to display the version number of MS-DOS that you are working with:

```
C>ver
MS-DOS Version  3.30
```

VERIFY

Internal
MS-DOS 2.X, 3.X, 4.X

Function: Turns the write-verify switch on or off

Format: VERIFY [ON|OFF]

Examples: verify
            verify on
            verify off

The VERIFY command is used to turn MS-DOS's write-VERIFY operation on or off. When VERIFY is on, MS-DOS performs a series of checks following each disk-write operation to verify that the data just written can be read without error. During verification, the system will run more slowly. This command serves the same purpose as the /v switch in the COPY command.

To turn VERIFY on, type **verify on**. To turn VERIFY off, type **verify off**. The current VERIFY state is displayed when you enter VERIFY with no parameters:

```
C>verify
VERIFY is on
```

VOL

Internal
MS-DOS 2.X, 3.X, 4.X

Function: Displays the volume label of the disk in the specified drive

Format: VOL [*d*:]

Examples: vol
vol b:

The VOL (VOLume) command is used to display the volume label of the disk in the specified drive. Simply type **vol** followed by the letter designator of the desired drive. The default is assumed if you do not specify a drive.

```
C>vol

Volume in drive C is MS-DOS_BIBLE
```

The DOS 4 version of VOL will also display the disk's serial number if one exists.

XCOPY

External
MS-DOS 3.2, 3.3, 4.X

Function: Provides enhanced file copying capability

Format: XCOPY[*d*:][*path*]*filename*[*.ext*][*d*:][*path*][*filename*][*.ext*][/A]
[/D:*mm-dd-yy*][/E][/M][/P][/S][/V][/W]

Example: xcopy *.* a: /e /s /a

XCOPY is a greatly enhanced version of the COPY command. It allows you to (1) selectively copy files that have their archive attributes set (see ATTRIB), (2) selectively copy files according to their date stamp, and (3) copy files located in the subdirectories of the specified directory. The following examples will demonstrate that XCOPY can also be much faster than COPY. Figure 3 shows the file structure used in the examples.

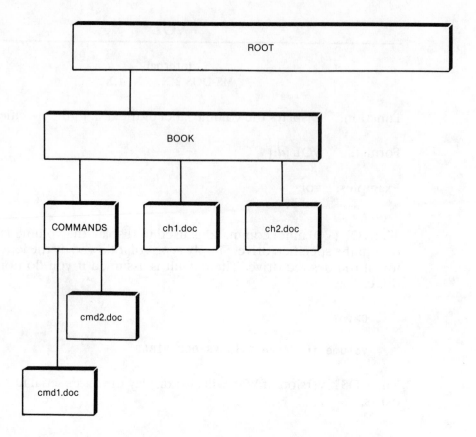

Figure 3. File structure for XCOPY examples.

XCOPYing Subdirectories

Assume that \BOOK is the current directory on drive C and that \COM-
MANDS is a subdirectory in \BOOK. A major limitation of COPY is that the
contents of \BOOK and the contents of \COMMANDS cannot be copied
with a single invocation of COPY. The /s switch provides XCOPY with the
ability to copy all files in all subdirectories below the specified source directory. The specified source directory in this example is the default BOOK.
Remember that since XCOPY is an external command, MS-DOS must be
able to read the command from disk before execution. (Internal and external
commands are discussed in the beginning of Part 3.)

```
C>xcopy *.* a: /s

Reading source file(s)...
CH1.DOC
CH2.DOC
```

```
COMMANDS\CMD1.DOC
COMMANDS\CMD2.DOC
        4 File(s) copied

C>
```

The nice feature of the /s switch is that it directs XCOPY to create the subdirectories on the target if they do not already exist. This capability makes XCOPY very useful in copying large multilevel directory structures.

Another feature of XCOPY is that it copies groups of files faster than COPY does. XCOPY reads as many source files into memory as is possible before making any copies. This minimizes disk access time and greatly speeds up the process.

XCOPY by Date

The /d switch allows you to selectively copy files that have a date stamp on or after a specified date. The date is specified in the format determined by the SELECT or COUNTRY command.

```
C>xcopy *.* a: /s /d:6-29-89

Reading source file(s)...
COMMANDS\CMD2.DOC
        1 File(s) copied
```

XCOPYing Archived Files

XCOPY can be used to selectively copy files that have their archive attributes set (see ATTRIB for a discussion of archive attributes). The /a switch directs XCOPY to copy a file if the archive attribute is set, leaving the attribute unchanged. The /m switch directs XCOPY to copy a file if the archive attribute is set, clearing the attribute in the process. The batch file "write.bat", discussed in chapter 4, uses the command "xcopy /m".

The /m switch was used daily in the writing of this book. At the end of each day, I would enter the following command:

```
xcopy *.doc a: /m
```

Since all of the files I worked on that day had their archive attribute set, this one command let me copy an entire day's work. Equally neat is that files not worked on were not copied. Also, since the /m flag cleared the archive bit, the files wouldn't be copied until I worked on them again.

Other Switches

The /e switch directs XCOPY to create a copy of any empty subdirectories specified in the command.

The /p switch produces the prompt:

```
path\filename.ext (Y/N)?
```

prior to each copy.

The /v switch directs MS-DOS to verify that each copy is performed accurately.

The /w switch tells XCOPY to wait for you to insert diskettes before searching for source files.

XCOPY versus BACKUP

Although there are strong similarities between XCOPY and BACKUP (e.g., subdirectories are copyable, archive attributes and dates are selectable), it is important to bear in mind the differences. BACKUP is used specifically to create backup copies of files. Files generated by BACKUP can be used with RESTORE only. No other MS-DOS commands can utilize these files. On the other hand, the files generated with XCOPY are conventional MS-DOS files.

P A R T

4

Appendixes

A

MS-DOS Interrupts and Function Calls

What Is an Interrupt?

An *interrupt* (int) is a signal, generated by either hardware or software, that alerts the central processing unit (CPU) that some function needs to be carried out. For example, each time a key is struck, the keyboard hardware generates an interrupt that tells the CPU that data was entered from the keyboard.

Each interrupt is assigned a unique number (e.g., the keyboard interrupt is "9") that the CPU uses to determine which *interrupt handler* must be used to process the interrupt. By convention, interrupt numbers are expressed in hexadecimal format. See chapter 13 for more information on interrupts, interrupt handlers, and CPU registers.

MS-DOS reserves for its own use interrupts 20H through 2FH. This means that programs designed to be portable across different implementations of MS-DOS should use interrupts 20H through 2FH only to perform specific tasks defined by the operating system. The most frequently used MS-DOS interrupt is interrupt 21H, the MS-DOS function dispatcher.

The MS-DOS Function Dispatcher

Interrupt 21H is the *MS-DOS function dispatcher*. The function dispatcher is responsible for carrying out most of the work done by MS-DOS. It does this by providing access to the *MS-DOS functions*. Each function performs a specific task, such as opening a file, sending a string to the display screen, allocating a block of memory, or determining which version of MS-DOS is running. Each function is identified by a function number.

In order to use the MS-DOS functions, a program must perform three tasks: (1) place the appropriate function number in the CPU's AH register; (2) place any parameters required by the function in other CPU registers, the register(s) used being determined by the particular function; and (3) issue a 21H interrupt. When the interrupt is issued, control passes from the program to MS-DOS. The operating system determines which function is to be executed by the number stored in the AH register. Any parameters are read from other CPU registers, after which the requested function is carried out. MS-DOS places any return parameters in specific CPU registers and returns control to the calling program. The program may then inspect the registers to determine the results of the function call.

Each of the MS-DOS functions is discussed in this appendix. For each function, there is a description of: (1) what the function does, (2) which parameters must be sent to the function and which registers must be used, and (3) which parameters are returned from the function to the calling program and which registers are used.

As an example of using functions, let us consider how an assembly language programmer might set up a program so that it could determine which version of MS-DOS was currently running. MS-DOS function 30H is used to obtain the MS-DOS version number. The description of function 30H in this appendix says that the function returns the minor MS-DOS version in the AH register and the major MS-DOS version in the AL register. In other words, if MS-DOS 3.30 is running, 30 is returned in AH and 3 is returned in AL.

```
                    ;Determines the version of MS-DOS running

                              ;Set up to issue interrupt
        mov     ah,30h        ;Requested service
        int     21h           ;call MS-DOS function dispatcher
                              ;
                              ;Read parameters returned
        mov     minor_num,ah  ;Save minor version number
        mov     major_num,al  ;Save major version number
```

Note: Those readers with little or no assembly language experience are referred to appendix E.

Interrupts and High-Level Programming Languages

Programs writtten in assembly language use explicit instructions (such as "int 21H") when issuing interrupts. Programs written in high-level languages (such as BASIC, Pascal, and C) do not use explicit interrupt instructions. Rather, high-level language commands (such as opening a file) are processed by the language's interpreter or compiler to generate the appropriate "int" instructions. In most cases, this arrangement is satisfactory for the high-level language programmer. The loss of "total machine control" provided by assembly language is offset by the ease of programming provided by the natural language structure of high-level programming languages.

In certain cases, though, it is desirable for the high-level language programmer to be able to issue explicit interrupts. The programs contained in this appendix are written in Turbo Pascal and Microsoft C. Both programs utilize explicit interrupts to illustrate how the MS-DOS functions can be accessed from high-level languages. Before getting to the programs, however, we need to discuss the use of interrupts to access the ROM BIOS.

Accessing the ROM BIOS

The ROM BIOS (read-only memory, basic input-output system) forms the interface between MS-DOS and the hardware. Programs also access the ROM BIOS through interrupts. For example, when a program needs to send a character to the display screen, the program may issue a call to the MS-DOS function dispatcher by using interrupt 21H. The dispatcher then accesses the ROM BIOS using interrupt 10H, and the BIOS goes on to display the character. In some cases (generally, increased speed of execution), it is desirable for the program to access the ROM BIOS directly. Program BRK_OFF.C (listing A-2) shows how this is done.

Since the ROM BIOS directly interfaces with the hardware, programs that access the BIOS directly tend to be not as portable as those that access the ROM through MS-DOS. You should refer to your computer system's technical manual for detailed ROM BIOS information.

ENVSIZE.PAS

ENVSIZE.PAS (listing A-1) is a program written in Turbo Pascal. The program counts the number of bytes actually stored in the DOS environment. You may find it useful in measuring how efficiently you are using the space reserved for the environment. The MS-DOS environment is discussed in chapter 11. The discussion of the SHELL command in Part 3 describes how to adjust the environment's size.

ENVSIZE.PAS uses the function `MsDos()`, a predefined Turbo Pascal function that can be used to access the MS-DOS function dispatcher. `MsDos()` takes as a parameter a Pascal record of type `registers`, which contains 10 integers. When `MsDos()` is called by the program, the function takes the first integer from the parameter record and places it in the AX register. The function then takes the second integer from the parameter record and places it in the BX register, and so on for each of the 10 integers (see listing A-1, lines 8–10). `MsDos()` then goes on to call the appropriate function. Upon return from the function, `MsDos()` takes the value stored in the AX register and places it in the first integer of the parameter record. The BX value is placed in the second integer of the parameter record, and so on. In this program, `dosreg` is declared as a variable of type `registers`.

The program begins (line 73) by calling procedure `vernum`, which will return the major number of the version of MS-DOS being used. Line 19 sets the AX field of `dosregs` to $3000 (Turbo Pascal denotes hexadecimal numbers by a leading "$" rather than a trailing "H"). The effect of line 19 is to place a value of 30H in the AH register and a value of 00H in the AL register. This establishes the conditions for a call to function 30H.

Line 20 is a call to the MS-DOS function dispatcher (interrupt 21H) with parameters passed in `dosreg`. On return from the function dispatcher, the major MS-DOS version number is stored in the AL register. Line 21 uses the Turbo function `Lo()` to assign the value in AL (the low byte in `dosreg.ax`) to `vernum`. The major version number is then returned to the main program module, which displays a message and terminates if `vernum` is less than 3.

The procedure `get_envaddr` uses MS-DOS function 62H to obtain the segment address of the program segment prefix and assigns the address to the variable `psp_seg` (lines 32–34). Procedure `vernum` must be called prior to calling `get_envaddr` since service function 62H is not implemented in versions of MS-DOS prior to 3.00.

Listing A-1. ENVSIZE.PAS

```
1 program EnvSize;
2
3 {This program determines the size of its MS-DOS environment.
4 The program uses service function 62H. Therefore, MS-DOS 3.0 or
5 later is required.}
6
7 type
8      registers = record
9                     ax,bx,cx,dx,bp,si,di,ds,es,flags: integer;
10                    end;
11 var
12     dosreg:     registers;
13     env_seg:        integer; {Segment address of environment}
```

```
14
15
16  {Returns the version of MS-DOS being used.}
17  function vernum : integer;
18  begin
19      dosreg.ax:= $3000;        {Set AH to 30H.}
20      MsDos(dosreg);            {Call MS-DOS}
21      vernum:= Lo(dosreg.ax); {Major version number in AL}
22  end;
23
24
25  {Obtains segment address of psp using service function 62H.
26  Reads segment address of environment at psp:002CH.}
27
28  procedure get_envaddr;
29  var
30      psp_seg : integer;
31  begin
32      dosreg.ax := $6200;
33      MsDos(dosreg);
34      psp_seg := dosreg.bx;
35      env_seg := MemW[psp_seg:$002C];
36  end;
37
38
39  {Returns the number of byte characters stored in the MS-DOS
40  environment. env_seg is global and contains environment's
41  segment address}
42
43  function get_size : integer;
44  var
45      count :  integer;   {Counts characters in environment}
46      firstZero,secondZero : boolean;{Flag records if last byte = 00}
47      env_ptr :  ^Byte;             {Environment pointer}
48  begin
49      env_ptr := Ptr(env_seg,$0);   {Start of environment}
50      count := 0;
51      firstZero := false;
52      secondZero := false;
53
54      while secondZero = false do     {Read environment}
55      begin
56      env_ptr := Ptr(env_seg,count); {Point to next byte}
57      count := count + 1;
58
59      if env_ptr^ = 0 then           {Byte of 00 read}
60      begin
61          if firstZero = true then   {2 consecutive 00's}
62          secondZero := true
63          else firstZero := true     {only 1 byte of 00 read}
64      end
```

```
65      else firstZero := false;        {00 byte not read}
66    end;
67
68    get_size := count;
69 end;
70
71
72
73 begin
74    if vernum < 3 then
75          writeln('MS-DOS 3.0 or later required.')
76    else begin
77          get_envaddr;
78          writeln('Environment Size: ',get_size,' bytes');
79    end;
80 end.
```

ENVSIZE.PAS will run under MS-DOS 2.1, and subsequent versions, with a few minor modifications. Change line 32 to:

```
dosreg.ax := $5100
```

The result is that MS-DOS now calls undocumented function 51H, which also returns the psp's segment address in BX. The other change (which is left to the reader) is to have the program check to make sure that MS-DOS version 2.1 or greater is running prior to calling the procedure `get_envaddr`.

MS-DOS function 51H is used in the program PSPEEP.PAS, which is presented in chapter 11.

Line 35 uses the predefined array `MemW` to assign the segment address of the MS-DOS environment to the variable `env_seg`. The value of `MemW[psp_seg:$002C]` is the value of the word stored at segment address `psp_seg`, offset address 2CH. As discussed in chapter 11, this is the memory location that stores the segment address of the MS-DOS environment.

The function `get_size` initializes a counter and two boolean flags (lines 50—52) before entering a loop (lines 54—65). On entering the loop, `env_ptr` points to the first byte in the MS-DOS environment. Each traversal of the loop increments the variable count and moves `env_ptr` to the next byte in the environment. The loop is exited when two consecutive bytes of zero are read. Two consecutive bytes of zero indicate that the end of the environment's character strings has been reached. Upon exiting the loop, the variable `count` stores the number of bytes stored in the environment. Note that this is not the storage capacity of the environment, but a count of the number of character bytes actually stored there. The value of count is assigned to **get_size**, returned to the program's main module, and displayed on the screen (line 78).

BRK_OFF.C

BRK_OFF.C (listing A-2), which is written in Microsoft C, uses the MS-DOS functions to capture any Ctrl-C or Ctrl-Break entered on the keyboard. The program also accesses the ROM BIOS to position the cursor on the screen.

Listing A-2. BRK_OFF.C

```
 1 /*This program illustrates how the MS-DOS service functions are
 2 *accessed using Microsoft C, version 4.0. The program implements
 3 *a keyboard routine that captures Ctrl-C.
 4 */
 5
 6 #include   <stdio.h>
 7 #include   <dos.h>
 8 #define          TRUE          1
 9
10 union    REGS     Regs;                  /*General registers*/
11 struct   SREGS    Sregs;                 /*Segment registers*/
12
13 char     message[] = "Ctrl-C disabled, press X to quit";
14
15 int      x_cur, y_cur;
16
17
18 /*Call to ROM BIOS which returns cursor's x coordinate in the Regs.h.dh
19 *register, the y coordinate in the Regs.h.dl register. These values
20 *are saved in global variables x_cur and y_cur. Prior to call,
21 *current page number is stored in Regs.h.bh.
22 */
23
24 void get_cursor_pos()
25 {
26   Regs.h.ah = 0x03;         /*Read cursor function*/
27   int86(0x10,&Regs,&Regs); /*Call BIOS*/
28   x_cur = Regs.h.dl;
29   y_cur = Regs.h.dh;
30   return;
31 }
32
33
34 /*Calls ROM BIOS to restore cursor position which has been saved in
35  *global variables x_cur and y_cur. Prior to call, Regs.h.bh
36  *contains active page number.
```

```
37  */
38
39  void reset_cursor()
40  {
41    Regs.h.ah = 0x02;          /*Set cursor function*/
42    Regs.h.dl = x_cur;         /*DL stores x value*/
43    Regs.h.dh = y_cur;         /*DH stores y value*/
44    int86(0x10,&Regs,&Regs);
45    return;
46  }
47
48
49  /*Calls ROM BIOS to display message at bottom of screen. Current
50   *position of cursor is saved prior to displaying message. Cursor
51   *position is restored after message is displayed.
52   */
53
54  void display_message()
55  {
56    Regs.h.ah = 0x0f;          /*Get active page*/
57    int86(0x10,&Regs,&Regs);   /*Call BIOS*/
58    get_cursor_pos();          /*Save cursor position*/
59
60    Regs.h.ah 0x02;            /*Set cursor function*/
61    Regs.h.dh = 0x18;          /*Row position*/
62    Regs.h.dl = 0x14;          /*Column position*/
63    int86(0x10,&Regs,&Regs);   /*Call BIOS*/
64    printf("%s",message);
65
66    reset_cursor();            /*To current position*/
67    return;
68  }
69
70
71  /*Calls DOS service function 02h to display a character on screen
72   *at current position of cursor. Prior to call, Regs.h.al contains
73   *byte data for character to be displayed.
74   */
75
76  void echo()
77  {
78    Regs.h.dl = Regs.h.al;
79    Regs.h.ah = 0x02;
80    intdos(&Regs,&Regs);
81    return;
82  }
83
84
85  /*Calls ROM BIOS, first to get the active page number in Regs.h.bh
86   *then to position cursor at 0,0. Then endless loop captures Ctrl-C.
87   *Loop is broken when "X" typed at keyboard. Other characters are
```

```
 88  *echoed to screen.
 89  */
 90
 91  break_off()
 92  {
 93    Regs.h.ah = 0x0f;                    /*Get active page*/
 94    int86(0x10,&Regs,&Regs);             /*Call BIOS*/
 95
 96    Regs.h.ah = 0x02;                    /*Position cursor*/
 97    Regs.h.dl = 0x00;                    /*  to 0,0 */
 98    Regs.h.dh = 0x00;
 99    int86(0x10,&Regs,&Regs);             /*Call BIOS*/
100
101    while (TRUE)                         /*Loop forever*/
102    }
103          Regs.h.ah = 0x07;             /*Input, no echo*/
104          intdos(&Regs,&Regs);          /*Call MS-DOS*/
105
106          if (Regs.h.al = '^C')
107                display_message();
108          else if (Regs.h.al != 'X')
109          echo();
110          else break;                    /*Break from loop*/
111    }
112    return;
113  }
114
115  main()
116  {
117    break_off();
118    exit(0);
119  }
```

The program declares **Regs** and **Sregs** (listing A-2, lines 10–11) to be variables of types **REGS** and **SREGS**, respectively. **REGS** is a predefined Microsoft C data type that contains eight integer fields, each of which corresponds to one of the CPU's general registers. **SREGS** is a predefined Microsoft C data type that contains four integer fields, each of which corresponds to one of the CPU's segment registers. As will be seen, these data structures perform the same role as the **register** variable used in the preceding Turbo Pascal program.

BRK__OFF.C begins (line 117) by calling **break_off()** (line 91). The first portion of **break_off()** positions the cursor at position 0,0 (the upper left corner) on the screen. In order to do this, the program accesses the ROM BIOS two times.

In Microsoft C, ROM BIOS accesses are carried out using the predefined function **int86()**. This function takes three parameters: (1) an integer that specifies an interrupt number, (2) a **REGS**-type data structure that contains parameters to be passed to the ROM BIOS, and (3) a second **REGS**-type data structure that will store parameters returned from the ROM BIOS to the calling program. The ROM BIOS video services are accessed using interrupt 10H. The number of the video function requested is passed in the AH register.

The first ROM BIOS call (line 94) is performed to determine the active display page. Since the ROM BIOS maintains a cursor position for each display page, the program needs to know which page is active before the ROM BIOS can be instructed to position the cursor. The active display page is returned in the BH register by video function 0FH. Accordingly, line 96 sets the AH field of `Regs` to 0902 (02H). Line 94 is a call to the ROM BIOS service using `int86()`. On return, `Regs.h.bh` contains the active display page number. Note that Microsoft C allows a program to access: (1) the high-order byte stored in a general register, for example `Regs.h.ah`; (2) the low-order byte stored in a general register, for example `Regs.h.al`; and (3) the two-byte word stored in a general register, for example `Regs.x.ax`.

Lines 96–99 position the cursor at 0,0. This is accomplished by calling video function 02H. Prior to the call, the *x* coordinate for the cursor is placed in the DL register, the *y* coordinate in the DH register. Function 02H also requires that the BH register contain the active display page number. This was accomplished by the previous ROM BIOS call.

Once the cursor is positioned, the program enters an infinite loop, which begins at line 101. The first part of the loop (lines 103–104) uses MS-DOS function 07H to read a character from the keyboard without echoing it to the screen. The MS-DOS functions are accessed using the predefined function `intdos()`, which does not take an interrupt parameter because all of the MS-DOS service functions are accessed via interrupt 21H.

Line 103 places 07H in `Regs.h.ah`. This will tell MS-DOS that function 07H is requested. Once MS-DOS is called (line 104), the operating system will wait until a character is entered at the keyboard. When a character is entered, MS-DOS returns control to the program and the byte value of the entered character is stored in `Regs.h.al`.

When control returns from MS-DOS to the program (line 106), BRK_OFF.C first checks to see if Ctrl-C was entered. Note that the ^C in line 106 is a single control character. Most word processors allow you to enter a literal control code character into text.

If Ctrl-C was entered, line 106 is evaluated as true and control is passed to `display_message()`. This function starts by repeating the call to ROM BIOS video function 0FH to determine the active display page. With the display page number back in `Regs.h.bh`, `display_message()` calls `get_cursor_pos()`, which uses ROM BIOS video function 03H to determine the position of the cursor. The cursor's coordinates are saved in the global variables `x_cur` and `y_cur` (lines 28–29), and control is returned to `display_message()`.

The function `display_message()` then uses ROM BIOS video service function 02H to position the cursor at row 18H, column 14H (lines 60–63). The C function `printf` is used to display a message saying that Ctrl-C has been disabled. Line 66 then issues a call to `reset_cursor()`, which uses video service function 02H to restore the cursor to the coordinates saved in `x_cur` and `y_cur`. Control is returned to **break_off()**, which repeats the infinite loop and waits for another character to be entered.

All of this happens (very quickly!) if Ctrl-C is pressed. We need to return to the infinite loop to see what happens if some other character is pressed. If, on return from MS-DOS function 07H, line 106 evaluates as false, the program checks to see if "X" was entered. If not, the program issues a call to **echo()**. If "X" was entered, the program breaks out of the infinite loop and returns to **main()**, where program execution terminates.

If neither Ctrl-C nor "X" was entered, **break_off()** issues a call to **echo()**. This function uses MS-DOS function 02H to display the character entered. Line 78 copies to **Regs.h.dl** the character returned by the previous call to MS-DOS. Function 02H is then called to display this character, after which control returns to **break_off()**, and the infinite loop is repeated.

The MS-DOS Interrupts

Interrupt	Description
Int 20H	***General program termination.*** This interrupt is one of several ways in which a program running under MS-DOS may terminate. The interrupt restores the terminate, Ctrl-Break, and critical error addresses, which are stored in the program's program segment prefix. This interrupt is a carryover from the early days of MS-DOS. Before issuing int 20H, CS must contain the psp's segment address. Most programmers use MS-DOS function 4CH to terminate because the function can be used to return an ERRORLEVEL value.
Int 21H	***MS-DOS function request.*** This interrupt is used to access the MS-DOS function calls, which are discussed in the next section.
Int 22H	***Program termination address.*** This interrupt points to the address in memory to which control is passed when a program is terminated. The address is stored in the program segment prefix of the program.
Int 23H	***Ctrl-Break address.*** This interrupt points to the address in memory of the routine that takes control when the user presses Ctrl-Break. The address is stored in the program segment prefix of the program.
Int 24H	***Critical error handler.*** This interrupt points to the address in memory of the routine that takes control when MS-DOS encounters a critical error. The address is stored in the program segment prefix. Prior to executing this interrupt,

Interrupt	Description
Int 24H (cont'd)	MS-DOS places an error code in the lower half of the DI register:

	Error Code	Description of Error
	0	Write-protected diskette.
	1	Unknown unit.
	2	Drive not ready.
	3	Unknown command.
	4	Data error.
	5	Bad request structure length.
	6	Seek error.
	7	Unknown media type.
	8	Sector not found.
	9	Printer out of paper.
	A	Write fault.
	B	Read fault.
	C	General failure.

BP:SI will contain the segment: offset address of the device header control block (see chapter 14) that was involved in the critical error.

Int 25H — ***Absolute disk read.*** This interrupt is used to read logical disk sectors into memory. Prior to calling the interrupt, the following registers must be initialized:

AL	Drive number containing the disk to be read (0=A, 1=B, etc.).
CX	Number of sectors to be read.
DX	Number of first logical sector to be read.
DS:BX	Segment: offset address of memory location that will receive the data to be read.

This interrupt destroys the contents of all registers except for the segment registers. If the read is successful, the carry flag will be zero on return. The carry flag will equal one on return if the read was not successful. If there is an error, the AL register will contain the MS-DOS error code. Refer to the discussion of int 24H for an interpretation of MS-DOS error codes. This interrupt does not pop the status flags on return.

The MS-DOS 4 version of int 25H supports a method for accessing sectors on disk partitions that are larger than 32 Mbytes. With this alternative method, the CX register is set to FFFFH (-1) prior to the call. AL contains the drive number and

Interrupt	Description
	DS:BX points to a 10-byte-long data structure. The first 4 bytes of the data structure contain the starting sector number. The fifth and sixth bytes contain the number of sectors to read. The final 4 bytes contain a segment:offset address of a data buffer that will store the data that is read.
Int 26H	***Absolute disk write.*** This interrupt is used to write data to logical disk sectors. Except for the fact that this is a write operation, its description is identical to that for the preceding interrupt 25H.
	The DOS 4 version of the interrupt supports a method for writing to large DOS partitions. The details are identical as described for reading with int 25H except for the fact that the data buffer contains data that is written to the disk.
Int 27H	***Terminate but stay resident.*** This interrupt is used to terminate the execution of a program while keeping the program resident in memory. Prior to executing the interrupt, the DX register must be set to the offset address of the program's end plus 1 byte. This offset is taken relative to the program's program segment prefix. Int 27H restores terminate, Ctrl-C, and critical error vectors. Therefore, it cannot be used to install critical error handlers. Programs that use int 27H are limited in size to 64 Kbytes. The preferred method for terminate and stay resident (under MS-DOS 2.X and subsequent versions) is MS-DOS service function 31H.
Int 28H	Used internally by MS-DOS (see appendix B).
Int 29H–2EH	Reserved for MS-DOS (see appendix B).
Int 2FH	***Multiplex Interrupt.*** This interrupt, implemented in MS-DOS 3.0 and later versions, is used to establish a multiplexing interface between two processes. A *process* is any program or command that is running. In *multiplexing*, the CPU runs one process for a period of time, halts the execution of that process and starts a second, halts the second and restarts the first, and so on, until both processes have finished executing. Int 2FH is used in the implementation of the command PRINT, which allows printing to occur in the background while another program is executing in the foreground (see PRINT in Part 3).
	Each program that runs under multiplexing (such as PRINT) is given a specific *multiplex number*. MS-DOS has reserved multiplex numbers 00–7FH for its

Interrupt	Description
Int 2FH (cont'd)	own use. PRINT has been given multiplex number 1. Multiplex numbers 80H–FFH are available for use by application programmers. There is no method for assigning a multiplex number to an application and, as is explained subsequently, each application must have a unique multiplex number. Therefore, IBM and Microsoft recommend that programs be written so that multiplex numbers are changeable.
	As if to emphasize the importance of changeability, MS-DOS assigns multiplex number B7H to a subfunction that determines if APPEND has been installed. IBM recommends that programs written to run under 3.3 and subsequent versions should use multiplex numbers in the range C0H through FFH.
	Each multiplexing program installs in memory an int 2FH handler. These handlers form a chain, similar to that formed by installable device drivers (see chapter 14). Prior to calling interrupt 2FH, a program places in the AH register the multiplex number of the handler that the program wishes to access. When MS-DOS receives control, the operating system scans the chain of int 2FH handlers until it locates one with a number matching the value stored in AH. MS-DOS passes control to that handler, which is then responsible for servicing the interrupt.
	Programs issuing int 2FH also place a *function code* in the AL register. The function code communicates to the handler the type of service requested by the caller. All int 2FH handlers are required to service a *get installed state* request (AL=00) from the caller. In response to this request, a return code is to be placed in AL:

	AL = 0	Handler not installed; okay to install.
	AL = 1	Handler not installed; not okay to install.
	AL = FF	Handler installed.

Interrupt	Description
Int 30H–3FH	Reserved for use by MS-DOS.

The MS-DOS Functions

The MS-DOS functions form the heart of the operating system. All of the functions are accessed by placing their function number in the AH register and issuing an interrupt 21H. See chapter 11 for examples of how functions are used in assembly language programming. The programs presented earlier in this apppendix demonstrate accessing the functions using Turbo Pascal and Microsoft C.

The "Reserved" Functions

Several of the functions are described as "reserved for use by MS-DOS." These functions are used by the operating system, but Microsoft and IBM refuse to officially document what the functions do. Thanks to the combined efforts of many determined hackers, the purpose of some of these functions is known. People who use these functions generally refer to them as "undocumented" rather than "reserved." Several of the undocumented functions are used in programs contained in this book. Appendix B describes some undocumented MS-DOS functions.

Error Codes

Many of the functions implemented in MS-DOS 2.X and later versions set the CPU's carry flag and return an error code in the AX register if an error occurs during the call. These same functions clear the carry flag if no error occurs.

Error Code	Meaning
01H	Invalid function number.
02H	File not found.
03H	Path not found.
04H	Too many files opened (no handles left).
05H	Access denied.
06H	Invalid handle.
07H	Memory control block destroyed.
08H	Insufficent memory.
09H	Invalid memory block address.
0AH	Invalid environment.
0BH	Invalid format.
0CH	Invalid access code.
0DH	Invalid data.
0EH	Reserved for use by MS-DOS.
0FH	Invalid drive specification.
10H	Attempted to remove current directory.
11H	Not same device.
12H	No more files.

The following error codes are implemented in MS-DOS 3.00 and subsequent versions:

Error Code	Meaning
20H	Sharing violation.
21H	Lock violation.
22H	Invalid disk change.
23H	FCB unavailable.
24H	Sharing buffer overflow.
25H–31H	Reserved.
32H	Network request not supported.
33H	Remote computer not listening.
34H	Duplicate name on network.
35H	Network name not found.
36H	Network busy.
37H	Network device does not exist.
38H	Network BIOS command limit exceeded.
39H	Network adapter hardware error.
3AH	Incorrect response from network.
3BH	Unexpected network error.
3CH	Incompatible remote adapter.
3DH	Print queue full.
3EH	Print queue not full.
3FH	Print file deleted (not enough space).
40H	Network name deleted.
41H	Access denied.
42H	Network device type incorrect.
43H	Network name not found.
44H	Network name limit exceeded.
45H	Network BIOS session limit exceeded.
46H	Temporarily paused.
47H	Network request not accepted.
48H	Print or disk redirection paused.
49H–4FH	Reserved by MS-DOS.
50H	File already exists.
51H	Reserved.
52H	Cannot make directory entry.
53H	Failure on int 24H.
54H	Too many redirections.

Error Code	Meaning
55H	Duplicate redirection.
56H	Invalid password.
57H	Invalid parameter.
58H	Network device fault.

MS-DOS Function	Description	Implemented in Versions
00H	***Program terminate.*** Used to terminate program execution. Restores the terminate, Ctrl-Break, and critical error addresses that were stored in the program's program segment prefix. This function is identical to int 20H. Any files that were opened with FCBs should be closed before using function 00H. Prior to the call, the CS register must contain the psp's segment address. Therefore, it is generally used in COM programs only.	1, 2, 3, 4
01H	***Read input with echo.*** When this function is called, MS-DOS waits for a character to be entered at the standard input device. The character is then echoed to the standard output device, and the ASCII code for the character is returned in the AL register. The function must be called twice to read extended ASCII codes (as generated by the function keys).	1, 2, 3, 4
02H	***Display output.*** Prior to executing this function, an ASCII value is placed in the DL register. When the function is called, the value in DL is sent to the standard output device.	1, 2, 3, 4
03H	***Auxiliary input.*** When this function is invoked, MS-DOS waits for a character to be input from the standard auxiliary device. The ASCII value for the character is returned in the AL register.	1, 2, 3, 4
04H	***Auxiliary output.*** An ASCII value is placed in the DL register prior to invoking this function. The function then sends the value in DL to the standard auxiliary device.	1, 2, 3, 4
05H	***Printer output.*** An ASCII value is placed in the DL register prior to invoking this	1, 2, 3, 4

MS-DOS Function	Description	Implemented in Versions
05H (cont'd)	function. The function then sends the value in DL to the standard printer device.	
06H	***Direct console I/O.*** The role of this function depends on the value stored in the DL register when the function is invoked:	1, 2, 3, 4
	If DL has a value of FFH, invoking function 06H directs MS-DOS to see if a character has been entered at the standard input device. If a character has been entered, the zero flag is set to 0 (cleared) and the ASCII value of the character entered is placed in the AL register. If a character has not been entered, the zero flag is set to 1 and a value of 00H is placed in the AL register.	
	If DL has a value other than FFH, the value in DL is sent to the standard output device. This function does not check for Ctrl-Break.	
07H	***Console input without echo.*** This function directs MS-DOS to wait for a character to be entered at the standard input device. The ASCII value of the character is returned in the AL register. This function does not echo the character to the display screen or check for Ctrl-Break.	1, 2, 3, 4
08H	***Read keyboard.*** This function is identical to function 07H except that it checks for Ctrl-Break.	1, 2, 3, 4
09H	***Print string.*** Prior to invoking this function, DS:DX is set to point to the segment: offset address of an ASCII string. The string must end with "$" (ASCII value 24H). Each character in the string (except the "$") is sent to the standard output device when the function is called.	1, 2, 3, 4
0AH	***Buffered keyboard input.*** This function is used to set up and utilize an area of memory as a buffer for input from the standard input device. Prior to invoking the function, you must do the following:	1, 2, 3, 4

1. Set DS:DX to point to the segment: offset address of the first byte in the buffer.

2. Specify the length of the buffer by placing a value in the buffer's first byte.

MS-DOS Function	Description	Implemented in Versions
0AH (cont'd)	When the function is called, MS-DOS places characters in the buffer as they are entered at the standard input device. The characters are stored beginning at the third byte of the buffer. Characters are stored in the buffer until carriage return (ASCII 0DH) is entered. If the buffer is filled to one less than the maximum, any remaining characters are ignored and the bell sounds until carriage return is entered. MS-DOS sets the second byte of the buffer to the number of characters entered (not counting carriage return). The buffer can be edited using the MS-DOS editing keys (see chapter 8).	
0BH	***Check standard input status.*** This function returns a value of FFH in the AL register if there are characters available from the standard input device. AL returns with a value of 00H if no characters are available.	1, 2, 3, 4
0CH	***Flush buffer, read standard input device.*** Prior to invoking this function, a value of 01H, 06H, 08H, or 0AH is placed in the AL register. When the function is called, the standard input device buffer is cleared and the MS-DOS function corresponding to the value in the AL register is invoked.	1, 2, 3, 4
0DH	***Disk reset.*** This function flushes all file buffers. Files that have been modified in size should be closed (functions 10H and 3EH). It is not necessary to flush a file that has been closed.	1, 2, 3, 4
0EH	***Select disk.*** This function selects the drive specified in the DL register (0=A, 1=B, etc.) as the default. The number of drives in the system is returned in the AL register. If a system has one diskette drive, the one drive is counted as two, since MS-DOS considers the system to have two logical diskette drives.	1, 2, 3, 4
0FH	***Open file.*** Prior to invoking this function, DS:DX must be set to point to the segment: offset address of an unopened file control block (FCB). When the function is called, the disk directory is searched for the file named in the FCB. If a match is found in the directory, the function returns a value of 00H	1, 2, 3, 4

MS-DOS Function	Description	Implemented in Versions
0FH (cont'd)	in the AL register and the FCB is filled as follows:	
	If the drive code of the FCB (offset 0) was set to default (00H), MS-DOS changes the code to match the actual drive used (1=A, 2=B, 3=C, etc.).	
	The current block field of the FCB (offset 0CH) is set to zero.	
	The record size field of the FCB (offset 0EH) is set to the default value of 80H.	
	The file size (offset 10H), date (offset 14H), and time (offset 16H) fields of the FCB are set according to information stored in the disk directory.	
	You must set the current record field of the FCB (offset 20H) before performing any sequential disk operations.	
	You must set the relative record field of the FCB (offset 21H) before performing any random disk operations.	
	You may modify the record size field if a file size of 80H bytes is not appropriate.	
	Function 0FH returns a value of FFH in the AL register if no match is made between the file named in the FCB and the entries in the disk directory. (The file control block is discussed in chapter 10.)	
10H	***Close file.*** This function must be used to update the disk directory whenever a file has been modified. Prior to invoking this function, DS:DX must point to the segment: offset address of an opened file control block. When the function is called, the current directory on the disk specified in the FCB is searched for the file named in the FCB. If a match is found, the file's entry in the directory is updated according to the information in the FCB and a value of 00H is returned in the AL register. A value of FFH is returned in AL if no match is found.	1, 2, 3, 4
11H	***Search for first match.*** Prior to invoking this function, DS:DX points to an unopened file control block (FCB). When the function is called, MS-DOS searches the current directory	1, 2, 3, 4

MS-DOS Function	Description	Implemented in Versions
11H (cont'd)	of the disk specified in the FCB for the first filename matching the filename specified in the FCB. The name in FCB may contain the wildcard characters "*" and "?". A value of FFH is returned in the AL register if no match is found. Otherwise:	
	A value of 00H is returned in the AL register.	
	An unopened FCB is created for the matching file at the disk transfer address (DTA). You may use MS-DOS function 2FH to obtain the current DTA.	
	DS:DX may point to a standard or an extended FCB (see chapter 10). The FCB created at the DTA will be of the same type. If the attribute byte of an extended FCB is set to zero, only normal files that match will be found. If the attribute byte of an extended FCB specifies hidden, system, and/ or directory entries, the search will find the specified types of entries that match, plus all normal files that match. If the attribute specifies volume label, only the volume label entry is returned. (See chapter 10 for a discussion of file attributes.)	
12H	***Search for next match.*** After function 11H has been used, this function is used to find additional directory entries matching the filename in the FCB at DS:DX. This function is used when the filename in the FCB contains wildcards. Prior to invoking this function, DS:DX must point to the segment: offset address of the FCB previously used by function 11H. If an additional match is found, function 12H creates an unopened file control block at the disk transfer area and a value of 00H is returned in the AL register. A value of FFH is returned in AL if no further match is found.	1, 2, 3, 4
13H	***Delete file.*** Prior to invoking this function, DS:DX points to the segment: offset address of an unopened file control block. When the function is called, MS-DOS searches the current directory of the disk specified in the FCB for an entry with a filename matching the one specified in the FCB. If a match is found, the	1, 2, 3, 4

MS-DOS Function	Description	Implemented in Versions
13H (cont'd)	file is deleted from the directory. If the filename in the FCB contains wildcards, all matching files are deleted. A value of 00H is returned in the AL register if any files are deleted. A value of FFH is returned in AL if no match is found.	
14H	***Sequential read.*** Prior to invoking this function, DS:DX must point to an opened file control block (FCB). The current block (offset 0CH) and current record (offset 20H) fields of the FCB determine a record within the file that is named in the FCB. The size of the record is determined by the record size field (offset 0EH) in the FCB. When the function is called:	1, 2, 3, 4

The specified record is read into memory at the disk transfer address (DTA).

The current block and current record fields are incremented to point to the next record.

The AL register returns a value of:

00H	If the read was successful.
01H	If an end-of-file mark is read, indicating no more data in the file.
02H	If there is not enough room at the DTA to read a record.
03H	If an end-of-file mark is read, indicating that a partial record was read and padded with zeros.

The DTA is set with MS-DOS function 1AH. The current DTA is returned with MS-DOS function 2FH.

MS-DOS Function	Description	Implemented in Versions
15H	***Sequential write.*** Prior to invoking this function, DS:DX must point to an opened file control block (FCB). The data to be written begins at the disk transfer address (DTA). The current block (offset 0CH) and current record (offset 20H) fields of the FCB determine a record within the file that is named in the FCB. The size of the record is determined by the record size field (offset 0EH) in the FCB. When the function is called:	1, 2, 3, 4

The specified record is written to the disk.

The current block and current record fields are incremented to point to the next record.

MS-DOS Function	Description	Implemented in Versions
15H (cont'd)	The AL register returns a value of:	

00H	If the write was successful.	
01H	If the disk is full and the write has been cancelled.	
02H	If there is not enough room at the DTA for one record; therefore, the write has been cancelled.	

16H	***Create file.*** Prior to invoking this function, DS:DX must point to an unopened file control block (FCB). When the function is called, MS-DOS checks the current directory of the drive specified in the FCB for an entry matching the file specified in the FCB. If a matching entry is found:	1, 2, 3, 4

The data in the existing file is released, making a file of zero length. The open file function (function 0FH) is then called.

If no match is found:

MS-DOS looks for an empty entry in the current directory. If an empty entry is available, MS-DOS initializes the file to have a length of zero and calls the open file function (function 0FH). A value of 00H is returned in the AL register. A value of FFH is returned in AL if there are no empty entries in the current directory.

A hidden file is created by using an extended FCB with the attribute byte set to a value of 02H (see chapter 10).

17H	***Rename file.*** Prior to invoking this function, DS:DX must point to the segment: offset address of a "modified" FCB. The FCB contains a drive number and filename beginning at offset 00H. The FCB contains a second filename beginning at offset 11H. When the function is called, MS-DOS searches the current directory of the drive specified in the FCB for an entry matching the first filename in the FCB. If a match is found:	1, 2, 3, 4

The filename in the directory is changed to the second filename in the FCB. If "?" characters are used in the second filename,

MS-DOS Function	Description	Implemented in Versions
17H (cont'd)	the corresponding positions in the original filename are not changed. A value of 00H is returned in the AL register.	
	If no match is found or if an entry is found matching the second filename:	
	A value of FFH is returned in the AL register.	
18H	Reserved for use by MS-DOS.	
19H	***Current disk.*** This function returns the number of the current default drive in the AL register (0=A, 1=B, etc.).	1, 2, 3, 4
1AH	***Set disk transfer address.*** This function is used to set the disk transfer address (DTA). Prior to invoking this function, DS:DX must point to the segment: offset address of the first byte in the DTA. MS-DOS establishes a default DTA at offset 80H in the program segment prefix if function 1AH is not invoked.	1, 2, 3, 4
1BH	***Allocation table information.*** This function returns information about the default drive's file allocation table (FAT). On return:	1, 2, 3, 4
	DS:BX points to the segment: offset address of a memory location that stores the first byte in the FAT.	
	DX contains the number of allocation units on the disk in the default drive.	
	AL stores the number of sectors per allocation unit.	
	CX stores the number of bytes in each sector.	
	In MS-DOS 2.0 and subsequent versions, this function does not return the address of the complete FAT, since the entire FAT is not stored in memory.	
1CH	***Allocation information for specific drive.*** This function is identical to function 1BH except that prior to invoking the function, the DL register contains the number of the drive from which the FAT information will be obtained (0=A, 1=B, etc.).	1, 2, 3, 4
1DH–20H	Reserved for use by MS-DOS (see appendix B).	
21H	***Random read.*** Prior to invoking this function, DS:DX must point to the segment:	1, 2, 3, 4

MS-DOS Function	Description	Implemented in Versions
21H (cont'd)	offset address of an opened file control block (FCB). The current block (offset 0CH) and current record (offset 20H) fields of the FCB must be set to agree with the relative record field (offset 21H). When the function is called, the record addressed by these fields is read into memory at the disk transfer address. A value is returned in the AL register as follows:	

00H	Read completed successfully.
01H	No data available in file.
02H	Not enough room in DTA to read one record; read cancelled.
03H	End-of-file mark encountered. A partial record was read and padded with zeros.

MS-DOS Function	Description	Implemented in Versions
22H	***Random write.*** Prior to invoking this function, DS:DX must point to the segment: offset address of an opened file control block (FCB). The current block (offset 0CH) and current record (offset 20H) fields of the FCB must be set to agree with the relative record field (offset 21H). When the function is called, the record addressed by these fields is written from the disk transfer address to the file specified in the FCB. A value is returned in the AL register as follows:	1, 2, 3, 4

00H	Write completed successfully.
01H	Disk full.
02H	Not enough room in DTA to write one record; write cancelled.

MS-DOS Function	Description	Implemented in Versions
23H	***File size.*** Prior to invoking this function, DS:DX is set to point to the segment: offset address of an unopened file control block (FCB). The record size field (offset 0EH) of the FCB must also be set prior to calling this function. When the function is called, MS-DOS searches the current directory of the drive specified in the FCB for a file that matches the filename in the FCB. If a match is found, the relative record size field (offset 21H) is set to the number of records in the file, and a value	1, 2, 3, 4

MS-DOS Function	Description	Implemented in Versions
23H (cont'd)	of 00H is returned in the AL register. A value of FFH is returned in AL if no match is found.	
24H	***Set random record field.*** Prior to invoking this function, DS:DX must point to the segment: offset address of an opened file control block (FCB). This function sets the relative record field (offset 21H) of the FCB to point to the record indicated by the combination of the current block (offset 0CH) and current record (offset 20H) fields.	1, 2, 3, 4
25H	***Set interrupt vector.*** This function is used to set the memory location that receives control when a specific interrupt is invoked. Prior to invoking this function, DS:DX is set to point to the segment: offset address of the first byte in the interrupt handling routine, and AL contains the number of the specified interrupt.	1, 2, 3, 4
26H	***Create a new program segment prefix.*** Prior to invoking this function, DX contains the segment address of what will be a new program segment. When the function is called, the first 100H bytes of the current program segment are copied into the first 100H memory locations of the new program segment. Offset 06H in the new segment is updated to contain the size of the new program segment. The addresses for the termination, Ctrl-Break, and critical error routines are stored in the new program segment beginning at offset 0AH. Programs written to run under MS-DOS 2.0 and subsequent versions should use function 4BH instead of this function.	1, 2, 3, 4
27H	***Random block read.*** This function is used to read a block of records from a file. Prior to invoking the function, DS:DX must point to the segment: offset address of an opened file control block (FCB). CX must contain the number of records to be read. The size of each record must be stored in the record size field (offset 0EH) of the FCB. The read starts with the record specified in the relative record field (offset 21H) of the FCB. The records are read into memory at the disk transfer address (DTA). A value is returned in the AL register as follows:	1, 2, 3, 4

MS-DOS Function	Description	Implemented in Versions
27H (cont'd)	00H Read completed successfully.	
	01H End-of-file mark encountered; no data in record.	
	02H Not enough room in DTA to read one record; read cancelled.	
	03H End-of-file mark encountered. A partial record was read and padded with zeros.	
	MS-DOS function 1AH is used to set the DTA. MS-DOS function 2FH returns the current DTA.	
28H	***Random block write.*** This function is used to write a block of records to a file. Prior to invoking the function, DS:DX must point to the segment: offset address of an opened file control block (FCB). CX must contain the number of records to be written. The size of each record must be stored in the record size field (offset 0EH) of the FCB. The write starts with the record specified in the relative record field (offset 21H) of the FCB. The data written is located at the disk transfer address (DTA). If CX equals zero on entry, no records are written, but the file size stored in the disk directory is adjusted according to the number of records specified by the relative record field. A value is returned in the AL register as follows:	1, 2, 3, 4
	00H Write completed successfully.	
	01H Disk full. No records written.	
	02H Not enough room in DTA to hold one record; write cancelled.	
	03H End-of-file mark encountered. A partial record was read and padded with zeros.	
	MS-DOS function 1AH is used to set the DTA. MS-DOS function 2FH returns the current DTA.	
29H	***Parse filename.*** This function is used to parse the information contained in a command line of the form "*d*: filename.ext" so that the information can be stored in a file control block (FCB). Prior to invoking this function, DS:SI points to the segment: offset	1, 2, 3, 4

MS-DOS Function	Description	Implemented in Versions
29H (cont'd)	address of the command line, and ES:DI points to the segment: offset address of what will be an unopened FCB. Parsing is controlled by the status of the first 4 bits in the AL register:	

> If bit 0=1, then any leading separator characters (see following text) are ignored.
>
> If bit 0=0, then parsing stops if a leading separator character is encountered.
>
> If bit 1=1, then the drive number in the FCB is not changed if the command line does not contain a drive number.
>
> If bit 1=0, then the drive number in the FCB is set to 00H if the command line does not contain a drive number.
>
> If bit 2=1, then the filename in the FCB is not changed if the command line does not contain a filename.
>
> If bit 2=0, then the filename in the FCB is set to eight blank characters if the command line does not contain a filename.
>
> If bit 3=1, then the extension in the FCB is not changed if the command line does not contain an extension.
>
> If bit 3=0, then the extension in the FCB is set to three blank characters if the command line does not contain an extension.

Filename separators are: . ; : = + SPACE and TAB. AL returns a value of 01H if either "?" or "*" appears in the filename or extension. AL returns FFH if the drive number is invalid. ES:DI returns the address of the first byte of the FCB. DS:DI points to the first character following the command line that was parsed.

MS-DOS Function	Description	Implemented in Versions
2AH	***Get date.*** This function returns the current date stored by MS-DOS. The CX register returns the year. DH returns the month (1=January, 2=February, etc.). DL returns the day of the month. AL returns the day of the week (0=Sunday, 1=Monday, etc.).	1, 2, 3, 4
2BH	***Set date.*** This function sets the current date stored by MS-DOS. Prior to invoking the function, the CX register stores the year, DH	1, 2, 3, 4

MS-DOS Function	Description	Implemented in Versions
2BH (cont'd)	stores the month (1=January, 2=February, etc.), and DL stores the day of the month. When the function is called, AL returns a value of 00H if the date entered was valid. AL returns a value of FFH and the function is cancelled if an invalid date is entered.	
	On machines with permanent clocks, the MS-DOS 3.3 and subsequent implementations of function 2BH resets the permanent clock's date. Unfortunately, PC-DOS 3.3 sets only permanent clocks whose memory address is the same as IBM's clock. 2BH has no effect on clocks with a different address.	
2CH	***Get time.*** This function returns the current time stored by MS-DOS. On return, the CH register stores the hours, CL has the minutes, DH has the seconds, and DL has the hundredths of a second.	1, 2, 3, 4
2DH	***Set time.*** This function sets the current time stored by MS-DOS. Prior to invoking this function, the CH, CL, DH, and DL registers are set, using the format described for function 2CH. AL returns a value of 00H if the time entered was valid; otherwise, the function is cancelled and AL returns FFH.	1, 2, 3, 4
	On machines with permanent clocks, the MS-DOS 3.3 and subsequent implementations of function 2DH resets the permanent clock's time. Unfortunately, PC-DOS 3.3 sets only permanent clocks whose memory address is the same as IBM's clock. 2DH has no effect on clocks with a different address.	
2EH	***Set/reset verify switch.*** Prior to invoking this function, the AL register must contain either 00H (verify off) or 01H (verify on). Each disk write is checked for accuracy when verify is on. The current state of the verify switch can be determined by using MS-DOS function 54H.	1, 2, 3, 4
2FH	***Get DTA.*** This function returns the segment: offset address of the current disk transfer address (DTA) in ES:BX.	2, 3, 4
30H	***Get DOS version number.*** On return, this function stores the major MS-DOS version number in the AL register and the minor	2, 3, 4

MS-DOS Function	Description	Implemented in Versions
30H (cont'd)	version number in the AH register. It can be assumed that a pre-2.00 version of MS-DOS is being used if AL returns a value of zero.	
31H	***Terminate and stay resident (Keep process).*** This function terminates execution of a program and keeps the program resident in memory. Prior to invoking the function, the AL register contains an exit code, and the DX register stores the number of paragraphs (16-byte blocks) of memory to be kept by the program. MS-DOS allocates this memory to the program; it will not be used for other purposes unless it is deallocated. There is no 64-Kbyte limit on the amount of memory that may be kept by the terminating program (compare with int 27H). The exit code passed in AL is retrievable with MS-DOS function 4DH.	2, 3, 4
32H	Reserved for use by MS-DOS (see appendix B).	
33H	***Ctrl-Break check or set.*** MS-DOS maintains a Ctrl-Break flag that determines when the operating system checks to see if Ctrl-Break has been pressed. If the flag is set, checking occurs each time an MS-DOS function is called. If the flag is not set, checking occurs only when input or output is requested. The AL and DL registers control this function. On entry:	2, 3, 4

AL=00H   The function checks the current Ctrl-Break state.

AL=01H   The function sets the Ctrl-Break state. If DL=0, state is set off. If DL=1, state is set on.

On return:

DL=00H   Ctrl-Break state is off.
DL=01H   Ctrl-Break state is on.
AL=FFH   Invalid value in AL on entry.

The MS-DOS 4 version of this function can also be used to obtain the identification number of the drive used to boot the operating system. Prior to the call, the value in AH is set to 5. On return, DL contains the boot drive's id number (1=A, 2=B, etc.).

| **34H** | Reserved for use by MS-DOS (see appendix B). | |

MS-DOS Function	Description	Implemented in Versions
35H	***Get interrupt vector.*** This function is used to obtain the memory address of an interrupt handling routine. Prior to invoking this function, the interrupt number is placed in the AL register. The function returns the interrupt's segment: offset address in ES:BX.	2, 3, 4
36H	***Get disk free space.*** This function is used to obtain disk information. A drive number (0=default, 1=A, etc.) is placed in DL prior to invoking the function. Information is returned as follows:	2, 3, 4

BX   The number of available clusters on the drive.

DX   The total number of clusters on the drive.

CX   The number of bytes per sector.

AX   The number of sectors per cluster. AX will store FFFFH on return if an invalid drive was specified on entry.

MS-DOS Function	Description	Implemented in Versions
37H	Reserved for use by MS-DOS (see appendix B).	
38H	***Retrieve or set country dependent information.*** Country dependent information includes specifications for a date format, a currency symbol, and a decimal separator. Countries are specified by a country code, which is typically the international telephone prefix for the country. Country dependent information may be retrieved with the MS-DOS 2.X implementation of this function. Country dependent information may be retrieved or set with MS-DOS 3.X and subsequent implementations.	2, 3, 4

Information is retrieved as follows: The AL register contains the code of the desired country. If AL is set to zero, the information for the current country is retrieved. The MS-DOS 2.X implementation of this function can specify country codes only in the range 0–255. In MS-DOS 3.X and subsequent versions, if a value of FFH is placed in AL, a 16-bit country code can be specified in BX. DS:DX is set to point to a memory buffer that

MS-DOS Function	Description	Implemented in Versions
38H (cont'd)	will store the returned information. The format of the returned information in MS-DOS 2.X is as follows:	

Offset	Value
0–01	Date/time format. A value of 00 specifies the USA standard (*hh:mm:ss mm/dd/yy*). A value of 01 specifies the European standard (*hh:mm:ss dd/mm/yy*). A value of 02 specifies the Japanese standard (*hh:mm:ss dd/mm/yy*).
2	ASCII code for currency symbol.
3	Byte of zero.
4	ASCII code for thousands separator.
5	Byte of zero.
6	ASCII code for decimal separator.
7	Byte of zero.
8–31	Reserved by MS-DOS.

The format for the information returned in the MS-DOS 3.X and subsequent implementations is as follows:

Offset	Value
0–1	Date format. A value of 00 specifies the USA standard (*mm/dd/yy*), 01 specifies the European standard (*dd/mm/yy*), and 02 specifies the Japanese standard (*yy/mm/dd*).
2–5	Null terminated currency symbol string.
7	ASCII code for thousands separator.
8	Byte of 00.
9	ASCII code for decimal separator.
10	Byte of 00.
11	ASCII code for date separator.
12	Byte of 00.
13	ASCII code for time separator.
14	Byte of 00.
15	Currency format. Bit 1 equals the number of spaces between the currency symbol and the value. Bit 0 equals zero if the currency precedes the value. Bit 1 equals 1 if the symbol follows the value.

MS-DOS Function	Description	Implemented in Versions
38H (cont'd)	16 Number of digits after decimal in currency.	
	17 Time format. Bit 1 equals zero if 12-hour format. Bit 1 equals 1 if a 24-hour format.	
	18–21 Case map call address (see following text).	
	22 ASCII code for data list separator.	
	23 Byte of 00.	
	24–33 Reserved by MS-DOS.	

The case map call address is the segment: offset address of a procedure that converts lowercase characters to uppercase. The function is used to set country information by placing a value of FFFFH in DX prior to the call. The function sets the carry flag and returns a value of 02 in AX if the country code is not valid.

39H	***Create a subdirectory.*** Prior to invoking this function, DS:DX points to the segment: offset address of an ASCII string that will be the path specifier of the new subdirectory. The string is terminated with a byte of zero. The function sets the carry flag upon return if an error occurs. The AX register contains information about any errors:	2, 3, 4

AX=03H   The path specifier was not valid or was not terminated with a byte of zero.

AX=05H   No room in parent directory for new subdirectory, the subdirectory already exists, or a reserved device name was used in the path specifier.

3AH	***Remove a subdirectory.*** Prior to invoking this function, DS:DX points to the segment: offset address of an ASCII string that is the path specifier of the subdirectory to be deleted. The string must be terminated by a byte of zero. A subdirectory must be empty before it can be deleted. This function cannot be used to remove the current directory. The function sets the carry flag if an error occurs.	2, 3, 4

MS-DOS Function	Description	Implemented in Versions
3AH (cont'd)	The AX register contains information about any errors:	

	AX=03H	The path specifier was not valid, was not found, or was not terminated with a byte of zero.
	AX=05H	The specified subdirectory was not empty, was not a directory, or was the root directory.
	AX=16H	The specified subdirectory is the current directory.

3BH	***Change current directory.*** Prior to invoking this function, DS:DX points to the segment: offset address of an ASCII string that is the path specifier of a subdirectory. The string must be terminated with a byte of zero. The function makes the specified subdirectory the current directory. The function returns a value of 03H in the AX register if the ASCII string is not a valid path specifier or if the string is not terminated with a byte of zero.	2, 3, 4

MS-DOS functions 3CH through 46H allow you to utilize disk files without the necessity of a file control block. When these functions are used, MS-DOS uses a *file handle* to keep track of files. A file handle is a hexadecimal number that MS-DOS places in the AX register when a file is created (function 3CH) or opened (function 3DH). The following handles are predefined by MS-DOS for peripheral devices. Devices do not have to be opened before reading or writing:

00H	Standard input device.
01H	Standard output device.
02H	Standard error device.
03H	Standard auxiliary device.
04H	Standard printer device.

3CH	***Create a file.*** Prior to invoking this function, DS:DX points to the segment: offset of an ASCII string that specifies a drive, path, and filename for a file to be created. The	2, 3, 4

MS-DOS Function	Description	Implemented in Versions
3CH (cont'd)	string must be terminated with a byte of zero. The attribute code for the file to be created is placed in the CX register (see function 43H). If the carry flag is not set on return from this function, the AX register contains the file handle. If the specified file did not previously exist, it is created in the appropriate directory. If the file did previously exist, it is truncated to a length of zero. The carry flag is set on return if an error occurred in execution of the function. AX contains information about any errors:	

AX=03H   The path specified was not valid.

AX=04H   The file was created, but there are no file handles available.

AX=05H   CX specified a directory or volume id attribute, or a directory previously existed with the same name.

MS-DOS Function	Description	Implemented in Versions
3DH	***Open a file.*** Prior to invoking this function, DS:DX points to the segment: offset of an ASCII string that specifies a drive, path, and filename of the file to be opened. The string must be terminated with a byte of zero. AL contains an access code that determines the manner in which the file is opened.	2, 3, 4

In MS-DOS 2.X, only the first two bits of AL are significant; the other bits should be set to zero.

Bit Setting	Access Mode
00	read-only
01	write-only
02	read and write

In MS-DOS 3.X and 4.X, other bits are used to determine the type of access to the file that other processes and other network users will have:

bit 7   = 0 if file is to be inherited by any child processes.

       = 1 if file is private to parent.

MS-DOS Function	Description	Implemented in Versions
3DH (cont'd)	bits 4–6 = 000 if network processes are denied access.	
	= 001 if read/write access is denied to network processes.	
	= 010 if write access is denied to network processes.	
	= 011 if read access is denied to network users.	
	= 100 if full access is allowed to network users	
	bit 3 Reserved (should equal 0).	
	bits 0–2 = 000 if read access for owner process.	
	= 001 if write access for owner process.	
	= 010 if read/write access for owner process.	

If the carry flag is clear on return, then AX contains the file handle. Any subsequent reference to the file is through the 16-bit file handle. On return, the file's read/write pointer is set to the file's first byte and the file's record size is set to 1 byte.

If an error occurs in execution of the function, on return the carry flag will be set and the AX register will contain one of the following error codes:

01	Function number invalid (file-sharing required).
02	File not found.
03	Path not found.
04	Too many files open; no handle available.
05	Access denied.
0CH	Access code invalid.

MS-DOS Function	Description	Implemented in Versions
3EH	***Close a file handle.*** Prior to invoking this function, the BX register contains a file handle that was returned from functions 3CH, 3DH, or 45H. The corresponding file is	2, 3, 4

MS-DOS Function	Description	Implemented in Versions
3EH (cont'd)	closed upon return if the carry flag is not set. The function flushes all internal buffers. If an invalid file handle was specified, the carry flag is set and a value of 06H is placed in the AX register on return.	
3FH	***Read from a file or device.*** Prior to invoking this function, BX contains a file handle and DS:DX contains the segment: offset address of a buffer in memory. The number of bytes to be read are stored in the CX register. When the function is called, the specified number of bytes are read into the memory buffer. If the carry flag is not set on return, the AX register contains the number of bytes read. If the carry flag has been set, AX stores an error code:	2, 3, 4
	AX=05H The file handle passed in BX was opened in a mode that does not allow reading.	
	AX=06H The file handle passed is not open.	
40H	***Write to a file or device.*** Prior to invoking this function, BX contains a file handle and DS:DX contains the segment: offset address of a buffer in memory. The number of bytes to be written are stored in the CX register. When the function is called, the specified number of bytes are written from the memory buffer. If the carry flag is not set on return, the AX register contains the number of bytes actually written. If the carry flag has been set, AX stores an error code:	2, 3, 4
	AX=05H The file handle passed in BX was opened in a mode that does not allow writing.	
	AX=06H The file handle passed is not open.	
	Note: If on entry CX stores a value of 00H, function 40H will set the file's size to correspond to the current position of the file's read/write pointer.	

MS-DOS Function	Description	Implemented in Versions
41H	***Delete a directory entry.*** Prior to invoking this function, DS:DX points to the segment: offset of an ASCII string that specifies a drive, path, and filename of a directory entry to be deleted. The string must be terminated with a byte of zero. The entry has been deleted if the carry flag is not set on return. The AX register stores an error code if the carry flag has been set: AX=02H File not found. AX=05H Access denied.	2, 3, 4
42H	***Move file pointer.*** MS-DOS establishes a "read/write pointer" for each created or opened file by using functions 3CH and 3DH. When a file is created (or opened), the file pointer is set to the first byte in the file. Each time a read or write is made to the file, the file pointer advances according to the number of bytes in the read or write. Function 42H is used to move a file's read/write pointer without making a read or write. Prior to invoking this function, the distance the pointer will be moved is stored as a 4-byte number in the CX and DX registers. The most-significant bytes are stored in CX. The file handle is stored in the BX register. The AL register is set to a value that determines the way in which the pointer is moved: AL=00H The pointer is moved CX:DX bytes from the beginning of the file. AL=01H The pointer is moved to its current location plus CX:DX. AL=02H The pointer is moved to the end of the file plus CX:DX. If the carry flag is not set on return, the new pointer location is stored as a 4-byte number in the DX and AX registers. The most-significant bytes are in DX. If the carry flag is set on return, AX contains an error code:	2, 3, 4

MS-DOS Function	Description		Implemented in Versions
42H (cont'd)	AL=01H	The number passed in AL on entry is not valid.	
	AL=06H	The handle passed in BX is not open.	
43H	***Change file's attribute.*** A file's attribute is determined by the bit pattern stored in the eleventh byte of the file's directory entry:		2, 3, 4

Bit	File Attribute If Bit Set (Equals 1)
0	Read-only file. Any attempt to write to such a file will generate an error.
1	Hidden file. Such a file is not listed during a standard directory search.
2	System file. These files are used to boot MS-DOS and perform many other system operations.
3	Volume label. The filename and filename extension in this directory entry form the disk's volume id label. Each disk may have only one file with this attribute, and the file must be located in the disk's root directory.
4	Subdirectory. Files with this attribute are subdirectories.
5	Archive. This bit is set if a file has been modified but not copied by BACKUP.

Function 43H is used to change a file's attribute. Prior to invoking this function, DS:DX is set to point to the segment: offset address of an ASCII string that forms a file's path and filename. The string must be terminated by a byte of zero. AL must be set to 00H or 01H:

AL=01H	Prior to entry, CX is set to the byte value of the desired attribute. Calling the function changes the attribute of the file specified by the string at DS:DX.
AL=00H	Calling the function returns the byte value of the current attribute.

MS-DOS Function	Description	Implemented in Versions
43H (cont'd)	An error condition exists if the carry flag is set on return. Error information is returned in the AL register:	

	AL=01H	The entry value of AL was not 00H or 01H.
	AL=03H	The file specified was not valid, or the ASCII string was not terminated with a byte of zero.
	AL=05H	An attempt was made to modify the attribute of a directory or volume id label.

| **44H** | ***I/O control for devices (IOCTL).*** This function is used to send information to, and receive information from, input/output control channels. The function is also used to determine the input/output status of peripheral devices. A device (or file) is specified by placing a file handle in the BX register. File handles 0000H through 0004H are reserved by MS-DOS for specific peripheral devices (see the list in function 3BH). | 2, 3, 4 |

Function 44H is divided into 16 subfunctions. A subfunction is selected by placing a value of 00H–0FH in AL prior to calling the function.

If an error is encountered, upon return the carry flag will be set and AL will contain one of the following error codes:

	AL=01H	Invalid subfunction number, or Ctrl bit was set to zero.
	AL=04H	No handle available.
	AL=05H	Access denied.
	AL=06H	Invalid handle.
	AL=0DH	Invalid data.
	AL=0FH	Invalid drive number.

Device Information Subfunctions (00H and 01H)

	AL=00H	Get device channel information. This subfunction returns information in the DX register

MS-DOS Function	Description	Implemented in Versions
44H (cont'd)	that describes a device control channel. The device channel is specified by the file handle placed in BX. The interpretation of the value returned in DX is described in figure A-1.	
AL=01H	Set device information. This subfunction is used to set the device information of a control channel. The channel is determined by the file handle placed in BX. The information set is determined by a value placed in DX prior to calling the function.	

Control String Subfunctions (02H through 05H)

These four subfunctions are used to receive command strings from, or send command strings to, a device.

AL=02H	Read string from device. Prior to invoking this subfunction, AL is set to 02H, a file handle is placed in BX, DS:DX points to a buffer that will receive the read, and CX stores the number of bytes to be read.	
AL=03H	Write string to a device. Prior to invoking this subfunction, AL is set to 03H, a file handle is placed in BX, DS:DX points to a buffer that contains the string to be written, and CX stores the number of bytes to be written.	
AL=04H	Read string from a disk drive. This subfunction is identical to 02H except that a disk drive number (00H=default, 01H=A, etc.) is placed in BL prior to calling the subfunction.	
AL=05H	Write string to a disk drive. This subfunction is identical to 03H except that a disk drive number	

ISDEV=1 if channel is a device. ISDEV=0 if channel is a disk file.

If ISDEV = 1, then:

EOF   = 1 if end of file on input.

RAW   = 1 if operating in binary mode (no check for Ctrl-Z).

RAW   = 0 if operating in ASCII mode (checks for Ctrl-Z as end-of-file mark).

ISCLK = 1 if the device is the clock device.

ISNUL = 1 if the device is the null device.

ISCOT = 1 if the device is the console output.

ISCIN   = 1 if the device is the console input.

CTRL   = 1 if the device can process command strings. This bit cannot be set with function 44H.

CTRL   = 0 if the device cannot process command strings.

If ISDEV = 0, then:

EOF   = 0 if the channel has been written.

Bits 0–5 represent the channel's block device number (0=A, 1=B, etc.).

Figure A-1. Channel information sent (when AL=00H) and received (when AL=1H) is determined by the bit pattern of the 2 bytes in the DX register.

MS-DOS Function	Description	Implemented in Versions
44H (cont'd)	(00H=default, 01H=A, etc.) is placed in BL prior to calling the subfunction.	

Input/Output Status Subfunctions (06H and 07H)

These two subfunctions allow you to see if a device or a file is ready for input or output.

	AL=06H	Get input status. Prior to invoking this subfunction, 06H is placed in AL and a file handle is placed in BX. When the file handle represents a device, the subfunction will return FFH in the AL register if the device is ready for input; 00H is returned if the device is not ready. When the handle in BX represents a file, the subfunction will return FFH in AL until the end of the file has been reached, at which point 00H is returned.
	AL=07H	Get output status. This subfunction is identical to 06H except that it checks output status instead of input status.

Other Subfunctions

	AL=08H	Test to see if block device has changeable media. The function returns zero in AX if the media is removable, one if the media is fixed. This subfunction is implemented in MS-DOS 3.0 and subsequent versions.
	AL=09H	Test to see if a drive is local or is remotely located on a network. For local drives, the attribute word from the drive's device header is returned in DX. For remote drives, bit 12 in DX is set on return. This subfunction is implemented in MS-DOS 3.1 and subsequent versions.

MS-DOS Function	Description		Implemented in Versions
44H (cont'd)	AL=0AH	Test to see if a file handle is local or remote. For local handles, the device header's attribute word is returned in DX. For remote handles, bit 15 in DX is set upon return. This subfunction is implemented in MS-DOS 3.1 and subsequent versions.	
	AL=0BH	Change sharing retry count. This subfunction is used to reset the length of delay between retries and to set the number of retries that can be attempted in carrying out file-sharing operations. Prior to calling this subfunction, CX contains the number of delay loops (the length of the pause), and DX contains the number of retries. The default is delay loops = 1, retries = 3. This subfunction is implemented in MS-DOS 3.0 and subsequent versions.	
	AL=0CH	Change code page used by device. This subfunction is used to assign a different code page to a peripheral device. This subfunction is implemented in MS-DOS 3.3 and 4.X.	
	AL=0DH	Generic IOCTL request. This subfunction is used to perform the following tasks:	
		Get peripheral device parameters.	
		Set peripheral device parameters.	
		Read a track on a logical device.	
		Write a track to a logical device.	
		Format a logical device.	
		For details on the use of this subfunction, refer to the MS-DOS 3.2 (or subsequent) technical reference manual.	
	AL=0EH	Get last logical drive used. This subfunction is used to	

MS-DOS Function	Description	Implemented in Versions
44H (cont'd)	determine if a block device has more than one logical device assigned to it. On call, BL contains the block devices drive number (0 = default, 1 = A, etc.). On return, AL contains 0 if there is only one logical device assigned to the block device; otherwise AL contains the drive number of the last logical drive letter that used the block device. This subfunction is implemented in MS-DOS 3.2 and subsequent versions. The discussion of subfunction 0FH illustrates how subfunction 0EH might be used.	
AL=0FH	Assign logical device. This function is used to assign a logical device to a block device that is supporting more than one logical device. Prior to calling, BL contains the drive number of the logical drive to be assigned (1 = A, 2 = B, etc.).	

As an example, consider a system with one floppy disk drive. The single drive will be supporting logical drives A and B. Only one logical drive is assigned to the disk drive at a time. If A is assigned to the drive, and MS-DOS needs to access B, MS-DOS will display the prompt: `Insert diskette for drive B:` and `strike any key when ready.`

An application program can use subfunction 0FH, in conjunction with subfunction 0EH, to suppress this prompt. The following assembly language code illustrates this:

MS-DOS Function	Description	Implemented in Versions
44H (cont'd)	;insert this code prior to accessing drive B	

```
                            ;Get logical drive
        mov     ah,44h      ;MS-DOS function 44h
        mov     al,0eh      ;Subfunction 0eh
        mov     bl,1        ;Drive A
        int     21h         ;Call MS-DOS
        cmp     al,2        ;B already assigned?
        je      exit        ;If yes, exit

                            ;Set logical drive
        mov     ah,44h      ;MS-DOS function 44h
        mov     al,0fh      ;Subfunction 0fh
        mov     bl,2        ;Logical drive B
        int     21          ;Call MS-DOS

exit:
```

Both subfunctions 0EH and 0FH set the carry flag and place an error code in AL if an error is encountered.

45H	***Duplicate a file handle.*** Prior to invoking this function, BX contains a file handle. On return, AX contains a second file handle for the same file. Both file handles use the original file pointer; moving the pointer using one handle will move the pointer for the other handle. The carry flag is set on return if an error was encountered. AX contains information about any errors:	2, 3, 4

AX=04H   No free file handles available.
AX=06H   The handle passed in BX is not currently open.

46H	***Force a duplicate of a handle.*** This function is used to assign a specific file handle to an open file. Prior to invoking this function, BX contains a file handle and CX contains a second file handle. On return, the CX file handle will refer to the same file as the BX handle. If the CX handle initially referenced another file, that file is first closed. On return, both file handles use the original file pointer; moving the pointer using one handle will move the pointer for the other	2, 3, 4

MS-DOS Function	Description	Implemented in Versions
46H (cont'd)	handle. The carry flag is set on return if an error was encountered. AX contains information about any errors:	2, 3, 4
	AX=04H No free file handles available. AX=06H The handle passed in BX is not currently open.	
47H	***Get current directory.*** Prior to invoking this function, DS:SI is set to point to the segment: offset address of a 64-byte block of memory and DL contains a drive number (00H=default, 01H=A, etc.). On return, the memory block will contain an ASCII string that is the path specifier of the drive designated by DL. The string will not contain the drive letter and will not begin with a backslash. The string will terminate with a byte of zero. The carry flag is set on return if an invalid drive was specified.	2, 3, 4
48H	***Allocate memory.*** This function is used to allocate a block of memory to a process. On entry, BX contains the number of paragraphs (a paragraph is 16 contiguous bytes of memory) to be allocated. On return, AX contains the segment address of the allocated memory block. The carry flag is set on return if an error was encountered. AX contains information about any errors:	2, 3, 4
	AX=07H Memory control blocks destroyed. AX=08H Allocation failed due to insufficent memory. BX contains the largest block of memory available for allocation.	
49H	***Free allocated memory.*** On entry, ES contains the segment address of a memory block that has been allocated with function 48H. Function 49H returns the memory block to the system pool. The carry flag is set on return if an error was encountered. AX contains information about any errors:	2, 3, 4
	AX=07H Memory control blocks destroyed.	

MS-DOS Function	Description		Implemented in Versions
49H (cont'd)	AX=09H	The block passed in ES was not allocated with function 48H.	
4AH	***Modify allocated memory blocks.*** On entry, ES contains the segment address of an allocated block of memory and BX contains the number of paragraphs of memory to be contained in the modified block (a paragraph is 16 contiguous bytes). When the function is called, the specified block is adjusted to the size specified in BX. The carry flag is set on return if an error was encountered. AX contains information about any errors:		2, 3, 4
	AX=07H	Memory control blocks destroyed.	
	AX=08H	Modification failed due to insufficent memory. BX contains the largest block of memory available for allocation.	
	AX=09H	The block passed in ES was not allocated with function 48H.	
4BH	***Load and execute a program.*** Through the use of this function, a program can load and execute another program. The original program is called the *parent*; the program that is loaded and executed is called the *child*. MS-DOS commands can be executed from within a program by calling function 4BH and specifying COMMAND.COM (the MS-DOS command processor) as the child.		2, 3, 4
	Prior to invoking this function, a "function value" is placed in the AL register:		
	AL=00H	Load and execute a program. MS-DOS will construct a program segment prefix for the child, load the program, and execute it. MS-DOS sets the child's terminate and Ctrl-Break addresses to the instruction in the parent that follows the function 4BH call. Register contents are not preserved by this function.	
	AL=03H	Load overlay. MS-DOS does not construct a program segment	

MS-DOS Function	Description	Implemented in Versions
4BH (cont'd)	prefix. The child is loaded at a specified memory location but not executed. Control returns immediately to the parent.	

Prior to invoking this function, DS:DX points to the segment: offset address of an ASCII string that contains the drive, path, and filename of the file to be loaded (the child). The string must terminate with a byte of zero.

The third and final requirement prior to calling this function is that ES:BX must point to the segment: offset address of a memory block that contains information required by the function. There is one format for the block used with the execute function (AL=00H) and another format for the block used with the overlay function (AL=03H). In either case, the block must be set up prior to calling the function. The memory block formats are presented in tables A-1 and A-2.

When the parent first receives control, MS-DOS allocates all available memory to it. Before a child can be loaded with function 4BH, some memory must be deallocated with MS-DOS function 4AH. When this function is invoked, MS-DOS uses the loader portion of COMMAND.COM to load the child. The loader is located in the transient portion of the command processor, which is stored in the high end of memory.

The carry flag is set by this function if an error is encountered. The AX register contains information about any errors:

AX=01H	The number passed in AL was not 01H or 03H.
AX=02H	The file specified by DS:DX was invalid or not found.
AX=05H	Access denied.
AX=08H	There is not enough memory available to load the child process.
AX=0AH	The environment passed was larger than 32K bytes.

MS-DOS Function	Description	Implemented in Versions
4BH (cont'd)	AX=0BH The file pointed to by DS:DX contains inconsistent information.	

Table A-1. Load and Execute Memory Block (AL=00H)

Address	Parameter
ES:BX	A 2-byte word that forms the segment address of the "environment" passed to the child. The address is stored with the least-significant byte first. The child will inherit the parent's environment if a value of zero is stored at this address.
	The *environment* is a series of ASCII strings that are referenced by MS-DOS. The environment always contains a string that begins "COMSPEC=" followed by the path to COMMAND.COM. MS-DOS references the COMSPEC string when it needs to locate the command processor. Other strings located in the environment include any statements entered with the MS-DOS commands PATH and PROMPT. Each string in the environment is terminated with a byte of zero. The final string in the environment is terminated with 2 bytes of zero. The environment is limited to 32 Kbytes in size. MS-DOS stores the segment address of a program's environment at offset 2CH in the program segment prefix.
ES:BX+2	A 4-byte double-word pointer to the segment: offset address of a command line. The offset address is stored at ES:BX+2 (least-significant byte) and ES:BX+3 (most-significant byte). The segment address is stored at ES:BX+4 (least-significant byte) and ES:BX+5 (most-significant byte). The command line will be copied to offset 80H in the child's program segment prefix (psp).
	The 128 bytes beginning at offset 80H in the psp form the "unformatted parameter area." This is the location that MS-DOS commands examine for any information on a command line following the command's name. If the command **edlin sample.txt** is entered, MS-DOS loads EDLIN. EDLIN would then find the string "0B 20 53 41 4D 50 4C 45 2E 54 58 54 0D" beginning at offset 80H in the psp. The first byte in this string tells MS-DOS the number of characters in the command line. The first character in the command line is a blank (20H). The remaining bytes are the ASCII values of the characters in the string

Table A-1. (cont'd)

Address	Parameter
	"sample.txt". The string terminates with a carriage return (0DH).
ES:BX+6	A 4-byte double-word pointer to the segment: offset address of a file control block. The offset address is stored at ES:BX+6 (least-significant byte) and ES:BX+7 (most-significant byte). The segment address is stored at ES:BX+8 (least-significant byte) and ES:BX+9 (most-significant byte). The file control block will be copied to offset 5CH in the child's psp.
ES:BX+10	A 4-byte double-word pointer to the segment: offset address of a file control block. The offset address is stored at ES:BX+10 (least-significant byte) and ES:BX+11 (most-significant byte). The segment address is stored at ES:BX+12 (least-significant byte) and ES:BX+13 (most-significant byte). The file control block will be copied to offset 6CH in the child's psp.
	Offsets 5CH and 6CH in a program's psp are the starting addresses of 12-byte "formatted parameter areas." File specifiers contained in the command line at offset 80H are "parsed" and placed in the formatted parameter areas. (Refer to the discussion of MS-DOS function 29H for information on parsing.)

Table A-2. Overlay Memory Block (AL=03H)

Address	Parameter
ES:BX	A 2-byte word that contains the segment address at which the child will be loaded. The address is stored with the least-significant byte first.
ES:BX+2	A 2-byte word that stores the factor used to modify the memory addresses of any relocatable items in the child. The factor is stored with the least-significant byte first.

MS-DOS Function	Description	Implemented in Versions
4CH	***Terminate a process.*** This function is used to terminate a process passing a return code in the AL register. The return code can be read with an IF ERRORLEVEL within a batch	2, 3, 4

MS-DOS Function	Description	Implemented in Versions
4CH (cont'd)	file or by MS-DOS function 4DH. All files are closed by this function.	
4DH	***Retrieve the return code of a child process.*** This function retrieves a return code previously set by a child process. (See the function 4BH for a discussion of parent and child processes.) The function returns the return code set by the child in the AL register. The AH register is set according to the manner in which the child process was terminated:	2, 3, 4

AH=00H   Normal termination.
AH=01H   Terminated by Ctrl-Break.
AH=02H   Terminated by a critical error.
AH=03H   Terminate and stay resident.

MS-DOS Function	Description	Implemented in Versions
4EH	***Find first matching file.*** This function is used to search a directory for a filename matching one that is specified. The specified filename may contain the wildcard characters "?" and "*". Prior to invoking this function, DS:DX is set to point to the segment: offset address of an ASCII string containing the drive specifier, path specifier, and filename of the specified file. The string must terminate with a byte of zero. An attribute for the file is specified in the CX register (see function 43H). If the function finds a matching file, the current disk transfer address (DTA) is filled as follows:	2, 3, 4

Offset	Value
00H–14H	Reserved by MS-DOS for use by MS-DOS function 4FH.
15H	Attribute of file found.
16H–17H	File's time stamp.
18H–19H	File's date stamp.
1AH–1BH	File's size (low word).
1CH–1DH	File's size (high word).
1EH–2AH	Name and extension of file found, followed by a byte of zero.

The carry flag is set upon return if any errors are encountered. AX contains information about any errors:

MS-DOS Function	Description		Implemented in Versions
4EH (cont'd)	AX=02H	The string specified by DS:DX was not valid or was not terminated with a byte of zero.	
	AX=12H	No matching files found.	
4FH	***Find next matching file.*** This function is used to find subsequent matching files after function 4EH has been used to find the first match.		2, 3, 4
	Prior to invoking the function, the current DTA must contain the information returned by function 4EH. Function 4FH returns any matching files in the manner described for function 4EH. The carry flag is set on return if no subsequent matches are found.		
50H–53H	Reserved for use by MS-DOS (see appendix B).		
54H	***Get verify state.*** This function returns 00H in the AL register if the verify state is off, 01H in AL if the verify state is on. The verify state can be set with MS-DOS function 2EH.		2, 3, 4
55H	Reserved for use by MS-DOS.		
56H	***Rename a file.*** Prior to invoking this function, DS:DX points to the segment: offset address of an ASCII string that contains the drive specifier, path specifier, and name of a file to be renamed. ES:DI points to an ASCII string that contains the new path specifier and filename. Both strings must terminate with a byte of zero. This function cannot be used to change the drive specifier. The carry flag is set if an error occurs on execution. The error code is returned in the AX register:		2, 3, 4
	AX=02H	File not found.	
	AX=03H	Path not found.	
	AX=05H	Access denied.	
	AX=11H	Not same device.	
57H	***Get/set a file's time and date stamp.*** Prior to invoking this function, BX contains a valid file handle. If AL=00H on entry, then the file's date stamp is returned in DX and the file's time stamp is returned in CX. If AL=01H on entry, the file's date stamp is set to the value in DX and the file's time stamp is set to		2, 3, 4

MS-DOS Function	Description	Implemented in Versions
57H (cont'd)	the value in CX. A file must be closed before a new time/date stamp can be stored.	

The time and date stamps are passed using the format described in function 38H. The high-order byte is stored in DL (or CL), and the low-order byte is stored in DH (or CH).

The carry flag is set if an error occurs. The error code is passed in AX:

AX=01H	The entry value of AL was not 00H or 01H.
AX=06H	The file handle passed in BX is not open.

58H   ***Get or set allocation strategy.*** When a 3, 4
program requests that a block of memory be allocated to it (via function 48H), MS-DOS must search memory to find a block to allocate. There are three "strategies" that MS-DOS can use in selecting a memory block to allocate:

1. *First fit*—beginning at the low end of memory, search until a large enough block is found. Allocate that block.

2. *Best fit*—beginning at the low end of memory, search all of memory, keeping track of each block that is large enough. Allocate the block that is closest in size to the allocation request.

3. *Last fit*—beginning at the high end of memory, search until a large enough block is found. Allocate that block.

Function 58H allows a program to determine what the current allocation startegy is and to set the allocation strategy. To get the allocation strategy, place 00H in AL. The strategy code is returned in AX. To set the allocation strategy, place 01H in AL and one of the strategy codes in BX.

 Strategy Codes

00H	First fit
01H	Best fit
02H	Last fit

MS-DOS Function	Description	Implemented in Versions
58H (cont'd)	The function sets the carry flag if an error occurs. An error code of 01H is returned in AX if the function code sent is not valid.	
59H	***Get extended error information.*** Function 59H is used to obtain extended information on an error. The error must have occurred on an immediately preceding call to int 24H or to one of MS-DOS functions 2FH–62H. The BX register must be set to 00H prior to calling function 59H.	3, 4

On return, function 59H places in AX the MS-DOS error code for the preceding error (the int 24H error codes and the MS-DOS function error codes are listed at the beginning of this appendix). Function 59H also returns three types of information: (1) An *error class* is returned in BH. The error class contains some descriptive information about the nature of the error (see the following list). (2) A *recommended action* is returned in BL. The recommended action (see the following list) can be used by the program in attempting to recover from the error. (3) An *error locus* is returned in CH. The error locus (see the following list) describes the type of hardware that may have been involved in the error.

BH = Error Class

01H	Out of resource (such as storage).
02H	Temporary situation (such as locked file), which should be expected to end.
03H	Authorization problem.
04H	Internal software error.
05H	Hardware failure.
06H	System software problem.
07H	Application program error.
08H	File not found.
09H	Invalid file type.
0AH	File interlocked.
0BH	Wrong disk in drive or bad disk.
0CH	Other error.

BL = Recommended Action

01H	Retry; then prompt user to select ignore or abort.

MS-DOS Function	Description	Implemented in Versions
59H (cont'd)	02H Retry with delay between tries; then prompt user to ignore or abort.	
	03H Get correct information from user.	
	04H Abort program in as timely a manner as possible (close files, release locks, etc.).	
	05H Abort immediately; system is probably corrupted.	
	06H Ignore error.	
	07H Retry after user intervention.	

CH = Error Locus

01H	Unknown.
02H	Block device.
03H	Network related.
04H	Serial device.
05H	Memory related.

MS-DOS Function	Description	Implemented in Versions
5AH	***Create a temporary file.*** This function will create a file with a unique name in a specified directory. The function is useful for word processors and other programs that use temporary scratch files.	3, 4
	Prior to calling this function, DS:DX points to the segment: offset address of a path specifier string. The string must end with a backslash (\) followed by a byte of zero. On return from the function, DS:DX points to the file specifier for the new file. The file specifier will end with a byte of zero. The carry flag is set if an error occurs. AX holds any error code.	

AX   Error

03H	Path not found.
05H	Access denied.

MS-DOS Function	Description	Implemented in Versions
5BH	***Create new file.*** Prior to calling this function, DS:DX contains a pointer to an ASCII file specifier and CX contains a file attribute code. On return, AX contains a file handle that is used to access the new file. This function is identical to function 3CH, with the exception that the function call will fail if the named file already exists. The carry	3, 4

MS-DOS Function	Description	Implemented in Versions
5BH (cont'd)	flag is set and AX contains an error code if an error occurs.	

AX	Error
03H	Path not found.
04H	No handle available.
05H	Access denied.
50H	File exists.

MS-DOS Function	Description	Implemented in Versions
5CH	***Lock/Unlock file access.*** This function is used to temporarily gain exclusive access to a portion of a file. In a network environment, data may be unreliable if simultaneous access to files is not controlled, thus the need for file *locking*.	3, 4

A file is locked by placing 00H in Al prior to the call. Also prior to the call, the handle for the file to be locked is placed in BX, the high-order offset of the region to lock in CX, the low-order offset of the lock region in DX, the high-order of the length of the region to be locked in SI, and the low-order of the length to be locked in DI. On return, the carry flag is set and AX contains an error code if an error occurred. IBM and Microsoft recommend a call to function 59H if an error occurs.

AX	Error
01H	Function code not valid.
06H	Handle not valid.
21H	All or part of region already locked.

A locked portion of a file is unlocked with the same procedure as that described for locking, with the exception that AH is set to 01H prior to the call. Any region that is locked must be unlocked, or unpredictable results will ensue.

MS-DOS Function	Description	Implemented in Versions
5DH	Reserved for use by MS-DOS (see appendix B).	
5E00H	***Get machine name.*** This function is used only on computers running IBM PC Net or Microsoft Networks. Prior to the call, AX is set to 5E00H and DS:DX points to a memory	3, 4

MS-DOS Function	Description	Implemented in Versions
5E00H (cont'd)	buffer that will store the computer's network name.	
	On return from the call: DS:DX points to a character string that stores the computer's name; the string is terminated with a byte of zero; CH is set to zero if the computer's name is not defined; and CL returns the NETBIOS name number if CH is nonzero.	
	The carry flag is set and AX contains an error code if an error occurs.	
	AX Error	
	01H Function code not valid.	
5E02H	***Set printer setup.*** This function is used only on computers running IBM PC Net or Microsoft Networks. It is used to send a control string to a network printer. Once a network user invokes this command for a particular printer on the network, each file that the user subsequently sends to the printer is preceded by the same control string. This allows different users on the network, using the same printer, to each have their own control strings.	3, 4
	Prior to calling this function: AX is set to 5E02H, BX is set to the index number in the redirection list of the desired printer (see function 5F03), CX is set to the length of the control string, and DS:SI points to the control string. On return, the carry flag is set and AX contains an error code if an error occurred.	
	AX Error	
	01H Function code not valid.	
5E03H	***Get printer setup.*** This function is used only on computers running IBM PC Net or Microsoft Networks. It returns the printer control string sent with function 5302H. Prior to issuing the call, AX is set to 5E03H, BX is set to the index number in the redirection list (see function 5F03) of the desired printer, and ES:DI points to a buffer that will store the control string. Maximum	3, 4

MS-DOS Function	Description	Implemented in Versions
5E03H (cont'd)	length of the control string is 64 bytes. On return, CX contains the length of the control string and ES:DI points to the control string.	
	On return, the carry flag is set and AX contains an error code if an error occurred.	
	AX Error	
	01H Function code not valid.	
5F02H	***Get redirection list.*** This function is used only on computers running IBM PC Net or Microsoft Networks. It provides access to the network's system redirection list (see function 5F03H). Each entry in the list is indexed; the first entry is index entry zero.	3, 4
	Prior to calling this function, AX is set to 5F02H, BX is set to a redirection list index number, DS:SI points to a 128-byte buffer that will store the local device name, and ES:DI points to a 128-byte buffer that will store the device's network name.	
	On return, the following conditions exist:	
	The zero bit in BH is set to zero if the device is valid. The zero bit is set to 1 if the device is not valid.	
	BL is set to 03H if the device is a printer, to 04H if the device is a disk drive.	
	CX contains the parameter value that was stored using function 5F03. The contents of DX and BP are destroyed.	
	DS:SI points to a string that is the device's local name. The string ends with a byte of zero.	
	ES:DI points to a string that is the device's network name. The string ends with a byte of zero.	
	On return, the carry flag is set and AX contains an error code if an error occurred.	
	AX Error	
	01H Function code not valid. 12H No more files.	

MS-DOS Function	Description	Implemented in Versions
5F03	***Redirect device.*** This function is used only on computers running IBM PC Net or Microsoft Networks. It establishes an association between a local device name and a network name. The list of associations is called the *redirection list*. The redirection list is indexed. The first local name/network name pair on the redirection list is at index value zero. The redirection list is used by functions 5E02H, 5E03H, 5F02H, and 5F04H.	3, 4

Prior to calling this function, the following holds:

AX is set to 5F03H.

BL is set to 03H if the device is a printer, to 04H if the device is a disk drive.

CX is set to a parameter that will also be stored in the redirection list.

DS:SI points to a string containing the device's local name. The string ends in a byte of zero.

ES:DI points to three strings, each separated by a byte of zero. The first string contains the device's network name. The second string contains a network path specifier. Network path specifiers must start with two backslashes (\\). The third string is a network password that must be followed by a byte of zero. On return, the carry flag is clear if the function has executed successfully. The carry flag is set and AX contains an error code if an error occurred.

AX **Error**

01H Function code not valid, string in wrong format, or device already redirected.

03H Path not found.

05H Access denied.

08H Insufficient memory.

| **5F04H** | ***Cancel redirection.*** This function is used only on computers running IBM PC Net or Microsoft Networks. It removes an entry from the redirection list (see function 5F03H). | 3, 4 |

MS-DOS Function	Description	Implemented in Versions
5F04H (cont'd)	Prior to calling this function, AX contains 5F04H and DS:SI points to a string that contains either a local device name or a network path specifier (which must begin with "\\"). The string must be followed with a byte of zero. If a network path specifier is used, this function will close the connection between the local machine and the network.	
	On return, the carry flag is set and AX contains an error code if an error occurred.	
	AX Error	
	01H Function code not valid or string not valid.	
	0FH Redirection paused on server.	
62H	***Get program segment prefix.*** This function allows a program to locate its program segment prefix (psp). Prior to calling the function, AH stores 62H. On return, BX contains the segment address of the program's psp.	3, 4
63H	***Get lead byte table.*** This function obtains the system table of valid byte ranges for extended characters, sets the interim console flag, and gets the interim console flag. This function is implemented in MS-DOS 2.25 only. It is not supported by any other versions of MS-DOS.	2.25
	Prior to issuing a call, AH contains 63H, AL is set to:	
	00H If getting address of lead byte table.	
	01H If setting or clearing interim console flag.	
	02H If getting value of interim console flag.	
	If AL = 01H, then DL = 01H if setting the flag, DL = 00H if clearing the flag.	
	On return, if getting the address of the lead byte table, DS:SI points to the table. If getting the value of the interim console flag, DL is set to the value of the flag.	
65H	***Get global code page.***	3.3, 4

MS-DOS Function	Description	Implemented in Versions
66H	*Set global code page.*	3.3, 4
67H	*Set handle count.* As described in chapter 11, 20 bytes in the psp are used to store file handles. This sets a limit of 20 on the number of files a process can have open at a time. This function can be used to override this limit.	3.3, 4

Prior to calling the function, BX contains the desired number of file handles. On return, the carry flag is clear if the function succeeded. The carry flag is set and AX contains an error code if an error was encountered. This function is implemented in MS-DOS 3.3 and 4.X. DOS allocates a block of memory to store the new file handle table. The amount of memory allocated is rounded up to the nearest paragraph boundary. In addition, one paragraph of memory (16 bytes) is allocated to serve as a memory control block (see chapter 11).

Two bugs have been reported with the PC-DOS implementation of function 67H:

1. When an even number of file handles is requested, MS-DOS allocates an additional 64 Kbytes for the handle table.

2. When the value set in BX approaches FFFFH, MS-DOS attempts to allocate more memory than exists. This can cause the system to hang.

IBM is aware of these bugs, but Big Blue has announced no correction will be implemented until the next release of MS-DOS.

68H	*Commit file.* This function flushes all buffers associated with a file handle and updates the file's directory information. Prior to calling the function, BX contains the file handle. On return, the carry flag is cleared if the function succeeded. The carry flag is set and AX contains an error code if an error was encountered. This function is implemented in MS-DOS 3.3 and 4.X.	3.3, 4
6CH	*Extended open/create.* This function, first implemented in MS-DOS 4, provides extended control over the processes of file	4

MS-DOS Function	Description	Implemented in Versions
6CH (cont'd)	creation and file opening. Prior to the call, CX contains the attribute of the new file. This value is ignored if an existing file is being opened.	

The action of the function is controlled by the setting of bit fields in the BX and DX registers, which occurs before the call is made.

BX Register

Bit Field	Value/Action
0–2	0 = open/create for reading only
	1 = open/create for writing only
	2 = open/create for reading and writing
3	Reserved
4–6	0 = deny all sharing access
	1 = deny read/write sharing access
	2 = deny write sharing access
	3 = deny read sharing access
	4 = allow all sharing access
7	0 = child processes inherit file handle
	1 = child processes do not inherit file handle
8–12	Reserved
13	0 = int 24H enabled
	1 = int 24H disabled
14	0 = disable file commit (function 68H)
	1 = enable file commit
15	Reserved

DX Register

Bit Field	Value/Action
0–3	0 = return error if file exists
	1 = open file if it exists
	2 = open file and truncate if it exists
4–7	0 = return an error if file not found
	1 = create file if file not found

MS-DOS Function	Description	Implemented in Versions
6CH (cont'd)	The function will disable the critical error handler (int 24H) for any I/O involving the handle returned from the call, if bit 13 in BX is set to 1. This allows the program issuing the I/O request to handle any critical error that may occur. If a critical error occurs during I/O, the carry flag is set, and AX contains an error code on return.	
	Bit 14 of BX is used to enable or disable file commit, which is discussed above under function 68H.	
	If the call was successful, function 6CH places a file handle in AX. CX is set to 1 if a file was opened, 2 if a file was created and opened, and 3 if an existing file was replaced and opened. AX contains an error code if an error was encountered on the call.	

B

Some Undocumented Features of MS-DOS

The term "undocumented feature" is applied to those interrupts and function calls that are utilized by MS-DOS, but whose use is not publicly sanctioned by Microsoft or IBM. Undocumented features are usually discovered by programmers scrutinizing the unassembled machine code that makes up MS-DOS.

There are two potential risks when using undocumented features. First, since there is no official description of what the feature does or how it does it, unpleasant surprises are always a possibility. Fortunately, the features presented here have been used by enough programmers for a long enough time that their behavior *seems* to be reasonably well understood.

The second potential risk is that Microsoft and IBM are not compelled to support the undocumented features in future versions of MS-DOS. In fact, for precisely this reason, the two companies have repeatedly warned programmers about using undocumented features.

Programmers must consider these risks whenever the use of undocumented features is being considered. Microsoft has published the MS-DOS Encyclopedia, which describes many of the undocumented features discussed here. However, the features remain officially "undocumented" and not fully supported by Microsoft or IBM.

Undocumented Interrupts

Interrupt	Description
28H	***The MS-DOS scheduler.*** Interrupt 28H is generated by MS-DOS to signal that DOS may be carefully reentered. (See chapter 13 for details.) The default handler for int 28H is simply an "iret" instruction. The interrupt appears to exist solely to provide TSRs with a safe access to MS-DOS.
29H	***Character output.*** This interrupt sends a character to the display device. The character is sent through ANSI.SYS if ANSI.SYS is installed. Int 29H is much faster than MS-DOS functions 2 and 9. Like these two functions, int 29H advances the cursor after a character is displayed. This makes it easier to use than int 10H. It would be interesting to see if int 29H can be used safely within a TSR. Best guess is that it could be used safely.
	If int 29H is used to sound the speaker (AL = 7), additional output with int 29H is suppressed while the speaker is sounding.

Undocumented Functions

Undocumented functions are called just like documented functions are. The function number is placed in AH, other registers are set as required, and interrupt 21H is called. Function 1FH is implemented in all versions of MS-DOS. Functions 32H through 53H are implemented in 2.X and later versions. Function 5DH is implemented in version 3.X and 4.X.

MS-DOS Function	Description
1FH	This function is almost the same as function 32H, described next. The difference is that the table is accessed for the default drive. The format of the table is slightly different under MS-DOS 1.X.
32H	***Get pointer to drive parameter table.*** On the call, DL contains a drive number (0=default, 1=A, etc.). On return, if AL is set to 00, the drive exists, and DS:BX points to the drive's parameter table. AL returns a value of FFH if the drive does not exist.

The format of the drive parameter table is as follows (offsets are in hexadecimal):

Offset	Function
00	Drive (0 = A, 1 = B, etc.).
01	Unit within drive (0, 1, 2, etc.).
02–03	Bytes per sector.
04	Sectors per cluster minus 1.
05	Number of times to left-shift (multiply by 2) bytes per sector to obtain bytes per cluster.
06–07	Number of boot sectors.
08	Number of FAT copies.
09–0A	Number of root directory entries.
0B–0C	Number of first sector containing data.
0D–0E	Total number of clusters minus 1.
0F	Number of sectors used by FAT.
10–11	Number of first sector in directory.
12–15	Offset and segment address of device driver's header.
16	Media descriptor byte (see chapter 14).
17	00 if the disk has been accessed.
18–1B	Offset and segment address of the next drive parameter table; set to FFFF FFFFH if last block in the chain.

MS-DOS Function	Description
34H	***Get address to INDOS flag.*** On return, the flag's address is stored in ES:BX. Refer to chapter 13 for details.
37H	***Get/set switchar.*** The switch character separates a command flag from the rest of the command. The default switch character is "/". To get the current switch character, set AL to 00. On return, the ASCII byte value for the current switch character will be in DL. To set the

MS-DOS Function	Description
37H (cont'd)	switch character, place a value of 01 in AL, and the byte value for the desired switch character in DL.
	In MS-DOS 2.X, function 37H can also be used to set or get the "forced \DEV\ flag". If the flag is set, device names must be preceded by "\DEV\". If the flag is clear, \DEV\ is optional. The flag is read with a value of 02 in AL. On return, DL equals 00 (flag set) or 01 (flag clear). The flag is set by calling the function with AL equal to 03 and DL equal to 00. Clear the flag with AL equal to 3 and DL equal to 1.
4BH	***Load program; do not execute.*** This undocumented subfunction of function 4B is used by DEBUG when it loads a program. On the call, AL contains a value of 01 and ES:BX points to a parameter block with the same format as that used by function 4BH, subfunction 0 (see appendix A). On return, the loaded program SS, SP, CS, and IP values are stored at ES:[BX+0EH].
50H	***Set current process id.*** Prior to the call, BX stores a process id number. The function designates that process to be current.
	A program's *id* is the segment address of the program's psp. MS-DOS stores the id of the currently executing program in an internal variable called the current process id.
	This function is important in TSRs that use file handles (see chapter 13).
51H	***Get current process id.*** On return, BX stores the current process id. This function is used, in conjunction with function 50H, in TSRs that use file handles. Function 51H is almost identical to function 62H. The only differences are that 51H is implemented in MS-DOS 2.X and function 62H is documented.
52H	***Return pointer to "invars".*** On return, ES:BX points to invars. Invars is a table of pointers used by MS-DOS. The name "invars" is a wholly unofficial one that is widely used (just like "INDOS").
	The value at ES:BX is a pointer to the drive parameter block for drive A. The value at ES:[BX−2] is the location of MS-DOS' first memory control block (mcb). Chapter 11 presents a discussion in which function 52H is used to locate the mcb chain.
	The device drive header for the NULL device is located at ES:[BX+22H]. This is the first header in the system's chain of device driver headers. The first 4 bytes of the

MS-DOS Function	Description
52H (cont'd)	header form a pointer to the next header in the chain. Refer to chapter 14 for details on the structure of device driver headers.
53H	***Generate drive parameter table.*** On the call, DS:SI contains the address of a bios parameter block (BPB) and ES:BP points to the area that will hold the drive parameter table (see function 32H). Refer to chapter 14 for a discussion of BPBs.
5DH	***Critical error information.*** This function has several subfunctions. Subfunctions are selected by placing a subfunction number in AL prior to the call.
	Subfunction 06H returns the address of the critical flag in DS:SI. The use of this subfunction is demonstrated in chapter 13. Subfunction 0AH sets extended error information. Prior to the call, DS:DX points to three words of error data. Extended error information is retrieved with function 59H. Subfunction 0AH can be used in TSRs that need to preserve and then restore the error information that existed when the TSR was called. Refer to the description of function 59H in appendix A for further discussion of extended error information.

C

Practical Batch Files

This appendix will show you how to create a menu and five batch files that combine many of the principles discussed in this book. The material presented here will provide you with ideas for customizing MS-DOS to suit your own needs. It also will demonstrate to you the convenience and flexibility offered by MS-DOS batch files.

The batch files given here require MS-DOS 2.00 or later versions. Since these batch files will be used during booting, you will need to store them on a diskette that has been formatted with the MS-DOS system files. The diskette must also contain the MS-DOS files SORT.EXE, MORE.COM,

TREE.COM, and CHKDSK.COM because these files will be utilized by the batch files. The menu and batch files will require approximately 3,000 bytes of disk storage space. (Please refer to chapter 4 for a discussion of MS-DOS batch files and to chapters 3 and 6 for a discussion of the commands used in these batch files.)

Before creating the batch files, we will use DEBUG to create a menu for controlling the batch files. Enter the DEBUG commands as they appear in the program listings. (DEBUG is discussed in chapter 15.) Note that the program listings assume that the root directory of drive C is used to boot MS-DOS.

```
C>debug
-e 100 ba
-e 14f ba
-f 101 14e 20
-m 100 14f 150
-m 100 19f 1A0
-m 100 23f 240
-m 100 37f 380
-m 100 32f 600
-e 100 c9
-e 14f bb
-f 101 14e cd
-e 240 cc
-e 28f b9
-f 241 28e cd
-e 7e0 c8
-e 82f bc
-f 7e1 82e cd
-e 16f "SAMPLE BATCH FILES"
-e 1c6 "from"
-e 210 "MS-DOS BIBLE"
-e 383 "1. SORT DIRECTORY ALPHABETICALLY (specify drive)"
-e 423 "2. SORT DIRECTORY BY DATE (specify drive)"
-e 4c3 "3. REPORT STATUS OF DISK (specify drive)"
-e 563 "4. EXIT BATCH FILES AND RETURN TO MS-DOS"
-rcx
cx 0000
:730
-n batmenu.txt
-w
Writing 0730 bytes
-q
```

You have just used DEBUG to create a file named "batmenu.txt". This file will serve as a menu for the batch files you are about to create. You can see what the menu looks like by entering the command **type batmenu.txt**.

Now you are ready to create the batch files themselves by using the command "copy con: [*filename*]". (See the discussion of COPY in Part 3 for details.) The first batch file is named AUTOEXEC.BAT and will be used to set the date and time and then display the menu when MS-DOS is booted:

```
C>copy con: autoexec.bat
echo off
cls
date
time
cls
type batmenu.txt
prompt ENTER A NUMBER (follow 1, 2, or 3 with a drive letter) $g
^Z        ←you enter Ctrl-Z
        1 File(s) copied
```

The next batch file is called "1.bat" and uses the MS-DOS filter SORT to alphabetically sort a disk's directory entries according to filenames. The batch file then uses the filter MORE to display one full screen of the sorted directory at a time:

```
C>copy con:1.bat
echo off
cls
prompt $n$g
echo SORTING DIRECTORY ALPHABETICALLY...STANDBY
dir %1: |sort |more
pause
echo off
cls
type batmenu.txt
prompt ENTER A NUMBER (follow 1,2, or 3 with a drive letter) $g
^Z
        1 File(s) copied
```

Batch file "2.bat" sorts directory entries by their date stamp. This is accomplished by sorting the directory entries according to the character in column 24 of each entry. The sorted directory is then displayed one screen at a time. This technique requires that all of the date stamps be for the same year. It will not work with different years; for example, 6-12-88 would be listed ahead of 12-14-86.

```
C>copy con: 2.bat
echo off
cls
prompt $n$g
echo SORTING DIRECTORY BY DATE...STANDBY
```

```
dir %1: |sort/+24| more
pause
echo off
cls
type batmenu.txt
prompt ENTER A NUMBER (follow 1, 2, or 3 with a drive letter) $g
^Z
        1 File(s) copied
```

Batch file "3.bat" uses the MS-DOS command CHKDSK to check a disk's status. This batch file also uses the command TREE, along with the filter MORE, to display information about the disk's directory and file structure. The information is listed one screen at a time:

```
C>copy con: 3.bat
echo off
cls
prompt $n$g
echo STATUS OF DISK IN DRIVE %1
echo **************************
vol %1:
chkdsk %1:
pause
cls
echo STRUCTURE OF DIRECTORIES AND FILES OF DISK IN DRIVE %1
echo ****************************************************************
tree %1: |more
echo off
pause
cls
type batmenu.txt
prompt ENTER A NUMBER (follow 1, 2 or 3 with a drive letter) $g
^Z
        1 File(s) copied
```

Batch file "4.bat" removes the menu from the screen and displays the standard MS-DOS system prompt. Any MS-DOS command may be entered once the standard prompt has been displayed:

```
C>copy con: 4.bat
echo off
prompt $n$g
cls
^Z
        1 File(s) copied
```

Our final batch file will display the menu whenever we enter the word "menu":

```
C>copy con: menu.bat
echo off
cls
type batmenu.txt
prompt ENTER A NUMBER (follow 1, 2 or 3 with a drive letter) $g
^Z
        1 File(s) copied
```

Having created the menu and the five batch files, you are ready to go. Type **menu** (or reboot your system) to display the menu. Now simply enter a number to select a batch file for execution. You may specify a drive for selections 1 through 3. For example, you might enter 1 B to get an alphabetical listing of the directory in drive B. The batch file selected will be executed on the default drive if you do not specify a drive letter.

D

Code Pages and Code Page Switching

This appendix looks at code pages and the principles and techniques involved in activating, or switching, the code pages. Display devices that support code page switching are listed, and important guidelines from IBM for using code pages are given.

Overview

A *code page* is a table that is used to convert stored numerical data into displayable characters. Designing a single code page that is appropriate for all languages is not possible, since languages differ in the character sets that they require.

Prior to MS-DOS 3.3, there were four different code pages used by MS-DOS. Each copy of MS-DOS had a single fixed code page. Copies of MS-DOS sold in the United States came with a code page appropriate for American English (code page 437). Similarly, copies sold in French Canada or Portugal came with the appropriate code pages (code pages 863 and 860, respectively). Given this situation, problems arose when software written to run with one code page was used with a copy of MS-DOS that had another code page.

To remedy this problem, a multilingual code page (code page 850) was introduced in MS-DOS 3.3. This single code page is designed to transfer data written in the following languages:

Belgian French	Norwegian
Canadian French	Portugese
Danish	Spanish
Dutch	Latin-American Spanish
Finnish	Swedish
Flemish	Swiss French
French	Swiss German
German	UK English
Icelandic	US English
Italian	

Software designers are encouraged now, and in the future, to use code page 850 as the standard, so that their software will have the widest possible audience. However, all of the pre-MS-DOS 3.3 software was written for code pages other than 850. Obviously this software is not going to disappear. To accommodate this base of existing software, *code page switching* was first implemented in MS-DOS 3.3.

What Is Code Page Switching?

Many printers and video display adapters support the use of downloadable fonts. This means that users may select character sets to be used with these devices. Code page switching basically allows the user, or the application programmer, to activate a particular code page for use with the display adapter, keyboard, and printer. The remainder of this appendix discusses the principles and the various MS-DOS commands involved in code page switching.

Code Page Switching Must Be Supported

Code page switching can be implemented only on devices that specifically support it. Support is provided in the form of code page information (cpi) files. Currently, there are two display adapters and two printers that support code page switching (table D-1). The code page information files for these devices are supplied with MS-DOS 3.3 and subsequent versions. The role of the cpi files is discussed in the next section.

Table D-1. Display Devices That Support Code Page Switching

Display Device	CPI File
IBM Proprinter Model 4201	4201.CPI
IBM Quietwriter III Printer Model 5202	5202.CPI
Enhanced Graphics Adapter	EGA.CPI
IBM Convertible LCD Adapter	LCD.CPI

Code page switching also requires support on the device driver level. MS-DOS 3.3 and subsequent versions supply a printer device driver (PRINTER.SYS) and a display driver (DISPLAY.SYS) that support code page switching. The device drivers must be installed in memory prior to implementing code page switching on printer or display devices. Refer to the discussion of DEVICE, in Part 3, for details on installing these drivers.

Hardware and Prepared Code Pages

A device that supports code page switching may have one or more code pages built into its hardware. These *hardware code pages* are prepared for use when the device's driver is installed in memory.

Code pages are also generated by the MODE command, using information contained in the cpi files. Code pages generated in this fashion are called *prepared code pages*. As an example, the following command generates code pages 437 and 850 for use by the display device (con). The code pages are generated using the file "ega.cpi":

```
mode con codepage prepare=((437,850) c:\dos\ega.cpi)
```

Refer to Part 3 of this book for details on using MODE to generate prepared code pages.

Switching Code Pages

There are three ways in which code page switching is actually carried out: (1) the CHCP command, (2) the MODE command, and (3) MS-DOS function 44H.

The CHCP command is used to select a specific code page for as many devices as possible. For example, the following command selects code page 850 for each device that has a code page 850 available to it:

```
chcp 850
```

Recall from the previous section that code pages are made available to a device in two ways: (1) during installation of the device's driver or (2) through use of the MODE command. The MODE command can also be used to select a specific code page for a particular device. The code page must have previously been made available for the device. The following command selects code page 850 for the display (con) device:

```
mode con codepage select=850
```

The use of CHCP and MODE to select code pages is discussed more thoroughly in Part 3 of this book.

Code pages can be selected from an application program by the use of MS-DOS function 44H, subfunction 0CH.

Some Code Page Programming Guidelines

IBM has published a list of guidelines for the applications programmer who uses code pages. Some of the more important guidelines are listed here. For a complete listing, refer to *IBM Personal System/2 Seminar Proceedings* (vol 5, no 6, May 1987).

1. Make sure that application programs will run on machines that do not support code page switching. One way to do this is to limit the characters used in displaying messages to a set of common characters.
2. Restrict the use of graphics characters to those in the common set.
3. If you must use a code page element for a control character, choose one that is not an alphabetic element in any of the code pages.
4. Construct a table of word delimiters that is not code page specific.

E

An Assembly Language Primer

This appendix is provided for those readers with little or no experience with assembly language programming. The information presented here is sufficient to follow chapter 13's presentation of terminate and stay resident programs and chapter 14's presentation of device drivers. You may also wish to consult any of the excellent books available on assembly language programming for MS-DOS computers.

What Is Assembly Language Programming?

Assembly language programming provides the programmer with direct access to, and control of, memory, the central processing unit (CPU), and the peripheral devices. Assembly language programmers like to say that they are "closer" to the computer than are programmers who use a high-level language (such as BASIC or Pascal). This increased intimacy with the computer allows assembly language programmers to write programs that execute faster and require less memory. In addition, programs that are closely linked to MS-DOS (such as device drivers and TSRs) are generally written in assembly language, since MS-DOS itself is written in assembly language.

The MS-DOS Hardware

Computers that run MS-DOS contain CPUs belonging to the 8088/8086/80x86 family of CPUs. These CPUs have internal storage devices called *registers*. Each register has a name that identifies it. There are six types of registers: segment registers, stack pointer registers, index registers, general-purpose registers, the instruction pointer register, and the flags register. Each of the registers is discussed in the following sections.

Segment Registers

The segment registers are used to identify a *memory segment*. A memory segment is a 64-Kbyte block of contiguous memory. Segment registers are used in conjunction with pointer registers and index registers to identify specific memory locations. The method used to accomplish this is discussed in the following sections.

There are four segment registers. The CS register is used to reference the portion of memory containing the program's code (the program itself). The DS register is used to access the portion of memory storing the program's data. The SS register is used to access the portion of memory known as the *stack*. The stack serves as a temporary storage area for information needed by MS-DOS or the program. The ES register is the extra segment register. It has various functions, some of which are discussed here.

Stack Pointer Registers

There are two stack pointer registers. These registers are used, in conjunction with the SS registers, to define the stack. The SP register, also called the *stack pointer*, is used, in conjunction with the SS register, to identify the *top of the stack*. Similarly, the BP register, also called the *base pointer,* is used, in conjunction with SS, to identify the base (bottom) of the stack.

Index Registers

There are two index registers. The **SI** and **DI** registers (source index and destination index) are used, in conjunction with one of the segment registers, to identify a memory location. SI is generally used with DS, and DI is generally used with ES.

General-Purpose Registers

There are four general-purpose registers: **AX**, **BX**, **CX**, and **DX**. As their class name implies, these registers perform many different functions.

The Instruction Pointer Register

The IP register is used, in conjunction with the CS register, to identify the memory location of the next machine instruction to be executed. The manner in which this is accomplished is discussed in the following text.

The Flags Register

The flags register contains nine 1-bit *flags*. These flags are used to record the status of certain machine operations.

Register Storage Capacity

Each of the registers stores 2 bytes, or 16 bits, of data. The general-purpose registers are actually composites of single-byte registers. Thus, AX is composed of AH, which holds AX's high-order byte, and of AL, which holds AX's low-order byte. Similarly, BH, BL, CH, CL, DH, and DL are each 1-byte registers.

Accessing Memory

Memory is accessed by combining the contents of one of the segment registers with one of the other registers. The value stored in the segment register is called the *segment address*. The value stored in the other register is called the *offset address*. The actual physical memory location is computed by multiplying the segment address by 16 and adding the offset.

For example, if CS stores a value of 22BH and IP stores a value of 100H, 22BH is the segment address and 100H is the offset. The physical address referenced by the two registers is computed as follows:

segment * 16 + offset = physical address
22BH * 16 + 100H = 22B0H + 100H = 23B0H

The physical address is usually written as the segment followed by a colon followed by the offset. Thus, in the example this would be:

physical address = segment:offset = cs:ip = 22B:100

Note that numbers in assembly language programs are decimal unless they are followed by an *H* or *h*, in which case they are hexadecimal (base 16).

Assembly Language Statements

Assembly language statements are stored in memory as *machine instructions*. Programs are executed as follows: (1) the instruction at address CS:IP is read and executed, (2) IP is incremented so that CS:IP points to the next instruction, and (3) steps 1 and 2 are repeated until the program terminates.

There are many types of assembly language statements. We will discuss the most common ones here. A *move* (written *mov*) copies data from a register or memory location to another register or memory location. Moves directly from one memory location to another memory location are not allowed. A "mov" is actually a copy, since the original data is unchanged. The following statements illustrate the use of mov.

Statement	Comment
mov ax,bc	;copy contents of register BX into register AX.
mov ax,temp	;copy contents of memory location "temp" in AX.
mov ax,00A2h	;copy a value of A2H into AX.

Compares (written *cmp*) are used to compare the value stored in a register or memory location against a value stored in another register or memory location. The following statements illustrate the use of cmp.

Statement	Comment
cmp ax,bx	;compare the contents of AX to that in register BX.
cmp dx,0060h	;compare the contents of register DX to 60H.

The results of a compare are recorded in the CPU status flags. Compares are used in conjunction with conditional "jumps," which are discussed next.

A *jump* (written *jmp*) is used to direct the computer to a memory location that contains the next instruction to be executed. Generally, instructions are executed in a sequential fashion: after a statement is executed, the statement at the next highest memory location is executed. Jumps provide a mechanism for program execution to branch to nonneighboring memory locations. Jumps are either conditional or unconditional. A conditional jump first checks the settings of the status flags. If they are set in a particular pattern, the jump is executed; otherwise, the jump is not executed. Unconditional jumps are executed without checking the status flags. The following statements illustrate the use of unconditional and conditional jumps.

Statement	**Comments**
jmp Init	;jump to memory address "Init".
	;this jump is unconditional.
cmp ax,bx	;compare AX contents to BX contents.
je exit	;if the contents are equal, jump to
	;memory address "exit".
cmp cx,0000h	;compare contents of CX to 0000H.
jg loop	;if contents of CX are greater than 0000H,
	;jump to memory address "loop".

A *call* (written *call*) is used to excute a set of instructions called a *procedure*. The first instruction in the procedure will generally have a label that is used as an access device. When a call is executed, MS-DOS places the contents of the IP register on the stack. Placing items on the stack is called a *push*. MS-DOS then places the offset address of the procedure being called in IP, and control is passed to the instruction at CS:IP.

The final statement in any procedure is a *return* (*ret*). This instruction directs MS-DOS to remove the IP value that was stored on the stack. Removing an item from the stack is called a *pop*. When the IP value is popped, execution continues with the instruction immediately following the original call.

A long call is identical to a regular (or short) call with one exception. With a long call, the called procedure lies outside the current code segment. When the long call is executed, MS-DOS pushes both the CS and IP values onto the stack and replaces them with the segment and offset addresses of the called procedure. When the called procedure terminates (with a far return), the old CS and IP values are popped and execution continues at the instruction following the long call.

Invoking an interrupt is similar to a long call, with one exception. Before the CS and IP values are pushed, the value stored in the flags register is pushed onto the stack. When the interrupt handler terminates (with an "iret" statement), CS, IP, and the flags register are popped, and execution continues with the instruction following the interrupt call. Interrupts are discussed further in appendix A.

F

ASCII Cross-Reference Tables

In addition to ASCII (see table F-1) and IBM ASCII extended cross-reference tables (see table F-2), this appendix explains how to convert from decimal to hexadecimal and vice versa. Table F-3 shows the extended ASCII code.

Table F-1. ASCII Cross-Reference

DEC X_{10}	HEX X_{16}	OCT X_8	ASCII	IBM GRA. CHAR.	Terminal Key *
0	00	00	NUL	(null)	< Ctrl-@ >
1	01	01	SOH	☺	< Ctrl-A >
2	02	02	STX	☻	< Ctrl-B >
3	03	03	ETX	♥	< Ctrl-C >
4	04	04	EOT	♦	< Ctrl-D >
5	05	05	ENQ	♣	< Ctrl-E >
6	06	06	ACK	♠	< Ctrl-F >
7	07	07	BEL	●	< Ctrl-G >
8	08	10	BS	▫	< Ctrl-H >
9	09	11	HT	○	< Ctrl-I >
10	0A	12	LF	■	< Ctrl-J >
11	0B	13	VT	♂	< Ctrl-K >
12	0C	14	FF	♀	< Ctrl-L >
13	0D	15	CR	♪	< Ctrl-M >
14	0E	16	SO	♫	< Ctrl-N >
15	0F	17	SI	☼	< Ctrl-O >
16	10	20	DLE	►	< Ctrl-P >
17	11	21	DC1	◄	< Ctrl-Q >
18	12	22	DC2	↕	< Ctrl-R >
19	13	23	DC3	‼	< Ctrl-S >
20	14	24	DC4	¶	< Ctrl-T >
21	15	25	NAK	§	< Ctrl-U >
22	16	26	SYN	▬	< Ctrl-V >
23	17	27	ETB	↨	< Ctrl-W >
24	18	30	CAN	↑	< Ctrl-X >
25	19	31	EM	↓	< Ctrl-Y >
26	1A	32	SUB	→	< Ctrl-Z >
27	1B	33	ESC	←	< Esc >
28	1C	34	FS	∟	< Ctrl-\ >
29	1D	35	GS	↔	< Ctrl-` >
30	1E	36	RS	▲	< Ctrl-= >
31	1F	37	US	▼	< Ctrl- ->
32	20	40	SP	(Space)	< SPACE BAR >

Table F-1. (cont.)

DEC X_{10}	HEX X_{16}	OCT X_8	ASCII	IBM GRA. CHAR.	Terminal Key *
33	21	41	!	!	! (Exclamation mark)
34	22	42	"	"	" (Quotation mark)
35	23	43	#	#	# (Number sign or octothorpe)
36	24	44	$	$	$ (Dollar sign)
37	25	45	%	%	% (Percent)
38	26	46	&	&	& (Ampersand)
39	27	47	'	'	' (Apostrophe or acute accent)
40	28	50	(	(	((Opening parenthesis)
41	29	51	)	)	) (Closing parenthesis)
42	2A	52	*	*	* (Asterisk)
43	2B	53	+	+	+ (Plus)
44	2C	54	,	,	, (Comma)
45	2D	55	-	-	- (Hyphen, dash, or minus)
46	2E	56	.	.	. (Period)
47	2F	57	/	/	/ (Forward slant)
48	30	60	0	0	0
49	31	61	1	1	1
50	32	62	2	2	2
51	33	63	3	3	3
52	34	64	4	4	4
53	35	65	5	5	5
54	36	66	6	6	6
55	37	67	7	7	7
56	38	70	8	8	8
57	39	71	9	9	9
58	3A	72	:	:	: (Colon)
59	3B	73	;	;	; (Semicolon)
60	3C	74	<	<	< (Less than)
61	3D	75	=	=	= (Equals)
62	3E	76	>	>	> (Greater than)
63	3F	77	?	?	? (Question mark)
64	40	100	@	@	@ (Commercial at)
65	41	101	A	A	A

Table F-1. (cont.)

DEC X_{10}	HEX X_{16}	OCT X_8	ASCII	IBM GRA. CHAR.	Terminal Key *
66	42	102	B	B	B
67	43	103	C	C	C
68	44	104	D	D	D
69	45	105	E	E	E
70	46	106	F	F	F
71	47	107	G	G	G
72	48	110	H	H	H
73	49	111	I	I	I
74	4A	112	J	J	J
75	4B	113	K	K	K
76	4C	114	L	L	L
77	4D	115	M	M	M
78	4E	116	N	N	N
79	4F	117	O	O	O
80	50	120	P	P	P
81	51	121	Q	Q	Q
82	52	122	R	R	R
83	53	123	S	S	S
84	54	124	T	T	T
85	55	125	U	U	U
86	56	126	V	V	V
87	57	127	W	W	W
88	58	130	X	X	X
89	59	131	Y	Y	Y
90	5A	132	Z	Z	Z
91	5B	133	[	[	[(Opening bracket)
92	5C	134	\	\	\ (Reverse slant)
93	5D	135	]	]	] (Closing bracket)
94	5E	136	^	^	^ (Caret or circumflex)
95	5F	137	_	_	_ (Underscore or underline)
96	60	140	`	`	` (Grave accent)
97	61	141	a	a	a
98	62	142	b	b	b

Table F-1. (cont.)

DEC X_{10}	HEX X_{16}	OCT X_8	ASCII	IBM GRA. CHAR.	Terminal Key *
99	63	143	c	c	c
100	64	144	d	d	d
101	65	145	e	e	e
102	66	146	f	f	f
103	67	147	g	g	g
104	68	150	h	h	h
105	69	151	i	i	i
106	6A	152	j	j	j
107	6B	153	k	k	k
108	6C	154	l	l	l
109	6D	155	m	m	m
110	6E	156	n	n	n
111	6F	157	o	o	o
112	70	160	p	p	p
113	71	161	q	q	q
114	72	162	r	r	r
115	73	163	s	s	s
116	74	164	t	t	t
117	75	165	u	u	u
118	76	166	v	v	v
119	77	167	w	w	w
120	78	170	x	x	x
121	79	171	y	y	y
122	7A	172	z	z	z
123	7B	173	{	{	{ (Opening brace)
124	7C	174	¦	¦	¦ (Vertical bar; logical OR)
125	7D	175	}	}	} (Closing brace)
126	7E	176	~	~	~ (Tilde)
127	7F	177	DEL	DEL	<Del>

* Those key sequences consisting of "<Ctrl->" are typed in by pressing the CTRL key and, while it is being held down, by pressing the key indicated. These sequences are based on those defined for the IBM Personal Computer series keyboards. The key sequences may be defined differently on other keyboards. IBM Extended ASCII characters can be displayed by pressing the <Alt> key and then typing the decimal code of the character on the keypad.

Table F-2. IBM ASCII Extended Cross-Reference

BINARY X$_2$	OCT X$_8$	DEC X$_{10}$	HEX X$_{16}$	Ext. ASCII
1000 0000	200	128	80	Ç
1000 0001	201	129	81	ü
1000 0010	202	130	82	é
1000 0011	203	131	83	â
1000 0100	204	132	84	ä
1000 0101	205	133	85	à
1000 0110	206	134	86	å
1000 0111	207	135	87	ç
1000 1000	210	136	88	ê
1000 1001	211	137	89	ë
1000 1010	212	138	8A	è
1000 1011	213	139	8B	ï
1000 1100	214	140	8C	î
1000 1101	215	141	8D	ì
1000 1110	216	142	8E	Ä
1000 1111	217	143	8F	Å
1001 0000	220	144	90	É
1001 0001	221	145	91	æ
1001 0010	222	146	92	Æ
1001 0011	223	147	93	ô
1001 0100	224	148	94	ö
1001 0101	225	149	95	ò
1001 0110	226	150	96	û
1001 0111	227	151	97	ù
1001 1000	230	152	98	ÿ
1001 1001	231	153	99	Ö
1001 1010	232	154	9A	Ü
1001 1011	233	155	9B	¢
1001 1100	234	156	9C	£
1001 1101	235	157	9D	¥
1001 1110	236	158	9E	P$_t$
1001 1111	237	159	9F	ƒ
1010 0000	240	160	A0	á

Table F-2. (cont.)

BINARY X_2	OCT X_8	DEC X_{10}	HEX X_{16}	Ext. ASCII
1010 0001	241	161	A1	í
1010 0010	242	162	A2	ó
1010 0011	243	163	A3	ú
1010 0100	244	164	A4	ñ
1010 0101	245	165	A5	Ñ
1010 0110	246	166	A6	a̲
1010 0111	247	167	A7	o̲
1010 1000	250	168	A8	¿
1010 1001	251	169	A9	⌐
1010 1010	252	170	AA	¬
1010 1011	253	171	AB	½
1010 1100	254	172	AC	¼
1010 1101	255	173	AD	¡
1010 1110	256	174	AE	«
1010 1111	257	175	AF	»
1011 0000	260	176	B0	░
1011 0001	261	177	B1	▒
1011 0010	262	178	B2	▓
1011 0011	263	179	B3	│
1011 0100	264	180	B4	┤
1011 0101	265	181	B5	╡
1011 0110	266	182	B6	╢
1011 0111	267	183	B7	╖
1011 1000	270	184	B8	╕
1011 1001	271	185	B9	╣
1011 1010	272	186	BA	║
1011 1011	273	187	BB	╗
1011 1100	274	188	BC	╝
1011 1101	275	189	BD	╜
1011 1110	276	190	BE	╛
1011 1111	277	191	BF	┐
1100 0000	300	192	C0	└
1100 0001	301	193	C1	┴

Table F-2. (cont.)

BINARY X_2	OCT X_8	DEC X_{10}	HEX X_{16}	Ext. ASCII
1100 0010	302	194	C2	⊤
1100 0011	303	195	C3	⊦
1100 0100	304	196	C4	−
1100 0101	305	197	C5	+
1100 0110	306	198	C6	⊫
1100 0111	307	199	C7	⊪
1100 1000	310	200	C8	⊔
1100 1001	311	201	C9	⊩
1100 1010	312	202	CA	⊥
1100 1011	313	203	CB	⊤
1100 1100	314	204	CC	⊫
1100 1101	315	205	CD	=
1100 1110	316	206	CE	⊹
1100 1111	317	207	CF	⊥
1101 0000	320	208	D0	⊥
1101 0001	321	209	D1	⊤
1101 0010	322	210	D2	⊤
1101 0011	323	211	D3	⊔
1101 0100	324	212	D4	⊢
1101 0101	325	213	D5	⊢
1101 0110	326	214	D6	⊓
1101 0111	327	215	D7	⊹
1101 1000	330	216	D8	⊹
1101 1001	331	217	D9	⌐
1101 1010	332	218	DA	⌐
1101 1011	333	219	DB	■
1101 1100	334	220	DC	■
1101 1101	335	221	DD	▮
1101 1110	336	222	DE	▮
1101 1111	337	223	DF	▬
1110 0000	340	224	E0	α
1110 0001	341	225	E1	β
1110 0010	342	226	E2	Γ

Table F-2. (cont.)

BINARY X_2	OCT X_8	DEC X_{10}	HEX X_{16}	Ext. ASCII
1110 0011	343	227	E3	π
1110 0100	344	228	E4	Σ
1110 0101	345	229	E5	σ
1110 0110	346	230	E6	μ
1110 0111	347	231	E7	τ
1110 1000	350	232	E8	Φ
1110 1001	351	233	E9	Θ
1110 1010	352	234	EA	Ω
1110 1011	353	235	EB	δ
1110 1100	354	236	EC	∞
1110 1101	355	237	ED	ϕ
1110 1110	356	238	EE	ϵ
1110 1111	357	239	EF	$\cap$
1111 0000	360	240	F0	$\equiv$
1111 0001	361	241	F1	$\pm$
1111 0010	362	242	F2	$\geq$
1111 0011	363	243	F3	$\leq$
1111 0100	364	244	F4	$\lceil$
1111 0101	365	245	F5	$\rfloor$
1111 0110	366	246	F6	$\div$
1111 0111	367	247	F7	$\approx$
1111 1000	370	248	F8	$\circ$
1111 1001	371	249	F9	$\cdot$
1111 1010	372	250	FA	$\cdot$
1111 1011	373	251	FB	$\sqrt{}$
1111 1100	374	252	FC	η
1111 1101	375	253	FD	^{2}
1111 1110	376	254	FE	■
1111 1111	377	255	FF	(blank 'F')

Abbreviations:

DEC = Decimal (Base 10)
HEX = Hexadecimal (Base 16)
OCT = Octal (Base 8)
ASCII = American Standard Code for Information Interchange

Table F-3. Extended ASCII Code

Key(s) Pressed	Extended ASCII Code Generated	Key(s) Pressed	Extended ASCII Code Generated
F1	0,59	Ctrl-F1	0,94
F2	0,60	Ctrl-F2	0,95
F3	0,61	Ctrl-F3	0,96
F4	0,62	Ctrl-F4	0,97
F5	0,63	Ctrl-F5	0,98
F6	0,64	Ctrl-F6	0,99
F7	0,65	Ctrl-F7	0,100
F8	0,66	Ctrl-F8	0,101
F9	0,67	Ctrl-F9	0,102
F10	0,68	Ctrl-F10	0,103
Shift-F1	0,84	Alt-F1	0,104
Shift-F2	0,85	Alt-F2	0,105
Shift-F3	0,86	Alt-F3	0,106
Shift-F4	0,87	Alt-F4	0,107
Shift-F5	0,88	Alt-F5	0,108
Shift-F6	0,89	Alt-F6	0,109
Shift-F7	0,90	Alt-F7	0,110
Shift-F8	0,91	Alt-F8	0,111
Shift-F9	0,92	Alt-F9	0,112
Shift-F10	0,93	Alt-F10	0,113

Hexadecimal to Decimal Conversion

Figure F-1 shows how the hexadecimal number 7D2F is converted to its decimal equivalent.

Each hexadecimal digit is always 16 times greater than the digit immediately to the right.

Decimal to Hexadecimal Conversion

The process is reversed when you convert decimal numbers to hexadecimal. Start by selecting the leftmost digit and determine its significance in the number (thousands, hundreds, etc.). Then the decimal is divided by the

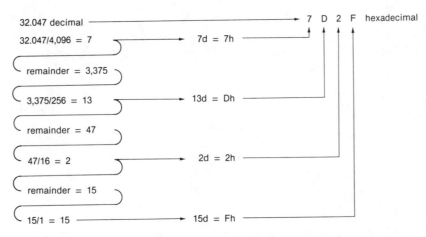

Figure F-1. Converting a hexadecimal number to decimal.

hexadecimal value of the first digit's relative position. That is, if the first digit is in the thousands position, divide by 4,096 (hexadecimal equivalent of 1,000 decimal). The result is the first hexadecimal digit. Then the remainder is divided by the hexadecimal value of the next digit's relative position (for example, divide the hundreds digit by 256 because 256 is the hexadecimal equivalent of 100 decimal). Figure F-2 shows how the decimal number derived in the previous example is converted back to hexadecimal.

Figure F-2. Converting a decimal number to hexadecimal.

Index

The Waite Group

100 Shoreline Highway, Suite 285   Mill Valley, CA 94941   (415) 331-0575

Compuserve: 74146,3515   usernet: bplabs!well!mitch   AppleLink: D2097

Dear Reader:

Thank you for considering the purchase of our book. Readers have come to know products from **The Waite Group** for the care and quality we put into them. Let me tell you a little about our group and how we make our books.

It started in 1976 when I could not find a computer book that really taught me anything. The books that were available talked down to people, lacked illustrations and examples, were poorly laid out, and were written as if you already understood all the terminology. So I set out to write a good book about microcomputers. This was to be a special book—very graphic, with a friendly and casual style, and filled with examples. The result was an instant best-seller.

Over the years, I developed this approach into a "formula" (nothing really secret here, just a lot of hard work—I am a crazy man about technical accuracy and high-quality illustrations). I began to find writers who wanted to write books in this way. This led to co-authoring and then to multiple-author books and many more titles (over seventy titles currently on the market). As The Waite Group author base grew, I trained a group of editors to manage our products. We now have a team devoted to putting together the best possible book package and maintaining the high standard of our existing books.

We greatly appreciate and use any advice our readers send us (and you send us a lot). We have discovered that our readers are detail nuts: you want indexes that really work, tables of contents that dig deeply into the subject, illustrations, tons of examples, reference cards, and more.

The Waite Group's MS-DOS Bible is a good example of The Waite Group formula for a computer book. Besides all of the basic information, you'll find facts, tips, boxes, and examples, with in-depth discussions that explain how the MS-DOS operating system works. If you want to explore MS-DOS from other angles, look for our other PC-DOS and MS-DOS books. *The Waite Group's Tricks of the MS-DOS Masters* is for power users and covers advanced MS-DOS topics and little-known tricks. *The Waite Group's Using PC-DOS*, a sister book to this one, combines a command reference section with tutorial chapters.

If you'd like to extend your programming experience into the fast and powerful C language, study our book *Microsoft C Programming for the PC*. This book teaches you how to use the Microsoft C Compiler to write programs for PC DOS systems. To understand how the PC DOS operating system works, look for *The Waite Group's MS-DOS Developer's Guide*, which presents a thorough discussion of assembly language programming techniques, MS-DOS memory management, the LIM EMS 4.0 specification, writing programs for the EGA and VGA, and much more. You can find a list of all our titles in the back of this book, and if you let us know what you want, we'll try to write about it. Thanks again for considering the purchase of this title. If you care to tell me anything you like (or don't like) about the book, please write or send email to the addresses on this letterhead.

Sincerely,

Mitchell Waite
The Waite Group

The Waite Group Library

If you enjoyed this book, you may be interested in these additional subjects and titles from **The Waite Group** and Howard W. Sams & Company. Reader level is as follows: ★ = introductory, ★★ = intermediate, ★★★ = advanced. You can order these books by calling 800-428-SAMS.

Level	Title	Catalog #	Price	

C and C++ Programming Language

Tutorial, UNIX & ANSI

Level	Title	Catalog #	Price	
★	C Primer Plus, Revised Edition, Waite, Prata, & Martin	22582	$24.95	
★★	C++ Programming, Berry	22619	$24.95	
★★★	Advanced C Primer ++, Prata	22486	$24.95	

Tutorial, Product Specific

Level	Title	Catalog #	Price	
★	Microsoft C Programming for the PC, Revised Edition, Lafore	22661	$24.95	NEW
★	Turbo C Programming for the PC, Revised Edition, Lafore	22660	$22.95	
★★	Inside the Amiga with C, Second Edition, Berry	22625	$24.95	

Reference, Product Specific

Level	Title	Catalog #	Price	
★★	Microsoft C Bible, Barkakati	22620	$24.95	
★★	Quick C Bible, Barkakati	22632	$24.95	
★★	Turbo C. Bible, Barkakati	22631	$24.95	
★★	Essential Guide to ANSI C, Barkakati	22673	$7.95	
★★	Essential Guide to Turbo C, Barkakati	22675	$7.95	NEW
★★	Essential Guide to Microsoft C, Barkakati	22674	$7.95	NEW

DOS and OS/2 Operating System

Tutorial, General Users

Level	Title	Catalog #	Price	
★	Discovering MS-DOS, O'Day	22407	$19.95	
★	Understanding MS-DOS, O'Day & Angermeyer	27067	$17.95	

Tutorial/Reference, General Users

Level	Title	Catalog #	Price	
★	The Waite Group's Using PC DOS	22651	$22.95	NEW

Tutorial/Reference, Power Users

Level	Title	Catalog #	Price	
★★	Tricks of the MS-DOS Masters, Angermeyer & Jaeger	22525	$24.95	

Tutorial, Programmers

Level	Title	Catalog #	Price	
★★	MS-DOS Papers, Edited by The Waite Group	22594	$26.95	
★★	OS/2 Programmer's Reference, Dror	22645	$24.95	
★★★	MS-DOS Developer's Guide, Revised Edition, Angermeyer, Jaeger, et al.	22630	$24.95	

UNIX Operating System

Tutorial, General Users

Level	Title	Catalog #	Price	
★	UNIX Primer Plus, Waite, Prata, & Martin	22028	$22.95	
★	UNIX System V Primer, Revised Edition, Waite, Prata, & Martin	22570	$22.95	
★★	UNIX System V Bible, Prata and Martin	22562	$24.95	
★★	UNIX Communications, Henderson, Anderson, Costales	22511	$24.95	
★★	UNIX Papers, Edited by Mitchell Waite	22570	$26.95	

Tutorial/Reference, Power Users and Programmers

Level	Title	Catalog #	Price	
★★	Tricks of the UNIX Masters, Sage	22449	$24.95	
★★★	Advanced UNIX—A Programmer's Guide, Prata	22403	$24.95	

Macintosh

Tutorial, General Users

Level	Title	Catalog #	Price	
★	HyperTalk Bible, The Waite Group	48430	$24.95	NEW

Tutorial/Reference, Power Users and Programmers

Level	Title	Catalog #	Price	
★★	Tricks of the HyperTalk Masters, Edited by The Waite Group	48431	$24.95	NEW